Anonymus

The Westminster Review

January and April 1874

Anonymus

The Westminster Review
January and April 1874

ISBN/EAN: 9783741178757

Manufactured in Europe, USA, Canada, Australia, Japa

Cover: Foto ©Thomas Meinert / pixelio.de

Manufactured and distributed by brebook publishing software
(www.brebook.com)

Anonymus

The Westminster Review

THE

WESTMINSTER REVIEW.

JANUARY AND APRIL

1874.

"Truth can never be confirm'd enough,
Though doubts did ever sleep."

SHAKESPEARE.

Wahrheitsliebe zeigt sich darin, daß man überall das Gute zu finden und zu schätzen weiß.

GOETHE.

NEW SERIES.

VOL. XLV.

TRÜBNER & CO., 57 & 59, LUDGATE HILL.

MDCCCLXXIV.

THE

WESTMINSTER

AND

FOREIGN QUARTERLY

REVIEW.

JANUARY 1, 1874.

ART. I.—THE DISESTABLISHMENT AND DISENDOWMENT OF THE CHURCH OF ENGLAND.

1. *Essays and Addresses, mostly upon Church Subjects.* By HENRY ALFORD, D.D., Dean of Canterbury. London: Macmillans. 1871.
2. *The Title Deeds of the Church of England to her Parochial Endowments.* By EDWARD MIALL, M.P. Second Edition, revised. London: Elliot Stock. 1871.
3. *Disestablishment: Is it Unconstitutional?* London: Society for the Liberation of Religion from State Patronage and Control. 1870.
4. *Disestablishment necessary for the well-being of the Church of England: a Paper read by Henry Clark, Esq., before the Members of the Liverpool Branch of the English Church Union, Jan. 16, 1871.* Published by request. J. Masters and Son, 71, New Bond-street, London.
5. *Verbatim Report of the Debate in the House of Commons, on the Motion of Mr. Miall, M.P., May 9,* 1871. Extracted from "The Nonconformist."
6. *Ecclesiastical Revenues, &c. Speech of Edward Miall, Esq., M.P., delivered in the House of Commons, July 2,* 1872. London: Elliot Stock.
7. "The Liberator:" *a Monthly Journal of the Society for the Liberation of Religion from State Patronage and Control, June,* 1873.—*The Debate on Disestablishment: Mr. Miall's Speech.*

8. *Three Essays on the Maintenance of the Church of England as an Established Church.* By Rev. CHARLES HOLE, B.A., Rector of Loxbear; Rev. RICHARD WATSON DIXON, M.A., Minor Canon of Carlisle Cathedral; and Rev. JULIUS LLOYD, M.A., Incumbent of St. John's, Greenock. To whom the Prizes offered by Henry W. Peek, Esq., M.P., were awarded by the Judges. London: John Murray. 1874.

"THE next term in the Free National Development," wrote the excellent and accomplished author of the "Essays on Church Subjects," "is the severance of the Church from the State."* When a dignitary of the English Church makes such an admission, it is clear that its disestablishment is only a question of time. Indeed, the movement for that purpose from a sectarian has become a national one; and the fact that Parliament is yearly invited to legislate for the purpose, clearly shows that, as in the case of the corn laws, the ballot, and the paper duty, the Government of the day—be it Liberal, or what is ironically called Conservative—will ere long be forced to adopt the measure as their own.

The question of the relation of the Church to the State has been treated successively after the theological and the metaphysical methods. Both these are now exploded, and it is now treated entirely on the inductive or experimental. The educated and intelligent of the defenders of the Establishment, even amongst its own clergy, have abandoned its defence on the old Scriptural grounds; they no longer put forward the arguments founded on Abraham giving tithes to Melchisedec, or on the legislation of the Jewish theocracy. If one did not know the ignorance of the Bible, which in England exists along with the blind and unreasoning idolatry of it, one would think it impossible for men gravely to assert—as it was the custom to assert—that the legislation recorded in the Pentateuch is of divine and universal obligation, and the permanent model for all States and communities. If this were so, it would of course involve the penalty of death to any pauper who should on a Saturday gather a few sticks for fuel, and also the registering in our Statute Book of the land law of the Hebrews,† which, however it might tally with the views of our extremest land tenure reformers, would not be equally acceptable to the country rectors and squires, who form the rank and file of the army of Church defenders. Lately indeed the Bishop of Ripon‡ aired some

* "Essays," &c., p. 166, art. "The Church of the Future."

† *Vide* Leviticus, chap. xxv. ver. 23 et seq.

‡ *Vide* "Breakers a-Head: Two Letters to the Bishop of Ripon." By Dr. Mellor.

of the old Biblical fallacies and platitudes, and it has been our fate to hear a sermon from a young curate, in which they were all reproduced with a sublime unconsciousness that they had been refuted and abandoned. The preacher, however, was not led into error by the working of his own mind; his sermon was one of those lithographed compositions supplied to the clergy at ten shillings and sixpence per dozen. In country parishes these form the chief part of the teaching the clergy give their hearers, and the use of them is rapidly destroying what little life and reality remain in the pulpits of the Establishment. With such rare and trivial exceptions the theological method of treating the Establishment question is abandoned even by the clergy. It received its death-blow when Chalmers rested his defence of the Establishment theory on purely practical and utilitarian grounds. Whately made a concession fatal to the Scriptural argument when, writing of the words attributed to Jesus in the Fourth Gospel—"My kingdom is not of this world"—he said they must be taken "as amounting to a renunciation of all secular coercion, all forcible measures in behalf of His religion."* It was reserved, however, for Dr. Newman to give the final blow to this delusive method of treating the question, which he does in these words:—

"There is no text in the New Testament which enjoins us to 'establish' Religion (as the phrase is) or to make it national, and to give to the Church certain honour and power; whereas our Lord's words, 'My kingdom is not of this world,' may be interpreted to discountenance such a proceeding."

This is decisive: but alarmed at his own admission, this master of dialectics attempts to qualify its force:—

"We consider that it is right to establish the Church on the ground of mere deductions, though, of course, true ones from the sacred text, such as S. Paul's using his rights as a Roman citizen."†

How St. Paul's exercise of his individual right justifies the giving by the State to one church out of several in a country "certain honour and power" to the injury of the rights "as citizens" of those who do not belong to it, Dr. Newman does not condescend to enlighten us.

The theological method being abandoned, was succeeded by the metaphysical mode of treatment. Of this method the theories of Arnold and Martineau are specimens; but they were

---

* See "The Kingdom of Christ."

† "Tracts for the Times," No. 85, 1838, republished in "Discussions and Arguments on Various Subjects." By J. H. Newman, sometime Fellow of Oriel College, p. 122.

ill adapted to the English mind, and never met with general acceptance.* A greater impression was produced by Mr. Gladstone's "The State, in its Relation to the Church,"† written when the author was "the rising hope of the stern and unbending Tories," and which Lord Macaulay's essay on it will preserve from the oblivion which would otherwise have been its fate.

"Mr. Gladstone's whole theory rests," said Lord Macaulay, "on the great fundamental proposition that the propagation of religious truth is one of the principal ends of government as government."

Or, to give Mr. Gladstone's own statement of his theory :—

"That the State in its best condition has such a conscience as can take cognizance of religious truth and error, and that the state of the United Kingdom was so far in this condition as to lie under an obligation to give an active and an exclusive support to the established religion of the country."‡

With the publication of this book the metaphysical phase of the controversy came to a close.

"Scarcely," says Mr. Gladstone, "had my work issued from the press when I became aware that there was no party, no section of a party, no individual person probably in the House of Commons, who was prepared to act upon it. I found myself the last man in the sinking ship. Exclusive support to the established religion of the country, with a limited and local exception for Scotland under the Treaty of Union with that country, had been up to that time the actual rule of our policy; the instances to the contrary being of equivocal construction and of infinitesimal amount. But the attempt to give this rule a vitality other than that of sufferance was an anachronism in time and in place. When I bid it live it was just about to die."§

In the meetings of ecclesiastical bodies such as Convocations, or the various Nonconformist Unions, and even by the Liberation Society itself, a formal profession of faith in the theological and metaphysical arguments continues, indeed, to be made by both the opponents of the Establishment and its supporters; but the real grounds on which the battle is now fought, and will be decided, is the practical and experimental one. This is, of course, the case in Parliament; and the Parliamentary debate gives the tone to all other discussions. It is on this ground alone that we propose to discuss the question, whether the English Church should be disestablished and disendowed, and, if so, in what manner the process should be carried out?

---

* Arnold's "Fragment on Church and State," *passim*. "Miscellanies." By Jas. Martineau, p. 105.

† London: J. Murray. 1838.

‡ "A Chapter of Autobiography." By the Right Hon. W. E. Gladstone, M.P., p. 7.

§ Ibid., p. 12.

The accomplished statesman who, after long years of patient and persistent advocacy of the policy of disestablishment, has fitly become—and we devoutly hope will continue—the Parliamentary spokesman of the party he has formed, in the motion which last session he submitted to the House of Commons thus clearly and concisely states the case against the English Establishment:—"The establishment by law of the Church of England,"* says Mr. Miall—

"1. Involves the violation of religious equality.

"2. Deprives the Church of the right of self-government.

"3. Imposes upon Parliament duties which it is not qualified to discharge.

"4. And is hurtful to the religious and political interests of the community."

Each of these topics, as Mr. Gladstone remarked, would require a volume for its discussion; and within the limits of this paper it is only possible for us to touch the fringe of each.

I. It must, we think, be conceded that the presumption is in favour of equality between all the Churches existing in a country; by equality we mean—to use the excellent definition given by Mr. Miall—"The equal position and status of all spiritual associations, so far as they are determinable by civil law, and their equal treatment, whether in the way of protection or restraint, by the legally expressed will of the nation."† That the existence of the English Establishment violates religious equality is a self-evident proposition, and the working of free institutions all over the world shows conclusively that religious equality is inseparable from their full development; that free institutions and an Establishment cannot permanently co-exist. "Religious liberty," says an ecclesiastical paper, *The Guardian*, "is one thing, and religious equality is another; the former is consistent with the existence of a National Church, the other is not." Mr. Gladstone also makes the following significant and noteworthy admissions:—

"When the State has come to be the organ of the deliberate and ascertained will of the community, expressed through legal channels, the inculcation of religion can no longer rest in full or permanent force upon its authority. When, in addition to this," he continues, "the community itself is split and severed into opinions and communions which, whatever their concurrence in the basis of Christian belief, are hostile in regard to the point at issue, so that what was meant for the nation

* The terms of the motion expressly included the Church of Scotland. The space at our disposal compels us to confine our remarks to the English Establishment. Possibly in a future article we may discuss the case of the Scottish Establishment.

† From "Religious Equality: a Lecture." By Edward Miall, M.P.

dwindles into the private estate as it were of a comparative handful, the attempt to maintain an Established Church becomes an error fatal to the peace, dangerous, perhaps, even to the life of civil society."*

This description was intended to refer to the Irish Church only, but it is equally applicable to the English Establishment, and in it we have the abstract phrase "the violation of religious equality" rendered into the concrete, and the practical evils and dangerous tendencies of such a violation pointed out. This violation of equality is no mere sentimental grievance; the bodies to whom Parliament delegates authority are ever in the discharge of their duty striving to perpetuate intolerance, either by violating the law or by disregarding its spirit for the benefit of the Establishment. The Elementary Education Act has been throughout dishonestly administered in the interest of the Establishment. Thus, to give a specific instance, when a dozen or more inspectors were being appointed under the Act, there were placed before Mr. Forster, as candidates for the vacancies, the names of gentlemen in every respect qualified, who had received an university education, who had taken honourable degrees, but who were Nonconformists; not one of them was appointed; all the inspectors appointed were members of the Establishment, though the schools they were to inspect belonged to all churches.† Out of 74, the total number of Government inspectors of schools, 45 are clergymen of the Establishment, pledged by esprit de corps to do everything in their power to favour and uphold it.‡

The administration of the Endowed Schools Act supplies another illustration. The spirit of that Act is no doubt that of religious equality, but its administration has been entrusted to Churchmen of decided opinions, ignorant to a great extent of the principles and feelings of Dissenters, and so far as their knowledge of either extended, inclined to disregard them. At the first appointment of commissioners, Mr. Gladstone was urged to appoint one Nonconformist, and afterwards, on a vacancy occurring, the application was renewed. On both occasions this very reasonable request was refused, and the result has been that the intention of the Legislature in favour of equality amongst the Churches has been disregarded, and the Act administered so as to secure the monopolies and privileges of the Establishment; and it seems probable that the ecclesiastical exclusiveness which the Act was intended to remove may be perpetuated. The 17th section of the Act required that the commissioners shall provide in their schemes for reforming schools that his religious opinions

* "Chapter of Autobiography," p. 30.

† Speech of Mr. H. Richard, M.P., at meeting of N.-E. Lancashire Nonconformist Association.

‡ "Report of Committee of Council on Education," 1872, p. 127.

or attendance upon any particular form of worship shall not in any wise affect the qualification of any governor. The purpose of this clause is evidently to place the governors on an equality as to their religion; but in scheme after scheme the commissioners, on the plea that being a minister or member of the Establishment is no disqualification, have contrived to give the dominant sect the entirety of the governing bodies, or where that was not possible, a majority in them.* As the result of extensive inquiries, we find that the proportion of Churchmen to Nonconformists appointed by the commissioners is ten to one. The Charity Commissioners have not only always endeavoured to defend and uphold the monopolies of the Establishment, but they have attempted to divert Nonconformist charities to its aid and support.† The limits of the space at our disposal, not want of further proofs, compel us to pass on to our next topic.

II. It is an easy task to prove that the Church of England is deprived of its right of self-government. Perhaps it would be more accurate to say its power of self-government; for an Establishment has no rights except what it derives from the laws establishing it. By self-government we mean those legislative, executive, and judicial powers which are possessed by all the Churches in the land, excepting only that one established by law. The possession of these powers by the Church of England would secure to it the selection of its bishops in an ecclesiastical manner —the decision of spiritual causes by spiritual persons—the conversion of Convocation from a debating society into a living, acting, energizing body; whereas now the bishops are appointed in truth and fact, though in a circuitous and anomalous manner, by the Premier of the day, and accordingly are sometimes imposed by force of law on a hostile clergy. The Queen is the head of the spiritual courts, which is as great an anomaly as if she were invested with the power of ordination. Convocation is not entirely silenced, but it is not permitted effectually to speak, much less to act.

Let us hear the testimony of some of the clergy on this matter. The subjection of the Church was thus sketched by Dr. Newman‡—as few but he could sketch it—while he was yet one of the Anglican clergy:—

"The civil power, which has cut us off from Christendom, has done,

---

* For cases in which this has been done, see "Nonconformists and their Rights as Citizens, especially as relates to the Endowed Schools Act." By Vigilans. E. Stock, Paternoster Row.

† Ibid.

‡ *Vide* Dr. Newman's "Historical Sketches," vol. i. p. 421 (Ed. 1872), art. "The Convocation of Canterbury, and Church and State in Discord." By Rev. Orby Shipley.—*Contemporary Rev.*, Sept. 1872.

it must be confessed, its utmost to reconcile us to our degradation. It has maintained, of course, our captivity as a first principle of the Constitution, but it has taken very great pains to keep us from fretting. If the Church was to exist at all in England it was like a law of the Medes and Persians, that she must exist for England alone; she must be a prisoner if she must be an inmate; but that being taken for granted, she has been accorded a most honourable captivity. Nothing has been denied her short of freedom; power, wealth, authority, rank, consideration, have been showered upon her, to make her as happy as the day is long. She has been like Rasselas in a happy valley, or like the crusader in Armida's garden; what want was unsatisfied? Yet even of our first parent it is said, under far more blessed circumstances, 'For Adam there was not found a help meet for him,' *Aliquid desideravere oculi*, which neither fawning beast nor painted bird could supply. He found a want in Paradise itself; and so upon this our poor Church of England, which is not in Paradise, this evil has fallen in spite of 'princes and other children of men,' that she has been solitary, she has been among strangers. Statesmen, lawyers, and soldiers have frisked and prowled around; creatures wild or tame have held a parliament over her; but she has wanted some one to converse with, to repose on, to consult, to love. The State, indeed, to judge by its acts, has thought it unreasonable in her that she could not find in a lion and an unicorn a sufficient object for her affections. It has set her to keep order in the land, to restrain enthusiasm, and to rival and so discountenance 'Popery;' and if she murmured, if she desired to place bishops in the colonies, or to take any other measure which tended to catholicity, it has used expostulation and upbraiding. 'Am I not,' it has seemed to whisper, 'am I not your own Parliament? pour your grief into my bosom. Have not I established you by law? Am I not your guide, philosopher, and friend? I am ready to meet all your desires. I will decide any theological point for you, or absolve vows and oaths for you as easily as I send soldiers to collect your tithes.' And if this did not succeed, then, in a gruffer tone, 'Are you not my own Church? Have not I paid for you? Have not I cut you off from Christendom to have you all to myself? Is not this the very alliance that you should take wages and do service? and where will you find service so light and wages so high?'"*

Again, a representative of another and opposite ecclesiastical party, the late Dean Alford, complains that—

"Any attempt at exertion for good under our existing State Establishment is made under the greatest possible difficulties. We are fettered on all sides. Not one proposed reform in ten ever struggles past the two guardians of the *Status quo*, the *Leo Piger*, and the *Leo Compitalis*. But suppose the desire for reform idly imagines it is about to be put in act, there awaits a foe hardly less formidable than those others. It must be fitted into the iron frame of precedent;

* "Essays, Critical and Historical," vol. i. pp. 310–11, art. "The Anglo-American Church."

whatever is to be done must only be done as it always has been done. . . . . What can be done in the present Church of England is also fatally hampered by law; technical difficulties are thrown in the way of almost every attempt at amelioration."

Of this he gives a specific instance :—

"The members of Convocation, feeling that the representation of the clergy in their house is inadequate and unfair, desire to remove the blot, and take the proper constitutional steps to do so. All is ready, and action is going forward. But the whole is frustrated and the reform deferred, no one knows how long, by a legal scruple. Surely the fetter on which there is such a strain cannot be far from breaking."*

We will add another illustration. A correspondent of *The Guardian*, referring to the day of intercession for missions, says :—

"Can any one possibly deny that, as far as the services authorized to be used in church are concerned, we met together for public prayer to Almighty God for the increase of the supply of missionaries, and separated without having offered up one direct prayer toward that end? The reason was obvious—there is no such prayer in the Prayer Book; and in drawing up such services the bishops are limited by law to what is contained in the Bible and the Prayer Book."†

The two pamphlets mentioned at the head of this paper: "Disestablishment: is it Unconstitutional?" and "Disestablishment necessary for the well-being of the Church of England," illustrate this state of things in detail. Each is written by a lawyer. The first, which is published by the Liberation Society, has, we happen to know, been pronounced by a very reverend dignitary of the Established Church to be unanswerable both in law and history. The Liberationist maintains that the Establishment, as regards its temporalities and equally as regards its doctrines and forms of worship, is the creation of Acts of Parliament. The writer of the other pamphlet, published by the English Church Union, does not deny this conclusion, and takes as his premises for his conclusion that disestablishment is desirable—the same premises which the Liberationist adduces to prove his conclusion, that disestablishment is constitutional. Both writers select the same legal and historical facts as illustrations of the subjection of the Church to the State; the Unionist thinking, we presume, he could not improve on them, often borrowing the very words of the Liberationist.‡ The result of this state of things is, that "it is the misfortune of the Church of England," as was recently

---

* "The Church of the Future," *ubi supra*, pp. 182–5.
† *The Guardian*, Jan. 10, 1873.
‡ Comp. the two pamphlets, *passim*.

said by a writer in *The Times*, "that neither its laity nor the mass of its clergy have the smallest voice in the management of its affairs." We have referred to the complaints of the clergy; as for the laity, their position is thus accurately described:—

"Their sole rights are, that they may enter into any church during divine service, and may take part in services rendered in Roman or Genevan fashion, at the caprice of the incumbent; also that they may be christened, married, or buried at their own parish churches, which privileges they share equally with Papists, Jews, Dissenters, and infamous persons. But *as against the clergy* the laity have no other rights. Endowments, freehold rights, and legal privileges, so far from belonging to the Church, are exclusively the property of the clergy, who are absolute masters of it."*

This is undoubtedly true, and is one great cause of the weakness and inefficiency of the Establishment. In the Free Churches the knowledge that everything depends on the exertions of their members, and that, if they wish to exist, they must work, fight, and pay for it, gives to these Churches life and continual impulse. On the other hand, the laity of the Establishment have neither representation in that which calls itself the representative body of their Church, Convocation, nor voice in the election of its members; and any suggestion that they should be represented in it is wholly repugnant to the clergy. The laity also are excluded from all share in the government of the congregations of which they are members; and, with exceptions so rare as to have no influence on the general state of the Church, they are universally and absolutely excluded from any choice in the appointment of their ministers. This is the result of the patronage system, which is an inseparable accident of the English Establishment. Mr. Bright lately hinted at what he called "the abolition of purchase in the Church," *i.e.*, the right of selling the patronage to livings. Except as part of a general measure of disestablishment and disendowment, such abolition is impossible. There are about 7900 livings, which are private property, and the lowest estimate of their annual value approaches closely to two millions of money. The owners of these would, of course, require compensation for the abolition of their rights, and they would have to be bought up at the public expense. It would not be justifiable, and even if it were, it would not be possible to pay out of the taxes the large sum of money which would be required for the purpose of carrying out a reform in what, though it proposes to be the National Church, is, in truth, only a combination of privileged

* "The Position of the Laity in the Church of England." London: W. Macintosh, 24, Paternoster Row.

but discordant sects. Purchase in the Church, therefore, with all its scandals, cannot be removed until the Church is disestablished. We need add nothing more to this division of our subject.*

III. That the establishment of the Church imposes upon Parliament duties which it is not qualified to discharge is a proposition easier of proof even than those we have before discussed. The composition of Parliament is itself a proof of it. We do not lay so much stress as do some Liberationists upon the fact that it is composed, not only of Churchmen whose membership is more or less a reality—less rather than more in the vast majority of instances, such as are earnest Churchmen being interdivided and in a state of internecine war with each other, but of Romanists, Dissenters of every denomination, Jews, and Secularists. Many of these non-Churchmen—the late John Stuart Mill, for instance—would give a far more careful consideration to ecclesiastical questions, because they had undertaken the duty, than the merely nominal Churchmen who form the great body of members of either House of Parliament. What we refer to in the composition of Parliament is that the House of Commons, "the centre of gravity in the Constitution," is made up, besides the official classes, of representatives of the landed, manufacturing, mercantile, and railway interests, lawyers on the look out for promotion, speculators who seek a Parliamentary position for the sake of the influence it gives them in promoting their often fraudulent schemes, and of wealthy nobodies who find the purchase of a seat in the House of Commons the only way open to them of obtaining social rank and influence. Such a body is not likely well to perform the functions of a collective head of the Church. Its members do not seek their seats on the ground of their fitness to deal with ecclesiastical questions; and a very small fraction of the voters of the United Kingdom give their votes on purely ecclesiastical grounds. Yet the House of Commons is the body which must settle what form of service it shall be lawful to use in the parish graveyard when a deceased Nonconformist is buried with his fathers, and whose consent was a condition precedent to the recent change in the portions of Scripture read in the public service of the Church. Seventeen measures relating to the internal affairs of the Church were brought into Parliament in the session of 1872, and the same number in 1873. Few, if

* See, on this question of patronage, "The Traffic in Church Livings in the English Establishment." By J. Charles Cox, Esq., J. P., published by the Liberation Society. And "The Cure of Souls by Purchase. By Promotion, by Merit." Manchester: Alex. Ireland & Co.

any, of these measures became law, owing to the disinclination of the House of Commons to deal with ecclesiastical questions, founded doubtless on the conviction entertained by the House of its utter unfitness to deal with them. The Bishop of Gloucester and Bristol refers to, and laments over, the increase of this feeling in Parliament, owing to which, he says, "we can hardly count on a continuance of those quiet and useful reforms which year by year are more urgently needed." The Bishop of Manchester wishes Parliament to pass an Act for the cheaper, simpler, and readier improvement of Church discipline. Already notices for the coming session are given in each House of measures which, if they are persisted in, will raise the question whether the Establishment is to continue—if, indeed, it be so—Protestant, or whether all Roman doctrine and ceremonial may be lawfully introduced into its churches. Parliament is thus asked to devote its time to the making special laws for the welfare of a religious establishment in which only two-fifths of British society are interested. Parliament will in all probability decline the labours which they are invited to undertake; but two things are equally clear—the one that the Church, being established by law, Parliament is the sole authority which can lawfully decide the questions raised by these motions; and the other, that Parliament is nevertheless, from its composition and its inherent excellences and defects, of all authorities the most unqualified to decide them. We are not justified in wasting our space in any further discussion of this topic.

IV. We can afford to give a few illustrations only of the fact that the Church as an Establishment is hurtful to the religious and political interests of the community.

(*a*) The right of patronage being private property, is of course saleable; hence the scandalous spectacle weekly and daily presented by the advertisements of livings for sale, specifying the age of the incumbent, the size of the house, the society, the hounds, and the fishing in the neighbourhood, the slightness of the duty, and the non-existence of dissent. "Is the Church," asked Bishop Ken, a hundred and fifty years ago, "grown so contemptible that it may be bought and sold for money? Is preferment a prize for the richest, not the worthiest?" The answer which must be given to both these questions is simply Yes. Mr. Cox, and also the author of "The Cure of Souls by Purchase,"* to whose publications we have before referred, show that at the beginning of 1873 one-tenth of the entire livings in the Church were in the market for sale or barter, which suggests this calculation,

* *Vide* the pamphlet *passim*, more especially p. 24, and the corroboration of it by Mr. Cox, *vide* "Traffic in Church Livings," p. 24, note.

"If one-tenth is in the market in one month, how long will it take to turn over the entire Church?" This traffic in the cure of souls is said by the Bishop of Exeter to be "increasing from day to day." No doubt he had in his mind the notorious Falmouth case. Falmouth is a rectory endowed with a house-tax levied by special Act of Parliament and producing yearly about 1600*l*. The advowson was the private property of a former incumbent, who had invested in the purchase the whole of his fortune. On his death it became necessary for his family to sell the living in order to regain their property; but, being vacant, it could not be sold. A gentleman, aged between seventy and eighty, was therefore presented, and the advowson, with the right of next presentation and the hope of its early enjoyment, found a purchaser. Age, and the probability of early death, not religious or intellectual fitness, were the qualifications required in this case for a pastor of souls.* Lately the advowson of the rectory of Liverpool was sold to the representatives of the ritualistic party, who bought it in order that the follies and vagaries of their bastard Romanism may be introduced into that ultra-Protestant—indeed Orange—community. It is amusing to read the following comments of one of the local Tory papers on the transaction; they equally apply to the Falmouth case:—

"A matter of 10,000*l*. was the one single condition essential to the bargain. It was no question of decency or competency; the propriety of bartering a spiritual charge for gold, or the probable feeling of the parishioners affected by the change, formed no element in the compact. It was a simple matter of hard bargaining; as thoroughly a matter of barter as if the transaction related to the good-will of a gin palace, or the purchase of a flock of sheep—not the metaphorical but the edible sheep. The rectory of Liverpool has changed owners, 'and there's an end on't.' But did it occur to the ecclesiastical hucksters what they were buying and selling? Nominally it is the advowson of the parish of Liverpool; literally it is the spiritual charge of a multitude of men. By sheer power of money a stranger, who has never spent four and twenty hours in the town, has acquired the highest ecclesiastical office in Liverpool; he is the arbiter of the religious teaching of a quarter of a million of people; the superior lord over a hundred district incumbents, and the immediate ruler of the two principal churches in the town."

These are noteworthy admissions from an organ of the party whose cry is "Church and State," and whose object—if they have one—is to uphold "our glorious Constitution in Church and State." Well may the Bishop of Exeter characterize such transactions as "shocking to the religious sentiment," and "de-

---

* *Vide* "The Falmouth Rectory Scandal and the Remedy for it." Published by the Liberation Society.

rogatory to the Church of Christ." We commend alike to the Tory journalist and the Liberal bishop the fact, that it is by disestablishment and disendowment alone that their Church can be purified from these evils. Here there is a proof of the injury to the religious interests of the community produced by the establishment of the Church.

(*b*) A greater proof even is to be found in its internal divisions. The existence within what professes to be one and the same Church of the Romanist, the Calvinist, and the Unitarian parties—to give them the names which most accurately describe them would be shocking to the religious sentiment of the country, were it not deadened by being accustomed to such a state of things. It is perfectly well known to all who do not from inattention or interested motives blind themselves to the fact, that the only bond of union between these opposing parties is that of the rank, wealth, and privilege which the establishment of the Church secures to them. Churchmen, lay or ecclesiastic, do not seem able to appreciate the injury done to the religion, the diffusion of which they seek, when a critical and sceptical age sees in one parish the mass set up again by men who have subscribed and assented to articles which teach "that the sacrifice of the mass is a fond thing, vainly invented;" while in the next parish the rector denounces these, his fellow ministers of the National Church, as—what in fact they are—Romanists in all but honesty and name, while he himself acts equally dishonestly as regards the doctrine of baptismal regeneration. While on a Trinity Sunday a very reverend dean—as we ourselves have witnessed—may be heard preaching in the Temple Church a sermon on the "Ineffable Mystery," which drew forth the apt comment that he had made a mistake in coming through Temple Bar, and should have stopped on the other side, and preached his sermon in Essex Street Unitarian Chapel, from the pulpit once occupied by Lindsay and Belsham. And all these are ministers, and speak in the name of one and the same Church, whose professed mission is to "declare Christ's truth to his people." To show that this is no caricature, but a faithful description of what may be heard and seen amongst us every Sunday, we borrow the following admissions from the *Church Review*. Referring to the contradictory theologies preached of late in Oxford University pulpit, our contemporary says:—

"What is the inevitable tendency of such an irreconcilable farrago of teaching from the same pulpit, to most or many of the same hearers, but either to confuse the intellect and blunt the moral sense, or to sow the seeds of infidelity, or to stir up strife and minister questions rather than godly edifying, or to make religion a mere butt for ridicule. Certainly it is not to produce the Christian unanimity which the apostle taught, 'Finally, brethren, be ye all of one mind.' The most contradictory doctrines upon vital points are preached by recognised ministers of the same Church. . . . One teaches that miraculousness is the character of Christianity; another that miracles 'are a vexed question,' and therefore doubtful. One that the Church cannot be a kingdom without dogma; another that creeds and confessions and one faith are obstacles to love and progress; one that modern sceptics have no faith; another that orthodoxy leads to unbelief; one that theology is not a fixed science, but must be changed to suit the times; another that there can be no new theology under the Christian dispensation; one that all men, without exception, will be saved; another that multitudes will be lost in unquenchable fire."

What a new force is given by this description to the old story of the University official who, after half a century's attendance at the University sermons, thanked God that, after all he had heard, he was a Christian still. The Liberal party in the Church, by way of defending their position, assure us, indeed, that a National Church must really comprehend the nation and represent all its opinions. It is sufficient to reply to this fallacy in the language of Dr. Newman, which for this purpose we gratefully appropriate :—

"To attempt comprehensions of opinion, amiable as the motive frequently is, is to mistake arrangements of words which have no existence except on paper for habits which are realities; and ingenious generalization of discordant sentiments for that practical agreement which can alone lead to co-operation. We may, indeed, artificially classify light and darkness under one term or formula; but nature has her own fixed courses and unites mankind by the sympathy of moral character, not by those forced resemblances which the imagination singles out at pleasure even in the most promiscuous collection of materials."*

The causes which produce the combination of such heterogeneous theologies in one and the same Church are innate in and ineradicable from the English Establishment, but they are fatal to the honesty and sincerity without which any profession of religion is vain. The maintenance of the promiscuous collection of materials of which the so-called National Church is composed is certainly one of the greatest evils its establishment does to the religious interests of the community.

(c) We are told by Guizot, the historian statesman, that "the Church of Rome has sometimes been the friend of freedom, the Church of England never." If this be so—and no candid reader of history will deny it—there is little need to elaborate our proof of the injury done by the Church Establishment to the political in-

* "History of the Arians," pp. 151-2. Edit. 1871.

terests of the community. Lest our Nonconformist sympathies should make us to judge unfairly between the Establishment and Dissent, we are glad to avail ourselves of the testimony of one who, standing outside both, may be trusted evenly to hold the scales between them—the writer of "The Struggle for National Education." In that very able work Mr. John Morley says:—

"The voice of history is clear and beyond mistake. There is not a single crisis in the growth of English liberties in which the State Church has not been the champion of retrogression and obstruction. Yes, there was one. In 1688, when her own purse and privilege were threatened she did for a short space enlist under the flag which the Nonconformists had raised in older and harder days, and immediately after, when, with their aid and on their principles, the oppressor had been driven out, she reverted by a sure instinct to her own base principles of passive obedience and persecuting orthodoxy. Yet this is the brightest episode in her political history. In every other great crisis she has made herself the ally of tyranny, the organ of social oppression, the champion of intellectual bondage. In the sixteenth century the bishops of the State Church became the joyful instruments of Elizabeth's persecution, and in their courts the patriotic loyalty of the Puritan was rewarded with the pillory, the prison, the branding iron, the gallows. In the seventeenth century, the State Church made her cause one with the cause of the Star Chamber and the Court of High Commission, with prerogative and benevolences, with absolutism and Divine Right. The Nonconformists shed their blood for law and ordered freedom. The Church, when she returned 'to exalt her mitred front in Court and Parliament' retaliated on them for their services in the great cause which she has always persecuted when she could, and always denounced when she could not persecute, and bitterly suspected when she has been unable to persecute and ashamed to denounce, by urging on the most vindictive legislation that defaced the English statute book even in those evil days of Restoration. She preached passive obedience with an industry that would have been Apostolic, if only its goal had been the elevation instead of the debasement of human nature. When that doctrine became inconvenient, she put it aside for a while, but as we have seen, she speedily relapsed into the maxims of absolute non-resistance when power and privilege once more seemed safe. The Revolution was no sooner accomplished than the State clergy turned Jacobite, deliberately repudiated the principles of the Revolution, which they had helped to make, and did their best to render the Hanoverian Succession impossible before it came to pass, and unpopular after. When George the Third came to the Throne and politics took a new departure, the State Church clung to her pestilent tradition. Her chiefs were the steadfast aiders and abettors in the policy which led to the loss of the American colonies; and then in the policy which led to the war with the French Republic. The evil thread of this monotonous tale has been unbroken, down to the last general election. That election turned upon the removal of an odious and futile badge of ascendancy from the Irish nation. The

Dissenters were to a man on one side and the dignitaries of the Church almost to a man on the other."

Mr. Morley might have shown in detail that the influence of the Establishment was exerted against the abolition of the slave trade and of colonial slavery, against the removal of Nonconformist, Roman Catholic, and Jewish disabilities, the repeal of the Corn Laws, the extension of the franchise, its protection by anonymous voting. With regard to the question to which Mr. Morley's work is devoted, it has been well said that "the educational history of England teaches as a matter of fact that, step by step, as the authority of the Church has been challenged, the area of education has been widened and its character reformed." We have already referred to the perversion of law and the violation of equality which have characterized the administration of the Elementary Education Act. We have only to add that the theory of that Act is the education of the children of the whole people under the management of the people themselves, acting by their elected representatives. The Establishment has done, and is doing, everything in its power to frustrate the intention of Parliament, and to prevent the popular management of national education, by resisting the universal establishment of School Boards; and its clergy are now engaged in a frantic struggle to get the control of the principal Boards, with the intention, if they can get the upper hand in them, of further maladministering the law in the interests of the Establishment. The continued existence of an institution which has opposed all the measures of reform which it is the glory of this nineteenth century to have carried, and which seeks to frustrate them after they are carried, is beyond all question hurtful to the political interests of the community.

Such are the premises upon which Mr. Miall submitted to the House the conclusion to which we entirely assent, that the Establishment by law of the Church of England ought no longer to be maintained. Mr. Miall might have also sustained two other objections to the Establishment. 1st. That it is a failure. 2nd. That it is unnecessary. We shall state these propositions more fully.

1st. The Establishment has failed to fulfil the purpose for which it was set up—viz., the supply of religious instruction and the means of worship to the whole people.

2nd. Whatever has been done towards remedying the failure of the Establishment to supply the religious wants of the people has been done by the voluntary principle alone, to which, therefore, the task may for the future be safely left.

The proof of these propositions is to be found in the history of the work done, and the progress made during the last forty-five years by the various Churches, Established and Nonconformist alike, in the great towns and in the country parishes of England and Wales.

Up to the commencement of the period we have named, "The Church of England," says Mr. Gladstone, "had been passing through a long period of deep and chronic religious lethargy," from which she was roused by the "political events which arrived in rattling succession." The events to which Mr. Gladstone refers were all, be it noted, destructive of those "exclusive claims on the part of the Establishment, which become positively unjust in a divided country governed on popular principles." All the while, however, that its foundations as an Establishment have been in course of being undermined, "the religious life throbs more and more powerfully within her." "During this same period," continues Mr. Gladstone, "the extension of the material and pastoral organization of English Nonconformity has been more rapid still."* It is to this period, therefore, that we shall look for the proof of our two remaining objections to the English Establishment. We will consider separately the two cases. 1st. Of the great towns. 2nd. The country parishes.

1st. In the great towns, say some of its defenders, "the Church is at her weakest," while others of its advocates point to these same towns as the great proof of the superiority of the Established over the voluntary principle. Let us look at the facts. To begin with the metropolis. At the time of Bishop Blomfield's appointment to the see of London, which was nearly cotemporaneous with the beginning of our period of forty-five years, the failure of the Establishment to supply the religious wants of the metropolis was as complete as it was evident. The Bishop proposed to form a "Metropolis Churches Fund," which Dr. Chalmers styled "a devout imagination impossible to be realized." The Bishop was a better judge of voluntary zeal than the great Presbyterian defender of establishments, and in eighteen years he collected for this fund 266,000*l.* This general movement gave rise to various local efforts, including "The Bethnal Green Churches Fund," by means of which ten churches were built and endowed. During the episcopate of Bishop Blomfield, he consecrated nearly two hundred churches, all of them built and endowed on the voluntary principle. Notwithstanding his labours, his successor, Bishop Tait, found that the growth of London was again leaving the provision for the Church's ministrations far in arrear. In 1863 the Bishop therefore boldly asked for a million to be raised in ten years, towards which at the close of the ninth year 430,000*l.* had been collected. The result, as compared with the original conception, is a failure, but it is sufficient for our

* "Chapter of Autobiography," pp. 23 to 28.

purpose. As an Establishment the Church has done nothing towards meeting the religious wants of the ever-growing population of London; whatever has been done has been done by the voluntary zeal and liberality of individuals amongst its ministers and members. Its wealth is mostly locked up in the excessive endowments of the City parishes, where it is wasted. Except in a few cases, regard to vested interests prevents these endowments being diverted to places where they might do some good. Had the Church been disestablished and disendowed forty-five years ago, its progress in the metropolis would certainly have been as great as—probably greater than—it has been. The progress of dissent in the metropolis, testified by the increased number of chapels and sittings during the same period, has been at least as great, if not greater, than that of the Establishment.

Let us now glance at the eighty-five towns of largest population in England and Wales, exclusive of the metropolis, containing an aggregate population of nearly six millions. In these the Establishment provides, on the average, within two-fifths of the means of public worship and instruction, and the other religious bodies a little over three-fifths. Here are some specific illustrations of this general statement. In one town, Brighton, the Establishment supplies such means for one-fourth of the population; in two, Bristol and Wolverhampton, for one-fifth; in seven of the largest towns, for one-seventh; in one, Salford, for one-eighth; and in two more, Sheffield and Newcastle, for one-ninth; and in one, Bradford, for only one-tenth of the population. What the Establishment fails to supply is supplied by dissent. In the fourteen largest towns the average provision of sittings by the Establishment is for about one-seventh of the population, against one-fifth provided for by Nonconformist Churches. In the older towns, such as Bath and Norwich, the Church supplies sittings for from 40 to 48 per cent. of the population. In newer towns and towns where the population is increasing, *e.g.*, as Cardiff, Bradford, and Merthyr, it supplies sittings for 7·7 per cent. only, while Dissenting Churches supply sittings for from 84 to 89 per cent. One cause of this difference between the Churches is to be found in the inelastic nature of the parochial system, and the legal fetters which prevent the free development of the Establishment, and its re-adapting its means and its machinery to the wants of the times. From these causes the Establishment, as such, does nothing to meet the wants of the growing populations, while it continues to supply an unnecessary amount of accommodation in places like Bath and Norwich, where the population is almost stationary, in others where it is decreasing, and in the City of London where it has migrated. What is true of the City holds good of Liverpool. So far as the churches in the old part of the town, supported by the corporation and the parish, at the ratepayers' expense, are concerned, they are for the most part nearly deserted on Sundays. At the same time the Establishment does nothing for the lower and more densely peopled districts of Liverpool, which are inhabited almost solely by Roman Catholics, whose contributions in support of their religion are a noble testimony to their self-denial. As a rule, indeed, the Establishment is strongest in districts where the wealthy reside, and Nonconformists abound in the poorer parishes. To revert again to London as an illustration. In St. George, Hanover Square, there were in 1865, 17 churches belonging to the Establishment and 8 to the Nonconformists. In the other parishes of Westminster, 22 Establishment and 10 Nonconformist churches. In the district of Islington there were 52 Nonconformist and 27 Established churches. In Hackney the Nonconformists possessed 40 churches, while those of the Established numbered only 15.

We have another fact to refer to in proof of the sufficiency of the voluntary principle to meet the religious wants of the large towns. In the twenty largest towns of England and Wales—excluding the metropolis—there were erected in the twenty-one years since 1851, by all the churches, established and non-established, together, but on the voluntary principle alone, 816 places of worship, containing 463,337 sittings; and while the population of these towns has increased at the rate of 43·5 per cent., the religious accommodation has been augmented at the rate of 46 per cent. It is instructive to note the rate of increase per cent. in the accommodation provided during this period of twenty-one years, by the different Churches. In the seventy-seven largest towns, the increase per cent. of such accommodation was, in the case of the Presbyterians, 150·9, showing how large is the emigration of Scotchmen to the southern side of the Tweed; Calvinistic Methodists, 140·5, showing how strong a hold the gloomy doctrines of Calvinism still have on the English mind, and pointing probably to a considerable Welsh element in the population of our largest towns; the Primitive Methodists, 108·6; the United Methodist Free Churches, 107·7. Against these the Establishment can only show an increase of 34 per cent., being equalled by the sect everywhere spoken against, the Unitarians, who show an increase of 34·4. The increase in the two Methodist bodies is most significant, as they are both—and more especially the Primitives—composed far more of the working and less of the wealthy classes than their parent body, the Wesleyan Methodists. The rapid progress of these bodies is an illustration of what *The Times*, in an unusual fit of candour, lately said of the work of Methodism generally:—

"The miracle we see before us this day is the fact of a body of near a million persons largely redeemed from the profligacy and irreligion of the age. The work Methodism is doing would not be done but for it, for the Church of England will not do it; all it does—perhaps all it can do—is to talk about it, declaim about it, write about it, argue about it, promise it, and invite people to do it; anything short of actually doing it."

The statistics* we have given sufficiently show that the Church of England, as an Establishment, has failed to meet the wants of our great towns; that what has been done to meet those wants, so far as it has been done by the Church at all, has been done on the voluntary principle, which has also supplied the means for the vast labours of dissent to do what the Church has left undone. So far as the great towns are concerned, therefore, the Establishment is a failure, and its further maintenance unnecessary.

2nd. We come next to the country parishes. Our readers will remember the picture of them given by Lord Selborne in the House of Commons—the Ecclesiastical Arcadia which he drew with such power, and coloured with such a Claude-like glow: the clergyman placed by the Church in every parish "to do the rural poor—who, according to the noble lord, are generally Church people—good in every possible way,"† and so doing it as to be regarded by them as a Providence in human form. It is difficult to realize the fact that an elderly lawyer should have so poetical an imagination. We have not, as in the case of the great towns, statistics at hand to substantiate our assertion; but, nevertheless, we think we can prove that the Establishment has failed to provide for the religious wants of the agricultural labourers; that it does not possess their confidence. We adduce, in the first place, the following admissions of its own ministers. In a remarkably outspoken sermon, lately preached before the University of Cambridge by the Head Master of Harrow, he propounded these suggestive questions:—

"Do we believe that the Church of England is a thoroughly popular Institution? Is it loved, clung to, appropriated by the masses of the people? Do they feel it to be their own? I do not say an Institution which is doing them much good; but their own, a society which shares their feelings, responds to their touch, lives and moves not only for them, but by them?"

Dr. Butler, in answering his own questions, frankly admits that "there is but too much reason to fear that the Church is losing her hold on the mass of the poor, and that the future is slipping from her grasp;" and that if this calamity—as the

* The source from whence our statistics is derived will be found in "Statistics of Religious Accommodation of England and Wales," 1872, published as supplements to *The Nonconformist*, Oct. 23, Nov. 6, Dec. 4, 1872; Jan. 5, Dec. 17, 1873. *Vide* also *The Liberator*, Feb. 1873.

† *Vide* "The Debate on Disestablishment," p. 18.

preacher naturally thinks it—is to be averted, "the poor must be disabused of all suspicion, however unreasonable, that the clergy hold a brief from the gentry to persuade them that subjection is the highest form of duty."*

We will next take Bishop Ellicott, from his position as Bishop, and his having reccommended the administration of a peculiar form of baptism to the leaders of the Agricultural Labourers' Union, he is not likely to be unduly hard on the clergy, or too sympathetic with the labourers. Speaking of the attitude of the clergy towards the uprising of the rural labourers, he admits "that many kindly palliations of a hard lot have been freely adopted, but anything like a systematic effort towards moral elevation, and improvement had never yet been made." Another Bishop—he of Oxford—at the recent Church Congress admitted that the Church had not always taught the duties of masters to their labourers as she ought to have taught them," and added—"perhaps we should not have come to our present pass if she had." Canon Ryle, himself a country clergyman, says, "There are hundreds of parishes in this land in which the Church of England is doing nothing practically for the souls of the people . . . . It is precisely here that our system fails and breaks down altogether." Another dignitary of the same rank and also a country clergyman—Canon Girdlestone—contends that, but "for the kindness of the clergy in the rural districts, the condition of the agricultural labourer would have been worse than it is," a statement which as regards many parishes we frankly admit to be true; yet the Canon acknowledges that "on the whole, it is true that the clergy have not taken the part which they ought to have taken in assisting the labourer to improve his condition;" and after surveying the life of an English peasant from his cradle to his grave, says, "Is this a happy, a just, or a proper state of things? Does it betray any large amount of 'paternal' feeling on the part of those [*i.e.*, the clergy] who might long since to a great extent have remedied it, and whose duty it was to make the attempt? Is it desirable to continue these so called 'paternal' relations."† At the Church Congress Mr. Llewellyn Davies owned "that the Church of England, greatly needs the help of Divine Grace to preserve it from an undue reverence for station and property, and to enable it to disown the ignoble task of bolstering up the privileges of the fortunate, and to claim the honours of a generous unworldliness, the sacred right of sympathy with the poor and the weak." Finally another clergyman, writing in *The*

---

* "The Relations of the Church to the Poor," Sermon before the University of Cambridge, Nov. 9, 1873, by H. Montagu Butler, D.D.

† Art. in *Macmillan's Magazine*, Sept. 1873.

Church Review, confesses "that the English people have more respect for Mr. Mill than all the clergy in the land." We leave the friends of the Establishment to reconcile these admissions of its ministers with the oft repeated assertion that it is the "Poor Man's Church." Let us now listen to the opinions of the working class. *The Labourers' Union Chronicle*, the organ of the rural labourers, contains almost weekly articles of great power on the relations between the Church and the Poor. We have space only for two extracts, but they are decisive.

"We have said that the labourer loves his Bible, and we say further, that he neither loves nor cares for the articles of the Established religion, nor the creeds of the Established Church."*

In another article commenting on the Bishop of Oxford's Church Congress speech—*The Chronicle* says:—

"The agricultural labourer wants not only higher wages, but he needs to be lifted up to a true, and noble, and intelligent manhood; and the Church, had it been a true Church, would long ere now have extended to him the hand that should have raised him. But this Church is itself dishonest and corrupt."

The subject is also discussed in *The Bee Hive*, which represents the working men of the towns, as *The Chronicle* represents those of the country. *The Bee Hive* says:—

"We know ministers of religion could not take money from the employing classes and put into the pockets of the employed; but they might have insisted on such a humane consideration and Christian regard for human welfare as would have so influenced men's dealings in regard to each other, as to have prevented the suffering and misery which have led to our present discussions."

It is well known that the leaders of the Labourers' Union are local preachers in the Primitive Methodist Church, which numbers amongst its members a large portion of the poor of our country parishes.

If we turn from England to Wales we find that the state of the Establishment cannot be better described than in Mr. Gladstone's words:—"What was meant for the nation has dwindled into the private estate, as it were, of a comparative handful." In fact, were a motion made in Parliament to extend to Wales the provisions of Mr. Gladstone's Irish Church Act, it would be impossible for him, with all his acuteness, subtlety, and power of reasoning, logically and consistently to justify the abolition of the Irish Establishment, and at the same time to uphold and defend the continuance of the English Establishment in Wales. While the alienation from the Establishment of the overwhelming majority of the Welsh people is so notorious as to render formal proof superfluous, it is equally true,

* *Labourers' Union Chronicle*, Aug. 10.

though not so generally known, that in Wales, where the Establishment is weakest, crime is weakest too. The small number of prisoners at Welsh assizes, the trivial nature of their crimes, and the contrast in this respect between the Principality and England, is often the subject of remark and congratulation by the Judges of Assize. We must close with the testimony of our own experience. These pages are written in one of the remotest parishes of Cornwall; and speaking with a knowledge of the facts gained by long residence in, and still longer connexion with the county, we unhesitatingly affirm that in Cornwall the Establishment is as weak as it is in Wales, and that, as in Wales so in Cornwall, with the weakness of the Establishment there co-exists a higher tone than common among the people, whom Mr. Bright has well described "as an industrious, a frugal, an intelligent, and a noble-minded population." Of the country parishes of Cornwall it may without exception be stated that their religious wants are supplied not by the Establishment, but by the voluntary labours of Dissent. Conversing on this subject lately with a friend, the incumbent of a large rural parish, made the following admission:—

"I am a Cornishman born, and have been a Cornish vicar five-and-twenty years, and if anybody tells me of the existence of a strong Church feeling in Cornwall, I don't believe it. I am excellent friends with all my parishioners, and they will do anything for me but come to Church."

At the last census this gentleman had the nominal care of 2174 souls, of whom seldom more than twenty avail themselves of his ministrations. His parish contains several Dissenting churches, the worshippers in which can be reckoned by the hundred. We will give another and a more precise illustration, which fairly represents the average state of things in Cornwall as regards the Establishment and Dissent. S——, a strictly rural parish of the extreme west, contained at the last census a population of 1182, scattered over 4471 acres. Taking Mr. Mann's estimate that sittings for 58 per cent. of the population is sufficient, the Establishment should in this case provide sittings for 685 persons. Towards this requirement it provides one church, which, supposing—what never occurs—every seat to be occupied, would accommodate at the most 400 persons, leaving a deficiency of 285 sittings, towards supplying which the Establishment neither does nor tries to do anything. What Dissent has done towards supplying the want appears from the following figures:—

Denominations.	Chapels.		Sittings.
Wesleyans	5	...	150
Bible Christians	1	...	700
	6	...	910

If we judge, not by the sittings provided, but by the number of services and of attendants on them, contributions to missions, Sunday schools, and other signs of religious energy and progress, we cannot help seeing that in S——, as in Cornwall generally, the religious life of the people is in the chapel and not in the church. Were the Establishment abolished, the small minority of the parishioners who avail themselves of its services—scarcely, if ever, exceeding 150 persons—would be absorbed by the various Dissenting churches, and no harm would ensue to the religious life or moral condition of the people. If like inquiries were made in other counties, we believe it would be found that the state of things existing in Cornwall prevails also in other parts of England to a much greater extent than is commonly believed.

From the admissions and opinions we have quoted, and the facts we have adduced, the conclusion, we think, follows that with regard to our country parishes, as well as our great towns, the Establishment is a failure, and its further continuance as such unnecessary.

It only remains for us briefly to point out the manner in which the disestablishment and disendowment of the English Church should be carried out. So far as disestablishment is concerned, we ourselves see no reason for departing from the precedent of Mr. Gladstone's Irish Church Act. We have seen an objection made to that part of the measure which provides for the recognition as a corporate body of the governing body of the Protestant Episcopal Church in Ireland, on the ground that it is a *quasi* re-establishment. We cannot appreciate this objection. There is not, in our judgment, any violation of equality in giving to any religious body which pleases to apply for it the conveniences afforded to associations, whatever be their object, by the power of acting "as one body politic and corporate, with perpetual succession and a common seal," to use the technical description of a corporation. If the Wesleyan Conference or the Unitarian Association were, for their own convenience, to apply for and obtain a charter of incorporation, they would be, in the eye of the law, simply corporations such as the North Western Railway Company or the Bank of England, and the conferring on them such legal conveniences would not involve the recognition by the State of any public ecclesiastical character in such corporations. When we come to disendowment, however, there must be a great departure from the Irish precedent.

Prior to legislation, there must be such an inquiry as Mr. Miall proposed in 1872 into "the origin, nature, amount, and application of any property and revenues appropriated to the use of the Church of England," in order that the public property in its possession may be clearly distinguished from property given by individuals to the Church of England *as it now exists.* Looking at the various phases the Church of England passed through in the reigns of Henry VIII., Edward VI., Mary, Elizabeth, and the two first Stuarts, it cannot, we think, be fairly said that any private endowments—if any there be given during those reigns—were given to the present Church of England; if there be such endowments, they are held by that Church by Act of Parliament, not by gift of the original donor, and may fairly be considered as part of the national property now in its possession. All the property in any manner given to or acquired by the present Church, *e.g.*, the vast number of churches, parsonages, and schools built within the last fifty years by individual gift or by voluntary subscription, must of course remain the property of the Disestablished Church.

The public property in possession of the Establishment may be classed under three heads.

1. The National Churches, *i.e.*, the cathedrals and old parish churches. 2. The tithe rent charge. 3. The estates—comprising under this last head the lands of the Bishops and Deans and Chapters (many of these being now in the hands of the Ecclesiastical Commissioners) and the parsonages and glebe lands of parochial Incumbents. With regard to the national churches it must in fairness be borne in mind that several of the cathedrals, *e.g.*, Hereford, Chichester, Exeter, Westminster, and we think Ely, have been either rebuilt or so much renovated by the voluntary contributions of members of the Establishment as to be in fact private and modern endowments. The same is true of many of the ancient parish churches. If Mr. Childers be correct in saying, as he did lately, that 2,000,000*l.* are now being spent yearly in the renovation, decoration, and beautifying of churches, it will soon be true of the greater part of such churches. With the exception of proved cases of this kind we think the churches should be vested in Commissioners, that the Episcopal sect should have a right of preemption or of occupation, on condition of maintaining them in repair; and that in parishes where the Episcopalians decline to purchase or cease to occupy or keep in repair the church, the Commissioners should be empowered to sell or let them on the same terms to any other denomination.

The great defect in the Irish Church Act is the manner in which, under the guise of commutation and other like devices, the Disendowed Church is permitted to retain a large portion of her wealth, and after her so-called "spoliation" remains the second richest Church in Europe; and we must profit by the experience gained during the passing of the Irish Act of the rapacity of ecclesiastics and the weakness of governments to insure that compensation in the English case shall be only for individual loss and not a re-endowment in disguise. We should, therefore, propose to deal with the tithe rent-charge in this way: on the death of each Incumbent the rent-charge should vest in the overseers, who should apply it to the local taxation of the parish, *i.e.*, the amount now raised in it for poor, police, county-highway, and in some and an increasing number of parishes the School Board rate. In the vast majority of parishes this would give a sensible relief to the now overburdened ratepayers. In some parishes the rent-charge would defray all the local taxation; in others even leave a surplus. In those cases where the surplus is of large amount, exceeding, say, 100*l.*, the excess over that sum should be paid to the Treasury as part of the general revenue of the country. Here is an illustration of the working of this plan in an ordinary case:—

Parish of S——.

Amount collected for Poor, Police, County, and Highway rate for the year 1872 .	£570 0 0
Amount at which the Vicar's rent-charge was assessed to Poor rate, 1872 . .	£321 0 0
	£249 0 0

In this case the relief to the ratepayers would be more than ten shillings in the pound.

Professor Fawcett* has pointed out that where farms are tithe free the landlords generally raise the rent by the amount which would otherwise have been payable as tithe rent-charge. In order to prevent our proposed benefit to the ratepayer being absorbed by the landlords in increased rents the question as to prohibiting by law any demand of higher rents, on the ground of the reduction of rates, would have to be considered. There remain the estates. With regard to the parsonages and glebes, we would give the church now holding them the right of purchase; in cases where this right was not exercised the Government should, on the death of the incumbent, resume possession of them for the purpose to which we shall presently allude. With regard to the episcopal estates the Government, on the death of each Bishop who shall be the lifeholder at the time the Act passes, should resume possession of them. With regard to the capitular estates, as they are held by Corporations, not sole, but aggregate, *i.e.*, the Dean and Chapter of each Cathedral or Collegiate Church, the more convenient course would be, on the dissolution of such corporations, which is a necessary part of disestablishment, for the Government at once to resume possession of the estates, paying to each member of the dissolved body for

* "Essays and Lectures on Social and Political Subjects," pp. 78, 9.

his life, an amount equal to his yearly share of the rents and profits. Those estates which have passed from Bishops or capitular bodies to the Ecclesiastical Commissioners would, subject to provision for any existing life interests, be at once resumed by the Government. There remains the question, How shall these large landed possessions be utilized for the public good? It is from this source that we should provide compensation for the owners of those advowsons which are private property, and whose rights would be abolished by disestablishment. No compensation, of course, would be payable in respect of advowsons which are held by the Crown, or by public officers, such as the Chancellor, or by Ecclesiastical or other Corporations, such as Bishops, Deans, and Chapters, or the Colleges of Oxford and Cambridge, in which no individual has any saleable right or interest. These, and any other *bonâ fide* claims for compensation which Parliament may sanction, should be provided for by the sale of a portion of these estates, as the natural fund from which to provide such compensation. This done, there would still remain large real estates. In conformity with the policy for many years advocated in this *Review*, we contend that these estates should not be sold or otherwise allowed to become private property, but should be, to use John Stuart Mill's phrase, "nationalized," *i.e.*, remain in the hands of the Government as the landowner, and be employed for the national benefit in such manner as the then state of public and parliamentary opinion shall sanction.

Since the foregoing pages were sent to press we have received the volume last mentioned at the head of this paper, containing "The Peek Prize Essays" on the maintenance of the Establishment. From the preface it appears that Mr. Peek, one of the Conservative members for Mid-Surrey, holds the opinion that, "though the mass of the people of Great Britain are, both by principle and by habit, deeply attached to their Church, great ignorance prevails as to its true relations to the State, and as to the grounds upon which such relation is to be defended and maintained."* He therefore gave the sum of seven hundred pounds to be paid to the writers of the three best essays on the maintenance of the Church of England as an Establishment. The award of the prizes was left to the Marquis of Salisbury, Rev. Dr. Hessey, late of Merchant Taylors' School, the Master of the Temple, and the Reader of the Temple. Out of 104 essays, the three published in the volume before us were selected as the best. The writer of the first, who received 400*l.*, is Mr. Hole, Rector of Loxbear, Tiverton; of the second, who received 200*l.*, Mr. Dixon, a Minor Canon of Carlisle; of the third, who received 100*l.*, Mr. Lloyd, whom we judge to belong to the Scotch

* "Peek Prize Essays," Preface, p. iii.

Episcopalians. None of these writers, so far as we know or remember, were previously known to fame. The passage explanatory of the donor's motives, which we have extracted from the preface, is a curious specimen of the "great ignorance" which, as the preface itself asserts, "prevails on the subject." "The people"—not, be it observed, of England only, but of *Great Britain*—are said to be "deeply attached to their Church." But to what Church? North of the Tweed there is an Established Church, to which English clergymen are in the habit of referring as the "form of schism established in Scotland;" while Scotchmen regard the English Prelatical Establishment as far too near akin to that Papacy which is an abomination to the Scottish mind. It cannot be said that the Scotch people are attached to the English Establishment; how far they are attached to their own is a question not under present consideration. On the very threshold of the volume we are therefore met by the fact, that Parliament maintains, in different parts of the Island, two Establishments, directly opposed to each other in the character of their doctrine and the theory of their Church Government; each Church asserting its own doctrine and government to be that alone divinely authorized "by Holy Scripture." This fact disposes of such pleas as those set up by Mr. Holo, that an Established Church maintains the safest guarantee of truth." As to Wales, we observe with amusement that, notwithstanding the fact of the prizes being offered was widely advertised in Wales,* not a voice from the Principality is raised in favour of the maintenance of the English Establishment. So much for its popularity with the *People of Great Britain.*

With regard to the essays themselves, they are the productions of clergymen, and exhibit the characteristics and defects of the clerical mind; they illustrate what we have said of the methods of treating the subject. The first two essays rest the defence of the Establishment purely on inductive and experimental grounds; the so-called scriptural arguments are not brought forward. In the third essay reference is made to the scriptural argument; chiefly, however, for the sake of combating the Nonconformist view of it. We regret that want alike of time and space prevents our refuting at length the arguments of these essays. We shall not, we hope, be thought presumptuous if we appropriate to ourselves the spirit of a grand passage of Hooker, where he says that he cannot stand to oppose all the sophisms of Romanism, only that he will place against them a structure of truth before which, as Dagon before the Ark, error

* "Prize Essays," Preface, p. iv., and the Welsh Advertisement in Appendix, p. 581.

will be dashed in fragments. This, we venture to think, we have done in the foregoing pages. We would refer the writers of these essays, and others like minded with them, to the recorded experiences of the working of a voluntary and unfettered Church which are just given to the world in the letters of the latest Christian martyr, John Coleridge Patteson. It is noteworthy how the missionary bishop, writing from the far distant Melanesian Islands, calmly contemplates as inevitable the disestablishment of the English Church, and refers his friends at home to the free development in the colonies of the Church, neither patronized nor controlled by the State, as at once an example, an encouragement, and a consolation under what he foresaw to be their approaching fate.*

We close this discussion with a few words on the present Parliamentary state of the question, and its future. It has now reached that position in which its debate is inconvenient to the leaders of both parties, inasmuch as neither party can say which of the two will earliest find it to their interest to make it a ministerial question. It will probably—as was the case with the Ballot—for some few years be annually brought forward, and be the subject of a division without serious debate. The position of the Liberal leaders is ambiguous. Mr. Gladstone says that the question will not be settled by him, but by younger men; but in his "Autobiography" he records, with regard to the Irish Church, that in 1865 he deemed the question "remote, and apparently without bearing on the politics of the day" (pp. 21, 22). Nevertheless, within three years Mr. Gladstone made the Irish Church the question of the day. Within another year he had disestablished and disendowed it. Events may again march as quickly, and it may be reserved for Mr. Gladstone to carry a similar measure affecting the English Church. Certainly his speech of last session was justly open to the criticism made on it, that it was very eloquent but did not ground his defence of the Establishment on any principle. "He deliberately," it was said, "left the back door open for escape at a future period; his policy was Janus-like, or in other words, double-faced." In fact, it has been truly said that on this question "the Liberal Ministry are without a policy."

With regard to the Conservatives, "Church and State" may be the cry of the rank and file, but their leader is cautious and reticent. Remembering his Reform manœuvres of 1866 to 1868, we should not be the least surprised to see him defeat the

* *Vide* "Life of John Coleridge Patteson, Missionary Bishop of the Melanesian Islands." By Charlotte Mary Yonge. London: Macmillan & Co., 1874.

Liberals on this question, in order that he may again "dish them," and carry the measure. We would recall to our leaders' minds the passage in "Coningsby" which says:—

"There is, I think, a rising feeling in the community that Parliamentary intercourse in matters ecclesiastical has not tended either to the spiritual or the material elevation of the humbler orders. Divorce the Church from the State, and the spiritual power that struggled against tyrannical monarchs and barbarous barons will struggle again in opposition to influences of a different form but of a similar tendency; equally selfish, equally insensible, equally barbarizing."*

Not without a purpose either was this ominous and pithy saying attributed to one of the characters in "Lothair." "Parliament made the Church of England, and Parliament will unmake the Church of England. The Church of England is not the Church of the English—its fate is sealed." Wherever it is necessary Mr. Disraeli can, *more suo*, refer to these passages to prove that he always was in favour of the separation of Church and State; that, in fact, it was ever one of the articles of the creed of so-called Popular and Constitutional Toryism.

Art. II.—The Metropolitan Police System.

We purpose in this article to bring before our readers the present state of that government of the metropolis which may be called for our purposes the metropolitan police system. Its administration is directed by the Commissioners at Whitehall Place; its judicial function is discharged in the metropolitan police courts. The working of this system as a whole has for a long time occasioned grave dissatisfaction: from time to time those who, by their habitual duties or by some special emergency, were compelled to observe its action, expressed their uneasiness in private; while at this moment the accidental arrest of some persons socially more conspicuous than the ordinary occupiers of a police dock has caused the public attention to be directed to the subject, has brought to light cases of noticeable significance, and laid bare a public danger. We take advantage of the state of the public mind to indicate that danger, to analyse the difficulty, and to point out the practical remedy for a state of things which, when known, can be satisfactory to no one, and with which

* "Coningsby," p. 260, Edit. 1853.

each one's dissatisfaction is precisely proportional to the extent and intimacy of his knowledge of the subject.

We will commence by a brief description of the police organization. We will take it first in its administrative, and then in its judicial aspect. The metropolitan police district has an area of 688 square miles. It contains the whole county of Middlesex, together with those parishes on the southern boundary of Hertfordshire, on the south-west of Essex, on the north-west of Kent, and along the north of Surrey which lie within the radius of fifteen miles from Charing Cross. But from this space must be excepted a district small in size, but by no means unimportant, lying at its very heart—the City of London—which, preserving its municipal integrity and independence, possesses also a separate police, judicial, and administrative organization. We mention this; we shall not again allude to it: with the praise or blame of the City police our article has nothing to do.

The area of metropolitan police activity is divided into twenty divisions, nineteen of which are land, each indicated by a letter of the alphabet, and one, wholly water, is the river Thames. The land divisions fall at once into two classes; nine town and ten country divisions. The town divisions are small in area, varying from a little under one square mile to a little over two square miles in extent, but densely peopled, and, lying around the centre of the circle, may be called "interior;" the ten country divisions narrow towards the interior, widen gradually towards the circumference, like the spaces in a wheel of ten spokes. They vary between fifty square miles, the extent of the smallest, up to eighty-four square miles, the area of the largest country division; and they may be called "exterior." Each division is under the charge of a divisional superintendent.

Each division is subdivided into smaller areas, called subdivisions, varying in size and shape according to local convenience. Where the population is dense, or specially difficult to manage, each subdivision is small; where the inhabitants are comparatively few, or are peaceable and orderly, it is of greater extent. Each subdivision has one or more police-stations within its limits, and the force within it is under the charge of an inspector. But to hold the organization well in hand there must be a closer control, and these subdivisions are themselves divided into sections. A section will contain a few streets, courts, and two or three hundred houses or so; or so many fields, lanes, villas, and more or less scattered houses or house-groups in the country sections. The number of the force posted in each section averages twelve. The men are quartered in a section house or in lodgings. They and the section are under the charge of a police-sergeant.

We may now, reversing our process for the purpose of getting a clear view, commence with the individual policemen. The whole police district is occupied throughout all its sections, town or country, by 7997 police constables, posted in small groups of about 12 men each, each group having charge of a section, and being under the command of a sergeant. Of police sergeants there are 903.

The sections with their constables and sergeants are, for purposes of common and united action, aggregated into subdivisions, each under the control of an inspector, and these subdivisions are again aggregated into divisions, each under the charge of a superintendent. The whole twenty divisional superintendents are held together by four chief, or district superintendents, and the total compound aggregate, as a whole and in its separate parts, is governed and administered by the commissioners.

Up to this point we have been dealing with the police system from within, we have shown how it is worked and bound together, we have now to show how it comes in contact with, and is brought to bear upon the general public, lawless and also law-abiding. We have now to deal with the 7997 individual policemen.

The whole metropolitan police district is divided into beats, so many beats to each section; but these beats are different as to size during the daytime from what they are by night. Night lasts for police purposes from 10 P.M. to 6 A.M. Day is from 6 in the morning till 10 at night. By day the beats are fewer and their respective areas larger in each section. By night the beats are smaller, more numerous, and patrolled by more men. The number of day-duty beats is 980, the number of night-duty beats 3500. The total length of beats along which by day and night the metropolitan police march in continual patrol is 6612 miles.

The day is divided into four watches: the night is one long watch. From 10 P.M. to 6 next morning, four-sixths of the whole body of constables are making their night duty rounds, in all the sections, country and town alike. The day duty in town districts is kept in four periods or watches by two sets of constables in two reliefs. The first relief in the early morning, and again during the earlier part of the afternoon, the second from 10 A.M. to 2 P.M., and again from 6 to 10 at night. In country sections, the watches last for eight hours; there is, therefore, a morning relief from 6 A.M. to 2 P.M., and an afternoon from 2 to 10 at night. Ceaselessly, along the outer or inner kerb-stones according to the time, of streets and squares, of lanes and roads, on round of duty, slowly—watchfully—on his path marked with most minute precision, paces each solitary man, alone yet part of one organic whole, just as through vein and artery, giving tone and health, or bearing disintegration and decay, pass in continuous circulation the corpuscles of the blood.

Each police constable patrols his beat with a mechanical yet ever varied regularity; the police-sergeant is here and there about his section; the inspector may be anywhere in his sub-division, while the divisional superintendent watches all. Now it is clear that the good working of the system with regard to the public depends on two conditions. On the sound judgment, watchfulness, and discretion of each individual policeman in each little emergency as it arises, and also on the discretion, judgment, and power of management which is possessed by the directors of organization at Whitehall. But whether the police system as a whole is employed in maintaining the freedom and free action of law-abiding Englishmen, high and low, respectable and rich, or poor and it may be discontented, or becomes an engine of repression, and we fall gradually into a police ridden people, depends upon another set of things: it rests with the character and idiosyncrasy, the firmness and discretion, or the weakness and vacillation of the Home Secretary for the time being, and who he may be depends upon the vote of the House of Commons; and who the members of that House may be, and what its nature as a whole, rests with us, the inhabitants of this United Kingdom, who have votes.

To return and complete our description. As each police constable being alone might easily be overpowered, and as the men of each section, or even division, might be inferior in numbers to some aggregation of roughs or criminals collected in a given spot, it is arranged that, by a method or plan easier to explain in detail *vivâ voce* than to set forth in writing, even if it were necessary or expedient, reserves of force can be gathered from all or any places where they are not at the moment wanted, and concentrated upon the disquieted area, and as the commissioners command the whole district, and the force is organized and united, while the roughs act in small areas, and have diverse and selfish interests, the peace of London may be held secure against violence. But when we look more closely into the moral basis on which this power rests (and so to look is what officials rarely or never will do), the power of so using a comparatively small but organized body against masses numerically far stronger, depends upon the respect in which the police are held, upon the general content amidst their rule and management, upon the content, discipline, and willing and loyal obedience within the force itself—such qualities can only flourish in a good and healthy soil—upon the general acquiescence and satisfaction of the *whole public, rich and poor,* and on the knowledge and intimate conviction on the part of the lawless, that the police themselves are law-abiding and incorruptible men, and that therefore these policemen, whether alone or few in number, may reckon on the support and assistance of the bystanders, or in times of grave perturbation, and such times may come, *or be brought on again*, on the fact that ordinary law worth citizens may be called to enrol themselves as special constables, and that, in such emergencies, they will come forth.

On this, in the last resort, rests our whole social edifice, this intricate structure of civilization ancient and yet new, for when in England order can only be kept by the constabulary, resting on the soldiers, and not on the citizens, behind and supporting the presence of the men armed to destroy human life, when in such a supposed case, they have to fire or to charge, with the last echoes of those volleys, before the blood-stains are washed out, either our freedom or our social structure will in effect have passed away, either repression must again and yet again repress, or in one crash of doom our paper credit wealth, our representative checks and counter-checks, our social comforts for the rich, our social hardships for the poor, our classes grinding one another, and comforted by our religious shams, the long-preserved continuity of our national life, snapped by the folly that could not learn and be wise in time, will sink to nothing out of sight, and vanish to that region where the ancient civilizations are.

To such a crisis we may, by an imperceptible process, come. If from a vague and indiscriminating irritability the general popular feeling, which till lately blindly approved, while those who knew were dissatisfied, now urges on an equally blind attack, and demands an ill-planned change; if to cure a too arbitrary and centralized system it requires as an improvement the more arbitrary control of a Minister of Police, and the still further adoption of the Continental system of minute and parental (so called) care and supervision of the public, instead of (as we shall show in detail can be done) infusing a healthy activity, on constitutional instead of arbitrary principles, for we intend to show what, in our judgment, is the exact nature and cause of the evil, and what is the exact thing to be done, and how to do it; if the popular feeling insists on any change, to do something, there is danger, either that our present police system may become paralysed and inefficient, or that our freedom may be placed among the things that are no more.

We have very roughly and slightly described the organization as a whole, and in its parts, and shown how it is held together and made to work. Let us now see how it is animated, and by what means information is diffused, and orders communicated throughout the mass. For this purpose is used the police telegraph, by which certain stations are connected with the central office at Whitehall Place, but this means of communication, though very perfect in the "interior" divisions, does not as yet extend to any place beyond the six-mile radius. For more regular purposes or for communication with more distant stations, the mounted police are employed.

Early every morning there is prepared at each of the twenty divisional stations an account of all occurrences of police interest during the previous twenty-four hours in the division. Fires, felonies, accidents, results of inquests, articles of value lost or found, instances of police misconduct, notices by policemen of their intention to resign, corpses recovered from the Thames, animals lost, stolen, or brought in, deserters, committals, absconded criminals. This is the Morning Report. With it is sent the Morning State, a complete record of the effective and non-effective members of each division, by which the central office knows in detail at all points the exact strength of the Force on which it can rely. The "Reports," and "States," with some other documents, are conveyed in despatch-bags by mounted policemen, now in process of being gradually superseded by despatch carts and driving policemen. The information, given in the most brief but clear form, is collected and put in type at once, and as the Morning Information is spread over the whole police district.

These Informations, a sort of printed journal of occurrences and Orders, are sent out from Whitehall four times a day, at 9.30 in the morning and at 1.30, 6.30, and 10.30 in the afternoon and night. On Sundays twice. At 6.30 P.M. daily, except on Sundays, are sent Police Orders, containing details of arrangements for traffic regulation, for boat races or similar events when they occur, promotions or degradations of policemen, transference from one station to another, dismissals, fines; also pawnbrokers' lists, convict lists, or a description of stolen property, and a hue and cry.

Four times a day regularly, and as often as necessity requires, in addition, there is communication between the central office and every divisional centre. And by this means notice of events, instruction, or warning of danger can be sent from any section in the district to the central office and thence to any other part. We have endeavoured to draw attention to the multifarious nature of the ordinary duties of the police, in order to show that they must either be men of intelligence and trusted with discretionary powers, or else, under a rigid mechanical discipline, be directed and governed from above. This agency of intercommunication, guided and controlled by the commissioners, is under the charge of the executive superintendent at Whitehall Place.

Besides, there is another agency, which we will only notice and pass on, as although important it does not come within the chief object of our article, we mean the Detective branch. "The strength of the detective force at Scotland Yard is 1 superintendent, 3 chief inspectors, 3 inspectors, 20 sergeants (one as clerk)." There are divisional detectives as well. Their functions we need not describe. There is also additional work, done by additional members of the force, directed and managed by the Commissioner at Whitehall Place, in the police supervision of the dockyards at Woolwich, Portsmouth, Devonport, Chatham, and Pembroke; and the difficult duties which late legislation has imposed in the working of the provisions of the Contagious Diseases Acts, on which the opinion of this review has been clearly expressed.

To sum up the duties of the police. They have to patrol the streets and roads, to answer questions civilly, to regulate traffic, to be on the alert in each emergency—a street row—a pocket picked—some one run over and hurt—an unowned dog—a fire, and its attendant crowd—a helpless or violent drunkard—a crawling cab—two buses "nursing" a rival—a street beggar at his trade—and all the thousand varying details of street life. Besides, to superintend public-houses and their frequenters, to watch the dangerous quarters, the thieves' kitchens, places like the New Cut and Ratcliff Highway, what burglaries are planned and foiled, what have succeeded and who accomplished them, all larcenies, and the guilty or innocent subjects of warrants, summonses, and cautions. Besides the police administration inspects and licenses stage and hackney carriages, and grants licences to drivers and conductors; inspects and regulates common lodging-houses, watches smoky chimneys, and warns and prosecutes those which smoke too much; takes charge of and restores when possible lost property, issues certificates to pedlars, licenses shoe-blacks to black shoes, licenses street messengers, keeps the doorways of many public buildings, preserves order at theatres, besides the work thrown on it by a Derby day or Boat race, a Hyde Park Reform Meeting, a riot, or by the visit of a Shah.

As to the organization of the police district, the co-ordination of its divisions and sections, all its routine and mechanical arrangements, all that appears on paper, its regulations—most minute—its instructions—so precise—its commissioners' reports, which testify to the satisfactory working of the whole system, the gratification of the public, and the "interior assent" of the force to all that is done *By authority*, or that authority may do: everything that skill, care, and organizing talent can do, has been done, all that inspecting, reporting, checking, and counter-checking, watching, supervising, keeping up a stringent and rigid discipline, can effect, has been accomplished; and yet—look out of the reports into the newspapers, let a man go about and use his own eyes, and his own ears—what is the reason of this difference? The machinery is perfect, but it is mechanical, repressive, lifeless routine.

We protest that we attack the system, not the men—the state of the law, not those who have to work that state, and make the best of it. They have a particular system to work, and they work that system well, so far as it goes. Divisional reports come in, informations and orders go out, and there is no hitch; the superintendents make things smooth to the commissioners, and the commissioner makes things smooth to the Government—*on paper.* They work the existing system and the system works, all goes well on the surface, and there is no one to see through and beneath into the real working and action of the whole thing. Take and read from the "General Orders and Regulations" its most admirable preface, read what is enjoined and provided as to apprehensions, evidence, gratuities, gossiping, numbers on collars and helmets, prisoners, public carriages, § 87, section houses, § 5, stations, § 7 and § 8, slang terms, command of temper—and any one who thinks will find occasion for reflection. We should not be in the least surprised if the commissioners on reading these remarks were simply ignorant of what there could be to blame. We will tell them. These and other little circumstances show that one fault of the system is that the men are *over-drilled.* They are not drilled too much in out-door evolutions, in carriage and alertness: they have only 14 days on joining the force, and about 20 *hours a year* afterwards (Report, p. 5). But they are bothered and hampered by vexatious minutiæ. We assert that any man who reads the regulations on gratuities and believes that they either could or would be carried out must know very little of human nature. But we expect to be told that they are carried out, because every reported breach of the regulation is severely punished, and very few breaches are reported. Just so. The rules work admirably to the official eye, but what of the thousand breaches which are found out and not reported? what of the ten thousand breaches which are not found out at all? We have no doubt that every infraction of any regulation which is reported to Whitehall Place, either, by a police officer or by one of the general public, is severely punished, but if every infraction of a regulation during one day was reported, Whitehall itself from Charing Cross to Parliament Street would not contain the informing throng.

With the exception of the black sheep in the body, we believe that to point out as we shall do whatever faults we have observed, will—if our criticisms are just though perhaps severe, they are certainly conceived in no hostile or unfriendly spirit, to a body of men with whom in the discharge of their difficult and trying duties we sympathize—be recognised as a valuable service, though it may be unpleasing at the time. And we do not deem ourselves hard on the Chief Commissioner, if we say that he seems to us to fail in that rare quality of estimating accuracy on paper, and routine order at its proper value. We think that he is judged by the public harshly for faults in the system which originated with his predecessor. Improvements have been introduced and adopted under his management, and the whole complexion of the management though it takes a tone from the superior officers, yet also gives imperceptibly a tone to them. To devise and carry out an effectual reform, men must be criticised from without. They must also be influenced from above. We are not at this moment alluding to Heaven, but to the Home Secretary. The public will expect much from the intellect and firmness of Mr. Robert Lowe, or, it may be, from the sound common sense and right judgment of Mr. Gathorne Hardy.

We can only glance at the system in its judicial aspect. The outer part of the district is under justices of the peace, its inner portion is under the metropolitan police magistrates. Of these there are 23 sitting in 13 police courts. They have a most difficult and laborious office to discharge. To be a perfect magistrate demands an almost perfect man. With testimony often of ignorant or untrustworthy witnesses, he must in the hurry necessary from the press of business deal a rough and ready justice by a sort of instinct. One point we direct attention to, and that is the tenure of office, and the relations between the Home Secretary and the magisterial bench, for this purpose we reprint a letter from *The Daily News* of Nov. 25. The charges made therein should be disproved, or the evils remedied.

THE POLICE FORCE.

To the Editor of the DAILY NEWS.

"SIR,—It is very easy to discover and denounce great abuses, and generally difficult to suggest a cure. This often arises from not discovering their root. There is not the smallest doubt that the police of the metropolis is in a most unsatisfactory state. But I think that, although Colonel Henderson cannot be considered an efficient or satisfactory chief, it would be very unjust to charge all the deficiencies and irregularities upon him. I have had, as you will acknowledge from the card I enclose, great opportunities of observing the conduct of this body, and I will venture to submit through you to the public some of my experiences.

"At a very early period of my career, I was instructed to prosecute a constable. The charge against him, which was fully substantiated, was that, being entrusted with warrants to apprehend the keepers of loose houses, he, instead of serving them, levied black mail, as a condition for not doing so. The case was heard before a magistrate not remarkable for either discretion or intelligence, but on this occasion he did what was right, convicting the constable. The result was that within three months the magistrate was dismissed, the policeman promoted.

"Several years ago I happened to be in Piccadilly at one o'clock in the morning, and saw a police-constable struggling with a drunken prostitute. She fell, and he threw himself heavily upon her stomach. I went up to him, and touching him upon the shoulder said, 'Why do you not get assistance, you will injure that woman.' He jumped up, and, seizing me by the collar, said, 'I take you into custody for obstructing me in the execution of my duty.' I cannot at this distance of time profess to give accurately all the incidents; but at one period a gentleman, then very high in the Government and now holding one of the greatest positions in the country, came up and expressed his indignation at the way in which the woman was being treated, upon which the constable, without touching him said, 'I take you into custody too.' 'What for?' said the gentleman, in great surprise. 'Oh, for many things; we know you very well.' The end of the affair that night was that some other policeman came up who probably knew one or both of us, and nothing more was done to either. There were, however, features which seem to me of great importance, and which I will proceed to relate. When the constable seized me, a tall, military-looking man, who had seen nothing of the affair, came up and said to the officer, 'I have seen all that took place; you are quite right. Here is my card. I shall be most happy to give evidence.' Well, I had taken the number of the police-constable, and next morning went to Marlborough Street to witness the end, and, if necessary, to give evidence. No charge was made, and it was stated that the woman had escaped. Being somewhat indignant at the whole affair, I wrote to Sir R. Mayne, stating the facts, and received the stereotyped reply that I could take out a summons. I merely answered that I should take my own course. I then got a message that the police-constable had been dismissed, which I believe to have been thoroughly untrue. Later than this event I was engaged in a case, in which, to my mind at all events, it was conclusively proved that the constables were in the habit of receiving bribes from the prostitutes frequenting Regent Street and its neighbourhood; and that those who did not or could not pay were sure to find their way into the station house.

"In the Pelizzioni case, with which I am quite familiar, a knife was found by the police in a place which made it impossible that the accused could have committed the deed if done by that knife. All mention of it was suppressed by them. He was convicted, and might have been executed. It was only upon a second trial that the fact was dragged out of them. I believe all of the constables engaged on that trial have since been promoted. I could give other instances, and I will briefly allude to one. There had been many robberies committed in a particular neighbourhood. The police were blamed. Beyond all question they 'planted' upon two or three perfectly innocent people of bad character, and charged them with an attempt at burglary. Two of the police were convicted of perjury. There were no funds to go on with other charges, and so, somehow or other, they escaped punishment. I dare say the public will ask, what remedy is there for this state of things: I can only answer that the first step is to make the police magistrates, who really stand between the police and the public, independent of the Government. Let them be placed upon the same footing as the judges. I will conclude with an illustration, supporting this view. An old magistrate, nearly related to myself, decided against the Government in some revenue matters. He received the opinion of the law officers of the Crown, with almost an order to be governed by them. He adhered to his own. The Government dared not dismiss him, but they shut out from him the change from a disagreeable jurisdiction to one more coveted, and practically, by this means, drove him to resign. I could relate many other incidents, but your space will not permit it, and I conclude by saying that in my opinion, formed upon no small opportunities of judging, the police are, as a body, utterly untrustworthy, and that the magistracy have not sufficient force and independence to correct the evil.—Yours obediently, S. L."

It is our duty now to present the practical reform and changes in the law itself, and in its administration which we deem necessary and desirable; and to become ourselves in due course the subject, and the willing subject of our readers' criticism. We have four principal suggestions to make.

The great difficulty in devising at the outset and in working afterwards such a system as the metropolitan police administrative and judicial arrangements, is that the police have such various and dissimilar duties to perform, and that there are so many and different classes and characters with which they come in contact. Let us endeavour in a rough and ready way to classify them.

1. They have to deal with habitual criminals, unruly vagabonds, and brutal roughs, with these they have to wage continual war.

2. They have to deal with vicious and disorderly people, persons who cannot be called criminal or anti-social in the same sense as the first class, but who, nevertheless, become with more or less frequency according to the individual instances, the subjects of police discipline and control; such are those who are the willing or remorseful examples of our terrible national vice of drunkenness, and all those who are the causes and consequences of prostitution and profligacy.

3. They have to deal with law-abiding and respectable citizens, rich and poor, in a thousand ways we need not specify, as particularly in the management of the streets and of street traffic. As to the whole subject of notices, it is clear that

the duty of reporting and serving a notice under the Smoke Nuisance Abatement Acts (there were 2356 reported cases in 1872), or the duty of licensing or summoning a cab driver, or omnibus man, or a case of street accident, is quite different, and requires quite other treatment from anything falling under classes 1 and 2.

4. They have to deal with political demonstrations, and agitations great or small. This is perhaps the most difficult of all their multifarious duties. Sometimes it brings them in relation to large multitudes of more or less orderly, and more or less excitable men, at times when party or class feeling is strong, and political passions on all sides run high.

5. They have to deal with riotous mobs, or mobs which may suddenly become riotous and dangerous to social freedom, to property, or even to life. And the chief difficulty in dealing with instances of the fourth class, is that there is always a danger in the complication of some peculiar emergency of such cases suddenly becoming an instance of this class.

I. Violent usage of the public at the hand of police-constables in making arrests, must, in all justice, and in order to an adequate comprehension of the question, be looked at with reference to the violent usage which constables are liable to, and do in fact receive from a certain portion of the public. The matter must be dealt with as a whole. The state of the law and the administration of the law is to blame. The interest at present manifested in the police system gives an opportunity for drawing attention to the proper remedy, but we have long felt indignant that a state of things so easily set right should endure. If the police had only to deal with persons falling under the first and second classes, or to those belonging to the third and fourth, the difficulty would probably never have been felt. A police-constable has to deal with all classes; he may infer, but he can seldom be *certain* in making an arrest to what class the individual to be arrested really belongs. Let us try to bring before our readers' mind an arrest of a person falling under our first class, that is, of an habitual criminal or a rough. Such people strongly object to be taken into custody, and they endeavour to make an arrest difficult. Let us see how they do so. They have a simple plan to which they usually have recourse. There is a part of the body which our social usages render it more seemly for us to indicate than to name, a blow upon which causes intense pain and temporary incapacity for activity. And your regular rough or habitual criminal on being taken up will infallibly, if he can catch the constable off his guard for a moment, administer to him a brutal kick, and if successful will make off. And therefore the object of the constable in effecting the apprehension is to incapacitate him from putting in practice his little game. He approaches warily, and darting his left hand under the prisoner's arm, seizes his collar, getting his knuckles against the prisoner's throat, while at the same instant he throws up and pinions with his right hand the prisoner's right wrist. Practice makes perfect. In a moment the rough is as safe as if he was in quod, for he must stand off, and sideways to the policeman, and he may kick as much as he chooses, but he can only kick the air, and unless there are pals around to effect a rescue, or there is an unusual disparity of weight and strength, he is securely marched away. Is this such a mode of making arrests as should take place in a civilized nation? It is a simple collision of physical force. Discipline is on one side, disorder and lawlessness on the other, but nothing higher than brute force has been brought to bear.

Though we reprobate his conduct, we do not pronounce indiscriminating censure on the rough. He knows that if he succeeds he has another day, or more perhaps, at large; and even if he is caught, magistrates, sanctioned by the public apathy, will deal very tenderly with his misdoing. One sturdy vagabond whose intelligent countenance we shall probably see at his post to-day has temporarily maimed several policemen, and permanently injured one so that he had to be pensioned off. For that case he was punished extra; for the others, the magistrate remarked to him that his conduct was extremely wrong, and must be put a stop to. It is actions not words that take effect with criminals. And it cannot be suspected that wrongs which do not stir the public conscience, will move the conscience or touch the heart of the criminal and the tramp. Neither do we greatly blame the magistrate, although we do blame him. He has to administer the law in accordance with public opinion, and the public, though always well meaning, are apt to take strange views when half informed as to the facts. It is with the thinking and governing classes that the true blame rests.

But all wrong-doing widens in its range, like the little splash whose ripples gradually spread over the quiet surface of the pool; and precautions which are necessary in the case of habitual and violent drunkards, are little by little made use of in ordinary arrests. There is a general tone of violence encouraged, and our judgment is that there is wonderfully little considering human nature, the circumstances in which, in out-of-the-way places, the police are placed, and the state of the law. For it is always hard in the case of an unknown person, as we said, to be sure of what sort he is. It is not alone the burglar, the smasher, the drunkard, and the tramp, who are more or less known, or recognisable, against whom the policeman has to guard. An apparently orderly person may have strong private reasons for dreading an arrest, and it may be worth his while to get away at almost any cost. He may be a well-dressed pickpocket, a forger, an embezzler of goods: your darkest criminal often passes for respectable until he is found out. So the policeman gets to take precautions in all doubtful cases, and generally to make himself secure.

Further, it is not assaults of this particular kind alone to which constables are liable. We believe that *Punch* remarked in his facetious way that the enjoyment which gave most pleasure at least cost, to such as were so inclined, was to punch a Bobby's head. And we will just mention a little incident, for the correctness of which in the details we vouch. A certain person sold his sister's bed and proceeded to drink the proceeds. She, naturally objecting, complained, and a policeman, whom we will call Policeman 1, proceeded to make the arrest. The man was violent and strong, there was a scuffle, he knocked the policeman down five times, and in the crowd which gathered he got away for the time. The policeman did his best to take him, he could do no more. He went back to the station, and reported himself unfit for duty. Policemen 2 and 3 were sent out to find the fellow and to bring him in. They came upon him up a court, arrested him, and walked him off. There met them on their way Policeman 4, animated by *esprit de corps*, and by a certain wild justice of revenge. *Instigante diabolo*, as the old writs used to say, he hit the prisoner a tremendous blow with his closed fist, and the man collapsed. Now Policeman 4 was very wrong, he took the law into his own hands, and we would have punished him severely if he had come before us. But yet we could not have helped feeling that something like this probably went on in the man's mind, he felt "This scoundrel, who has wronged his sister, and done all the damage he could to one of my comrades who never injured him, will go before a magistrate and get off scot free; shall he go altogether without getting his deserts? Let him take that!" And we believe that although the others felt that an illegal action had been done, still that the less said about it the better; for that a thorough blackguard had got what he would not have got at all, or only got by accident in a police-court—justice.

Violence reacts in violence, and wrong returns upon us from unexpected quarters; and when wrong is done and suffered no man may stand aside and say it cannot possibly affect himself. It may not or it may. At all events we all suffer from wrong-doing to which we were not parties, we all are gainers by noble deeds and lives in which we had no share. Vicarious suffering and vicarious benefit fills the world. That violence which the public acquiesced in while only law-breakers and law-guardians were the sufferers is now seen to spread far and wide. The surgeon or the merchant may be affected, respectability may be touched, and that which, while it was a question of principle disquieted the statesman and the philosopher, now disquiets to some extent society itself. This is the beginning; we do not look only to what is, but also to what may be. If the police became unmanageable, or were felt to be unworthy of the public trust and confidence, the anarchy of a single day would cost its thousands and undo the work of years.

We have to deal in legislation in this instance with criminal actions, which are easily definable, and to which we can mete out appropriate punishment. We suggest that wherever a person arrested, or about to be arrested, shall make an assault with intent to do grievous bodily harm, leaving bruises upon any person lawfully arresting him, and shall be convicted of doing so (in the way we shall hereafter point out), he shall receive punishment with the cat. Just as garroting at once disappeared (after that propitious garrotment of a member of Parliament), so these assaults on the police and simultaneously violent arrests by the police will vanish. As to pity for such criminals, the dastard craven who commits a brutal assault is not an Englishman, a freeman, or a man.

In each case the act *should be done*, and of such assaults the proof is always easy. In the case we mentioned the policeman's face and shoulders showed the effects of that scoundrel's blows. And the sure punishment of accomplished assaults will prevent attempts. For there is nothing your genuine vagrant and criminal is so careful of as his own stomach, nothing he guards so tenderly as his own skin. When he knows that a successful assault of a particular nature or violence means a flogging, he will be careful not to make an attempt which, if successful, would produce a thoroughly disagreeable result.

With the cessation of violent assaults on the police, police violence will also disappear. For it will be unnecessary and inexcusable. Of course in arresting a violent drunkard the policeman must use precaution. We wish, and the Legislature can cause, that a policeman's uniform should be his sufficient protection. But this suggestion which we have made must be taken with and accompanied by our third suggestion.

II. The internal discipline of the police, and the relations between the commissioners and the force, will be the subject of this suggestion.

We mentioned that police orders are sent out every evening.

Let us make an extract from one of these orders, and show the form in which they appear (altering names, dates, and numbers); we only give as an example what is of continual occurrence.

DISMISSAL.—K. P.C. 937 Smith; no pay.

By this order a police constable is sentenced to be dismissed.

FINES, &c.—C. P.C. 756 Brown, 10s. and cautioned.
L. P.C. 643 Jones, transferred to another Division.
M. P.C. 630 Robinson, cautioned.

REDUCTION.—H. P.S. 941 Green; to 1st Class P.C.; pay as P.S. to 10th.

and so on, and to these orders is subscribed the name of an assistant commissioner.

Now the point to which we wish to direct our readers' attention is this. Here is a policeman dismissed the force, and several fined, transferred, or reduced in rank. Police-constable Brown has been fined ten shillings and cautioned. Jones is removed from Lambeth and transferred to another division. Robinson, of the Southwark division, is cautioned without a fine. Police sergeant Green has been degraded to the rank of a police-constable of the 1st class, but receives his pay as sergeant up to the day before the order. Police-constable Smith of the Stepney division is dismissed, and the pay due to him forfeited. It may be supposed that the man in each case knows what he is punished for; nevertheless, to the body, as a whole, each order appears as an exertion of arbitrary power. *Stet pro ratione voluntas.* There is no reason given. And so the effect of each sentence in the way of warning or example is lost. There is not the least doubt that the commissioners as well as the whole force would much prefer that the ground of each sentence was briefly stated. The power of dismissal without cause expressly assigned being, where it might be expedient, retained. And the reason why it is not set forth plainly is not far to seek. The commissioners would be liable to an action for libel. In fact, actions have been brought against them before now.

We would therefore strongly urge that since the police orders, although published, only circulate among the police force; it should be enacted that such orders be held to be of the nature of privileged communications, and that no commissioner should be liable to an action for libel, unless the plaintiff was prepared to prove malice and the absence of *bonâ fides* on his part. Arbitrary power there must be to some considerable extent in the government of such a force, as there is in the case of the captain of a ship, but the power as, under present conditions, it is exercised, is represented as irrational besides.

For tyranny ever lurks near irresponsible power, and in the police administration cases of great hardship have occurred. We will give one instance, which took place in the time of the late Chief Commissioner, the process is the same now; we select this case because we have verified the facts, and we use it to illustrate the method of procedure.

Sergeant S—— was temporarily incapacitated for duty by injuries received; during his illness Sergeant M—— was placed in charge of the section. He made an unwarrantable arrest under circumstances which caused great local indignation. Many complaints were made, and among others an anonymous letter was written to the Chief Commissioner, bringing certain charges against Sergeant M—— and demanding his dismissal from the force. The accused when shown the letter, declared that it was written by Sergeant S——, and he was believed. It seems to us that in police cases generally, to be accused and for the accusation to be credited, is the same as to be condemned without redress. So then at 12 o'clock on a Saturday night, the inspector of the subdivision with Sergeant M—— called on Sergeant S——, and required him to appear at 7·30 next (Sunday) morning before the superintendent. After a few words, the superintendent, as one may say, found a true bill, and ordered him to present himself at Scotland Yard next morning. There, after two hours' inquiry, careful indeed, but one-sided, before an assistant-commissioner, he was suspended for a month, pending Sir Richard Mayne's decision, who had just gone away from town. On his return, three weeks afterwards, Sergeant S—— was summoned at 11.30 P.M. to appear before the commissioner next morning. A short inquiry, and he was dismissed the force. Twelve years as a constable, eight years' as a sergeant, twenty years' good service stood him in no stead against an accusation based on mere opinion. But it may be said he was guilty; the inspector and Colonel (then Captain) Labalmondiere, and the commissioner believed him to be so, and he got his deserts. It is the arbitrary method of procedure we wish to call attention to. There is no security against prejudiced judgment. But was he guilty? The local bench of magistrates believed him innocent, and petitioned to that effect. Influential neighbours exerted themselves, everything was done. The commissioner refused to reconsider his judgment, or *even to produce the letter* until compelled. Then, by comparison of handwriting, the best-known expert certified in a report that it was impossible that the writing could be by the same man; and after an investigation of all the circumstances the Home Secretary, compromising a matter of plain justice, awarded Sergeant S—— from the police fund 100*l.*, but did not give him his good service pension or restore him to the force. Either he was guilty or he was not. There is sufficient moral evidence to satisfy any impartial person that Sir R. Mayne afterwards knew that he had been wrong and made a blunder.

We believe that the arbitrary exercise of almost irresponsible authority is the reason of the discontent and insubordination lately shown to the public by the mutiny. It is not the being under irresistible power, but the consciousness that power firmly grasped is exercised with careful justice that causes content, loyalty, and discipline. We have taken an old case, which came before us in investigating this subject, as an example, in other cases we should do harm. We would remark that a probable reason of a policeman's anger at having his number taken, is that he will become subjected to fine, probably to dismissal, practically without redress.

III. Our next suggestion concerns the judicial side of the police system: we regard it as of very great importance. The offences and charges which become the subject of magisterial action in the police courts we may divide for present purposes into two classes—1st, those in which both the plaintiff and defendant are members of the general public; or if a policeman is plaintiff he appears only as having served a notice or a summons, in fact, merely as putting the law in motion; and, 2nd, those in which a police-constable is charged with having used unnecessary violence in making an arrest, or in which he has been the subject of violence himself. We propose that all such cases of charges against or by the police should be tried in the following way.

Let there be a Central Police Court, in which a magistrate, to be called the chief police magistrate, shall sit to judge such offences with a jury, and let them have sole jurisdiction in all such cases throughout the whole metropolitan police district. The power of inflicting flogging ought not to be entrusted to the discretion of any one, or even two magistrates, but it may fairly and constitutionally be lodged in a magistrate with a jury of free Englishmen. And where a policeman has made a violent arrest, the complaint against him should not be heard in some private room in an office, before officials who may select the evidence they please to receive, but before a magistrate and jury in open court. We have no doubt that those policemen who feel themselves guilty will prefer the present system: we are quite sure those who know themselves to be innocent will prefer the one we suggest.

As to the jury, we will cause that jurymen offer themselves voluntarily. At present, merchants, professional men, tradesmen great and small, to all of whom time is valuable, and it is of moment that they may know that they are free and able to keep the business engagements which from time to time they make—these and other persons also are liable to be summoned suddenly on a jury, and left hanging about a court, which is the most provoking part of the system, waiting day after day until their attendance is required. Let it be made law that any one whose name is on the jury panel at present may be permitted to place his name on the jury of the chief police magistrate's court, stating the period during which he is willing to be summoned. Let him say, for example, on any day in the months of or . Let the names be drawn out by chance one after another, and assigned to particular days, each jury to sit for a whole day; and to prevent the possibility of packing, let every drawing take effect at not less than fourteen days after the date of drawing. No one then can tell what cases he may have to try; and every juryman, after discharging this duty for one whole day, should be exempt from the liability to be summoned to serve on any other jury during the next twelve or perhaps twenty-four months. We would enable any one who suffers or may suffer from the present system, and who is inconvenienced and harassed by its uncertain operation, to substitute the voluntary discharge of a duty in a mode by which he may select the time during which he can perform his public duty without injury to his private business. We have merely sketched here the principle we suggest. We have thought it out in detail; but a review is not the place for bringing forward details which are of necessity dull, especially where a principle can be carried out in many forms.

We shall now touch upon the remedies which we have for wrong-doing and excess of duty and assaults by the police, and also on what, in our judgment, ought to be the state of the law. If a man has been assaulted with violence, or illegally arrested by the police, he may complain to the Chief Commissioner, and ask him for redress. This seems to be perfectly satisfactory to the official mind; but in the old days, although the law was sometimes overborne by the violence of king or barons, or by the injustice of political parties, the English Nation never permitted the rights of Englishmen to lie at the discretion of any official. That was a Continental peculiarity abhorred by English freedom. When an Englishman was wronged, he did not go to the official persons who presided over the body which had done him the wrong, and crave from their courtesy or discretion that they would help him. No; but he went before a jury of his countrymen, and the judges of the land, and demanded justice from them as his birthright. It may be said that he can do so now. Technically he can, but practically he cannot. For many reasons in most cases a criminal prosecution would be inapplicable, and a civil action is useless. 'Where is the good of bringing an action against a constable on four-and-twenty shillings a week? The aggrieved person may, either by complaining (for the Commissioners will take action on any valid complaint), or else by bringing an action, ruin the police-constable in fault, but that is not what we want. We want a law so enacted and administered that under it offences will have a tendency to cease. We want a law which will not be called upon, because, by its mere enactment, it will have done the work required to be done. The Garroting Act is not useless, because garroting, immediately on its enactment, ceased. Rather on that account it is eminently good. It is not only an instance of *post hoc*, it is *propter hoc* as well.

We propose that any one who is aggrieved by the police may come before the Central Police Court and demand damages *against the department*. Let the Commissioners take care not to enlist or retain in the force men who will offend. A jury will not be prone to give damages unduly, because they must come out of the rates, which the body from which the jurymen are drawn have to pay; but in cases of real wrong they will give damages, and do justice to their fellow citizen, as they are sworn. Let damages assessed by the jury be given and paid, as the force are now paid, three-fourths out of the rates and one-fourth out of the imperial revenue.

IV. We are, for our own part, thoroughly convinced of the importance of our three first suggestions; this one we make with diffidence. We are sure that it is good in principle, but whether it is expedient to be carried out *at present* we have some doubt. We are indebted for the idea to a very valued friend.

Continued routine work has a tendency to convert a man into a machine. Even if it does not demand great physical or intellectual exertion, still, if it is monotonous, it becomes a heavy and oppressive toil, especially if it involves the observance of many minute and harassing regulations. It is proverbially true that, "All work and no play makes Jack a dull boy."

"*Apollo*"—that is, the policeman—"*semper arcum tendit*," his attention is ever on the stretch. The same round of duty goes on through the whole seven days of the week. We hold that unceasing work of any kind, day after day, without an express provision for periodical intermission, is injurious to the well-being of the workers. A great improvement was introduced some time ago, under a Conservative Administration. The number of the police was increased, and as we are informed, every policeman was given four holidays in each month. The result was that, owing to the way in which the leave was spent, the majority of the leavetakers were incapacitated from work on the following day. The conclusion drawn therefrom is that the principle of the regulation was bad. Now we submit that such a deduction is not correct.

By the present regulation (Leave, p. 137, § 1), "Leave is to be granted to every man twice a month, one day to be invariably on Sunday." This is a good rule, but it is not based on any principle. The principle we advocate is that no man be compelled to work for more than six consecutive days; but we would recognise, and *expressly recognise*, the fact that the necessities of the national life of a civilized nation require that many occupations and processes should go on without any interruption. At present our Sunday legislation, dating as to statute law from the religious and moral reign of King Charles II., is based on a commandment promulgated in a religion we do not profess, and on the custom deduced therefrom by the Christian Church or Churches. We take the fact that England does observe a rest of one day in every seven, and that on the whole we find it good in practice; we place this on a sure ground apart from theological belief. The form we would let our proposal take in enactment is, When any man has worked during the working portion of six consecutive periods of twenty-four hours each, let him have by statute a right to rest during the next following period of twenty-four hours. And as it is perfectly certain that employers would take care to make their servants renounce this right, we propose that no work or occupation may go on incessantly unless this proviso is observed.

This law, we maintain, is just in such a nation as ours is, which practically observes the Sunday, and yet contains men of many religious beliefs. Under it whoever wished to keep his Sunday for religious worship would make his six periods begin with 12 o'clock between Sunday night and Monday morning, his seventh period then would be Sunday. But men who did not care to observe that day would make their time begin at some other point, and so their period of relaxation would be Monday or Tuesday, or any other day, which they could spend as they chose.

We make, however, one proviso. We have a moral purpose chiefly in this enactment. We wish to provide seasonable or regularly recurring relaxation for all who deserve it. But if a man passes his day in drunkenness or other degradation, and is thereby incapacitated for work, we do not wish to do an injury to him. He is best under continual work. If, then, a man is unable to work on the day following his rest, we take from him the benefit of our law for a certain period, to be settled.

We have inserted this suggestion, though it may be Utopian, and perhaps it would be difficult to carry it through Parliament.

Our first three suggestions, we believe, may and will be carried; as to this, we submit the thought to consideration. It is capable of wide application. Its principle concerns our railway companies and all occupations requiring continuous work. There are processes, especially in the manufactures of iron and glass, in which the employment of many persons is endangered by the competition of nations who can carry on continuous work, such as we tolerate by a violation of principle in our railways, or which we refuse to notice in other cases.

Small matters frequently occurring become of more importance in the general working and effect of a system than things which, though of great moment in themselves, are also rare. And though space prevents our entering fully on this aspect of our subject, we may not pass it altogether by. The police system shares in a tendency which has been for some time manifested generally in our legislation. Just as Parliament has undertaken to superintend *the details* of all possible subjects, ranging from minutiæ of ecclesiastical discipline to the regulation of salmon fisheries and the healthy state of prostitutes, so the police system tends steadily to interfere more and more with the free activity of our daily life; and by so doing it becomes proportionately less efficacious in the discharge of its proper duties. By incurring responsibility which ought not properly to belong to it, the police neglect duties and work which no one except themselves can discharge. The police system, like our late legislation, is becoming fidgety and fussy.

This fidgetiness and fussiness is a great and growing evil. Instead of Parliament being the supreme authority to which all yield a willing and loyal assent, it is tending to become a supporter of the advocates of one theory against others. And the wider the interference the less is the effective control. It is so by natural law—the expression of facts—which Parliament, like everything natural or artificial, must exemplify. And so more and more, day by day, is pressed upon us the conviction, that the only security for our cherished freedom, and for our independence and responsibility, in a word, for our national life, is to be found in watchful exertion, carried on under well-grasped principles, in defining and limiting the range of legislative interference (not of legislative authority), and so in making such interference effective and responsible within that range.

A well-devised law requires some thought to perceive its meaning and action; a command bad in principle is often clear. High protective duties create smuggling, smuggling creates coast-guards; then hasty legislators set to work to increase the stringency of the repression, but wise legislation creates low duties and free trade. Prostitution and drunkenness are terrible evils; legislators before now have punished fornication and drunkenness by death, and produced demoralization and appalling reaction against good order and religion. And yet we do not advocate a *laisser faire* legislation. Good legislation never leaves evils alone, but it takes them in hand in an effective way. We may not touch upon the questions now, but we are persuaded that the present state of the law as to the sale of indecent and obscene publications directly tends to aggravate the evil it is meant to put down. We would undertake to prove this (with every proper diffidence personally towards those who support opposed views: it is not we but our principles that are right)—we would prove it face to face, and convince any impartial person, though we should probably provoke a storm of anger at first. We do not propose that the sale of such publications should be treated as a legitimate trade. We differ as to the best mode of causing it to cease. And what we say of this we say of other more complex matters, such as the state of the law as affecting prostitution, and of other more easily discussed questions, such as the licensing system as relating to public houses, and the whole great and difficult question of the Poor Law. There are tendencies in our recent legislative action towards either ignoring or stamping out evils, rather than towards altering the conditions under which the evil exists.

We have had a good deal of heroic legislation—so-called. Let us hope that under which ever party Government is to be carried on, we may enter on an era of legislative action, much needed to consolidate our power, which by heroic people may be called *humdrum*. We wish to see some quiet unostentatious humdrum legislation, grappling with the many evils before us. We offer our suggestions on the police system as a sample.

As to the effect of the legislative action we have sketched in outline. Let us observe what, in its present state and under the proposed reform, a man who may contemplate entering on the occupation of a police-constable has now in contrast to what he would have before him under our law.

There are two ideals which the nation might aim at in police administration. The one to carry out completely among us the Continental police system, by organizing a *Gens d'armes régime;* the other, to reanimate and make effective the old office of conservators of the peace. The one institutes an organized mass of men trained to carry out with exactness, in a mechanical way, many and minute regulations, referring at every moment to the central authority in each emergency for direction; by this the men become more and more machines, and for human action is substituted a system, precise, strict, drilled, and dead. The other institutes a disciplined multitude of rational and self-governed men, responsible each one and each rank to the nation for intelligent action in a carefully defined range of duty, each one free within limits, and each one limited exactly, guided and governed by a central responsible authority, prescribing the course of action of each one, and of the whole, and that authority itself intelligent, limited, and free. Both ideals are before our Government, both are partly followed, and it is not perceived that they are antagonistic.

Which ought England to adopt? Which would offer most inducement for enlisting to the set of men we wish to attract.

At present a man who joins the force must be prepared to suffer brutal violence, and to use violence which is only necessary because the law and the magistrates will not protect him. We are obliged to look chiefly to a physical standard of height and strength, and not to ability for the duty, and this narrows the area of selection. There should always be men of tall stature in the force, and they must all be strong. But with the protection the law we propose would give, we might, by having a larger number to select from, require a higher standard of intelligence. At present—we quote from an able article in *The Globe* of Nov. 14th :—

> "It may be very well to say that in taking a person into custody a policeman is only administering the law. Stripped of the disguise of language the thing bears quite another aspect. In all cases where there is an actual conflict of physical strength, the execution of the law becomes in effect a personal quarrel. The temper of the policeman is aroused all the more quickly because the encounter is undertaken for no purposes of his own."

The fact is he is compelled to use physical force, and not moral power, and we do not get as good men as we might. We repel the very men we ought to attract. Physical force must always be behind in the last resort; for moral power alone, in dealing with a criminal whose very existence as a criminal proves that he, as far as he can, repudiates its influence, would be absurd. But it makes an immense difference whether we bring physical or moral power first to bear—whether we use physical force in the first or in the last resort. In the one case we take hold of the violent man and control him by force; in the other we compel him by fear of a greater evil to control himself. The difference in the way of educating the disorderly classes is immense.

At present a man, by joining the force, subjects himself to arbitrary and irresponsible power. He may be dismissed at any moment, and no reason will be given, or he may be condemned unheard; he may do duty for many years, and be promoted and become entitled to a good service pension, and yet he may be suddenly dismissed and forfeit that pension which he deserved. And all this may be just, and we believe the Commissioners act justly in intention in most cases; but there is no safety from injustice and wrong. We denounce the system with all our might. Men who will not be either the victims or the instruments of arbitrary and irresponsible power will not join, and they are the very men we ought to do our utmost to attract.

At present he must submit himself to that which all Englishmen specially hate: a system of minutely regulated drill. We do not mean that there is too much of military evolutions, rather there might well be more—if there is drill at all, the force might be taught company drill; but there is an unnecessarily minute regulation of things best left alone, and the tone and tendency of the system is to depress individual action, instead of calling out and directing it. There is not, in our judgment, enough of discipline; there is far too much of drill.

Yet, after all, the individuals composing the bulk of the force discharge their arduous duties well. Let the tone and tendency of the system be changed, and the men, freed from the evil-encouraging conditions, will rapidly improve. Still better men will enlist; for the force even now is not unattractive, and with little changes might be made popular to a high degree. It is little things that harass. There is in the system surface perfection on paper in the reports and apparent working, covering the seeds of disintegration and decay. Turn to page 4, line 17—25, and see how that grave mutiny, whose significance was pointed out by all the daily press, and notably by *The Times*, is slurred over and treated as a trifle of no consequence in Colonel Henderson's last report. In his reports and in the reports to him printed with them, the force is excellent in discipline, contentment, and efficiency. We admit that the great majority of the men are better than the system deserves, but there is too much wrong-doing going on. And as the strength of a chain is measured by the strength of its weakest link, so the violence and illegality to which the public are liable is to be measured by that of the "blackest sheep" who is tolerated in the police-fold.

We do not wish to hold a brief against the police; but if we were challenged, and if we could prove facts without delivering individual policemen (not more guilty than others who escape our knowledge) into the hands of authority, we could bring heavy charges against the force. Some are incorruptible under any stress of temptation. Some create occasion for wrong. The mass are, like other classes, what circumstances have made them.

But wrong-doing goes on. There is by some constables brutal violence used against prisoners; there is perjured evidence supported by the oaths of suborned men; there is black mail levied on cabmen, on public-houses, on brothels, and on prostitutes. Is it not enough? Those who know and are behind the scenes know that we speak truth.

To sum up. It is not in the courts of equity or in the courts of common law that English law and government come in contact with the toiling multitudes in their daily lives. It is through the county court judges, the police courts, the magistrates, and justices of peace, and the local and metropolitan police. It would be a great day for England—greater than the day of any party triumph in the House—when Parliament takes action, or when the nation compels Parliament to make the force such as we would have it, and as it might easily be made. Which party will see the political capital which can be made of this? Which party has insight into the sources and springs of permanent power?

Art. III.—Christian Missions to the Heathen.

1. *Reports of the Church Missionary, S.P.G., Baptist, Wesleyan, &c., Missionary Societies for* 1872.
2. *Reports of the Religious Tract Society and the Society for the Promotion of Christian Knowledge,* 1872.
3. *Under His Banner: Papers of the Missionary Work of Modern Times.*
4. *Church Missionary Atlas,* 1873.
5. *Annals of the Propagation of the Faith.*

WE are not among those, if such there be, who look upon all kinds of Christian missions to the heathen with unmixed disfavour. On the contrary, we are inclined to wish some of these enterprises a much greater amount of success than at present seems likely to fall to their lot. We should like to learn that the natives of Melanesia were united as one man in defence of the Athanasian creed; that the Gold Coast was peopled by Particular Baptists; that the Dyaks of Borneo were everywhere identifying the Pope with the Beast, and that the Virgin was appearing to little boys and girls all over Madagascar. In other words, we should learn with pleasure that a higher form of religion had supplanted, even though but temporarily, a lower one; and we deem Christianity, in any shape, higher than the creed of the savage. Nor are we insensible to the indirect benefits which have resulted to mankind from a cultivation of the missionary spirit. As every one knows, it has been a means of stimulating discoveries and increasing our geographical knowledge, from the days of Columbus to those of Livingstone. And it cannot be denied that, quite irrespectively of the religion which he brings with him, the missionary, even though working to the present unsatisfactory plan of missions, is a civilizing influence; a kind of amateur ambassador from the higher to the less-favoured races; sometimes, it is true, causing very disastrous results, but much more often to be credited with beneficial ones. John Smith, formerly a linendraper's assistant, now a fluent and fervent young Wesleyan minister, finds himself possessed by "a call" to convert the heathen, gets the recommendation of his superintendent, is approved by the quarterly meeting, passes the necessary examination, and is shipped off to South Africa. Some of his former fellow-apprentices, who are what the world calls "making their way" at home, that is to say, are on the high road to lucrative businesses of their own, to common councillorships, and other positions of vantage, regard him as an amiable visionary, and smile when his name is mentioned. Yet if any of these gentlemen were to visit the Grahamstown district some dozen years hence, he would very likely find Smith at the head of a station—a man whose name is known a hundred miles around, who enjoys considerable influence with contending chiefs, who has prevented more than one petty war, and saved ever so many Kraals from being burnt, and cattle from being carried off, and miserable witches from being tortured—master of several barbarous dialects, into every one of which he has translated the most stirring hymns of Wesley's collection, and surrounded by some eighty or ninety Fingoe and Pongoe lads and girls reading and writing and washing themselves under his direction. Now here, it must be admitted, is no insignificant result: many men who have been trumpeted by fame, as among the wisest and the best of their epoch, have not done much more than this for mankind. And if the object of missionary societies be to dot little oases or centres of benevolence of this kind about the heathen world, with people to look after them and to insure their continued existence, then these societies must be held to be a complete success. But we are sure that their object is a great deal in advance of this; and, indeed, unless it were, even this much could not be achieved. It is no less than to convert the whole heathen world. In reference to this larger object, it is a fair question to ask how far the means employed have proved successful in the past, and are likely to prove successful in the future. And if it should turn out on inspection, as we fear it will, that, viewed in proportion to the efforts made, the result has been, and will probably continue to be, unsatisfactory, the inference will be either that the object aimed at is hopeless, or that a wrong method of proceeding has been adopted. The latter is the conclusion which we shall presently invite the reader to consider.

The mass of excellent persons who crowd the Missionary meetings at Exeter Hall, and similar gatherings in the provinces, are dominated by hopes and expectations, natural enough in their case, but which experience has shown to be erroneous. They feel themselves to be in possession of a religion which, to their minds, carries its miraculous origin stamped on the face of it, and which must necessarily command unqualified acceptance on the part of all those who fairly consider it. It is true, they say, that there are unbelievers in Christian countries, or rather persons who have persuaded themselves that they do not believe: people who have never taken the trouble to examine the claims of Christianity; others whose wicked hearts are offended by its purity, and who decline to submit their passions to its control; others, again, proud, stiff-necked philosophers, run away with by their "science falsely so-called." But these are, after all, happily exceptions. The average supporter of missions cannot conceive that revelation, if fairly brought under the notice of the untutored negro or New Zealander, or even of the Mahometan or Buddhist, will fail to carry conviction. These people are heathens simply because the bulk of them have never had an opportunity of being anything else. Let them only be got at, on a sufficiently extensive scale, and whole nations will discard their religious errors. It is a matter of history that Christianity is capable of producing this wholesale conviction, the entire Roman Empire, and the nations dependent upon or connected with it, having been converted in a comparatively short space of time. Why, it is asked, should not the effects produced in Europe, in the first centuries of our era, be reproduced in Asia and Africa in the nineteenth and twentieth? So the cry is for more money, more missionaries, more Bibles, more awakening and alarming tracts, that the happy consummation may be attained as soon as possible.

As long as notions such as these are held by the bulk of the religious subscribers to these societies, it is idle to hope that missions will be conducted on a right method. It becomes the duty, therefore, of every dispassionate friend to the cause to do his best to dispel them; and the Archbishop of Canterbury might be worse employed than in drawing up against next "Mission Day" a special prayer for the preliminary conversion to common sense of the innocents who hold them. It is by no means true, then, in the present day that the mere exhibition of the Christian system necessarily carries conviction. As a general rule, nowhere are nations or races, or even moderate-sized towns, converted offhand to the faith. The causes of this marked falling off in what may be termed the attractive force of Christianity in relation to heathenism we are unable to determine with any approach to accuracy; but we can see that the result is strictly in accordance with a law of vast application, which seems to hold good of religions. Every one of these that has met with any success in the world has exhibited a particular kind of vitality in its youth, which, as a general rule, has not distinguished its maturer age. And intimately connected with this phenomenon is this other one—namely, that each religion seems to chime in with the temperament of certain races, which are, however, not necessarily connected by the closest family ties with the people who originated it. But to pursue this subject further would lead us away from that which we have in hand. Suffice it that as a matter of fact Christianity did, in a comparatively short period, overspread a certain area inhabited by nations for which it must be supposed to have had a particular affinity. It is true that some of the Teutonic peoples and the Slaves were not brought into the fold till a later period. Lithuania, indeed, only became Christian in the fourteenth century. But it has been well remarked, "Whatever may be the cause, Christianity is the religion of the Roman Empire in the widest sense of those words" (that is to say, including the disciples of the Roman—the Teuton and the Slave), "and it is the religion of very little besides."* In Africa and Asia its flourishing settlements have been swept away, and all attempts to extend it beyond certain limits have been failures. These limits may be defined with tolerable precision as including the countries and their offshoots which have drawn their civilization from the Roman Empire. Similarly, Mahometanism in a very short space of time swept over a large area inhabited by peoples widely differing from the European in race and in civilization. In Europe it has never been anything but an intruder. For centuries after its first triumphs, it has remained quite stagnant within certain bounds, until recently it has exhibited signs of vitality in Africa, converting, it is said, whole tribes in the interior. But this phenomenon we take to be very much on a par with the conversion of the Swedes and Lithuanians. Maho-

* *Saturday Review*, Dec. 28, 1872.

metanism, on being for the first time brought into contact with these races, is proved to have a sort of affinity for them. The people throw off their old creeds in masses and almost spontaneously, the chiefs and kings probably setting an example which is easily followed. The conversions seem to be genuine. And all this is done without millions of Medjidés being subscribed annually for the purpose, or days of special prayer being appointed at Constantinople and Teheran. We conclude that no Western nation which has adopted Christianity will ever turn to Mahometanism, and we take it that there is just as little chance of any existing Mahometan people embracing Christianity. The Reformation is one among many other illustrations of what we would seek to convey. As Lord Macaulay has remarked, "The geographical frontier between the two religions has continued to run almost precisely where it ran at the close of the Thirty Years' War, nor has Protestantism given any proofs of that 'expansive power' which has been ascribed to it." The fact is that the Reformation, like every other religious movement, expended its chief provision of this particular power at a comparatively early period; or it would perhaps be more correct to say that the materials upon which it could work having been exhausted, the power was thenceforth latent: the result being that, speaking roughly, the Reformation *took* with the Teutonic nations, and did not take with any others.

In short, the history of religions resembles in some points the history of some diseases, though we must not be understood to hint at any resemblance between the *natures* of the two things compared. Certain conditions must have been necessary for the rise of these diseases, and we are always imperfectly informed, and sometimes indeed entirely ignorant, as to what these were. They have almost always spread with the greatest rapidity shortly after their first appearance, and it is a recognised fact with regard to some of them that they have taken most strongly when fairly launched in a new scene of action. Yet they are liable to be stopped at what might almost seem to be an imaginary line, as for instance a narrow river or creek, and within such limits as these to become endemic and gradually milder in form. Not but that they are capable of breaking out afresh under favouring conditions; but at each reappearance, the physiognomy of the disease, even when not visibly affected by human action, is somewhat changed. Sometimes they altogether disappear, as it is probable that all existing epidemics will disappear, to make place for diseases of a now unknown, but it may be hoped of a milder type. It would probably be impossible, in the present day, by any exercise of ingenuity, to reproduce the sweating sickness in England; but granting that the requisite conditions were discovered, it might again be made, as in the times of our ancestors, to depopulate the island; while, granting the theory of infection, a single shipload of persons seized with the malady in sight of Madras or Calcutta might spread it through the whole of India.

If from the physical we turn to the moral world, we shall find great religious movements running a very similar course. A certain atmosphere, a certain disposition of the human mind are necessary for their spread; and, favoured by those, they will for a time spread with almost inconceivable rapidity, without the aid of force. But beyond a certain line, they will be sporadic, or from some cause will ultimately fail to establish themselves. Just as a line indicating some difference of soil will be the limit to the spread of cholera, so often an ethnological line will be the limit to the spread of Christianity or of Protestantism. Then they cease, as a rule, to be epidemic; yet they are capable of fresh outbreaks wherever a fresh set of susceptible constitutions is submitted to their influence. In these cases, however, the old symptoms are seldom or never exactly repeated. The Christianity which subjugated Russia was not in all respects the same Christianity as that into which Ethelbert, King of Kent, and his subjects were baptized by Augustine. The protest against the domination of Rome which is known by the name of Old-Catholicism assumes a very different form from that fulminated by the men of the sixteenth century. Mahometanism, indeed, owing to the simple character of its chief dogmas, appears to be less subject to this law. Yet we may be sure that the creed with which parts of Africa are being impregnated will develop variations due to altered conditions. From this we gather that if ever —circumstances being favourable—the Brahmins and Buddhists embrace Christianity in large numbers, it will not be exactly the Christianity preached in Rome, or in London, or in St. Petersburg, or at Constance. It may be, for aught we know, some form of Arianism, or Unitarianism, or even Manichæism, or more probably some entirely new type of the creed, naturally evolved by circumstances, and consequently suited to the recipients. But in order that a new religion of any kind should career through a population, it is necessary, we repeat, that their constitutions should be susceptible to its influence. Let this condition be present, and a single boatload of pious Christians will send the religion of the cross, as a fire is sent through dried grass, from the mouths of the Indus to the mouths of the Ganges—from the Hindoo Koosh to the extremity of Ceylon.

Now it has been made obvious to sensible people that this preliminary condition nowhere presents itself to the Christian Missionary of modern times, and therefore all expectations of wholesale conversions produced by the mere "power of the word" must be given up. We have attempted to take heathendom by storm—perhaps it was only right that the attempt should be made—and we have failed. We have been in the position of a troop of children attempting to set fire to a damp plantation growing in a morass, by applying to it here and there a lighted lucifer match. All over it there are cracklings heard and little "centres of light" visible; and in places, by the burning of a bough or two, small openings are made, which, if neglected for a year or two, will be found to be covered by fresh boughs. At the few spots where a real clearing has been effected, it is found that the soil had been previously drained for some other purpose, and the light of the sun let in, and the wood rendered susceptible to the action of fire. Now, granting that the particular operation—the burning of the plantation—is for some reason desirable, a grown-up man who watches all this sees at once the only way in which it can be undertaken with a chance of success. His plan has this additional advantage, that it does not include the occasional chance consumption of a rick, or a barn, for which the children's parents are invariably made to pay.

But before considering what we venture to think the most hopeful scheme of missionary enterprise, it is necessary to justify our opinion that the existing scheme has upon the whole proved a failure. A brief glance at the history and present position of modern missions will therefore not be out of place.

The great maritime discoveries of the fifteenth century proved the means of reviving the missionary spirit in the Church of Rome; and the Church, in its turn, reacted upon the spirit of discovery. As new regions were added to the world, the necessity was felt of carrying thither the tidings of the true religion. And the zeal for proselytism, thus awakened, became an additional motive force, urging men on to still further adventures. The Reformation, which shortly followed, could not be other than an exceedingly strong stimulus to Roman Catholic enterprise of this kind. To make up for the territory lost to the Faith, there was reason to hope that fresh territory might be conquered. No more efficient soldiers than the Jesuits have have ever been enlisted for a campaign of this kind. As to the numbers of their converts, it is as impossible to form a correct notion as it is to pronounce upon the lists of the slaughtered in ancient battles. We hear of the existence of four hundred thousand native Christians in Japan, in the year 1596; of twenty thousand Chinese baptized in the single year 1664; of three hundred thousand Chinese Christians living in 1723; and, on better authority, of one hundred thousand Indians living under the control of the Jesuits in South America in 1767; with much more to the same effect. Doubtless in all this there is exaggeration; yet it has never been disputed that the Jesuit missions have exhibited, in a higher degree than any others, the result which we think destined to follow upon all missions of the existing type—*temporary* success. There can be no doubt that they persuaded a great number of heathens all over the world to call themselves Christians; and in some cases kept them and their descendants faithful to the name for a long period. And there can be no doubt that no other body of men has succeeded in doing the like. Now of two things one. The bulk of these conversions were either real or nominal. If they were nominal only, as many Protestants assert, we have nothing further to say. Here is no success to show, in the sense that we attach to the word. If, on the other hand, a considerable portion of them were real, as most Catholics affirm, then we are entitled to ask what has become of the descendants of these converts in the present day? If persecutions be pointed to as the cause of the disappearance of the Catholic Church in some countries, and its enfeebled condition in others, we are entitled to recall the persecutions under the Roman Empire from Nero to Diocletian; and to ask whether, far from stamping out or even weakening the power of Christianity in Europe, these were not among the chief agencies for increasing it. At any rate, whatever may have been the real condition of these monuments of Jesuit enterprise, when they stood, we can see clearly where they stood. In their character of religious outworks they were built upon the sand, and scarcely a trace remains of their foundations.* Yet, with all this, there can be doubt that Roman Catholic missions have been, upon the whole, the most successful; among other reasons, because they have often been conducted with more worldly wisdom than marks those of their Protestant rivals. The question indeed arises whether the kind of religion which they succeed in propagating is a very great advance upon that which it supplants. We hear that Roman Catholic natives of India are permitted to indulge in processions and ceremonies in no respect differing from those of the heathens around them, except that wax figures of Jesus and the Virgin are substituted for wax figures of other deities, while the European priest beats a drum. We know that on the reredos of the Roman Catholic Church at Pekin, Jesus and his Apostles are represented in Chinese dresses, and with strongly-marked Chinese countenances. Elsewhere, coal-black saints are exported to coal-black communities—not improbably contracted for with English firms, and shipped out in company with the figure-heads of local divinities. It is averred by travellers that, in the South Sea Islands, highly-coloured pictures of the Crucifixion are circulated by the priests, and that groups of mockers, judiciously distributed about the foot of the Cross,

* Except in India, of which, however, we are not now speaking. Why Roman Catholicism has not disappeared in India admits of an easy explanation.

are made to do duty as Protestants. Not that we are prepared, by-the-bye, to brand these proceedings as altogether deceitful and dishonest. On the contrary, we think that a good deal might be said for them, as indeed a good deal may be said for almost anything in the matter of religion. But the question is, What do the converts take, in the shape of belief, by their conversion through such agencies as these? And we fear the answer must be that they are only turned over from one system of idolatry to another. What else indeed can these people take, in any case, from missionaries who, in want of food, pray to the sacred heart of Mary, and whose prayer is answered by the gift of a shark; and who subsequently obtain from St. Francis Xavier a shower of rain to quench the thirst engendered by eating the flesh of the shark?* For our part, seeing what it is that these men themselves believe, we understand that such a belief may here and there make way with the lowest classes of heathens. And we rejoice at this (as we stated at the outset) precisely to the extent that we deem the incoming creed superior to the outgoing one: that is to say, with pleasurable emotions of a very subdued character. But it is a fair question to put to those reverend gentlemen who are so eloquent at Exeter Hall on the successes of Christian missions to the heathen, whether the results obtained by these Roman Catholic missionaries are held by them to be a part of these successes? We hardly see how they can be, because a large portion of the time of these same reverend gentlemen, when not expatiating on missions, is employed in informing us that the Pope is Antichrist, the man of sin, the false prophet; the Roman

* "We were in all twenty-three persons on board. I began by putting all my people on rations, consisting of a few spoonfuls of rice and a little bit of dried cocoa; then we began to offer a novena to the Sacred Heart of Mary. Our good Mother sent us, on the very festival of her Nativity, an enormous shark, which supplied us for several days with an additional provision of fish. But the torment of thirst became only the more insupportable. We therefore had recourse to St. Francis Xavier, who obtained, on the same night, a heavy fall of rain, sufficient to satiate every one's thirst, and to fill, if not the casks, at least all the boilers and pots on board."—Letter of the Rev. Father Montiton, of the Congregation of the Sacred Hearts, in "Annals of the Propagation of the Faith," Sept. 1873, p. 314. On the same page we are informed how an old woman, at the point of death, was immediately restored to "perfect health" by the "great sacrament of baptism." In another part of this same number we are told how the most fearful judgments overtake those who resist the missionaries. They are attacked by apoplexy; they die suddenly in the vigour of youth and flourishing health; they fall down stone dead; they are covered with a hideous leprosy; their flesh, corrupted and infected, falls off their bones; they fall into the deepest poverty, illness, lawsuits, and unforeseen accidents; their wives poison themselves with opium; their fathers fall into ditches and get killed; sharks drag them into the water and tear off their legs. The apostates fare, if possible, still worse—as they are labouring in the fields, landslips occur which swallow them up alive, &c., &c.

Church the great whore, the great Apostacy; its presiding genius the dragon.* If people are still serving under the devil, it does not seem a great triumph for the children of light to watch their exchange from one regiment into another. Of course, the same remark holds good from the Roman Catholic point of view. If either Romanists or Protestants succeeded in their enterprise of converting the whole heathen world, the adherents of the unsuccessful creed would still be bound to another enterprise, that of endeavouring to upset almost everything that their rivals had accomplished.

For some time after the Reformation we do not hear much of Protestant Missions. This was only natural: the Protestant nations had not began to found colonies, and so to acquire a practical interest in the conversion of the heathen. Leaving aside for the present the operations of the Dutch in Ceylon, and some others of the same kind, we may say that it was not till the beginning of the eighteenth century that anything like a systematic effort was made in this direction.

To about the same time are to be referred the foundation of the Society for the Propagation of the Gospel in England, and the departure of the first Danish Missionaries for India. Since that period there have sprung up in England alone the Church Missionary, the London, the Wesleyan, the Baptist, and more than thirty other missionary societies; as well as the Society for Promoting Christian Knowledge, the Religious Tract, and the Bible Societies, whose efforts have to a considerable extent been directed to the same channels. The income of the principal among these associations (omitting many smaller ones) is given as 995,993*l.*, or about a million sterling, for the year 1871. Of this sum it is calculated that about two-thirds or 607,590*l.* was devoted exclusively to foreign and colonial missions in the following proportions: Church Societies, 440,810*l.*, Nonconformist ditto, 367,918*l.*, Mixed, 183,055*l.* But this after all does not nearly represent the total outlay, for the gratuitous labour given, and the funds voluntarily raised by native Christians, have to be taken into account. Thus we read how, at Calcutta, "An ample income has been provided for the perpetual support of a native pastor (of Trinity Church) and this in a great measure by the contributions of the people

* It may be said that these absurd expressions are only heard from the lips of "Evangelicals." But these are precisely the main supporters of missions. Their organ is quite correct in saying, "The gifts of Ritualists to missionary work are very small compared to the gifts of Evangelicals. . . . Ritualists take a share, and that not a very large share, in one society, the S.P.G., while Evangelicals support both the Church Missionary Society and the Colonial and Continental Society, and a host of smaller organizations."—*Record*, Oct. 31, 1873.

themselves." At Ellore, the Evangelistic agents are paid "by a voluntary rate." At Mirat, the congregational offerings in money and grain amounted last year to Rs. 109, "notwithstanding their poverty." From the Tonga group of islands alone, the Wesleyans, according to their published report for 1870, obtained a sum of 6000*l*. In many places churches and schools are gratuitously built. We think we should be below the mark in estimating the total amount spent on missions to the heathen, in England, and through the instrumentality of England, at a million sterling annually. The number of persons actively and professionally employed in propagating the faith on behalf of three English Societies alone are as follows: S.P.G. 468 ordained missionaries, 855 catechists and lay teachers; Church Missionary 2589 clergy and lay teachers; Wesleyan 1071 ministers and assistant missionaries, 4341 paid agents, catechists, &c., 25,548 unpaid agents, as Sabbath-school teachers, &c. We are not in a position at present to ascertain what may be the amount spent, and the number of persons employed on missions by other Protestant countries. We should, however, suppose that the United States does not lag very far behind England. According to Hoole's Year Book of Missions for 1847, the receipts of American Missionary, Bible and Tract societies amounted at that time to a sum not far short of a quarter of a million. Germany, Holland, Sweden, Denmark and Switzerland, have before now greatly distinguished themselves in the cause. Taking all sorts of Christian missions together, Greek Church, as well as Catholic and Protestant, we should say that not less than one hundred thousand human beings are engaged in some capacity or other, in the work of converting the heathen, and that several millions sterling are spent annually on behalf of the cause: no small portion of this sum having gone to the purchase of countless religious tracts and Testaments, which have been showered, thick as snowflakes, upon every portion of the habitable globe.

What, we must ask, is the outcome of this century and a half of gigantic efforts? Here are agencies at work which Paul and his associates, if they could rise from their graves and behold them, might well suppose capable of fulfilling a dream like that of the benevolent Heber, and spreading the gospel from the mountains of Greenland to the shores of India. Of course, a considerable number of converts can be exhibited on paper. From a return recently presented to Parliament, we learn that in India, Burmah, and Ceylon the number of Protestant communicants in 1872 was 78,494, while the converts young and old are given as over 300,000. We are not at all disposed to underrate this result. It constitutes, indeed, the most brilliant page in the whole history of our Missionary enterprise. It amounts, however, to this; that after a century of supremacy in the Peninsula, we are able to count one inhabitant in every six hundred as a nominal adherent of our creed, while one in two thousand is induced to participate in the one essential rite enjoined by that creed upon every grown up Christian; a rite deemed, we believe, essential to salvation, at any rate in the highest degree obligatory, by all Christians who do not happen to be Quakers. And, further, this balance-sheet requires a little more careful consideration than is likely to be bestowed upon it at enthusiastic meetings in Exeter Hall, where the mere sound of "Three hundred thousand converts!" is sure to make the rafters ring with plaudits. Is it quite certain that whatever is solid about it is entirely due to Missionary agency, and not partly, or perhaps chiefly to other agencies? We gather from these returns that comparatively little progress was made before 1852. Since that year the native Christians have more than doubled, and the communicants have nearly quadrupled. Now it was precisely during these twenty years, 1852-1872, that the railway system in India may be said to have been inaugurated, and the telegraphic system established, irrigation works set on foot, postal communications enormously developed, a scheme of education introduced, a code of laws framed; in short, the "progress of India" has become an accepted phrase, and is written in statistics too well known to need being recalled here. It is at any rate a noteworthy fact that this period of enlarged civilization, of assimilation to Great Britain, should correspond to that in which the number of adhesions to the creed of the dominant and civilizing race has largely increased. We do not insist on this point, which nevertheless merits consideration, and will just glance at one or two other points. Is it, or is it not, a fact that nearly the whole of the converts are drawn from the lowest classes of the population?* We, at any rate, have constantly heard the fact asserted. Not once or twice, but scores of times, have we been informed by men who had spent their lives in India, that they had hardly ever known a case of the conversion of a native of rank. We do not cite this as a reproach to missions, but as a circumstance which, if true, gives rise to reflections. Again, what is there of really "solid" about these conversions? It is impossible to say, but it is certainly strange to hear old Indians, themselves not unfriendly to the principle of missions, constantly declaring that nothing in the world would induce them to take a converted native for a servant. Further,

* It is plain that it is in the southern part of the Presidency of Madras, and among the low-class aboriginal population which abounds there, that the bulk of the converts are to be found.

these three hundred thousand "converts" are represented to us as a vast array of heathens rescued from darkness, and destined continually to increase, both by propagation and the influence which they will exert on those outlying. Is this so sure to be the case under all circumstances? Sixty-six years ago, Sydney Smith wrote what, *mutatis mutandis*, is not wholly inapplicable to the present day: "Nothing is more precarious than our empire in India. Suppose we were to be driven out of it to-morrow, and to leave behind us 20,000 converted Hindoos: it is most probable that they would relapse into heathenism."* We believe that in the supposed contingency the result predicted by Sydney Smith would assuredly ensue. We believe that if we were to leave India next year, and no other civilized power, as Russia for instance, stepped into our place, a hundred years hence scarcely a trace of Christianity would be found in the peninsula. We believe that the same sort of consequences would follow our departure as would follow in England if we were suddenly freed after a long period of Mussulman rule. The converts to the Koran—and there would be a number of these among the lower classes—would rapidly die out and be at length extinguished in the person of the last genuine native Mahometan, just as we read the other day of the death of the last Muggletonian; and the mosques would be used as music-halls in the towns, and places for storing potatoes in the country. This is an opinion not volunteered without evidence but amply supported by facts. Take the following from a missionary work: "When Dr. Caldwell went first to Endeyengoody (which means 'the home of the shepherd') he found among the inhabitants of six villages, which forty years before had embraced the Gospel, only one man who had remained steadfast."† In the same book we find the following on the subject of Ceylon, a case strictly in point:—

"The history of the peninsula is, in its general outline, the history of the island . . . . Portuguese and Dutch, each have held it, and each have done their best to evangelize it. When the Dutch were driven out of the island in 1795, they left some 350,000 Christians behind them: the converts of the Portuguese mission were supposed to be hardly fewer in number. The Treaty of Amiens finally made the island over to the British Crown, and in 1811 the non-Roman Christians had dwindled down to 150,000. The Scriptures had been largely translated into Singalese and Tamil in the last century, and the churches, both Portuguese and Dutch, which still remain, bear testimony to the zeal of those nations."‡

* "Indian Missions," *Edinburgh Review*, 1808.

† "Under His Banner," p. 48.

‡ *Ibid.* p. 64. We may remark that some accounts represent nominal Protestant Christianity as still more widely spread over the surface of Ceylon in

It would thus appear that at the end of the last century there were to be found in the island of Ceylon alone a greater number of nominal Protestant Christians (and what is to be our guarantee that the bulk of the converts of the Church Missionary and other Societies in the present day are of a different complexion?) than eighty years later are comprised in the whole of India, together with Ceylon. In 1811 they had decreased by more than one-half. In the present day there are in the island, according to the missionary reports, 20,000 members of the Church of England, 2187 Wesleyans, and 647 Baptists, with probably some few others, though whether these figures include the 18,000 whites resident in Ceylon we do not know. This comes, we are told, of the island having been "neglected." In other words, these people when left to themselves invariably go back. A similar lesson is taught by the Jesuit mission in Paraguay, which we have already mentioned. Half a century after its expulsion very little of the religion which it had introduced and fostered was to be discovered, but the useful knowledge which it had brought with it remained. We are further of opinion that if England left India to itself to-morrow, with nine-tenths of the lower classes (the educated are hopeless) communicants of some religious body, and the remaining one-tenth members of the Society of Friends, in less than a hundred years the general public would be Christians in name only. The island of Ceylon, to which we have just called attention, will furnish an illustration on this head. When Bishop Chapman arrived there in 1845, he found extensively prevailing a singularly compounded creed, in which the remains of Christianity peeped through the idolatry which enveloped it, just as the remains of one fish are sometimes to be seen through the transparent body of a larger fish by which it has been devoured. Other numerous illustrations will present themselves when we turn our eyes to other parts of the missionary field.

A useful little Atlas published by the Church Missionary Society serves to show in a general way what this field is, and what settlements have been made upon it. The heathen regions are of course in the darkest black, and Protestant countries and settlements are picked out in yellow. Passing out of Europe and the United States, Canada, &c., we find a band of yellow encircling Australia, and the same colour filling in Tasmania and

---

the 17th century. We are told of one district where, in 1663, out of 278,000 inhabitants, 180,000 professed Christianity; of another district, where there were 62,000 Christians, &c. We may add, that when the Dutch came, the Portuguese converts deserted to them largely, and it is only fair to say that the Roman Catholics left in the island in 1705 could hardly have approached the figure given above.

New Zealand. In the case of these countries and some others, such as Newfoundland, there can be no pretence that Christianity is overspreading, or has overspread them, in the same sense in which it spread over Europe in the early centuries. Nations professing that creed have taken forcible possession of them, and have extended themselves, not with a direct view of opening out Heaven to the heathen, yet possibly with that result, by the sharp and ready method of improving them off the face of the earth. In the course of a comparatively short time it is certain that the whole of Australia will figure on missionary maps as "yellow;" and it is equally certain that this would have happened if not a single missionary had ever landed on that vast island. It may be our duty to try and convert the natives of the interior, and the thirty thousand Maories still left in New Zealand, before proceeding to elbow them out of existence, but it will be over their graves, rather than through their ranks, that Christianity will career triumphant. The work will have been largely indebted for its accomplishment to the "sword," or, in modern language, to the rifle, and is being greatly furthered in the present day by the use of ardent spirits, especially among the converts. A grog-shop having been opened within easy distance of a flourishing church and congregation, we will leave an archdeacon to relate the result:—

> "The enemy has come in like a flood and swept away many of my hopes. The last year has been one of cloud, though not without *some sunshine*, enough to keep us from thinking that our work is in vain. The cause of all this retrogression is the unresisted importation of spirits and a corresponding amount of intemperance. . . . . Meanwhile, however, *our services are well attended*, and that by many who, while acknowledging the error of their ways, *are unable to withstand their besetting sin*."*

In other words, these interesting converts yielded to temptation the moment it was put in their way, and after being beastly drunk all the week, came to church on Sunday, just as they would have come to almost any other kind of rendezvous. We believe, by the way, that these missions to the Maories have been from first to last utter failures. Many of the most promising converts, with whom the Christian dogmas had seemed to take in the most satisfactory fashion, who were in the habit of weeping at passages in the sacred narrative, who could tell all about sanctification and justification, suddenly became possessed with Hau-Hauism, an amalgamation of Romanism, Wesleyanism, cannibalism, and Church doctrines, with some new rites or practices superadded, such as that of "barking like a

* Archdeacon Clarke's letter, "Proceedings of Church Missionary Society, 1873-1874," p. 176. The *italics* in this and other quotations are our own.

dog." Well might the bishop write in 1863, "Our native work is a remnant in two senses, a remnant of a decaying people, and a remnant of a decaying faith." He adds, with laudable candour, that all the horrors perpetrated were the "works of baptized men."* Within the last year or two we hear of a new superstition spreading in the Southern Island, that of Tamaihawaism, and the Christians are going over to it in numbers.† Now these Maories are the very people of whom Bishop Selwyn wrote in 1842: "We see here a whole nation of pagans converted to the faith . . . . another Christian people added to the family of God . . . . all, in a greater or less degree, bringing forth and *visibly displaying in their outward lives some fruits of the influences of the Spirit!*" On reading this we are irresistibly reminded of Theodore Hook's well-known lines on a wine-vault under a chapel, "There's a spirit above and a spirit below," &c.

We do not believe that Protestant Missions have everywhere been so unsuccessful as they have proved in New Zealand. On the contrary, as we remarked at the beginning of this article, we believe that both from them and from Roman Catholic Missions much good has resulted in certain districts; while we cling very strongly to the opinion that the great proportion of this good is only indirectly due to them and does not wholly result from what is their professed aim, conversion to Christianity. Reverting to the Atlas, we find what may be called three groups of spots coloured yellow, indicating localities the circumstances of which are altogether different from those of Australia, New Zealand, or British Columbia. They are places where the white man has not carried Christianity in his cartouche-box, as the French soldier is reported to carry civilization in the folds of his flag. They are regions which the native inhabitants, aboriginal or imported, are likely for some time to keep for themselves.‡ These are almost entirely islands: (1) Islands of Polynesia, including if we may be allowed to do so, the Sandwich family; (2) British West India Islands, with Jamaica at their head; (3) Sierra Leone, still under British rule, though surely not destined long to remain so, where, however, there were in 1860 but 130 white inhabitants to 41,000 coloured people, seven-eighths of whom were Christians. These are localities which enable us to judge what becomes

* "Under His Banner," p. 249.

† "Of Christianity the Maories have adopted only the outward form. Instead of the old pagan rites and ceremonies they now have Christian forms; biblical history is to the Maori only a new edition of traditions, which he exchanges for, and perhaps also mixes up with, his own ancient traditions."—Von Hochstetter's "New Zealand." English edit., p. 210.

‡ Speaking generally, Fiji will doubtless be assimilated, *i.e.*, swallowed up by the whites, in a comparatively short time.

of Christianity in the hands of ignorant swarthy races left virtually to themselves; a most important subject of inquiry in relation to the value to be put on missionary enterprises.

In Jamaica, which may be taken as in some degree a type of the West Indian islands, the whites, as is well known, are but a handful in the midst of the emancipated slaves and their offspring. The population is a population of black and "brown" people. For years past they have been operated upon chiefly by the Wesleyans and the Baptists, the most fanatical of Protestant Churches, the Churches which, by the help of processes widely differing from those of Rome, share with Rome the faculty of stirring to its depths an uneducated nature, such as that of the negro. To roll about the ground foaming at the mouth and biting the grass under a sense of "wrath," and to see the devils figuratively, perhaps literally, sneaking away when exhaustion has set in, is to these people a congenial religious observance; to get dipped in a tank, amidst a cannonade of hymns, is a mode of conversion suited to the sable or mahogany "inquirer." What has been the result? Under a thin veneer of Christianity, Quashee is still an unmitigated heathen. It is impossible not to read this between the lines of the missionary reports themselves, abounding as they are in such expressions as "gracious visitations of the Holy Spirit," "sound and saving conversions," "great success of the Gospel," "richness in faith and good works." "It is not the fact," writes the Rev. James Watson, one of the oldest missionaries in the island, "that the religious portion of the community are retrograding or deteriorating; but the vicious, the criminal, and the ignorant, being more numerous, neutralize the good that has already been done, cast it into the background, and in fact *give character to the whole island population.*" This state of things is thus accounted for further on, "Beyond localities blest by the faithful labours of Christian missionaries, there are idleness, licentiousness, cunning, malice, and crime of every phase, rampant and strong, and setting at defiance decency, law, and religion. It is plain that the outstanding heathenism of 300,000 people must to some extent neutralize and cast into the shade the character and conduct of the 100,000 who have embraced Christianity, but it is altogether unfair to reason from such premises that missions have been a failure in Jamaica."* According to this theory, the "heathens" do all the mischief, and the Christians are like sheep in the midst of wolves. We believe this to be an entirely erroneous account of the matter. We believe that all are virtually heathen alike, the professing Christians, as a class, quite as much as any other class in the community. In confirmation of what we assert we will not go so

* "Report of the Wesleyan Methodist Missionary Society for 1867," p. 65.

far back as to the Commission of 1866, but will quote from an interesting book of travels which has appeared quite recently.

"Professedly a Christian, it may be doubted whether one negro in a thousand attaches a correct meaning to even the most simple ordinances of religion. In some districts of the island, indeed, these are travestied at midnight meetings held under leafy booths erected for the purpose, which are carefully concealed from the knowledge of the parish minister. At these 'singing meetings' a woman sanctifies the bread and administers the elements. Hymns are sung, words are spoken, mysterious rites are observed. The worshippers grow more and more excited as the fires burn out, and the night grows old; and the meeting ends as might be expected, in licence and debauchery."*

Further on we are told that at wakes "a white cock is sacrificed over the grave to propitiate the manes of the deceased" (p. 83), and of course similar orgies often follow. Their regular services seem to be not much more edifying. "The scenes that occur at the native Baptist chapels throughout the island are almost blasphemous in their absurdity."(p. 86.)

Here is the account of "revivals," given by an English clergyman and missionary, one of the really right sort, who was setting a good example and teaching a useful lesson by "resuscitating a thrown-up sugar estate."

"Not the least interesting part of his conversation was his account of the revival meetings, which a few years back took place amongst the negroes of his district. For seven days and seven nights the people would not leave the chapel. Religious frenzy seized all classes. Some fed on grass; others crawled on all-fours like beasts; others went about *prophesying that Obeah was hidden under the threshold of the church.* Immorality under such circumstances was much more rife than religion." (pp. 74, 75.)

Talking of Obeah, it seems that the superstition is believed in by "Christians" as well as "heathens," as indeed may be gathered from the above.

"The practice of Obeah amongst the humbler classes is still unfortunately as prevalent at the present day, despite the severely penal laws against it, as it was in the beginning of the century." (p. 140.) . . . We are informed that three Obeah-men, who were not apprehended at the time we left Lucea, had received 10*l.* for their services, and that for some months past they have had other and well-paying customers in Lucea, *some of whom are among the most earnest in professions of Christianity.*†

The degree to which these converts are Christianized might be illustrated by many other passages from the pen of the same

* "Letters from Jamaica." Edmonston and Douglas, 1873, p. 84.

† P. 142, quotation from a Local Journal.

acute observer. It was almost impossible, he was told by a clergyman, to make a negro believe in hell. Some may think that this is no discredit to the negro; yet it must be remembered, the boast is that these people have been brought to receive what Wesleyans and Baptists call the "Gospel," and hell is a very important part of this Gospel.

"Death to the negro has no terrors. He dies because his time has come. But he dies like a dog; without a regret, and without a pang, confident that, if there be a heaven, he will find admission there; and that if there is not, he has finished his course, and drunk all that he will ever be allowed to drink of the pleasures and pains of life." (p. 82.)

Yet he is terribly afraid of "duppies" or ghosts.

"Nothing will tempt the negro to go out of sight of the light burning in his hut on a dark night. His fear peoples every bush and every tree with ghostly forms." (p. 83.)

He is at the same time a firm believer in his Bible, indeed to such an extent that he will endeavour to kiss his thumb instead of the book when about to give a false oath (which he invariably does when occasion requires) in a Court of Justice. (p. 81.) "Bob," one of the author's drivers, was, we doubt not, a fair example of these students and worshippers of the inspired writings. He not unusually indulged in "an extra glass of rum and water at night." When he did not wish to travel, he would himself break off a horse's shoe or cut the harness, and pretend that an accident had happened. Yet, "no matter how pressed we were for time, *he would read his Bible for an hour every morning.*" (p. 39.)

We have only space for two other short extracts. Here is an aged female Christian's idea of Heaven.

"Don't you think it will be delightful to be in Heaben, Massa?—Noting to do, no work, no boderation, no cleaning, no noting; but always to fold me hand, *and to sit down chattering with me Saviour.*" (p. 37.)

At the weekly markets in the country towns it seems that the women troop in, in their gayest attire, and this includes an apron decorated with texts of scripture, religious verses, &c. Here is a specimen of one of these inscriptions, which the author copied.

"Once the world was all to me,
But now it turns its back on me,
O you freckle-hearted young man!
I lay my eye at Jesus feet,
Till I find my secret love!" (p. 93.)

Such are the Jamaica Christians! And we have only time to

observe that the religious condition of some of the other islands (as St. Lucia, and Trinidad) seems to be still more lamentable.

Let us glance, for we can do no more, at the South Seas. What good has resulted from the most successful missions there? And how much of this good is to be traced directly to their *religious* teaching? There can be no doubt that owing to the appearance of white people among them, the natives have thrown away some barbarous customs and learnt some useful arts. They no longer sacrifice human victims, nor do they eat human flesh. Cattle, horses, pigs, and other domestic animals, as well as many useful plants, have been introduced among them. They have been taught to dress themselves and to build houses. On the other hand, it is fair to observe that European diseases and European drinks have been imported; and that the population of many of the islands has decreased in a most frightful ratio. Now we do not debit missionaries with all the evil which has been wrought, nor, on the other hand, can we credit them with all the good. We agree with the writers who, in an amusing series of sketches, have lately recorded their experiences of these regions, that "there is good reason to believe that the mere intercourse with higher races would have abolished cannibalism and human sacrifice without the necessity of any *religious* teaching."* Two other passages from the same book illustrate this view very forcibly, and we quote them because they record the opinions of sensible missionaries themselves:—

"'The young missionaries,' said one of them to me, 'have a new work to do. The old ones who first introduced Christianity captivated the minds of the natives by their superior accomplishments. These men, cried they, can build ships without outriggers, make leaves speak (write), and many other wonderful things; let us believe all they tell us and we shall be able to do the same! But after this first rush there comes a reaction, when they find that they do not gain all the advantages they expected; and we young missionaries will have to try and plant a *real* religious feeling in their hearts.'" (p. 292.)

Another missionary repeats the same story:—

"'The old missionary, who was looked on as a kind of god by the natives, because he was surrounded by the superior inventions and appliances of civilization, which they had never seen before, and could scarcely understand, could alter, or at least keep down anything he disapproved of. Now that the reaction has come, and the natives have discovered that the priest is only a man, and a person not more ingenious and wonderful in invention than a layman, but rather the contrary, the missionary has lost most of his power and is puzzled how

* "South Sea Bubbles." By the Earl and the Doctor. P. 271.

to act. In fact, the native wants to improve his body, which he cares a great deal about, and the missionary to save his soul, which he cares nothing about, even if he believes he has one.'" (p. 208.)

Here, we believe, is the plain truth of the matter. The savage recognises in the white man a superior being, a kind of god. This indeed does not prevent him from beating the god about the head with tomahawks or shooting him with poisoned arrows when the latter comes, or is supposed to come, with hostile intent, just as we should put a rifle ball through a "superior being" in a like case. But where he appears as an instructor, he is to the savage like another Saturn come down from Heaven to teach agriculture, sometimes we fear like another Bacchus unfolding the virtues of the grape. The native will throw aside his old customs and smash up his old idols, because he believes *in the white man* and wants to learn his cunning devices, which appear to him supernatural. If the king or queen can be secured, a permanent change is brought about, and here the converts, owing to their insular position, not being so much exposed to the attacks, or the example, of neighbouring peoples retaining the old institutions, are not so apt to fall back into pure savagery.* This is how sacrifices, cannibalism, and idolatry have been put down, and we see no religious influence, properly so called, in the result. Half a dozen infidel and hard-swearing but ingenious mariners, would in a few years produce the same result on any savage island where they had happened to be shipwrecked, and had avoided being eaten. So far from this being a violent supposition, it is by no means unlike what took place in the Sandwich Islands, where 40,000 idols were destroyed in a few days before a single missionary had landed there. Lately we heard of Sir Garnet Wolseley addressing a collection of Fantee Chiefs, and informing them that Europeans did not slaughter their captives, or cut off the heads of their dead enemies. We may be sure that when the Fantees return from "fighting" beside the British, in what we doubt not will be a victorious campaign, this lesson will have sunk into their minds. The missionaries who labour among them will be more usefully employed in reminding them hereafter how the British, who never adopted such customs, nevertheless pounded the Ashantees with their Gatlings, and destroyed the capital, and slaughtered everybody right and left, handsomely, in fair fight, visibly moving under Divine guidance and protection, than in attempting to show them (which, by the way, they could not very well do) that these venerable and national practices were dis-

* Yet they do sometimes. Williams the Martyr of Erromanga relates that on one occasion the inhabitants of a converted island, *in his absence*, solemnly met together and re-established idolatry and the old system.

tinctly forbidden in a mysterious Book which they carried about with them. In answer to all this it will doubtless be said that, but for the desire to save immortal souls the vast majority of the South-Sea islands, and other out-of-the-way places, would not enjoy the advantage of any white residents at all. We admit the fact, and respect the motive. What we contend is, that the best means are not adopted to secure the wished-for result; in other words, that more immortal souls will ultimately be saved, or as we should prefer to put it, that more people will be converted to Christianity, and to Christianity of a more genuine and durable kind, if a different system of approach were followed out from that which is generally dictated by the chiefs of the staff at the London Mission-Houses. We say "generally," because the London Mission really does seem to have an inkling of the right way. This Society is, we believe, principally in the hands of the Congregationalists or Independents, long honourably known as one of the most liberal of English sects.*

"From what I have seen and been told, the London Society seems to be of a very liberal nature. It seems to care more for 'results' than for doctrines, and sends out its emissaries with a free permission to teach almost any form of Christianity best suited to themselves or their natives. This very 'easiness' tends to keep men of very extreme or narrow ideas out of their ranks, and is one great reason why they get on so much better than most other sects."†

The Society is represented as virtually giving these instructions to its young missionaries:—

"Learn the language, get up a school, improve the people how best you can; teach them any form of Christianity that is likely to suit them; keep clear of native politics. God bless you!"‡

These men "do not fanatically try to force the natives into their own groove, but patiently try to make them peaceful and happy." They avoid "abstract and disputed dogmas," and under these circumstances we can readily understand that "The London Mission has certainly had great success." We heartily wish these "wonderfully good, intelligent, liberal, practical men" a still greater measure of success.

What, indeed, we again ask, has been the outcome of the purely dogmatic and religious instruction given to these people?

* We need hardly say that this is the sect which counts Dr. Davidson among its ministers. At the recent meeting of the "Congregational Union of England and Wales," held at Ipswich, some papers were read, amid general applause, on the subject of Inspiration, which show an immense advance on the part of the younger members. A friend, a literary man of distinction, has just called our attention to a remarkable letter on the same subject, admitted into the *English Independent* (the organ of the body), for Oct. 30th.

† "South Sea Bubbles," p. 291. ‡ *Ibid.*

What sort of Christianity is it that they have been made to imbibe? On this head we have two accounts, at first sight widely differing from each other, but both of them, we believe, substantially correct. We have the reports of the Wesleyan and other missionaries of that class. According to these there are ever so many thousands of inquirers, persons who have been baptized, communicants, native teachers, congregations of converts who are able to give a good account of the sermon, and answer rather abstruse questions about the "Gospel scheme." Discarding the conventional language used here and there of these converts and their conversion, the above is the result which may be justly claimed by the Missions. On the other hand, we have the reports of such visitors as Captain Beechey, Daniel Wheeler, Commander Wilkes, Herman Melville, and quite recently of "the Earl and the Doctor." The evidence of the four first-named will be found referred to in a previous number of the *Westminster Review*, and we shall not reproduce it here.* Moreover, it may be said, that nearly thirty years have elapsed since the visit of the most recent of these travellers. We shall, however, quote two short passages from the last-named book, which records observations made within the last few years. They entirely confirm the reports of previous writers; and, moreover, one of these passages shows us how the view of the missionary and the view of the man of the world, so seemingly divergent, may nevertheless be reconciled.

"I am afraid that the South Sea natives are apt to live two lives—a Church and a natural one—and naturally the missionary reports the Church one. I was much struck with this in one island where I attended divine service, and saw all the chief ladies of the land dressed out to the nines, taking notes of the sermon with big pencils on fools-cap paper, and looking as if butter would not melt in their pretty lips . . . . The next day I saw the identical saintly creatures madly executing the most improper gambados, all as wild, savage, and amorous as they were in the days of Captain Cook."†

Again:—

"If they were to state, as they might do with truth, that three women out of four, from the Island Queen downwards, had not the smallest notion of chastity, shame, or common decency; that the people were in the constant habit of going off in groups of fifty or sixty for the purpose of drinking themselves mad on orange rum, and committing the most fearful bestialities; that their old lascivious dances were as well known as ever, and that five minutes' excitement turned church-members into frantic savages, there might be a slight falling-off in the subscriptions."‡

Here we have the Jamaica Christian over again. Indeed,

* *Westminster Review*, July, 1856. "Christian Missions, their Principles and Practice." † "South Sea Bubbles," p. 237. ‡ *Ibid.* p. 303.

converts from the low races are everywhere much the same. They resemble the being in the fairy tale, in "Christabel," a beautiful maiden by day and a monster by night. To the missionary it is given to see the face of the "wise virgin" modestly bent over the hymn-book, or eagerly raised to the pulpit. The traveller obtains a glimpse of the lascivious postures, the wild orgies of the rum-drinking Menad!

A remarkable confirmation of our views as to the quality of the Christianity imbibed by these savages comes to us as we write, in the shape of a letter in a daily paper, on the subject of Fiji. The writer, Mr. Hyndman, has a personal acquaintance with these islands. Now there is no part of the globe which has been made a greater subject of missionary trumpeting than this same Fiji. The Wesleyans, in their last report, boast of having 58 missionaries, native and English, on the group; 29,223 members, and 57,037 scholars. Mr. Alderman MacArthur, speaking in the House of Commons on June 13, 1873, quoted "an official statement made by Mr. Clarkson, the treasurer of the government in Fiji, showing the population as 150,000 (of whom 2000 are whites), while the number of attendants at public worship was 107,250." That is to say they are more regular church-goers than the English. Well might Mr. MacArthur, impressed by all this amount of "worship," add triumphantly, "That country which lately was so deeply degraded by the most dreadful crimes, now contained a population advancing in education, civilization, and Christianity!"*

This is how these church-goers were employed a month after Mr. MacArthur's speech:—

In July a battle occurred between some of the settlers, together with a number of the lotued (Christianized) Fijians, and the Kai Tholos (devil tribes or mountaineers) of Na Thula. The former were victorious, the Christian Fijians finishing off the wounded "under circumstances of great cruelty."

"As soon as the battle was over, the friendly natives slipped out of their Christianity and, in spite of the protests of a missionary, prepared an elaborate bukola (cannibal) feast out of the remains of their foes. The beating of the great wooden cannibal drum bade friends for hours to the entertainment. It is far from improbable that whether the Fijians remain split into factions, or make common cause against the white man, they will throw off the new religion and fall back on their old rites, as so many of the tribes of New Zealand did during the Maori Wars."†

We have said that the above narrative confirms our general

* "Hansard's Debates," vol. ccxvi. p. 936.

† *Pall Mall Gazette*, Nov. 6, 1873. The *Fiji Times* relates the same story.

views, but we ought to add that it refutes our assumption that these converts never revert into pure barbarism, an assumption based simply on a desire not to overstate the case against missionaries.

We wonder whether these interesting warriors are back again in their pews; or whether, indeed, during these transactions, they ever gave up "sitting under" their accustomed ministers and fathers in the faith? Possibly, in the words of Archdeacon Clarke, the services were all the time *well attended* by many who acknowledged their error, *but were unable to withstand their besetting sin!*

Negative as the *religious* results of missions in the South Seas must be pronounced to be, still worse are the accounts which reach us from Western Africa. We will beg the attention of the reader to a few extracts from a discussion held at an Anthropological Society's meeting (in 1865, we think), a brief report of which we happen to have preserved; and we particularly call attention to the passage in italics. This is how African Christians are spoken of by competent observers:—

"Mr. HARRIS read a short paper founded on his own personal observation, in which he expressed his decided convictions that African Missions were failures. . . . The conversions were all hollow and insincere . . . the native boys who had been sent out of the Mission schools were thorough liars, thieves and drunkards, as compared with the uncontaminated negro boys. This he would vouch for, as he had employed many boys of both kinds. . . . On the other hand, the Mahometan proselytism was comparatively successful, probably because it was a simpler religion, avoiding argument and abstaining from denouncing other creeds. *If the money expended on Christian Missions in Africa were devoted to the establishment of model farms, and to the payment of good mechanics and agriculturists to teach the natives useful arts, he considered that they would speedily find improvements making larger strides in Africa than could with truth be said at present.*

"CAPTAIN BURTON said that Mr. Harris had laid before them a photograph which he (Captain Burton) could say from his own knowledge was exactly and disgustingly true. The native pagan of Africa was not a nice animal, but he was infinitely superior to the African converted to Christianity. No people could be worse, more immoral or everyway disgusting than the native Christians of Sierra Leone. . . . The Christian Missions were the curse of Western Africa, and the only antidote to it was the spread of Islamism, which was in reality spreading all along that coast. . . . African travellers rarely read the missionary advertisements from the Coast of Africa, which were mostly written in London *ad majorem populi injuriam*.

"Mr. WALKER speaking from his own experience could say that if the missionaries at Abbeokuta were to be relied upon, they had not saved even one soul. . . . He could say that in the Gaboon, with which he was acquainted, Christianity had receded; a community of converts there known as Jesus Christ Town, having for some years past degenerated into a society of thieves, liars, forgers, and prostitutes."

Such was the language held to the meeting, on the subject of missions, by those present who could lay claim to a practical experience of them. Something not altogether unlike it has recently been uttered by Governor Pope Henessy, in relation to the very locality then principally under discussion, Sierra Leone and the West African coast. We have heard the same kind of statements in a modified form from other experienced persons, friendly to missions, who deem it part of our duty to convert savages and idolaters into Christians, while admitting with a sigh of perplexity that in most cases which have come under their eye, conversion is by no means identical with improvement.

Yet the reason of all this, and of the failure of missions in a religious point of view, lies on the surface. In what has preceded we have already indicated it; and as we are not unfriendly to these enterprises, if only a little common-sense could be imported into them, we shall take the liberty of pressing it. Religious missions have been almost everywhere comparative failures, either because the Gospel has been tendered to classes—such as Mahometans, Jews and educated Buddhists—upon whom it is quite hopeless to attempt to make an impression, or, because in cases where it really might make way, a wrong method has been adopted.* The seed has been sown upon soil incapable of causing it to fructify, or else it has been sown upon soil which has not been duly prepared. If people will persist in the former undertaking, they must go their way. It is of the latter that we would speak here. There must, we say, be *preparation of the soil.* To receive, with anything like understanding, the Protestant system of belief requires some degree of mental culture on the part of a convert; and to preserve it, when so acquired, from deterioration requires a considerable amount of culture. This is what the great English and American Missionary Societies, with some happy exceptions, have never understood. Wishing them well, yet we are not of them, and can speak quite disinterestedly of their interests. We would remind them of the old proverb that lookers-on often see most of the game. They have always contemplated the setting forth of their own leading dogmas

* We have purposely passed by the question of missions to those who already possess an elaborate religious system of their own, and have confined ourselves to the lower races. *Why* the case of the Buddhists, &c., is hopeless may be gathered from Prof. Max Müller's able lecture in Westminster Abbey, delivered since the above was written.

as the one great object to which all others are mere accessories. If the unfortunate heathen is taught to read, it is mainly that he may read "The Sunday Party," or "The Spirit's Teaching," or, if there be a rival Romish mission in the neighbourhood, "Popery opposed to Truth" or "Scripture Light and Romish Darkness" in his own language. If he is taught his notes, it is that he may sing "Rock of Ages." If he is taught a trade, it is that he may be able to support himself without hanging on to the Mission, and not make the Mission look ridiculous by going back to his heathen relatives who had cast him off. And then these good people are amazed to find that the man stuffed with so many texts and tracts, and with his head addled by so many mysterious dogmas, can on occasion lie and steal as before. They are astounded to hear of a parcel of Hindoos going off with the New Testament, which they have been taught to read, and identifying Jesus with their own Guru, or religious teacher; or at a Maori tribe solemnly accepting the Old Testament, to the exclusion of the New, and justifying the most savage acts of barbarism in war by a reference to the cases of Jael and Sisera, Samuel and Agag.*

At the risk of some repetition, we must here observe that widely different as were the circumstances attending the spread of the Gospel in the first centuries of our era, from those which we observe at present; yet there was one condition precedent to success, which is common to both periods, and that is precisely the one we are insisting on. In order that the seed should bear fruit fifty and a hundredfold, it is requisite that it should fall upon good ground. Apart from what we have ventured to call the mysterious atmospheric conditions which, in the days of the Apostles, made the ground *good* for the reception of Christianity, there were certain other favouring circumstances which can be distinctly noted. We have only space to allude, in passing, to one or two of these. The races which may be said to have capitulated to Christianity, the highest of then known creeds, were, in many respects, the most highly endowed races then existing in the world. Can any one say the same, in the present day, of the Negro and the New Zealander? Even as it was, the creed began immediately to deteriorate in their hands, and sunk into something like idolatry, which lasted for more than a thousand years. The Reformation never would have had a chance of establishing itself if it had not been for a great preliminary increase in knowledge and culture. And this, by the way, should warn us—as so many other examples warn us—of what would certainly, in time, follow the conversion of any

* These incidents are recorded in "The Report of the Religious Tract Society for 1672," and the New Zealand papers.

ignorant race in the present day. Again, and this has been more than once pointed out, the Apostolic Missionary had a comparatively easy task when preaching to the heathen. In point of simple credulity, he was on a level with his hearer. He believed in ghosts and angels, and dreams and divination, and demoniacal possession; he believed in the whole heathen mythology, in the wars of the Titans, the conquests of Bacchus, the thefts of Mercury; he believed that Jupiter had taken the form of a swan, and that Io had been changed into a cow—only he considered that these gods and goddesses were devils, and that Jesus had put an end to their reign. The introduction of a new and more powerful Deity into the heathen Pantheon, who should supersede all others, was not an absolute novelty in mythology: had not Jupiter grown up and dethroned Saturn? It is impossible to take up this line with the Mahometan or the Buddhist. And in approaching the inferior races now-a-days, the preacher finds himself in a world of ideas which is not his own. No accommodation is possible between teacher and taught. The West African is called upon to acknowledge that all the accumulated beliefs and practices of thousands of years, the natural productions of the mental condition and circumstances of his race, pressed upon him with all the force accruing from ages of successive inheritance—that all this is so much nonsense. He is called upon to take in exchange a highly complex system evolved by other races, and in other climes, and embracing such conceptions as Trinity in Unity, the Atonement, Justification by Faith, Imputed Righteousness, and the metaphysics of Paul.

The truth has recently been told, in such terms as we venture to hope may at last arrest attention, by that eminent public servant and friend to missionary exertions—Sir Bartle Frere. In his reports to Government, in his book on Indian missions, in a speech at the Church Congress held at Bath, he has pointed out the right road, and the responsibility of failure will rest upon those who decline to follow it. In one of his reports he thus expresses himself:—

"If I might presume to advise the Bishop and the Missionaries I would introduce a far larger industrial element into their schools. Every one should learn a trade or mechanical art of some kind, or sufficient of agriculture to support himself. The teaching might be such as a good native artizan or mechanic or cultivator could impart, to which might be added tentatively, and with caution, instruction in European methods, and the use of European tools, which are not invariably adapted to African habits and necessities. Every boy should, I think, be taught to make himself useful in building a hut, in cultivating, in managing a boat or fishing canoe; washing, and mending his own clothes and shoes, and his nets and fishing tackle, &c."

Of one of the missionaries of the Church Society, he speaks as one "who has had the usual effect of exciting the admiration without securing the imitation of the people around him."

At the Bath Congress he spoke of "the futile attempt to make any great impression upon Heathendom unless they carried with them that civilization which they justly thought was the direct product of Christianity." He would bid the Bishop, when he had made a start, to "come back and look among our manufacturing population, our scholars, our doctors, and our nurses" for people to take back. Sir Bartle Frere further alluded to the London missions (to which we have already referred), and to the Moravian missions, as illustrating his remarks; and he might have spoken of the Americans in Ceylon, and especially of the course pursued by Rajah Brooke, as still further confirming the soundness of his views. We had marked for quotation numerous passages from the reports lying before us, in which evidence to a like effect is, as it were, wrung from the witnesses; but the length to which this article has already reached will prevent us from citing them. Yet we cannot help noticing one passage, in which the Bishop of Sarawak favours us with his opinion. The small capitals are not ours.

"I should be rejoiced if his highness the present Rajah saw his way to carry out the original design of Sir James Brooke, in the first foundation of the mission, which was to receive the children of the principal people for education and for instruction in the SIMPLE ARTS OF LIFE in the mission school."*

In plain language *religious* missions are admitted by their most intelligent friends to be complete failures.† To use a homely

---

* "Report of Society for the Propagation of the Gospel for 1871," p. 120.

† We cannot help giving here an illustration of the way in which one religious denomination, while puffing its own successes, will constantly pooh-pooh the efforts of its rivals and treat them as virtual failures. This is how a publication of the Society for the Propagation of the Gospel handles the work of Nonconformist missionaries in Madagascar. "The morality of the people is still of the lowest type, and becomes not the more attractive *by being lacquered over with a thin varnish of Christian phraseology.*" Further on we read of "this semi-heathen island, which is steeped in the foulest sensuality, *while it repeats the intolerant shibboleths of the seventeenth century.*"—*Under His Banner*, pp. 193, 194.

In the same publication we have an extraordinary story of a Chinaman who found the Athanasian creed intelligible. His name, which we would wish to make known as widely as lies in our power, was Foo Ngyen Khoon. He seems not only to have understood the creed, but to have been greatly agitated on hearing it read. "Why did you never teach me this before?" he exclaimed. "*This is the thing to teach the Chinese!*" Ibid. p. 92.

The above incident was related, with great approval, by an ex-missionary bishop (M'Dougall) in the Lower House of Convocation. This, then, is the kind of instruction which the High Church clergy would impart to the heathen! Has it never occurred to any of those who are so hard upon the phrase, the cart has been everywhere put before the horse. The suggestion made by Sir Bartle Frere is in reality one for the *secularization* of these societies. From agencies for the direct propagation of a higher faith, they would become agencies for the conveyance of worldly instruction, with the view, indeed, of paving the way for the reception of a higher faith; but their primary object would soon become their chief concern. Eton and Harrow, though managed by clergymen and furnished with chapels, are schools for teaching Latin and Greek, and not schools for teaching religion. So it would be with these missionary stations and schools. Under a thin veneer of episcopal supervision and dogmatic teaching they would be institutions for teaching people to build houses and boats, to cultivate land, to compound medicines, and to mend clothes. We think that all sensible people would have reason to be satisfied with such a change; Christians, because they ought to see that it would furnish them with the only *possible* chance of carrying out their ends: Infidels, because they must admit that, in any case, it is a good thing to teach savages to roll up pills, to build and to plant, to dig and to sew.

That there would be a great difficulty in bringing about the change of programme is clear. The chief supporters of these institutions are to be found among the so-called religious: in other words, among people who in matters of religion yield to their emotions, and (with some rare exceptions) do not consult their reason. Their delight is to hear of so many heathen being rescued from the bottomless abyss at such and such a station; and it would be tame work, in place of this, to have to read an account of the number of coats and trousers which the heathen have been taught to cut out. Still, we do not despair of the change being sanctioned, when it is seen, as surely it must before long, that the only way to evangelize the lower races is to educate them; when it is discovered that the "short cut" which has hitherto been attempted, is in reality, like many other short cuts, a road leading away from the point of destination. When this truth shall have dawned upon the religious, the *modus operandi* will of course present other difficulties. In India, as we have seen, the path is being cleared for the missionaries, though some of them are so blind to their own interests as to cry out against the godless system of education which is being enforced there.* Just as the nations brought under the dominion of Roman ideas were the only ones who embraced Christianity,

Nonconformists in the matter of *intolerant shibboleths*, that the Athanasian creed itself might, in the estimation of some, merit that appellation?

* In point of fact, a large part of the missionary success obtained in India has been due to secular schooling—to the adoption (for other purposes) of the very plan we are recommending.

so, of a surety, will the races in India which are brought under the dominion of English ideas be the only ones likely to embrace it in the present age. When that preliminary shall have been accomplished, England, if compelled to part company with India, may leave behind her the Christian moral system, not in the stage of a sickly exotic, but in the form of a flourishing plant safely rooted in prepared soil.

With regard to some other localities, such as the Pacific Islands, parts of Africa, Madagascar, Borneo, &c., we are of opinion that a number of the existing stations and isolated points of contact with the heathen should for the present be given up, and efforts be concentrated upon a few properly appointed centres of illumination. *Non multa sed multum* should be the motto of missionary societies. These centres should be located—there is no use in disguising the matter—on spots favourable to commercial intercourse between the natives and the foreigner. Dreadful as it may be to some to think of missionary stations being turned into trading stations, yet if the conclusion be arrived at that the first thing to be done is to instruct our intended converts in the arts of Europe, it will be obvious that the best stimulus to such instruction will consist in opening out a market for their industry, for their produce and the wares to which we have taught them to communicate a value by their labour. At the same time it ought to be distinctly understood that these benevolent adventurers must proceed to traffic and to convert, at their own risk; and that the Home Government will not feel bound to rescue them if they are captured, or to avenge them if they are eaten.

In what has preceded, we have written in what we believe to be the true interest of missions, which must, we repeat, to a certain extent and within certain limits, command the sympathy of all right-thinking people. For example, we should look with doubtful feelings on the conversion to Christianity of a Mahometan; but as these conversions are the rarest of occurrences, we are not called upon to examine closely their supposed advantages. On the other hand, there is a clear gain to humanity whenever people are attracted into a theological creed admittedly superior to their old one. From this point of view dogmatic Christianity may be looked at, either as a transitional phase of belief, or a permanent resting-place for the human mind. It is in the former character that we, of course, contemplate it. We are desirous that people should ultimately get to Edinburgh, and we are of opinion that the best way for them—at any rate a very good way—lies through London. Let those who want to get these people into London and to settle them there, take some account of our counsel, as far as relates to that portion of the road in which we have a common interest.

Art. IV.—The Working Classes.

1. *Histoire des Classes Ouvrières en Angleterre.* Par M. Nadaud, Ancien Représentant du Peuple. Paris: E. Lachaud, Editeur. 1872.
2. *Work and Wages Practically Illustrated.* By Thomas Brassey, M.P. London: Bell and Daldy. 1872.
3. *Our New Masters.* By Thomas Wright ("The Journeyman Engineer"). Strahan & Co. 1873.

THE most superficial observer can hardly have failed to note the fermentation now working in the lower strata of English society. For good or for evil, those composing the base of the social pyramid have awakened to a sense of the fact that their labour underlies, and therefore upholds the whole superstructure. They have discovered, also, that the source of political power lies below; and that, unlike all other influences, moral and intellectual, it *works upwards.* A new discovery in physics; a new law evolved from a congeries of freshly arranged facts, or a new conception born on the quiet heights of contemplation, may be dropped upon, to permeate, by a process of gravitation, the busy multitudes below. But in all that touches man's wants and rights, this law is reversed. When the masses see at all, they see microscopically and clearly. They feel strongly; and with no abstract difficulties to perplex, and with no conflicting interests to paralyse, they act swiftly. With extraneous aid sometimes; checked by opposition often; cajoled and betrayed; erring from miscalculation or passion; and always with an accompaniment of fear or contempt, even when courted, they have advanced and are now progressing. Act follows thought; and slowly but surely *they raise themselves.* From serfdom into the higher range of feudal service, and from feudal domination to personal freedom, the "working men" have struggled, and struggle still. The first break in the meshes was made in 1247, when privileges in kind, the chief characteristic of feudality, gave place to the payment of money wages. In 1350 the "free" labourer was first specifically noticed by the Legislature. Meanwhile the growth of manufactures in towns, was developing a strong spirit of independence, which was attempted to be repressed by a quick succession of measures enforcing the subjection of labourers to the arbitrary power of their employers. In 1360 a confirmatory law was passed, rendering the "Statute of Labourers" of 1350 more stringent, by the attempt to fix under heavy penalties, a maximum rate of wages. Further efforts were made in 1363 to control the labourer by a species of sumptuary law; and in 1376, the Commons made complaint that masters were obliged to give their labourers high wages to prevent their running away. In 1378 the growth of manufactures, the result of the Flemish immigration, excited the jealousy of the sister industry—agriculture, and complaints were again made in the Commons, "that persons engaged in agriculture fled into cities, and became artificers, mariners, and clerks, to the great detriment of husbandry."

About this time *the worm turned.* Wat Tyler was the clumsy exponent of a long repressed discontent, and henceforth the dread of "going too far" introduced a new element into the councils of the dominant class.

This sketch sufficiently indicates the measure taken of the working man in the political economy of former times, and marks clearly enough the slough of degradation out of which he has gradually and persistently *raised himself.* From slavery and servile dependence, he has now assumed an attitude in regard to capital which by comparison may appear aggressive. We say *by comparison*, because it has yet to be shown that the demand for higher wages is *intrinsically* wrong, or that the mode of enforcing a fair demand has been unnecessarily stern. If the spirit exhibited by the "working classes" in the attainment of their rights has been an exclusive, a narrow, and a bitter one, it would be hard to deny that they, like Shylock, have had "Christian example" for such a course; but equally hard to prove that they, like him, have done anything to "better the instruction." We by no means intend to say that there exists amongst even the leaders of Trades Unions any acknowledged personal feeling in regard to "turning the tables" upon the generic employer; but we maintain that traditional feelings—untraced, unmeasured, and unacknowledged, and existing altogether apart from the exciting cause, may be, and are, hereditarily transmitted. Some one has defined an intuition to be an idea of which the origin has been forgotten; in such case, the feeling we have described may be called "intuitive." It is the old story, *mutatis mutandis*, of the wolf and the lamb. The reasons for the animosity are all wrong, but there is an ingrained dislike that prompts and excuses, and so helps to make the action right; and like Irish hatred of English rule, the proximate and quoted cause is not the real one.

The antagonism between capital and labour now existing in this country, is as unnatural as it is unfortunate. "Is't not as if this hand should tear this flesh?"—but the feeling is not born of to-day. Its origin may be found, as we have shown, far back in history. The masters have had their "innings," the men are now going in for theirs; and an altered commercial relationship, sound and healthy in itself, is taking place, while there still exists a residuum of the old feudal spirit on the one side, and a transmitted feeling of class oppression on the other. Neither section is at ease. Masters cannot yet understand that the old notion of patronage and kindness must be "levelled down" into a purely commercial relation between wages and work. They speak of ingratitude and insolence when, in the face of kindly conceived supplementary additions to wages in kind, labour talks of "rights." They forget that the very existence of such a feeling, condemns as selfish and interested what they imagined they were giving in a spirit of pure philanthropy. On the other hand, workmen are not yet habituated to their newly acquired power and importance. Unaccustomed to ride, they have found themselves suddenly placed in the saddle. Moreover, along with an awakened sense of *right*, their Trades Union organization has imparted to them a sense of *might*; and if they do not yet quite realize the fact, it will sooner or later come home to them that the People's Representation Act of 1867 has placed the political power of this country in their hands. All this puts them into a state of fermentation and vague expectation, which alarms society, but which is perfectly natural and innocuous if left to work its own cure. Even the agricultural labourer, the least intelligent, the most apathetically contented, and most under the influence of the old feudal supremacy, has been warmed to self-assertion, with a result upon the minds of those employing them much akin to that produced upon the workhouse officials when little Oliver Twist plucked up courage "*to ask for more!*"

However foundationless it may be, according to our estimate, we must not shut our eyes to the fact that much distrust prevails in the minds of many well-meaning and intelligent persons as to the future of the working classes, and through them of this country; and this doubt and anxiety will probably exercise considerable influence on the results of the next general election. The questions are asked—Whence arises the prevailing ferment? What direction will it take in spreading? What are the compensatory principles at work? What the guiding agencies? What the ameliorating and reassuring influences?

To aid us in the solution of the problem which these questions help to make up, we have had of late several characteristic publications, each in its own province and in its own way, throwing light upon this important and interesting subject. The "Histoire des Classes Ouvrières en Angleterre" has the especial advantage of conferring upon us the "giftie,"

"To see oursels as ithers see us;"

and from the point of view at once of foreigner and handicraftsman. M. Nadaud's experience of English workmen was not picked up as a bird of passage, nor in dilettante fashion. He for years became "one of us;" worked as a journeyman mason; mixed with English workmen in England, and tested their wants and wishes by contact and colloquy. His honourable career abroad has been testified to in a preface by Louis Blanc, and he claims the friendship and acknowledges certain obligations to Mr. T. Hughes, M.P., Mr. Ludlow, and others, whose names are familiar in this country in connexion with working-class interests. The opinions of these gentlemen are perfectly well known, but because their lights upon this subject have by no means been hidden under a bushel, we confess that we should have preferred to have heard M. Nadaud speak from his own platform; and that we should have attached more value, as well as interest, to the results of his own research, pure and simple. *Noscitur ex sociis*, however, may, in the best sense of the phrase, be applied to M. Nadaud's mixing in such society; but we take it that his opinions are valuable to Englishmen only to the extent that they are those of an operative foreigner, and we fear in his case—owing perhaps to the objective influence which Goethe speaks of as insensibly changing a man's nature—that however valuable his conclusions may be to his own countrymen (and the work was written for them), they will lose value to readers in this country in proportion as they merely reflect the opinions of eminent English economists.

Mr. Brassey's work is cast in a different mould. He regards the same problem from the opposite point of view; and, with a more restricted outlook, sets before the public the experiences of his father, the late Mr. Brassey, in a field peculiarly his own. The position of that eminent and successful contractor as a master was an exceptional one, inasmuch as his operations were on a scale so gigantic and so scattered over the world, as to lead him to merge the individual workman in the class; and even to lose sight (as it were) of human nature, and to deal with the working class as a concrete machine rather than as a section of humanity. The chief value of the book is derived from this experience. From its exceptional nature it helps to supplement and confirm rather than to contrast with the experience of those who estimate the class by the individual sample.

The work entitled "Our New Masters" may be supposed to supply the link by which the chain of evidence would be completed. It has, however, the drawback, from which M. Nadaud's History is free, that it is written by one whose views as a "Journeyman Engineer" must necessarily be microscopic. As the worst picture of a battle would be drawn by one immersed in the thick of the fray, so a real "Journeyman Engineer," or any one having a close but restricted experience, would not thereby be entitled to a confidence extending beyond his personal knowledge and testimony. The several witnesses we have cited may, however, collectively help us to answer the question, What are the real characteristics—what the aims—and what the future of the English working classes?

That the working man of this country has distinguishing qualities no one who knows him at all can deny. He is more stolid than his French competitor, and less torpid than his ancestors of the Teutonic race. He differs from the Swiss and the Italian in a marked manner; and even within the limits of Great Britain he stands prominently out from his Celtic brethren. Probably we are not wrong in saying that he combines, and by combining modifies and improves, the peculiarities of all who have conquered and peopled this land. To this we may ascribe the influences of race or blood, and call him a more harmoniously built-up specimen of humanity than any of those races who excel in particular ways. How much he owes to each race Max Müller would trace in our mixed language, the basis of which he characterizes as unmistakeably Teutonic. Hence, while M. Nadaud ascribes the English workman's independence, his love of liberty, his obedience to law, and the elements generally of his social progress to Protestantism, we would go deeper still, and ascribe that Protestantism to his "race." The manifestation of the religious feeling takes form and colouring from peculiarities of race, modified by intellectual development. The graceful Pantheism of the Greek was the natural birth of temperament and the surroundings of his everyday life. Buddhism could have had no existence except amongst the inhabitants of India, and Mahomet no followers except amongst dwellers in the East. The Southern imagination alone gives its full significance and value to religious ceremonies which are mere ecclesiastical upholstery and theatrical tinsel, to the colder northern temperament. The early Christianity of the aboriginal Briton was a species of Congregationalism, compared with the faith imported by Augustine and his "forty monks" in 597; and it is questionable whether the latter system ever found a congenial reception in the Anglo-Saxon mind. Priestcraft in the early history of this country has always had a political significance; and piety been made a convenient cloak to policy. It has been a useful adjunct to kingcraft; but the steady Anglo-Saxon nature has always chafed against the doctrine of Church infallibility, from the time of Bede to that of the Reformation; and when M. Nadaud says:—"Les droits politiques d'un peuple ne sont, on le voit, que le fruit mûr que la religion a produit.

Telle religion, telle constitution." He forgets that the principles of the English Constitution were asserted at Clarendon, and endorsed and extended at Runnymede, and that the religion of 1164 and of 1215 was not the Protestantism to which he assigns the English love of freedom, but Roman Catholicism. He is nearer the truth, however, when subsequently he states that:—

"L'Anglais, dirigé dans toutes ses actions par un grand bon sens, est d'un caractère fier et audacieux, quoique en apparence calme. Les marques de déférence qu'il montre à ses lords ne procedent pas d'une idée de crainte, ni d'un sentiment de servilisme. Ce qu'il vénère ce n'est pas la personne de ses maîtres, *c'est la loi*, pour laquelle il a une sorte de fétichisme."

English freedom is the natural offshoot of Anglo-Saxon blood, race, temperament. It is no extraneous parasitical plant, but the natural indigenous growth of a congenial soil. Its roots are in the earliest stages of English national existence, and its life will be conterminous only with the Anglo-Saxon race. Throughout history it has flourished under tyranny—been fostered under oppression, fought for in the field and asserted in the Senate, until it has set England in the eye of the world as—

"A land of settled government:
A land of just and high renown,
Where freedom broadens slowly down
From precedent to precedent."

It is to race and blood therefore that we must look for the true exponents of social development; and from the experience of the past, we may venture to read the future. No education, no training, no "unfolding" (Entwickelung) could develop into a similar entity the mercurial Frenchman and the impassible Teuton. No effect of religious systems, no action of law, no academic influence will impart the flash of Irish wit to the Flemish boor; nor will they ever supplant the Anglo-Saxon love of athletic sports by the Bardic proclivities of the Welsh; nor convert the shrinking dread of the pure Celt into the craving of the Teutonic race, whenever and wherever it touches upon the sea, to take to the water like ducks.

The laws of a people are more intimately interwoven with their national life, and are consequently more strongly characteristic than even the religious *system* they may adopt. If the origin of law be enforced or protected custom, and customs grow naturally out of the combined character and circumstances of the people generating those customs, then a mixture of races means also the gradual adoption of the best customs of each. If the fusion take place by a continuous stream of several races, an absorbing and conforming process will be at work, as in the United States of America. But if, as in most cases of conquest, and particularly when, as in Britain, the conquering races *settle*, and putting in force their own laws and practising their own usages, there will then be, instead of absorption and conformity, discontent, discussion, and finally, modification and improvement. Nor will the process itself be valueless in its educational influences. The elements of social and political life are excited, and the end is the assertion and prevalence of a spirit of civil liberty and equality.

In England this was an often repeated process, and with accumulating results. Romans, Saxons, Danes, and Normans each successively laid the "red hand" upon the soil; and each wave of invasion brought new phases of manners, customs, and law. No conquered people at once can coalesce cordially with the victors, and when the hand is tied and liberty of action restrained, speech at least is free to criticise the usages and polity of the conquerors. Acquiescence is not submission; the Anglo-Saxon intellect has developed best under the influence of counter-irritants; and grumbling is one form after all of liberty. Ajax set the tongue of Thersites agoing, and speedily had the worst of the encounter!

The characteristics of the British workman, we maintain therefore, were developed, and may be found far back in history. They belong to him by hereditary descent, and may and will be, we trust, transmitted to his descendants. What he has been, so in the main, we believe he will continue to be, a sturdy assertor of his birthright of liberty, but not blinded nor misled by passion, nor unmindful of justice and of law. Contrasted with the history of the classes above him, he will not suffer by the comparison. He has been struggling since the Heptarchy against a dominant spirit, and against laws embodying that spirit. In making these laws he has had no voice: and but small hope by legitimate political or social action to amend acknowleged abuses. And yet he has on the whole patiently and persistently, and in the main with dignity, asserted his rights, and made his wants and influence beneficially felt. He has suffered often from a prevalent, false, and selfish political economy, and from a narrow and unjustly exclusive social philosophy. At times, as we have said, he, like the worm, has turned; he, like the best of humanity, has erred; he, like those above him boasting higher intellectual advantages, and subjected to less temptation, has sometimes lost hope and resisted. But how seldom! Test him by the rigour and pungency of his irritations; judge him fairly in the face of his wrongs, and the verdict will surely be a penalty mitigated on the plea of extenuation.

We wish we could believe that the political power conferred upon the working classes in 1867 was conceded in the spirit of trust and hope with which we think they ought to be regarded. We fear, however, that the boon only fell to them because of the strife and jangle of competing parties. As regards the Conservatives, it was a bid for place and power. As regards the new constituency, it was a "leap in the dark," so far as the use they would make of the privilege without previous training, and when taken by surprise. On the whole it was a just measure passed in a way so reckless and so unprincipled, as to make the angels weep to see the interests of millions dealt with as by a throw of the dice!

The indecent haste with which this measure was settled by the party in power,* is the more to be regretted because it is by the members of that party that charges have been made against the class to whom they have handed over the political power of the country. It is stated by them and others, and currently believed by a large number of well-meaning persons, that the working classes are drunken, reckless, vicious, and immoral; tending in politics to Republicanism, and in morals to pauperism, vice, and crime. That they are ignorant and irreligious, and therefore that they are in one word "*dangerous.*" There is, however, an amusing variation in this heavy bill of indictment. When the artisan becomes known as the "Conservative working man;" and falls under clerical influence, or competes, in deference for "a lord," with the model agricultural labourer; or more especially *when his vote is wanted*, his whole social and moral status becomes changed. He is then petted and praised. He becomes the bulwark of the constitution; the pride, as he is the pillar, of England's industrial greatness. His virtues then are his own—his vices and weaknesses are the transient consequences of a vicious civilization for which he is not responsible. If, generically, he is a wild beast, and in his natural state to be feared, yet when tamed by the influence of the "Bible and Beer," and the judiciously administered commendation of the aristocracy, he is humble, docile, and useful. Both these aspects are so partially true, that they cannot be met by a curt denial.

"The lie that is all a lie
May be met with and fought outright;
But the lie that is half a truth,
Is a harder matter to fight!"

We take it, however, that the typical British workman is a fair

---

* Sir John Pakington has publicly stated that this, the most important measure of the Reformed Parliament, was determined upon at a Cabinet meeting *in ten minutes.*

average specimen of humanity, neither very "dangerous" nor at all a paragon of perfection. The "dangerous" theory may have gained support from the fact that he lives essentially in a "glass house." Unlike the classes above him, all he does, and is, may be seen and discussed. His door is always open, and his "short and simple annals" may be recited, for aught he cares, in every market-place. He at least is no hypocrite. He conceals nothing, and partly from genuine openness, and partly from want of delicacy, he "washes his dirty linen" indifferently in public or in domestic privacy, with supreme disregard to the comments of "Mrs. Grundy." Most of his characteristics, therefore, may be readily noted, and as "men's evil manners live in brass," and as there is "more detraction at one's heels than fortune before," scandal may easily be manufactured, and spread unchallenged. The "paragon" theory is simply a political euphuism. It is at best a hollow friendship with "the mammon of unrighteousness" for party purposes. The natural language of Mark Antony to the "rabblement," except "for a purpose," is that of "honest Casca!"

The English workman excels in all occupations requiring a combination of coolness and intelligence. The peculiarities of his mixed genealogy are the foundation of his industrial success. He unites much of the Teuton steadiness with something of the Celtic fire; avoiding the stolidity of the one, and the nervous irritability and infirmity of purpose of the other. He inherits also, with his Scandinavian frame, his Saxon steadiness, and his aboriginal spirit, physical strength and endurance; courage, patience, perseverance, and intelligence. Perhaps to his native coal and climate he owes (besides industrial pre-eminence) his bright fireside influences, bringing in their train cleanliness and the domestic virtues. He lacks, on the other hand, the taste and *savoir faire* of the Gaul, and he is too hardy to understand the sensuous *far niente* enjoyment of the Italian peasant. His failings, like his virtues are robust, and lacking the opportunity, perhaps the desire, for a flow of small gratifications, he takes to his pleasure seriously, and makes of it a matter of business. In plain speaking, he inherits with other specialities a taste for strong waters, and is inclined to excess. Abroad he has got the name of an habitual drunkard, and it seems to be a part of the programme of the "United Kingdom Alliance" similarly to take away his character at home. Is this charge true?

No one denies that a large amount of drunkenness exists in this country. So alive is society *intellectually* to the evil of it, that no social question, except that of the religious difficulty in regard to education, subtends so large an angle of public attention. The "United Kingdom Alliance" has done at least so much good in the cause of sobriety that by the habitual use of exaggerated statements, it has awakened the community to entertain the question whether England is to be drunk or enslaved. If vague generalities emphatically enunciated; and vigorous denunciations persistently repeated; and the hardy use of coincidences as direct consequences; and the grand simplicity of the logic that all human vice and misery flow from "drink;" and that all human nature is to be fitted to the Procrustean dimensions of the Permissive Prohibitory Bill;—if all this narrow earnestness, glib talk, and loud assertion could bring home conviction to the mind of the public, the "United Kingdom Alliance" would have accomplished a great work, and the millennium would be at hand. But to terrify is not to convince; and to persuade timid people that no remedy will influence human nature but the impossible one of strained legislation, is simply to drive society dazed with iteration, to adopt the aphorism of the Bishop of Peterborough. We wish we could be sure that the Sir Wilfrid Lawsonites have not discredited and prevented the working of what Dr. Chalmers beautifully calls "the expulsive power of a new affection," in the hearty application of the persuasive influences of healthy amusements, comfortable houses, social clubs, reading-rooms, free libraries, and general culture. These counter attractions are not unfortunately heroic enough in their treatment, and swift enough in their effect, to suit the impatient philanthropy of the gentlemen of the Alliance. Amendment by such agency would be too slow, and too little seen, in its action. It would only "grow like the summer grass fastest by night, unseen but cressive in its quality," and nothing short of the brutum fulmen of law will satisfy their craving for tangible results.

How it is that the "United Kingdom Alliance" has got hold of the public imagination, to the extent they have, may be easily explained. In the first place they deceive themselves. They are philanthropists of one idea, and habitually fix their thoughts and shape their acts to one end. They, therefore, naturally exaggerate the importance of their aim, and distort the perspective of all its surroundings. They are earnest to the extent of fanaticism; and the fever of enthusiasm is infectious. On the other hand, the well meaning but socially indolent portion of the public incline to acquiescence in order to evade importunity. To avoid the examination of such a question is a gain; and to have its logical complications and its statistical difficulties presented in the neat form of a syllogistic conclusion, seems an agreeable division of ethical labour. Then again, "Constant dropping wears a stone," and the resolute persistency of an extensive and energetic organization has so wearied the impatient, and scared the weak, that judgment in the great case of national drunkenness has been allowed to go by default. Moreover it is the business of no disinterested person to defend so degrading a vice. Everybody, even the victims of self-indulgence themselves, hate and decry it. As an abstract question of truth and justice it may interest a few; and some, like ourselves, may take up the pen to remove as best we may, the unmerited aspersions cast upon a large class in connexion therewith. If it were not for this, we should gladly let the end condone the means; and wish the members of the Alliance God-speed in their chief object, at the same time lamenting their sadly mistaken appliances and the reactionary effect of their exaggerations.

There are, in fact, no reliable statistics on "drunkenness;" nor can there be until an accurate definition be given as to what it really is. Its conventional designation is as slippery as an eel. It changes like a chameleon, and is as chromatic in its variations as a dissolving view. From the "slightly elevated" phase to that of "lighting a pipe at a pump handle," we may easily reckon up more than two dozen epithets, showing a power of lingual fusion equal to the insensible blending of the gamut from the strings of the violin. Police reports are the uncertain source of what we know of the "increase of drunkenness;" but the number of "apprehensions" is rather evidence of police vigilance than of the variations in the rate of drunkenness;" the number of "convictions" may be taken equally as evidence of the condition of magisterial digestion, or whether the bench reflects the "Minos, Rhadamanthus, and Æacus" vein of justice, or the philanthropy which despises "Charity Organization," and is loose enough to take into consideration the "wife and children at home!" Given the proclivities of the chief magistrate of any town, and we may safely predicate the comparative amount of its drunkenness. There would as naturally be an "increase of drunkenness" if Sir Wilfrid Lawson were mayor, as that it would dwindle under the presidency of Sir Michael Bass; and both instances would simply mark the sympathy of subordinates with the known opinion of those in authority.

The current utterance of the "United Kingdom Alliance" would lead the world to suppose that drunkenness was the root of all social evil. It is said to be the cause of pauperism, vice, and crime. It is stated that four-fifths of the pauperism of the country is due to the love of drink. So long as "pauperism, vice, and crime" were on the increase, that increase was cited as the clear proof that drunkenness must have increased also; and from the increase of drunkenness thus proved, was established the indisputable fact that its concomitant and inevitable results were spreading fast and far. Let us admit the logic and accept the conclusion. The case therefore may stand thus:—that a large proportion of the pauperism and crime of the country results from drunkenness. Surely then, a diminution of pauperism and crime would show that (at least) drunkenness had *not* increased.

On January 1, 1863, the number of paupers (exclusive of vagrants) receiving relief in England and Wales was 1,142,624. On the 1st of January, 1873, the number was 890,372.

In the year 1862 the number of criminal offenders convicted in England and Wales was 15,312. In the year 1872 it was 10,862: while during the decade linked within the above dates the population rose from 20,590,356 to 23,356,414 (or 13·4 per cent.), and the deposits in the Post Office Savings' Banks alone, swelled from 4,993,124*l.*, in 1864, to 19,318,339*l.*, in 1872. Again, as regards education, which, inefficient as it has proved, under the denominational system (turning out in England and Wales during 1872 no more than 8319 6th standard children as the finished product) nevertheless indirectly trains to habits of order and inculcates a sense of propriety and of self-respect, and so tends to good citizenship. In 1862 the number of children present at the annual inspection was 906,158, and in 1872 it had risen to 1,737,002, or nearly double. All these "facts and figures" prove incontestably that the moral status of the community of which the working classes form the widest and deepest strata, and who are confessedly the most vulnerable as regards "pauperism, vice, and crime," *has advanced immensely.* And yet it is in the face of this moral and economic progress that the charge is made against those classes that they have become more drunken, more absolutely pauperized, and more politically "dangerous!"

We have already said that there are no reliable statistics whatever in regard to drunkenness. The police reports from large towns, we repeat, are evidence of influences very different from the results they primarily affect to establish. But dismissing them as insufficient testimony regarding the main issue, we may learn with advantage what they do prove as to collateral and subordinate facts.

Liverpool has the unenviable notoriety of being the most drunken town in the kingdom. In analysing the statistics of this populous place, we go therefore to the most instructive evidence we can obtain. In the year ending September, 1870, the number of apprehensions of persons "drunk," was 22,925. In the year ending September, 1872, the number of apprehensions dropped to 18,810; but the notable fact in connexion with this statement is, that of this large number only 2972 *were householders,* and this without any disturbing effect from the operation of the Licensing Act.* Further, it is a significant fact that inasmuch as of the total number of 18,810 cases, no less than 15,694 transgressors were *lodgers,* the prevailing intemperance does not attach to the socially responsible population. It is a surface malady rather than a deep-seated constitutional disease. It is not the pith and core of society that is tainted—the fathers of families—the payers of rates, and voters at elections, that swell the register of drunkenness, but the unsettled residuum, the waifs and strays having loose ties, floating here and there, probably young, undeterred by domestic influences, and without homes in the proper sense of the word. They sleep in lodgings, and make the public-house, or music-hall, or dancing saloon, the resorts of their leisure. It is there they seek for society, shelter, amusement; and there they are constrained (at least in public-houses) to drink in order that the comforts they thus enjoy may be paid for. Unless they "give their orders" they must "turn out," and the result of giving their orders is that they get "overtaken by liquor," and caught by the police. Under the "heroic treatment" of the Alliance, these resorts might be forcibly closed; but where would the unfortunate lodgers go for warmth, shelter, and society?

The next point worthy of consideration is the fact as shown in the table giving the *accumulation* of offences amongst those apprehended. The real state of this terrible Liverpool picture of intemperance is this,—that 10,697 persons, by the return of September, 1872, out of a population of 505,200, have each "got drunk" *once in twelve months.* It is weak and foolish to get drunk at all; but considering that the bulk of the transgressors are "lodgers," driven to hot rooms and amongst loose associates, and into a vitiated atmosphere of opinion; considering "hocussed" drink, excited discussion, foolish habits of "treating," vicious betting of "glasses round," the conceit of being "manly," and Delilah seductions, the wonder really is that the outward and visible sign of the inward social folly is not more blatant than it is. And bad as it undoubtedly is, more amazing still that two-thirds of it all consists of only *a single slip!*

But it is said that the quantity of alcoholic liquors annually

* The new Licensing Act received the Royal Assent on August, 1872. On the 25th September the justices made the order for *early closing* to come into effect on the 25th October, 1872. It is obvious therefore that there could be no new element introduced to disturb the comparison up to September, 1872, from the operation of the new Act.

consumed is enormous, and that consequently there must be excessive drinking, and a vast amount of drunkenness not dealt with by the police. It is said that 100,000,000*l.* are spent each year in drink; that we drank ourselves out of the Alabama difficulty; that our financial prosperity is only another name for social rottenness; and that such "self-imposed taxation" is degrading.

We will not enter into the question as to the quantity of intoxicating liquor which may be good for any one. To some it is poison, to others it is food. A given quantity is maddening to many; while to different temperaments the same quantity merely restores exhausted brain power. Dr. Chambers calls the desire for it "*instinctive*,"* and speaks of total abstinence as a "fallacy;" while unscientific declaimers quote individual examples of benefit as a criterion for the whole human race.

The allusion to quantity and cost raises the question of the relative venality of *politic drinking* and of *absolute drunkenness*. It raises the question also of the sin of such politic drinking, as against the social loss and inconvenience of the last stage. It further raises the question as between the "well-to-do" middle class consumer in snug bar-parlours and the working man; between the toper and the tipsy man; the man who has time to habitually tipple, and so "season himself" up to the capacity to carry off indefinite "ports," "sherries," and "brandies" in cabs, and the man whose circumstances make him huddle his drinking into a short space of time at the end of the week. As it is, the self-indulgent working man flouts public opinion, and the whole class is maligned; while the politic drinker adroitly preserves his own character and that of his class. Again, the man who takes a few glasses of wine every day, at or after dinner, because "he likes it," or because it "agrees with him," shows a certain power of self-restraint, as compared with him who would mass the hebdomadal quantity together, and so get drunk; but there is another, and we incline to think a truer, version of this arrangement. Such politic drinking is evidence of a more ingrained and constantly operative habit *of self-indulgence*. It may arise from the coolly calculated epicureanism that avoids excess in order that gratification may be prolonged. In this way no law is broken, no social nuisance is caused, no reputation is

* "Is it not right to call the desire for alcohol 'instinctive' when it is stated by the Editor of the 'Band of Hope Review' (on the authority of the famous teetotal lecturer Mr. Gough) that of half a million of persons who had taken vows of abstinence in the United States, 350,000 broke them? truly an awful outburst of nature! Have the same proportion ever violated vows of chastity, or any other similar solemn obligation?" "Digestion and its Derangement," by T. K. Chambers, M.D.

lost. He who practises it is not a drunkard, but he may be, and often is, *a sensualist.*

It is a common platform argument to condemn the English artisan in comparison with his foreign competitor. It is said that the workman abroad is more sober, more intelligent, more diligent, and more ingenious than the same class here. We very much doubt the truth of this current notion. It must always rest upon opinion, and each one's opinion on the subject must be formed by his own immediate surroundings. The general impression is, that the inhabitants of wine-growing countries are sober; but as regards the French artisan, at least, we have reason to doubt the correctness of this idea. We believe that in this, as in the counter idea as regards the Englishman, no allowance has been made for deterioration on the one hand, and of improvement on the other. We think it might easily be proved that the ouvrier of the present day fails as much in the matter of sobriety as he does in the violence of his political opinions and in the laxity of his morals. The modern Communist is not a satisfactory element in French social life. In Paris and the other large towns of France, he is no longer content with the thin "vin du pays," but has become a consumer of alcohol in a more concentrated form. Even the flâneurs of the boulevards, the habitnés of the cafés, and "Jacques Bonhomme" in general, take to Vienna beer, absinthe, cognac, and methylated spirits, to the discredit of eau sucrée and café noir. The sobriety of the German is essentially that of temperament, muddled by thin beer and revived by schnaps. He soaks, as he smokes, quietly and steadily. His enjoyment is spun out into a subdued contentment; and what he gains in decency of demeanour he pays for in time. His vice chronically smoulders, while the Englishman's flares up periodically, sharp and short. The Swiss workman is no model of sobriety.* He imbibes large quantities of the cheap wine of the country, and in the large towns often transgresses. On the whole, we incline to believe that whatever difference there may be between the foreign and the English workman in outward manifestation, may be accounted for by a more ubiquitous, officious, and official police. With a climate forbidding much reliance on out-door amusements; with small appreciation of the beauty of colouring, of form, or of variety; with no sensibility to the delicate influences of climate in itself; the English artisan naturally centres his enjoyments upon the

---

* We have the authority of an English officer high in rank, and a close observer, and who has resided some years at Lausanne, that during the short period of his residence he had seen more drunkenness there than he had in England during the whole of his life.

more robust animal gratifications. An æsthetic Pantheism is impossible in perennial fogs, and with the thermometer under 50°; and equally futile would be the attempt to invest his Lares and Penates with any ideal grace in houses whose chief characteristic is typhoid fever. His bright coal fire is suggestive of cooking, or of warmth to enable him to endure his ill-fitting doors and damp floors. He is "in the way" by his own hearth. His wife and he are hardly companions. Their short and simple aims and cares are soon discussed to be dismissed; and uncultured, and with no internal resources, what remains? His interest is stirred and his attention taken up by his Union and his workshop politics; his ideas find more fitting scope with his mates at the public-house; and yet, in spite of the impossibilities of an out-door life, and in spite of want of the attractiveness of home life, the story of Liverpool vice shows that it is not the householder that swells the annals of drunkenness. Give him the surroundings of the Frenchman and the Italian, and what might he not become? We may, as Burns tells us, *partly* compute "what's done," but, after all, the highest merit may lie in "what's resisted."

Then again, society can never be brought to treat the drunkard as a sinner. It may use hard words, but there is always a smile to counteract their pungency. The head condemns the vice, but the heart looks upon it as a "merrie failing,"—one to be treated with a jesting forbearance; for is not the tipsy man's jollity contagious? Angels may weep to see the aberrations of inebriety, but humanity always laughs. On the stage the eccentricities of drunkenness never excite disgust and reprobation. Sir Toby Belch is a universal favourite. Tipsiness "draws," in theatrical phrase, like some other reprehensible exhibitions, and to "draw" means public approval. The stage may "catch the manners living as they rise," and probably burlesques with their inane puns, coarse wit, vicious conceits, and indelicate costumes, *do* hold up a mirror to the tastes of the age; but it cannot be said that such representations "shoot folly as it flies." Rather do they tend to foster by familiarizing, and by familiarizing to spread the small vices and follies of society, and notably the prevalent vice of drinking. Why will the middle and upper classes offer a constant temptation to domestic servants to acquire a taste for stimulants? Why is a poor man to be always rewarded for small service with "a glass?" and why to him is "a glass" made to be evidence of small hospitality on the part of superiors, except that there is a vitiated condition of feeling and opinion in the educated classes? and *the working men know it!*

But with whom does the sin lie—the tempter or the tempted?

Surely with the cultivated intelligence, which, "looking before and after," gauges the evils of drink and the sin of self-indulgence, and yet persists in leading on the poor and ignorant, whose existence is merely material! Nothing but "law," say the members of the "Alliance," will reach and restrain the working men; but how as to the classes above them? Surely *they* are amenable to reason—*they* do not need "the sword of the Lord, and of Gideon;" *they* might be induced to withdraw this stumbling-block in the way of their blind brethren, and so help to build up a breezy, healthy public opinion. As it is, the working classes have a right to infer from what they see and know, on the part of those above them in the social scale, that they sanction, if not absolutely encourage, initiatory drinking; and that, in the main, they only reprobate the excess when it comes "betwixt the wind and their nobility," or affects their pockets through the payment of Poor Rates.

The connexion of pauperism with intemperance is no doubt a close one; but the loose and exaggerated statements* made on this relation only tend to defeat their own purpose. It is idle to ascribe 75 per cent. of the pauperism of the country to intemperance; and the common sense of the country knows it. It is as true to human nature to regard drunkenness as the result of poverty; and it would be wiser to look for a remedy, not in coercion, but in moral tonics. When self-indulgence, passion, want, despair, one or all, point to the commission of crime, drink supplies the spurious courage required for its perpetration, and applies the anodyne to assuage the pangs of conscience when perpetrated. And when care and anxiety and hunger bring sickness, and "home" means a starving wife and drooping children, and is the centre of hopelessness and misery, then drink brings the temporary oblivion which may ward off madness. Earth would be a happier sphere if the enigmas of life were no deeper than "drink," and reached no farther than the public-house!

There is no mistaking the dread and dislike of all classes to the social sore of pauperism. The poor themselves hate all connected with it, and the rich shrink from its concomitants as from a leprosy. The very terms "Poor Law," "Parish," "pauperism," "poorhouse," have in them the ring of social degradation. And yet there is no more valid reason to be assigned for this feeling beyond that given by Shylock for his hatred of Antonio—"a lodged hate, and a certain loathing." The disgrace has been so ingeniously indoctrinated, that the poor will in many cases beg "*to keep themselves off the Parish!*" It is politic, unquestionably, to foster this detestation, as such a feeling is a

* See "Convocation Report on Intemperance."

stronger deterrent than the scrutiny of the Poor Law officers. And yet the true interpretation of the hated system is that of a "National Benefit Society." Every householder pays the Poor's Rate, and by the same warrant earns the right to relief in case of destitution. His rate is as much "Club money" as is the voluntary subscription to some private sick fund. The Poor Law prescribes *compulsory* payment, but then it provides in return a *national guarantee*. There is a sliding scale of contribution, and the wealthy are honorary members; but the case of "the widow's mite" establishes the true criterion of merit in paying. If the poor man subscribes in proportion to his means, why should he have the finger of scorn pointed against him? Why should he be stigmatized as a social Pariah if he is compelled to "go upon his club?" Poverty is no crime. It oftentimes has been, and may at any time and with all persons be, honourable. Variations take place in the worldly circumstances of every one, and without a reserve to fall back upon, pauperism might suddenly be the lot of any of us. No social degradation attaches to the reduction of household expenditure in case of trade fluctuations, bad harvests, losses from accident or bad debts, or family misfortune, or professional incapacity. From highest to lowest, each grade may drop into a lower grade without stigma; and except amongst the witless and worthless, without remark. But when the *very poor*, whose lives have been a chronic struggle for the supply of the barest necessities, succumb to sickness or accident, and slide out of the "lowest deep" of self-support into the "lower deep" still of parish relief—the true meaning of which, as we have said, is a resort "to their Club"—the managers of that Club (to wit society) set up a howl of opprobrium, call him bad names, and put him under a ban of disgrace for ever after. "Once a pauper always a pauper;" for the same cruel judgment is passed upon those who slip into destitution, as upon those of the weaker sex who slip into unchastity; *and the punishment of both is for life!* If the applicant be personally unworthy, let him be treated accordingly. Keep him close—work him hard—feed him meagrely; but why not leave to the personally worthy, but socially unfortunate, his self-respect, and a feeling of honourable poverty? Why should not the lowest poor, like the higher poor, be able (in spirit) to say in respect of Fortune's changes, as Horace has said, for him and for all the world:—

"Si celeres quatit
Pennas, resigno quæ dedit, et mea
Virtute me involvo, probamque,
Pauperiem sine dote quæro."

We have already shown that pauperism has been gradually

diminishing. Unfortunately, however, the *cost* of the smaller amount, owing to the increased expense of living, has been gradually growing. For the year ending Lady-day 1870 the amount expended was 7,644,307*l.*; for the year 1871, 7,886,724*l.*; and for 1872, 8,007,403*l.* The increase, therefore, in the expenditure has been 120,679*l.*, while the reduction in the number of persons has been from 1,085,661 to 981,042 on the 1st of January each year, and from 973,294 to 877,005, on the 1st of July respectively: while, by the latest return (to September 29th, 1873) the number was reduced to 755,664. Passing from the numerical aspect of the question to its more important moral bearing, we find that out of the enormous total of 981,042 persons in receipt of relief on the 1st January, 1872, *not more than* 39,512 *were male able-bodied adults;* and that of the total of 877,270 on the roll of July 1st, 1872, not more than 26,058 were male able-bodied adults: and further, that the bulk of this latter number *were relieved on account of the temporary sickness of themselves or of their families.* Lastly, to show the real gravamen of the indictment brought against the working classes on this question of pauperism, 289 of the total of the able-bodied male adults receiving out-door relief were relieved in the metropolis, leaving only 416 *for all the rest of England and Wales.* The residue consists of females—principally widows, children under sixteen, vagrants (who ought to be under police supervision), and lunatics.

These statistics, showing as they do the real status of the English working classes, are worthy of the gravest consideration. Children under sixteen and lunatics cannot be held to be morally responsible for their condition. To what extent their parents may have neglected to make provision for those dependent upon them in case of their death, it is impossible to say; but we take this simple and high ground on behalf of the working classes, that the payment of a poor's rate is, and ought to be, considered as such a provision; and that to brand all suffering from family unavoidable sickness as *paupers* is unjust and cruel. How far collateral support of widows and orphans ought to be enforced is another question, and one which ought to be probed to the bottom. The ties of relationship are in this respect very loosely regarded amongst the poor; and we think that Boards of Guardians ought to exert themselves to draw them closer. Family influence would be brought to bear most beneficially upon the thoughtless, the idle, and the improvident, if it was felt that the results, in a money point of view, would be brought home to all blood relations.

The money consideration is an important one in the abstract; but there is no evading the fact that the aged, the impotent, and the immature of society *must be fed.* If the entire number of the incapable non-producers were to be removed to-morrow from the pauper roll, and were supported by relations, the burden would be *shifted* but *not obviated.* Nothing short of the miracle which would convert impotence into health and vigour, and endue infancy with the strength of maturity, could prevent these "*fruges consumere nati*" from reducing the aggregate store of the commonwealth. The how and by whom these classes are supported is an important moral consideration; but so long as they are incapable as producers, we maintain that society as a whole does not suffer. The 8,000,000*l.* annually expended might, no doubt, be more economically disbursed through a natural and domestic process of relief, as compared with the Poor Law system, but it would, in most instances, be attained by an expenditure of *time* in lieu of *money.* The marked change made in the number of persons relieved in the town of Elberfeld, by the substitution of a minute superintendence of the poor by voluntary and almost pastoral visiting and interest, may be accounted for in two ways; first, that money was saved by a more costly expenditure of time (as in the Prussian military system), or second, that as the organization was confined to one town, there is nothing in Mr. Doyle's report to show that the original recipients were not "harried and worried" out of its limits by an obnoxiously searching investigation. The very poor have "their feelings" as well as the rich; and the efforts of an army of amateur relieving officers, prying and spying, with much zeal but little tact, may have driven the deserving poor out of the town. In this case the change of locality is only an advantage snatched by Elberfeld at the expense of some other places, and the material question still remains as to the effect of systems relatively on the "producing" powers of the consumers.

The true principle of the English Poor Law system, purged of prejudice and sentiment and hereditary disgust, is the socially and economically healthy one of *mutual assistance.* The Poor's Rate is an assurance fee, or the contribution to a compulsory "National Benefit Society." Why not acknowledge it as such; and by presenting the option to each ratepayer of merging his Poor Law liability in a new and higher range, by a slightly advanced payment, lift him out of the obnoxious category of pauper association, and give him the nationally assured results of an economical Benefit Society, worked by existing national machinery?

But if not as a class morally debauched by intemperance, nor deeply tainted by pauperism, is not the English artisan mentally inert and untutored? Is he not illiterate, and in comparison with his foreign competitor, industrially inapt and merely mechanical? Illiterate? Yes! Unintelligent? No! He has little book-learning, and shows small signs of careful "instruction;" but in all that evidences "education," in its widest meaning—development, unfolding (Entwickelung), the natural process by which the acorn becomes an oak—the British workman is not in this respect behind the same class in any other country, excepting America. His Anglo-Saxon temperament, or in other words, his peculiarities of "mixed race," eminently fit him for success in the world's industrial race. It is not the happy thought, flashing as by inspiration through the mind, which revolutionizes the world's habits, and writes fresh pages in a nation's industrial history; but the patient, persistent, indomitable courage that tries and tries again, and wont know failure, nor acknowledge defeat. It was this quality of Watt's which turned out the steam engine all but perfect; and thus it was that George Stephenson adapted it to locomotion. Similarly, in every new process that has left its mark upon civilization, from the days of Newcomen to the last triumph of ocean telegraphy, English intellect and English energy has been foremost in the van of improvement, and even now directs and controls the material progress of every civilized country. This aptitude to invent and perfect—to apply and to diffuse—we take to be due, not to the system of elementary school "telling, cram and mechanical drill," as Mr. Joseph Payne describes our "denominational system," but to inborn qualities, developed and brightened by practical use. That he is illiterate we have admitted. After thirty-nine years' experience of our denominational system, and with an annual expenditure at the present time of 1,120,000*l.*, augmented by voluntary subscriptions of 570,975*l.* per annum, we have only turned out in all England and Wales, in 1872, 8819 children capable of passing the 6th Standard; while the annual increase of the population is some 300,000! In the face of these figures what can we do otherwise than admit that illiteracy is the rule? But does the disgrace attach to the system, or to those who suffer? And if the English artisan, under existing difficulties, has so far distinguished himself in the world's race, we may be sure that (to use Carlyle's colloquial expression) he has not yet "struck 12 o'clock!"

We deprecate all empirical processes, and all partial measures. We hold that nothing short of general and systematic culture will suffice to train the mind to the use of its fullest and choicest powers, and that what is ungrammatically called "technical education" (by which term instruction in science as applied to industry is meant) is empirical and partial, and therefore delusive.

The argument in support of this charge against the English workman is, that foreign competition is pressing keenly and closely upon us; and that this is owing to the fact that foreign workmen are better instructed in technology than the same class in England; and the inference is drawn that to keep our trade we must technically educate our artisans.

Admitting the pressure of foreign competition in many small and comparatively unimportant branches of industry, we may remark that the extent of this competition has been exaggerated, and its causes erroneously stated. If, for example, English makers of locomotives happen to be full of orders, and foreign makers are disengaged, because their engines as a rule are less perfect than ours, and it suits them to undertake an urgent commission in a short time, and (to gain a new market) for less profit, the registered fact that foreign engines are sent into this country proves nothing as regards the main question, either of economy of manufacture or of the intelligence of workmen. Again, because wages are lower on the Continent than in this country, and because the hours of work are longer, and there are protecting duties, both fiscal and indirectly from carriage, the fact that we are undersold by native manufacturers in their own, or even in neutral adjacent countries, proves nothing as regards the relative intelligence of foreign and English artisans. Further, the fact that there is a large importation into this country of "fancy goods," of articles of vertu, of fabrics whose peculiar value rests upon colour, taste, and variety of design, only proves that the Frenchman has a more finely organized temperament than the Anglo-Saxon—has a livelier appreciation of sensuous beauty, and greater aptitude than his rival, in embodying that beauty in variety of design. If each race follows the bent of its natural gifts, and freely exchanges the products to which various minds and hands are best adapted, all are benefited. Individual aptitude creates a natural division of labour, and peculiar advantages of race and climate work out the good of all, through the sound principle of Free Trade.

A "Report on Technical Instruction in Germany and Switzerland," made to the French Ministry of Agriculture, Commerce, and Public Works, was laid before the British Parliament in 1869. We briefly summarize the results of that valuable inquiry as follows:—

1. That the primary schools in those countries are entirely without training *in the technicalities of Trade.*

2. That the aim of their middle-class schools is *General Culture*, with the subordinate aim of particular and practical trade application and illustration. Thus, the study of chemistry as an abstract science is promoted by practical illustrations, taken

from the application to the arts of dyeing, calico printing, bleaching, metallurgy, &c. The study of pure mathematics is aided and utilized by examples of calculations applied to the industrial arts, such as building, machine making, navigation, &c.

3. That although in France technology is more attended to, it is at the expense of general culture; and that, except in the case of the art of decoration, the results, as shown in agriculture and in all other branches of industry, are not such as to give the palm of superiority to special over general training.

4. That the opinion of the Commissioners appears to be, that apprenticeship is the time, and the workshop the place, for what we call in this country technical education.

The economy of manufacturers generally demands the minutest division and subdivision of labour. It demands also, more and more urgently, the substitution of machine for manual labour. It further reduces the condition of the labour left, more and more completely to the nature of the single machine it feeds and watches. The successful working of a large manufactory depends upon the merging of the *individual* into the *system.* A man may not only be tied to a single machine, but to the production of a single article, and kept working in a single room full of similar machines. His excellence as a workman is to be automatic. Thought, theory, inventive skill, and novel scientific applications are for him quite out of place. They may do for Nuremberg toy makers, or a Baden domestic clock establishment, or for a French designer, but for the gigantic mechanical organizations of this country, whose trade life breath is division of labour, they would be elements exotic, disturbing or destructive. Take the case of a machine maker. In a large establishment each man is a "turner," a "borer," a "filer," a "shaper," a "fitter," &c. His excellence consists in being one of these, *and nothing more.* Take the case of a cotton "hand" in a gigantic Lancashire factory. He or she is a carder, slubber, rover, spinner, piecer, winder, warper, weaver, &c. The work of each begins and ends within the narrowest possible limits. From each and all is demanded complete concentration of attention. It would be pleasant, no doubt, for them to understand the theory of mechanics, or the physiology of the cotton plant, or the commercial history of the trade of which they are infinitesimal parts; but practically such knowledge would be useless. Take the case of a shipwright. Would the science of naval architecture, involving a knowledge of the mathematics, of "stability," of "isochronous rolling," of "metacentres," or the laws of the resistance of fluids, make him a better plate-riveter or carpenter? In all these cases the want in England is of a *general culture,* which shall lift men *out* of the dull round they tread, and the precise groove which trade economy compels them to work in; and not of a special instruction in schools, which, as compared with workshop practice, would be mere child's play. As it is, the culture of the elementary schools is, in a measure, sacrificed to the supposed necessity for sectarian training. If we further restrict its operation to special, as opposed to real culture, we run the risk of further waste of the too little time the children of the working classes can devote to mental development.

It would be foolish and short-sighted to turn a deaf ear to the alleged pressure of foreign competition; but more foolish and short-sighted still to neglect the law of natural selection, of special aptitudes, and of the equalizing action of Free Trade. The Englishman's intelligence is objective, slow, and persistent. That of the foreigner subjective, mobile, versatile, and refining. What, then, is the process to bring the former within reach of the intellectual influences affecting the latter? The answer is ready and clear—*general, not special, culture* for the young, with patient waiting for results. We can neither eradicate nor neutralize the effects of half a century of indifference to culture all at once. But the intelligence is there to be acted upon; and with the Education Act of 1870, properly amended, we have no fear for the intellectual future of the working classes.

Passing from what the working classes *are*, we may find further assurance as to their future from an inquiry as to what they have *done*; and their chief work has been in reference to the relation existing between Capital and Labour. The economic terms respecting this relation have been superseded by the generic and practical one of *Trades Unionism*.

The gigantic organizations existing under this designation are evidence of the possession of remarkable qualities on the part of the working classes of England. They number at the present time over 900,000 members. They form a federation of trade interests spreading over the whole of England and Wales, unique in its constitution and influence. This union of "Unions" has been built up by a rare combination of courage, perseverance, and class fidelity, which testifies clearly to the convictions of the working classes as to their interests, and their consistency in promoting them. The working of this vast organization, up to its present stage of development, proves, on the part of the leaders, the possession of honesty, zeal, temper, and forbearance. Against legal injustice, amidst public opprobrium, through good report and through evil report, the steady growth and increasing influence of Trades' Unionism has gone on to falsify the predictions of failure and mischief. Checks have been sustained, mistakes redeemed, misfortunes borne, and false steps retraced, all with the practical and characteristic firmness of the Anglo-Saxon race.

The story of this organization is authentically related in the Report of the Royal Commissioners, appointed to inquire into the "effects produced by such Trades Unions and associations on the workmen and employers respectively." Men, masters, and disinterested observers have all given evidence, and the balance has been fairly determined by the Commissioners in the Report. The crucial question has been held to be, "whether Trades Unions are advantageous to workmen," and the Report says, "Treating it as a question of wages only, we think it doubtful whether the nett earnings of the workmen connected with unions have not, on the whole, been diminished rather than increased through the agency of the unions." We concur in the justice of this remark. Admitting that the law of supply and demand is, in the long run, paramount in its influences, we must grant also that the expenses of such an organization must be so much money loss to the workmen, *as an association.* But we question whether the operation of the natural law could be sustained in its integrity at a less cost *to individuals.* Many writers seem to think that the law of supply and demand would produce its natural effects without any action on the part of the individuals concerned. They presuppose that, if there be no union there is no agitation, no ferment, no demands on the part of individuals in particular shops, and in different localities. What the public does not see and hear, it is inclined to ignore; and hence they do not recognise, or at least do not admit the fact, that the price of labour must be adjusted precisely like the price of all other commodities; that the "market value" is ascertained only by a perpetual conflict of opinions and interests, and only finally adjusted by the inexorable logic of actual plethora or proved scarcity. Can any one of common sense believe that the law of value can be ascertained without antagonism and without risk? or that agreement can be come to except after bargaining, and through the operation of the dread of results? Every time that a merchant claims an advance, or resists a decline, in the price of what he has to sell *he strikes*, and by so doing suffers inconvenience and loss, at least of interest; and in case he makes a mistake and overstands the market, a loss in price also. If 50 or 500 others, acting upon, or being resisted by *opinion*, also "strike," the aggregation of isolated efforts brings about a similar result to that of a concerted combination of effort, which is an union strike. In both instances, if the precise condition and ultimate position of the market could be accurately predicated, no dislocation of business would take place, and no loss ensue; but our contention is, that in case of such dislocation, there may be quite as much loss to bring about a proper adjustment by the natural accretion of individual efforts, as by a preconcerted union of efforts. No political economist doubts that "price" is determined by the ratio of supply and demand; but the chapter in political economy has yet to be written which shall determine the easiest and most certain mode of finding out what the ratio really is, and whether its exponent in price can be best adjusted by the chaffering of the mart, the migration of labour, or the demands of Trades Unionism.

Again, the law of political economy leaves *time* an indefinite element in the calculation of results. It determines also the *average*, but is silent and inefficacious as to the mode of producing that average. "In the long run" is a saving phrase for the political economist; but it may mean starvation to a workman. A certain value in the long run may be made up by two great oscillations, or by fifty small ones, or by a dead level without change; and when Mr. Brassey says of Trades Unions, that "Their organization and united action may secure an advance of wages at a somewhat earlier date," he justifies their action as practical machines. The exigences of human life, and the necessities of the manual labourer, call for the earliest practical realization of results; and Mr. Brassey tells us Trades Unionism effects this; and early realization means also the absence of violent fluctuations. It is no satisfaction to a workman with a large family to know that his sufferings will be compensated by counterbalancing advantages to his descendants. It is better for both, and for society, that the advantages (subject, of course, to all other disturbing causes) should be equalized; and Trades Unions do this by the same process by which speculation also "insures an advance at a somewhat earlier date," and prevents it getting so high as it otherwise would. Take the case of a deficient harvest. Supply and demand might continue equal, and prices remain unaltered until famine stared the consumers in the face. Panic would then ensue, and political economy justify its law by running price up to an extravagant height. But speculation, by anticipating scarcity, prevents it; and by raising prices sooner, and not letting them advance so high, is a real boon. In both cases the *average* might be the same, but how different the effect to society! And so with wages under the action of Trades Unionism.

Again, the action of Trades Unionism, without militating against the operation of economic law, may obviate the supposed necessity to strike at all. Moral force is an important and beneficent social element; but, like most things worth having, it must be bought with a price. Unless founded upon the fear of a resort to physical force, it would not exist. It is the underlying dread of something to follow—appealing to, and perhaps exaggerated by, the imagination—that gives the single policeman his superiority against odds. He is the representative, for the time, of the whole force of law; and again, law, nothing in itself, means the united power of the military backed by the whole community. In like manner, *the fear* of a resort to a strike on the part of the masters may prevent the necessity for its occurrence. The delegate or agent, like Talbot,

"—— is but shadow of himself,"

"his substance, sinews, arms, and strength" lie in the Union that is ready at his call *to strike!*

Capital is simply accumulated or stored labour. Unionism is labour banded together for a fixed purpose. Capital and labour, therefore, meet on fairer terms when the latter meets the former in the concrete. It is the old story of the bundle of sticks: separate, the sticks are easily broken; united, they defy aggression. The interests of both are identical *theoretically*. Capital is useless without labour, and labour can do little without the binding and supporting power of capital; but there is no law but the highest (not necessarily put in force in such circumstances)—that of neighbourly love—to insure a fair division of the profits which are due to the working of both. It is only when that which is put in force by the workmen themselves—the law of equality through Unionism—steps in that the balance is struck. With every disposition to credit the capitalist with good feeling and right-mindedness, we yet think that the fear of a resort to a strike will often induce him to concede to labour some extra portion of his profits; and the power manifested by union will quicken the disposition for an amicable arrangement if a strike actually takes place. When the strength of united labour is guided by those in whom it can repose confidence, the masters each and all gain an unacknowledged advantage as between themselves. *The men take care that all the masters are put upon an equality as regards labour.* They may also be saved much anxiety and expense, in having the labour market ruled by firm hands, and by the prevention (when strikes occur) of its migration under the natural law of supply and demand. A case in point is now before us. If the agricultural labourer had possessed intelligence enough in time gone by to have agitated generally for a larger share than he has had of the profits arising from land, Mr. Joseph Arch would have remained in obscurity, and the farmers would long ago have settled the account with the landowners. If, further, Unionism was more than a name amongst the labourers at the present time, the proposition for a wholesale exportation of labour would have been still-born. Mr. Arch is, however, working to give full validity to the natural law of supply and demand; and if successful, the result will be that the farmer will be compelled to pay higher wages when he has become embarrassed for labour, and to pay a still higher rate than he need have done, in order to induce the emigrants, or a portion of them, to return. This state of things fully exemplifies the inconvenience and loss from the operation of the natural law of *individual strikes*, as compared with that of Trades Unionism working by the influence of moral force.

Within our present limits we can only deal with the broad principles of Trades Unionism.* We have not shut our eyes to their abuses nor to the hardship inflicted by details, nor to the cruel blunders of some of the smaller unions, like that at Sheffield and that of the Manchester brickmakers. But we do not take "the indisposed and sickly fit for the sane man," and particularly because, supplementing our approval of the broad principles of Unionism, we have confidence in the temper, tact, judgment, and right-mindedness of the present leaders of these organizations. Such influence as they possess has always been exerted on behalf of law, order, and sobriety; and a word from these men carries with it a force upon such rough material as is to be found in the mining districts, and amongst the iron-workers of the "Black country," far beyond any power of preaching, which, in fact, they never hear! Such men are forming a most valuable and potent public opinion within the bounds of Trades Unionism, just as these organizations in their internal working and outward effects exert a most beneficial educational influence. And this alone would furnish a sufficient guarantee against their members becoming "dangerous." M. Nadaud, who enters fully, and with a Frenchman's zest for organization, into this phase of the history of the working classes, says:—"Les *Trades Unions* sont une école où les ouvriers s'instruisent tous les jours, et où ils apprennent à se gouverner par euxmêmes." And again:—"Aussi les Trades Unions sont

* There is perhaps the less necessity to speak of the *principles* of Trades Unionism, as they have been emphatically endorsed by the example of the Masters in establishing the National Federation of employers. Those who have long, as a body, denounced Trades Unionism, now when success has justified its action, have put upon it the mark of their approval. We cannot but regret this action, because the equilibrium which was *restored* by Trades Unionism, will again be disturbed, and again require readjustment at the hands of the men.

devenus, nous ne cesserons le répéter, une école de bonne mœurs. Ces hommes espèrent tout du travail car ils regardent l'aumône comme une humiliation des plus dégradantes, et ils y échappent dans bien des cas."

We can hardly over-estimate the beneficial influences of the educational process going on within and beyond the vast organization of Trades Unionism. No less than 900,000 persons, mostly heads of families, are daily and hourly subjected to its developing and beneficial power. It furnishes to their thoughts, to their workshop talk, and to their leisure resources, the "expulsive power of a new affection" to the low enticements of the public-house. Compared with this process of self-culture through self-government, the passing of *one-thirtieth* of the annual addition to the population through the 6th Standard, as the result of our elementary school system, is poor indeed; and the empirical nostrum of the "United Kingdom Alliance" for making men sober by Act of Parliament simply absurd.

We have spoken of the "right-mindedness" of the leaders of Trades Unionism. Their possession of this quality has been proved by their advocacy in favour of the settlement of wages and other trade disputes by means of Boards of Conciliation and Arbitration. Had they shown the disposition ascribed to them of fomenting and prolonging disputes, and of fostering a spirit of ill-will between capital and labour, and of selfishly battening upon the suffering of the workmen, they would have repressed, not encouraged, a reference to these tribunals. But to their honour be it said, their voice as a rule has been on the side of a speedy and peaceful settlement of all differences. And not only when action has been taken, but at conferences and in council, they have (we believe we may say invariably) advocated justice and forbearance, conciliation and firmness. When they have put out the "hand of steel" they have not hypocritically, but from policy, covered it with the "silk glove!" The discipline they have established amongst the rough, uncultivated mining population, the confidence they have won from those whose battles they fight, and the respect they have obtained from the employers generally, mark their prevailing characteristics, and show the success of their policy. If it were not for Trades Unionism, and not for the firm guidance of these institutions, arbitration would be difficult, if not impossible. The establishment of regularly constituted Boards is evidence of the growing faith in the suitability of such appliances, and their tendency to repress *à priori* extreme demands. They curb the violence of temper, and prevent unnecessary irritation. They offer "a golden bridge to a flying enemy." Pride, presumption, and

I 2

error are glad of a loophole for retreat from impossible conditions and immoderate pretensions. Without it, obstinacy obscures justice, and good feeling is lost through injustice. It is, therefore, on all accounts desirable to resort at once to the decision of an eligible umpire; and all who are friendly to the progress and well being of the working classes must rejoice that the dominant good sense of their leaders favours a resort to arbitration, and that they have the will and power to hold those they control fairly and honourably to the decision of the umpires.

But, after all, Trades Unionism and Boards of Conciliation and Arbitration can exist only in the face of an abnormal antagonism. They presuppose and are founded upon the error that labour and capital have naturally divergent and hostile interests. They may be, and we think are, admirable curatives, as medicine may be for disease; but the wise physician looks to remove *constitutional* disorder. Arbitration may settle wages disputes when they arise; but may not such dispute be altogether prevented? "What is truth?" "What is a pound?" have been puzzling questions; and we may add to them "What is a fair day's wage for a fair day's work?" If we could find any "fulcrum" in any fixed standard for these things, it would be easy to move away the difficulty that besets the relations between Capital and Labour.

Manual labourers often confound the wages *rate* with the *net receipt.* Dock labourers, with a wages rate of 4*s.* per day, may be worse off, owing to irregular employment, than another class in the steady receipt of 18s. per week. The "cost of living" is an acknowledged element in political economy so far as it may reduce the supply of labour. But how is the standard of living to be determined? King Lear wasn't mad when he expostulated against nature's need being taken as the measure of his requirements, and stated a bald fact when he said—

> "Our basest beggars
> Are in the poorest thing superfluous."

The supply of such need is not altogether a question of the support of life. It involves questions of relative management. Habit teaches a refinement of economy which is a sort of second nature in its instructive operation; and observation has led us to believe that any given class in France would, partly from habit and partly from intuitive aptitude, and partly from natural appreciation of what is "superfluous," be able to live daintily on the waste and leavings of a class in England immediately above them. "The mother of invention"—necessity, and that which suggests the best practical definition of man, as distinguished from other animals, namely, "cookery," supply all deficiencies; and it is this wonderful frugality, combined with skill, and supplemented by the larger application of female middle-class labour, added to natural resources, that have given to France her recuperative power under the heavy blows lately dealt to her.

If nature's needs, then, are no measure of value for wages remuneration, what is? Mr. Hoby sometime ago, in a court of justice, defined the value of a pair of boots to be "what he could get for them;" and although his price covered all sorts of adventitious considerations, such as fashion and reputation on his side, and folly and superfluous means on the side of the buyer, yet he was not far wrong in his definition. Why, then, should not the working man consider his day's wages to be "What he could get for it?" And if so, does not this presuppose perpetua haggling and the necessity for driving hard bargains, and the formation of Trades Unions, and the establishment of Boards o Conciliation and Arbitration?

All these arrangements, we are happy to believe, belong to, and are useful in a state of transition only. So long as capital and labour are in a state of antagonism all such inventions are useful to eke out imperfect arrangements. But if, and when, the two opposing elements be brought into fusion and unity: when that which calls for perpetual discussion shall have been assimilated, then all such machinery becomes cumbrous and out of place. And we feel little doubt that such fusion and identity of interest may be brought about naturally, and all differences be made self-adjusting, by the principles of co-operation and industrial co-partnery.

The associations formed under the principle of co-operation have struggled (like Trades Unionism) against restrictive and unjust laws from their earliest formation, until 1871, when they were set free from legal impediments, and a fair field opened to their enterprise in any direction they chose to take. In spite of all obstruction, their progress has been sure and rapid. In April, 1851, at the first Congress held at Bury, eighty-three stores were reported to be at work, besides some twenty productive associations. By the end of the year 174 stores, thirty-five productive associations, and fourteen flour mills were in successful operation. In 1865 there were no less than 441 registered societies, with a share capital of 1,164,333*l.*; and in 1870 this number had sprung up to 749, possessing a capital of 2,034,261*l.*, without including such associations as those of the Civil Service Supply, now located near the Mansion House, the one in the Haymarket, and the Agricultural and Horticultural Associations, all registered under the Joint Stock Companies Act. The capital of 2,034,261*l.* appears to have had a "turn over" of 8,204,466*l*., realizing a net profit of 555,435*l*., or 27 per cent. The latest statistics as returned to Parliament are stated to be incomplete; but they show in 1871 a capital of 2,521,000*l*., doing a business to the extent of 9,439,471*l*. per annum, and realizing a profit a little short of 800,000*l*. The members are not, however, content with retail profits. They have tapped a new and profitable spring. A "Wholesale Society" has been formed in Manchester for the supply of the various and rapidly increasing retail establishments. That society has a capital of 140,000*l*., and does a business to the extent of 1,250,000*l*. per annum. During the last eight years its trade reached 4,000,000*l*. sterling, and in the same period the bad debts were only 200*l*.*

The most successful of these associations have been those engaged in "distribution." There is a simplicity in this process which is eminently suited to the genius of co-operation. The margin of profit is large, the skill required small, their adaptability to any locality good, and the wants they supply unrestricted. Moreover, the custom of the shareholders at once starts them into success, and continues to assure to them a certainty of prosperity. We have been told by the best authority on such subjects, that the average "turn over" of a West-end shop is 5000*l*. per annum; that the advance upon wholesale price is 30 per cent., and that the expenses are 10 per cent.; leaving 20 per cent., or 800*l*. as the cost for "distributing"—with all expenses paid, about 4000*l*. of goods. The Civil Service Supply Association Limited, against which so strong an objection has been made by shopkeepers, and which turns over 800,000*l*. per annum, therefore, does the work of some 200 West-end shops, and saves its customers 160,000*l*. per annum. A few figures may help us to realize the large sum annually paid in this country for merely handing goods over the counter, or for obtaining a vicious credit for the payment of such goods. The census of 1871 shows that the number of families in England and Wales was 5,049,016; and taking the annual expenditure of each family for articles merely weighed and measured, or transferred, by unskilled labour, to be 20*l*. each, we have over 100,000,000*l*. thus laid out; and the cost, in profit, after paying expenses to the consumers, 20 per cent., or 20,000,000*l*. It is evident, therefore, with every allowance for error in the estimate, co-operation has a wide field available for work and saving. To the working classes, however, the advan-

* The fifth annual Co-operative Congress, held at Newcastle-upon-Tyne, April, 1873.

tage yielded by these associations is not limited to the money saving. Co-operation means ready money payment; it means also the self-respect and general interest arising from the possession of property; and it *may* mean, and too often it is to be feared does mean, *absence of adulteration.*

Under such circumstances, it appears to be only a question of time for the principle of Co-operation to spread rapidly within the limits of "distribution." It is very doubtful, however, how far it may prove successful when applied to "producing," or "manufacturing." Such concerns generally require more vigorous and autocratic management than could be made available in a co-operative establishment. Moreover, it is unlikely that the workmen who find the labour could themselves subscribe the whole of the required capital. If the capital of non-workers is used, the chief aim of such association, *i.e.*, the combination of capital and labour in the same hands, would be defeated.

On the other hand, the admission of the manual labourers to a participation in the profits of businesses mainly or entirely carried on with capital not contributed by those labourers, seems to us to offer the readiest and most promising solution of the difficult problem of the due relations of capital and labour, *so far as the fluctuations of trade control them.* Although this arrangement would solve much of the difficulty existing, it would leave untouched such cardinal points as the proportion of profit normally due to labour, to management, and to capital. If these could be fairly settled, all the rest would be adjusted by the self-acting process of Industrial Co-partnerships—that is, so long *as business was remunerative.* It is always pleasant to divide a surplus; but to apportion a deficiency, particularly when on the one hand there is a nomadic element, and on the other one fixed and responsible, is another matter altogether. A sort of assurance fund becomes essential, and the due arrangement of the liability of the profitable years—"the well-favoured and fat-fleshed kine"—to supply the hunger of their "ill-favoured and lean-fleshed" followers and devourers, has to be properly determined. Again, it would seem just that labour should have a voice in the management of the business, in the profits of which it is to participate, not by favour but of right. The settlement of this point may prove troublesome, as well as the arrangement of some of the broad principles upon which the business is to be carried on. For example:—in cotton spinning there may accrue a fair profit from the "hand to mouth" operations of the factory, and a heavy loss arise from operations which may be put into the category of ill-advised speculation. No doubt a practical separation of what may be called the "merchant" part of the business might be made, so that the profit or loss attaching to the results of labour, in its close contiguity with capital, could be kept distinct. These and other similar impediments will, no doubt, work themselves into easy going train. As regards their due and satisfactory adjustment, we see no insurmountable obstacle, and only one obstruction—namely, the very natural, because so long fostered, feeling of superiority on the part of capital, and, we must reluctantly add, of a certain amount of class pride and prejudice.

When capital will meet labour hand to hand; and, on terms of equality in regard to their mutual working, will recognise the purely commercial nature of the relation between them; and eliminate from merely business transactions all notions of patronage; and "do good, hoping for nothing in return" in the shape of servility and wages pliability; all the obstacles in the way of Industrial Co-partnerships will vanish. And when Trades Unions have brought about this condition of mutual respect, and a feeling of identity of interests—and we are persuaded they will sooner or later do this—then will their mission be accomplished, and, like the Anti-Corn Law League, they too may be dissolved.

Taking a broad view of the industrial condition of England at the present time, the mind is arrested, and with no satisfaction, by the unsettled relations between Capital and Labour. These relations are unhappy, and the antagonism arising from the prevalent feeling of divergent interest, painful, but of no evil augury. The principal agencies bearing upon and influencing these relations are Trades Unionism and Co-operation—the one flushed with success and in full maturity of power, but adapted only to a transitional state; the other an infant Hercules, full of vitality and promise, and holding the germ of the natural solution of the relations of Capital and Labour.

Both these agencies are of original working class conception; both show proof of capacity for organization; and both in their action testify to the possession of mental and moral qualities, as well on the part of the managers as the members. Mr. Brassey, in speaking of Trades Unions, falls into the common error of supposing that because the Guilds of the Middle Ages were "the forerunners of the Trades Unions of to-day," that therefore they were the origin of such associations; and M. Nadaud uses the same argument. It would be, however, more correct to say that the ancient Guilds were the origin of our modern Chambers of Commerce; and equally so, of Friendly Societies. They were formed principally for mutual assistance in sickness and difficulty, and as trade barriers to a domineering feudal spirit. Except in London, there is no evidence to show that their members belonged to particular handicrafts. The avowed object of Trades Unions is opposition to, not association of men with, masters; and when Mr. Brassey states that "there is a general tendency amongst the Trades Unions to ignore the interest of the master, as if his property was not essential to their own prosperity," he states the true case in a wrong connexion. We entirely dissent therefore from the view that Trades Unions have descended from the old Guilds, except on the ground that there is an M in Macedon and another in Monmouth. Both may be called associations, but with entirely different objects, and comprised of altogether different classes. We are the less willing to take from the working classes the merit of originating both the agencies particularized, because we see in the fact of their possessing the remarkable qualities requisite for their conception and working out, a guarantee for the future. A class having the foresight, patience, courage, and ability brought to bear upon Trades Unionism and Co-operation *ab initio*, is not likely to be led far by passion nor to be long blinded by prejudice; but, pursuing their true interests calmly and rationally, will act with due reverence for law, order, and the general well-being of society.

In conclusion we would state our conviction that the present political and industrial status of the working classes is healthy, and their future more than hopeful. What they have achieved has been under heavy discouragement, and with discredited means; but it has been done well, and with temper and discretion. They have won for themselves the consideration of observant and thoughtful men; they are attaining to a feeling of self-respect; they are becoming cultured; and are awakening to a sense of class responsibility. They are entitled to a verdict of acquittal on the chief counts of the indictment against them. History allows it, and truth awards it. What they claim is merely justice, and their bond. There is no whining plea that society should—

"Be to their virtues very kind,
But to their faults a little blind,"

but simply *just!*

If there "ariseth a little cloud like a man's hand," it is not from the masses.

The element of mischief most to be dreaded is the feeling towards them of the classes higher in the social scale. If the working classes feel that they are not understood and not appreciated; that they are misconstrued and maligned; that their interests are not fairly represented; that they are not dealt with in a fair spirit of trust and forbearance; if they be isolated and estranged by pride and neglect; or sought for to be cajoled; or hardened by want of sympathy: then, when they awaken to the sense of their full power, they may, in "bettering the example," be "dangerous;"—*but not else!*

Art. V.—John Stuart Mill.

Autobiography. By John Stuart Mill. London: Longmans, Green, Reader, and Dyer. 1873.

THE present memoir which John Stuart Mill has bequeathed to the world contains, not the narrative of a life, but the growth of a mind. We find none of the smaller incidents and details that make up the history of the individual, and which readers commonly look for with a pardonable curiosity and interest, greater or less in degree, according to the importance of the place the author of the biography has filled in public estimation. It is not therefore surprising that those who had expected a graphic picture of an entire career, intellectually remarkable, should feel some disappointment, and conclude that the real memoir has still to be written. Against any expectation of this sort Mr. Mill in the first words of the autobiography has done his utmost to guard. He wrote it, he tells us, not with any conception of self-importance, but because education is now a subject of more profound study among us than at any former period of our history, and the experiment, as it might well be called, of which he is an example, may tend to economize the tasks of the young, and save the many early years that are little better than wasted; because it might interest and help those, who in an age of transition are searchers for truth, to see how one engaged in the same pursuit has profited by a readiness to learn and to unlearn in his forward course; and last, but not least, because he desired to acknowledge the debt which he believed that in his moral and intellectual development he owed to others.

The absence of any minute record of passing events affecting himself or the persons and objects immediately around him, cannot be regarded as a defect. It is obviously the very condition under which the work is prepared. We see that the author rigidly adheres to the purposes indicated. He does not permit himself to be diverted by any matters, however interesting they might have been to himself, but which he looks upon as valueless to the world. His evident design is, first to convey by the testimony of experience of no ordinary kind, a great lesson on the extent of teaching or education that it is possible for the mature mind to communicate to the immature; and again, on that never-ceasing process of education which continues from youth to manhood, and thence to the latest period of life, which it is the business of every mind to gather for itself.

In order that this education should have its proper and beneficent influence on character, he shows that it must not simply operate on the reasoning powers—that there is needed the culture of the feelings as well as of the reason; that the work is moral as well as intellectual. Having dwelt on the process for reaching more perfectly that condition of mental equilibrium the best suited for forming a right judgment of the result of conduct and action, we learn the effect which his labour to attain, and his progress toward that condition, had in confirming or modifying his earlier views of the great subjects affecting mankind, sociological and economical principles, law, religion, and political government.

Although it is difficult to assent to the judgment Mr. Mill pronounces upon himself, that in powers of apprehension and memory, and in activity and energy of character, he was rather below than above par, yet it is impossible not to perceive from the facts stated to what an incalculable degree he was indebted to the early training of his father, which enabled him, as he says, to start with the advantage of a quarter of a century over his contemporaries.

James Mill must be regarded as one of the most remarkable men of his own or any other age. Born without any of the advantages of fortune, and educated by the aid of one of the Barons of the Exchequer in Scotland, after whom he named his son, he went through the studies of the University of Edinburgh, and was licensed for a preacher, but finding himself unable to believe the Church doctrines, he left the profession. Holding, and always fearlessly asserting, opinions both in politics and religion more odious at that time to the influential and wealthy of this country than they have been either before or since, he maintained himself and his family by his work as a tutor and an author. Amidst the perpetual interruptions of settled labour, caused by this necessary struggle for existence, added to the time employed in the education of his children, he planned and in about ten years completed the "History of India." In this work he comments with great severity on many of the acts of the East India Company in their government, and expresses unqualified hostility to their commercial privileges. A book full of opinions and modes of judgment of a democratic radicalism, then regarded as extreme,—he might, as his son truly observes, have expected it at some future period to win for him reputation, but certainly not advancement. The Directors of the East India Company, feeling a far deeper personal responsibility in the exercise of their powers than perhaps can be expected from the members of an executive government, whose attention is at best divided between considerations of party exigency and regard for the public good, perceived in the author of the History the qualities of a public servant of inestimable value, and disregarding his adverse criticisms, appointed him to an important office in their establishment. It is an event rare in the dispensation of public patronage, and should be ever remembered to their honour. The Autobiography contains very much relating to the character and works of James Mill, which deserves an attentive perusal, and there are few who will not agree in the judgment, that his place was an eminent one in the literary and political history of his country. He died in 1836. "The eighteenth century," Mr. Mill observes, "was an age of strong and brave men;" and he was a fit companion for its strongest and bravest. The last of that century, as Brutus was called the last of the Romans, he had continued its tone of thought and sentiment into, without partaking of the reaction which was the characteristic of, the first age of the nineteenth.

It was the good fortune of Mr. Mill that his education from his earliest years was conducted by such a teacher. The account of the progress which he made is full of instruction for a people now entering upon the work of National Education, and who are almost everywhere treating the mere instruments of knowledge as its substitute. While this Autobiography was in the press, an address was delivered by one who has given as much study to the subject of Education as any one living, pointing out the utter insufficiency of an educational method which assumes that the power to read will develop the love of reading—the ability to understand and appreciate what is read, to choose the worthy and reject the unworthy, elevate the taste, arm it against temptation, and ennoble life!* What is needed is the training of the mind, "to observe nature, animate and inanimate, to watch and classify ordinary social arrangements, to trace the relation of cause and effect, to think of the consequences of different kinds of actions, and to guide conduct accordingly; to forego immediate enjoyment for the sake of greater good to oneself or others." We perceive in the Autobiography, how these, the true objects of Education, were attained, the mechanical part being subordinated

* See "Professor Hodgson's Address as President of the Educational Department, Social Science Congress, Norwich," (*Transactions*). 1873.

and acquired almost unconsciously. Mr. Mill tells us that he had no remembrance of the time when he began to learn Greek. He had been told that it was when he was three years old. His earliest recollection on the subject was that of committing to memory what his father termed vocables, being lists of common Greek words, with their signification in English, which he wrote out for him on cards. Of grammar, until some years later, he learnt no more than the inflexions of the nouns and verbs, but, after a course of vocables, proceeded at once to translation :—

"The only thing besides Greek, that I learnt as a lesson in this part of my childhood was arithmetic : this also my father taught me ; it was the task of the evenings, and I well remember its disagreeableness. But the lessons were only a part of the daily instruction I received. Much of it consisted in the books I read myself, and my father's discourses to me, chiefly during our walks. From 1810 to the end of 1813 we were living in Newington Green, then an almost rustic neighbourhood. My father's health required considerable and constant exercise, and we walked habitually before breakfast, generally in the green lanes towards Hornsey. In these walks I always accompanied him, and with my earliest recollections of green fields and wild flowers, is mingled that of the account I gave him daily of what I had read the day before. To the best of my remembrance this was a voluntary rather than a prescribed exercise. I made notes on slips of paper while reading, and from these in the morning walks, I told the story to him ; for the books were chiefly histories, of which I read in this manner a great number : Robertson's histories, Hume, Gibbon ; but my greatest delight, then, and for long afterwards, was Watson's Philip the Second and Third. . . . . Next to Watson, my favourite historical reading was 'Hooke's History of Rome.' Of Greece I had seen at that time no regular history, except school abridgments and the last two or three volumes of a translation of Rollin's Ancient History, beginning with Philip of Macedon. But I read with great delight 'Langhorne's Translations of Plutarch.' In English history, beyond the time at which Hume leaves off, I remember reading 'Burnet's History of his Own Time,' though I cared little for anything in it except the wars and battles ; and the historical part of the 'Annual Register,' from the beginning to about 1788, where the volumes my father borrowed for me from Mr. Bentham left off. I felt a lively interest in Frederick of Prussia during his difficulties, and in Paoli, the Corsican patriot ; but when I came to the American War, I took my part, like a child as I was (until set right by my father) on the wrong side, because it was called the English side. In these frequent talks about the books I read, he used, as opportunity offered, to give me explanations and ideas respecting civilization, governments, morality, mental cultivation, which he required me afterwards to restate to him in my own words. He also made me read, and give him a verbal account of many books which would not have interested me sufficiently to induce me to read them of myself. Among others, 'Millar's Historical View of the English Government,' a book of great merit for its time, and which he highly valued; 'Mosheim's Ecclesiastical History,' 'McCrie's Life of John Knox,' and even 'Sewell and Rutty's Histories of the Quakers.' . . . Two books which I never wearied of reading were 'Anson's Voyages,' so delightful to most young persons, and a collection (Hawkesworth's, I believe) of 'Voyages round the World,' in four volumes, beginning with Drake and ending with Cooke and Bougainville. Of children's books, any more than playthings, I had scarcely any, except an occasional gift from a relation or acquaintance; among those I had, 'Robinson Crusoe' was pre-eminent, and continued to delight me through all my boyhood. It was no part, however, of my father's system to exclude books of amusement, though he allowed them very sparingly."

The Latin and Greek stories were carried on from his eighth to his twelfth year. Among other authors he read much of Cicero. His strongest predilection was for history, especially ancient, and writing histories was throughout his boyhood a voluntary exercise. A spontaneous attempt at a continuation of Pope's Iliad, led to a command of his father to continue his attempts at English versification. Experimental Science, especially Chemistry—not by actual experiment, but as treated in scientific works—was also one of his greatest amusements. In this course of instruction a method was adopted in which the mind was actively employed without being overtaxed.

"Most boys or youths who have had much knowledge drilled into them have their mental capacities not strengthened, but overlaid by it. They are crammed with mere facts, and with the opinions or phrases of other people, and these are accepted as a substitute for the power to form opinions of their own; and thus the sons of eminent fathers, who have spared no pains in their education, so often grow up mere parroters of what they have learnt, incapable of using their minds, except in the furrows traced for them. Mine, however, was not an education of cram. My father never permitted anything which I learnt to degenerate into a mere exercise of memory; he strove to make the understanding not only go along with every step of the teaching, but, if possible, precede it. Anything which could be found out by thinking I never was told until I had exhausted my efforts to find it out for myself."

Once he had used the word idea, and his father instantly asked what an idea was, and expressed displeasure at his ineffectual attempts to define the word. On another occasion, he used an expression—still commonly repeated by not less than nine out of ten of the so-called instructed classes—that something was true in theory, but false in practice; provoking the indignation of his father, who, after making him vainly strive to define the word theory, explained its meaning, and showed him the fallacy of the vulgar form of speech he had uttered. In and after his twelfth year the objects of instruction were chiefly regarded—not the aids and appliances of thought, but the thoughts themselves. The reading of the scholastic logic, then begun, was accompanied and followed by the numerous and searching questions of his father in their daily walks.

"It was his invariable practice, whatever studies he exacted from me, to make me, as far as possible, understand and feel the utility of them. . . . I well remember how, and in what particular walk in the neighbourhood of Bagshot Heath (where we were on a visit to his old friend Mr. Wallace, then one of the mathematical professors at Sandhurst), he first attempted, by questions, to make me think on the subject, and frame some conception of what constituted the utility of the syllogistic logic; and when I had failed in this, to make me understand it by explanation. The explanations did not make the matter at all clear to me at the time; but they were not, therefore, useless; they remained as a nucleus for my observations and reflections to crystallize upon; the import of his general remarks being interpreted to me, by the particular instances which came under my notice afterwards. My own consciousness and experience ultimately led me to appreciate, quite as highly as he did, the value of an early practical familiarity with the school logic. I know of nothing, in my education, to which I think myself more indebted for whatever capacity of thinking I have attained. The first intellectual operation in which I arrived at any proficiency was dissecting a bad argument, and finding in what part the fallacy lay; and though whatever capacity of this sort I attained, was due to the fact that it was an intellectual exercise in which I was most perseveringly drilled by my father; yet, it is also true, that the school logic and the mental habits acquired in studying it, were among the principal instruments of this drilling. I am persuaded that nothing, in modern education, tends so much, when properly used, to form exact thinkers, who attach a precise meaning to words and propositions, and are not imposed on by vague, loose, or ambiguous terms. The boasted influence of mathematical studies is nothing to it, for in mathematical processes none of the real difficulties of correct ratiocination occur. It is also a study peculiarly adapted to an early stage in the education of philosophical students, since it does not presuppose the slow process of acquiring, by experience and reflection, valuable thoughts of their own. They may become capable of disentangling the intricacies of confused and self-contradictory thought, before their own thinking faculties are much advanced; a power which, for want of some such discipline, many otherwise able men altogether lack; and when they have to answer opponents, only endeavour, by such arguments as they can command, to support the opposite conclusion, scarcely even attempting to confute the reasonings of their antagonists; and, therefore, at the utmost, leaving the question, as far as it depends on argument, a balanced one."

There was no author to whom James Mill had thought himself more indebted for his own mental culture than Plato, or whom be more frequently recommended to young students; and to the value of this recommendation his pupil bears the like testimony. By the Socratic method, the man of vague generalities is constrained either to express his meaning to himself in definite terms, or to confess that he does not know what he is talking about. The perpetual testing of general statements by particular instances, the siege in form laid to abstract terms, the distinctions which limit and define the thing sought, and separate it from the cognate objects, Mr. Mill pronounces to be an education for precise thinking which is inestimable, and one which, even at that early age, took such hold of him as to become part of his own mind.

High as the cultivation of the intellect stands, it is not that alone that is needed for the creation of a better ideal of humanity. In the parental intercourse there had been, if not a want of tenderness, at least the absence of its display. His father, Mr. Mill remarks, resembled most Englishmen in being ashamed of the signs of feeling, and starving it by want of demonstration. He found that intellectual culture required correction by joining other kinds of cultivation with it. Poetry, art, music, to which he had not before been unsusceptible, began at an early period to fill a large place in his thoughts. In this part of his self-education he encountered, in his circle of friends, an opposite theory. There were those who, if possessed of strong susceptibilities of temperament, yet found them more painful than pleasurable—as standing rather in their way than the contrary; and who, therefore, regarded the pleasures to be derived from the fine arts as impediments, rather than aids in the formation of character. Mr. Mill considered it too much a part of the English habit, derived from social circumstances, to count the sympathies for very little in the scheme of life,—to see little good in cultivating the feelings, and none at all in doing so through appeals to the imagination. He more than once adverts to this side of English life—the absence of enlarged thoughts and unselfish desires, the low and petty objects on which the faculties are, for the most part intent, and the habit of taking for granted that they are always the motives of conduct; and the effect of this, in lowering the tone of feeling, making people less earnest, and causing them to look on the most elevated objects as unpractical, or too remote from realization, to be more than a vision or a theory.

Several incidents in the Autobiography are introduced to show the wholesome and vivifying power which the fancy and imagination can exercise over the will. Between his eighth and twelfth years he spent intervals of time at Ford Abbey, the occasional abode of Mr. Bentham, and he regarded these visits as fruitful in his education. Elevation of sentiments in a people are nourished by the large and free character of their habitations. The mediæval architecture and the spacious and lofty rooms of Ford Abbey, so unlike the cramped externals of English middle-class life, gave the sentiment of a larger and freer existence. The house and grounds in which it stood, secluded, umbrageous, and full of the sound of falling waters, were to him in themselves a sort of poetic cultivation. Again, two or three years later, Sir Samuel Bentham and his wife, whom he refers to as "a daughter of Dr. Fordyce, and a woman of much knowledge and good sense of the Edgeworth kind," invited their brother's young friend and disciple to their residence in the South of France, at the Château of Pompignan, on the heights overlooking the plain of the Garonne between Montauban and Toulouse. He spent nearly a year in this visit, accompanying his hosts in an excursion of some duration to the Pyrenees. This, his first introduction to the highest order of mountain scenery, gave a colour to his tastes through life. After adverting to the lectures on chemistry, zoology, and logic which he attended in the winter at Montpelier, he adds that the greatest, perhaps, of the many advantages which he owed to this episode in his education was, that of having breathed for a whole year the free and genial atmosphere of continental life, though at that time he did not estimate or consciously feel the advantage he was deriving. It was not until long afterwards that he learnt to appreciate the general culture of the understanding, which results from the habitual exercise of the feelings, and is thereby carried down into the most uneducated classes of several countries on the Continent in a degree rarely equalled in England.

The impulse and force given to the cultivation of new tastes and sympathies, served to elevate the ideal of a noble and unselfish life which his previous teaching had done much to form. Of his earliest historic readings he says, "the heroic defence of the knights of Malta against the Turks, and of the revolted provinces of the Netherlands against Spain, excited in me an intense and lasting interest." His father was fond of putting into his hands books which exhibited men of energy and resource in unusual circumstances, struggling against difficulties and overcoming them. The interest which in boyhood he had taken in the wars and conquests of the Romans culminated in an engrossing contemplation of the struggles between the patricians and plebeians, and in his juvenile essays he vindicated the Agrarian Laws, and upheld the Roman Democratic party. In his fifteenth or sixteenth year, in 1821 or 1822, after his visit to France, he read the history of the French Revolution. Then, he says:—

"I learnt with astonishment that the principles of democracy, then apparently in so insignificant and hopeless a minority everywhere in Europe, had borne all before them in France thirty years earlier, and had been the creed of the nation. As may be supposed from this, I had previously a very vague idea of that great commotion. I knew only that the French had thrown off the absolute monarchy of Louis XIV. and XV., had put the King and Queen to death, guillotined many persons, one of whom was Lavoisier, and had ultimately fallen under the despotism of Bonaparte. From this time, as was natural, the subject took an immense hold of my feelings. It allied itself with all my juvenile aspirations to the character of a democratic champion. What had happened so lately, seemed as if it might easily happen again; and the most transcendant glory I was capable of conceiving was that of figuring successful, or unsuccessful, as a Girondist in an English Convention."

This admiration of great and persistent effort in a worthy cause, which with advancing years he came more and more to regard as of incalculable value, in bringing the memory and imagination to the aid of conduct, had been early rooted in his mind."

"Long before I had enlarged in any considerable degree the basis of my intellectual creed, I had obtained, in the natural course of my mental progress, poetic culture of the most valuable kind, by means of reverential admiration for the lives and characters of heroic persons; especially the heroes of philosophy. The same inspiring effect which so many of the benefactors of mankind have left on record that they had experienced from 'Plutarch's Lives,' was produced on me by 'Plato's Picture of Socrates,' and by some modern biographies, above all by 'Condorcet's Life of Turgot'—a book well calculated to rouse the best sort of enthusiasm, since it contains one of the wisest and noblest of lives, delineated by one of the wisest and noblest of men. The heroic virtue of these glorious representatives of the opinions with which I sympathized, deeply affected me, and I perpetually recurred to them as others do to a favourite poet, when needing to be carried up into the more elevated regions of feeling and thought."

It is interesting to trace the abiding influence of the remembrance of great examples, and of the memories of an heroic past, in the fact which Mr. Mill mentions, that upwards of thirty years after the impressions, of which he speaks in the foregoing extract, had taken root, the thought of completing and giving to the world as a volume the "Essay on Liberty," first arose in his mind, in mounting in 1855, the steps of the Capitol.

We have described Mr. Mill in his youth, as a disciple of Bentham, but this he does not appear thoroughly to have become until, in 1821 or 1822, he read the Traité de Législation, which he terms an epoch in his life. The standard of "the greatest happiness," the exposure of the fallacy contained in such sounding expressions, as "law of nature," "right reason," and "moral sense," burst upon him with all the force of novelty. The classification of offences and punishment under the guidance of the ethical principle, of pleasurable and painful consequences, seemed to place the moralist and student of jurisprudence upon an eminence, from which he could survey a mental domain of vast extent, affording the most aspiring prospects of practical improvement in human affairs. It opened to him a grand conception of the changes to be effected in the condition of mankind through that doctrine. Before this time the book which had contributed most largely to his education in the best sense of the word, was his father's History of India. In this he was not alone. There are others living who acknowledge, as he does, their debt to this work, and to its disquisitions on society and civilization, on institutions, and acts of government, for a multitude of new ideas, and for a great impulse and stimulus as well as guidance in their future studies.

After the Traité de Législation followed the reading of most of the other works of Bentham; of Locke's Essay, an abstract was made, and discussed, and the other principal English writers on mental philosophy were also read. In 1822 he wrote his first argumentative essay, on the aristocratic prejudice which is supposed to attribute to the rich, moral qualities superior to those of the poor, and in the winter of the same year he gathered together and formed a small society of young men called the Utilitarian Society.* In 1823 his father obtained for him an appointment in the office of Examiner of India Correspondence in the service of the Company.

The constant occupation in the India House had the necessary effect of abridging his opportunities of gratification afforded by a country life, and by travel. The latter was now restricted to the short annual holiday.

"I passed (he says) most Sundays throughout the year in the country, taking long rural walks on that day even when residing in London. The month's holiday was, for a few years, passed at my father's house in the country: afterwards a part or the whole was spent in tours, chiefly pedestrian, with some one or more of the young men who were my chosen companions; and at a later period, in longer journeys or excursions, alone, or with other friends. France, Belgium, or Rhenish Germany were within easy reach of the annual holiday: and two longer absences, one of three, the other of six months, under medical advice, added Switzerland, the Tyrol, and Italy to my list. Fortunately, also, both these journeys occurred rather early, so

* A title borrowed from Galt's "Annals of the Parish."

as to give the benefit and charm of the remembrance to a large portion of my life."

In a chapter entitled "Youthful Propagandism," we are told of the efforts which were made to propagate the main tenets of Utilitarian Radicalism in the columns of the *Globe and Traveller*, the *Morning Chronicle*, and finally in the *Westminster Review*. His part in the first appearance of this Review, had been that of reading through all the volumes of the *Edinburgh Review*, and making notes of the articles which he thought his father would like to examine for the purpose of his intended paper. This article, of James Mill, treated the *Edinburgh Review* as the political organ of one of the two aristocratic parties constantly endeavouring, without any essential sacrifice of aristocratical predominance, to supplant each other. The *Quarterly Review* was the subject of an article, as a sequel to that of the *Edinburgh*. Mr. Mill was one of the most active of the very small number of young men who, drawn around his father, had imbibed from him a greater or smaller portion of his opinions, and were supposed to form the so-called Bentham school in philosophy and politics. The chief characteristics of their creed were in politics, an almost unbounded confidence in the efficacy of two things; representative government and complete freedom of discussion; and in psychology the formation of all human character by circumstances, through the universal principle of association, and the consequent unlimited possibility of improving the moral and intellectual condition of mankind by education. It was in the spirit of what Mr. Mill terms youthful fanaticism that these opinions were seized by the little knot of young men of whom he was one. For himself, he conceives that the epithet of "reasoning machine" was not altogether untrue, or may be said to be as applicable to him as it could well be to any one, for two or three years of his life:—

"Ambition and desire of distinction I had in abundance, and zeal for what I thought the good of mankind was my strongest sentiment, mixing with and colouring all others. But my zeal was little else, at that period of my life, than zeal for speculative opinions. It had not its root in genuine benevolence, or sympathy with mankind, though these qualities held their due place in my ethical standard. Nor was it connected with any high enthusiasm for ideal nobleness. Yet of this feeling I was imaginatively very susceptible: but there was at that time an intermission of its natural aliment, poetical culture, while there was a superabundance of the discipline antagonistic to it, that of mere logic and analysis. Add to this, as already mentioned, my father's teaching led to the under-valuing of feeling. It was not that he was himself cold-hearted or insensible; I believe it was rather from the contrary quality; he thought that feeling could take care of itself; that there was sure to be enough of it if actions were properly cared about." . . . .

"From this neglect both in theory and in practice of the cultivation of feeling, naturally resulted, among other things, an undervaluing of poetry, and of imagination generally, as an element of human nature." . . . . "As regards me (and the same thing might be said of my father), the correct statement would be, not that I disliked poetry, but that I was theoretically indifferent to it. I disliked any sentiments in poetry which I should have disliked in prose, and that included a great deal. And I was wholly blind to its place in human culture, as a means of educating the feelings; but I was always personally very susceptible to some kinds of it. In the most sectarian period of my Benthanism, I happened to look into Pope's Essay on Man, and though every opinion in it was contrary to mine, I well remember how powerfully it acted on my imagination."

A time came when something more was felt to be needed. The attainment of a condition of physical comfort alone, in which the pleasures of life would no longer be kept up by struggle, and in the midst of privation, could afford no sufficient hope of human happiness. What had been founded in a large degree on the intellectual and abstract conception of aggregate results, had to be converted into an exercise of genuine benevolence, and sympathy with individual distress and suffering. For the mere rational conviction that such and such things were good and evil, and the proper objects of praise and blame, reward and punishment, higher and deeper motives were substituted. At the same time in external things, a sense of vague and general admiration of grandeur and beauty was concentrated and intensified by examples brought into immediate contact with the mind and eye. The experiences of the time led him to adopt a theory of life which, while admitting that all rules of conduct must be tried by their tending to promote happiness as the end of life, yet that end could not be reached by its direct and sole pursuit, or by making it the principal object of desire. This has given occasion to a singular criticism. "He found," say the objectors, "that it was not a safe or successful course to pursue happiness as a direct end, therefore," they add, "it follows, that it is not the proper end and aim of life, and the utilitarian principle fails!" This is a confusion of two things entirely distinct from each other, the particular and the general happiness, and the diverse methods of their pursuit. Nothing in the theory that the happiness of the individual should not be the direct end of his existence, would forbid the direct pursuit of ordinary pleasures. He may attend the performance of a play of Shakspeare, or listen to a composition of Mendelssohn, set out on a spring day for a woodland walk, or ascend an Alpine hill, with a direct view to the enjoyment which such a use of his time will produce. But if one passes his life in seeking nothing else but his own direct and personal enjoyment, if he does not look beyond this to a higher and nobler purpose of existence—a purpose into which the idea of its bearing upon his individual happiness does not enter, except as a sense of the performance of duty in the promotion of the good of others, which is attended with an unsought pleasure—the narrow objects he has pursued will ultimately fail him, and the time will come of decaying natural powers, and of blunted capacities for the accustomed enjoyment. Breadth of affection is an element in its durability. "When people who are tolerably fortunate in their outward lot do not find in life sufficient enjoyment to make it valuable to them, the cause generally is, caring for nobody but themselves. To those who have neither public nor private affections, the excitements of life are much curtailed, and in any case dwindle in value as the time approaches when all selfish interests must be terminated by death; while those who leave after them objects of personal affection, and especially those who have also cultivated a fellow-feeling with the collective interests of mankind, retain as lively an interest in life on the eve of death as in the vigour of youth and health."* "I do not," he said, in concluding his address to the University of St. Andrews, "attempt to instigate you by the prospect of direct rewards, either earthly or heavenly; the less we think about being rewarded in either way, the better for us. But there is one reward which will not fail you, and which may be called disinterested, because it is not a consequence, but is inherent in the very fact of deserving it; the deeper and more varied interest you will feel in life, which will give it tenfold its value, and a value which will last to the end. All merely personal objects grow less valuable as we advance in life; this not only endures but increases."

He was also now led to give its proper place to internal culture, as among the prime necessities of human well-being. We have seen how much of the pleasure he had before enjoyed had been derived from the love of rural objects and natural scenery. He now found in the poetry of Wordsworth, the expression not alone of outward beauty, but of "states of feeling, and of thought coloured by feeling, under the excitement of beauty."

"In them I seemed to draw from a source of inward joy, of sympathetic and imaginary pleasure, which could be shared in by all human beings; which had no connexion with struggle or imperfection, but would be made richer by every improvement in the physical or social condition of mankind. From them I seemed to learn what would be the perennial sources of happiness, when all the greater evils

* Utilitarianism. Its Meaning, p. 20.

of life shall have been removed. And I felt myself at once better and happier as I came under their influence." . . . . "I needed to be made to feel that there was real permanent happiness in tranquil contemplation. Wordsworth taught me this, not only without turning away from, but with a greatly increased interest in the common feelings and common destiny of human beings."

This part of the Autobiography introduces the acquaintance with Frederick Maurice and John Sterling, the former a disciple of Coleridge, and the latter of Coleridge and Maurice, and both were of use in his development. Nothing is more interesting than the account Mr. Mill gives us of his intimacy with them :—

"With Sterling I soon became very intimate, and was more attached to him than I have ever been to any other man. He was indeed one of the most loveable of men. His frank, cordial, affectionate, and expansive character; a love of truth, alike conspicuous in the highest things and humblest; a generous and ardent nature, which threw itself with impetuosity into the opinions it adopted, but was as eager to do justice to the doctrines and the men it was opposed to, as to make war on what it thought their errors; and an equal devotion to the two cardinal points of Liberty and Duty, formed a combination of qualities as attractive to me, as to all others who knew him as well as I did. With his open mind and heart, he found no difficulty in joining hands with me across the gulf which as yet divided our opinions. He told me how he and others had looked upon me (from hearsay information) as a made or 'manufactured' man, having had a certain impress of opinions stamped on me, which I could only reproduce; and what a change took place in his feelings when he found, in the discussion on Wordsworth and Byron, that Wordsworth, and all that that name implies, 'belonged' to me as much as to him and his friends."

From a brief view of the sources and method of Mr. Mill's education, and the primary effect it had on his mind and character, we pass to the opinions of his mature years, and then to some of the results of those opinions upon his labours in moral and political science, as well as in practical politics.

And first, on the subject of religion, the Autobiography supplies us with a less perfect account of the opinions of Mr. Mill than it is understood we may expect from some hitherto unpublished essays which will be soon before the world. What is to be collected from the work before us cannot, however, properly be passed over in silence. The views of James Mill are clearly stated.

"My father had been early led to reject not only the belief in Revelation, but the foundations of what is commonly called natural religion. I have heard him say that the turning-point of his mind on the subject was reading Butler's Analogy. That work, of which he always continued to speak with respect, kept him, as he said, for some considerable time, a believer in the divine authority of Christianity; by proving to him that whatever are the difficulties in believing that the Old and New Testaments proceed from, or record the acts of, a perfectly wise and good being, the same and still greater difficulties stand in the way of the belief, that a being of such a character can have been the Maker of the Universe. He considered Butler's argument as conclusive against the only opponents for whom it was intended. Those who admit an omnipotent as well as perfectly just and benevolent maker and ruler of such a world as this, can say little against Christianity but what can, with at least equal force, be retorted against themselves. Finding, therefore, no halting place in Deism, he remained in a state of perplexity, until, doubtless, after many struggles, he yielded to the conviction that, concerning the origin of things, nothing whatever can be known. . . . . These particulars are important, because they show that my father's rejection of all that is called religious belief, was not, as many might suppose, primarily a matter of logic and evidence; the grounds of it were moral still more than intellectual. He found it impossible to believe that a world so full of evil was the work of an Author combining infinite power with perfect goodness and righteousness."

While he impressed upon his son from the first that the manner in which the world came into existence was a subject on which nothing was known—

"He at the same time, took care that I should be acquainted with what had been thought by mankind on these impenetrable problems. I have mentioned at how early an age he made me a reader of ecclesiastical history; and he taught me to take the strongest interest in the Reformation, as the great and decisive contest against priestly tyranny for liberty of thought."

In this negative state of opinion on religion which one of the critics of the Autobiography gravely attributes to the want, on the part of both father and son of a comprehension of the higher mathematics, Mr. Mill grew up.

"I looked (he says) upon the modern exactly as I did upon the ancient religion, as something which in no way concerned me. It did not seem to me more strange that English people should believe what I did not, than that the men I read of in Herodotus should have done so. History had made the variety of opinions among mankind a fact familiar to me, and this was but a prolongation of that fact."

Of unbelievers (so called) as well as of believers, Mr. Mill observes, there are many species, including almost every variety of moral type, many of the best of the former being more generally religious in the best sense of the word, than those who exclusively arrogate to themselves the title. They repudiate all dogmatism, and especially dogmatic atheism, which they regard as absurd;

but they deny that beings endowed with reasoning faculties are justified in permitting themselves to receive as true the character and acts commonly attributed to an Omnipotent Author of all things, who created the human race with the infallible foreknowledge, and therefore with the intention that the great majority of them were to be consigned to terrible and everlasting torment.

"Though they may think the proof incomplete that the universe is a work of design, and they assuredly disbelieve that it can have an Author and Governor who is *absolute* in power as well as perfect in goodness, they have that which contributes the principal worth of all religions whatever, an ideal conception of a Perfect Being, to which they habitually refer as the guide of their conscience; and this ideal of good is usually far nearer to perfection than the objective Deity of those who think themselves obliged to find absolute goodness in [one whom they are taught to believe is] the author of a world so crowded with suffering and so deformed with injustice as ours."

In this aspect, the argument, however orthodox believers are disposed to repudiate it, ought to be regarded even by them according to its manifest design, as an effort to vindicate the Divine Ideal. It is the belief of those who thus argue that a low and imperfect conception of the Being which is adored, radically vitiates the standard of morals, and causes fictitious excellences to be set up and substituted for genuine virtues. It is true that—

"Christians do not in general undergo the demoralizing consequences which seem inherent in such a creed, in the manner, or to the extent which might have been expected from it. The same slovenliness of thought, and subjection of the reason to fears, wishes, and affections, which enable them to accept a theory involving a contradiction in terms, prevents them from perceiving the logical consequences of the theory."

Another cause through which such consequences are avoided may be found in the great counteracting principles that are embodied in the Christian doctrine, and which teach forbearance, love of others, and self-sacrifice. These, the fundamental teachings of Christianity, apart from dogma, few would appreciate better than Mr. Mill. He found in them the corroboration of the doctrine he advocated. "In the golden rule," he says, "of Jesus of Nazareth we read the complete spirit of the ethics of utility. To do as you would be done by, to love your neighbour as yourself, constitute the ideal perfection of utilitarian morality."

Mr. Mill attributes one bad consequence to this part of his education. In giving him an opinion contrary to that of the world, his father thought it necessary to give it as one which could not be prudently avowed to the world. This lesson of keeping his thoughts to himself at that early age was attended with some disadvantages, though his limited intercourse with strangers, especially such as were likely to speak to him on religion, prevented him from being placed in the alternative of avowal or hypocrisy. Looking at the present advance in the liberty of discussion since the time of which he was speaking, he thinks that few men of his father's intellect and public spirit, with such intensity of moral conviction, would now withhold his opinions from the world, unless in cases, becoming fewer every day, in which frankness would risk the loss of subsistence, or be an exclusion from a sphere of usefulness to which the individual was particularly suited. On religion—

"The time appears to have come, when it is the duty of all, who being qualified in point of knowledge, have on mature consideration satisfied themselves that the current opinions are not only false but hurtful, to make their dissent known; at least, if they are among those whose station or reputation, gives their opinion a chance of being attended to. Such an avowal would put an end, at once and for ever, to the vulgar prejudice, that what is called, very improperly, unbelief, is connected with any bad qualities either of heart or mind. The world would be astonished if it knew how great a proportion of its brightest ornaments—of those most distinguished even in popular estimation for wisdom and virtue—are complete sceptics in religion; many of them refraining from avowal, less from personal considerations, than from a conscientious, though now in my opinion a most mistaken apprehension, lest by speaking out what would tend to weaken existing beliefs, and by consequence (as they suppose) existing restraints, they should do harm instead of good."

As years have passed on, the evidences of the truth of this view of the progress of thought have multiplied. Mr. Mill mentions the well-remembered collision of his friend Frederick Maurice with orthodox opinion, and the penalty to which he submitted rather than recognise a doctrine utterly inconsistent with a Divine benevolence. Between himself and Sterling the distance in opinion we find was always diminishing. Still later the author of "Literature and Dogma," setting out from a starting-point as distant as the poles, and pursuing an entirely different route, has sought like him to raise an ideal conception of a true Divine Guide. What is the object of that moral and intellectual culture which Mr. Mill has laboured to prove the most suitable for mankind, other than that they should be taught to know, "the best that has been thought and said in the world?" In what does the Ideal of Perfection, to which he refers as the best guide of the human conscience, differ from that "Enduring Power, not ourselves, which makes for righteousness?"

Turning to philosophy let us see what was the especial object which Mr. Mill had in view in his examination of that of Sir William Hamilton. And here the first thing that strikes the reader is, that even in his most abstract works, those apparently of a nature purely speculative, and falling within the region of metaphysics, he had chiefly, if not wholly, in view a great and practical end. He did not seek merely to establish a barren theory of remote application, but to assert a truth which to the extent to which it was accepted and influenced conduct, might have a practical result in the consideration of the conditions of human existence. It was nothing less than this which led him to attack the foundation of a system, that theoretically denies the effect of the conditions of existence upon the moral as well as the intellectual state of society, and thus goes far to discourage and cripple real efforts for improvement.

"The difference between these two schools of philosophy, that of Intuition and that of Experience and Association, is not a mere matter of abstract speculation; it is full of practical consequences, and lies at the foundation of all the greatest differences of practical opinion in an age of progress. The practical reformer has continually to demand that changes be made in things which are supported by powerful and widely-spread feelings, or to question the apparent necessity and indefeasibleness of established facts; and it is often an indispensable part of his argument to show, how those powerful feelings had their origin, and how those facts came to seem necessary and indefeasible. There is therefore a natural hostility between him and a philosophy which encourages the explanation of feelings and moral facts, by circumstances and associations, and prefers to treat them as ultimate elements of human nature; a philosophy which is addicted to holding up favourite doctrines as intuitive truths, and deems intuition to be the voice of Nature and of God, speaking with an authority higher than that of reason. In particular, I have long felt that the prevailing tendency to regard all the marked distinctions of human character as innate, and in the main indelible, and to ignore the irresistible proofs that by far the greater part of those differences, whether between individuals, races, or sexes, are such as not only might, but naturally could be produced by differences in circumstances, is one of the chief hindrances to the rational treatment of great social questions, and one of the greatest stumbling blocks to human improvement. My father's Analysis of the Mind, my own Logic, and Professor Bain's great Treatise, had attempted to re-introduce a better mode of philosophizing, latterly with quite as much success as could be expected; but I had for some time felt that the mere contrast of the two philosophies was not enough, that there ought to be a hand-to-hand fight between them, that controversial as well as expository writings were needed, and that the time was come when such controversy would be useful."

The treatise on Liberty Mr. Mill regards as likely to survive longer than anything else he has written, with the possible exception of the Logic. It stood pre-eminent in his estimation, not only from its intrinsic importance, but as the last and most elaborate result of the joint labours of himself and his wife, and consecrated to her memory. None of his other writings was either so carefully composed or sedulously corrected. "After it had been written as usual twice over, we kept it by us, bringing it out from time to time, and going through it *de novo*, reading, weighing, and criticising every sentence."

The joint revision, which was to have been the work of the winter of 1858-9, was frustrated by Mrs. Mill's death. Its publication was his first undertaking after that event. It is, he says, the text-book of a single truth—the importance to man and society of a large variety in types of character, and of giving full freedom to human nature to expand itself in innumerable and conflicting directions. A danger was that the growth of social equality, and of a submission to public opinion, should impose on mankind an oppressive yoke of uniformity in opinion and practice. The doctrine of Individuality, the right and duty of self-development, asserted by insulated thinkers from age to age, worked out in the labours of Pestalozzi, and having among its promulgators Wilhelm von Humboldt, Goethe, De Tocqueville, and others less known but not less ardent in its cause, was with modifications and differences of detail embodied in this work. It was, moreover, in direct conflict with Positivism. Agreeing with Comte that from the necessity of the case, the mass of mankind, even including their rulers, must accept many of their opinions on political and social matters, as they do on physical, from the authority of those who have made those subjects their especial study; that Europe during the Middle Ages had greatly profited by the distinct organization of the spiritual power, and the moral and intellectual ascendancy once exercised by priests would naturally pass into the hands of philosophers, he yet repudiated with his utmost energy the conclusion that a corporate hierarchy should be formed of the latter. He could not see in such a body any bulwark against oppression, or security for good government. The "Système de Politique Positive" he regarded as the most complete system of spiritual and temporal despotism which had ever emanated from the human brain, except possibly that of Ignatius Loyola. "The book stands a monumental warning to thinkers on society and politics, of what happens when once men lose sight in these speculations, of the value of Liberty and Individuality." The Essay on Liberty has recently been the subject of an able and appreciative article by Mr. John Morley,* to which we may refer our readers.

* *Fortnightly Review*, August, 1873, pp. 234-256.

On Political Economy, especially in the distinction between the laws of the production and distribution of wealth, Mr. Mill's later views were a material modification of his earlier ones. The capacity to learn and unlearn, which he regards as essential to real progress, one of his reviewers describes as a constant state of vacillation, and an absence of any firm standing ground. Mr. Mill had no fear of such reproaches. In the days of his most extreme Benthamism he tells us that he had seen little further than the old school of political economists, into the possibilities of fundamental improvement in social arrangements. He subsequently became less indulgent to ordinary social opinion, and less willing to be content with secondary and more superficial improvements. Any diminution of the evil involved in the fact that while some are born to riches, the vast majority inherit nothing but poverty—except such amelioration as might result from a voluntary restraint on the numbers of the latter—had before appeared chimerical. While still repudiating the tyranny of the society over the individual which most Socialistic systems involve, he came to look forward to a time when the division of the produce of labour will depend less on the accident of birth, and it will be more common for all to labour strenuously to procure benefits that shall not be exclusively their own, but shall be shared by the society of which they are members. The capacity of all classes to learn by practice to combine and labour for public and social purposes, and not solely for narrowly interested ones, had always existed, and was not hindered by any essential difficulty in the constitution of our nature. Why should it be more difficult to persuade a man to dig or weave for his country than to fight for it? In the gradual formation of such opinions, and their publication in the second and third editions of the Principles of Political Economy, we must not pass over the share which Mr. Mill attributes to his wife. No one who knew him will feel surprise at the place which her memory fills in the Autobiography. Few narratives appeal more powerfully to every mind sensitive to human affections than the story of their partnership of thought, of feeling, concurrent labour, and entire existence; and in truth there seem to have been qualities existing in each which made their association with one another eminently valuable. One happily possessed that which the other needed. The chapter on Political Economy which Mr. Mill believes has had the most influence on opinion,—that on "The Probable Future of the Labouring Classes," he informs us is entirely due to his wife. She pointed out the need of such a chapter, and the imperfection of the book without it. It certainly deals with that part of the subject in which the reflections of an acute woman, conversant with the social necessities of the people around her, would be likely to be of great value. Thoroughly sensible of the folly of premature attempts to dispense with the inducements of private interest in social affairs, they welcomed all experiments, such as co-operative societies, which whether they succeeded or failed, would be an education for those who took part in them, by cultivating their capacity for acting upon motives pointing directly to a more general good. Speaking of this work, he says:—

"It was chiefly her influence that gave to the book that general tone by which it is distinguished from all previous expositions of political economy that had any pretensions to being scientific, and which has made it so useful in conciliating minds which those previous expositions had repelled. This tone consisted chiefly in making the proper distinction between the laws of the production of wealth, which are real laws of nature, dependent on the properties of objects, and the modes of its distribution, which, subject to certain conditions, depend on human will. The common run of political economists confuse these together, under the designation of economic laws, which they deem incapable of being defeated or modified by human effort; ascribing the same necessity to things dependent on the unchangeable conditions of our earthly existence, and to those which, being but the necessary consequences of particular social arrangements, are merely co-extensive with these: given certain institutions and customs, wages, profits, and rent will be determined by certain causes; but this class of political economists drop the indispensable presupposition, and argue that these causes must, by one inherent necessity, against which no human means can avail, determine the shares which fall, in the division of the produce, to labourers, capitalists, and landlords. The 'Principles of Political Economy' yielded to none of its predecessors in aiming at the scientific appreciation of the action of these causes, under the conditions which they presuppose; but it set the example of not treating those conditions as final. The economic generalizations which depend, not on necessities of nature, but on those combined with the existing arrangements of society, it deals with only as provisional, and as liable to be much altered by the progress of social improvement."

An observation is often made that Mr. Mill was not a practical politician. Indeed, his more virulent detractors have not shrunk from attributing to him an "utter incapacity to grapple with practical legislation or the real business of life." The ground of this conclusion is not very difficult to discover. It arises from a radical difference in the sense of duty. To those who measure the value of the business of life, and the practical character of those who undertake it, by the immediate prospect of success, by the probability of their acquiring some personal distinction or profit, in fact, by the question whether the work is likely "to pay," Mr. Mill's labours will naturally appear mistaken and absurd. We can fancy the supreme contempt with which such critics must have read in the Autobiography, "the idea, that the use of my being in Parliament was to do work which others were not able or not willing to do, made me think it my duty to come to the front in defence of advanced Liberalism, on occasions when the obloquy to be encountered was such as most of the advanced Liberals in the House preferred not to incur." Mr. Mill was one of those who are dissatisfied with human life as it is, and whose feelings are wholly identified with its radical amendment. With such there are two main regions of thought, one that of ultimate aims, the constituent elements of the highest realizable ideal of human life; the other that of the immediately useful and practically attainable. Some test of the value of these criticisms may be found by selecting one or two of the principal subjects within the domain of politics, to which a portion of the labours of Mr. Mill have been directed. For this purpose let us take, first, the general question of Government, in the aspect in which it is presented to modern inquirers; and secondly, the legislation affecting the proprietorship or occupation of land.

First, on government, Mr. Mill thought that in his father's "Essay on Government," the premises were too narrow, and included but few of the general truths on what, in politics, the important consequences depend. He was dissatisfied with the answer to the criticisms of Macaulay, and thought a better reply would have been, "I was not writing a scientific treatise on politics, but an argument for Parliamentary reform." His progress in logical analysis subsequently helped him to a different conception of philosophical method as applicable to politics, of the pedantry of adopting and promulgating a systematized political creed. He acquired a conviction that the true system of political philosophy was something much more complicated and many-sided than he had previously had any idea of, and that its object was to supply, not a set of model institutions, but principles from which the institutions suitable to any given circumstances might be deduced. This train of thought produced a clearer conception than he had ever before had of the peculiarities of an era of transition in opinion, and he ceased to mistake the moral and intellectual characteristics of such an era for the normal attributes of humanity. He looked forward to a period of unchecked liberty of thought, and unbounded freedom of individual action in all modes not hurtful to others, combining the best qualities of the critical with the best qualities of the organic times.

A complete view of his most matured opinions on the subject will be found in the Considerations on Representative Government. The problem stated is the combination of complete popular control over public affairs, with the greatest attainable perfection of skilled agency. James Mill, as well as his son, were in comparison with others who hold democratic opinions, comparatively indifferent to monarchical or republican forms: and, in this work, the existence of a constitutional monarchy—with an hereditary king—is considered, as in many cases, a favourable condition for the attainment of good government. He may, by his position, have an interest in raising and improving the mass, under circumstances such as those which make up a great part of the history of the English Parliament. In other cases where none, or only some fraction of the people feels a degree of interest in affairs of State necessary to the formation of a public opinion, and the suffrage is only used by the electors to serve their private interest, or that of the locality, or of particular persons, of whom they are adherents or dependents, the selfish and sordid factions of which the assembly is likely to be composed, if struggling for the Presidency or chief place in the Government, would, as in the case of Spanish America, keep the country in a state of chronic revolution and civil war. A despotism of illegal violence would be exercised by a succession of political adventurers, and representation would have no effect but that of preventing that stability of government by which some of the evils of a legal despotism are mitigated. In such a case, the struggle for place—under an hereditary king—would be far less mischievous. The tranquillity of Brazil, as compared with that of the other parts of the South American continent, is an illustration of this argument. In our own government, Parliament virtually decides who shall be Prime Minister, or who shall be the two or three individuals from whom the Prime Minister shall be chosen, without nominating him, but leaving the appointment of the head of the administration to the Crown, in conformity with the general inclinations which the Parliament has manifested. This initiative method, in the formation of the executive government, seemed to Mr. Mill to stand on as good a footing as possible. In this conclusion he will have the sympathy of most of the English people, who will not readily be persuaded that the periodical election of a President would be an improvement in Government.

The evil effect produced on the mind of any holders of power, whether an individual or an assembly, by the consciousness of having only themselves to consult, was the consideration which appeared to him of the greatest weight in favour of a second chamber. Without it the majority in a single assembly, might easily become overweening and despotic. It was this which induced the Romans to have two Consuls. In every polity there should be a centre of resistance to the predominant power. If any people, possessing a democratic representation, are, from their historical antecedents, more willing to tolerate such a centre of resistance in the form of a second Chamber or House of Lords than in any other shape, this constitutes a strong reason for so constructing it. It did not, however, appear to him the best or most efficacious shape. Of such a body, the construction of the Roman Senate seemed to be the best example. He suggests how a chamber of statesmen might be formed of the heads of the Courts of Law; those who had been Cabinet Ministers; the more distinguished chiefs in the Army and Navy; the diplomatic servants of long-standing; governors of colonies and dependencies. In England it was highly improbable, from its historical antecedents, that any second chamber could possibly exist which is not built on the foundation of the House of Lords; but there might be no insuperable difficulty in adding the classes mentioned, to the existing body, in the character of peers for life.

It is in the constitution of the Representative Assembly that his hopes of good Government depend, and he devotes a chapter to the consideration of its infirmities and dangers. The greatest among these is the delivery over of the management of public affairs to the representatives of a numerical majority alone, and the placing of all the unrepresented classes at their mercy. It is as possible, and as likely, for this numerical majority, being the ruling power of a democracy, to be as much under the dominion of sectional or class interests, or supposed interests, as any other ruling power. The constituencies to which most of the highly educated and public-spirited persons in the country belong—those of the large towns—are in great part either unrepresented or misrepresented. This had been thought irremediable, and from despairing of a cure, people had gone on for the most part to deny the disease. An attempt to obtain a somewhat more true representation, proposed by Earl Russell in one of the Reform Bills, met with no support. The late Mr. Marshall subsequently suggested the method of the cumulative vote, to rescue at least some portion of a constituency from the tyranny of the numerical majority. This system is now tolerably well understood from the experience of the school board elections, and consists in enabling the electors of every constituency, having more than one representative, not only to give, as before, one vote to each person to be chosen, but, instead of that, to give all their votes to one, or distribute them as they please among the candidates. The effect of this system may be made clearly intelligible in a few words, which will show also its infirmities, as a vehicle for bringing into the elected body any complete expression or representation of the individual thought or study of the members of a large community. Thus suppose 100 persons are about to elect a committee of 4 to settle some business which concerns them, and that 21 out of the 100 place their confidence in A, while 51 prefer B, C, D, and E, as those through whom their interests will be better secured. Under the old system, the latter might have elected the whole committee; and not only the 21 desiring to be represented by A, but as many as 28 others might have been excluded from any voice in their deliberations. With the cumulative system, every voter may give his 4 votes to any one or more candidates, and thus 21 persons may give their single candidate 84 votes; the other 79 persons cannot altogether poll more than 316 votes, one of their candidates at least must, therefore, be left with no more than 79 votes, and the election of the candidate of the united 21 is thus secured. It will be thus seen that though it is a great improvement on the exclusive majority system, it yet requires that the holders of opinions differing from the majority shall combine and adhere rigidly together in voting for the same person in order that their success may be certain. If one or two of the 21 had failed to poll for their candidate, the efforts of all the rest of the 21 might be thrown away; or the 79, not submitting to direction, may, if there were more candidates than 5, have less representatives than they are entitled to by their numbers. Meetings, verbal and written communications, and the guidance of party leaders are necessary; and every sort of manipulation may thus be brought to bear. If the voter does not approve of the candidates presented to his constituency, he is helpless; and if he does, he cannot, without placing himself in the hands of the party leaders or agents, be certain that his vote will have any effect.

The method of popular election, which has since been known under the various appellations of the Minority, Personal, Proportional, and Preferential, system, had been put forward in a crude form in 1857,* and in its matured shape in 1859.† This system effected the object that Mr. Mill had thought desirable as an antidote to the exclusive representation, and therefore exclusive rule of local majorities, and was at the same time subject to none of the infirmities and inconveniences of the cumulative system, inasmuch as it enabled every single elector, while he exercised the most extensive choice practicable, to give an independent vote, with the certainty that it will not be thrown away. The scheme was made known to Mr. Mill in 1859, after the publication of his "Thoughts on Parliamentary Reform," and it immediately obtained his assent and adoption. After a careful

* "The Machinery of Representation." Maxwell, 1857.

† "A Treatise on the Election of Representatives, Parliamentary and Municipal." Longmans, 1859.

examination of the proposed plan, in a letter* suggesting an alteration in a matter of detail, he said that it appeared to him "to have exactly, and for the first time, solved the difficulty of popular representation, and by so doing to have raised up the cloud of gloom and uncertainty that hung over the futurity of representative government, and therefore of civilization." In a conversation on the subject which took place a few weeks afterwards Mr. Mill expressed his belief and expectation that the idea of such an improvement as was proposed would soon have a prominent place in the minds of statesmen and reformers; and those who were present have not forgotten that almost his first inquiry was, whether the plan had been brought to the attention of Mr. Gladstone. "Had I met with the system," Mr. Mill says, in his Autobiography, "before the publication of my pamphlet, I should have given an account of it there. Not having done so, I wrote an article in *Fraser's Magazine*, reprinted in my miscellaneous writings, principally for that purpose. In his "Considerations on Representative Government," he devotes the greater part of a chapter to this subject.† After explaining the mode in which the votes would be given and counted, and referring to Mr. Fawcett's pamphlet on the system, he explains its immediate result, that all parties sufficiently numerous to be entitled to be represented would be sure of being so; that the representation would be real and not merely nominal, or what is called "virtual;" that the tie between the elector and representative would commonly have a strength, value, and permanence now unknown; that while localities would secure adequate attention, general and national interests would be paramount; that every person in the nation honourably distinguished among his countrymen would have a fair chance of election, and with such encouragement such persons might be expected to offer themselves in numbers hitherto undreamt of; that when the electors were no longer reduced to Hobson's choice, the majorities would be compelled to look out and put forward men of higher calibre, and their leaders could no longer foist upon the people the first person who presents himself with the catchword of the party in his mouth, and three or four thousand pounds in his pocket; that it would correct the tendency of representative government towards collective mediocrity; that though the representatives of the majorities would be the most in number, they must speak and vote in the presence and subject to the criticism of their opponents, and before the public.

* March 3, 1859.

† Chapter vii. "True and False Democracy; Representation of All, and Representation of the Majority only."

"The multitude have often a true instinct for distinguishing an able man when he has the means of displaying his ability in a fair field before them. If such a man fails to obtain any portion whatever of his just weight, it is through institutions or usages which keep him out of sight. In the old democracies there were no means of keeping out of sight any able man: the bema was open to him; he needed nobody's consent to become a public adviser. It is not so in a representative government; and the best friends of representative democracy can hardly be without misgivings that the Themistocles or Demosthenes whose counsels would have saved the nation, might be unable during his whole life to obtain a seat. But if his presence in the representative assembly can be insured, or even a few of the first minds in the country, though the remainder consists only of average minds, the influence of these leading spirits is sure to make itself sensibly felt in the general deliberations, even though they be known to be in many respects opposed to the tone of popular opinion and feeling. . . . . This portion of the assembly would also be the appropriate organ of a great social function, for which there is no provision in any existing democracy, but which in no government can remain permanently unfulfilled without condemning that government to infallible degeneracy and decay. This may be called the function of Antagonism. In every government there is some power stronger than all the rest; and the power which is strongest tends perpetually to become the sole power. Partly by intention, and partly unconsciously, it is ever striving to make all other things bend to itself, and is not content while there is anything which makes permanent head against it, any influence not in agreement with its spirit. Yet, if it succeeds in suppressing all rival influences, and moulding everything after its own model, improvement in that country is at an end, and decline commences. Human improvement is a product of many factors, and no power ever yet constituted among mankind includes them all; even the most beneficent power only contains in itself some of the requisites of good, and the remainder, if progress is to continue, must be derived from some other source. No community has ever long continued progressive, but while a conflict was going on between the strongest power in the community and some rival power: between the spiritual and temporal authorities; the military or territorial and the industrious classes; the king and the people; the orthodox and religious reformers. When the victory on either side was so complete as to put an end to the strife, and no other conflict took its place, first stagnation followed, and then decay. The ascendancy of the numerical majority is less unjust, and on the whole less mischievous, than many others, but it is attended with the very same kind of dangers, and even more certainly; for when the government is in the hands of one or a few, the many are always existent as a rival power, which may not be strong enough ever to control the other, but whose opinion and sentiment are a moral, and even a social, support to all who, either from conviction or contrariety of interest, are opposed to any of the tendencies of the ruling authority. But when the democracy is supreme, there is no one or few strong enough for dissentient opinions and injured or menaced interests to lean upon.

The great difficulty of democratic government has hitherto seemed to be, how to provide in a democratic society what circumstances have provided hitherto in all the societies which have maintained themselves ahead of others—a social support, a *point d'appui*, for individual resistance to the tendencies of the ruling power; a protection, a rallying point, for opinions and interests which the ascendant public opinion views with disfavour. For want of such a *point d'appui*, the older societies, and all but a few modern ones, either fell into dissolution or became stationary (which means slow deterioration) through the exclusive predominance of a part only of the conditions of social and mental well-being.

"Now, this great want the system of personal representation is fitted to supply, in the most perfect manner which the circumstances of modern society admit of. . . . . The representatives who would be returned to Parliament by the aggregate of minorities, would afford that organ in its greatest perfection. A separate organization of the instructed classes would, if practicable, be invidious, and could only escape from being offensive by being totally without influence. But if the *élite* of these classes formed part of the Parliament, by the same title as any other of its members—by representing the same number of citizens, the same numerical fraction of the national will—their presence could give umbrage to nobody, while they would be in the position of highest vantage, both for making their opinions and counsels heard on all important subjects, and for taking an active part in public business. Their abilities would probably draw to them more than their numerical share of the actual administration of government; as the Athenians did not confide responsible public functions to Cleon or Hyperbolus (the employment of Cleon at Pylos and Amphipolis was purely exceptional), but Nicias, and Theramenes, and Alcibiades, were in constant employment both at home and abroad, though known to sympathize more with oligarchy than with democracy. The instructed minority would, in the actual voting, count only for their numbers, but as a moral power they would count for much more, in virtue of their knowledge, and of the influence it would give them over the rest. An arrangement better adapted to keep popular opinion within reason and justice, and to guard it from the various deteriorating influences which assail the weak side of democracy, could scarcely by human ingenuity be devised. A democratic people would in this way be provided with what in any other way it would almost certainly miss—leaders of a higher grade of intellect and character than itself. Modern democracy would have its occasional Pericles, and its habitual group of superior and guiding minds."*

Subsequently in Parliament, in moving, as an amendment to Mr. Disraeli's Reform Bill, the introduction of clauses for the distribution of seats according to the proportional system, Mr. Mill brought it forward in an expository and argumentative

* "Considerations on Representative Government." 3rd edit. p. 149-152.

speech.* The House was, however, as might be expected, unprepared for its consideration. The debate is not, however, uninteresting, as much perhaps for what was not, as for what was, said. Mr. Mill, in his Autobiography, adds on this subject :—

"I was active in support of the very imperfect substitute for that plan, which in a small number of constituencies, Parliament was induced to adopt. This poor makeshift had scarcely any recommendation, except that it was a partial recognition of the evil which it did so little to remedy. As such, however, it was attacked by the same fallacies, and required to be defended on the same principles, as a really good measure; and its adoption in a few parliamentary elections, as well as the subsequent introduction of what is called the Cumulative Vote in the elections for the London School Board, have had the good effect of converting the equal claim of all electors to a proportional share in the representation, from a subject of merely speculative discussion, into a question of practical politics, much sooner than would otherwise have been the case."

The view which Mr. Mill took of the absolute need of this change in the method of creating representative bodies, is in no small degree justified by the attention which it has since received in our own† and in nearly every other country where free institutions exist.‡ Its fundamental principle is, in fact, a corollary of that of Individuality. It puts forward in a practical shape the necessity of freedom for individual action. It liberates every voter from the condition of being an instrument of those around him, and enables him to bring all he knows and feels,—his maturest judgment, to his aid in the choice of the man in whose hands he would place power. We know that there are many who are ignorant or stupid, and to whom this discretion would be of little use. It is enough to say that they would be no worse off than they now are, and could do far less harm in corrupting and degrading the constituency of which they are a part. On the other hand, there are large numbers whose intelligence and public spirit ought not to be wasted and lost to the nation. A careful observer of the English mind and manners, and one who certainly takes no optimist view of the present or future conditions of society, in his latest publication, remarks that "no nation in the world possesses anything like so large a class of intelli-

* "Hansard's Parliamentary Debates," 30 May, 1867, vol. clxxxvii. pp. 1343-1362.

† See "The Debate on Mr. Morrison's Bill—Hansard's Parliamentary Debates," vol. ccxii. pp. 890-926.

‡ "The Election of Representatives, Parliamentary and Municipal." A Treatise. By Thomas Hare. 4th edit. Appendices A to O, pp. 292-380. See also on the Empirical Character of the Three-cornered Constituency Clause, and the Cumulative Vote.—Ibid. pp. 16-19. Longmans, 1873.

gent, independent, and vigorous-minded men in all ranks of life, who seriously devote themselves to public affairs, and take the deepest possible interest in the national success and well-being;" while he truly adds that, "the character of our public men is the sheet-anchor on which our institutions depend. So long as political life is the chosen occupation of wise and honourable men, who are above jobs and petty personal views, the defects of Parliamentary Government may be endured; but if the personal character of English politicians should ever be seriously lowered, it is difficult not to feel that the present state of the constitution would give bad and unscrupulous men a power for evil hardly equalled in any other part of the world."* The safeguard surely is to place it distinctly and certainly in the power of every intelligent and vigorous-minded elector to give a vote which shall secure the return of a wise and honourable man.

Secondly, on the Land Laws. A pamphlet, entitled "England and Ireland," published before the season of 1868, after an argument to show the undesirableness, for Ireland as well as for England, of separation, contained a proposal for settling the land question by giving to the tenants a permanent tenure, at a fixed rent, to be assessed after due inquiry by the State:—

"If no measure short of that which I proposed would do full justice to Ireland, or afford a prospect of conciliating the mass of the Irish people, the duty of proposing it was imperative; while if, on the other hand, there was any intermediate course which had a claim to a trial, I well knew that to propose something which would be called extreme, was the true way not to impede, but to facilitate a more moderate experiment. It is most improbable that a measure conceding so much to the tenantry as Mr. Gladstone's Irish Land Bill, would have been proposed by a Government, or could have been carried through Parliament, unless the British public had been led to perceive that a case might be made, and perhaps a party formed, for a measure considerably stronger. It is the character of the British people, or at least of the higher and middle classes who pass muster for the British people, that to induce them to approve of any change, it is necessary they should look on it as a middle course; they think every proposal extreme and violent unless they hear of some other proposal going still further, upon which their antipathy to extreme views may discharge itself. So it proved in the present instance; my proposal was condemned, but any scheme for Irish Land Reform, short of mine, came to be thought moderate by comparison. I may observe that the attacks made on my plan usually gave a very incorrect idea of its nature. It was usually discussed as a proposal that the State should buy up the land and become the universal landlord; though, in fact, it only offered to each individual landlord this as an

* "Parliamentary Government." By James Fitzjames Stephen, Q.C. *Contemporary Review*, Dec. 1873, p. 3.

alternative, if he liked better to sell his estate than to retain it on the new conditions; and I fully anticipated that most landlords would continue to prefer the position of landowners to that of Government annuitants, and would retain their existing relation to their tenants, often on more indulgent terms than the full rents on which the compensation to be given them by Government would have been based."

With regard to the English land system, Mr. Mill says that the criticisms of the St. Simonians had some effect in showing the very limited and temporary value of the old political economy, which assumes all the rules affecting private property and inheritance as indefeasible facts, and the abolition of entails and primogeniture—the freedom of production and exchange, as the *dernier mot* of social improvement. The question here, as in other subjects, was the way in which all practicable ameliorations could be justly and wisely aided, by the promulgation of sound principles and adopting the means best suited to lead to their application. Asserting emphatically the value of private property as the root of industry, the ultimate object appeared to be that of uniting the greatest individual liberty of action with a wide diffusion and accessibility of the ownership of land—the raw material of the globe. With this view Mr. Mill took the chief part in framing the programme of the Land Tenure Reform Association, to which he gave his name and cordial support. We find in this programme the result of a careful study both of what he thought desirable, and what he deemed at once possible—the distant ideal, and the course to be immediately taken towards its accomplishment, or to bring us nearer to a better condition of things. It contains all that is comprehended in the words "free land" as recently interpreted, but it does not stop there. Concurring with those who believe that merely opening the ownership of land to competition in the money market, however valuable it may be in one of the aspects of economical improvement, would do but very little towards placing it under the control of the workman or giving him a direct interest in it; he regarded it as an indispensable condition that some part of the land of the kingdom should be placed within the reach of the industrious labourer, so as to be attainable in the shape of property of reasonable duration. The programme of the Association consists of ten articles. The earlier clauses contain the old tenets of the "free land" reformers. We will take the clauses in their inverse order, the last seven being especially the work of Mr. Mill. A prominent object, we find, is the mental culture of the classes which have the least opportunity for such improvement, by encouraging and fostering their tastes for rural scenery, for history, and art. The things to which he felt himself so greatly indebted—the love of nature and of beauty, and the cultivation of the power of recalling in the imagination what is memorable and great in former ages, he would bring home to all, as things not to be forgotten in the daily struggles for material results. The programme (X.) claims the preservation of all natural objects or artificial constructions attached to the soil, of historical, scientific, or artistic interest; that (IX.) the less fertile lands, and especially those within reach of populous districts, should be retained in a state of wild natural beauty, for the general enjoyment of the community, and the encouragement in all classes of healthful rural tastes, and of the higher order of pleasures. The next clauses deal with land already belonging to the public, or dedicated to permanent uses, not of a private character. They ask (VIII.) that land of which Parliament alone can authorize the inclosure shall be retained for national uses, compensation being made for manorial and common rights; that (VII.) lands belonging to the crown, to public bodies, or charitable and other endowments, be made available to be let for co-operative agriculture, and to small cultivators, as well as for the improvement of the dwellings of the labouring classes; and no such lands to be suffered (unless in pursuance of those ends, or for exceptional reasons) to pass into private hands. To protect such lands from alienation to private uses, which is rapidly taking place; to obviate all legal impediments to a voluntary dedication of land to public objects, and to secure their prudent and productive administration under skilled district agents of local appointment, exercising their powers without partiality to any class, Mr. Mill approved the action of the Association in the preparation and introduction of the "Public Lands and Commons Bill," of 1872.* His view of endowments it is known differed materially from that of Turgot. It forms the subject of the first article in his "Dissertations and Discussions."† Notwithstanding, he observes, the reverence due to that illustrious name, it is now allowable to regard his opinion of that subject as the prejudice of the age. Mankind are dependent for the removal of their ignorance and defect of culture, mainly on the unremitting exertions of the more instructed and cultivated, to awaken a consciousness of this want, and to facilitate the means of supplying it. "The instruments for the work are not merely schools and colleges, but every means by which the people can be reached, either through their intellect or their sensibilities, from

* See "Hansard's Parliamentary Debates," vol. ccxii. p. 583. (Erroneously printed as "Commons' Protection, &c., Bill.") 3 July, 1872.

† "The Right and Wrong of State Interference with Corporation and Church Property." Published in *The Jurist* for May, 1833.

preaching and popular writing, to national galleries, theatres, and public games. Here is a wide field of usefulness open to foundations."

His article on this subject, first published in 1893, shadowed forth the policy which has now, in spite of the opposition of bodies and persons interested in retaining local patronage, and influence arising from the power of dealing with estates, and selecting beneficiaries, been partially adopted by the Government and Parliament. The only point as to which Mr. Mill's opinions had undergone a change was on the question of the utility of endowments being held in the shape of land. In the essay referred to, he spoke of the evils of allowing land to pass into mortmain—adding that trustees ought to have no concern with the money, except applying it to its purposes. Their time and attention should not be divided between their proper business and the management of landed estates. He now felt that the only objections to the application of the produce of land to the uses of endowments would be obviated altogether by separating the management of the property from the administration of its income. If the management were placed under competent local agents, having charge of large districts, responsible alike to the public and the several institutions, and always accessible to the offers of cultivators and tenants of all classes, vast tracts of land in the country, and extensive areas covered with houses in cities and towns, would be opened to co-operative associations and others, whom the prejudices of private owners, in favour of fewer or more wealthy occupiers, might exclude. The Bill therefore proposed to repeal the mortmain Act of George II., which prevents land only from being devoted to charitable uses, leaving all other property to be so disposed of. It is not surprising that the House was unprepared for such a measure. It is only after repeated agitation that it is likely to succeed; but such tentative proceedings are obviously the practical course. A reform bill was introduced many successive years before it passed. It will, some day, probably be thought worth while to appoint a committee or commission to examine the subject. It will be found that nothing could be more moderate or just than the proposed measure: it secured the interests of the objects of the trust, and left the trustees unencumbered with alien duties, and at liberty to employ their undivided attention exclusively to the business of making the best use of the fund.* The great im-

* This subject is discussed in a Paper read at the Social Science Association, on the 27th Jan. 1873—"On Lands held by Corporations, and on the Policy either of their Alienation or of Providing for their Management with regard to the Public Utility."

pediment in the way of measures such as these, is the fact that almost every constituency contains a few persons, forming a compact body of much influence, whose importance in the locality may be lessened by the withdrawal of public property from their control. Mr. Fitzjames Stephen, in the article before referred to, points out the power of a small knot of persons in a constituency to turn the balance against any candidate who has the courage to take an independent view differing from them.*

The two next articles of the Land Tenure Programme (V. VI.) are for the encouragement of co-operative agriculture and the tenancies of small cultivators. Of the remaining clause (IV.), proceeding from Mr. Mill, the claim of the State to intercept by taxation the unearned increase in the rent of land; it is unnecessary here to say much. It has, perhaps, been subjected to more adverse criticism than any other part of the programme; but it exhibits the elaborate care with which, in any great change, he endeavoured to guard existing interests. All who have read or heard the explanation which Mr. Mill has repeatedly given of this suggestion know well that not the value of one farthing, of any realized or existing property, would be taken thereby from any proprietor. To characterize the proposal, therefore—as has been done recently—as one involving the virtual confiscation of the estates of the great landowners, and whereby, as regards the present, most landed proprietors would be reduced to ruin, is a gross misrepresentation.

So much space has been occupied in thus attempting to convey a just idea of the vast field over which Mr. Mill's labours have extended, and upon which his autobiography is full of interest and instruction, that a multitude of subjects must still remain untouched. Of his work on the Subjection of Women, and in the cause of extending to them the political franchise, we need not speak. They have been more or less discussed in most houses and families.

In December, 1859, appeared "A Few Words on Non-Intervention,"† in which he pointed out the situation of Great Britain, "as an independent nation, apprehending no aggressive designs, and entertaining none, seeking no benefits at the expense of others, stipulating for no commercial advantages, and opening its ports to all the world; yet, finding itself held up to obloquy as the type of egotism and selfishness, and as a nation which thinks of nothing but outwitting and outgeneralling its neigh-

* *Contemporary Review*, December, 1873, pp. 6, 7.
† *Fraser's Magazine*, vol. lx., p. 766.

bours. This was the continental estimate of English policy. What was the cause of this? First, was it not our common mode of argument for or against any interference in foreign matters, that we do not interfere in this or that subject 'because no English interest is involved?' Secondly, how is the impression against us fostered by our acts? Take the Suez Canal—a project which, if realized, would give a facility to commerce, a stimulus to production, an encouragement to intercourse, and therefore to civilization, which would entitle it to high rank among the industrial improvements of modern times. Assume the hypothesis that the English nation saw in this great benefit to the world a danger, a damage to some peculiar interest of England—such as, for example, that shortening the road would facilitate the access of foreign navies to its Oriental possessions, that the success of the project would do more harm than good to England—unreasonable as the supposition is. Is there any morality, Christian or secular, which would bear out a nation in keeping all the rest of mankind out of some great advantage, because the consequence of their obtaining it may be, to itself, in some imaginable contingency, a cause of inconvenience? If so, what ground of complaint has the nation who asserts this claim, if in return the human race determines to be its enemies? In the conduct of our foreign affairs in this matter, England had been made to appear as a nation which, when it thought its own good and that of other nations incompatible, was willing to prevent others even from realizing an advantage which we ourselves are to share." The subsequent history of the Suez Canal has proved the errors of English diplomacy here pointed out. The remainder of the article on the few and rare cases—if any—in which interference in the domestic affairs of one nation by another is permissible, has probably not been, and will not be, without its influence in the subsequent and future history of the world.

Mr. Mill's sympathy with the downtrodden and oppressed, whether as slaves, while there still existed a slave power in America, or in the condition of their emancipated brethren in Jamaica, is well known. He saw from the first, as many clear-sighted persons in our country did—though perhaps they formed a minority—that the Civil War in America "was an aggressive enterprise of the slave owners, under the combined influences of pecuniary interest, domineering temper, and the fanaticism of a class for its class privileges—to extend the territory of slavery." A passage in his article on "The Contest in America,"* justifying the determined course taken by the North, is

* *Fraser's Magazine*, Jan. 1862.

worth quoting as an emphatic rejection of a misplaced feeling of humanitarianism—a feeling which in a fitting case no one would have respected more than he. He says:—"I cannot join with those who cry Peace, Peace. I cannot wish it should be terminated on any conditions but such as would retain the whole of the territories as free soil. War in a good cause is not the greatest evil which a nation can suffer. War is an ugly thing, but not the ugliest of things; the decayed and degraded state of moral and patriotic feeling which thinks nothing *worth* a war is worse."

There are some who say they find in this Autobiography evidence of self-sufficiency and self-glorification, and that it is defaced by egotism! Such charges appear amazing, not only to those who remember Mr. Mill's entire freedom from self-assertion, and readiness to attribute to others even the merit of works or suggestions proceeding from himself, but to the readers of the Autobiography, who find throughout instances of the same self-abnegation. He is only bold and uncompromising in the assertion of what he deems right. Instead of egotism, he is, at other times, charged with sentimentality and weakness in ascribing such praise to others. One distinct proof of the absence of any thought of self-sufficiency or egotism is found in a passage in the Autobiography which has probably no parallel in any other personal memoir: "Whoever," he says, "either now or hereafter, may think of me, and of the work I have done, must never forget that it is the product, not of one intellect and conscience, but of three." It is a painful example of the low pitch to which literary criticism may at this day sink, to read a comment on it such as this: "All touches of natural affection have been sedulously kept under or suppressed; his brothers and sisters are only mentioned as annoyances or checks to progress."* So far from

* The tone of complacent triumph with which the author of an Article in *Fraser's Magazine*, for Dec. 1873, acquaints his readers of the "rapid change of the public mind concerning Mr. Mill," and of the "startling *collapse* of his reputation which has happened," since, as he says, Mr. Mill's admirers met the "mildest protest" against his fame with "clamour and abuse," might provoke a smile. He has probably reiterated this announcement so many times that at length he fancies himself "the public," as the three tailors in Tooley Street styled themselves, "We, the people of England." It will, however, be a somewhat curious chapter in the literary annals of the day, if he should inform his readers in some future paper when and whence this "mildest" of protests issued, and who were the "audacious" delinquents who tried, and how, to put down discussion. Was it put down because the answer was so complete that nothing was left to be said? At present, however, those who listen to every breath relating to the venerated object of their regard, have heard only of one unjust attempt to cast reproach on a pure and honourable life, which, when indignantly challenged, was found to be utterly unsupported by even the pretence of evidence. It cannot, however, but be regretted that a periodical

his brothers and sisters being mentioned as hindrances, Mr. Mill tells us expressly that, from the discipline involved in teaching them, which after his eighth year his father required, he derived the great advantage of learning more thoroughly, and retaining more lastingly, the things which he was set to teach. The insinuation that natural feeling was wanting, leads us to borrow a passage from the current number of the *Workman's Magazine* (p. 385): "It was our good fortune," says the writer, "to know Mr. Mill in early life. One of our class-fellows at University College was James Bentham Mill, a younger brother of John, and we (the younger ones) soon became very intimate friends. Strong mutual sympathies led to interchanges of visits during the long vacations and after we had left the college, so that we had frequent opportunities of seeing and conversing with the elder brother in his pretty cottage home at Mickleham, where the whole family spent all the summer months for several years. . . . John Stuart Mill was, of course, then unknown to fame, but we well remember the impression he made on us by his domestic qualities, the affectionate playfulness of his character as a brother in the company of his sisters, and of the numerous younger branches of the family."

Without further noticing comments such as that which has led us to introduce this reminiscence, it seems strange, as a correspondent of the *Spectator* touchingly remarks, "to hear accused of heartlessness and coldness in his affections the man over whose grave a chorus of friends has just been pouring the strains of sorrowing love and gratitude, to hear of the 'meagre nature,' 'the want of homely hopes,' 'the monotonous joylessness' of him whose delight in nature and in music, whose knowledge of flowers, whose love of birds, whose hearty happiness in country walks with friends, whose long genial talks with those friends, have been so variously and beautifully delineated."

We are able to add to that chorus another strain issuing from the voices of some who, a few years ago, visited him in his southern home, and there learnt his genial powers of participation and sympathy with various and dissimilar tastes. Mr. Mill's fondness for natural studies and appreciation of historic associations had taken him much through Provence and Languedoc, parts of which they visited with him. None failed to be struck with the uncommon degree of affection and reverence with which he and his step-daughter were met in their neigh-

---

so high in character as *Fraser's Magazine* should have admitted into its columns an Article that, first misrepresenting Mr. Mill, both as respects his words and works, then proceeds to draw unfounded inferences from them, which nothing but a prurient imagination could have suggested.

bourhood, and journeying with them was made doubly pleasant from their cordial and warm reception by those to whom they were known. Mr. Mill's conversation carried all vividly back to the Roman and mediæval days, of which the ruins in the country round Avignon reminded him. Under his guidance every spot became replete with interest: "One day we traversed the hills above Vaucluse"—we copy from the journal of one to whom Mr. Mill was before unknown—"over the mountains, among the wildest stony paths, through gorges, over dwarf box, lavender, thyme, cistus, rosemary, fragrant as it was crushed under our feet, botanizing, talking, till finally we descended, as the day closed, to Petrarch's fountain. Whether visiting the flourishing town of Carpentras, or ascending Mont Ventoux, he directed attention to a multitude of interesting objects, taking himself the most laborious part and exhibiting no symptom of fatigue." "Apart from the charm of his converse," writes another, "there was the unceasing kindness with which he pointed out to one the rarer flowers, to another the geological formation, and again the peculiar construction of the several ancient remains; and all saw and felt his delight at having brought them to the summit of the hill, on which stands the excavated and almost deserted town and castle of Les Baux, at a moment when they could behold the beauties of the lovely light of sunset shedding its glory over the valley of the Rhone."

"The life of one," says the writer we have quoted, "who lives and strives in opposition to the ideas of his age, will scarcely be expected to be a very bright and cheerful one; but it is noble instead, and many a one will feel that for such nobleness he would exchange all that the world calls pleasant." We have gathered enough from Mr. Mill's works, and the testimony of others, to show that a career of unselfish devotion to the highest object on which man can be employed—the welfare of his fellow creatures—is consistent with every rational enjoyment of life, while it incalculably increases the capacity to enjoy it.

Art. VI.—Third-Class Passenger Traffic.

THE most effective method of allaying the agitation which has begun in favour of governmental management of the English railways is probably that of removing, as completely as possible, all causes of just complaint of their management by their present owners. Now, one of the most reasonable complaints against them is, that railway travelling in England is excessively expensive: as a matter of fact the sum which, on an average, would enable a passenger to travel 100 miles in England, would enable him to travel 140 miles in France, and 288 in Belgium. As England is the country in which railways originated, as English contractors, English engineers, and even English labourers have been employed in building various railways out of England, and as iron and coal are cheaper here than anywhere else, the fact that the cost of railways in England, and therefore of travelling upon them, is so much greater than that of railways and of railway travelling on the Continent, is at first sight not less astonishing than it is deplorable. Our railways—about 15,400 miles in extent—have cost the extravagant sum of 553,000,000*l.*, or at the average rate of 35,944*l.* per mile. This amazing outlay affords an adequate explanation of the great cost of travelling by rail in England. But notwithstanding this outlay, the present market value of English railways considered as a whole is 10 per cent. greater than that sum, exorbitantly great as it is; and both the receipts and profits which they yield are on the whole steadily increasing.

Now, if the English railways are already worth more than the amount of their original cost, and if the aggregate profits to their shareholders are really increasing, the companies may reasonably be asked to lower their present scales of fares, and especially to give increased facilities of locomotion to the labouring classes. We say if the value and profits of the railways are increasing, for we freely recognise that asking the managers of an unprosperous business to lower their prices and to adopt the principle of "small profits and quick returns," might be justly described as a demand that they should incur a risk of serious loss; but the request has a very different aspect if the business is already prosperous and on the increase. Then the adoption of that principle may be rightly regarded as a judicious and prudent speculation, justifiable by appeal to experience in similar cases. Moreover, any business which ministers to a want felt at one time or another by almost every member of the community is, as a general rule, sure of success in proportion as it acts unreservedly on the principle of exacting a very small percentage of profit on each transaction, and especially of enforcing in every case payment in cash. Now the business of a large railway company is a business of precisely this kind. Of the different modes of locomotion as yet possible on land it offers the very best; it can offer it at a cheaper rate than that at which any other practicable kind of conveyance can be supplied; everybody wants to travel somewhere, at some time or other; and everybody expects and prepares to pay cash for doing so. Here, then, are all the conditions for insuring the possibility of doing a large and successful business. Moreover, the steady and general rise in value of railway property provides an ample margin for covering even considerable risks in the shape of experimental lowering of fares, and the supply of additional facilities of rapid locomotion. The people, therefore, who through their representatives have granted to the several railway companies important privileges, without which they neither could have begun, nor can continue to carry on their business at all, may fairly claim that the charges for travelling by railway shall be adjusted in strict accordance with the principle in question. Indeed, not only are the people as a whole fully warranted in insisting on this claim, but, as we have shown, the railway shareholders will, owing to the very nature of their business, best consult their own interests in the long run—*i.e.*, during a not very long series of years they will realize the largest amount of profit—by granting this claim as completely as possible.

To their lasting credit, not only for possessing real insight and appreciation of true commercial principles, but for having the courage to act upon them, the directors of the Midland Railway Company began in April, 1872, the sensible practice of conveying third-class passengers at "parliamentary fares" by all trains. We say "to their lasting credit," for this bold and beneficent innovation was determined on in face of the disapproval, and even condemnation, pronounced by the chief managers of other great lines. Happily the prophecies of failure were falsified. In the course of the first half-year of 1873, the Midland Railway Company carried the enormous number of 8,403,272 third-class passengers, or 1,139,510 more than were conveyed by the same company during the corresponding half-year of 1872. There was a decrease of 4592 first-class, and of 346,325 second-class, during the same period. If we deduct the total of this decrease from the increase of third-class passengers, we find that the actual or net increase in the number of passengers carried during the half-year was 788,593. It would be impossible to depict, and difficult even to imagine, the manifold and very beneficent results, in the shape of business, mental development, health, and general enjoyment, produced by enabling upwards of three-quarters of a million of people within the space of a few months, to avail themselves of the advantages of locomotion. If only the great boon of cheap travelling can be conferred on the public by the railway companies without involving them in loss, the public may, as we have said above, justly claim it from them; but how much more powerful do the reasons for the claim become, if it can be shown that one of the consequences of its concession will consist of an increase of profit to the companies themselves! That an increase of profit will be obtained from running third-class carriages with all trains, may be considered as already fairly proved by the actual experience of the Midland Company. Comparing the first half of 1873 with the first half of 1872 (the first quarter of which elapsed before the experiment in question was begun), we observe that the increase in the amount earned in 1873, by carrying third-class passengers, was 50,478*l.* On the other hand, there was a decrease in the earnings from carrying first-class passengers of 706*l.*, and in those from carrying second-class of 40,969*l.* These sums, deducted from the former, leave 8803*l.* as the net increase of earnings of the passenger traffic during the first half of 1873. It must be borne in mind, however, that this sum is far from representing the full amount of the increase in earnings, consequent on the change in question, for as that change was effected in the beginning of the second quarter of the year 1872, and as third-class passengers were therefore, during that quarter, already conveyed by all trains, a comparison of the results obtained during the first half of 1872 and of 1873 respectively, is, in so far as the second quarter of 1872 is concerned, a comparison only of the results obtained during two different but similar periods by the working of the same system; a correctly instructive comparison of the earnings during a period in which third-class passengers were conveyed by all trains, with those during a period before that practice was adopted, would be made by placing side by side the earnings of the first quarter only of 1872 and 1873 respectively; then the pecuniary advantage of the change in question would doubtless become more strikingly apparent even than it does in the shape of the figures already given. But we have not at hand the data requisite for that comparison, and can therefore only ask our readers to bear in mind the fact just mentioned, when considering the import of the amount of the increase in the earnings, during the first half of 1873, beyond those of the first half of 1872. We have only to add, in respect to the experiment in question on the Midland Railway, that, as stated by the chairman of the company, another satisfactory feature of that experiment consists in the fact, that while it has been effected the passenger train mileage has been reduced: in the first half of 1872 it was 3,532,800: but in the first half of 1873—notwithstanding the net amount of earnings had increased—the passenger train mileage decreased, and was only 3,275,669. Moreover, whereas the earnings per train per mile, during the first half of 1872, were 3*s.* 9¾*d.*, they were 4*s.* 6*d.* during the first half of 1873, and thus yielded an increase of 8¼*d.* per train.

The wise policy boldly exemplified by the Midland Railway Company, has been adopted more or less completely by several other companies, and with results which decisively demonstrate the expediency, even from the shareholders' point of view only, of running third-class carriages with every train, as a general rule, on every railway in the kingdom. The experiment has been tried on the North Staffordshire line, and comparing the passenger traffic during the first half of 1873 with that of the first half of 1872, we find that "the first-class remained pretty much as it was before. There had been a falling off of 50,000 passengers in the second-class department, and an increase of 284,000 in the third, with an increase of 4377*l.* in the revenue. This showed," as the chairman justly remarked, "how great a boon had been conferred on third-class passengers by the new arrangements." The report of the directors of the Lancashire and Yorkshire Railway Company is to the same effect. In the first half of 1872 that company conveyed 13,891,278 ordinary, and 5706 contract passengers, for the sum of 498,140*l.*; but in the corresponding half-year of 1873 the same company conveyed 15,054,008 ordinary and 6139 contract passengers, for the sum of 537,378*l.* During the latter period the increase in the number of ordinary passengers was thus 1,162,730; in the number of contract passengers, 433; and in the amount of money, 39,232*l.*—the increase in the number of passengers being at the rate of 8⅓ per cent., and in the amount of money 8 per cent. It would be found, however, that this increase of the number of passengers had been confined to those who travelled third-class: in the first-class passengers there was a diminution of 902; and in the second-class passengers of 479,209; while the third-class passengers had increased 1,643,021. The changes in the passenger traffic on the North Eastern Railway are of a similar kind. In the half-year ending June, 1872, this railway carried 588,666 first-class passengers, 1,544,024 second-class, and 7,361,200 third-class. In the corresponding half of 1873 the numbers were—559,673 first-class, 878,843 second-class, and 9,758,425 third-class. It thus appears that during this period there was a decrease of 28,993 first-class and of 670,181 second-class passengers, and that the increase in the number of third-class passengers was no less than 2,397,225. These important and very significant changes in the passenger traffic were accompanied, notwithstanding the great decrease in the number of second-class passengers, by an increase of revenue from it during the first half of 1873 to the extent of 73,000*l*. So great have been the changes in the passenger traffic of this company that, as stated by its chairman, "out of 100 persons who now travel by the North Eastern 86 travel third-class."

The chief competitors of the Midland Railway—viz., the London and North Western and the Great Northern, have been forced in self-defence to convey third-class passengers by nearly the whole of the trains running on those lines. In respect to the London and North Western line we can only state the general results experienced during the first half of the years 1872 and 1873 respectively. They are as follows:—

	1872.		1873.		Increase.
Number of Passengers...	17,360,857	...	19,290,085	...	1,929,228
Receipts from Passengers	£1,505,520	...	£1,624,093	...	£118,573

It thus appears that the increase in the number of passengers carried was nearly two millions, and as the number of trains carrying third-class passengers on the London and North Western line has been greatly increased, we may fairly assume that the greater part of the increase of nearly two millions in the number of passengers and of nearly 120,000*l*. of revenue, is due to the fact that third-class passengers are now conveyed by a considerable proportion of the fast trains.

Turning to the Great Northern Railway and comparing the experience of the first half of 1873 with that of the first half of 1872, we find the facts to be as follows:—In 1873 there was an increase of 21,508, or 7 per cent., of first-class passengers; a decrease of 125,664, or 25 per cent., of second-class passengers; an increase of 699,835, or 68 per cent., of third-class passengers. If the decrease in the number of the second-class be deducted from the aggregate increase in the number of the first and third, the net increase in the number of passengers carried is seen to be 595,679. The increase of income from the passenger traffic was no less satisfactory. There was an increase of 2711*l*., or 25 per cent., in the receipts from the first-class; a decrease of 19,575*l*., or 29 per cent., in those from the second-class; and an increase of 47,404*l*., or 46 per cent., in those from the third-class. After the amount of the decrease in the second-class receipts is deducted from the amount of increase in those of the first and third there is left a net increase of 30,578*l*. Surely this result, at the very threshold of the experiment too, is sufficiently satisfactory; and, in view of it, we cannot help feeling some surprise at the ungracious manner in which the able chairman of the company reluctantly recognises and acquiesces in the success of running third-class carriages with all trains as an established fact. He said at the last meeting of shareholders:—"I think our neighbours the Midland were rather hasty in coming to the conclusion of carrying third class passengers by every train. I think if they had only confined themselves to three or four trains a day in carrying third-class passengers, they would have found it better to their advantage. . . . However, they did not see fit to act in that way, and the result has been as I have stated." Nevertheless, the public has cause to be thankful that the Great Northern Railway Company is presided over by a gentleman who is sagacious enough to descry the path along which, for the sake of self-preservation, the company must proceed, and who has the resolution to enter on it, although that resolution is a virtual reversal of his own judgment, while the success consequent on its adoption is a practical condemnation of the policy he had recommended.

The influence of the admirable example of the Midland is already making itself felt on the Great Eastern and on the Great Western lines; but in one respect, at least, the manner in which that influence is manifesting itself is so remarkable that it ought, we think, to become generally known. Imitating the Midland Railway Company the Great Western announces in large type, on large placards, posted at its principal stations:—

"THIRD-CLASS TICKETS ARE ISSUED BY ALL TRAINS;"

But, unfortunately, here the likeness of the conduct of the Great Western to that of the Midland stops; for immediately following this satisfactory announcement is printed in type so small that middle-aged people, sitting in the carriages at the stations where the placards are placed, need the aid of spectacles in order to read it:—

"EXCEPT THE FOLLOWING EXPRESSES, VIZ.:—

The 9.0 a.m., 10.15 a.m., 11.45 a.m., 4.50 p.m., 5.0 p.m., and 9.0 p.m. (Limited Mail) Trains from Paddington, and the corresponding Up Trains leaving Bristol at 7.50 a.m., 12.9 p.m., 2.45 p.m., and 12.40 a.m. (Limited Mail), New Milford at 2.45 a.m. and 8.10 a.m., Weymouth at 6.35 a.m. and 12.30 p.m., and the Branch Trains running in connexion with them."

As many of the working classes are obliged to be frequent travellers even by the Great Western Railway, and as both time and money are alike precious to them, they were, no doubt, immensely elated when they read that big letter announcement, "Third-class tickets are issued by all trains;" but our readers will imagine their disappointment when they came to scrutinize the placard, and thus to learn that there are fourteen trains running daily on the main line, besides all the trains running on the various branch lines in connexion with these main line trains, by which third-class passengers are not allowed to travel! Surely these numerous exceptions to the general statement in the big letter announcement degrade it to the level of a mere advertisement trick; and, if so, the sooner it is withdrawn the sooner will the public cease to be misled, and the better for the credit of the Company which now puts it forward. It is the more vexatious and disappointing, because while working men whose time is in a pre-eminent degree not only money but very life, have especial need to travel quickly, the trains they are excluded from are precisely those which ought to convey them—viz., "the expresses." We say "ought" for the reason already mentioned—viz., that inasmuch as Parliament grants great and exclusive privileges to each of the railway companies, they owe it to the people which Parliament represents to convey third-class passengers by those trains now that experience has shown they can do so not merely without loss but with the certainty of an ample and increasing profit to the shareholders. It is, indeed, to be regretted that a great public company like that of the Great Western Railway should condescend to make use of a delusive artifice in advertising, in order to seem, at first sight, on a level with its rivals; but in common with "the million," who are compelled to travel by it, we feel that it is much more to be regretted that the Directors of this important line have not the courage to adopt in its entirety the bold, beneficent, and successful policy of the Companies which they merely affect to imitate. We are sorry to be obliged to add, however, that great and persistent pressure will, seemingly, have to be applied to them before they consent to adopt it, for at the last half-yearly meeting of the Company, its Chairman, Sir Daniel Gooch, said:—

> "I was never an advocate for carrying third-class passengers by all trains. I do not think it was a wise step that the railway companies took when they commenced this system. . . . We have not adopted it so far as express trains are concerned, and I hope it will not be done."

Sir Daniel Gooch seems to regard the results of the partial experiment already tried of giving increased facilities of locomotion to third-class passengers on the Great Western line as condemnatory of the innovation. He complains of it thus:—

> "It involves us in a very large expenditure in lengthening stations; it has also, I believe, involved us in a large loss of revenue, for if you look at the facts you will find that in the last six months we carried 7100 more first-class passengers than in the corresponding half-year,

and we took 6424*l.* less in money—that arises, no doubt, from the passengers travelling shorter distances. But we come to second-class, and there we lose 315,403 passengers and 47,467*l.* We carried in third-class 2,081,334 more passengers, and took 82,728*l.* more in receipts. The result is this, we carried in the half-year 1,772,277 more passengers for 28,828*l.* of revenue, which is something like 4*d.* per passenger. I contend that that has been a heavy loss to us in money, in the punctuality of the trains, and in every way, and that the railways were unwise to act as they have done in creating such a large change at one time."

A man who espouses a bad cause undertakes a difficult task; but it becomes incomparably more difficult if he is obliged to defend that cause by weapons which may be readily turned against himself. Sir Daniel Gooch is unfortunate in having to express his opinions concerning third-class passenger traffic, and at the same time to defend them by a statement of facts; for while his opinions point in one direction his facts point in the other. Referring to the recent increase of third-class trains on the Great Western line, he says,—"it has, I believe, involved us in a large loss of revenue;" and he expresses this belief in face of the fact which he states immediately afterwards—viz., that the revenue from the passenger traffic during the half-year in which third-class passengers were carried by all trains except the expresses, was 28,828*l.* *more* than it was during the corresponding half-year of 1872—a period preceding the date when the change, such as it is, in favour of third-class passengers was effected. But the result of the experiment is not fairly indicated by that sum: though the receipts from the first-class passenger traffic during the period in question fell off to the extent of 6424*l.*, there were 7160 more first-class passengers carried than during the corresponding half-year of 1872. This diminution cannot therefore be ascribed to the increase of facilities for travelling in the third-class; but, as stated by Sir Daniel Gooch himself, "arises, no doubt, from the [first-class] passengers travelling shorter distances." It is clear, therefore, that the sum representing this change in the first-class passenger traffic cannot be included in a correct estimate of the result of running third-class carriages with all trains except the expresses. Now during the first half of 1873 as compared with the first half of 1872, the increase in the number of third-class passengers was 2,081,334, and the increase in the amount received from them was 82,728*l.*; but simultaneously the decrease in the number of second-class passengers was 315,463, and the decrease in the receipts from them was 47,476*l.* Having deducted the amount of the decrease in the number of second-class from the amount of the increase in the number of third-class passengers, and the amount of the decrease of the receipts from the second-class from the amount of the increase of receipts yielded by the third-class passengers, we find the correct result to be a net increase of 1,765,871 passengers, and of 35,252*l.* of revenue. Seeing this handsome increase of revenue as an accompaniment and direct consequence of the change in question, the shareholders, who are now rejoicing in the receipt of a 5⅞ per cent. dividend, will, we imagine, be scarcely disposed to look on that change in the light in which it is regarded by their chairman. It still remains for him to prove to them that the change has entailed upon them "a heavy loss in money," and we cannot help thinking that he will need to resort to much statistical conjuring in order to enable himself to do so. During the first 14 weeks of the second half of 1873 the total gross earnings were 1,537,084*l.*, or 88,898*l.* more than they were during the corresponding weeks of 1872; and if, as may be fairly assumed, the proportion between the increase of expenditure and that of receipts continues the same during the two periods, the dividend to be declared at the next half-yearly meeting of shareholders will be at least as great as, and will be probably greater than the last one.

Sir Daniel Gooch's complaint that the change has "involved the Company in very large expenditure in lengthening stations," is indeed quite intelligible; but this expenditure cannot be rightly regarded as forming part of the alleged "heavy loss:" it is simply a prudent investment of additional capital in order to provide the conveniences absolutely necessary for the transaction of a rapidly growing and at the same time thoroughly sound business. Any merchant or manufacturer at the head of a great and thriving concern, who is unwilling to enlarge his establishment and appliances for carrying it on to such an extent as may be found necessary for its efficient conduct, is rightly looked upon by his rivals as a man whose business energy is flagging and whose spirit of enterprise is becoming extinct. In such a case competition effects a transfer of the business in question from the hands of the man who has passed the meridian of mental vigour to those of men whose enterprising energy proves them to be still in the ascendant. But in the case of the chairman and directors of a great railway company like that of the Great Western, which possesses a monopoly of a large part of the carrying business throughout the West of England, the stimulant and corrective influence of competition cannot be brought to bear upon them; and unless it happens that among the shareholders there is at least one who is sagacious and far-sighted enough to urge upon the managers that a thoroughly enterprising, courageous, and liberal administration of the business confided to them will rove at once the most profitable and the most permanently conservative of the Company's interests, the only efficient corrective of the conduct of those managers is public opinion. The chairman and directors of the Great Western Railway seem to be especially in need of its invigorating influence. An increase of passenger traffic to the extent of 3,500,000 a year, consequent on running third-class carriages with all trains, except the expresses, is likely indeed to tax their energies severely, and perhaps, therefore, we ought to feel no surprise when we hear their chief spokesman deploring the "large change at one time," which has entailed upon them an amount of work seemingly beyond their strength. But while uttering this complaint, he should not be allowed, we think, to mislead the Great Western shareholders and the public at large as to the nature of the consequences of the large increase of third-class passenger traffic which, as it seems, he dislikes and deplores: it has not involved the company "in a large loss of revenue," but, on the contrary, has considerably increased it; "the very large expenditure in lengthening stations" is in reality a profitable investment; "the heavy loss in the punctuality of the trains," which indeed all travellers by the Great Western suffer from and deplore, therefore, quite as feelingly as Sir Daniel Gooch himself, he will surely be able to remedy when he and his co-directors have been duly invigorated by the tonic influence above-mentioned; and the "heavy loss in every way" which he also alleges and mourns over, as a consequence of the "large change at one time," will probably be seen by himself, when he recovers from the mental shock produced by that change, to be a figment of his imagination as unreal as the loss of revenue of which he complains.

We are credibly informed that until a few years ago third-class passengers on the Great Western line were regarded as consisting in great part of thieves and vagabonds, and that, as a whole, they were looked upon with scarcely less suspicion than aversion, and we know that until last year a minimum amount of facilities was afforded them for travelling on that line. It is to be hoped, however, that the prejudices against them which its officials have long entertained, but which have been already, in great measure, overcome, will soon wholly disappear, and that Sir Daniel Gooch becoming convinced of the soundness of the policy inaugurated by the Midland, will adopt it in its entirety on the line over the administration of which he presides.

Referring to the Great Western Railway we venture here on a slight digression before completing our remarks on third-class traffic. There seems to be a strong and justifiable feeling in the minds of most persons in the suburbs, access to which is afforded mainly by that line, that its directors are intent on secluding those suburbs as far as possible from metropolitan invaders, by refusing them facilities for cheap and frequent transit to and fro; and to prove the truth of this suggestion, several persons have directed our attention both to the table of suburban fares, which certainly are unreasonably high, and to the time table, which shows how reluctant the directors are to facilitate the movement, and thus to encourage the settlement of people along their line. For example, the first station out of London, (*i.e.*, the first beyond Westbourne Park, where the tickets are collected), viz., Acton, which is now a widespreading suburb whose inhabitants are, for the most part, obliged to be in London daily during business hours, is actually prevented from communicating with London by means of the Great Western Railway during some hours of each day. During nearly the whole of the three busiest hours of the morning, it is impossible for any one in London to reach that suburb unless he undertakes the journey by omnibus or makes the long circuit from Broad Street, City, by the North-London Rail; for no Great Western train from London stops at Acton between 8.38 and 11.25 a.m., an interval of nearly three hours. And again no down-train stops at that station between 11.25 a.m. and 1.42 p.m., another interval of more than two hours and a quarter. We may also mention that during the period between 7 and 8.25 p.m.—a period in which a large class of persons are desirous of going home—no train stops at the first, and therefore the one which might be the most conveniently accessible, suburb on that line. The arrangements of the up-trains evince the same policy: all persons who find it inconvenient to go to town so early in the day as 10.3 a.m., must nevertheless do so, or else remain per force at Acton until 12.10, unless they choose to spend an hour in omnibus or to go by the North-London to Broad Street, where, if they want to go to the West End, they are still miles from their destination. The number and time-arrangements of the trains which run on Sunday are doubtless significant of the policy above indicated, but perhaps also indicate that a majority of the directors are in respect to passenger traffic, at least, strict Sabbatarians. Precisely on the only day when the hundreds of thousands of toiling Londoners have time in which to get out into the country in order to refresh themselves during a few hours by its beauty and pure air, the number of trains by which they can reach the country directly westward of the metropolis would be ludicrously, if it were not deplorably small. As we have adverted to the week-day communication with the first station out of London we may mention, that no one living in Acton can leave for London between 9.3 a.m. and 3.9 p.m., or again between 4.58 and 8.7 p.m. But the greatest grievance of all complained of by the residents along the Great Western line is that no train leaves Paddington for any station on that line on Sunday night after a quarter past nine o'clock! This primitive arrangement by which all persons living along that line are not allowed to remain in the metropolis later than 9.15 p.m., has continued precisely the same during the whole of the last thirty years, and, we must confess, reflects great credit on the truly paternal government of the Directors, who evidently exercise jealous care for the preservation of the traditional habits and morals of the people confided to their charge.

Returning from our digression we observe that the chairman of the Great Eastern Railway seems in respect to third-class passenger traffic to be in sympathetic accord with the chairman of the Great Western. At the last half-yearly meeting of the Great Eastern shareholders, Mr. Lightly Simpson said—

"You will remember that in April, 1872, the Midland commenced carrying third-class passengers by every train, and other lines have followed their example. The result up to the present time has been a large increase in third-class traffic, and a material falling off in second, so that, on the whole, while largely increasing our quantities and affording great facilities to the public, it has not materially benefited our receipts. The practice is now continued by our neighbours, and I do not think at this stage we are prepared to say what our course of action will be; but we shall certainly hark back if we find our revenue is at all diminished thereby."

Passing to the railways south of the Thames we find the whole group wholly undisturbed by the startling innovation of running third-class passengers by express trains, which is producing the great revolution in passenger-traffic on the lines running northward already indicated. On the other hand, one of the subjects which exercised the minds of the shareholders of the South Eastern Railway at their last meeting was the expediency of raising the fares of that line; but the proceeding was evidently regarded as a very hazardous one, and probably will not be adopted. The chairman (who is by no means in favour of the policy adopted north of the Thames) "quite agreed with those who argue that there is a mode of increasing passenger fares which results in obtaining less money."

The question of fares was not even mooted at the last meeting of the shareholders of either the London, Chatham, and Dover line, or of the South Western line; but "the unsatisfactory state of the dividends" yielded at present by the London and Brighton line, caused a lively discussion of the subject of fares at the last meeting of the shareholders of that railway. One of them, Mr. Morrin, proposed that an advance of 5 per cent. upon the average be made upon the passenger fares, that the fares by excursion trains be increased, and "that no abatement upon 'return' penny-a-mile tickets be henceforth allowed." The proposal was, however, met by a decided negative, the experiment of raising the fares had already been tried, and had resulted in such a diminution of passenger traffic, and consequently of revenue, that the directors recognised the wisdom of retracing their steps as speedily as possible, and are not likely to be tempted to repeat their costly error. "In June, 1868, when the fares were raised, they carried 8,000,000 passengers; in 1869 they carried only 7,782,000; but that year the fares were reduced, and they carried 8,891,000; the next year, 9,970,000, and in 1872 they still progressed, and carried another million passengers." The Chairman remarked respecting Mr. Adams, who made this statement, that "he deserves great credit for having years ago predicted the result when others thought very differently," and mentioned the following facts in respect to the traffic receipts during the period in question:—

"When the fares were increased in 1868 and 1869, the traffic receipts for the twelve months were 1,274,000*l.*, but in 1869 and 1870 they were only 1,283,000*l.*, showing during the twelve months during which the increased fares were in force an increase of only 9,000*l.*; in fact, practically they had been stationary. Then they began to reduce the fares, and although it took some little time before that alteration produced an effect upon the traffic, still in the next twelve months, 1870 and 1871, the traffic increased by 37,000*l.*, bringing it up to 1,320,000*l.* for the half year. Then the operations of the reduced scale got into full work, and the result was that in the next two years the receipts increased from 1,320,000*l.* to 1,520,000*l.* In other words, when they increased the fares they did not increase the traffic; but when they reduced them they increased the receipts 100,000*l.* a year, for two years successively, and that rate of increase was now being maintained in a satisfactory manner."

With such an experience as that, it would be nothing short of insanity again to attempt a raising of the fares.

These important experiences, though not identical with those which we have previously dwelt upon, and which had exclusive reference to the effects of largely increasing the facilities of locomotion of third-class passengers, nevertheless point in the same direction, and afford powerful encouragement to railway directors generally to rely on the millions rather than on the thousands of passengers for the augmentation of their receipts and profits to an extent likely to prove permanently satisfactory.

There is only one other point to which we will invite the reader's attention before closing this article: we refer to the expediency of granting return tickets to third-class travellers. This boon is required in order to complete the beneficent revolution we have been considering, and indubitable success of which we think has been fairly proved by the evidence we have adduced. It is difficult to imagine that the reasons which prove it to be expedient to grant return tickets to first and second-class passengers do not apply with equal force in respect to the third. The benefit to the labouring classes of granting third-class return tickets would be incalculably great, and we believe that, excepting the Passenger-Tax, the sole objection to doing so consists in a traditional indisposition, astonishingly vital in England, to give due heed to the rightful claims of the lower classes even when doing so would be followed by a reflex action eminently advantageous to those initiating the movement.

We have only to add, in conclusion, that due consideration of the facts we have mentioned, both by the various railway companies who have not ventured to practise the system which those facts prove to be eminently judicious as well as beneficent, and by the public at large, will tend, we believe, to insure the speedy adoption of that system on every railway in the United Kingdom. For the sake of the toiling millions in this metropolis, who, by breathing the sea-air from time to time, would derive from it fresh supplies of health and vigour, and indeed of life itself, we appeal especially to the shareholders of the chief railways south of the Thames to "better the instruction" afforded by the several experiments we have described, and thus to confer on those millions an estimable boon, while at the same time benefiting themselves.

Art. VII.—Medical Charity: Its Extent and Abuses.

1. *Reports of the Committee and Sub-Committees appointed to inquire into the subject of Out-Patient Hospital Administration in the Metropolis.* London: 1871.
2. *Our Medical Charities and their Abuses, with some Suggestions for their Reform.* By William O'Hanlon. Manchester: 1873.
3. *Hospital Out-Patient Reform. No.* 1. *Facts and Figures.* By H. N. Hardy. London: 1873.
4. *Letters to the Governors and other Subscribers of St. George's Hospital.* By One of Their Number. London: 1872.
5. *Letters to the "Times" and "Lancet" on Famine, Fever, and Public Charities.* By Sir Charles Trevelyan, K.C.B. London: 1873.
6. *Sanitary Economics: or Our Medical Charities, as they are, and as they ought to be.* By A. P. Stewart, M.D. London: 1849.
7. *Low's Handbook to the Charities of London for* 1873. London: 1873.
8. *Second Annual Report of the Local Government Board.* 1872-3. London: 1873.
9. *Metropolitan Asylum District. Abstract of the General Account of the Managers for the Half-year ending 29th March,* 1873.
10. *Contrasts dedicated to the Ratepayers of London*. London: 1873.
11. *Hints for the Subscribers to the Metropolitan Free Hospital.* London: 1873 (Printed for Private Circulation).

"THE poor always ye have with you," is a saying which, so far as history records, has been applicable to man in all ages, in all countries, under every variety of social and political condition, and it is true still. Enthusiastic social reformers may predict a future for humanity when crime will be unknown, when the production of all that is needful for the satisfaction of the material wants of every member of the human family will be always assured, and when the distribution of what is produced will be so wise and equitable that those forms of suffering denoted by the terms "poverty" and "destitution" will no longer constitute a distinctive feature of human life; but there are, unfortunately, too many and too good reasons for fearing that that future is still very far off, that this generation and many after it are sure to have the poor still with them, and, therefore, that charity in its multiform aspects will long continue one of the most important among the many beneficent agents of civilization.

But there are two kinds of charity: one seeing clearly into the character and conditions of its objects, the other blind; one wise, the other foolish; one beneficent, the other injurious. Clairvoyant, wise, and beneficent charity raises its objects, develops their resources, trains them to habits of self-help, and calls forth in them a spirit of independence; but blind, foolish, and injurious charity, even while temporarily benefiting its recipients, permanently degrades them: not perceiving the real nature of its applicants, it gives to those who are not really in need, and those who may be needing only temporary help, it converts into permanent pensioners on its bounty; moreover, it gives to those who clamour most, and neglects those who, being too modest or too feeble to make themselves heard amid the crowd of competitors for its favours, suffer in silence; it discourages thrift and prudence; it induces habits of carelessness, improvidence, and helplessness; and it both generates and fosters that spirit of dependence which is the chief source of pauperism in this country.

Surely, then, it behoves all classes, above that of the pauper himself, thoroughly to acquaint themselves with the twofold nature and opposite effects of charity! For by thoroughly understanding that nature and those effects we shall be enabled, while promoting the cultivation and development of true charity to an extent commensurate with the real necessities of suffering humanity, to restrain—if not wholly suppress—that spurious charity which, as a worker of evil, is one of the greatest enemies enlightened philanthropists have to contend against at the present day. As a slight contribution to the elucidation of this difficult subject, the following pages will, we hope, prove useful to those who concern themselves in bettering the condition of the poor.

Charity presents itself in so many aspects that it would be impossible for us to treat profitably of each within the compass of an article; we propose therefore in this article to deal only with medical charity, and mainly with it in so far only as it is observable in the British metropolis.

The amount known to be expended in the shape of medical charity in London is astonishingly great, and is increasing every year. Great, however, as that amount is, the aggregate sum of all that is expended privately, and of which no record exists, must also be enormous. Moreover, several of the public institutions engaged in the administration of medical charity give either inadequate or unsatisfactory information respecting their income and expenditure, and none at all respecting their accumulated funds. The income of the great majority of the medical charities consists mainly of donations, annual subscriptions, and occasional legacies; but that of the three largest hospitals—viz., Guy's, St. Bartholomew's, and St. Thomas's—is derived almost entirely from real and funded property, the produce of endowments. In nearly all cases the income of the several institutions exceeds the expenditure; and the surplus—very often a considerable one—is invested year by year as it occurs. The aggregate amount of such investments becomes in many instances a very important reserve fund—in some instances so large indeed as ultimately to yield the largest proportion of the income of the institution in question. We regret that the information given concerning these invested funds is in many cases notably deficient, and in many others is withheld altogether. Perhaps experience proves that the less the charity-giving public knows of the existence or extent of "invested funds," the more easily are its benevolent feelings excited, and the more abundant are its subscriptions; and therefore that, as a matter of policy, a minimum amount of information concerning those funds is volunteered to the public, to which urgent appeals for help are continuously made in the public journals.

We present below a tabular statement concerning the metropolitan hospitals, dispensaries, and asylums; but for want of sufficient data we are obliged to present it in a very defective state. Moreover, we are far from claiming that the list here given of 79 hospitals, of 43 dispensaries, of 5 asylums for lunatics, and 4 asylums for idiots and imbeciles, is complete even as respects number merely, for we believe there exists in the metropolis many small medical charities of which we have no knowledge; indeed, there must be such, for new ones are constantly springing up. In the list here supplied we have endeavoured, in the case of the hospitals, to state the number of beds appropriated to patients in each, the number of in-patients and of out-patients respectively treated during each year, the yearly income and expenditure, and the amount of invested funds. It will be observed that only in respect to the amount of income is the statement, even in appearance, approximately complete. We give the fullest information we can under the other headings—defective though it be—for what it is worth, and, indeed, as we shall find, it is worth a good deal.

In compiling these tables we have taken the facts from the last published reports of the hospitals themselves, in all cases in which we are able to obtain those reports; and in the majority of cases the reports we have used are those published this year, and which relate to the year 1872. In respect to the few hospitals of which we have not received the reports, we have depended on "Low's Hand-book to the Charities of London for 1873," which in most cases refers to the state of the medical charities in question in 1871, instead of in 1872. In respect to about the half of the dispensaries we have also depended on that work. We have expended much time and care in endeavouring to make the analysis here presented as accurate and as complete as possible; and though we are painfully conscious that it is far from being complete, it is, at all events, sufficiently so to form an adequate basis for the argument which we shall hereafter build upon it.

Table showing the number and names of the Metropolitan Hospitals, the number of Beds, and the number of In- and Out-patients treated in each; also the amount of Income, Expenditure, and Invested Funds of each.

No.		Beds.	In-patients.	Out-patients.	Income.	Expenditure.	Invested Funds.
		No.	No.	No.	£	£	£
1	Cancer Hospital	60	647	836	9,156	6,470	...
2	Charing Cross Hospital	160	1,363	15,934	9,925	6,102	[illegible]
3	Chest, City of London Hospital for Diseases of the	160	773	13,574	9,864	8,734	...
4	Chest, Hospital for Consumption and Diseases of the	210	1,169	12,583	17,168	14,383	30,331
5	Chest, Infirmary for Consumption and Diseases of the	...	...	1,913	653	467	...
6	Chest, National Hospital for Consumption and Diseases of the (Ventnor)	24	169	18	9,318	9,139	...
7	Chest, National Sanitorium for Consumption and Diseases of the	...	...	...	—	...	...
8	Chest, Royal Hospital for Diseases of the	...	158	6,309	4,048	3,891	6,300
9	Chest, North London Hospital for Consumption and Diseases of the	22	230	7,910	2,734	2,963	7,650
10	Children, Belgrave Hospital for	...	111	878	949	994	...
11	Children, East London Hospital for	38	300	7,634	3,765	3,363	6,945*
12	Children, Evelina Hospital for	100	297	6,815	3,447	3,358	...
13	Children, Hospital for Sick	127	844	11,910	12,390	7,716	19,000
14	Children, North Eastern Hospital for	...	119	10,940	1,011	1,376	6,014
15	Children, Royal Infirmary for	...	101	5,339	2,108	1,763	4,398
16	Children, Victoria Hospital for Sick	43	353	3,600†	3,536	2,060	2,734
17	Children, Home for Sick	12	...	...	...	...	...
18	Crippled Boys' Industrial Home	...	...	...	1,192	...	...
19	Cripples' Home	100	100	...	4,929	3,760	5,398
20	Cripples' Nursery	50	...	...	1,870	...	...
21	Dental Hospital	...	...	16,539	863	747	453
22	Dental Hospital, National	...	...	5,787	230	...	...
23	Fever Hospital, London	...	...	...	...	...	...
24	Fistula, St. Mark's Hospital for	...	...	1,071	3,113	2,919	10,634
25	German Hospital	100	1,310	16,347	7,195	6,083	33,700
26	Great Northern Hospital	...	919	23,563	3,708	3,416	...
27	Guy's Hospital	710	6,000	65,000	46,000	...	...
28	Hip Disease in Childhood, Hospital for	70	60	...	1,991	1,073	920
29	Homoeopathic Hospital	...	695	6,925	3,928	7,891	6,500
30	Incurables, Hospital for	137	137	377	21,448	...	34,814
31	Incurables, British Home for	130	120	149	10,154	8,896	90,978
32	Jews Hospital, Spanish and Portuguese	...	63	1,700	1,943	1,844	...
33	King's College Hospital	170	1,620	33,111	10,709	9,348	80,359
34	Legs, Hospital for Diseases of	...	...	10,000	394	600	600
35	Lock Hospital	150	610	4,580	9,894	5,665	636
36	London Hospital	600	5,927	64,285	33,977	36,689	180,793
37	Lying-in Hospital, British	40	165	663	1,737	1,161	3,100
38	Lying-in Hospital, City of London	...	631	143	2,039	1,460	9,910
39	Lying-in Hospital, General	—	—	—	—	—	—

* This sum includes the value of the Hospital buildings.

† In the "Medical Report" of this Hospital, the number of "Attendances" only is stated—viz., 10,931. We presume the "Cases" would form about a third of that number.

No.		Beds.	In-patients.	Out-patients.	Income.	Expenditure.	Invested Funds.
		No.	No.	No.	£	£	£
40	Lying-in Hospital, Queen Charlotte's	...	633	628	3,078	1,913	9,000
41	Metropolitan Convalescent Institution	390	3,191	...	6,424	...	8,000
42	Metropolitan Free Hospital	30	277	30,634	4,790	3,938	...
43	Middlesex Hospital	310	1,[illegible]	20,171	34,403*	7,800	160,000
44	Nervous System, Hospital for Diseases of	...	...	1,000	1,914	1,080	—
45	Nervous Diseases, National Hospital for the Special Treatment of	30	...	7,000	686	975	...
46	North London, or University College Hospital	160	1,777	17,283	12,901	12,461	40,000
47	Ophthalmic Hospital, Central London	...	...	6,617	1,079	437	637
48	Ophthalmic Hospital, Royal London	...	1,300	18,700	4,628	...	...
49	Ophthalmic Hospital, Royal South London	...	...	3,646	1,150	828	400
50	Ophthalmic Hospital, Royal Westminster	36	361	9,257	2,031	1,480	8,281
51	Ophthalmic Hospital, Western	...	60	1,911	877	553	...
52	Orthopædic Hospital, City	...	...	1,140	2,036	869	1,002
53	Orthopædic Hospital, National	26	...	1,983	1,867	1,469	...
54	Orthopædic Hospital, Royal	...	1,174	...	3,210	2,836	168
55	Paralysed and Epileptic, National Hospital for the	100	...	2,323	5,670	4,201	...
	" " " Various special Funds of	...	...	...	6,708	...	...
56	Poplar Hospital	...	292	2,774	2,377	2,318	1,746
57	Royal Free Hospital	178	1,439	46,362	7,077	...	...
58	Royal Surrey County Hospital	60	...	...	2,164	...	—
59	St. Bartholomew's Hospital, including House at Highgate	710	6,000	100,000	40,000	...	...
60	St. George's Hospital	350	3,654	18,813	32,768	31,490	101,668
61	St. George's Convalescent Hospital	...	659	...	4,192	...	...
62	St. Mary's Hospital	168	1,777	20,783	13,676	9,676	16,851
63	St. Thomas's Hospital	620	6,000†	65,000	39,000	—	...
64	Sea Bathing Infirmary	...	...	...	...	...	...
65	Seamen's Hospital	160	2,321	1,671	7,088	8,738	109,000
66	Skin Diseases, British Hospital for	...	...	3,591	2,424	981	3,500
67	Skin Diseases, Hospital for	—	—	10,000	...	...	...
68	Skin Diseases, National Institution for	...	...	...	...	...	...
69	Skin Diseases, St. John's Hospital for	14	...	...	347	...	...
70	Small Pox Hospital	104	—	...	8,000	...	...
71	Stone, St. Peter's Hospital for	...	60	2,000	1,187	1,033	—
72	Throat, Hospital for Diseases of	...	181	3,134	2,948	2,316	...
73	West London Hospital	63	407	21,240	2,791	2,272	...
74	Westminster Hospital	191	1,802	23,279	8,[illegible]	8,141	13,391
75	Women, Hospital for Diseases peculiar to	—	...	...	370	...	100
76	Women, Hospital for	...	222	3,178	6,048	...	—
77	Women and Children, Samaritan Hospital for	...	262	6,672	4,278	3,070	...
78	Women's Hospital	10	103	3,[illegible]	1,001	608	...
			68,383	830,019	359,627		

* Including amount of Samaritan Fund, 233*l*., and of Legacies received during 1872—26,082*l*.
† Stated conjecturally.

Table showing the number of Patients, the Income and Expenditure, and the Invested Funds of the Metropolitan Dispensaries.

No.	Name.	No. of Patients.	Income.	Expenditure.	Invested Funds.
			£	£	£
1	Bloomsbury	4,848	1,197	...	...
2	Brompton Homœopathic	400	...	...	...
3	Camberwell, Provident	...	...	...	...
4	Camden Town	1,000	1 [illegible]	199	...
5	Chelsea, Brompton, and Belgrave	5,[illegible]	1 [illegible]	565	...
6	City	13,390	1,320	1,160	2,000
7	City of London and East London	5,181	919	...	...
8	Clapham	...	371	481	...
9	Clare Market, Public Dispensary	4,784	860	629	8,000
10	Ear, Royal Dispensary for Diseases of	7,000	300	...	...
11	Eastern	3,707	480	...	8,228
12	Farringdon, General	27,160	894	640	...
13	Finsbury	6,000	641	665	650
14	Haverstock Hill Provident	...	...	...	...

No.	Name.	No. of Patients.	Income.	Expenditure.	Invested Funds.
			£	£	£
15	Holloway and North Islington	8,469	1,154	861	...
16	Islington and North London Provident	...	...	...	...
17	Islington	14,654	830	894	...
18	Kensington	8,053	674	696	...
19	Kilburn, General	...	700	...	...
20	Metropolitan	8,497	741	810	...
21	North-West London, for Children	4,306	827	189	...
22	Paddington, Provident	...	...	...	...
23	Provident, Medical	...	...	...	...
24	Queen Adelaide's	43,048	430	...	1,250
25	Royal Maternity Charity	3,253	1,631	1,440	...
26	Royal Pimlico	5,402	666	679	...
27	Royal South London	8,766	1,274	1,059	...
28	Rupture Society	646	443	...	7,600
29	St. George's and St. James's	6,983	430	460	300
30	St. John's Wood	...	500	...	...
31	St. Marylebone, General	6,340	723	633	1,250
32	St. Marylebone, Provident	...	...	...	...
33	St. Pancras and Northern	6,175	44	45	...
34	Skin Diseases, Western Dispensary for	...	800	...	...
35	South Lambeth	2,801	621	491	...
36	Surgical Aid Society	...	2,337	1,768	1,700
37	Surrey	8,139	3,014	—	17,415
38	Tower Hamlets	1,879	351	...	...
39	Truss Society	8,114	3,894	...	...
40	Western City	704	154	...	1,000
41	Western	...	...	...	...
42	Western General	28,311*	1,473	1,142	...
43	Westminster General	12,000	480	497	1,100
		253,065	30,628		

* This number includes 21,650 "Temporary Cases."

The following summary statement represents approximatively the total number of persons, exclusive of paupers, who, during the year 1872, were recipients of medical charity in the metropolis:—

Total number of In-patients as recorded in Table No. I.	58,382	
Estimated number of In-patients of hospitals from which we have no return, say	1,618	
Total number of In-patients..........................	———	60,000
Total number of Out-patients as recorded in Table I...	830,019	
Total number of Dispensary Patients as recorded in Table II.	253,065	
Estimated number of Out-patients of 6 Dispensaries and of 11 Hospitals from which we have no return, say.......................................	56,215	
Total number of Out-patients	———	1,140,000
Total number of In- and Out-patients............		1,200,000

We believe that the total number of patients here given will prove to be nearly correct. Whatever amount of error it may contain is likely to consist mainly of omissions. Several hospitals and dispensaries report, not the number of *patients* treated during the year, but the number of times patients have attended; and as of course one patient may attend several times, the number of attendances is no reliable index of the number of patients treated; but in all cases in which attendances and not patients are reported we have made a careful estimate of the probable number of patients treated, and have recorded that number so that exaggeration has been scrupulously excluded. Therefore the total number of patients here stated represents the aggregate number of patients attending the various hospitals and dispensaries mentioned in the tables; and as we know several dispensaries not mentioned in Table II. exist in the metropolis, it is certain that, if the reports actually published are true reports, the number of persons in receipt of gratuitous medical relief must, in fact, be greater than that which we have stated.

The hospitals from which in respect to out-patients we have obtained no return are 11 in number, and there are 6 dispensaries mentioned in Table II., exclusive of the Provident Dispensaries, the patients of which are not enumerated. It seems to us probable that if the number of out-patients of these hospitals and the number of the patients of the dispensaries were added together the total would be near upon 125,000. However, to insure that we understate rather than overstate the number, we have estimated them at less than half of that number; and for the sake of obtaining a round number as a total, we have stated them at 56,215. The statistics of the Provident Dispensaries we have omitted altogether, as they do not properly come within the category of medical *charities*.

The aggregate income for 1872 of the whole of the medical charities concerned in affording medical relief during that year to 1,200,000 persons was as follows:—

Income, stated, of 70 Hospitals supported by Endowments, Legacies, Donations, and Subscriptions	538,627	
Income, not stated, of 8 Hospitals of the same class	20,378	
		568,000
Income, stated, of 35 Dispensaries supported by Endowments, Legacies, Donations, and Subscriptions	30,626	
Income, not stated, of 1 Dispensary, say.........	1,374	
		32,000

Besides this enormous sum of £600,000 provided and administered by voluntary agency, there was a compulsory levy in the shape of poor-rates on behalf of Pauper Patients during 1872 as follows:—

Proportion of Poor-rates paid for the ordinary Medical Relief of the Poor		41,031
Paid by the Metropolitan Parishes through the agency of the Metropolitan Asylum Board for—		
Hampstead Hospital	2,859	
Homerton Small-pox Hospital	5,356	
Homerton Fever Hospital	0,391	
Stockwell Small-pox Hospital	6,513	
Stockwell Fever Hospital	4,698	
		24,817
Total sum contributed for providing gratuitous Medical Relief of the Poor, exclusive of Lunatics and Idiots, during 1872		£665,848
Cost of Lunatics:—		
In St. Luke's Hospital supported by voluntary agency	0,000	
In Bethlem Hospital supported by voluntary agency	30,000	
Pauper Lunatics, chiefly in Colney Hatch, Hanwell, and the City of London Asylum, and paid for by poor rates, the amount of which in 1872 was	159,530	
		198,530
Cost of Idiots and Imbeciles:—		
In Earlswood Asylum, supported by voluntary agency	20,857	
In Leavesden Asylum*	37,510	
In Caterham Asylum*................................	44,123	
In Hampstead Hospital*, say	21,510	
		130,000
Total amount contributed by voluntary and compulsory agency to provide for the gratuitous medical aid of all kinds afforded by, or in, the metropolis in 1872	£994,378	

* These Asylums are paid for by the metropolitan parishes through the agency of the Metropolitan Asylum Board.

In estimating the yearly cost of the Hospitals and Asylums under the direction of the Metropolitan Asylum Board we have taken the cost, as stated officially, for the half-year ending March 29th, 1873, and have doubled it.

We have just explained that the tables given above do not comprise every medical charity in the metropolis, and we are by no means sure that we have not considerably understated the amount expended in the gratuitous support and medical care of lunatics; but we are quite certain that the total sum—nearly a million of pounds—here shown to have been provided by the metropolis during 1872, as payment for the medical care and needs of a part of its population suffering from diseases of various kinds, is not more, but less, than the sum actually contributed. On examining the results here presented, and bearing in mind that the population of the metropolis within the police circle is now nearly 4,000,000,* we observe that those results may be concisely expressed in round numbers as follows:—

An amount equal to nearly eightpence per head of the whole population is spent annually in supporting idiots and imbeciles.

An amount equal to one shilling per head of the whole population is spent annually in supporting lunatics.

An amount equal to three shillings per head of the whole population is spent annually in the voluntarily gratuitous medical relief of patients not afflicted with mental disease.

An amount equal to fourpence per head of the whole population was spent in 1872 on the compulsorily gratuitous medical relief of persons not afflicted with mental disease.

These statements are based on the assumption that the income and expenditure of the voluntary medical *charities* equal each other, as is the case with the income and expenditure of the institutions under the direction of the Metropolitan Asylum Board. The *ordinary* expenditure of the voluntary medical charities, in the majority of cases, is, however, less than the income; but for reasons which we shall hereafter mention, we consider it expedient to regard the amount of income as the measure of the expenditure.

Unfortunately we have no means at present available by which we can learn what proportion of the population of the capitals of Ireland and Scotland are recipients of medical charity, what is the aggregate cost of all its forms in each of those capitals, and what is the average cost of it per head of all its recipients: we say "unfortunately," because if a just comparison of the number in proportion to the population receiving

* Allowing for the known increase of London we assume that its population at the end of 1872 was 3,939,470.

medical charity, and of the cost of it per head in Dublin and Edinburgh could be made with the number and cost in London, such a comparison would, we believe, be very instructive, and would probably show that both the number and cost per head are much greater in London than they are either in Dublin or Edinburgh.

But even in Manchester, where wealth abounds in a maximum degree, the cost of voluntary medical charity is, in proportion to the population, far less than it is in London, if the value of the land and buildings occupied by the charities both in Manchester and London be not taken into account. Mr. O'Hanlon, whose admirable paper on the Medical Charities of Manchester was read to the Manchester Statistical Society last February, has shown that, according to "the most recent available reports," the present annual expenditure in medical charity in that city, exclusive of the annual value of the land and buildings occupied by the various institutions, is 85,655*l.* Now this sum divided equally among the whole population would yield to each member of it 1*s.* 4¾*d.*; whereas, exclusive of the amount paid by the metropolitan parishes for pauper patients, and exclusive of the value of the land and buildings occupied by the London Medical Charities, their aggregate income during 1872 was 600,000*l.*, which, divided equally among the whole metropolitan population, would yield 3*s.* to each person. It thus appears that, in proportion to the population, more than double the amount spent in Manchester is spent in London in the shape of voluntary medical charity. In Manchester one person in every five receives such charity; and if the total amount expended were divided equally among its recipients, each would receive 6*s.* 4¾*d.*; but in London, although the number of recipients in proportion to the population is much greater than in Manchester—being in fact three persons out of every ten, the sum available for voluntary medical relief in London during 1872 would, if divided equally among the 1,200,000 recipients of it, yield 10*s.* to each of them.

Let us now glance at this question of cost in another aspect. We possess no information respecting the actual cost per week of in-patients of the several London hospitals; we have reason to believe, however, that the cost is very much greater in some hospitals than it is in others. We doubt if in any London hospital separate accounts are kept of the cost of in-patients and of out-patients respectively. But there are institutions which afford medical relief to out-patients only, and there are institutions which take charge of in-patients only: the former are the dispensaries; the latter are the convalescent hospitals and the asylums for the insane or imbecile. We have no information of the weekly cost per head of inmates of the convalescent hospitals; but we have precise and authoritative information on this point concerning several asylums.

During the half-year ending the 29th of March, 1873, the weekly cost of each inmate of Leavesden Asylum was 7*s.*, and at the Caterham Asylum during the same period it was 7*s.* 7*d.* At the Fisherton Asylum the weekly cost is 11*s.* At Earlswood the cost in 1865 was 12*s.* 4*d.*; but in 1872 the cost had risen to 17*s.* 6*d.* For reasons which will become apparent hereafter, we shall ignore the increased cost of the inmates of Earlswood since 1865. Now the average cost per week of each inmate at these four Asylums is 9*s.* 5¾*d.*, and the average cost means the cost of maintenance of the patients including their clothing, maintenance of the officers including their salaries, as well as the medical and other charges. As the in-patients of the London hospitals find their own clothing, it might be supposed that their cost in other respects would not exceed the average cost of patients in the asylums just mentioned—say 9*s.* 6*d.* each per week. But in order that we may make a liberal allowance for each patient in the London hospitals, we will assume it to be 12*s.* 6*d.* each per week, or 2*d.* more than the cost in the most costly of the asylums—viz., that of Earlswood; and as every one can testify who visits that establishment that its provisions, administration, and style are first class, it will be admitted, we think, that the in-patients of no hospital supported by public charity ought to cost more per head than do the inmates of Earlswood. The average length of time during which patients remain in the Manchester hospitals is about four weeks; and we shall assume that patients remain, on an average, the same length of time in the London hospitals. The total number of in-patients of the voluntary London hospitals during 1872 was, as we have shown, about 60,000. The weekly average cost per head of this number being 12*s.* 6*d.*, and the *average* length of their stay in hospital being four weeks, their total cost would be 150,000*l.* Deducting this amount from the total cost of the in- and out-patients—viz., 600,000*l.*, we find the remainder to be 450,000*l.* to provide for the treatment of 1,140,000 out-patients, and this sum divided equally among them would yield close upon 7*s.* 10½*d.* to each.

The ascertained average cost of treating patients at seven different dispensaries in Manchester was 2*s.* 6*d.* each, and this we understand is a greater sum than they are supposed to cost in London: certainly, 2*s.* 6*d.* per patient is in our opinion amply sufficient to pay all expenses of carrying on a thoroughly efficient dispensary. The reports are now lying before us of three dispensaries—viz., "The Royal South London," "The

Islington," and "The Chelsea, Brompton, and Belgrave." The first refers to the year 1869. In that year the total expenditure of the institution was 1004*l.* 8*s.*, and the number of patients treated by it in the same year was 7000; dividing the money spent by the number of patients treated, we find that the cost of treating each patient was 2*s.* 10¼*d.* The report of the Islington Dispensary refers to 1872. In that year the total expenditure was 998*l.*, and the number of patients treated was 14,654; the treatment of each of these cost, therefore, 1*s.* 4¼*d.* The report of the "Chelsea, Brompton, and Belgrave" also refers to 1872. The expenditure that year was 566*l.*, and the number of patients treated was 6697; in this case division of the money spent by the number of patients treated shows that they cost 1*s.* 8¼*d.* each. Adding the cost in these three cases together and dividing the total by three we find the aggregate number of patients treated at the three dispensaries—viz., 28,351 cost 1*s.* 11¾*d.* We entertain a strong opinion that the treatment of patients at the dispensaries is, as a general rule, quite as skilful, careful, and successful as is the treatment of the out-patients of hospitals: therefore, in assuming the average cost of both classes of patients in the metropolis to be 2*s.* 6*d.* each, we believe we over-estimate the necessary cost, and certainly we do not under-estimate it.

Now we have shown that, exclusive of the value of the land and buildings occupied by the metropolitan medical charities, their income in 1872 was 600,000*l.*; that, assuming the total cost of the 60,000 in-patients treated during that year to have been, as it might have been, 150,000*l.*, there would have remained a balance of 450,000*l.* available to defray the cost of the treatment of the out-patients, including those treated at dispensaries; and that the average cost per head of the treatment of out-patients, including those treated at dispensaries, is not in many institutions, and ought not generally to be, more than 2*s.* 6*d.* But if the sum just mentioned of 450,000*l.* be appropriated for the treatment of such patients, then the treatment of the 1,140,000 of them in London during 1872 must really have cost 7*s.* 10¾*d.* each! If, on the other hand, they did not really cost, at the utmost, more than 2*s.* 6*d.* each, or collectively 142,500*l.*, then the amount of the difference between that sum and the sum mentioned above as available for the treatment of the class of patients in question—that is to say, 307,500*l.*—was subscribed in excess of what was needful for the treatment of the whole of the patients who were treated through the agency of the voluntary medical charities in the metropolis during 1872. How that vast sum was actually appropriated is a question we must leave the givers of medical charity to ask, and the administrators of that charity to answer.

In stating the aggregate income of the London medical charities, we have done so without regard to the value of the land and buildings occupied by them. It is manifest that if to the income already stated 5 per cent. on the value of the land and buildings in question were added, that income would be enormously increased. We have no means of knowing, even approximatively, what the value of those lands and buildings is. But the value of those belonging to the medical charities of Manchester seems to have been fairly ascertained, and Mr. O'Hanlon has given a separate statement of the value of those belonging to each charity. The total value of the whole of them appears to be 839,810*l.*, and 5 per cent. on that amount is 41,990*l.* 10*s.* Now, seeing that the amount of medical charity administered in Manchester is, in proportion to the population, considerably less than that administered in London, we may fairly assume that the value of the land and buildings used by the charities in London is quite as great in proportion to its population as is the value of the lands and buildings used by the charities of Manchester in proportion to its population. The population of London is about 7¾ times that of Manchester. Multiplying the alleged value of the lands and buildings of the Manchester medical charities by 7¾, we find that the value of the lands and buildings of the metropolitan medical charities is 6,508,527*l.*—or, say in round numbers, six millions and a half! Five per cent. on this sum is 325,000*l.*, which, added to the income of those charities as already stated—viz., 600,000*l.*, bring up the total income to the respectable sum of 925,000*l.* This amount divided among the 1,200,000 recipients of medical charity in London would yield to each 15*s.* 5*d.* The total number of medical men in London is about 3500, and the enormous sum just mentioned would suffice to insure to each of them 264*l.* a year, irrespective of any private practice they may have.

Being unable to do more than hazard a conjecture concerning the value of the property occupied by the 76 hospitals and 37 dispensaries the incomes of which we have endeavoured to state, we must content ourselves by mentioning the value of the land and buildings of only one—a very important one certainly—viz., St. Thomas's. The land on which that magnificent hospital now stands was bought—and very cheaply it is said—from the Metropolitan Board of Works for 95,000*l.*, and 5000*l.* was given for the roadway. The buildings were estimated to cost, according to the original contract, 330,000*l.* To furnish and complete the establishment in every respect, in the style in which it is finished, can scarcely fail to bring up the total cost to 500,000*l.* We may add that the hospital is designed to contain 600 beds; that if the land, buildings, furniture, &c., should cost half a million, each bed will cost 833*l.* 6*s.* 8*d.*, the interest on which is 16*s.* a week, or 3*s.* 6*d.* a week more than the total cost of the food, nursing, &c., of each patient. So that, supposing the current weekly expenses per head of the patients in St. Thomas's is limited to 12*s.* 6*d.* (and this is supposing a good deal), the charge of 5 per cent. interest on the capital sunk in providing each bed, when added to that 12*s.* 6*d.*, will swell the weekly cost of each patient to 1*l.* 8*s.* 6*d.* The cost of Poplar Hospital is at the rate of 30*l.* a bed, the weekly interest on which is 7*d.*; so that a patient may be provided with the same quality of food, nursing, and general care in Poplar Hospital for 13*s.* 1*d.* per week as that which in St. Thomas's will cost 1*l.* 8*s.* 6*d.*—or, in other words, the sum which provides 100 beds in St. Thomas's would provide 217 beds in Poplar Hospital.

Though unable to give any authentic information concerning the cost of the various metropolitan hospitals and dispensaries supported by endowments or voluntary contributions, we can give the cost of the hospitals and asylums under the direction of the Metropolitan Asylum Board. The following statements respecting these institutions are official:—

Name.	Number of Beds.	Cost of Land, Construction, and Furniture.
Stockwell Fever Hospital ...	176 ...	53,000
Homerton " " ...	200 ...	45,000
Stockwell Small-pox Hospital ...	102 ...	40,000
Homerton " " ...	102 ...	32,000
Leavesden Asylum ...	1,809 ...	157,000
Caterham " ...	1,882 ...	160,000
	4,271	£487,000

In consequence of the outbreak of relapsing fever in the metropolis during 1870 the managers of the above hospitals and asylums caused a temporary hospital to be erected at Hampstead for the reception of patients suffering from that fever. The hospital was afterwards enlarged, and used as a small-pox hospital. When it was no longer needed for small-pox cases it was thoroughly disinfected, and is now used for the reception of 580 imbeciles. The cost of this hospital we are unable to state, but it can scarcely have been less, we presume, than 33,000*l.* This would bring up the total cost of the hospitals in question to 520,000*l.*; and, in fact, we learn that "the total amount raised by the managers for the purchase of land and the erection and fitting up of their several establishments has been somewhat over half a million, which is repayable, with interest, in equal instalments spread over sixty years."

If to the conjectural estimate given above of the cost of the medical charities supported by endowments and voluntary contributions we add the actual cost of the institutions under the management of the Metropolitan Asylum Board, we find the total cost to be above seven millions of pounds; and even this sum does not include the cost of either the County Lunatic Asylums—Hanwell and Colney Hatch, or of the City of London Lunatic Asylum, or of the workhouse infirmaries.

In closing these remarks on the cost of the land, buildings, and furniture of the various medical institutions above adverted to, we cannot help directing attention to an astounding contrast of the total sum expended on the hospitals and asylums under the management of the Metropolitan Asylum Board with that expended on St. Thomas's Hospital: leaving the Hampstead Hospital out of the account, we see that the six other hospitals built by that board at a total cost of 487,000*l.*, contain collectively 4271 beds; whereas St. Thomas's Hospital alone has cost about the same sum, and will contain only 600 beds!

In writing the preceding pages we have had three objects in view: *First*, to show what is the proportion of the metropolitan population which is habitually receiving medical charity; *Secondly*, to show what is the annual cost of that charity; and *Thirdly*, to show that the total cost of the 60,000 in-patients, and of the 1,140,000 out-patients, who were under treatment during 1872 was extravagantly great—was, in fact, at least 300,000*l.* more than it ought to have been, even on the assumption that there is no extravagance in respect to the land and buildings occupied by the charities—an assumption which will itself perhaps be held to be very extravagant indeed. But we shall now proceed to inquire whether the 1,200,000 recipients of medical charity in London are really and truly proper objects of such charity in any rational sense of that term.

On the census night, April 3rd, 1871, the population of London was, within the tables of mortality, 3,251,804; within the Parliamentary boundaries, 3,008,101; within the limits of the Metropolis Local Management Act, 3,264,530; within the London School Board District, 3,265,005; within the police circle, 3,883,092. The police circle comprises a considerable number of important centres in which there must be medical charities, consisting chiefly of dispensaries, but comprising also a few hospitals not included in the list given in the beginning of this paper. We know, for example, that Acton and Ealing have each a dispensary of their own. Croydon, also within the police circle, is so large that we feel sure it must have at least one medical charity of its own. Hackney, Stepney, Fulham, Stoke Newington, Bow, Bromley,

Greenwich, Deptford, Woolwich, Wandsworth, Putney, Tooting, Streatham, Hampstead, and Lewisham are several among the numerous suburbs in which dispensaries are almost sure to exist; and it will be observed that none of these places are represented in the tables we have given. Therefore, if we take the number of the population within the metropolitan police circle as the basis of comparison with the number of patients treated gratuitously during the year 1872, we shall certainly under-estimate the proportion of the London population receiving such charity in that year. We prefer, however, to understate our case, and hence take the number of the population within the police circle as our standard. The population of the United Kingdom is increasing at the rate of 705 per day; and as the metropolitan population forms about an eighth of the whole, its increase is at the rate of about 88 per day. Allowing for this increase, we find that the total population within the police circle at the end of 1872 was 3,930,466; we therefore speak of it in round numbers as 4,000,000. We have shown that the number of patients treated during 1872 was 1,200,000. Now 1,200,000 constitutes exactly 30 per cent., or three-tenths of the whole population in question; and it is, in fact, highly probable that if we knew what is the number of patients treated gratuitously in the various suburban centres just adverted to, we should find that the total number of the recipients of medical charity really forms a third of that population. But assuming it to be only three-tenths, this enormous proportion cannot fail to strike with astonishment any one who considers it for the first time. Indeed it seems at first sight incredible that in the wealthiest metropolis in the world medical charity should have assumed the colossal magnitude which it actually presents; and, as a matter of fact, such incredulity is in a certain sense justified, for the enormous development which metropolitan medical charity has attained is a phenomenon of recent years.

The extraordinarily rapid increase in the number of persons receiving gratuitous medical relief in proportion to the increase of the general population is exemplified by the following facts. In 1830, at eight hospitals which at that date supplied advice and medicines to out-patients, the total number of such patients was 46,435; but in 1869 it had arisen to 277,891. This more than fivefold increase took place during a period in which the metropolitan population had only a little more than doubled. The rapid increase in the number of out-patients at St. Thomas's and at St. George's Hospitals fairly exemplifies what has taken place, and what is still taking place, at the medical charities generally. Until 1834, St. Thomas's Hospital was without an out-patient department. At that date the practice of prescribing for and supplying medicines to out-patients began; and the number of out-patients increased so rapidly, that in 1842 it was found necessary to add to the professional staff a second assistant-surgeon and two assistant-physicians. In 1858 the total number of out-patients at this hospital was 38,268; in 1861 the number was nearly 42,000; and in 1869 it had reached nearly 66,000. During the seven years between 1863 and 1870, the number of out-patients at St. George's Hospital rose from 14,853 to 18,923, being an increase of nearly 30 per cent. The Royal Albert Hospital at Devonport "was established in 1861, on the ordinary principle of a free hospital; but before it had been six years in operation, the number of its out-patients was found to be so increasing that it threatened to absorb the whole revenue derived from subscriptions, and to leave nothing for the in-patient department, which consisted of fifty-five beds." Mr. O'Hanlon shows that "the average number of patients treated annually at St. Mary's Hospital (Manchester) during the periods of five years ending 1861, 1866, and 1871, were 5161, 7463, and 10,537 respectively. The earliest year referred to in the published table is 1856. In that year 2149 patients were received; in 1871 the number was 12,002, the population having increased 12 per cent., but the patients 450 per cent." The number of patients "under treatment in 1836 at all the hospitals and dispensaries in Manchester and Salford was 34,835. The population of Manchester and Salford and the suburbs in 1831 was 261,584, and in 1841, 339,734. Assuming the rate of increase to have been uniform during the intervening ten years, the population in 1836 was 300,600. In that year, therefore, one person in every eight and a-half was in receipt of charitable medical relief. Making the calculation in the same way—viz., on the basis of the published reports, we have in 1872 one in every four and a-half in receipt of charitable relief. No doubt, the increased supply of charitable medical institutions has increased the demand for their assistance; yet the fact remains the same, that the proportion of the population which, by applying for medical charity, confesses its inability to make suitable provision for a time of sickness has almost doubled within the last ten years."

Statistical facts respecting the whole administration of medical relief, other than that in the shape of private practice, in a town like Manchester are much more easily obtained than they could be in respect to the whole administration of medical relief afforded in the metropolis, and Dr. O'Hanlon has furnished a very instructive analysis of those facts as they present themselves in Manchester. He gives valid reasons for assuming that in Manchester and Salford there are from 20,000 to 22,000 paupers, and that about "40,000 working men are attended solely by their own club-doctors in time of sickness." He estimates moreover, that the number of "the middle and upper working classes who, in all cases, pay the ordinary medical fees," to be about 120,000. "Deducting these," he remarks, "along with the members of the friendly societies and the paupers—or say a total of 180,000—from the whole population, we find that the 95,000 patients treated by the various hospitals and dispensaries are derived from the remaining 330,000, and bear the proportion of one to every three and a-half. Whilst then, there are at the bottom of the social scale at least 20,000 paupers, there is immediately above these a stratum of 330,000 persons, in which one in every three and a-half is either unable or unwilling to make any provision for a time of sickness." In this estimate the paupers, the "working-men who are attended solely by their own club-doctors in time of sickness," and "the middle and upper working-classes who in all cases pay the ordinary medical fees," amounting as they do to 180,000, form more than a third of the whole population of Manchester; but let us deduct a third only as representative of the three classes just mentioned from the 3,939,470 of the metropolitan population, and assume that the recipients of medical charity are derived from the remaining two-thirds—viz., 2,626,311, we find that those recipients form nearly 46 per cent. of that number, or nearly one in every two, whereas in Manchester the proportion is only two out of every seven. In both cities these facts present a very serious aspect, but in London they are especially grave.

It is of course impossible that the condition of things implied by these statistics can exist without making itself felt by all who concern themselves practically with the administration of the medical charities, even if they have never looked beyond the immediate horizon of their own several and special centres of activity; but when once the subject is forced on their consideration, and their attention is consciously directed to an examination of the character and social position of the applicants for medical charity, they find that that charity is being administered to persons occupying positions in the social scale which become gradually higher as time advances; so high, indeed, that only the repeated observations in different parts of London, and in different provincial towns of men whose veracity is indubitable, constrain us to believe that persons whose incomes enable them to command many luxuries, are in the habit of obtaining all the medical aid they require from an hospital or dispensary. "At a conference on out-patient hospital relief, summoned by the Charity Organization Society, Dr. Meadows stated it to be 'unquestionably the fact that the poor are now being gradually ousted out of the consulting room by well-to-do persons,' and that he knew 'as a fact that persons in the possession of incomes of 1000*l.* a-year, come as out-patients to receive advice, and that the wives and daughters of men almost as wealthy actually borrow their servants' clothes, in order to apply as out-door patients.'" These must, we presume, be very exceptional cases; but those we are now about to mention are almost as remarkable. A correspondent of the *Medical Times and Gazette* of May 10th, 1873, affirms that the seven following instances of persons who are able to pay for medical attendance, but who have applied for and received out-door gratuitous medical relief, are cases which have occurred in his own practice:—

"(1.) The wife of a gentleman who resides in one of the best houses in a suburb, and has a private income of 800*l.* a-year; (2.) the wife of a gentleman who, besides other means of living, has a salary of 400*l.* a-year; (3.) the daughter of a musical instrument maker, who has two establishments and employs a number of hands; (4.) the wife of a grocer in business; (5.) a lady living on her household property; (6.) a publican doing one of the largest trades, if not the largest trade, in his neighbourhood; (7.) a tradesman just now recovering from an illness, during which he stated that in the event of his death he had his family comfortably pvroided for."

The chairman of the conference just referred to, Mr. W. H. Smith, mentioned that some years ago he had taken the trouble to investigate the position of the persons registered as out-patients in one large hospital, and found that "20 per cent. of them 'had given false addresses, so that it was impossible to trace them.'"

In Manchester, Mr. O'Hanlon finds, he says, "that out of 6359 patients admitted in 1871," at the Eye Hospital, "4400 to 4500 were agents, colliers, factory operatives, joiners, moulders, mechanics, &c., and probably, therefore, in receipt of high wages." Dr. Thorburn, of the Southern Hospital [Manchester], a gentleman who has had considerable experience in the management of several of the Manchester hospitals, states, "that out of every 100 patients 10 are paupers, and therefore inadmissible by the rules of all the hospitals, 20 are 'unable to pay,' 50 are 'able to pay by a little effort,' and 20 are 'decidedly able to pay.'" Thus, according to Dr. Thorburn, only one-fifth of these applicants were fit objects for gratuitous medical relief. Mr. O'Hanlon undertook a careful investigation of the position of the patients who applied for medical aid at three of the medical charities at Manchester, and he supplies the following very valuable statement of facts which he elicited. He says:—

"The questions asked were these:—the name of the applicant, address, occupation, wages, number of children, and the amount of their earnings. This information was obtained, in a more or less imperfect form, from 63 patients at the Infirmary, from 36 at the Hulme Dispensary, and 65 at the Southern Hospital. As these cases were not in any way selected, some idea may be obtained from them of the general character of those who are in the habit of receiving medical charity.

"The following were the weekly family earnings, as given by 144 of the patients; in 16 cases the information on this point is defective, and 3 patients refused to make known their income:—

Under 10*s.*	10*s.* to 15*s.*	15*s.* to 20*s.*	20*s.* to 25*s.*
10	11	25	38
25*s.* to 30*s.*	30*s.* to 35*s.*	35*s.* to 40*s.*	40*s.* to 50*s.*
18	17	12	6
50*s.* to 60*s.*	60*s.* to 65*s.*	91*s.*	Domestic Servants.
2	1	1	3

"The patients, as a rule, were very reluctant to give any information about their earnings. In a large number of cases it is evident they greatly understated them, and in others, those received in a time of sickness were given as normal ones. Joiners were said to be in receipt of 20*s.* a week, colliers 25*s.*, packers 18*s.* and 20*s.*, painters 15*s.*, and compositors 20*s.* Case 1, at the Southern Hospital, said his wages were 20*s.* a week, and the visitor employed to call at his house, found him living in a shop of a weekly rent of 10*s.*, and evidently doing a good trade in glass and earthenware. He had spent 40*l.* in doctors' bills, and was thus driven to apply for gratuitous medical relief. Had he been a member of a provident dispensary, he would have been able to obtain the assistance he required without difficulty or any loss of self-respect. Number 16 said he was a carter, earning 18*s.* per week; upon inquiry he was found to be the owner of a cart and horse, and to rent a shop, for which he paid 6*s.* 6*d.* a week. Number 32 is an engraver, and would rather pay any reasonable sum than be known to have applied at the hospital. Number 36 is a secretary, paying 16*l.* a year for his house, and when the visitor called his wife came to the door in a silk dress. Number 23, at the infirmary, earns 20*s.*, but his children, living at home, earn 71*s.* besides. Number 26 earns 20*s.* weekly, and his children living with him 41*s.* Number 29 earns 25*s.*, and the children 18*s.* 6*d.* Number 36 is a coach-builder, and said we had no right to ask what he earned. Number 53 has 30*s.* coming in weekly. Number 1, at the Hulme Dispensary, has 41*s.* Number 5 earns 30*s.*, and has four children working, but would not tell what their wages are. Number 27 earns 15*s.*, and his children 47*s.*

"One of the rules of the Chorlton Dispensary is this:—that

'those in receipt of more than the following scale of weekly income or earning, shall not be considered proper objects of the charity;' and we must suppose that it was adopted only after careful investigation:—a single woman, 10*s.*; a single man, 12*s.*; a married couple, without children, 16*s.* For every child in the family, an increase of 2*s.* If this rule be acted upon by the Southern Hospital, out of the number of patients by whom the requisite information was given, 30 would have been refused and 23 admitted; but if the occupations of the 23 be taken as affording a clue to their earnings, probably only 11 would have been admitted, and 42 refused. Thus, only 20 per cent. of those 53 patients would have been considered by the committee of the Chorlton Dispensary to be fit objects for charity; and this agrees with the opinion of Dr. Thorburn in his pamphlet, as to the proportion suitable cases bear to the whole number of applicants.

"Out of 33 cases at the Hulme Dispensary, from whom the requisite particulars were obtained, 17 would have been refused and 16 received, but out of these 16 there are 5 or 6 who, on investigation, would in all probability have been found to be inadmissible. Out of the 47 at the infirmary, where the full particulars were given, 31 would have been refused and 16 received; but these numbers would doubtless have been altered to 35 and 12 upon proper inquiry.

"Taking the 144 patients who gave information about their trades, we find that 5 were servants, 6 were seamstresses or charwomen, 11 worked in factories, 38 were labourers, carters, or tailors, 74 were joiners, painters, mechanics, masons, colliers, bricksetters, packers, or shopkeepers, and 10 were clerks and warehousemen.

"In 22 cases from the Southern Hospital, in which the rent paid by the patients was ascertained, 1 paid 2*s.* weekly, 5 paid 3*s.* to 4*s.*, 1 paid 4*s.* to 6*s.* 6*d.*, 8 paid 4*s.* 6*d.* to 6*s.*, 3 paid 6*s.* to 7*s.*, 1 paid 7*s.* to 8*s.*, 1 paid 9*s.* to 10*s.*, and 2 were lodgers."

About four years ago an attempt was made to induce the workmen of a large factory in the metropolis to add something from themselves to a subscription of fifteen guineas per annum, already given by their employers, to a neighbouring dispensary; the whole of the letters of admission available for this amount being constantly in use, and many more being required. It was found that a penny a month from little more than half the men usually at work would raise the subscription to forty guineas per annum, which would entitle them, according to the published scale, not only to as many letters as they could require for themselves and their families, but also to a certain number for their friends beside. Notwithstanding these advantages, the subscription was started with considerable difficulty, and the collection of the pennies became gradually so irregular and unsatisfactory, that at the end of two years and a half it had to be entirely dropped, a small balance of the subscription for 1871-2 still remaining unpaid. It thus appears that *a farthing a week* was considered too heavy a charge for medical advice *and medicine*; not because they were not wanted, for the full complement of "letters" was in constant requisition, nor because a penny a month could not be afforded by each man, for even a labourer at 18*s*. per week could not possibly miss a penny a month, but simply because every trace of the principle of independent self-help had been undermined and abolished by the facility presented to the men of getting what they needed at other people's expense.

Medical pauperism, as we have now described it, certainly prevails in the metropolis and in all the large towns of Great Britain on an immense scale; and the question arises, Does this special kind of pauperism tend to induce complete pauperism on a scale sufficiently large to cause any appreciable rise in the poor-rates? It may perhaps be impossible to present absolutely indisputable proofs that it does, but facts and considerations bearing on the subject compel every one, we believe, who gives due attention to it to conclude that the habit of receiving gratuitous medical relief and that of receiving parish relief stand to each other, in a vast number of instances, in the relation of cause and effect. We believe that many patients visit dispensaries and the out-patient department of hospitals chiefly for the purpose of persuading, if possible, the physicians who prescribe for them to give certificates that they are not in a fit state to work, that they are in urgent need of specially nourishing food, wine, &c., the gift of which they then solicit from the benevolent. We also believe that many make use of their prescription-papers as evidence that they are under medical treatment in order to establish a claim for help of various kinds. Our own experience justifies the expression of this opinion, and Dr. Stewart* expressed himself long ago to the same effect. He says—"My long-cherished and firm persuasion is, that the offer of gratuitous advice and medicine draws to the dispensaries many who are mere candidates for public or private charity. I have been led to this conclusion from having been often asked, in a way that plainly showed it was the main errand, for a certificate of ill health, either couched in general terms or addressed to some benevolent individual; at other times for a few lines to the Board of Guardians; but oftener far for a recommendation to the District Visiting Society."

All physicians and surgeons of dispensaries and of the out-

* "See his pamphlet mentioned at the head of the Article."

patient departments of hospitals cannot fail to be impressed with the striking change in the demeanour of many patients who have become habitual recipients of medical charity. When they apply for it on the first occasion they evince shame and compunction, apologize for coming to the hospital or dispensary at all, and in some cases, indeed, give satisfactory proofs that they have maintained their independence as long as they could; but when once they have experienced how easy it is to get medical advice and medicine without paying for either, and when they find in the waiting-room many persons whose positions in life are similar to their own, their views respecting medical charity are modified: they begin to think themselves quite proper objects of it, and soon, instead of the hesitating diffidence and apologetic manner which they manifested when applying for gratuitous relief in the first instance, they evince a comfortable self-assurance and consciousness of being entitled to the medical aid they ask for, which could scarcely be more pronounced if they had paid a guinea on the occasion of each visit. It is readily conceivable that they who have become habitual recipients of medical charity, and have thus deadened their feelings of independence, are easily tempted to take the further step of applying for parochial charity also. "The workman," it is said, "has too often learned at the hospital the first lesson of dependence. He begins by taking physic, and then food from charity."* And again, in the report of one of the hospitals occurs the following passage:—"For some years there has been a growing conviction amongst philanthropists that indiscriminate medical charity greatly tends to pauperize classes who would not think of receiving any other form of benevolent assistance, and that, by gradually undermining their independence, it leads them afterwards openly to solicit pecuniary aid." Facts have recently been communicated to us concerning the working of a suburban dispensary which confirm in a very striking manner the truth of the above statements. We are unable to prove that the large amount of pauperism of the City of London is chiefly due to the influence of the medical charities, but the fact is notorious that gratuitous medical relief to an excessive extent and an extraordinary amount of pauperism exist side by side. The medical charities of the City are said to attend to about 300,000 out-patients each year; and though the population of the City, according to the last census, was only 74,732, the cost of the pauper relief within the City amounted, during the parochial year 1871-1872, to 164,063*l.*

It is manifest that if medical aid is supplied free of cost to

* "Reports of the Committee and Sub-Committee appointed to inquire into the subject of Out-patient Hospital Administration in the Metropolis," p. 14.

the community, or even to the so-called working-classes only, the employers of labour ought, at any rate, to get it cheaper than they otherwise could do. It is, indeed, well understood by political economists, and was conclusively proved in the Report of the Royal Commission on the Poor Laws in 1834, that the charitable gifts of this and of former ages have the effect of supplementing wages, or, in other words, of lowering them, and thus of benefiting to a corresponding extent the employers of labour—at least, until by competition among themselves, they are induced to transfer the benefit, wholly or in part, to *their* employers, the various sections of the public. Viewing the subject from this point of view our readers will perceive that a large proportion of English workmen accept in the form of medical charity a portion of their wages, the whole of which would otherwise be paid to them in money by those who employ them. Having never been led to look on medical charity in this light, and to understand the real nature of its indirect but no less indubitable influence, "men whose ordinary income is two or three pounds a week expect," we are told by competent authorities, "to have letters of recommendation given them to the neighbouring institutions." An employer of several hundred workmen by subscribing with seeming liberality to the hospital nearest to his business establishment accomplishes two objects, the reflex influence of which on himself is eminently satisfactory: he acquires social importance as a beneficent patron of a charitable institution, and the privilege, possessing substantial value, of giving letters (commonly called "governors' letters") of recommendation which insure to their holders reception in the hospital as soon as there is room, and whatever surgical or medical treatment may be necessary, of the best kind, without charge. A physician having adequate opportunities of knowing the facts stated recently at a public meeting that the well-known brewers, Messrs. Truman, Hanbury, and Co., subscribe a considerable sum annually to the London Hospital, and thus secure medical and surgical attendance gratuitously for all the men employed in their large establishment, and not only for the men, but for their wives (whom the hospital actually supplies with medical attendance during their confinements!) and families.

In some cases the head of a factory, besides subscribing to, takes a more active part in the administration of the medical charity in his immediate neighbourhood—becomes, for example, the treasurer and chairman of a dispensary in which all his workmen, who are not so seriously maimed or suffering as to need treatment as in-patients of a hospital, may obtain all the medical aid they require, either at the dispensary itself, or, if unable to go to it, at their own homes. We do not affirm that, as a matter of fact, a gentleman assuming such a position does so in consequence of having made a deliberate calculation of the benefits, social and pecuniary, which he will derive from the dispensary of which he is the chief official. Nevertheless the arrangement insuring medical treatment to the men whom he employs without costing them anything, works beneficially for him: should they demand an increase of wages to which he may not feel disposed to assent, he is able to point out to them that among the items of their cost of living the doctor's bill, unless in very exceptional cases, does not appear either for the workman himself or for his wife and family. Moreover, as treasurer of the dispensary, to which he sometimes makes pecuniary advances, he occupies a commanding social position, both at the dispensary committee, at which he is chief, and at the annual dispensary dinner, where his praises are often chanted in tones which, to him at least, are sweetest music. But whether or not large employers of labour who contribute to the support of hospitals and dispensaries are conscious of the advantages accruing to themselves from doing so, certain it is that they value and use freely the privilege of giving "governors' letters" to persons in their employ, and thus in effect keep down their nominal wages at a level lower than that to which they would otherwise rise; and it is notorious that in this way many subscribers secure for their domestic servants, for their workmen, and for the wives and families of the latter, an amount of medical aid far greater than could be procured from private practitioners for a sum equal to that of their hospital or dispensary subscriptions.

The employers of labour on a large or small scale are not, indeed, to be blamed for making use of the medical charities in the manner here indicated, for, as a general rule, they are unmistakably invited to do so by the managers of those charities; and the arrangement by which, in return for a subscription of a certain amount, the privilege is obtained of nominating a certain number of patients for treatment at the hospital or dispensary to which the subscription is given assumes the character of a simple matter of business. Many of these charities publish a scale of prices on the payment of which the subscriber is "entitled to recommend" for treatment a number of patients proportionate to the amount paid; and not only are such scales of prices published, but the privileges of recommending or nominating patients are especially adverted to, as inducements to subscribe, in letters canvassing for subscriptions. For example, in a letter we have recently received from one of the hospitals, we are informed that "a subscriber of 1*l.* 1*s.* is entitled to one in-patient letter as well as to five out-patient letters, and so on in proportion." It is not difficult to understand that patients sent by subscribers to so-called "medical charities" in conformity with these arrangements are scarcely likely to be refused admission whatever may be their circumstances, and however able they may be to pay for the medical aid they may require.

In looking still more closely into this matter, we arrive at the conclusion that the benefit reaped in the first instance by the employers of labour, and ultimately in some degree by the several sections of the public who employ those employers, is conferred chiefly by the members of the professional staffs of the different medical charities—men who are confessedly among the hardest worked of the community, and who are certainly the last whose earnings ought to be lessened in order indirectly to benefit either the employers of labour, or that part of the public from whom they receive their orders. Certainly, if the system continues, we seem likely to reach a state of *medical* communism, at all events; a state in which Physicians, Surgeons, and General Practitioners—their private practice having of necessity come to an end—will be compelled to ask from the Commonwealth the means of existence in the shape of salaries for work the same in kind as that which they have hitherto done for the public for nothing, but on a larger scale. In that case the practice of medicine will become a vast Government-department with its 20,000 or 30,000 officials; and perhaps the devout believers in the perfection of government-agency will hail with enthusiastic satisfaction the prospect of a transformation subjecting the whole profession to the commands of the Medical Department of the Privy Council until a full grown "Secretary of State for the Medical Department" is duly inaugurated and takes his seat as a member of the Cabinet.

We have now demonstrated, we think, that the system of medical charity practised alike in London and in the provinces is characterized by very great and rapidly growing evils, and the question which urgently needs an answer is, Do those evils equal or exceed the good which the system confers? Good and evil are so generally, and so inextricably mixed, and beneficent institutions can be so rarely carried on without producing injurious influences of some kind, that we should not willingly condemn the system in question, simply on the ground that it does harm as well as good: before condemning it we ought to be assured that the evil is greater than the good which it works. The avowed object of medical charity and its *raison d'être*, is the supply of medical relief to persons urgently needing it, and unable to pay for it. We have shown that a large proportion of those who apply for it are not fit objects of it, and ought not to receive it, and the question still needing an answer is, Do those persons who are urgently needing such relief and who are unable to pay for it really obtain it in any such measure as fairly to counterbalance the enormous expense, the degradation of large numbers of the community previously independent into recipients of charity, the great extension of pauperism, and the serious loss sustained by the whole medical profession which result from the existing system? We are sorry to be obliged to answer this question in the negative, in so far at least as out-patients are concerned. The crowds of those attending at the hospitals and dispensaries each day, being so great as they are, it is impossible that they can receive such careful attention as is necessary in order to enable the physician or surgeon to prescribe for them with a fair chance of adequately benefiting them. This part of our subject has been recently discussed in the *Pall Mall Gazette* in a manner which renders it unnecessary for us to do more than quote the remarks in question.

"Believing it expedient to give the poor every possible facility for obtaining medical and surgical relief, the authorities virtually throw open the doors of both hospitals and dispensaries to all comers. It is true that admission to some of these charities is by means of letters of recommendation given by subscribers, but the great majority of patients are received and prescribed for without their claims to gratuitous relief being submitted to scrutiny of any kind. The consequence is the out-patient waiting-rooms of the different institutions, unless exceptionally large and exceptionally well-ventilated, are, as a rule, crowded to excess, and during the summer months almost to suffocation. The so-called* 'casualty' patients who attend St. Bartholomew's Hospital are now attended in a new building, consisting of a large well-ventilated room capable of seating about 6000 patients, but even this large room is often so overcrowded in summer that the heat and unpleasant atmosphere are much complained of. The three waiting-rooms at the Royal Free Hospital are frequently so much crowded that the patients hang about the yard of the hospital, and even during the present temperate weather,* when passing through the rooms while the patients were waiting in them, we found the air was sickeningly offensive. The crowding at the Children's Hospital at Great Ormond Street is reported to be such that it has been necessary to prohibit the patients from sitting on the steps of the adjoining houses. At the Metropolitan Free Hospital, during the early part of each week, not only is the waiting-room so densely packed with patients that any one would find it a somewhat difficult task to force a passage through it, but the lobbies and staircases are equally crowded. At this hospital the men are seen before the women, so that many of

* The article from which these passages are quoted was published June 4, 1873.

the latter often wait several hours before reaching the consulting-room.

"Considering the average length of time which patients have to wait before they are prescribed for, and the frequently crowded state as well as the insufficient ventilation of the rooms in which they are pent up meanwhile, we cannot help thinking that many of them, besides losing their time (which in a large proportion of cases is equivalent to losing their wages for the day), experience hygienically more harm than good from their visit to the hospital.

"A day's proceedings in the casualty consulting-rooms of St. Bartholomew's Hospital was thus depicted three years and a half ago by the *Lancet*:—'Two of the house physicians attend, one to the males and the other to the females and children, whilst the old cases are generally seen by the physician of the week before. As the requirements of the department must be measured by the heaviest day's work, we may take Tuesday, October 12, 1869, as an example of what is done. On that day one physician was required to see and prescribe for 125 men, and the other physician for 164 women and 62 children. There was also a considerable number of old cases. After some hours of steady work, it was found necessary to hurry over the remainder in order that the house physicians should attend the physicians in the wards. On the morning in question 120 patients were seen and dismissed in an hour and ten minutes, or at the rate of thirty-five seconds each. Who shall say what mistakes are made? None can tell.' Since 1869 a slight change has been made in the arrangements of the medical staff occupied in seeing the patients who fill the 'casualty' out-patient room of St. Bartholomew's. The medical officers who now see these patients have been especially appointed for the purpose, and are styled 'casualty physicians.' These gentlemen either alone, or, on especially busy days, with the aid of the junior assistant physician, see the whole of the 'casualty patients,' and, while prescribing for the great mass of them, select those whose maladies appear to be decidedly grave or interesting for treatment by one of the 'senior assistant physicians,' to whose department they are accordingly transferred. In this department the patients are examined and treated more carefully than those in the 'casualty' consulting-rooms, and are, moreover, made use of as subjects of study for the pupils, several of whom usually attend the practice of each of the 'senior assistant physicians.' When visiting, recently, the out-patient consulting-room, we noticed that the number of students present varied from eight to twelve, and that about a dozen patients were admitted into the room together: one of these was being attended by one of the senior assistant physicians, who was surrounded by the students, for whose instruction he made remarks concerning the case; another was being prescribed for at a separate table by, apparently, a senior student; and the rest of the patients 'assisted,' as the French say, at the proceedings. The change we have mentioned in the arrangement for the treatment of the great mass of out-patients, who are now treated by the 'casualty physicians,' is rather one of form than of substance; the inherent evils of the system remain essentially the same as before. The defenders of the present arrangements for the treatment of the out-patients as a whole insist that, as the 'casualty physicians' act as filters and thus collect and transfer to the care of the 'senior assistant physicians' all really severe cases, the whole body of patients receive good and effective treatment according to their needs. We admit that, given the large crowd of patients received at the hospital each day, and given the present number of physicians who now attend to them, the workers are skilfully organized, and the work is done perhaps in the most effective manner possible. But it is precisely against the admission of this vast crowd that we protest; and so long as its magnitude remains what it is, we protest against the limitation of 'assistant' and 'casualty' physicians to the insufficient number now employed in ministering to that crowd."

At King's College Hospital, according to a writer in the *Medical Times and Gazette*, the physician and his assistant sit at two small tables two or three feet apart in the out-patients' room, and as many as twenty patients, admitted into the room at the same time, arrange themselves in two groups, one around each table. This picture, with its accessories, which for want of space we abstain from reproducing, assures the spectator that the out-patients at King's College fare much the same as those of St. Bartholomew's.

We resume our quotation from the *Pall Mall Gazette*:—"Despite every argument advanced in favour of the present system," continues the writer, "the fact remains, that it is still customary to 'clear off' the great majority of the patients at a rate which, if adopted in the private consulting-rooms of physicians, would, we believe, very much astonish those who go to them; indeed, it not unfrequently happens that 200 patients are seen by one physician in the course of two hours and a half, so that the average length of time given to each patient is forty-five seconds. Referring to the Royal Free Hospital, the *Lancet* states:—'As the times of the physicians' and surgeons' entrance and exit are entered in the porter's book, we are enabled to note exactly the time spent by them in the performance of their duty. Thus Mr. Hill saw 208 patients, and was present in the hospital four hours and ten minutes. Supposing the whole of this time to have been occupied in seeing out-patients, he would have given on an average seventy seconds to each patient. On the same day Dr. O'Connor saw 318 patients in three hours and twenty minutes, or at the rate of thirty-seven seconds each. On another day in the same week Mr. Hill saw 240 patients in two hours and fifty minutes; and Dr. O'Connor 276 in three hours and forty minutes. Mr. de Meric saw 135 patients in three hours, and Dr. Cockle 150 patients in three hours and ten minutes.' This passage was written in 1869, but it is an accurate representation of the facts of to-day. For example, Dr. O'Connor now sees, on an average, 275 out-patients twice a week—namely, on Wednesdays and Saturdays, and he occupies about three hours and a half on an average each time in seeing the whole 275, or about forty-six seconds in hearing the complaints of and in prescribing for each patient. We have not informed ourselves concerning the ordinary rate at which out-patients are now seen at St. Thomas's Hospital, but when this charity was carried on at the Surrey Gardens the whole of the duty of prescribing for the medical part of the 'out-patients,' as distinguished from the 'casualty patients,' devolved on one man—Dr. Clapton—who had no assistance whatever. He attended four days in every week, and had sole charge of about 5000 patients every year. At the Metropolitan Free Hospital, which passes through its portals about 30,000 patients a year, the system familiarly spoken of to each other by hospital physicians as that of 'clearing off' or 'knocking off' the patients is thoroughly exemplified. The number of new patients in proportion to the number of old ones is probably greater at this hospital than at any other in London; and inasmuch as the new ones claim the physician's attention considerably longer, as a rule, than the old ones do, it must be admitted that the average rate at which the old and new, counted together, are seen and prescribed for—namely, about one per minute, proves that this hospital is quite worthy to take rank with St. Bartholomew's and the Royal Free in respect to the rapidity with which its patients are disposed of.

"We venture to think that our readers will conclude from the facts we now lay before them that the system in question has not even the justification of achieving what its designers and supporters intend and believe it to achieve—namely, the efficient medical relief of those members of the lower classes who are at the same time both diseased and destitute. To such sufferers the proffer of the sort of help above described is little better than grim mockery. Mr. Holmes, whose long experience at St. George's Hospital adds great weight to his opinion, may well say, as he does, 'Very much of the assistance given is merely nominal,' and is both 'a deception on the public and a fraud upon the poor.' Referring to St. Bartholomew's Hospital, the *Lancet* says: 'This superb hospital opens its capacious doors freely and widely, and by the reputation of its staff attracts the poor, invites their confidence, and excites their hopes of cure; but they are dismissed as if the main object were to get rid of a set of troublesome customers rather than to cure their ailments. The whole proceeding is unworthy of the place.' A physician of another of the London hospitals recently said to us, 'We are all disgusted with the system; it is worse than absurd; it is a living lie from one year's end to another. But we are powerless; if we attempt reform we encounter the worst kind of opposition, and our position as medical officers is likely to be rendered so thoroughly uncomfortable as to be practically untenable.'"

Considering the numerous and great evils of the system of medical charity we have now described, as well as its signal and acknowledged failure, considering also its enormous cost—between five and six hundred thousand pounds a year, exclusive of the value of the lands and buildings occupied in working it, and inclusive of them between eight and nine hundred thousand pounds a year in London alone, the reader can scarcely fail to ask, How comes it that such a system continues to obtain every year even more than the immense sum which is necessary to maintain it? The charity-giving public, which it is to be presumed is solely intent on lessening suffering, cannot be supposed to be the willing agent in developing and supporting an organization which, while exerting an indisputably baneful influence on large classes of the community fails in great measure to accomplish the special object for which it is designed; the general public in so far as it possesses real knowledge of the subject is interested to discourage rather than support a system which works more evil than good, and which tends, by multiplying the number of those who constitute the idle and dependent classes, to increase the amount of the poor rates; and, though certain members of the medical profession may find that their active promotion of medical charity as now carried on may conduce to their own personal advancement, the great body of medical men suffer so seriously from the effects of the system in question that it is not likely to receive any aid from them: indeed, they are fully aware of the great injury which it does them, and many of them denounce it as their greatest enemy.

The fact is, each hospital and dispensary may be correctly likened to a living organism, the growth of which is proportionate to the amount of food it obtains, and which as it grows has a larger bulk and greater energies to sustain, and therefore a correspondingly increasing appetite. Hospital chairmen and treasurers, hospital committees, and hospital secretaries—and in like manner all dispensary officials—believe in the vast importance of their mission, and in the necessity, therefore, of extending the sphere of their activity as far as possible. Being themselves convinced of the greatness, if not sacredness, of the cause they represent, they possess the chief requisite for success in labouring to convert others to their own faith. Moreover they are equipped with the incalculably great power of being able to appeal not merely to the benevolent feelings, but to the "eternal interests" of a people, whose religion teaches with the sanction of Divine authority, "He that giveth to the poor lendeth to the Lord." A large body of men, and of women too, thus inspired and thus armed, who work without ceasing for the development and enlargement of their respective establishments, and especially for the augmentation of their incomes, which are at once the source and measure of their power and influence as hospital officials, can scarcely fail to animate society at large with their own spirit, and thus insure its zealous co-operation in providing for the needs of the ever-increasing crowd of the "medically destitute." Our readers will easily understand, that to those persons who eagerly engage in such work, *hospitalism*, as we venture to call it, becomes a sort of religion. Just as to an enthusiastic Roman Catholic or English Protestant, the colossal figure of the Church to which he is devoted eclipses the object for the achievement of which it was organized, and, causing him ultimately to lose sight of that object, converts him into a slavish devotee of the organization itself, so hospital and dispensary officials are wont to forget that the promotion of the welfare of humanity is the sole *raison d'être* of charitable institutions of every kind, and instead of learning by experience and observation whether the effects of medical charity, indiscriminately administered on the vast scale it has now attained, are or are not really beneficent, they blindly dedicate their energies to the development, extension, and strengthening of the institutions with which they are severally connected. Hence the eagerness with which subscriptions are constantly asked for, and especially the unremitting efforts to accumulate a capital, the interest of which may alone suffice to support the institution on behalf of which those efforts are made, so that it may acquire an independent existence, and its officials may be enabled to direct and control it from within, without reference to those who contributed the funds for its formation.

The multiplication of medical charities is rarely effected by means of offshoots, but, as a general rule, is a phenomenon of "spontaneous generation." All the wisest, that is, the most conservative, physiologists doubt the occurrence of this phenomenon; but sociologists, even the wisest of them, often mention it as a fact quite familiar to them. The process of spontaneous generation, by which medical charities are produced, may be said to present a threefold form. 1st. There is the simple or homogeneous type, in which, born of pure compassion for suffering humanity, the idea of beginning a dispensary or small hospital in a neighbourhood, the poor of which are thought to be medically destitute, is simultaneously developed in the minds of a few philanthropic laymen, and of two or three medical men. Co-operating to achieve this object, they quickly embody their idea, give it a local habitation and a name, and then appeal to the benevolent public for its sustenance, and seldom, indeed, do they appeal in vain. This simple type, originated by noble motives, and presenting the co-ordinate and harmonious working of the lay and professional element, is admirable so long as it lasts, but unfortunately it rarely preserves its characteristic features beyond the lifetime of its founders. 2nd. A wealthy man or woman, animated perhaps by genuine philanthropy, perhaps by a desire to make atonement for "sin," or perhaps by a longing only for worldly distinction either during life or after it, provides funds to found an hospital. In any case the property is almost certain to be vested in the hands of laymen, and the chief manager of it, whether under the name of governor, treasurer, or secretary, most generally assumes despotic authority. 3rd. A considerable number of hospitals are founded for the treatment of special diseases, by physicians and surgeons mainly intent on exemplifying their special knowledge of and special skill in the treatment of those diseases, and thus of insuring their own professional advancement. But in whatever way hospitals originate—whether from selfish or disinterested motives in their founders—they are sure, sooner or later, to exemplify the same principles and methods of growth and extension which we have shown to be generally characteristic of hospitals established by voluntary agency.

We do not hesitate to affirm that, as a general rule, the establishment of an hospital in any given district multiplies indefinitely in that district the demand for the gratuitous medical aid which hospitals afford, and that the proportion of the population of that district which consents to compromise its independence by accepting medical attendance and medicines without paying for them—in other words, to become medical paupers—continuously increases; on the other hand, the greater and more rapid the increase, the louder and more urgent become the cries for more funds in order to meet the increasing demands for the charity administered. And thus the evil proceeds in an ever-widening circle—action and reaction developing the social malady to the gigantic proportions it has now attained. In short, given the origination and enlargement of hospitals and dispensaries from the motives and by the organizations and methods which obtain in this metropolis, and any man possessing these data and capable of reasoning logically can easily foretell the inevitably continuous increase on an immense scale of the numbers of those who become dependent on hospitals and dispensaries for all the medical aid they require. But while reasoning *à priori* on the data just named enables us to prophesy that great and continuous increase, the fact itself is indisputably demonstrated by experience ranging over many years; and, if we look for it, evidence of its truth may be found in every town in which an hospital or dispensary granting gratuitous medical relief has been established. Moreover, the magnitude of the increase is so astonishingly great as to cause very serious apprehension in the minds of all who duly consider how baneful are its influences on the economical, social, and moral conditions of millions of the British people.

We have often heard it asserted that the hospitals and dispensaries which are chiefly supported by voluntary contributions are in a state of chronic bankruptcy, and we have been asked whether such is not the case. Certainly, if we were to infer their pecuniary condition from the character of their ever recurring appeals in the daily journals for help, we should be constrained to believe that many of them are either approaching, or are actually entering on, the stage of dissolution. But these appeals, so affecting when listened to by the charitable public, have a very different significance to those who interpret them by the light of the facts which a study of the growth and pecuniary management of hospitals reveals. Feeling deeply interested in the whole subject of medical charity, we have long watched carefully in expectation of the demise of first one and then another of those hospitals, which, judging from their cries for help, seemed to be struggling for existence most desperately; but to our surprise the death of each of them was always seemingly postponed *sine die*, and at length by a careful examination of their balance-sheets, we have arrived at the conclusion that it is precisely those which cry out most piteously and most frequently that are really in the most flourishing condition. Taking up a few of the reports for 1872 which first present themselves to our hands, let us see what is the income and what the expenditure of the hospitals to which those reports severally refer.

The most usual phrase by which the public is appealed to is, "Funds are most urgently needed." The Royal Hospital for Diseases of the Chest, City Road, thus advertises for further help. Now, according to its balance-sheet for 1872, its income that year was 4045*l.* 19*s.* 4*d.*, and its expenditure was 05*l.* 9*s.* 2*d.*, so that its clear gain during that single year was

1240*l.* 10*s.* 2*d.*: a new hospital is decided upon, and 1000*l.* is placed to the credit of the building fund.

The Hospital for Consumption and Diseases of the Chest, Brompton, expended during 1872, 14,032*l.*, but its income was 21,861*l.* and thus yielded the satisfactory surplus of 7801*l.* But the public is informed that the pressure for admission sadly increases beyond the capabilities of the hospital, that "with the view of extending the operations of the charity, the committee have in addition temporarily fitted up a South Branch;" that "this useful charity is almost entirely dependent on voluntary contributions;" and that subscriptions and donations will be thankfully received.

The National Hospital for Consumption recently established at Ventnor, received during 1872, 9215*l.* 5*s.* 3*d.*, its ordinary expenditure was 3937*l.* 4*s.* 9*d.*, and it cleared during the year 6088*l.* 9*s.* 7*d.*, which it devoted to the extension of its premises.

The income of the Children's Hospital in Great Ormond Street exceeded its expenditure in 1872 by 3296*l.*, and seeing that the invested funds of that hospital were already 19,000*l.*, we presume that it has a handsome surplus every year; but its committee, as we observe in the *Times* of December 1st, 1873, still continues its appeal and "very earnestly solicits contributions."

St. Mary's Hospital received during 1872, 13,576*l.* 10*s.* 7*d.*, and expended for maintenance 9875*l.* 18*s.* 6*d.*, the balance in favour of the hospital being 3700*l.* 15*s.* 1*d.* During the same year, the Charing Cross Hospital also received 1823*l.* more than it expended. King's College Hospital had a surplus of 1326*l.*, and already 20,339*l.* in the shape of invested funds; and the German Hospital had a surplus of 1332*l.* and invested funds to the extent of 93,700*l.*

The London Hospital balance-sheet for 1872 shows a deficit of 11,503*l.*, and it seems that there was a deficit at the end of the preceding year of 3668*l.* The hospital is already immense, containing as it does 600 beds, and it appears at first sight remarkable that in presence of such a deficit the managers should determine on building a new wing to their already large establishment, capable of containing 200 more beds. But the fact is by a special effort made during last year either the whole, or nearly the whole sum of 100,000*l.* was forthwith raised for the purpose of building the new wing and increasing the income of the hospital. It is supposed that the erection of the new wing will not cost more than 25,000*l.*, so that there will be 75,000*l.* which can be used either to endow it or to augment the general resources of the establishment. The funded property and investments, on mortgage, &c., of the hospital now amount to 196,792*l.*; and we understand that in about twenty years hence the hospital will become greatly enriched by the falling in of a large number of valuable leases. The managers can therefore contemplate with perfect equanimity these temporary deficits, seeing that although a part of their regular income consists of annual donations and subscriptions, the public promptly responded to their special call to contribute 100,000*l.*, and that the time can scarcely be far distant when their fixed income will be so large as to render them either independent or nearly so of further aid from without. Meanwhile we learn from their advertisement in the *Times* that "the demand for admission is continually increasing," and that "contributions are earnestly requested."

We might show in detail from balance-sheets of many other of the most important hospitals that, as a general rule, their funds are steadily increasing, and that, in fact, the bounty of the public seems to be inexhaustible. In glancing down the columns of the tables given at the beginning of this article, our readers will observe that, as a general rule, the income of each hospital and dispensary is stated, but that in many cases no information concerning expenditure is given. Still the expenditure of 50 hospitals is mentioned. In 43 cases out of the 50 the income exceeded the expenditure, and in the remaining 7 cases the expenditure appears to have exceeded the income. In the latter cases the aggregate expenditure was 56,723*l.*, while the aggregate income was only 41,361*l.*, so that there was an aggregate deficit sustained by these 7 hospitals of 15,862*l.* Nearly the whole of this deficit was sustained by two hospitals only—the "London" and the Seamen's Hospital; the deficit of the former being 11,503*l.*, and of the latter 2652*l.* There was therefore an aggregate deficit of only 1207*l.* to be borne by the other 5 hospitals whose expenditure exceeded their income. What is the significance, from our present point of view, of the deficit apparent in the balance-sheet of the London Hospital has already been explained. On the other hand, the aggregate income of the 43 hospitals the incomes of which exceeded their expenditure was 261,944*l.*, and their aggregate expenditure was 169,947*l.*—the excess of the income over the expenditure being 91,997*l.* Moreover, the aggregate income of the hospitals the expenditure of which is not stated was 198,798*l.* Now, if the income in these cases exceeded the expenditure in anything like the same proportion as that in which the income exceeded the expenditure in the cases of the 43 hospitals previously mentioned, the total excess must be indeed enormous. The outlay in advertising must be admitted to be well spent.

It will have been observed, probably, that throughout this article we have spoken of the income and expenditure of the hospitals supported by voluntary contributions as one and the same, although the difference between them from a certain point of view is so great as we have just shown it to be. We have done so because, though the *ordinary* expenditure, as stated, is much below the income, yet the *extra-ordinary* expenditure, in a considerable proportion of cases, absorbs the whole income of the year: as the influx of patients continually increases it becomes necessary from time to time to enlarge the hospital or to build a new one, and sometimes in the course of these operations debts are contracted which are liquidated year by year from the surpluses in question. Or, on the other hand, they are accumulated as a building-fund to be afterwards appropriated. We fully bear in mind that a portion of the excess is saved and held as "Invested Funds;" but as the interest derived from these funds lessens in no degree the alleged need of further supplies and the urgency of the claims on the charity-giving public to give ever more and more, the practical result is, that all which is annually contributed is annually disposed of; and, as we have already said, the appetite for more increases in proportion as the supplies themselves increase.

Though in order to present a comprehensive view of the medical charity of the metropolis, we have included in that view the asylums for lunatics and idiots, a discussion of matters connected with those asylums scarcely enters into the plan of the present article, the more especially as the county asylums, and those under the control of the Metropolitan Asylum Board, are, in our opinion, both very efficiently and very economically conducted, and as of all forms of human suffering none possesses a claim at once so imperative and so indubitable on our compassion and on our help as that of mental alienation and infirmity, these asylums, if ably and economically conducted, may be justly regarded as being at once the most absolutely necessary, and of all forms of medical charity, those which offer the least temptation to abuse. But one of these institutions—the one which is mainly supported by voluntary subscriptions, the givers of which neglect to supervize their application—viz., the Asylum for Idiots at Earlswood, claims from us a few remarks, because it illustrates in a striking manner the method of growth characteristic of voluntarily supported medical charities, the consequences of irresponsibility on the part of its managers, and the significance of the advertisement-appeals just referred to. This magnificent asylum was opened for the reception of patients in 1855, or nearly nineteen years ago. According to the Report of the institution, published in March last, the income for 1872 was 28,535*l.*, which was only 1697*l.* in excess of the expenditure. But we observe among the charges, 1454*l.* 6*s.* 7*d.* for "Furniture (wear and tear);" 11*l.* 13*s.* for "Furniture, Office (wear and tear);" 386*l.* 13*s.* for

"Plant and Machinery (written off);" and 500*l*. for "Building Depreciation (written off)." These four charges for "wear and tear," and "building depreciation," during one year, amount to the enormous sum of 2352*l*. 12*s*. 7*d*. Now is it credible that this large amount is fairly chargeable for "wear and tear" and "depreciation" of an establishment built and furnished only 19 years ago, and ever since maintained in perfect condition, regardless of expense? It seems to us, that on the debit side of the account of such an establishment, the charges for "wear and tear" ought to be those only of the moneys actually expended during the year to which the account refers; and that all additions of substantial furniture should be regarded as capital, and treated as such. We have the best of reasons for stating, that the greater part of the land, 170 acres, now belonging to the Asylum, was bought under peculiarly favourable circumstances, that it would now sell for very much more than was given for it on behalf of the Asylum, and that it continues to rise in value. Moreover, the palace-like Asylum itself was built during a period of depression in the building trade, and cost about 40 per cent. less than it would cost now. Under these circumstances, a statement of the sum which the land, buildings, machinery, furniture, &c., actually cost in the aggregate, is obviously an under-statement, and therefore a misstatement, of their present value; and we have very good authority for saying, that the gradual increase in their value more than compensates for any depreciation in the worth of the furniture, machinery-plant, &c., by "wear and tear." Now the account as rendered shows a surplus of income over expenditure of 1697*l*. But if we add to this sum the aggregate of the sums charged on account of "depreciation" and "wear and tear"—viz., 2352*l*., we find that the real surplus last year was 4049*l*., which, added to what was stated to be the capital at the end of 1871—viz., 96,138*l*., would make the present capital 100,187*l*. But during the nineteen years which have elapsed since the Asylum was opened, the practice of writing off a large sum yearly on account of "depreciation" and "wear and tear" has, we believe, been persisted in, although, as we have shown, the land purchased has steadily increased in value, and the land and buildings together would now sell for more than they cost. This being the case, it is manifest that to arrive at a really accurate estimate of the capital now belonging to the Asylum, we must learn what is the aggregate of the sums which have been written off each year during the past nineteen years, and must add that total amount to the 100,157*l*. already mentioned. Not having the accounts for those years before us, we can only conjecture what that total amount may be, and we believe we shall be within the mark if we state it to be 20,000*l*.

If it is, then the actual capital now belonging to the Asylum is at all events 120,000*l.*

We must now add that this large capital would have been very much larger even than it is if during recent years the establishment had been conducted with any reasonable regard to economy. In 1865 the total annual outlay was a sum which if divided by the total number of patients then in the asylum gave 12*s.* 4*d.* as the weekly cost per head of the whole of them. In 1869 the weekly cost per head had risen to 16*s.* 11¼*d.* And lest that enormous increase should be to any extent ascribed to an increase in the cost of food of late years, we must state that the food supplied cost a farthing less weekly per head in 1869 than it cost in 1865. Each year since there has been an increasing expenditure. During last year the average number of patients was 533, and the expenditure, including the charges for "wear and tear" and "building depreciation," was 26,857*l.* 18*s.* 2*d.* If we divide this sum by the number of inmates, we find that each of them cost last year 50*l.* 7*s.* 9½*d.*, or at the rate of 19*s.* 4½*d.* a week! If those charges are not considered as a part of the expenditure, each inmate then cost 45*l.* 19*s.* 6¼*d.* during the year, or at the rate of 17*s.* 8*d.* a week. Moreover, it must be borne in mind that although each inmate cost that large sum, he lives rent free. Among the items of expenditure no charge for rent occurs; but if such a charge were made at the rate of say 3 per cent. on only 100,000*l.*, that sum would be equal to 2*s.* 2*d.* per head, and that sum added to the lowest of the two weekly sums already stated would make the weekly cost of each idiot last year 19*s.* 10*d.* But leaving this item of rent out of the account, let us glance for a moment at the annual extravagance now going on at Earlswood. The increase in the weekly cost of each idiot in 1872 beyond what each cost in 1865 is 5*s.* 4*d.*, even if the charges for "building depreciation" and "wear and tear" be excluded from the account of expenditure in 1872. If we multiply this sum by 533, the average number of inmates in 1872, we find that the weekly increase of cost is 142*l.* 2*s.* 8*d.*; and again, if we multiply this by 52, we find the yearly increase of cost to be the enormous sum of 7390*l.* 18*s.* 8*d.* Or, in other words, if the establishment were only conducted as economically as it was in 1865 there would be an addition to the yearly surplus of that large amount. Moreover, the number of inmates of the asylum was about 140 more in 1872 than it was in 1865, and there can be no doubt but that in such an establishment the cost per head might easily be considerably lower when the number of inmates is 553, than it could be when the number was only 412, the average for 1865. An additional proof of the extravagance in question rests in the fact that in certain other well-conducted asylums the weekly cost of the inmates per head is considerably less than it was in Earlswood, even in 1865. We have already stated that the inmates of the asylum at Fisherton cost 11*s.* a week each; that those of the Caterham Asylum, which contains 1800 patients, cost only 7*s.* 7*d.*, and that those of the Leavesden Asylum cost only 7*s.* a week. If in the face of these facts it pleases the supporters of Earlswood to continue lavishing on each idiot there 17*s.* 8*d.* a week, exclusive of rent for him, or 19*s.* 10*d.*, including it, there are, we believe, no means of preventing them from doing so, and we can only regard their costly indulgence as a form of mental eccentricity, the more deplorable because probably it is neither curable nor capable of being subjected to any effective control. The truth is Earlswood is a sort of high-class boarding-house for the very minute proportion of its patients whose friends pay for them handsomely, and the style and order of the establishment are kept up conformably to that idea, instead of on a scale befitting an institution which mainly depends for its support on public charity. It is clear from the facts we have adduced that, with its present income, Earlswood could amply provide for a much larger number of idiots than it receives at present, but in accordance with the principles which, as we have pointed out, determine the development of medical charities, the managers of Earlswood, perverted by the enthusiasm of "hospitalism," think more of the institution itself than of the object for which it was founded; we have visited it, and thoroughly endorse the observation of a writer in the *Athenæum* for 9th of August last, who says:—"It is impossible not to notice that it is the building which visitors are expected to admire—the building, with all its magnificent fixtures and fittings, and that in Earlswood's theory of its own existence the patients exist for the glory of the Asylum, rather than the Asylum for the good of the patients."

The following are the terms in which this magnificent and already wealthy charity, which has lately become so prodigal as we have shown it to be of its immense resources, appeals in the *Times* systematically for further help:—"The Board earnestly solicit additional CONTRIBUTIONS to meet present expenses and to provide for the contemplated increase. This institution derives no benefit from the Hospital Sunday Fund."

In connexion with the system of advertising for funds, we may mention that it has long been the practice of what *The British Medical Journal* appropriately calls "the advertising hospitals," to publish in the newspapers the number of *attendances*, which means the number of times which patients have attended at any given hospital within a certain period. If on an average each patient attends three times the proportion of attendances to patients is of course as 3 to 1. Very often the proportion is much greater. Now the general public knows nothing of the difference between *attendances* and *patients*, and the imposing array of figures representing *attendances* seemingly magnify enormously the amount of medical relief administered, and do in fact impose on the credulity of the public, to which urgent appeals for funds are, as we have seen, continuously made. The attention which has of late been directed to hospital administration by the Charity Organization Society, and by the Hospital Out-patient Reform Association, has already produced one beneficial effect—viz., that of causing the advertising hospitals to withdraw to a great extent at least those misleading announcements of *attendances*. But the practice still lingers and would, we believe, revive in full force were it not for the restraining and wholesome influence of dawning public opinion on the subject.

This article has already exceeded the limits assigned to it; we are therefore unable on this occasion to describe and discuss the various plans which have been suggested as means of remedying the grave abuses of voluntary medical charity which we have now exposed. Indeed, no remedy, however efficacious, can be applied until the public has been thoroughly imbued with a knowledge of those abuses, and thus induced to resolve that they shall be abolished. But powerful interests intervene to prevent the public from obtaining that knowledge. The physicians and surgeons who have the fullest information on the subject—viz., those who are officially connected with the several hospitals and dispensaries, are precisely those whose professional interests are best promoted by maintaining a "discreet silence." And if any of them should, within the walls of the hospital attempt a reform of the abuses which he encounters, he does so at his peril. What his fate is likely to be is sufficiently indicated by the treatment of Dr. Mayo, who was dismissed from St. Bartholomew's hospital in 1869. "Expecting to have in the casualty out-patient room and wards of the hospital exceptionally good opportunities of extending his experience, Dr. Mayo purchased the post of house-physician; but no sooner was he installed than he found he was expected to see, in the course of a morning, as many as from 300 to 400 casualty patients, besides having to go the rounds of his wards, and he was not long in coming to the conclusion that to prescribe for new patients at the rate of one hundred per hour, or forty seconds a-head, was unprofitable for himself, dangerous for them, and altogether a shameful farce. He refused to see more than fifty new cases, and was in consequence dismissed from his office by the unanimous vote of the governors of the hospital.

"The senior students of the hospital, however, took the matter up, and, in a crowded meeting, passed resolutions of sympathy with Dr. Mayo, and also one to the following effect:—

"That this meeting believes that the defects in the present administration of St. Bartholomew's Hospital call for Parliamentary inquiry, and permanent Government supervision, in the interests of the public."*

It will probably be admitted that these brave "senior students of the hospital" had the best possible means of judging of the reality of the abuses which exist in it, and that they were wholly justified in believing that the defects in the present administration of that hospital "call for Parliamentary inquiry, and permanent Government supervision, in the interest of the public;" but neither their expression of opinion, based on ample observations, concerning the maladministration of the hospital, nor their expression of sympathy with the victim to the conservators of notorious abuses, availed to re-instate Dr. Mayo in the position from which he had been expelled, and his fate constitutes an impressive warning to all officially connected with St. Bartholomew's, of the penalty to be exacted from any one who may be rash enough to attempt even the smallest instalment of reform of the existing system.

The Metropolitan Free Hospital vigorously enforces, it seems, what has been happily termed by Mr. Jodrell, "obsequious mutism" from its professional staff. We have been informed that several of its physicians have at different periods attempted to effect improvements in the administration chiefly in respect to the treatment of out-patients, and that each attempt has been stifled by a request conveyed to the innovator for his resignation; and though in some of these cases, if not in all, the request was not complied with it was none the less effective in deterring each member of the professional staff from introducing any improvement in the management of the hospital—a management wholly in the hands of a small and irresponsible committee of laymen, the chief of whom are its chairman, Mr. Joseph Fry, and its secretary, Mr. George Croxton. But one of the physicians of this hospital, Dr. John Chapman, finding how unavailing were the efforts of any of its medical staff to effect even the smallest measure of improvement from within, felt the strong necessity, on public grounds, of calling public attention to the gross abuses of the out-patient system as exemplified in the

* See article in *Public Health*, No. 3, vol. i., "On Hospital Reform, in Connexion with the Out-patient Department." By H. Nelson Hardy, F.R.C.S. Ed.

London hospitals generally, and therefore in the "Metropolitan Free" as one of them, and yielding to his sense of duty, encountered the same fate as that which had previously befallen Dr. Mayo. The story of the disgraceful conduct in this affair of the managers of the Metropolitan Free Hospital has been concisely told by one of its governors, and one who has taken a leading part in the movement for hospital reform generally, Mr. T. J. P. Jodrell. Availing ourselves of his letters, published in the *Pall Mall Gazette*, as well as of other sources of information, we present to our readers the following brief statement of the facts of the matter.

In the *Pall Mall Gazette* of the 4th of June, 1873, there appeared what Mr. Jodrell designates "a temperately written article" on "The Treatment of Out-patients at the London Hospitals and Dispensaries." In that article a description was given of the crowded state of the Out-patients' waiting-rooms of the London hospitals; and St. Bartholomew's Hospital, the Royal Free Hospital, the Children's Hospital in Great Ormond Street, as well as the Metropolitan Free Hospital, were especially adverted to in a passage which we have already quoted at page 200. Shortly after the publication of the article the physicians and surgeons of the Metropolitan Free Hospital were summoned to meet the Managing Committee, nominally to confer on the general interests of the hospital, but mainly in consequence of the appearance of that article. Of the members of the medical staff who obeyed the summons, the only three who could be reasonably suspected of having written the article—viz., Dr. Fotherby, Dr. Drysdale, and Dr. Chapman—were successively interrogated respecting its authorship. Dr. Fotherby was asked if he knew who had written the article and answered, "No, I do not." Dr. Drysdale was asked if he had written it and answered, "No." He was then asked if he knew who had written it, and again he answered in the negative. Dr. Chapman entered the room after Drs. Fotherby and Drysdale had already been questioned, and was immediately asked if he wrote the article. After protesting against the propriety of the question, but finding it useless under the circumstances to insist on his privilege of silence respecting the authorship of an anonymous article, he avowed that he was the author.

"The general committee, it seems, were not satisfied with this humiliation of their medical staff, for their next step was to get them to pass a vote of censure on their offending brother. For that purpose a meeting was summoned of the medical committee, at which a resolution was come to 'expressive of the deep regret of that committee that an article calculated to do such serious injury to the hospital in the opinion of the charitable public should have emanated from one of their colleagues, and their great surprise that he should deem it consistent with the feeling of honour to continue to hold the appointment of assistant-physician to a public charity which he deliberately and anonymously in the public press disparages.' It is a significant circumstance that though the medical committee comprises the whole medical staff of eleven members, five only were present on this occasion, the three surgeons, and the two other assistant-physicians, one of whom only, with the three surgeons, signed the resolution, and he, Dr. McNalty, a very young man, not yet admitted a member of the College of Physicians. The three principal physicians were conspicuously absent. Yet on the authority of this resolution alone the general committee founded its mandate to Dr. Chapman to resign his office, and on his refusal to do so, dismissed him.

"It will be observed that the resolution does not impute to Dr. Chapman any falsification of fact; nor was this possible; for not only were the facts to which his comments referred indisputably true, as I can myself testify from having paid a personal visit to the hospital at the hour when the patients were there, but they were facts which must have been as well known to the general committee and to every member of the establishment as to Dr. Chapman himself. His offence was not that he had published what was untrue, but that by an article in the daily press he had directed public attention to matters which men in general would regard as abuses, but in which the general committee, though equally cognizant of them, by a strange obliquity of judgment could see no abuse at all; for in their last annual report, published a few months before, after noticing that much had been said and written on the subject of hospital out-patient reform, they undertake "to assure the governors that the abuses complained of have no existence in this hospital." There is nothing in all this to surprise any one who considers what the constitution of the governing body of this and most other London hospitals really is. Whatever they may be in theory, they are substantially and in practice close corporations with all the instincts well known to belong to such bodies—idolatry of old traditions, repugnance to all change, insensibility to public opinion out of doors, and extreme jealousy of any appeal to it. * * * * With respect to the article in question, I am told that three of the most eminent men in the profession, whose names I only forbear to mention because I have not the honour of being personally acquainted with them, have expressed the opinion, in which I cordially concur, that there is nothing in the article itself which a medical officer of any of the hospitals mentioned in it might not with propriety have written. To have thrown away the services of such a man for such a cause is to proclaim the gagging system in its most absolute and obnoxious form. Let the public and the profession be upon their guard. If benevolent people are too busy or too indolent to exercise personal control over the institutions which they support, they are only the more interested in keeping open every channel by which the truth can reach them."*

We observe that the medical journals have expressed themselves in terms of indignant reprobation, both of the conduct of the managing committee, and of the four members of the professional staff who degraded themselves by passing the "vote of censure" which the managing committee needed as their pretext for the action they were intent upon.

"If," says the *Medical Times and Gazette*, "the resolution [of those members] was intended to obtain the favour of the General Committee or of any of its members, all we can say is, that the procedure was simply pitiable. . . . If honorary medical officers to medical charities are to be subjected to the treatment which Dr. Chapman has suffered, the public will certainly be the losers, for there will very soon be no medical charities. But we hold that the precedent is a most dangerous one, and should arouse the indignation of the whole profession. . . . We only hope that the subscribers to the hospital will convene a meeting to express their opinion of this unprecedented piece of petty tyranny."

"The treatment of Dr. Chapman," says the *Lancet*, "by the committee of the Metropolitan Free Hospital is a severe satire upon the name of that institution;" and it asks, "why were not all the members of the medical staff present," when the medical committee passed its vote of censure, in order "to vindicate the liberty of medical men to speak the truth and to help to make institutions what they pretend to be? We are still not without hope of the Metropolitan Free Hospital. There is a body of governors who may yet vindicate the name and fame of the institution which is sadly lowered by the incident upon which we comment."

"Five out of eleven medical officers agree," observes the *Medical Press and Circular*, "to a resolution condemning the conduct of one of their colleagues—outside the hospital. Where are the other six? Their wisest course would be at once to issue a repudiation of the judgment of the other five. . . . An appeal to the governors at large should be made, and if the power of the press should not suffice to kindle interest enough to replace the clique that has too long ruled the Metropolitan Free Hospital by a committee of independent gentlemen, then farewell to all hope of hospital reform."

Mr. Jodrell has expressed his belief that "in the particular

* *Pall Mall Gazette*, Nov. 12, 1873: Letter by T. J. P. Jodrell.

abuse of authority" in question, the Metropolitan Free Hospital "stands quite alone;" but our readers have seen that that hospital had a precedent for its abuse of authority in the conduct of St. Bartholomew's described above. St. Bartholomew's by virtue of its enormous endowment is placed for the present, at least, beyond the reach of any influence which can be exerted by public opinion; and many years will probably elapse before that opinion will compel Parliament to institute a searching investigation into the working and defects of that hospital. But the Metropolitan Free is almost wholly dependent for its existence on the contributions of the charitable public, and as it is to be presumed that they have no wish to sanction the perpetration of gross abuses, as well as of contemptible tyranny, in the persons of its officials, we think it worth while to show that that hospital is urgently needing a sweeping reform in several respects.

Dr. J. Murray, Assistant Physician and Joint Lecturer on Pathology at Middlesex Hospital, whose recent death has elicited a widely and very strongly expressed feeling of professional regret for the loss of one who gave promise of being among the most effective promoters of medical science, visited the Metropolitan Free Hospital in 1868, and published a report of his observations during his visit in *The British Medical Journal* for December 12th of that year. In our account of the hospital we shall avail ourselves freely of Dr. Murray's description, but shall supplement it as we may judge necessary in order that it may be a faithful representation of the institution in 1873.

"The hospital, as it at present stands," in Devonshire Square, Bishopsgate, City, "is composed of two old private houses communicating one with the other, and is an example of that short-sighted and pernicious system, unfortunately too common, which attempts to combine economy with the modern requirements of a hospital. . . . The wards are seven in number, with from two to six beds in each, and containing altogether about twenty-seven beds. . . . Two of the wards are set apart for the sick poor of the Jewish community.

"There are no bath rooms, and only two sitz-baths supplied for the use of the patients." Incredible as it may seem, we believe, nevertheless, that up to the present time no means of giving a patient an ordinary warm bath, in which the whole body can be immersed, exist in the establishment.

"The water-closets are amongst the worst features of the hospital," there are two; they are both dark; and "there is no attempt to obtain ventilation from the external air."

One of the garrets "is used as a lumber and *post-mortem* room. It is needless to remark that this arrangement ought not to continue a single day longer." It does continue, however, to the present time. "Into this place the bodies are brought up by the porter, with the assistance of the nurse. The floor at our visit was bespattered with blood, as were also two pair of calico-covered steps.

"There is no operating room: the surgeon's out-patient room, or the ward being used for the purpose." The effects of this procedure on the nervous system, and through it on the special maladies of the patients in the adjoining beds, our readers will readily imagine.

"Instruments are certainly not plentiful in the hospital. There are a few catheters, scalpels, tongue depressors, and such like; but otherwise the hospital is badly found in this respect. The surgeons at one time, we believe, were required to bring their own instruments; and we are told this necessity not unfrequently still exists.

"The nursing arrangements are very bad . . . The scrubbing and washing are done chiefly by the nurses; a scrubber and general servant doing the rest. The nurses take their meals in the wards. The under-nurses wear no regular dress, and look most untidy to say the least of it."

"The out-patient department is the leading feature of the institution. . . . . *The out-patient waiting-rooms are totally inadequate for the purpose.* They are confined to the old house, and occupy the ground and first floors . . . . . they are very dirty, *and far too small; the staircase,* which also leads to the wards above, *is equally dirty, and generally crowded with male and female out-patients.*" We beg the reader's special attention to the words of this paragraph, which we have put in italics. They are almost identical in form, and completely so in meaning with those for the use of which Dr. Chapman was dismissed from the hospital; and their literal truthfulness is moreover confirmed by Mr. Jodrell, who paid a special visit to the hospital in order to inform himself on the point.

"This hospital," says Dr. Murray, "adopts the system, in its annual reports, of publishing the *attendance only* of patients throughout the year; which may mean anything, and not the number of *new cases alone.* This plan is apt to mislead the public." Since Dr. Murray wrote, even the Metropolitan Free Hospital has been reluctantly constrained to give the number of *new cases* as part of a tabular statement printed along with its "Reports;" but in the Reports themselves it is still the "*attendances* of out-patients" only which are given, and these, the charity-giving public is told, in the Report published in 1873, "reached the unusually large total of 88,749." The new cases are stated to have been during the same year 38,465. But the value of these figures will be better understood by the reader when he has learnt the meaning of the "marking off" system which is practised at this hospital. In order to lessen somewhat the amount of labour to be got through, a practice is adopted of dismissing many of the new out-patients as soon as they have been prescribed for only once: the physician after writing his prescription places a cross below it: the dispenser after giving the medicine prescribed takes from the patient the prescription paper on which this cross is placed, and the patient is dismissed. If there were no cross in the paper the patient would retain it, and would be admitted for continuance of treatment as an "old patient." Many of the patients who, after having been seen only once, have their prescription papers taken from them, require of course further treatment, and are again admitted, if they apply for it, as many do. But all patients who thus give up their papers, and who, nevertheless, return to the hospital for further treatment are counted as *new patients!* It is manifest that by the practice of this absurd system the number of so-called "new cases" is greatly increased; and therefore that those who put faith in the published statements of the number of "new cases" treated at the Metropolitan Free Hospital are deluded.

In connexion with delusive reports of the number of "new cases," we may mention on the authority of Dr. Murray, another glaring example of the style of advertising adopted by the managers of this hospital. The garret ordinarily used as the *post-mortem* room, "and the two rooms now transformed into a ward for children's diseases, were opened as a cholera ward during the late epidemic in the east of London; and a special sum of money —100*l*., we believe—was granted to the hospital by the Mansion House Relief Fund, to assist in defraying expenses. Although a number of out-patients were treated for diarrhœa here, as at all hospitals, these wards were, however, on *no occasion* required for cholera patients." But in their annual report the managers published the following remarkable statement:—"The demands on the resources of the hospital during the prevalence of cholera were excessively heavy, and to the prompt assistance rendered in upwards of 5000 cases, may be attributed, in great measure, the almost total absence of fatal cases *within* and around its walls. Through the liberality of the public, your Committee were enabled, at the outbreak of the malady, *to set apart three rooms for the reception of cholera patients, which being no longer required for that purpose*, are being converted and fitted for the special treatment of sick children."

"The financial management of the hospital" seems to have puzzled Dr. Murray a good deal, "because of the loose manner in which the annual reports are prepared;" but at all events he seems to have grappled effectually with one part of that "management"—viz., the charge for "drugs and dispensary expenses," exclusive of dispensers' salaries, entered in the balance sheet for 1867, of 1795*l.* Dr. Murray discusses this charge at length, compares it with the charge for the like things in several other hospitals, and having regard to the number of patients at those hospitals observes:—"A ratio, more or less constant, is apparent in all similar accounts we have examined of numerous London hospitals—a ratio which is greatly exceeded by the Metropolitan Free Hospital." In proof of the justness of his reasoning, and of the necessity that the supporters of that hospital should look into its accounts, we may mention that when in 1867 the charge for drugs and dispensary expenses, *exclusive* of dispensers' salaries, was, as he says, 1795*l.*, the number of "attendances" of patients was 78,987; and that though the average yearly number during the three years—1870-1-2—was 2445 *more* than in 1867, the average charge during those three years for drugs and dispensary expenses, "*including* salaries of dispenser and assistants," dropped down to 872*l.*, which is 923*l.* a year less than the sum Dr. Murray objected to!

We too are a little puzzled with the "financial management" of the hospital. According to the "Cash Statement" for 1871, the income during that year, together with balance at bankers, was 4039*l.* 13*s.* 6*d.*, the expenditure was 2999*l.* 1*s.* 7*d.*, and the surplus or excess of income over expenditure was 1040*l.* 11*s.* 11*d.* But notwithstanding this surplus a "Loan from Bankers" of 1500*l.* is introduced on the credit side of the account, and on the debit side is introduced this item—"Building Fund 2516*l.* 11*s.* 5*d.*" And then at the foot of the account we are informed that the "Liabilities, Dec. 31st," 1871, were 2063*l.* 7*s.* 6*d.*, and that the "Balance against the Hospital" was 2040*l.* 7*s.*, no word being vouchsafed as to the amount of the Building Fund! According to the "Cash Statement" for 1872 the income was 4790*l.* 7*s.* 7*d.*, and the ordinary expenditure was 3958*l.* 17*s.* 6*d.*, so that there was a surplus of 831*l.* 10*s.* 1*d.* Out of this surplus, 750*l.* was devoted to repaying half of the "Loan from Bankers;" 46*l.* 6*s.* 6*d.* was charged to "Building Fund;" and the balance remained "at bankers." But notwithstanding this apparently prosperous state of the finances the "liabilities" are increased: at the end of 1871 they were stated as 2063*l.* 7*s.* 6*d.*, and as the loan was not mentioned separately, we concluded it to be a part of those liabilities. In the last "Cash Statement" the liabilities are stated to be 2396*l.* 7*s.* 3*d.* *exclusive* of the loan, the part still remaining to be repaid being stated as an additional liability. Now the loan was a liability at the end of 1871, and ought to have been treated as such then, as well as at the end of 1872. If it was, by being included in the general statement of liabilities, then the liabilities have increased from 2063*l.* 7*s.* 6*d.* to 3146*l.* 7*s.* 3*d.* in twelve months; if it was not, the liabilities at the end of 1871 were understated, and therefore misstated. Moreover, if the items of expenditure included in the "cash statement" do not represent the cost of the hospital during the year, but merely a number of accounts which it pleased the managers to pay, it is worthless to subscribers to the hospital, who desire to learn whether its income is more or less than its expenditure. Again, if it be expedient to mention in detail in the cash statement such an item as "omnibus and cab hire, 1*l.* 14*s.* 10*d.*," it is expedient to mention what the liabilities amounting to 3146*l.* consist of. And further, if such sums as 2516*l.* 11*s.* 5*d.* are disposed of in one year by being charged to "building fund," it may be fairly presumed that a subscriber to the hospital is entitled to know what is already the amount of that fund. But in these important points the report is obstinately silent. After giving careful consideration to the accounts, we are obliged to pronounce them, as Dr. Murray did, "loose" and unsatisfactory, and seemingly designed while affording a minimum amount of information, to impress the inspector of them with the conviction that the hospital has a heavy debt, and is in urgent need of pecuniary help.

Dr. Murray reports that at the time he wrote, the members of the professional staff made an effort to secure their representation, if by only one of their number, at the weekly board of management, and passed an unanimous resolution to that effect; but of course the effort was abortive; and so long as the managing committee continues practically despotic and irresponsible as it is now, the honorary members of the medical staff who are the best qualified advisers concerning the needs and administration of the hospital will be resolutely excluded from any share in its management. It is probable that great as was the crime with which Dr. Chapman was charged openly—viz., that of adverting to the crowded state of the waiting-rooms, a greater one, but one which could not be openly brought against him, consisted in the fact that not only had he expressed a strong opinion at the hospital that the members of the medical staff ought, *ex officio*, to be members of the committee of management, but that by his articles in the *Pall Mall Gazette* concerning the "Abuses of Medical Charity," he had proved himself to be a dangerous person, who under one pretext or another must be immediately got rid of.

The description, mainly in the language of Dr. Murray, which we have now given of the Metropolitan Free Hospital, proves conclusively that it requires, as he said, "radical reform." The building itself is thoroughly unsuitable for the purposes of an hospital; its hygienical conditions are notably defective; it has no operating room, and no *post-mortem* room; its out-patient rooms are so small, that patients are crowded together in the lobbies and staircase, as well as in the rooms themselves; it has no bath-room, and no means of giving an adult a complete bath on the premises; it "is badly found," Dr. Murray says, in respect to instruments and the ordinary appliances of an hospital; its "nursing arrangements are bad;" the members of its staff "are expected," as he says, "to see thousands of patients, for whom it is impossible to prescribe in the time allotted to each; its managers adopt a system of advertising the number of "attendances" instead of patients, and of announcing as "new cases" a large number which are really old ones—a system which cannot fail to mislead the public; the annual reports of the hospital are proved to be unreliable by the fact that in one of them the rooms which had been set apart for cholera patients were referred to in language which was untruthful—a procedure which Dr. Murray euphemistically designates "trying to make capital;" the hospital accounts are so managed as to be unintelligible, and any one who studies the two "cash statements" last published can only assure himself of the seemingly paradoxical fact, that though the income exceeds the expenditure by several hundreds of pounds, the debts of the hospital increase to a similar extent each year; and, finally, the government of the hospital, which is nominally representative, and which goes through the ceremony of election at the "annual meetings of the governors," is really an absolute despotism, intolerant, like all despotisms, of even the most temperate criticism: as Mr. Jodrell observes, in language at once terse and true, "the general meeting is a sham, the annual election is a sham, the responsibility of the governing body is a sham, and the results such as might be expected from a body which is elected practically by co-optation, and responsible virtually to nobody."* With these indications of the condition of the Metropolitan Free Hospital, and the character of its management, we earnestly commend them both to the serious consideration of its supporters, and no less earnestly do we ask the charity-giving public as a whole, to meditate on the evil effects exemplified not only in this hospital, but in hospitals generally, of giving money without the greater gift of personal superintendence of its application.

* Letter on the Metropolitan Free Hospital in the *Pall Mall Gazette* of Nov. 12th, 1873.

Contemporary Literature.

The Foreign Books noticed in the following sections are chiefly supplied by Messrs. Williams & Norgate, *Henrietta Street, Covent Garden*, and Mr. Nutt, 270, *Strand.*

THEOLOGY AND PHILOSOPHY.

NO one can deny the praise of sincerity to Prof. de Lagarde's brief but pregnant essay "On the Relation of the German State to Theology, Church, and Religion."[1] Although in part exclusively adapted for German readers, the remainder is of such general interest, and couched in a style of such unusual individuality, that we cannot refrain from giving a specimen of its contents. It deserves notice, that the outlines of the work were written down and obtained a limited circulation as long ago as 1859; the gravity of the late political crisis in Germany led to its republication with important additions. Let us first hear the author on the subject of Protestantism. "Protestantism is a historical development, which can only be rightly estimated from the study of the sixteenth, not from the public opinion of the latter half of the nineteenth century. There is no doubt from the writings of the Reformers and the formularies of the Lutheran as well as the Reformed Church, that Protestantism aimed at being, as we still call it, a Reformation, and that, therefore, it recognised the Catholic Church in essentials, and only put away abuses." "Science (if such an imposing expression is allowable) has advanced the assertion, that the Reformation had two principles, the formal and the material, *i.e.*, the religious authority of the Bible, and justification by faith in Christ." But both these principles were principles of controversy, not of dogmatics. The Reformers appealed to the Bible, as an authority equally recognised by their adversaries, in order to get rid of certain obnoxious doctrines, and justification by faith was only a mode of denying that grace could be obtained by such mechanical means as indulgences and almsgiving. But considered as principles neither the one nor the other were or could be consistently carried out. The one because a sincere appeal to the Bible would show that doctrines which the Reformers regarded as essential to Christianity were of later origin, *e.g.*, infant baptism, the keeping of Sunday, the abolition of the Law, the Trinity. And the other, because it would have involved the destruction of the scholastic theology, which except in isolated points the Reformers retained. "The strength of Protestantism consisted in its opposition to the dominant Church; since its recognition at the Peace of Westphalia, the last trace of this has vanished, the last pretext for existence been removed. . . . . What yet remains of it owes its existence not to an uninterrupted development from the time of

[1] "Ueber des verhältniss des deutschen Staates zu Theologie, Kirche und Religion." Von Paul de Lagarde. Göttingen: Dieterich.

Luther, but has been artificially produced, because people were conscious of incapacity for supplying the wants of the age. . . . . I roundly deny that Lessing, Goethe, Herder, Kant, Winkelmann, have been at all influenced in essentials by the Protestant system." And what is the Catholicism of modern times? "The Catholicism with which the Reformers struggled has been for more than four centuries dead, or if you prefer it, in course of dying. What is now called Catholicism is a new production, originated by Protestantism, but not by it alone; it has preserved the Catholic formulæ of dogma, but made essential alterations in several important points, by which it has exhibited its incompatibility with the new developments of history. The Vatican Council of 1870 is not at all an episode in the Catholic, but the closing act in the period of formation of the neo-Catholic Church. It bears the same relation to neo-Catholicism as the assembly of Nicæa to Catholicism. . . . . By the consolidation of the European States Catholicism became a negative instead of a positive idea," and the deadly enemy of modern civilization. The author next examines the foundation common to Catholicism and Protestantism. His conclusion is that of Strauss, "Christianity is for us entirely out of the question." This view is justified by a historical criticism of Christianity, which is sharply distinguished from that genial exposition of the laws of the spiritual life, which has received the name of "the Gospel." But Prof. de Lagarde does not look at religion merely through the spectacles of an antiquarian. Each nation, he thinks, has a special providential mission, and requires a special national religion. Impartial observers are agreed that the existing forms of religion are effete; how are we to provide one for Germany? Religions are born, not made. All that the State can do is to purify men's ideas of what religion is; all that the individual can do is to exhibit the Gospel in action. The State ought at once to abolish, or rather assign to the sects, the theological faculties in the universities, which are out of place in seminaries of science; and to substitute for them professorships of the study of religious phenomena. It ought also to encourage the natural growth of religion by promoting the ideal aspects of life, especially as ideality is now almost extinct in the rising generation of Germany. But the individual can do even more; he can exhibit the essential elements of the Gospel personified by Jesus in his own life and character. The essay rises at its close into a strain of unsought eloquence.

Conscientious considerations, and the recent works of Strauss and Lagarde, have led a young but not unknown professor at Basle, Dr. Overbeck, to publish an essay "On the Christian Character of the Current Theology."[3] In the most essential points he agrees with Lagarde, though he differs from him more or less in his view of the history of Christianity, and is not prepared to accept Lagarde's suggestions. His subject is the Christianity of the current theology, but he prefaces it with the inquiry whether theology has ever been

[3] "Ueber die Christlichkeit unserer heutigen Theologie." Streit und Friedensschrift von Franz Overbeck. Leipzig: Fritzsch.

really Christian, and whether the interests of knowledge and of faith have not always been diametrically opposed. No conviction is more essential to a religion than that of the falsehood of all other religions:—none is more completely destroyed by science. True, a professedly Christian theology arose at a very early period. This was only natural, considering the highly-refined form of culture which preceded Christianity, and which that religion could not hope to destroy. A compromise was the only alternative, but the theology in which this compromise issued was jealously watched and constantly suspected by the true believers. It is useless to distinguish between what is essential in Scripture, and what is not. The very idea of a life of Christ destroys the religious value of the record. Historical criticism at best will only result in a religion for scholars, as destitute of warmth and colour, as of influence on the masses. The author then examines the claims of the two great contending parties to be called Christian. He doubts whether there is any radical difference between them, either in Biblical criticism, or in their views of life. With regard to the party of Apologists (answering to our own "Christian Evidence Society"), the author remarks that the historical argument for Christianity, on which they lay so much stress, is the most rotten of all (except, indeed, that from natural history). The deeper thinkers of the school seem to have had a dim perception of this, *e.g.*, Pascal, who admits that there must be a strong desire for the truth of Christianity, if the historical argument is to be effectual. To excite such a desire, however, he appeals to ascetic views of life from which modern apologists would shrink, though these ascetic views are of the very essence of the Christian religion. In fact, the main difference between the two parties in German Protestantism is this, that the one has the shell, but not the kernel, the other neither shell nor kernel, neither the form nor the spirit of Christianity. The Apologists imagine that they can defend the orthodox doctrine by scientific, *i.e.*, irreligious, means; the Liberals that after it has been destroyed, they can rebuild it through criticism. The latter are fond of using Lessing's well-known phrase, "the religion of Christ." But Lessing was well aware (see fragment in "Werke," Bd. xi.) though he does not speak it out plainly, that to talk of the religion of Christ is practically to place oneself outside the pale of Christianity, because such a notion is based on the discovery of the true humanity of Christ, a discovery which, though sanctioned by criticism, stultifies the primitive ages of the Church. It is true that the Church also speaks of the "imitation of Christ," but the reference here is not so much to Christ's personal views, as to his tragic fate, and the ascetic ideal founded upon it. But what at once condemns the attempts of Liberals to pass themselves off as Christians is their view of the world, which is diametrically opposed to that of primitive Christianity. From the 4th century down to the Reformation nothing in the grand style has existed in the Church, which has not issued from or stood in some connexion with the cloister. And even before the first of these epochs, the opposition between the Christian principle, on the one hand, and the world and culture on the other, is as pronounced as anywhere in the ascertained history of Paul, not to say of Christ. If any further argument is needed, there is the systematic limitation of popular religious ceremonies in the early Church, which is not disproved by the reaction within the Catholic Church towards the Paganizing of Christianity. This can only be explained on the hypothesis that aversion to the world is the most vital part of Christianity. The author then proceeds to question the propriety of popularizing liberal theology. Important as this subject is, we are unable to give the reader even an idea of Dr. Overbeck's mode of treatment. Certainly if it is true of Germany, it is no less true of England, as the works noticed in these pages prove, that popular liberal theology suffers from artificialness and unreality. The next section deals with the relation of critical theology to positive Christianity and culture, which are shown to be under almost equal obligations to it. The office of criticism is to elicit historical facts; it is absolutely indifferent to the practical inferences which may be drawn from those facts. It is as much opposed to a volatilized Christianity as to an enervated culture. Dr. Overbeck's practical suggestions may be thus summed up. Christianity cannot be separated from an ascetic view of life. Such a view is equally repugnant to the Orthodox and the Liberals of the day. Both therefore have as good or as bad a right to call themselves Christians; neither party has any right to exclude the other from the National Church. But though the Liberal is to be unmolested for his rejection of the "creed outworn," he is not to disturb the minds of naïve believers, who will long form the majority of the congregations, and whose religious wants can only be satisfied by that very creed. The ordination oath must therefore be so framed as to guard the liberties of both parties. In the church the clergyman is to preach the doctrines of the formularies; out of church, he may give stronger meat to those who crave it, and speak and write without restraint. By thus legalizing the ancient distinction between the esoteric and the exoteric, the clergyman will be transformed from a mere teacher of a private theology into a genuine priest of religion. Space forbids us to give the criticism which these remarkable works well deserve. A few suggestions may however be ventured. Thus, in Professor de Lagarde's criticism of ecclesiastical Christianity, we regret his extreme depreciation of Paul. The difference, both in form and content, between the dogmatic system of Paul, and the "good tidings" of Jesus, is undeniable, but this ought not to have blinded the critic to the points of contact between Paul and Jesus, nor to the merits of the immortal genius through whom the Gospel, however adulterated, became an universal religion. A similar remark applies to Professor Lagarde's criticism of the early Christian writers. We are also disposed to differ from him in our estimate of Protestantism. The Catholic doctrines, left by the Reformers, seem to interfere now with the sincerity of a Christian's devotions, just as penance and indulgences did in the times of the Reformers. They are also too often inconsistent with the original documents of the Christian religion; and on both grounds we seem to be justified in rejecting them, and yet retaining the name of Protestant. Dr.

Overbeck, on the other hand, seems to us to be fairer to Paul than Professor Lagarde, but more unfair to Jesus. He seems, if we rightly understand him, to ignore the distinction between the asceticism of Jesus, and that of A'Kempis or St. Francis. The latter condemn the world as radically evil; the former condemns the present world, but anticipates its sudden regeneration, Satan being cast out within a few years or months. But both Jesus and the modern philanthropists aim at a kingdom of God upon earth. Orthodox and Liberals are fundamentally at one in cherishing this ideal; may they not both be distinguished as followers of Jesus—as Christians? We must also differ from Dr. Overbeck on practical points. His suggestion for the relief of the clergy seems only applicable to places where modern ideas have either not penetrated at all, or to a very limited extent. Fancy an English clergyman adopting it in a manufacturing town! A moderate use of "accommodation" may be justifiable, but Teutonic morality forbids its development into the "economy" apparently advocated by Dr. Overbeck. It is an almost hopeless puzzle; and even Professor Lagarde, with his admirable straightforwardness, is not much more successful in solving it. His language about preparing for a new religion, seems open to misapprehension. Does he wish for a new "German" religion distinct from the "Evangelical?" Or does he merely recommend the study of religious phenomena as a means of purifying men's minds from effete forms of thought? Probably he wishes us to return to the Gospel, purified of its temporary accretions; but this is not clearly expressed.

A natural transition leads us to Mr. Leslie Stephen's[3] clear-sighted "Essays on Freethinking and Plainspeaking," which have already most of them appeared in *Fraser* and the *Fortnightly*. The work is the outcome, not only of meditation, but of practical experience, and does not admit of such detailed criticism as the works of Profs. Lagarde and Overbeck. It has points of contact with both. Like the latter, Mr. Stephen considers Christianity inseparable from a pessimistic view of the world; like the former, he anticipates a new religion, the "path-finder" of which, however (to use an expression of Prof. Lagarde), is not so much historical criticism as the new view of the world generated by Darwinism. The most conclusive of his essays seems to us to be the first, against the position of the Broad Church clergy. Those who take a different view of the genesis of belief and of the essence of Christianity may be disposed to take a somewhat different view of the practical course to be adopted by the freethinking laity. Some pages of the work may seem slightly unsympathetic in tone, but the Essay on Darwinism and Divinity proves that Mr. Stephen fully appreciates the ennobling instincts of which some of the old dogmas are the envelopes.

Mr. W. W. Smyth[4] is of opinion that the doctrine of Evolution

---

[3] "Essays on Freethinking and Plainspeaking." By Leslie Stephen. Longmans.

[4] "The Bible and the Doctrine of Evolution." By William Woods Smyth. H. K. Lewis, Gower-street.

may be shown to be in harmony with the Bible, "not by accommodating each to the other, but by accepting both in their simplest and most manifest sense" (Preface). He tells us himself that "little argument has been used, but many things stated in a variety of ways," and that he hopes his work may serve as "stepping-stones." His main thought seems to be that, so far as the teaching of the Bible and the philosophic interpretation of Science cover the same ground—for instance in the cosmogony—there is no discrepancy between them; that both where the Bible comes into contact with Science and where it does not, the principle of Evolution reigns; and that this creates a strong presumption that what the Bible says on subjects beyond the ken of science is true. This may or may not be sound reasoning. Mr. Smyth may or may not have properly understood Mr. Herbert Spencer or Mr. Darwin; as theological critics, we are chiefly concerned with the other class of facts on which he builds, those which depend on the literary criticism of the Bible. Let us do him the justice to admit that he has observed at least two facts of Biblical theology which are generally denied by orthodox writers. We refer first to the expressions in Genesis i., in which the genesis of vegetables and fish is ascribed to the inherent virtue of earth and water, respectively. But Mr. Smyth has failed to observe that these expressions are derived, like several other features of the narrative, from an original myth of heathen complexion, and are qualified for the benefit of Jewish theists by the emphatic dictum in the first verse, and by the expression "after his kind," which certainly points in the direction of separate creations. But how can any thinker accept such a story as in "complete congruity" with the teachings of philosophy or science? The other point on which Mr. Smyth is right is this, "that creation out of nothing and action at a distance are myths (?) which have no foundation in scripture or science whatsoever" (p. 131). But two successful hits are not enough to make up for the blunders with which the book is literally strewed; above all, for the nonsense about Preadamites (p. 177), about the days of Genesis i. and ii. (p. 163), about the renewing powers of the patriarchs (p. 298), and about the prophetic character of the record of the Deluge (p. 281), &c. In one place he even says, "the scientific interpretation of the Bible shows the 'higher critics' to be always wrong" (p. 180), a passage which proves at least that the author lays no claim to the Christian virtue of humility.

An attempt of a considerably higher value in the same direction is made by Mr. G. Henslow,[1] who obtained one of the Actonian prizes for the year 1872. It is important to remember the origin of the work, as it accounts for a slight timidity of expression which does not really detract from its usefulness. Apologetic theology has for one of its functions that of correcting the received religious views in accordance with the best philosophy of the time; if it is to accomplish

[1] "The Theory of Evolution of Living Things, and the Application of the Principles of Evolution to Religion, etc." By the Rev. G. Henslow, M.A., F.L.S., F.G.S. Macmillan and Co.

its end it must not fly too violently in the face of the notions it has to correct. Whenever an outspoken expression of opinion is necessary, Mr. Henslow is not backward to deliver it, and it is a sign of the times that one of the lecturers at the Victoria Institute should have given up the traditional idea of creation, which even Schleiermacher thought almost essential to Christianity. The first part of the essay is devoted to the exposition of the evidence for evolution; the second considers its relations to religion. From the latter we learn that the author does not "at present see any evidence for believing in a gradual development of man from the lower animals by ordinary natural laws; that is, without some special interference, or, if it be preferred, some exceptional conditions which have thereby separated him from all other creatures," &c. (p. 108). An interesting chapter is devoted to the evidence of the wisdom and beneficence of the Creator. The error of the Bridgewater Treatises consisted in adducing merely relative evidence of this. "An Ichneumon fly, had it reasoning powers, might easily conclude that caterpillars were beneficently designed for its use, as being the place in which it should lay its eggs. On the other hand, the caterpillar would have a very different view." The essayist prefers to trace such evidence in creation as a whole; or rather, in those great principles which govern the evolution and development of all beings in the world. We must recognise the fact that the wisdom of God in nature is synonymous with the will of God. This may seem, he remarks, "very like cutting the Gordian knot, but when once we get beyond positive evidence, and try to investigate causes and motives, we are attempting to escape beyond the confines of the human intellect" (p. 104). With regard to the mixture of good and evil in the world, the author maintains that it is not a "fatal" result of undirected natural forces, but designed in its ultimate bearings to surround man with "inideal" circumstances, and so render his life on earth probationary. This principle of Inideality, on which the author lays great stress, is illustrated by two examples,—rudimentary organs, and imperfect conditions of existence, neither of which can be accounted for except by evolution. It may perhaps be objected by some readers that too small a place is given to the goodness and beneficence of the Creator. But so little had been said on physical evils by previous writers on Natural Theology, that the author deemed it necessary to advert to them in greater detail, and to show that they could be accounted for as conducive to the probationary condition of man.

Mr. Samuel Smiles has chosen a fine subject for his new book,* the tragic story of the Huguenots (why add *in France?*) after the revocation of the Edict of Nantes. He has gone conscientiously to the best published sources, and succeeded in producing a work which will be interesting to all students and admirers of that subtle compound of opposites—the French character, and which fills, for the present at any rate, a gap in English literature, the existence of which was not quite creditable to our national Protestantism. It may be asserted,

* "The Huguenots in France after the Revocation of the Edict of Nantes, with a Visit to the Country of the Vaudois." By Samuel Smiles. Strahan and Co.

without fear of contradiction, that nobler episodes than the insurrection of the Camisards, and the reconstitution of the Protestant Church through the almost superhuman labours of Antoine Court, cannot be found in any period of ecclesiastical history. But Mr. Smiles will, we think, be the first to admit that his work has but a provisional value. Protestantism in France demands a broader and more critical treatment, and cannot be properly understood from a collection of episodes. It is pleasing to notice that the author does full justice to the noble efforts of Voltaire in behalf of the Huguenots Calas and Sirven, though he adds, with an implication of questionable morality, that "David, the judge who had first condemned Calas went insane, and died in a madhouse." The utility of the volume would have been increased, had the author given some of the facts relative to the historical antecedents of the recent discussions in Paris, which for ability and width of range, may probably take the precedence of all other councils and synods from the Nicene to the Vatican. It is hardly fair of the author to refer for "the best account of the proceedings" to the able but onesided essay in *Blackwood's Magazine* for January. He ought at least to have balanced it by the calm, historical sketch by M. Etienne Coquerel, in the *Theological Review* for October, 1872. The latter part of the book is made up (literally) by a loosely written account of a visit to the country of the Vaudois, which first appeared in "Good Words," and is every way inferior to the portion on the Huguenots.

The author of "A Dominican Artist," and other graceful works of Catholic religious history, has given us an equally graceful sketch of "The Revival of Priestly Life in the Seventeenth Century in France."[7] Putting aside all questions as to the healthiness of the particular form of religion, we gladly and fully admit the moral elevation and historical and psychological instruction to be gained from this volume. The chief figures on the canvas are Charles de Condren and Cardinal de Bérulle, the founders of the Oratorians, St. Vincent de Paul and the Lazarists, Jean Jacques Olier and the Seminarists of St. Sulpice.

Certainly there is something more attractive, as the biographer truly remarks, in the winning human kindness of St. François de Sales and St. Vincent de Paul, but the sterner character and practical wisdom of De Condren, was no less valuable as a complement to the milder qualities of his friends. All these orders—the Oratorians, the Lazarists, and the Sulpicians—did good service to the Gallican church; the first in the furtherance of the highest objects of the priesthood, not forgetting the culture of the intellect in a Christian spirit; the second, in the evangelization of the poor, especially the rural poor, and the raising of the tone of the clergy; the third, in the direct training of priests. But there is a foresight in the wide conception of the Oratorian body which is akin to genius, and a liberality which deserves recognition, whatever opinion be held as to the carrying out

---

[7] "The Revival of Priestly Life in the Seventeenth Century in France." A sketch by the author of "A Dominican Artist," &c. Rivingtons.

of their motto, that knowledge is to be sought "Non tam circa scientiam quam circa usum scientiæ." A fine saying is told of a devout woman on her deathbed: "J'adore tout ce que Dieu est . . . Je me sépare de l'être présent, et me retire dans l'être inconnu de Dieu." (P. 77.)

The fame of Ludwig Häusser rests upon his lectures, which are said to have produced a powerful impression in Germany. Those here published[1] form part of a course on the history of the three centuries 1571—1789, which Häusser used to deliver at Heidelberg in the winter months. It is important to bear this in mind, for it shows that Häusser's interests were more political than theological, and excuses a certain superficiality in his treatment of the religious aspect of his subject. The method of editing which Dr. Oncken intended to adopt was the same which he applied to Häusser's lectures on the French Revolution; and which then met with general approval. This was to collate as many notes as possible of hearers of the lectures and then to fill in the details from Häusser's manuscripts. Unfortunately Dr. Oncken's appeal for notes of the lectures on the Reformation was unresponded to; added to which, he found but little bearing upon the subject among his friend's papers, so that he was "compelled to have independent recourse to the literature referred to, to a far greater extent than was necessary in the former case." (Preface.) This is not quite satisfactory, but as the lectures do not lay claim to originality, and Dr. Oncken is a warm friend of the author, it is not likely that any serious misrepresentation has occurred. The result is what we should hardly have expected from a German professor, a popular work of a high class, but still distinctly popular. Those who go to these lectures expecting to receive an impulse to original inquiry, such as was so powerfully given by Niebuhr's lectures on the History of Rome, will be disappointed. But the ordinary reader will be so much the more grateful for a book which unites the *abandon* of personal teaching with the accuracy of a work based on profound study. The author is a patriotic German; yet he devotes a large share of attention to the history of the Reformation in France and England. He is an enthusiastic Protestant, yet he is as fair to the character of Charles IX. as to that of Coligny, as considerate to Queen Mary as to the Lord Protector Oliver. The translation is in idiomatic English, and, so far as we have compared it with the original, is substantially accurate: a great advance upon those hybrid German-English works with which the theological market is inundated. It is, perhaps, worth mentioning that the first volume of Von Sybel's *Historische Zeitschrift* contains a remarkable paper by Häusser, exposing the misstatements of Lord Macaulay's essay on Frederick.

Mr. A. D. Crake[2] has produced a sketch of Church history for the

---

[1] "The Period of the Reformation, 1517 to 1648." By Ludwig Häusser. Edited by Wilhelm Oncken, &c. Translated by Mrs. G. Sturge. In two volumes. Strahan and Co.

[2] "History of the Church under the Roman Empire, A.D. 30—476." By the Rev. A. D. Crake, B.A. Rivingtons.

general reader, based on some original reading, and on the works of Fleury, Mosheim, Gibbon, Bingham, Professor Bright, and Canon Robertson. The flowing style will recommend it to many readers, but will not compensate for the want of criticism and of any but the most ordinary scholarship. Mr. Craise would have done well to work carefully through such a book as the "Lehrbuch der Kirchengeschichte für Studierende," by Professor Kraus (a moderate Roman Catholic), which from its orthodoxy and ample collection of references would have been invaluable to him in his present stage.

The painful subject[10] of the religious history of Ireland is treated by Mr. Godkin with judicial impartiality, relieved by a profound sense of humour. There is no attempt to palliate the misgovernment of the English, though it is fully admitted that the fault was not all on one side. The only weak part of this most enjoyable work is the introductory chapters, in which are many strange things to a philologist or historical critic. Mr. Godkin is severely condemnatory of the "Root and Branch" system defended by Messrs. Carlyle and Froude.

Dr. Eitel's[11] brief but accurate description of Buddhism has deservedly reached a second edition. We commend his comparison of the lives of Buddha and Christ to theologians, who, like Canon Westcott, suppose that Orientals may be converted by the "facts" of Christianity without its dogmas.

Mr. J. M. Capes[12] has given us a lively picture of the "Tract" movement from the undergraduate side, and of the conversion of one who was never really converted.

A fourth edition of the "Sketch of the Character of Jesus,"[13] by Dr. Schenkel, the well-known eloquent and accomplished Heidelberg professor and leader of German Liberal Protestants, has just appeared. The author claims with justice to have made the first published attempt at an historical sketch of Jesus,—not of the life, but the personality or character. The muses of poetry and history it has been well said are allied and yet distinct, or, as Novalis puts it, in words adopted for a motto by Dr. Schenkel, the history of Christ is as much a poem as a history. Hence the conception of the "Characterbild Jesu" is somewhat different from that of Renan's "Vie de Jésus," and even of Keim's "Geschichte Jesu von Nazara." Dr. Schenkel's work is not original; he builds on the researches of others, especially of his colleague, Dr. Holtzmann, but is in the best sense of the word popular. A certain political tinge, which injured it in some circles of the "Fatherland," will only add to its interest among ourselves. The

---

[10] "The Religious History of Ireland, Primitive, Papal, and Protestant." By James Godkin. Henry S. King & Co.

[11] "Buddhism: its Historical, Theoretical, and Popular Aspects." By Ernest J. Eitel, M.A., Ph.D. Second Edition. Trübner.

[12] "To Rome and Back." By the Rev. J. M. Capes, M.A. Smith, Elder and Co.

[13] "Das Characterbild Jesu." Von Dr. Daniel Schenkel. Vierte verm. u. verb. Auflage. Wiesbaden: Kreidel.

fourth edition claims to be not only enlarged, but thoroughly re-written. It would require a more minute examination than we can at present give to tell how far this is the case; but several new chapters have been added, and reference has been made to the latest literature, with the important exception however of Sir R. Hanson's Life of Jesus. It is really strange, and an evidence of the provincialism of German scholars, that Dr. Schenkel should have failed to read the able and thorough review of this work (the only independent English contribution to the subject) by Prof. Weizsäcker in the *Academy*, (vol. ii. pp. 221, etc., 241, etc.).

Of works like the present, written in a lucid, popular style, but not with popular superficiality, we may say with Mr. Dixon in his thoughtful little essay,[14] "though the young thinkers may not adopt [its] conclusions, they will be wiser men by the acquaintance of the author." A readable translation of substantial accuracy, from the third German edition, was published by Messrs. Longman in 1869, which we recommend to our readers.

In recent popular theology, one of our most important books, in spite of its unpretending exterior, is Mr. Philip Wicksteed's excellent translation of Dr. Oort's "Bible for Young People."[15] How it would have rejoiced Goethe, whose early partiality for Genesis is well-known, and who has given us in a few pages perhaps the best abstract of that book, incomplete as it is, which we possess, to see such delicate sympathy with the beautiful legends of the Israelites, coupled with such genuine but lightly-worn learning, and uncompromising loyalty to the moral sense of our own times! Yet we are not sure that even the young Goethe would have succeeded in digesting all the contents of this book, and we cannot help wishing for an abridged edition, containing only the stories and the moral lessons, for the benefit of children. True, that it is never too soon to cultivate a child's sense of truth, but simple as the criticism is which is here applied to the Hebrew legends, it is perhaps too profound for those who have not yet learned historical perspective, and developed a feeling for literature. An English child, at any rate, ought, we think, to have sucked the marrow out of such books as Mr. Matthew Arnold's edition of the Later Isaiah, and Freeman's Child's History of England, before he can be expected to receive a healthy stimulus from such a volume as this. There are some sensible remarks to the same purport on p. 13 of the author's preface. It would be out of place to enter into a criticism of details. The reputation of Oort, and still more of Kuenen, to whom the work was submitted for revision, is a sufficient guarantee of accuracy, so far as accuracy is obtainable in Oriental archæology. Its point of view is, of course, that of the higher Rationalism, which refuses to treat the Bible as different in kind from other sacred books,

---

[14] "The Right Honourable W. E. Gladstone and Dr. Strauss." By J. M. Dixon. Hull: Fisher, Walker and Brown.

[15] "The Bible for Young People." By Dr. H. Oort, and Dr. T. Hooykaas, with the assistance of Dr. A. Kuenen. Vol. I. Prepared by Dr. H. Oort. Authorized Translation. Williams and Norgate.

or to extenuate the moral defects inseparable probably from the one-sided character of Hebrew culture. To be complete, it should perhaps be followed by a sketch of the development of the other great religions, with an account of their sacred books, in the same style and for the same class of readers.

Mr. Herbert Spencer's "Sociological Tables," of which a section[16] relating to England has already been published, promise to be a valuable contribution to the study of the history of social progress. Their purpose cannot be better described than in Mr. Spencer's own words in his Provisional Preface:—

"In preparation for the Principles of Sociology, requiring as bases of induction large accumulations of data, fitly arranged for comparison, I some five years ago, commenced by proxy, the collection and organization of facts presented by societies of different types, past and present: being fortunate enough to secure the services of gentlemen competent to carry on the process in the way I wished. Though this classified compilation of materials was entered upon solely to facilitate my own work, yet, after having brought the mode of classification to a satisfactory form, and after having had some of the tables filled up, I decided to have the undertaking executed with a view to publication: the facts collected and arranged for easy reference and convenient study of their relations, being so presented apart from hypotheses, as to aid all students of social science in testing such conclusions as they have drawn and in drawing others. The work consists of three large divisions. Each comprises a set of tables exhibiting the facts as abstracted and classified, and a mass of quotations and abridged extracts, otherwise classified, on which the statements contained in the tables are based. The condensed statements, arranged after a uniform manner, give in each table or succession of tables, the phenomena of all orders which each society presents—constitute an account of its morphology, its physiology, and (if a society having known a history) its development. On the other hand, the collected extracts, serving as authorities for the statements in the tables, are (or rather will be when the work is complete) classified primarily according to the kinds of phenomena to which they refer, and secondarily, to the societies exhibiting these phenomena; so that each kind of phenomena, as it is displayed in all societies, may be separately studied with convenience."

Thus it will be seen that the Tables themselves together with the corroborative matter furnished by the classified extracts go far to establish a sort of *Historia Naturalis* such as Bacon desiderated as the foundation of social inquiry. For the arrangement of the Tables, it appears that Mr. Spencer himself is responsible, but for their contents and for the collection of the materials on which they are based he is indebted to the labours of his assistants. That these labours have not been slight may be inferred from the fact that the social phenomena of the English race from the earliest times down almost to the present day are condensed into seven Tables, while the extracts on which the

---

[16] "Descriptive Sociology, or Groups of Sociological Facts," classified and arranged by Herbert Spencer. English, compiled and abstracted by James Collier. London: Williams and Norgate, 1873.

statements in the tables are based occupy a printed space at least five times as great, and Mr. Spencer assures us that even these are only a selection from the mass of materials gathered together for the purpose. In a design so vast it is as easy as it would be superfluous to discover faults of detail; indeed, Mr. Spencer himself admits that ideal perfection of arrangement has occasionally been sacrificed to typographical convenience, but in such a case, "well begun is half-done," and if the outline be firmly and accurately traced the rectification in detail may well be left to future inquirers. There can be no doubt that the arrangement of the Tables is excellent; by reading the columns vertically we can trace the gradual growth and increasing complexity of the various parts into which the social organism is divided; while, by reading horizontally across the tables we gain a conspectus of the social phenomena simultaneously presenting themselves at the successive critical epochs of English history, and that this arrangement should be successfully preserved throughout such a vast aggregation of heterogeneous data is in itself no slight proof of the skill with which the outline has been devised. We have said that criticism of detail is out of place; but the scheme, however praiseworthy its conception, and, however valuable its results, is open to one or two general objections which can scarcely be entirely overcome. In the first place it may be said, not without considerable truth, that the phenomena here presented as sociological facts are so various and heterogeneous, that to exhibit them in a statistical or even a tabular form, is to assume a great deal that stands in urgent need of verification and proof; even the scheme of arrangement in which they are exhibited is in itself an assumption which can only be justified by an independent examination of the data which it presents. We all know how a skilful advocate can so marshal the facts at his command as to support a foregone conclusion, and while we are far from attributing any such purpose to a thinker so cautious and positive as Mr Spencer, yet it is obvious that his whole hypothesis of a Social Organism with its concrete metaphors borrowed from Biology, is a conception not yet placed beyond the reach of dialectical debate. It is therefore, perhaps too much to say that the facts collected and arranged in these tables are presented "apart from hypotheses," though it is true, no doubt, that independent inquirers can use the data furnished in testing their own conclusions. In the second place, the problem of arranging the almost infinite phenomena of a society so highly organized as that of England in the later stages of its development is one which is well-nigh insoluble from its overwhelming complexity. The phenomena of a primitive or barbaric society are simple and easy of interpretation: those of a progressive society, especially in its later stages, are of infinite variety and complexity, and can scarcely be tabulated rightly until they are thoroughly interpreted and understood. While doing full justice to the industry and ability with which Mr. Collier, Mr. Spencer's assistant in the tables before us, has accomplished his task, we cannot resist the conclusion that he has been far more successful in the collection and arrangement of the earlier and comparatively simple data with which he has had to deal than with those of a later date and a more complex character. It is impossible to test in detail the execution of so heterogeneous a work, but in regard to the earlier portion we may note that Mr. Tylor, no mean authority in such a case, has expressed his approval of the skill and industry with which the data relating to his own field of inquiry have been collected and arranged. When, however, we come to the later stages of English society, and to its complex literary and æsthetic productions we cannot think Mr. Collier has adequately conceived the magnitude of the task required of him. It is one thing to determine the facts of primitive society, and the data may be drawn from any accessible source; but the case is altogether altered when we have to deal with the problems of literary and artistic development; here the distinction between fact and opinion, between data and hypothesis almost vanishes, and it is only given to the highest criticism to disengage the primary facts and to present them as data to the social philosopher. Hence in collecting his data on such points, Mr. Collier should have trusted only to the best and most widely recognised authorities; whereas we find him putting as much trust in ephemeral and anonymous literature, the authority and credentials of which it is impossible to verify or to test, as in the judgments of those who are recognised as masters in their art. Here it is not his execution but his method which is at fault; his industry is conspicuous throughout; but whereas in the earlier part of his compilation his work is effective and complete, in the latter part it is a conspicuous failure from an inadequate conception of the problem to be solved. It matters not what authority is given for the mode in which the ancient Britons buried their dead, provided the statement can be verified and tested; but it matters a great deal what authority is given for an estimate of the literature of the last century, or of the poetry of the present day; the former is a fact which can be variously interpreted but cannot, if properly attested, be denied; the latter is at best but an opinion, the value of which can only depend on the estimate we form of the authority of the person by whom it is uttered. Data thus loosely determined can only mislead when presented in a tabular form; and for this reason we are inclined to consider the earlier tables, which rest on less questionable data, as far more valuable than the latter. Notwithstanding the serious defects we have pointed out, however, there can be little doubt that in the skilful arrangement of the tables, and in superintending their careful compilation, Mr. Spencer has conferred a great benefit on all students of social phenomena.

Whatever Mr. G. H. Lewes writes on philosophical subjects is deserving of the most respectful attention; for he has shown in his "History of Philosophy" a genuine interest in philosophical inquiry, while his researches in Biology attest his familiarity with the methods of scientific investigation. His new work, "Problems of Life and Mind,"[17] of which as yet only an instalment has been published, will

[17] "Problems of Life and Mind." By George Henry Lewes. First Series. The Foundations of a Creed. Vol. I. London: Trübner and Co.

surprise many who are familiar with the "History of Philosophy;" for its first aspect is that of a determined attempt to rehabilitate much that the Positive Philosophy was supposed to have banished for ever under the name of Metaphysics. But on a closer inspection it becomes manifest that the contrast is due not so much to a change as to an extension of view. Mr. Lewes does not propose to apply to the problems now presented for solution any other method than that which science recognises in its more special and concrete inquiries, but he maintains that what he boldly, but justly, calls the Empirical Method, must be applied, and can be applied with success, to the problems which all sciences present for solution, but none pretend to solve. What Comte rejected as Metaphysics Mr. Lewes would discard as "Metempirics," while he restores to Metaphysics its old meaning of the "general laws of Being," and maintains that in this sense it deals with problems which are as real and as capable of definite solution as are those of any other science. The distinction is important and instructive; for whereas Comte's criterion tends arbitrarily to divide lines of inquiry which are equally legitimate if scientifically pursued, that of Mr. Lewes, if applicable at all, is equally applicable in all parts of the field of inquiry, and will discriminate methods which are legitimate from those which are not. The term "Metaphysics" is now so much discredited by the loose and ambiguous use of it sanctioned by Comte and his followers, that we are thankful to Mr. Lewes for giving us the term "Metempiric," which can start on its career unencumbered with misleading associations; this is no doubt an advantage, but the difficulty still remains that both Comte and Mr. Lewes are applying to their opponents a criterion which in reality begs the whole question in dispute. We may tell the so-called Metempiricist that he has failed to prove his conclusion, but we fail to shake his conviction so long as our canons of proof are framed so as to exclude his own; until we stand on a common ground discussion is useless between us; and as he at least professes to start from principles common to us both, it is incumbent on us to show in each particular case at what point and for what reason we cease to follow him; and at this point we must either agree with him or he with us, or all argument is at an end. Thus the whole question turns, as Mr. Lewes would doubtless admit, on the possession of a common criterion of proof. Mr. Lewes proposes the Empirical criterion, and though he reserves the discussion of the tests of certitude for a subsequent volume, and may therefore have arguments to adduce which his opponents would be unable to refute, it is obvious that, so far as he has hitherto gone, he is proposing a criterion which is open to attack on strictly scientific grounds. The empirical theory of knowledge, even in the modified and guarded form in which Mr. Lewes presents it, and the theory of "Reasoned Realism" on which it is based, cannot be said to be placed beyond the reach of discussion and debate; but it is only when it is regarded as axiomatic that we can legitimately brand the theories of opponents who reject its criterion as metempirical figments. We cordially sympathize with Mr. Lewes's chivalrous endeavour to rescue Metaphysics from the undeserved contempt into which it has fallen, and we wish we could believe that he had succeeded in placing Empirical Metaphysics on a foundation from which even his opponents would be unable to dislodge it; but we confess that we rose from the study of his work with somewhat of the disappointment which Socrates is related to have felt at the teaching of Anaxagoras. To extend the scientific method to the study of Metaphysics is a tempting programme, nor can we determine from the mere fragment before us whether the plan is likely to be successfully fulfilled; but after all it is a reversal of the perhaps inevitable order; for till Metaphysics has given its sanction to the conceptions with which Science deals we never can be quite sure that the scientific method is itself legitimate. If, on the other hand, it be maintained that the method of science is to be sanctioned by a rational Psychology, it is precisely at this point that the assault of opponents is most difficult to meet and repel. That Mr. Lewes has not overlooked the difficulty here pointed out is evident from his taking as his motto the pregnant sentence of Stuart Mill—"England's thinkers are again beginning to see what they had only temporarily forgotten, that the difficulties of Metaphysics lie at the root of all Science; that those difficulties can only be quieted by being resolved; and that until they are resolved, positively whenever possible, but at any rate negatively, we are never assured that any knowledge, even physical, stands on solid foundations"—and we are far from saying that he does not see his way to an ultimate solution. For this reason we shall look for his succeeding volumes with great interest—indeed it is almost an injustice to criticise his general theory in its present development. It is almost needless to say that, putting aside the general theory, the whole volume is full of the most suggestive speculation presented in the happiest manner: if the problem of philosophy be as far from solution as ever, the search has revealed many treasures by the way, and we cordially commend the work to all who are interested in philosophical speculation. Though directly affiliated to the system of Mr. Herbert Spencer, as the author gratefully acknowledges, the speculations of Mr. Lewes have a stamp and flavour of their own. All who are interested in the problems and methods of scientific inquiry should study and ponder the portion of the work entitled "The Limitations of Knowledge." The chapter on "Ideal Constructions in Science" is both novel and profound, and we know not where the "Use and Abuse of Hypotheses" has been more adequately treated than in the chapter bearing that title; the account of Demonstrations and Axioms is a real and solid contribution to the controversy on this much-debated topic; and the last chapter on the "Place of Sentiment in Philosophy" is as suggestive a piece of writing as we have met with in modern philosophical literature. We cannot acquit Mr. Lewes of a relapse into "Metempirics" in his use of the term "Unknowable" as a positive conception; the "Unknowable" is a region whose hither boundary is always receding before the advance of positive knowledge: it is a legitimate term in the speculations of those who, like Mr. Herbert Spencer, would posit the existence of ranges of Being behind phenomena with which the mind can never come into contact, but as the object of Mr. Lewes's endeavour is to demonstrate the non-existence of such a region, the "Unknowable" with him becomes simply the "Unknown," and is not entitled to a separate name. In this sense nothing is unknowable save that which is expressed in terms which are mutually destructive, and it seems to us an illegitimate restriction of the range of scientific inquiry to treat any problem as insoluble simply because we have not yet the data necessary for its solution. The Mechanical Equivalent of Thought, or the Calculus of Mental Operations, are expressions which indicate problems scientifically legitimate, though at present they are wholly incapable of solution; to call them unknowable is either to erect simple ignorance into a necessary limitation of knowledge, or to use a term which can scarcely fail to mislead. We may require that all fresh problems shall be presented for solution in terms which science can accept, but we can never set an absolute limit to the problems which under these conditions may be attempted. We are not without hopes that in his subsequent volumes Mr. Lewes will be found to have anticipated and removed many of the difficulties which we have ventured to suggest; and the commencement of his undertaking is so instructive that it may well be that its conclusion will be even more satisfactory. We shall gladly welcome the continuation of a work which cannot fail to interest all serious students.

Professor Bain has collected into a volume "The Minor Works of George Grote,"[16] and prefaced them by a critical account of his writings and speeches. Copious analyses are given of Grote's speeches in Parliament, and one of his political pamphlets on the "Essentials of Parliamentary Reform," published in 1831, is reprinted at length. The other writings here reprinted are the product chiefly of Grote's historical and philosophical studies, and have great interest as indicating the course of the author's reflections, and exhibiting the seeds which bore such splendid and abundant fruit in his greater works. The pamphlet on Plato's Timaeus is well known to students of ancient philosophy, but as it has, we believe, been long out of print, and was never extensively circulated, Professor Bain has done very wisely in including it in the present volume. The review of Niebuhr's "Greek Heroic Stories," which was published in this *Review* in 1843, gains considerable interest when read in the light of the fuller discussion of the same subject, in two celebrated chapters of the "History of Greece," and it is worthy of note, that the remarkable illustration of the normal growth of a myth in modern times, furnished by Goethe's story of the Florentine amour of Lord Byron, is given in the earlier essay. Grote's keen and sustained interest in metaphysical speculation, is attested by several valuable papers, of which not the least remarkable is the well known review of his friend Stuart Mill's "Examination of Sir W. Hamilton's Philosophy;" while the activity and freshness of his mind to the last is shown in some very acute remarks,

[16] "The Minor Works of George Grote, with Critical Remarks on his Intellectual Character, Writings, and Speeches." By Alexander Bain. London: John Murray.

written in 1871, when his last illness was upon him, on M. Taine's work, "De L'Intelligence." The editor has prefaced his selection from Grote's writings with an Introduction, containing long abstracts and summaries of the author's principal speeches and works, interspersed with critical remarks, not very adequate or profound: the summaries are too long, the criticism is too slight, and too exclusively from an identical point of view, and the style is not attractive. Take, for example, the following extract from the account of Mr. Grote's reading of the Posterior Analytics of Aristotle:—

"Mr. Grote follows this treatise through its numerous windings and repetitions, and succeeds in making plain the author's drift, even when he is crude and inconsistent. There is some confusion of thought in applying the syllogistic designation, the middle term, to intermediate links in physical cause and effect, and the celebrated four causes are brought in to explain the meanings of knowledge. Generally speaking, Aristotle has a good grasp of the main conditions of demonstration: he is less steady, but still very knowing, in the niceties of definition. From our present logical point of view we can see distinctly what he is aiming at and where he misses, and the interest of the work consists in tracing the struggles of an original mind."

This is ludicrous and grotesque, nor can we believe Grote would have sanctioned such a style of criticism. One little mystery and misconception is cleared up in the present volume. It has lately been stated, that Grote was the author of a now forgotten work, entitled, "Analysis of the Influence of Natural Religion on the Temporal Happiness of Mankind, by Philip Beauchamp," and interest in the work has been somewhat revived, by references to it in Mill's "Autobiography," though the secret of its authorship is not there revealed. It appears that Grote's share in the work was confined to its arrangement for publication, and that the real author was Jeremy Bentham, who was in the habit of confiding many of his manuscripts to his younger friends, with a view to their publication. The original papers in Bentham's handwriting are still extant, and in the possession of Mrs. Grote.

The indefatigable Professor Bain has contributed to the International Scientific Series a small treatise on "Mind and Body" and the theories of their relation."[1] It will be found a useful handbook to those who are content or obliged to study philosophy in handbooks. But the use of handbooks has its limits, and these are perhaps reached when it is found possible to give a history of theories of the soul from the earliest times in less than sixty widely printed pages, of which the Pre-Socratic philosophers occupy barely one. There are not wanting indications that psychology in England is about to take a new departure: the reviving interest in Kant, and the gradual recognition of his true relation to Hume and the earlier Sensationalists, the speculations of Mr. Herbert Spencer, and the new ground already partially broken by Mr. G. H. Lewes in the work

---

[1] "Mind and Body. The Theories of their Relation." By Alexander Bain, LL.D. Professor of Logic in the University of Aberdeen. London: Henry S. King and Co.

noticed above, all seem to point in their various ways to a coming abandonment of the old standpoint of Empirical Dualism and the resumption of some form of Monism still in a sense Empirical, in which the purely Empirical and purely *à priori* hypotheses will meet in a new synthesis. If this be so a revolution in psychology is imminent, and treatises which, like the present, are based in the main on the old Empirical hypothesis will gradually become obsolete. Meanwhile, however, and probably for a long time, the treatise of Professor Bain will be found valuable and instructive by those for whom it was probably intended—viz., candidates for competitive examinations.

Mr. Abbott, of Trinity College, Dublin, gives a new translation of "Kant's Theory of Ethics,"[30] consisting of the whole of the "*Grundlegung zur Metaphysik der Sitten,*" and select portions of the "*Kritik der Praktischen Vernunft,*" and of the "*Philosophische Religionslehre.*" He has been induced to undertake the translation by experience of the unsatisfactory character of the work of Mr. Semple, who has traversed much of the same ground. We have compared the two works with selected passages of the original, and there can be no doubt that Mr. Abbott's translation is written in English, while Mr. Semple is content with that detestable jargon which so often does duty for English among students of German philosophy: but we do not think that Mr. Abbott has been very successful in fixing the charge of misconception of Kant's meaning on his rival. "When Kant," he says, "speaks of a maxim as not being without contradiction *conceivable* as a universal law, Mr. Semple speaks of it as not *fit* to be a universal law. The question must then arise, what is the test of this fitness? And no further answer being given, it seems not unfair to say, as English critics have said, that this is ultimately placed by Kant himself in the consequences resulting. There could not be a more fundamental perversion of Kant's doctrine." If this be so, the encouragement to such perversion is given more by Kant himself than by any translator: for he himself tests the conceivability of the maxim by a consideration of the consequences of acts done in accordance with it, nor is it otherwise inconceivable than because in practice it is self-destructive. Mr. Semple's translation may be wrong, in fact it is wrong, but Mr. Abbott's does not remove the difficulty, nor are we acquainted with any satisfactory solution.

Professor F. A. Lange republishes the first or historical part of his valuable and learned "Geschichte des Materialismus"[31] in an enlarged and improved edition. The new volume, though it contains only half the work, is almost as large as the single volume of the former

---

[30] "Kant's Theory of Ethics, or Practical Philosophy." Translated by Thomas Kingsmill Abbott, M.A. Fellow and Tutor of Trinity College, Dublin. London: Longmans.

[31] "Geschichte des Materialismus und Kritik seiner Bedeutung in der Gegenwart." Von Friedrich Albert Lange. Zweite, verbesserte und vermehrte Auflage. Erstes Buch. Geschichte des Materialismus bis auf Kant. Iserlohn, Baedeker.

edition, and we are promised in the second volume a critical estimate of the progress of modern science and its relation to Materialism, together with a formal exposition of the author's own point of view. The present volume is a great improvement on the former edition, which was designed primarily, as the author declares in both editions, for an immediate and temporary purpose; for besides being expanded and improved throughout, it is furnished with abundant illustrative and explanatory notes, indicating the sources and materials of each successive section; the want of such illustrative notes was a great defect in the former edition. It is also an advantage that the historical and critical parts should be published in separate volumes, for they will interest different classes of readers. We shall look for the second volume with much interest; for there can be little doubt that Mr. Lewes is right when he says "Science itself is in travail. Assuredly some mighty new birth is at hand. Solid as the ground appears, and fixed as are our present landmarks, we cannot but feel the strange tremors of subterranean agitation which must, ere long, be followed by upheavals disturbing those landmarks." If this be so, a criticism of the problems and methods of modern science by one whose competency for the task is well established cannot fail to be of interest.

Such a criticism will not be found in the series of rhapsodies entitled "The Newest Materialism,"[m] by Mr. William Maccall. Mr. Maccall tells us that he never had any taste or faculty for dialectics: he certainly has not, but he has rather a turn for vigorous invective. We commend to him his prescription for others:—

"Mr. Mill, by the inexorable directness and faultless limpidity of his speech, forces back to reality the brain which has been bewildered by a vapoury, chaotic pictorialism. He is the Priessnitz of literature, and much is a Priessnitz of literature needed when there has been a reckless revel in furibond and fantastic phrases. If, then, you know any one who has been ensnared by the clumsy and cantankerous circumlocutions of the Carlyle apes—for whom, however, the great and good man they outrageously imitate should not be held responsible—send him to the physician Mill."

Mr. Maccall has made us acquainted with such an one, and he was, we believe, a friend of Mill's; if so the remedy has been applied, and, so far as we can see, applied hitherto in vain.

---

[m] "The Newest Materialism: Sundry Papers on the Books of Mill, Comte, Bain, Spencer, Atkinson, and Feuerbach." By William Maccall. London: Farrah.

POLITICS, SOCIOLOGY, VOYAGES AND TRAVELS.

IT is always refreshing to meet with a genuine student and follower of Mr. Cobden doing his utmost to gather up the different truths which his great master was among the first to vindicate in this country, and to diffuse them abroad in the dress likely to be most attractive to a new generation. The life of a statesman like Mr. Cobden necessarily wears at the time something of a desultory and disjointed appearance. He is pledged to so many great causes and engaged in so many movements at the same time, that it is difficult to ascertain what is the relative value they have for him, or how far he is promoting that of which he is the only earnest supporter, or simply giving one additional prop to that which scarcely needs his aid. The previous publication of Mr. Cobden's speeches and writings has done much to bring into their proper relation with each other his central beliefs, and what may be called his accidental opinions. The plan of writing a series of essays on the topics most interesting to Mr. Cobden, and on which his views were most pronounced, is that adopted by Mr. Thorold Rogers.[1] The work is an extremely interesting one, both from the lucidity with which the joint opinions of Mr. Cobden and Mr. Rogers are presented, and the actual importance and variety of the topics discussed. These topics cover a tolerably wide field, though the more significant ones in relation to Mr. Cobden are those of the Corn Laws, the Land Question, International Relations, Financial Reform, and Commercial Diplomacy. Mr. Rogers says, "The school which Cobden—I will not say founded, for all who have assisted the solid progress of good government and national prosperity have belonged to it—strengthened, affirmed that freedom was the natural condition of the individual, and that restraint must always be justified in order to be defended. In the presence of an outrageous and serious wrong, the old Corn Law, it assailed the principle of protection to agriculture with irresistible force. But it was the accident of a fact which caused the assault to be made on this position. It attacked every kind of protection, on the ground that the assistance given to one interest was an injury, a restraint, an indefensible control on other interests, which were depressed, impoverished, and dwarfed in consequnce." The essay on International Relations will be found to contain on every page of it truths of the highest moment. It is there shown conclusively that war is a necessary consequence of the existence of despotically or aristocratically governed States. So soon as governments come into the hands of the people, war becomes "an anachronism and an impossibility." For if a war is to take place, the persons who make it are also those who immediately feel it; and also in popularly governed States, the two great causes of war, dynastic rivalries and occupation for the standing armies needed to feed

---

[1] "Cobden and Modern Political Opinion. Essays on Certain Political Topics." By James E. Thorold Rogers. London: Macmillan. 1873.

monarchical pride or ambition, are out of the way. Mr. Rogers says, for instance, that there is nothing which the French nation detests more than the sacrifice which war entails on it. "War has been the passion of French monarchs and French statesmen from the days of Francis I. to those of Napoleon III. Mr. Cobden has proved in the clearest manner that the French people were eagerly anxious not to excite the hostility of the English people at the beginning of the Revolution. It is certain that the last vote of confidence which a plébiscite gave the late Emperor was accorded from a belief that the policy of the French government would be peace. The same may be said of other nations."

The publication of Professor Fawcett's Speeches in the House of Commons[2] is due to the lateness of the hour at which the discussion on the Indian Budget came on in the past session, and the consequent impossibility of the debate being adequately reported. Thus the speeches on Indian Finance are the most important speeches in the volume, that being a subject to which Professor Fawcett has given an amount of attention which is, unfortunately, rare in English statesmen; and it being extremely difficult to diffuse among Englishmen an intelligent knowledge of the facts concerned. Professor Fawcett takes a truly statesmanlike view both of the true difficulties of governing India and of the sole agencies by which those difficulties can be overcome. He notices, for instance, the incessant errors that flow from false and misleading parallels drawn between the situation of India and England. Local taxation may be a good thing in England because it is bound up with local government; but in India, says Professor Fawcett, we allow the people to have no representative institution, either local or imperial. The decentralization scheme has done nothing whatever to increase local self-government, but, on the contrary, the local taxes which it has necessitated have more than any other taxation ever levied in India been imposed in utter disregard of the wishes, the wants, and the habits of the people. Professor Fawcett goes on to point out that the result of substituting local for imperial taxation is that the state of taxation in India is likely to become more and more concealed from the House of Commons, and thus to escape the criticism of public opinion. As an instance of this he cites the case of the constant reference in the House to the Imperial Income Tax in India, and of numerous articles written against it in the leading English newspapers; and yet an act was passed to levy a far more burdensome income-tax in Bombay, which scarcely attracted any attention at all in this country. It was for a long time unnoticed in the House, and scarcely any reference was made to it in the public press. Professor Fawcett notices one special disadvantage to India arising from the abolition of the East India Company, a disadvantage already prophesied in a memorable paper prepared by Mr. J. S. Mill—that of no influential persons in this country being sufficiently at leisure to give their whole attention to

[2] "Speeches on some Current Political Questions." By Henry Fawcett, M.P. London: Macmillan and Co. 1873.

the wants of India, and sufficiently single-minded to secure that so often as Indian and English claims come into competition, those of England be not invariably preferred. Professor Fawcett is of opinion that the Council of the Secretary of State for India has, for some reason or other, not fulfilled the expectations formed of it. The reason seems to be that the pressure of the Secretary of State is too strong for it, and—as Professor Fawcett notices—the Secretary of State is only the servant of the Cabinet, and the Cabinet the servants of an Assembly in which England is represented, and India is not. Professor Fawcett strongly recommends that the sittings of the Council be open to the public, so that, in the case of a protesting member being unsupported in the Council, the merits of his protest should be reconsidered elsewhere. Among specific reforms advocated is the adoption of the same economic system of government for Bombay and Madras (that is, by Lieutenant-Governors appointed in India by the Viceroy, and usually chosen from the list of distinguished Indian officials) as in the Punjaub, the North-West Provinces, and Oude. These last are more than twice as populous as the former, and the extravagance of Indian Government is one of the chief causes of the deficit in the revenue, and of the discontent which mistaken remedies for this deficit occasion. The immediate dependence of the governors of Bombay and Madras on the Secretary of State rather than on the Viceroy, and the isolation of the different portions of the Indian army, are also evils of no small magnitude.

Mr. Freeman's[5] modes of reasoning are unlike those of other and perhaps baser men. The method and tone are Conservative, but few Conservatives would venture to embark in an imitation of them, as the conclusions are as often as not startlingly Liberal, or rather Radical. Nevertheless, the Liberal who distrusts Mr. Freeman's methods, and the Conservative who dislikes his results, have both much to learn from all that Mr. Freeman writes. He is always erudite, and never flags in laborious research or in political zeal. From whatever curious and out-of-the way sources he extracts his information, it is never allowed to moulder as a mere instrument for the gratification of an antiquarian curiosity, but is at once directed to the destruction of some mischievous idol, or the propping up some novel creation only supported as yet by an insignificant minority. Mr. Freeman's six lectures, delivered before the Royal Institution in the present year, which together with the Rede Lecture on the "Unity of History," delivered the year before at Cambridge, are now illustrated with voluminous notes, and bound in one volume, entitled "Comparative Politics," afford numberless instances of the author's characteristic qualities. It is doubtful whether Mr. Freeman has any respect for kings or not. There is no man who dislikes more the theory of kings having a "right divine to govern wrong." He labours

[5] "Comparative Politics. Six Lectures read before the Royal Institution in January and February, 1873." By Edward A. Freeman, M.A., Hon. D.C.L. London: Macmillan. 1873.

to prove with almost excessive pains and anxiety that the Teutonic nations have invariably cared only for the office of the king, that is, for the usefulness of his functions, and not for the individual personality of particular kings. On the one hand, there is no strict law of hereditary succession; on the other hand, the kingly office is not put up to indiscriminate competition among the whole people. Our fathers felt, with the practical mind of the Roman, that the rule of men could not be safely trusted to the chances of mere hereditary succession. The sentiment of kingly descent was satisfied if the king came of the divine stock, while some degree of fitness for his office was secured by a free choice among those in whose veins the sacred blood of Woden flowed.—"Kingship was an office; it was an office which, like any other office, the nation gave and the nation could take away." The readers of Mr. Freeman's other works will remember how fond he is of illustrating this position from repeated examples in the history of England; and how firmly he believes it to represent the sound constitutional doctrine in England at the present day. The volume contains some extremely interesting researches into the history of Private War and the development of Early Criminal Law, which took its place; also into the nature of the English Peerage. Mr. Freeman contrasts peerage in England with the institution of a nobility in foreign countries in a variety of ways, but especially by pointing out that "in an English peerage the primary idea is political power; rank and privilege are mere adjuncts. The peer then—not a mere noble, but a legislator, a counsellor, and a judge—holds a distinct place in the State, which his children can no more share with him than any one else."

If the copious military literature that is now issuing from the press is an index to the scientific spirit in which military studies are for the future to be conducted in this country, the augury ought to be a hopeful one—so far as hope can be connected with the thought of war at all. In his "Studies of the New Tactics of Infantry" Major von Scherff[4] notices that the general adoption of the rifled musket, soon followed by that of the rifled cannon, has impressed a very different character upon the tactical literature of all European armies from that of the previous period. It seems that the conditions of attaining the maximum of attacking power are (1) the greatest mobility, (2) the greatest possible security from the effects of the enemy's fire, and (3) the greatest possible development on the part of the attacking force of its own fire at the moment of actual collision. To satisfy these conditions Major von Scherff believes that individual skirmishing order, as opposed to formation in masses, has become the only battle formation for infantry.

We have the pleasure of noticing a singularly practical and handy little book on "Elementary Military Geography,"[5] compiled "for non-

[4] "The New Tactics of Infantry." By Major W. von Scherff. Translated by Colonel Lumley Graham. London: Henry S. King. 1873.

[5] "Elementary Military Geography, Reconnoitering, and Sketching." By Lieut. C. E. H. Vincent, F.R.G.S. London: Henry S. King. 1873.

commissioned officers and soldiers of all arms." It must be of the greatest use in the field as (what it professes to be) a "portable key."

The story of the events that happened in and near Paris during the period of the Government of the National Defence, that is, from the 30th of June to the 31st of October, 1870, detailed by M. Jules Favre,[6] and very well rendered into English by Mr. H. Clark, will be found to present as vivid, and no doubt as truthful a picture of the time from the French point of view as could be desired. An interesting feature of the work is the collection at the end of it of a large number of original documents, entitled "Pièces justificatives," including letters, proclamations, circulars, and official reports; letters from French, Prussian, or other quarters. The interview of M. Jules Favre with Count Bismarck, and the circumstances amidst which it took place, are described with much effect. They met in a little manor-house, called la Haute Maison, situated on a little wooded hill. The Count professes or pretends to be a little nervous about the possible presence of franc-tireurs, which leads to a preliminary conversation as to the right of employing such auxiliaries. When the conversation is fairly opened, Bismarck says, "I only ask for peace. It is not Germany which has disturbed it. You declared war without any cause, with the direct intention of taking our territory. In thus doing you have been faithful to your past. From the time of Louis XIV. you have not ceased to aggrandize yourself at our expense. We know that you will never give up this policy; that you will only regain your strength to commence a fresh war. Germany has not sought this occasion; she seized it for her own security, and this security can only be guaranteed by a cession of territory. Strasburg is a constant menace to us. It is the key of our house, and we desire to have it." M. Jules Favre gives a lively description of the Count's personal appearance, and says rather naïvely, "He certainly regarded me as a negotiator quite unworthy of him, but he had the politeness not to let this be seen, and appeared interested by my suavity."

Colonel Wright, the translator of two important military works by Count Hermann von Wartensleben[7] and Major A. von Schell,[8] respectively, on the Prussian Campaign of 1870–1871, notices that it is characteristic of the first period of the German-French war—the campaign (as he describes it) "against the *Imperial* Army," that notwithstanding the great breadth of front on which the French troops assembled in the first instance, still both sides aimed at the greatest possible co-operation of all their forces. In the latter period, on the other hand, that against the *Republican* army, the armies on both sides engaged in separate campaigns, each more or less depending on the other. These

---

[6] "The Government of the National Defence, from the 30th of June to the 31st of October, 1870." By M. Jules Favre. Translated by H. Clark. London: Henry S. King. 1873.

[7] "The Campaign of 1870–1871. Operations of the First Army under General von Manteuffel." By Count Hermann von Wartensleben. London: Henry S. King. 1873.

[8] "The Campaign of 1870–1871. Operations of the First Army under General von Goeben." By Major A. von Schell. London: Henry S. King. 1873.

considerations point to the value of studying, for the latter half of the war, the campaign as conducted under each separate commander apart by itself. The works translated by Colonel Wright supply the materials of this study. The first of them gives a survey of the campaign under General von Manteuffel, from the capitulation of Metz to the fall of Peronne. The narrative is founded on the head-quarter war-documents, and much that it describes was personally witnessed by the author. The second work is a sequel to the first, and describes, from like authorities and sources, the further operations of the first army under General von Groeben.

Mr. de Tracy Gould[9] has bestowed a valuable service on the increasing number of students of Roman Law in this country in translating from the Dutch the important treatise of Professor Gouldsmit. The book is a thoroughly good one, not only from the quantity of ground it covers and the number of references by which every proposition is supported, but from the conception it presents of Roman Law as a still living and indestructible system. English students have their attention so exclusively fixed upon the elementary treatises of Gaius and Justinian, that they have only a very dim notion of what the real substance of the law, as conveyed in the Pandects, really was. The present work will open a new field to many such students, though, from the extraordinary magnitude of the subject, it cannot do much more than deal thoroughly with introductory matter.

The "Legal Hand-book for Architects, Builders, and Building-Owners"[10] will be, no doubt, found a highly useful work for those for whom it is intended. The multiplication of such books and the apparent demand for them are of themselves sufficient indications of the need of popularizing law. It may be that a Code would not of itself dispense with such supplementary aid as the works of Mr. Jenkins and Mr. Raymond, but it would afford a common type upon which all such books would be constructed.

There cannot well be a better chosen subject than the English Land Laws[11] upon which to base a lecture or series of lectures delivered at a Working Men's College. The laws are interesting retrospectively as bound up with the mode of development of the English Constitution; they are interesting prospectively as connected directly or indirectly with every great measure of improvement which engages the attention of far-sighted politicians. The present work of Mr. Wilkinson is indeed a somewhat disappointing one, owing to the humble estimate the lecturer seems to have formed of the political curiosity and voracity of his audience. The lectures are almost exclusively devoted to describing the technicalities of the law of what is called "real property" in England. This matter is of course important

---

[9] "The Pandects: a Treatise on Roman Law, and upon its Connexion with Modern Legislation." By J. E. Gouldsmit, LL.D. Translated from the Dutch by R. De Tracy Gould, M.A. London: Longmans. 1873.

[10] "A Legal Hand-Book for Architects, Builders, and Building-Owners." By Edward Jenkins, Esq., and John Raymond, Esq. London: Henry S. King. 1873.

[11] "Short Lectures explanatory of our Land Laws, delivered at the Working Men's College." By Thomas Lean Wilkinson. London: Henry S. King. 1873.

enough as part of a course of permanent instruction to a law class, but as there were only three lectures in the course, and they are said to be "explanatory" of the land laws, we repeat that the little book is disappointing.

The "Opinions concerning the Bible Law of Marriage, by one of the People,"[12] will be read as a curious specimen of misplaced ingenuity, devoted to the support of what are believed to be at once morality and orthodoxy. The work ought to command general attention, as it is dedicated to the "Anglo-Saxon people speaking the English tongue." The purpose of the work is to establish that plurality of wives was never sanctioned in any part of the history contained in the Old Testament. The ulterior object of the argument seems to be to prevent Utah, so long as polygamy is recognised, being admitted into the Union. "In short," says the author, "the question of admitting the territory of Utah as a state into our Union must be tried and decided chiefly on this issue—Whether polygamy is not a sin against God's law of equality in marriage, and therefore an outrage on the inalienable rights of humanity, which outrage would, if allowed, infallibly destroy the freedom of women and the republican equality of men."

There are few questions more important in that stage of civilization to which England has now arrived, when immense populations become crowded into contracted centres of industry, than that of the healthy and economic disposal of sewage. An interesting pamphlet[13] is published by Scott's Sewage Company, giving an account of the process of Major-General H. G. D. Scott. The principle of this process seems to be the application of lime in such a way as to destroy the noxious gases of sewage and to act as a preventive against sewer emanations generally. The method of operation is that of precipitating the solid matter in sewage by rapid combination with it. The material so deposited is capable of being dried and manufactured into cement. The organic matter can be removed by burning. The pamphlet contains a quantity of evidence of the highest authority in favour of the different parts of the process.

Whether looked upon as a supplement to the general history of England, or as an essential part of the history of English law, a "History of Crime in England,"[14] if thoroughly worked out and built up, at every point, out of contemporary records, cannot be regarded as other than a work of the utmost value. Mr. Luke Owen Pike's work, of which one volume is now published, covering the period from the Roman Invasion to the accession of Henry VII., will be found to satisfy most of what is required in a book of this nature. If there is any defect, it is one which, depending as it does rather on the nature

---

[12] "Opinions concerning the Bible Law of Marriage." By one of the People. London and Philadelphia: Trübner and Co. 1871.

[13] "The Sewage Question and the Lime and Cement Process of Major-General H. G. D. Scott, C.B." Part I. Printed for Scott's Sewage Company, Limited. London: 1873.

[14] "A History of Crime in England, illustrating the Changes of the Laws in the Progress of Civilization." By Luke Owen Pike, M.A.

of the subject-matter than on the discretion of the author, may seem irremediable. This defect is that of want of convenient arrangement. The strictly chronological method which is almost inevitable in what professes to be history above all else, when extended to a vast number of matters of the greatest possible variety, is almost intolerable. The reader's attention becomes hopelessly wearied and distracted, as well as disappointed by being made to pass arbitrarily from one class of topics to another, and never being allowed to follow a single matter to its close. This characteristic is not peculiar to Mr. Pike's work, but is common to that and the most celebrated works on the same class of subjects, such as Hallam's works and Reeves' History of English Law. A choice must be made between two methods. Either a complete general history must be written which will have a continuity of interest of its own, and yet which will comprehend in their proper places the changes in the constitution, or in criminal law, or in any other part of the law. These will then be subordinated to the general history and read with a proper relish. Or another method may be adopted, which is that of tracing from first to last the history of each several branch of the criminal law, or other branch of the law, as the case may be. This may, no doubt, involve some repetition, but a skill in the use of cross references will avoid much of this. We have thought it necessary to make these remarks, not from a wish to depreciate the value of Mr. Pike's labour, but from so great an appreciation of that value, that we grudge any want of economic management which may fail to render his book as popular as it deserves to be. Mr. Pike's researches are far too original and exhaustive to afford to be treated as desultory snatches of history and philosophy to be taken up and thrown down as the suggestions of an idle moment dictate. Perhaps the most interesting part of the work is that comprised in the chapter at the end, entitled, "References and Notes." We think Mr. Pike has solved very happily the question of what to do with notes. He puts them altogether at the end of the book, and makes, as he says, the notes refer to the text instead of the text to the notes. In this way any one who wishes to know the authority for any statement has only to look to the marginal reference in the corresponding chapter of notes, and he will there see all the authorities set out in full. On the other hand he can, if he likes, follow the reverse process, and read the notes and references in the first instance, only using the text in order to see the conclusions the author draws from them.

Mr. Philip Vernon Smith's "History of the English Institutions"[11] belongs to a highly useful class of works, which are getting largely multiplied in the present day; that of books dealing with somewhat recondite subjects, and prepared by the best scholars, and yet intended to be used, in the course of education, by persons as yet wholly unacquainted with the subject. The difficulty of imparting enough without clogging the pages with matter which, from one point of view, cannot be regarded as superfluous, is extreme. The series of "Histo-

[11] "History of the English Institutions." By Philip Vernon Smith, M.A. London: Rivingtons. 1873.

rical Handbooks," of which Mr. Smith's is one, is edited by Mr. Oscar Browning, and judging both from the topics of the forthcoming treatises and the names of the authors, is likely to form a very considerable contribution to the historical and political education of the coming race. Mr. Smith's book is accurate, complete, erudite, and, in fact, all that a really good book of the kind ought to be, if it were not that a little want of skill in general arrangement imparts to the work too much of a dislocated or even desultory appearance, which the real unity which pervades it makes it by no means deserve.

The reappearance in a new and popular shape of Lord Russell's work on the "History of the English Government and Constitution,"[16] will encourage those who have not yet done so to study the features of the transition period in English political thought, between that of genuine Whiggism and that of modern Liberalism. Lord Russell has sides allying him to both, though chiefly to the former.

Mr. Manley Hopkins,[17] a writer already well known to the readers of the literature of our marine commerce, increases their obligations to him by a most useful book, intended to help master mariners in the intelligent study of the legal and commercial side of their duties. This class of men are commonly not only thoughtful and studious, because of the amount of enforced leisure they enjoy, but are also commonly considerably cultivated by the study of scientific navigation. They are therefore a class of men for whom it is a worthy and a hopeful task to investigate the rules, and the reasons for the rules, which must guide their conduct in the many difficult positions in which they may find themselves, apart from all questions of mere seamanship. The first chapter is occupied with a definition of the position of the master mariner's legal position and duties, and a suggestion of the various classes of difficulties to which he may be exposed "in port," together with his relation to English and foreign law. These difficulties, and the various modes of avoiding them, or of extricating himself from them, are minutely discussed under the heads of Agency and Agents, Average, Bottomry, and other methods of raising money, Bills of Lading and the Charter-party, Stoppage in Transitu, and Collision.

The writer of the spirited and admirable little book[18] on the duties and position of English women repudiates, at the outset, all notion of being a champion of the rights either of men or women as against the opposite sex, and strikes the true note when she insists on the identity of those rights and of the interests to be served by the recognition of them. It is high praise, after the exhaustive way in which the subject of the position of women has been treated elsewhere, to say that L. F. M. has found a new and most convincing reason why English women are bound, in a sense in which they never were bound before, to be up

---

[16] "An Essay on the History of the English Government and Constitution from the Reign of Henry VII." By John Earl Russell. New Edition. London: Longmans. 1873.

[17] "The Port of Refuge." By Manley Hopkins. Henry King and Co.

[18] "English Matrons and their Profession." By L. F. M. London: Sampson Low and Co. 1873.

and doing lest, having nothing in political matters, that which they have should be taken from them. Assuming it to be universally conceded that all governments tend to increase the area, and the amount within that area, of their legislative power—that they are habitually kept in check by the counter force of their subjects, and that these propositions are pre-eminently true in England—she points out that, since the last Reform Bills, in England the Government has come to consist of nearly all the men in the country, and the subjects of quite all the women. The results of this state of things are clearly pointed out, and the future results are indicated, if the subject population do not bestir itself to fulfil the ancient rôle of the English nation, and insist on the concession of its rights to personal liberty, trial by jury, to the unmolested enjoyment of property, and representation in Parliament, to equal laws, to freedom from liability to reckless and unnecessary imprisonment or abuses at the hands of the police, to free trade, and the absence of restrictions on labour. To those who dread the effect on women of entering upon so great a struggle, L. F. M. addresses the warning, that "politics have a great deal to do with women," and that "being a law-abiding race, we all learn to look upon ourselves to a great extent, and on each class of our fellow-subjects, as being of necessity and by nature that which our laws first said we were; and also a strong Government actually stamps each class of its subjects with the character which its regulations about them presuppose them to have; and moulds them into that nature which it assumes them to possess." So that if we suffer laws to continue which assume the weakest and most unfortunate women of the land to be useful and necessary in their degradation, the unmarried mothers of children to be the only parents of those children worth troubling ourselves about, or desirable to punish—customs to abide which treat all girls as incapable or unworthy of the education useful for boys—all "ladies" as superior to or incapable of honest work—all women as unfit for professional occupations—and fresh enactments to be made which treat women as unreasonable beings, incapable of choosing their own modes and hours of labour,—the women, girls, and "ladies" will come more and more to look upon themselves in the same light in which they are thus authoritatively presented. With the example of the political intrigues, and the domestic vice and misery of the East before them, L. F. M. urges English women to seize upon the occupation for which their most active suppressors deem them to be created. And she shows how impossible it is for any woman to be the wife and mother and mistress of the ideal English home, unless she receive the education, the freedom, the political interest, and the equality before the law which are believed by some of the community to be destructive of all the arts and graces which go to make up the true English matron. The call, then, is as loud to men, and to as yet indifferent women, as to the more discontented and active women of the day. And to all alike the motive for concession and for demand is the highest possible—a straining after the highest good of the nation. It need scarcely be added that a theme so loftily conceived, and so thoroughly worked out, is not marred by the want of any of the grace or brilliancy which are the frequent gift of educated and patriotic women.

"The Pilgrimage of the Tiber"[*] is a full and elaborated description of the course of the river, which embraces an unsurpassed continuity of the most beautiful and varied scenery that is to be found even in Italy, based on a journey from its mouth to its source, made by the writer and Mr. C. J. Hemans, in order to weld together their previous knowledge of a large portion of the ground before writing the book before us. To artistic readers the illustrations, and notably the charming little tail-pieces, will add much to the attractions of the wealth of mediæval art-lore which Mr. Davies betrays. To many the chief charm of the book will lie in a chapter on the popular songs of the Tiberian district, which opens up quite a new field of interest in Italy. It appears that the peasantry of that region, rude and uncultivated as they are, possess a faculty of lyrical composition "which often matches Horace and Catullus in subtlety of rendering, in neatness of form and finish, breathing a fragrance and delicacy of sentiment quite unknown to their time and age." These popular songs are chiefly love-songs, but they are wholly free from all coarseness, although existing side by side with a stream of printed ballad literature which consists of little else but the vulgar recitals of adventure and crime. A comparison of the impromptus of to-day with the poems of Cima da Pistoia, Dante da Maiano, Guido Cavalcanti, and others, gives probability to the surmise that the literary revival in Italy in the thirteenth century owed its birth in large measure to the native poetic gift of the peasantry, and to the store of little lyrics already accumulated among them. Whether the advance of Italy will educate this wild and lovely faculty to death it is impossible to guess; but at all events it is a desideratum that a complete collection of all songs now current should be made, and much poetic delight must surely be destined to be further bestowed on the world by a race which produces Beatrice di Pian degli Ontani, a shepherdess and the wife of a shepherd, who improvises on any subject given to her in stanzas of six interrhymed lines and a couplet in a fashion represented by the following translation made by Mr. Davies:—

"It is no marvel, youths, your song is shorn
 Of that fine tone which makes the poet burn;
Within my house there is no master born,
 Nor any school where I my task might learn.
If you would go to school where I did gain
My power, mount yonder crags through hail and rain:
If you would read, as I, the muses' tome,
Go dig the ground and fetch the fuel home."

Mr. Davies gives most glowing and pleasant descriptions of his travels and the scenery through which he travelled, and enlivens and enriches his pages by laying under contribution every source of

---

[*] "The Pilgrimage of the Tiber." By William Davies. London: Sampson Low and Co. 1873.

interest, historical, artistic, and social, ancient, mediæval, and modern, which was likely to reward his search.

Wrapping himself in the dignified cloak of an editorial "we," Mr. Smith[30] gives with considerate naiveté an account of an eccentric expedition which he made in the summer of 1871 in Norway. It is to be presumed that Mr. Smith's former "wanderings in search of gipsy lore" had so enamoured him of gipsies that a holiday trip had no charms apart from their company; any other motives are inconceivable for his encumbering himself with the two gipsy men and their sister, who proved such wild, and sometimes such almost intolerable companions. Any one who proposes travelling in Norway may, however, gain much minute economical and topographical information from the book, as well as a very effectual warning, should there be the man who needs it, not to go and do likewise. Readers anxious to form an idea of the beauties of Norwegian scenery will find more vivid descriptions elsewhere. The excitement caused by the appearance of the donkeys of the party in a land where donkeys are not known, is one of the leading features of the expedition.

Mr. Blackburn's beautifully printed and well illustrated "Sketch of Life in the Hartz Mountains,"[31] may probably attract to follow in his steps more people than will be diverted from any such plan by his warning at the end of the volume against the discomforts which are to be encountered in the search after the very moderate pleasures and excitements of the region. To tell the truth, Mr. Blackburn writes in a blasé tone, which has the effect of leaving his readers' minds impressed with the conviction that things are much better than he paints them; and so his descriptions of the grandeur of the neighbourhood of the Brocken, and of the quaintness of the toy-like villages of the Hartz, are doubly attractive. For architects, geologists, and lovers of the picturesque, there would seem to be ample and stimulating food; and for those who only want simplicity in the human beings around them, and freshness and exhilaration in the air, the Hartz Gebirge can also cater well. The drawbacks to pleasure appear to consist in a somewhat meagre culinary idea, and in a surfeit of hobgoblins and spectres—in story at least—though not a shadow of them is to be seen on the Brocken, generally speaking.

While the United States were collecting the necessary knowledge for their great Pacific railroad, and then carrying out the scheme, Canada was from time to time dreaming of a rival or a sister line, but was constantly deterred from the work. At last British Columbia made it one of the conditions of her junction with the Dominion in July, 1871, that such a railroad should be made in ten years. Immediately surveying parties left Victoria for various points of the Rocky Mountains. Their reports were laid before the Canadian "House" in April, 1872, and in that summer the engineer in chief thought it well to go

---

[30] "Tent Life with English Gipsies in Norway." By Herbert Smith. Henry S. King and Co. 1873.

[31] "The Harz Mountains: a Tour in the Toy Country." By H. Blackburn. London: Sampson Low and Co. 1873.

and examine the route with his own eyes. The Rev. G. M. Grant[12] went with him as secretary, and it is to that gentleman's diary, kept under great difficulties in such rough travelling, that we owe a very interesting volume. It is so little written in extenso that to do more than to praise its style, to say that no page is dull, and to give a very few facts from it, is not possible. To those interested in emigration questions it will be important to hear of land about fifty miles west of Lake Superior, where a family who had arrived there two months before had cereals up, and roots and vegetables, all doing well, where, sixty days earlier, there had been stumps, undergrowth, and tall trees; and also of land, such as is repeatedly spoken of, where cereals return from a hundred to two thousand per cent. of grain. Of course all is cheap, some is only a few dollars for a hundred acres. The tone as to missionary efforts and as to the right mode of dealing with the Indians, is manly, generous, and religious without cant.

Mr. Winwoode Reade[13] is already known as a writer on Africa, and that fact, together with the certain unusual amount of public interest felt in Africa just now, may tend to incline many to read his new book. This consists of a republication of his travels, essays on the slave trade, African exploration, and the progress of Islam in Negroland; several tales intended to illustrate the manners and customs of the natives; and finally, his recent travels. Mr. Reade says that the tales are the only parts of his volumes which are fictitious; but he tells in the other part of his book how he encouraged certain Africans in the belief that white men were cannibals; and it is scarcely probable that he is more careful to tell plain truth to his countrymen. On the face of it the book is full of "touched up" pictures; and the whole style is characterized by a levity and a want of refinement which makes it anything but a pleasure to read.

Captain Clements Markham's object in the publication of a volume on the Arctic Regions[14] is to give the public a correct knowledge of the whole line of frontier separating the known from the unknown region around the North Pole. The obvious method is that which he has adopted—the historical. He gives a sketch of the adventures and discoveries of early navigators in those seas, comparing and correcting their conclusions, and showing how far more recent knowledge and present scientific speculation verifies early tradition and assertion. In the hope of arousing a spirit of national enterprise to overcome the obstacles raised by nature to the satisfaction of either scientific or commercial curiosity, Captain Markham closely investigates the probabilities and difficulties of each proposed route to the Pole, and encourages adventure by the recital of the varied and important scientific results to be obtained from Arctic exploration, and of the generally underrated ease and pleasure of life at the Pole. The volume is as in-

[12] "Ocean to Ocean." By the Rev. G. M. Grant, of Halifax, N.S. London Sampson Low and Co. 1873.

[13] "The African Sketch Book." By Winwoode Reade. London: Smith, Elder and Co. 1873.

[14] "The Threshold of the Unknown Region." By Clements R. Markham, C.B., F.R.S. London: Sampson Low and Co. 1873.

teresting and exciting as the pen of an enthusiastic and well-informed writer can make it.

While Captain Clements Markham accumulates grave reasons why Arctic exploration should be taken up as a national duty, Captain Wells[30] contributes his share to the sort of literature which has as great an influence on the public mind as any other, and which is sure to educate a number of enthusiastic volunteers for Arctic service. His descriptions of exploration as well as of whale and seal hunting in northern seas are really enticing, and the suggestions of exciting discoveries which are partially made of lands, in latitude 79°, where large herds of reindeer fatten enormously in valleys green with pasture, and broad lakes reflect the bright sky, are enough to fill both young enthusiasts and grave speculators with the spirit of adventure which, and which alone, will ever lead to the solution of Arctic problems. Nor are these the only interesting portions of the volume. Captain Wells has found the art of seizing upon the picturesque parts of ancient travels, and recounts them with an ardour and a pointedness which greatly enhance the value of his work.

Under the rather modest disguise of a title apt to land his book among mere casual "Travels," Lieutenant-Colonel Marshall[31] contributes a most valuable quota to the study of the primitive condition and manners of mankind. In fact he seems, partially blinded by a superstitious and absorbing faith in phrenology, to be scarcely aware at how many points he is touching and throwing light upon the labours of other men. He has compiled a most painstaking series of chapters, founded upon personal observation and research, describing the exact condition, mental, moral, and physical, of a tribe living in the Nilagiri mountains in Southern India, who seem to approach very nearly to what is believed to have been one of the earliest conditions of human society. These Todas live in small village-communities, in which individual males own the buffaloes which are the sole property of the people, but the produce of the buffaloes is common property till all wants are supplied, surplusage being divided in the ratio of the property in the beasts. They appeared to have emerged from the stage in which the female line was the line of inheritance, although groups of men and women still usually live together in common as husbands and wives, every man who belongs to the group owning himself father of all the children. Yet at the same time such things as single married pairs are not unfrequent, and apparently two people are more especially the husband and wife of each other than they are of the rest of the group. During a stage prior to their settlement in the Nilagiris they were infanticidal, probably owing to the difficulty experienced by a totally idle race in finding food to fill all the mouths that came. The custom is quite gone out now, but Mr. Marshall believes that they present the singular spectacle of a race producing

---

[30] "The Gateway to the Polynia." By John C. Wells, R.N. London: Henry S. King and Co. 1873.

[31] "A Phrenologist among the Todas." By William E. Marshall. London: Longmans. 1873.

more boys than girls, in the proportion of four to three. They admit no question as to their origin or their future; they *know* that they came from the earth and will go to rejoin their friends where the sun sets. Living a simple life, and having simple natures, they have elaborated no words for sin or punishment, but use, with a mild meaning, some words imported from Hindu. They burn their dead with buffaloes and other necessaries for the next life, and pray that the deceased may there as here have milk to drink. Grain, to the extent of their needs, they levy from a neighbouring tribe as rent for the land; but that other tribe, a shrewd and clever people, also manage to secure the reversion of most of the young bull calves of the flocks, which are not wanted by the Todas, and which nevertheless are too sacred for them to eat. For details, for statistical tables, for a grammar and vocabulary, which are very interesting to a comparative philologist, as well as for much phrenological lore, the reader must turn to the book itself. Mr. Marshall will not disappoint any expectations. His photographic illustrations are particularly interesting and valuable.

It must be pleasant to any Englishman to read the approving and hopeful way in which Herr Oscar Flex[27] speaks of English rule in Assam. He is assured that the Assamese must rejoice in the change from native and from Burmese dominion to that of the English, who give them a law by which all are equal before the seat of justice. The Assamese are a well-made race, mentally and physically, and have been quick to learn wisdom from the rush and the speculation that accompanied the earliest development of tea-planting in Assam. It is to be feared, however, that some of them have also learned folly, and hasten to get rich in order to be idle. That it is easy to get rich in Assam is clear when once it is understood that her wealth in tea-producing power is as nothing in comparison with the mineral resources, of which as yet no advantage has been taken. Coal, on each side of the Burrumputr, sulphur, salt, gold, all are at hand, while the plains produce abundance of cotton, opium, tobacco, and all manner of fruits and animals. It is a great field for further cultivation of all sorts, mental, moral, and physical, with good soil for each description. Herr Flex gives a number of vivid pictures of a planter's life in Assam.

Few items of political knowledge seem less accessible than any insight into the interior of the Russian political circle. A volume describing its distinguished persons[28] is, therefore, particularly welcome. Whether this volume is written by a native Russian or not is hard to say, for it takes the most unbiassed stand in relation to the different schools of thought, which it describes in sketching the prominent figure in the school, and it discusses exalted personages with great freedom; and yet other evidence would go to prove that none but a Russian born would so fairly, minutely, and comprehensively de-

27 "Pflanzerleben in Indien." Von Oscar Flex. Berlin. 1873.

28 "Distinguished Persons in Russian Society." Translated from the German by F. E. Bennett. London: Smith, Elder and Co. 1873.

scribe the various shades of national political life. Some of the persons sketched are the Grand Duchess Helena, who tried to raise the standard of taste at the Imperial Court; Count Peter Schouvaloff, head of the secret police, and at the present day "the most powerful and influential man" in the empire; Countess Antoinette Poludoff, a vivacious maiden lady, the leader of the most bigoted party of the "orthodox" church as against Catholicism; the Counts Adlerberg, who are merely Imperial favourites from generation to generation; the Militins, the two brothers who, rising from the middle class, have been the leaders in the reform of the army, in the abolition of serfdom, and the effort to make the freed serfs owners of the land they lived on, as well as in many other radical reforms; Prince Gortschakoff, the somewhat conservative and somewhat effete, but peaceful Chancellor; Count Protassoff, the hussar officer who was pitched upon by the Emperor Nicholas to bring all his dominions within one ecclesiastical fold, and who has unpityingly striven to bring about the desired end; Walnieff, spoken of as a likely ambassador to England, a man of high character, and bearing a good reputation throughout his administrative career in difficult days; General Ignatieff, the blundering devotee to the idea of panslavism; and others, including the leading authors and journalists.

Mr. Ralston[29] continues his long labour of giving to the English as faithful a picture of Russian peasant life as may be drawn from the legends, fairy stories, fables, and Russian popular literature in general. The present volume is a complete repertory for such members of society as, while they feel themselves profoundly and incredibly incapable of spinning "a story," yet must perforce satisfy the clamorous demands of the little ones in their own and their neighbours' houses. Not that all Mr. Ralston's collection are fit for juvenile ears, for no one would spoil the dreams of the children with the horrible corpse and vampire literature which seems to abound in the dismal plains of Russia. Still much may be got from the store; and rumour says that most of the tales here printed have already been rehearsed before and tested by a crowd of little invalids. Onother sections of society Mr. Ralston makes worthy claim for attention, most of all on the comparer of folk-lore generally. Each chapter, or group of stories, is preceded by valuable remarks and comments which are full of information about those lower sections of the Russian nation among whom these stories are current coin.

Herr P. Lerch's[30] characteristically exhaustive pamphlet of fifty-five pages long, on Khiva, discusses the ancient name of the country, the course and delta of the Amu, the question of the Oxus, the doubt whether the Oxus was a contributary to the Caspian Sea before the tenth century of our era, the value of the testimony of various travellers throughout the whole region, whether it is possible once more to divert

---

[29] "Russian Folk-Tales." By W. R. Ralston, M.A. London: Smith, Elder and Co. 1873.

[30] "Khiva. Seine historischen und geographischen Verhältnisse." Von P. Lerch. St. Petersburg. 1873.

the Amu into the Caspian Sea, and the tales of more modern travellers. A careful history of Kharezm, or the territory now known as Khiva, is of course not omitted. Published at St. Petersburg, and in the Russian interest, the tendency of the little work is to picture Khiva as so wretched, poor, miserable, and insignificant, that it gains all, and Russia gains little by its absorption, although the actual subject is scarcely entered upon further than to intimate that the only possible advantage to Russia may be scientific — an advantage which the Russian scientific societies have not been slow to follow up.

Mr. Goodman[31] is an artist who, having formed a close friendship with a Cuban artist in Florence, resolved to settle in Santiago. His knowledge of Cuban society, to which he had complete access through his friend, was acquired in a residence of three years' duration, and the interest of his sketches of life in Cuba is greatly heightened by the fact that he was there when the insurrection broke out, and came away from the island in company with Cuban friends who were active in its first outbreak. The description he gives of the minute, vexatious, and capricious nature of the Spanish rule in Cuba would of itself be enough to convince any one who might remain doubtful which side to espouse in the struggle which is desolating the beautiful island. Looking at everything rather from the artist's than the politician's or the philanthropist's point of view, Mr. Goodman does not discuss the questions of Cuban independence or Cuban slavery. But on the latter subject so photographic a writer could not have failed to throw some light. The condition of the slaves seems to have been just such as was familiar in Southern America among somewhat gentle, lazy masters; well fed, not overworked, treated with contemptuous kindness, but whipped savagely sometimes, the negroes kept their equanimity of nature, and fawned upon their owners.

SCIENCE.

WE have before us the first portion of the second volume of Professor Wiedemann's great work[1] on Current-Electricity. The general scope of the work is nothing less than to classify and describe the phenomena of galvanic electricity in the same ample and critical spirit in which the phenomena of frictional electricity have been discussed by Riess in his classical work on the more early development of the latter branch of electrical science. The fundamental plan of the work appears to be to postpone all investigation of theories until the vast mass of experiments has been thoroughly sifted. This would undoubtedly be sound policy in an elementary treatise, but Wiedemann's work on galvanic electricity is studied and consulted by others than mere

---

[31] "The Pearl of the Antilles." By Walter Goodman. Henry S. King and Co.

[1] "Die Lehre vom Galvanismus und Electromagnetismus." Von Gustav Wiedemann. Braunschweig: Vieweg und Sohn. 1873.

students, and the defective and brief theoretical explanations which accompany the description of the phenomena in the first portion of the work are somewhat unsatisfactory. Nor is the literature and history of the science so extensively given as we are entitled to expect in a work of such pretensions. We have in vain looked for a description of Sir William Thompson's reflecting galvanometer, although the chapter on the various kinds of apparatus for electro-magnetic and electro-dynamic measurements is otherwise very complete, and enters into the practical requirements of electricians with great thoroughness. These few points, to which objection might thus be taken are, however, insignificant when compared with the profound learning, the wide practical experience, and the clear, critical perception which the author displays in this work, probably the greatest which has yet been produced on this branch of Physics. Hardly a single paper has ever been written on current electricity, which has materially contributed to the extension of the science, of which the results are not given in the proper place. Especially admirable appeared to us the chapters on magnetization and determining magnetic moments, which certainly surpass for completeness and lucid exposition every other publication on these subjects. The author has unfortunately given only so much of terrestrial magnetism as is required for reducing galvanic and magnetic results to absolute measure; this is much to be regretted, for the intimate connexion of current-electricity and terrestrial magnetic phenomena have been placed beyond doubt, and further researches will most probably tend to establish more definite laws on this connexion than have as yet been discovered.

Some interesting papers, written by Mr. Proctor in a very popular style for the *Cornhill Magazine* during the last three years, have been collected and published under the name, "The Borderland of Science."[1] We are somewhat at a loss to understand the choice of this title. There are in all sixteen distinct essays contained in this volume, of which thirteen treat on subjects principally astronomical aud geological, which form the very essence of those sciences, and are centres of scientific labours. Thus essays on the Sun, on Jupiter, Saturn, and Mars, on Meteors and Star showers, on Earthquakes, on coal, on flying and flying-machines, are certainly on essentially scientific subjects, and do not belong to the "borderland" of science. On the other hand, "Gambling Superstitions," "Coincidences and Superstitions," and "Notes on Ghosts and Goblins," are things which have no relations whatever to scicuce, although Mr. Proctor has certainly given a scientific colouring to his talk about them. A certain class of readers are attracted by such a title, and this seems to be its sole justification; while to admit even for an instant, that these subjects are worthy of the attention of scientific men, cannot but do mischief somewhere. Apart from this, there is here and there in these essays a style of writing which must be repugnant to an intellectual reader anxious to obtain only sound information. In order to exhibit the more recent discoveries about the constitution

---

[1] "The Borderland of Science." Richard A. Proctor, B.A. London: Smith, Elder and Co. 1875.

of the Sun, Mr. Proctor takes his readers with him on "a voyage to the Sun." Such sentences occur in the description of this "voyage:" "We were interested (and Y. was not a little amused) to observe that most of the meteors were rotating as steadily as though they were of planetary importance," etc.—"Y. in particular wished to escape from the fierce light and the dazzling colours," etc.—"X. was desirous of penetrating deeply beneath the photosphere; he suffered himself, however, to be overruled, though exacting from us a promise," etc. etc. We regret that a writer of Mr. Proctor's tact should not see that this style adds in reality nothing to the attraction of a popular scientific essay, while it greatly interferes with its dignity.

To all students of chemical analysis, especially to those who have not the advantage of the personal instruction of a teacher, we recommend most strongly a small work on chemical analysis by Dr. Classen,[3] of Bonn. It is undoubtedly the most practical and useful little book which has appeared for a long time on a subject on which there is at present no scarcity of treatises of different standards. Dr. Classen begins by placing the most common salts, such as the chlorides, sulphates, carbonates, &c., of the alkaline and earthy metals, and further on, various other metals, either pure or in their most common salts, before the student, with a full description of the manner of demonstrating the existence of their constituents, and the chemical reactions of these latter. This brings at once life into the student's work, and when afterwards the course of analysis really and systematically begins, the mind has already grasped a great number of primary facts of which the further operations are only so many repetitions, enlarged by new additions to the store of knowledge already gained. Another great advantage to the student of this book is, that he is made very early acquainted with the reactions of organic substances. In fact, there is not here that hard line drawn between inorganic and organic analysis which is seen in other treatises, and for which, in the present state of chemical research there is no justification, while from a practical point of view, the student is generally more anxious to test his experience on organic substances than on mineral bodies. The chapter on the Alkaloids is extremely complete and well-arranged for such a small treatise.

What is Feng-shui?[4] This question, says Mr. Eitel, has been asked over and over again for the last thirty years. For since foreigners were allowed to settle on the confines of this strange empire of China this same question has been cropping up continually here and there. It appears from the author's statements that Feng-shui is in the Chinese mind another name for natural science, but we are inclined to think that it is also another name for the effect and influence of physical agencies. The author says that whenever foreigners purchase a site, or build a house, or pull down a wall, or

---

[3] "Grundriss der analytischen Chemie." Erster Theil: "Qualitative Analyse." Bonn: A. Marcus. 1873.

[4] "Feng-shui; or, the Rudiments of Natural Science in China." By Ernest J. Eitel, M.A. London: Trübner and Co. 1873.

when it is proposed to erect telegraph poles, innumerable difficulties are placed in the way of these undertakings on account of Feng-shui. When mortality was frightful among the Hongkong troops quartered in Murray Barracks, and the colonial surgeon proposed the planting of bamboos at the back of the buildings, the Chinese remarked that this measure was in direct accordance with Feng-shui; and when it was found that disease was actually checked thereby, they looked upon it as a proof of the virtues of Feng-shui. There is thus no doubt that Feng-shui embraces all physical science and its laws. The author has, therefore, endeavoured to collect Chinese science materials, and gives an outline of the results of his labours in a series of very well-written chapters on the laws of Nature, the numerical proportions of Nature, the breath of Nature, that is, the Atmospheric agencies which influence health, and the history and literature of Feng-shui. The author has produced a thoroughly interesting pamphlet, which will undoubtedly be quoted henceforth as a source of most valuable information on Chinese knowledge of physics.

There are two works before us on Furnaces and their Phenomena. M. Gruner's[1] work on the phenomena of blast furnaces has been translated by Mr. Gordon, who has thus given us a most valuable addition to a branch of scientific literature, which is of the highest importance, not only in a technical aspect, but also in a purely scientific view. Practical men need not be reminded of a work which discusses questions of technical economy, and answers them on the basis of a series of the most careful observations; but we would call the attention of scientific chemists to these papers, which will reward a perusal by the great number of facts bearing upon the chemical and calorific phenomena of the blast furnace. Another smaller work[2] is a pamphlet by M. Carl Heuleux on Hoffmann's Furnaces. The writer appears somewhat too enthusiastic about the merit of these furnaces, and damages his own cause by a zeal which is simply unintelligible. He urges the alteration of the patent laws in Germany, and mixes unfortunately his opinions on this subject so much with the impartial scientific consideration of the furnace in question, that the whole leaves no very clear impression on the reader's mind as to the aims of the author.

We have already had on more than one occasion to indicate, as a characteristic of the popular scientific literature of the day, that the preparation of its constituent parts is no longer left exclusively to people who, with more or less power of writing, set themselves to compile popular or elementary treatises. Of late years some of our chief authorities and most original workers in science, and especially in Natural History, have deigned to descend from their thrones in order to communicate to general readers an outline of those branches of knowledge

[1] "Studies of Blast Furnace Phenomena." By M. L. Gruner. Translated by L. O. B. Gordon. London: Henry S. King and Co. 1873.

[2] "Der Hoffmann'sche Ringofen." Von Carl Heuleux. Berlin: Polytechnische Buchhandlung. 1873.

to which they have specially devoted themselves. We have now to notice another little book entering into this category—namely, Sir John Lubbock's treatise "On the Origin and Metamorphoses of Insects,"[7] originally published in *Nature*, and now reprinted in a small cheap volume. This little book, which is written in the spirit of the theory of evolution of organic forms, commences with a short sketch of the classification and habits of insects, and in the following chapters the form and structure of the larvæ of insects, the influence of external conditions upon them, the nature and origin of metamorphosis, and the origin of insects as a class are discussed. It does not seem to us that Sir John Lubbock has here made much progress towards the explanation of the phenomena of metamorphosis as displayed by insects, most of the conclusions at which he arrives as to the cause of metamorphosis being either assumptious, or restatements of the facts in a new form. Nevertheless, as a summary of the phenomena of insect metamorphosis, his little book is of great value, and will be read with interest and profit by all students of natural history. With regard to the origin of insects generally, our author, accepting the theory of the origin of species by natural selection, and holding fast by the still older theory that the forms through which animals pass during their individual development are truly ancestral, reproducing the mature forms of their progenitors, points out with justice that "many beetles and other insects are derived from larvæ closely resembling *Campodea*" (a genus of the Thysanura), and inquires "why should it be regarded as incredible that insects as a group have gone through similar stages?" "Again," he says, "other insects come from vermiform larvæ much resembling the genus *Lindia*" (a Rotifer), and he concludes "that the insects generally are descended from ancestors resembling the existing genus *Campodea*, and that these again have arisen from others belonging to a type represented more or less closely by the existing genus *Lindia*." The whole chapter on the origin of insects is most interesting and valuable. The illustrations to this little volume are numerous and good.

It is rather difficult to understand what object Mr. St. George Mivart proposed to himself in publishing his little book entitled "Man and Apes."[8] From a perusal of the work, and especially from its concluding paragraph, we should judge that its main purpose was to demonstrate that man did not originate from "the much-vaunted Gorilla;" but so far as we are aware, no one has ever asserted that man did originate from the gorilla—except Carl Vogt, and he only ascribed such an origin to the negroes. Mr. Mivart's book is divided into two parts: the first, which strikes us as being, for the most part, unnecessary, consists of a sketch of the classification and natural history of the Quadrumana, illustrated with numerous wood-cut

---

[7] "On the Origin and Metamorphoses of Insects." By Sir John Lubbock, Bart., &c. &c. 12mo. London: Macmillans. 1874.

[8] "Man and Apes: an Exposition of Structural Resemblances and Differences bearing upon Questions of Affinity and Origin." By St. George Mivart. Sm. 8vo. London: Hardwicke. 1873.

figures, chiefly of ancient date, and often of very indifferent quality. The second part contains a detailed comparison of the structure of man with that of the Anthropoid apes, indicating the points in which each of the principal forms of those creatures approaches or recedes from the genus *Homo*. The results of this investigation, he thinks, are quite in accordance with his conception of the origin of species by their emergence "from a latent and potential being into actual and manifest existence," without there being necessarily "any genetic affinity between the resembling forms."

We need hardly do more than call our readers' attention to the appearance of a new edition of Sir Charles Lyell's work on the "Antiquity of Man,"[9] the book being already too well-known to require any lengthened notice. The veteran geologist, the last now remaining among us of that brilliant band who, in years long past, placed England foremost in the race of geological investigation, continues with almost the energy of youth the study of his favourite science; and from time to time gives the public the benefit of his laborious researches, in the form of new and carefully revised editions of those valuable works, for which we are indebted to his pen. It is little more than a year since the last edition of the "Principles" made its appearance; and we have now another stout octavo volume, much of which has undergone careful revision, whilst some parts have been almost entirely recast. Without careful comparison of the two books, it would, of course, be impossible to indicate precisely what has been done to the present edition; but the more important points indicated by the author in his preface consist in the description of the caverns of the Lesse, in Belgium, explored by M. Dupont with such important results; the revision of the chapter relating to the Brixham Cavern and Kent's Hole; the notice of the remarkable skeletons and other remains discovered by M. Rivière in caves near Mentone; and the thorough revision of the chapters relating to the crag-beds of Norfolk and Suffolk, and to the action of ice.

We have also received the tenth edition of Professor Page's "Introductory Text-book of Geology,"[10] and the second edition of the same author's "Advanced Text-book of Physical Geography."[11] Both of these are excellent little books of their kind, and the author appears to keep them well up to the present state of knowledge.

In his essay on what he calls the "Physical Basis of Mental Life,"[12] Major Noel appears as a very candid supporter of the doctrines of phrenology. He commences by arguing in favour of the special loca-

---

[9] "Geological Evidences of the Antiquity of Man, with an Outline of Glacial and Post-tertiary Geology, and Remarks on the Origin of Species with Special Reference to Man's Appearance on the Earth." By Sir Charles Lyell, Bart., &c. 8vo. London: Murray. 1873.

[10] "Introductory Text-book of Geology." By David Page, LL.D., &c. Tenth and enlarged edition. Sm. 8vo. Edinburgh and London: Blackwood. 1873.

[11] "Advanced Text-book of Physical Geography." By David Page, LL.D., &c. Sm. 8vo. Edinburgh and London: Blackwood, 1873.

[12] "The Physical Basis of Mental Life." A Popular Essay. By R. R. Noel. 8vo. London: Longmans. 1873.

tion of mental powers in the brain, the physical basis of mental life. From various considerations, most of which will find pretty general acceptance, he indicates that the broad peculiarities of character are innate. He describes, at considerable length, the structure and development of the brain in man; and indicates that the skull, being as it were moulded upon the brain, the surface of the former must necessarily give an approximate idea of that of the latter; although he recognises the fact that certain parts of the bony case are much thickened, rendering it difficult to obtain "a perfectly accurate knowledge of the development-forms of the brain by an examination of the head." But whilst maintaining that the quantitative development of different parts of the brain, or the total amount of brain, is no absolute guide, "power or energy of mental life" not being measurable by sign or quantity alone, he holds that "the *relative size* of different parts of the head will give the key to the relative strength of different categories of mental life." Exercise tends to increase the size of the part of the brain implicated in any prevalent form of mental energy, and thus character becomes fixed and intensified. In the author's analysis of the various mental functions, he seats them in the same parts of the head as ordinary phrenologists; but he gives a tone of generality to his views, and recognises clearly that the positive mapping of the whole surface of the head into distinctly circumscribed "organs" (for which Gall is not responsible) has done very much to discredit phrenology in the eyes of scientific men. In his closing remarks the author says: "Regions of the head, or groups of correlated faculties—I mean correlated in reference to their genesis, historical development, and analogy of character—is about all that forty years of observation, for the purpose of testing the principles of phrenology, has confirmed to my mind." We fancy that few will be found to object to this very limited adherence to phrenology, except, perhaps, upon metaphysical and so-called theological grounds. But if phrenology goes no further than this, it can only claim to be a sort of more or less precise statement of principles which are generally recognised, and which always have been recognised by artists; and the majority of phrenologists most certainly overstep considerably the bounds of their science.

We have seldom taken up a periodical with so much pleasure as the present,[11] which is the modest first-fruits of scientific research at the great University of Cambridge. First-fruits perhaps we ought scarcely to say. We have not forgotten the "Journal of Anatomy and Physiology," which is in some measure, though not exclusively, the result and evidence of Cambridge activity. But the present report is an actual record of particular work done in the physiological laboratory of Cambridge only, and this beginning of great things too long neglected, we owe to Professor Michael Foster. We do not enter at length into the things done, for it is the doing of them at all which most pleases

[11] "Studies from the Physiological Laboratory at Cambridge." Cambridge, 1873.

us. But we may say that the papers seem quite up to the mark of a high class "Archives," and we doubt not that succeeding numbers will keep up a standard that will draw a new kind of attention to the school from which they come. The first number contains papers on embryology, on innervation, on the physiology of the pancreas, and on minute anatomy.

We have put this little book[14] to the best of tests; it has lain for some weeks upon the table during this autumn, and we have referred to it whenever the subject of winter climate arose in the course of consultations. It has answered very well to our requirements, and has offered generally useful information concerning those places where delicate invalids generally betake themselves during the damp cold season of the year. The object of the author is to combine medical and other information in one handbook, so that all material points should be duly considered in deciding the place of resort. We all know how often a poor patient is banished to some far-off land in the most careless and irresponsible way. The medical adviser often knows nothing of the toil or the length of the journey, or of the many discomforts to be borne when the journey is over; and so fatigued and dispirited, more harm may be done an invalid by the change than could have happened to him at home. Dr. Reimer makes such carelessness impossible for the future. At the head of each chapter he puts a concise account of the season when each resort is most useful, by what routes it is reached, what accommodation it affords and at what prices, who are the best physicians, and so forth. Then comes a careful scientific survey of climatic and other conditions, such as average temperature, moisture, and the like; of the topography and prevailing diseases; and finally, he often makes a useful comparison between the place described and others which resemble it or seem to resemble it. We can recommend this handbook as being as convenient as it is unpretending.

Not only every physician but every physiologist, and every man of letters, will be glad to have Dr. Rolleston's address in its present useful form.[15] It received a warm welcome at the time of its delivery, and it was felt that the existence of a ceremony which resulted in an address of so much power and brilliancy was thereby amply justified. In Dr. Rolleston's oration we have not a more or less valuable scientific sermon adorned with tags and dictionary quotations, but it is penetrated throughout with that power and directness of thought and language which is the best result of academical culture. It is the earnest work of a scholar and a man of science, not the effusion of a sententious philosopher who has written up to a special occasion and published his address "at the request of many friends." All that Dr. Rolleston does has a purpose, and generally more than one.

Dr. Maudsley is a very considerable writer,[16] and we may think it

[14] "Klimatische Winterkurorte." Von Dr. Hermann Reimer. Zweite Auflage. Berlin, 1873.

[15] "The Harveian Oration for 1873." By George Rolleston, M.D. London, 1873.

[16] "Body and Mind." An enlarged and revised edition, with other Essays. By H. Maudsley, M.D. London, 1873.

well worth while to submit his writings to careful criticism both in respect of their intrinsic merit, and as expressive of the dominant thought of the day. In this place, however, such criticism is impossible. If we may speak shortly of Dr. Maudsley, we should speak of him as a highly finished author, by which we mean not only an elegant writer, but a complete thinker and an instructed physician. His merit consists less in flashes of originality, or in the winning of new fields of knowledge, and more in a mastery of that knowledge which is already won, and in a faculty of so organizing the various kinds of that knowledge as to leave the impression of novelty upon the reader. Many men have said Dr. Maudsley's things before him, but perhaps none have put them all so well together. Moreover, Dr. Maudsley's style is in like manner an accomplished style. He allows himself no rough periods, no inadequate or flimsy language, and no tracts of scanty or inappropriate reflection. He is always philosophical, always judiciously fervid, always restrained and courteous, so much so that even his antagonists are disarmed by his calm and sympathetic treatment of them. We were amused no little to see in the strangely ill-written and unbecoming article on Dr. Strauss in the October number of the *Edinburgh Review*, that the writer quoted Dr. Maudsley with an air of approval, which showed his unconsciousness of the iron hand below Dr. Maudsley's velvet glove. Perhaps there are few men who have more right to be politely scornful of such a writer than Dr. Maudsley himself. Unobtrusive as these essays may seem, yet to the making of them there has gone a wide reading, an impartial education of the judgment, and a minute cultivation of style which do much honour to the author, and will do much service to his own generation. The lecture on Conscience and Organization, and two essays, on Hamlet and Swedenborg, are added in the present edition. Both these latter essays are very interesting, and that on Hamlet shows an adequate literary culture, aided and enlightened by a psychological knowledge which has never been brought to bear on the play before.

It is proverbially difficult to distinguish between facts and inferences and to remember that we are too often guilty of basing upon inference a superstructure which we fondly suppose is built upon the rockiest of facts. Modern physiologists are well aware that the tongue is not essential to speech,[7] and they securely realize that knowledge now so familiar to them is in truth of but recent discovery. Moreover, it seems likely that this which is so familiar to them is probably new to the general public, and that Mr. Twisleton is amply justified in writing a popular book to enlighten those whose studies have not lain in the direction of physiology. For it appears that Roman Catholics have flattered themselves, even up to the present time, and that Dr. Newman in particular has flattered himself, that one miracle of the early Church at least is beyond all cavil. Certain persons known as the African Confessors were persecuted for the faith by the Vandal Huneric near the end of the fifth century. The particular atrocity

[7] "The Tongue not Essential to Speech." By the Hon. Edw. Twisleton. London, 1873.

which was perpetrated upon these wretched victims was the excision of their tongues, the punishment being intended no doubt to have a practical meaning for the false babblers. They were henceforth to have no power of spreading their detestable opinions by word of mouth at any rate. Yet in spite of this, we are told upon the evidence of a body of respectable witnesses, that in after years they were heard to speak as before. Clearly, then, here was a miraculous interposition of God, who granted speech to these believers for the confusion of their enemies. So respectable are the records of this so-called miracle that even the infidel Gibbon was silenced, and the Roman Church if it could not say much for some thousand or so of the rest of its miracles, had one left at least for its comfort and support. Now it turns out that Gibbon was rightly confounded and the early witnesses spoke the truth, but unluckily the facts when granted turn out not to be miraculous at all. In support of this latter view Mr. Twistleton quotes much evidence, the chief and strongest part of which he finds in the records of those who have talked in an equally miraculous way after the excision of their tongues by modern surgeons. But for all the interesting details of these cases and other things we must refer our readers to Mr. Twistleton's entertaining volume.

This pamphlet by Dr. Blanc[18] is sound and useful so far as it goes, and this is some comfort after the crude speculations to which writers on Cholera have lately treated us. We certainly recommend the little book to the attention of our readers, for it contains some new illustrative facts which are valuable, and the chapters on treatment bear the mark of a thoughtful and experienced physician.

On receiving this volume[19] our first feeling was one of regret that we should be called upon to review a compilation which no doubt had cost the author a great deal of trouble, but of which the only use seemed to be the profit which it might bring to the pocket of the publisher. There are several excellent treatises well known to the profession, which deal more or less adequately with medicine as a whole, and we certainly regarded the attempt to produce a smaller volume as a new effort in the direction of cram. However, as we have turned the book over we have grown more amiably disposed towards it, and we have certainly concluded that the author is a clear-headed and well instructed physician. We suppose that students now-a-days will not "wade through" Watson or Tanner, still less through Aitken, and Dr. Roberts' book is no doubt far more manageable. It will sell therefore, no doubt, among students, and if it helps on the cause of cram we have the examiners to thank. On the other hand, we must admit that the book cannot be accused of a very bare or scanty handling of its subjects; it seems equally done throughout, and science and practice are judiciously blended. Moreover, bulk is reduced quite as much by the avoidance of unnecessary detail as by the abridgment of more valuable matter. On the whole we think that the book will be a gain to students, and it certainly will not lead them

---

[18] "Cholera." By Henry Blanc, M.D. London, 1873.

[19] "A Handbook of Medicine." By F. T. Roberts, M.D. London, 1873.

astray. Our only fear is lest such handy compendiums encourage in them the notions that medicine is a thing of cut and dried diagnoses, and of appropriate remedies for each. It would be unfair to blame Dr. Roberts for following his predecessors in giving an anatomical classification of diseases, a method which seems to us not only vicious in itself, but to have great power for evil in narrowing the student's conceptions. The necessary consequence is that gastralgia, let us say, is put with actual dyspepsias and away from neuralgias elsewhere, as asthma is divided again from angina, and so on all through the nosology. To arrange diseases on a natural basis in accordance with their observed affinities may be very difficult, indeed it may be impossible, for we have never tried to write a system of medicine; but we must surely come to it in time, and if that time is not yet, well, we have a little longer to lament the inadequacy of our knowledge of the natural history of disease.

Perhaps no department of human affairs owes more to the doctrine of final causes than the treatment of disorder and disease by means of mineral waters.* Because it has pleased Providence to mix certain salts with the water of a spring, therefore it is indicated as a medicine for some kind of suffering humanity. Were we to approach the matter anew we should do so in a somewhat opposite frame of mind. We should think that a chance medley of salts, whose ocurrence and combination was due to nothing more than the characters of the strata through which a given spring found it way, could not meet the special views of complicated and varying maladies, except by the most extraordinary hazard. However, if we are to look at the matter otherwise—if given a special spring, there must be something for it to cure—then perhaps the task could not be better done than in the book before us. The volume, which consists of 850 large pages, contains, as we may fairly suppose, all the latest and best information upon a subject which, if important at all, certainly deserves an elaborate handling. To secure the best treatment of each separate watering-place the chief local doctors have been entrusted with the several chapters which relate to them respectively. We do not profess to have read the book, but we have read a good deal in it, and we cannot but feel much encouraged to find that no invalid need despair of finding a spring for his relief; nor, on the other hand, need any spring despair of finding invalids, for the list of diseases which are curable even by the least of them is very comforting. A distinguished physician once said to the writer, that the prescribing of medicine is invaluable as a regulation of the nursing, even when otherwise useless; and so it is with watering-places, the drinking of the waters, whether otherwise useful or not, is a famous regulation of the patient. Given a beautiful valley or upland, fine air, wholesome food, sufficient exercise, freedom from anxiety, the postman and the doctor, and you may well throw in a daily glass of a mild purgative or ferruginous water to serve as a central motive. The introduction by the editor is intelli-

* "Handbuch der Balneotherapie," redigirt von Dr. Th. Valentiner. Berlin, 1873.

gently written, and well worth reading in its way; but the effort to give an accurately scientific character to the chief subject of the work assumes to us, we must admit, the air of elaborate trifling. But we may be prejudiced or unenlightened.

Marienbad is one of those watering-places which have gained great celebrity during the last few years, and Dr. Jagielski has published a small book,[21] in which he gives us a sketch both of Marienbad itself, and of the value of its springs. The situation seems to be airy, sheltered, and beautiful, so that we are not surprised when the author tells us (page 3) that "the so-called 'air cury' produces the most surprising effects, so that mere residence and open air exercise in Marienbad and its environs is often a sufficient remedy." Accommodation in the way of hotels and reading-rooms is apparently all that can be desired, and Marienbad is therefore, no doubt, a welcome and delightful retreat for all who wish to escape from the confusing turmoil of populous towns. Any one who thinks he has earned such a holiday may have every hope that his own disease will be discovered among those over which the Marienbad springs exercise so beneficial an influence, and he could not, we are sure, do better than consult Dr. Jagielski before he goes, and go again to thank him on his return for his complete restoration.

We are much pleased to see this new edition of Dr. Althaus's admirable work[22] upon our table in so short a time after the appearance of its predecessor. The present is no re-issue, but a genuinely new edition. It is a much handsomer volume, and the text has been modified and enlarged so as to include all the latest and best work on the subject. Nor is the quantity of new matter to be measured by the mere multiplication of the pages, but it is introduced by way of revision and substitution, as well as of addition. A great number of interesting questions arise which it is impossible in this place to discuss, or even to summarize. We may state, however, that Dr. Althaus has made important changes in the first chapter on physics, where the conductivity of the different tissues, the rheostat and other things have been fully re-considered. The chapter on diagrams also has received considerable additions, among which we may refer to the remarks on the electric probe, and on faradization as a means of ascertaining death. In the fifth chapter electrolysis, always a strong point with the author, has been still further developed, and a section on mental diseases has been added. In this section, while quoting Arndt's few cases, Dr. Althaus has made no reference to the long series of therapeutical investigations of this kind made in the West Riding Asylum, the results of which were published in the second volume of the Reports of that institution. On the whole we think that Dr. Althaus still keeps his place as the leading exponent of medical electricity in this country, and that in each edition he advances upon himself and becomes a more and more trustworthy guide as he is led the more by his own larger and larger experience, and the less by such

---

21 "Marienbad Spa." By Dr. Jagielski. London, 1873.

22 "Treatise on Medical Electricity." By Julius Althaus, M.D. 3rd edit.

visionary writers as Remak and Benedikt. Did space permit, the present writer would willingly break a lance with Dr. Althaus on some points of difference between them—differences which depend in great part upon issues of fact, but also in no slight degree upon verbal or dialectic misunderstandings, to which the writer's inaccurate or imperfect explanations have probably given rise.

HISTORY AND BIOGRAPHY.

FOUR biographers and two translators have been engaged in producing for English readers the present biography of Alexander von Humboldt.[1] The work was originally undertaken in commemoration of the centenary of Humboldt's birth, and is a very worthy memorial of the author of "Cosmos." It is the first and only adequate biography that has yet appeared, although many attempts had previously been made to record the life and trace the process of development of his master mind. There were many reasons for previous failures. Humboldt himself was painfully shy of communicating anything relating to family affairs, and cordially detested all biographies. In respect for this well-known prejudice, his relatives and friends published immediately after his death a protest against the publication of confidential letters. It has, however, been found impossible to maintain this prohibition. The editor is of opinion that posterity has a just right to the letters of men whose public career is connected inseparably with the history of their country. Others have thought so too, and the result is, that a vast proportion of Humboldt's unpublished letters have been placed in the Editor's hands by friends of the late Baron, amongst whom may be mentioned the Empress-Queen Augusta. The present biography, therefore, has been compiled under circumstances peculiarly auspicious. It is impossible for us to follow in detail the varied incidents of Humboldt's life. Born at Berlin in 1769, he began his travels in 1790 with George Forster, and visited the Rhineland, Holland, and England. His tour through this country was rapid, but left a vivid impression upon his mind. Long years afterwards he spoke with pride of having heard Burke, Pitt, and Sheridan all speak in Parliament the same night. In 1795 he visited Italy, and subsequently Paris, where he made the friendship of Aimé Bonpland. In 1799 he obtained the fulfilment of a long-cherished plan—namely, that of undertaking a journey to the tropical regions of America, in a ship fitted out at his own expense. For this visit a permit from the King of Spain was necessary, and this being obtained, Humboldt sailed on the morning of June 5th, 1799, from the harbour of Corunna, in the *Pizarro*. He was accompanied by Bonpland, and they were well provided with scientific instruments. The expedition

---

[1] "Life of Alexander von Humboldt." By J. Löwenberg, R. Ave-Lallemant, and A. Dove. Edited by Karl Bruhns. 2 vols. Translated by Jane and Caroline Lassell. London: Longmans, Green and Co.

occupied five years, and was of incalculable value to science. This part of the biography is admirably treated by Löwenberg. Humboldt and his friend passed from Camana to Cuba, and on to Quito. In June, 1802, they ascended Chimborazo to a height of 18,570 feet above the level of the sea, at which height the atmosphere was so rarefied that blood started from their eyes and lips. They next went on to Assuay, over the magnificent road of the Incas, which lies, a porphyry causeway, across the Andes. In 1803 they reached the capital of Mexico, and the next year they investigated the Cordilleras. In May of that year they reached the United States, and in August landed in Europe, where their arrival spread great and universal joy. The rich collection of botanical specimens which they brought with them is unique, and of the highest value. It contains 6300 species of plants. For some time after this expedition Humboldt lived in Paris, pursuing in conjunction with Gay-Lussac, his investigations of the magnetic equator. In 1816 he was again in London, but the period from 1808 to 1826 was spent for the most part in Paris. This portion of Humboldt's life has for biographer M. Ave-Lallemant, who describes it as a "time of unobtrusive industry in a foreign country, which, succeeding to years of study and travel, was to be followed by the most important epoch of the life, passed in his native city." This final epoch was certainly different from the eventful periods which had preceded it. Henceforth he was to lead a life of comparative tranquillity and contemplation. M. Dove observes truthfully—

"He became increasingly the ideal representative of scientific progress, even in the details of close investigation, while at an earlier period he had been a leader in the path of inquiry."

And again—

"It is precisely as the representative of the scientific knowledge of the age, that he was so highly honoured by his contemporaries; the honours profusely showered upon the author of 'Cosmos' may after all be regarded merely as the homage offered by the men of the nineteenth century, proud of the grand achievements of modern science to their own comprehensive genius impersonated in a manner not granted to every age, in a living representative gifted with a mind alike distinguished for power of arrangement and universality of comprehension."

The last ten years of Humboldt's life was one perpetual scene of homage paid to scientific genius. Long trains of visitors filed towards the "plain two-storey house with a dull pink front" where the illustrious author lived. America sent a large and enthusiastic contingent of admirers, who worshipped, interviewed, and recorded their impressions in fervid eulogies. To one of them, said Humboldt, "You have travelled much, and seen many ruins, now you have seen one more." "Not a ruin," was the reply, "but a pyramid." And so the American admirer goes away in a fever of delight to record his conversation, yet with sufficient self-possession to observe that he passed a live Prince upon the stairs.

The end came on May 6th, 1859. Humboldt's intellect had remained clear to the last. All honour was done him at his death by the whole civilized world, and the centenary of his birth, which followed so closely upon his death, was celebrated by those who had known and loved him.

The concluding section of this biography is the best. It is affectionate and yet just. We shall conclude our notice of this valuable work with the following extract:—

"The achievements for which science is indebted to Humboldt are of a character to be easily enumerated. However exaggerated may be the modesty that led him in a moment of depression to assert: 'I know that in the realm of science I shall leave behind me but a faint track,' it is yet true that the track he has left in the world of thought of his century is neither so deep nor so marked as to permit his name to be applied to the whole or even a part of this high road of progress. Nor do we find a sufficient cause for the splendour of his name in the countless services he rendered to science by the powerful influence he was able to exert in inciting others to labour. It is to be expected that a just estimate of the value of his achievements, now confined to the student of individual branches of science, will in a future age become universal."

Mr. Mackay in writing the present biography of the author of the "Institutions of the Law of Scotland,"* has done a good work and one of some difficulty. To form the living picture of a man removed by nearly two centuries from our own time, and to do this with deficient information as to those minute particulars which biographers generally have at hand, is the task which Mr. Mackay has set before himself. Unfortunately most of the Dalrymple papers were destroyed by a fire at Castle Kennedy, but there is still ample matter for an account of Skeir's public acts, and for an estimate of his character as a statesman, judge, and author. James Dalrymple, the son of a Scotch laird, was born in 1619. Both his parents were descended from noted adherents of the Reformation, and their son was sent to the University of Glasgow, in the year in which Charles I. was crowned at Edinburgh. At this University he attained the position of Regent, and married in 1643 Margaret Ross; the condition of celibacy obligatory upon a Regent being remitted in his case. In 1648 he was admitted Advocate, and during the next few years he twice visited Holland upon important commissions, and became acquainted with Milton's antagonist Salmatius. In 1657 he was admitted to the bench by the Council, and his appointment was confirmed by Cromwell. Upon the Restoration he went to London and was received with favour by the king and knighted. He, however, shortly afterwards refused to sign the declaration which Charles had required from all persons in public trust, and placed his resignation in the king's hands. This, however, was practically not accepted, and he resumed his seat as a baronet. In 1670 Stair was appointed one of the Commissioners for the union of the two kingdoms. Mr. Mackay traces his legal career until his fall, which occurred in 1681. Both he and Argyle had refused to vote on the infamous Test Act; Argyle was committed to prison and condemned to death. Stair retired to his country seat in Galloway, and employed his leisure in the preparation of his

* "Memoir of Sir James Dalrymple, First Viscount Stair. By Æ. J. G.

great work, the "Institutions of the Law of Scotland." Of this work Mr. Mackay writes:—

"It forms a complete body of law or *corpus juris* for Scotland. A master-mind was required even when the law was less complex than it now is, to grasp the various parts and unite them in a complete whole; but given such a mind, the work done is one that may endure, though many and even most of its parts should be altered by the changes which time brings to every system of positive jurisprudence—for it represents Scotch law as it existed when first moulded into shape by the great lawyers of the sixteenth and seventeenth centuries from which the existing law has been and the future law will be developed. Perhaps the traits which most deserve admiration are the consummate order or arrangement of the work, which once apprehended can never be forgotten, and the concise clearness of the expression."

Stair was not, however, left to the quiet enjoyment of his literary leisure in Galloway. In 1682 he was compelled to leave the country, having entered into a conflict of jurisdiction with Claverhouse, who had been commissioned to put down Conventicles. In Leyden, to which he now withdrew, he appeared as an author in a new field by the publication of his "*Physiologia nova Experimentalis*," a work not of much importance, though exhibiting, Mr. Mackay thinks, independent thought and close observation. Whilst still in Holland, Stair was tried and condemned for treason. He was subsequently pardoned, and returned to England with William of Orange in 1688. Two years later he was created Viscount of Stair. Mr. Mackay does not disperse the cloud which hangs over the name of Stair in connexion with the massacre of Glencoe, but he coincides with Mr. Paget in attributing the greater part of the guilt of that crime to William. There were, however, many other charges brought against Viscount Stair in his later years, and his family became notoriously detested. These charges would have tried the spirit of most men. They tried his; and in 1695 he died at Edinburgh. Of his character Lord Macaulay has spoken in his history with unmixed severity. Mr. Mackay has been a more charitable historian, and has certainly been more minute in his investigation of Stair's life. Scotchmen at any rate may be glad to receive a careful and kindly biography of one who, whatever his faults, was the founder of the law of their country.

Mr. Fitz-Patrick's "History of Louis II., Prince of Bourbon," generally known as the great Condé,[1] is written in a measured and dignified style. Although the author's opinions are in many cases open to objection, and although he writes from a Roman Catholic point of view, there can be no question that he has the power of depicting clearly and instructively the characters and events which marked the unhappy period of the Fronde. This period of the Fronde lasted from 1648 to 1654. The Fronde was the French party which during the minority of Louis XIV. opposed the regency of the Queen-mother and Mazarin. In this regency the party of the Fronde saw continued the despotism of Richelieu under other forms. The taxes which were laid upon the people were immense, and aroused the anger

---

[1] "The Great Condé, and the Period of the Fronde." A Historical Sketch. By Walter Fitz-Patrick. 2 vols. London: T. Cautley Newby.

not only of the vulgar sufferers, but of princes of the blood. At the head of the Fronde stood the Coadjutor De Retz. These troubles are well related by Mr. Fitz-Patrick, but it is for the character of the "great Condé" that he reserves his chief power. This prince had defeated at the battle of Rocroi the Spaniards when he was only twenty-two years of age, and bore the title of Duke of Enghien. He brought the disastrous period of the Fronde to an end, and became an enemy of Mazarin, who had still sufficient strength to shut him up for a year as prisoner at Vincennes. Upon his release he entered into negotiations with Spain, and was enabled to march against Paris. In 1652 he had an engagement with Marshal Turenne in the Faubourg St. Antoine. This was not, however, decisive, and Condé withdrew to the Netherlands. In 1650 he returned to France, and after the death of Turenne he commanded the French army in Germany. His later years though painful through ill-health were passed in retirement at Chantilly, where he enjoyed intercourse with Corneille, Bossuet, Racine, Boileau, and Boundalone, and died at Fontainebleau in 1687. We have said that some of Mr. Fitz-Patrick's views are open to grave objections. They are certainly remarkable. He says that the "evening of Condé's life was gilded by the glow of a splendid prosperity," yet at the very time his wife, the "devoted," "heroic" Princess of Condé, was pining away in imprisonment in the stern old castle of Chateauroux, for an offence of which she was then believed innocent and is now known to have been so. Mr. Fitz-Patrick, though he says that "in an age of licentiousness and impiety Condé had been notorious as a *roué* and a scoffer," and that when that age had passed away his irreligious sentiments remained unchanged, is yet anxious to claim him for the Roman Catholic Church. It pleases Mr. Fitz-Patrick to relate that in 1685, the year of his death, he publicly returned to the "bosom of Christianity," and he asserts that his submission to the church was "a severe blow to infidels." We have already indicated the fact that the book is written from a Roman Catholic point of view. We will not say that this entirely spoils Mr. Fitz-Patrick's work, but it certainly colours and distorts his view of historical events. Thus, in speaking of the massacre of St. Bartholomew, the excesses of the Spanish Inquisition, and Louis XIV.'s oppression of the Huguenots, he does not explicitly attempt to justify these atrocities, but he naively remarks: "It should be remembered that in a system based upon the doctrine of infallibility repression of dissent is not what it is in systems based on freedom of judgment, a glaring violation of fundamental principle." To which we will only add that we sincerely hope it may be eternally fixed upon the memories of each and all.

M. De Flandre gives to the world two large volumes[1] which M. Petit has written in defence of the unfortunate Mary Stuart. In his eyes she is only unfortunate, and the present work is an appeal against

---

[1] "History of Mary Stuart, Queen of Scots." Translated from the Original and Unpublished MS. of Professor Petit. By Charles de Flandre, F.S.A. Scot. London: Longmans, Green and Co.

the prevailing belief in her guilt. "For twenty years," says M. Petit, "M. Mignet in France, Mr. Froude in England, and Professor Von Raumer in Germany, have swayed the minds of the people, and the few voices raised in Mary's defence have been drowned and lost amid the outcries of her slanderers." Once more, therefore, M. Petit raises his voice. He says that he has ransacked the libraries of Paris, London, and Edinburgh; he has certainly included some curious documents in his large and handsome volumes. He says that he writes not for those who read for pleasure, and indeed there is not much pleasure to be got out of his book. This is of less consequence, as it matters, he says, little to him whether the public hold his views or not. The writing of the book has met with special encouragement from the Empress Eugénie. The motto which the author has chosen for his title page will sufficiently warn the reader that he is not treading the trustworthy paths of history under M. Petit's guidance. "D'aller faire le neutre ou l'indifférent sous prétexte que j'écris une histoire serait faire au lecteur une illusion trop grossière."

Yet if M. Petit is under the fascination which attaches to personages who have occupied a great portion of the world's attention, our next authoress is not less so. Mrs. Abel's book[1] is, however, one which can be read with pleasure. The first edition of her "recollections" appeared in 1844, and her daughter has just revised and published the third edition. Mrs. Abel was at the time of Napoleon's stay at St. Helena a little girl, residing with her father, who was a navy agent upon the island, in which capacity it was his duty to act as purveyor to the Emperor. It happened upon Napoleon's arrival at St. Helena that he greatly admired the "Briars," the residence of Mrs. Abel's father, and expressed a wish to remain there. It was accordingly arranged that he should stay at this cottage until his residence at Longwood was fit to receive him. During this time he seems to have conceived an attachment, not rare between great men and children, to the authoress of this book. The interest of the book depends upon the childish freedom with which a little English girl was permitted to converse with the great enemy of her nation. Once, indeed, having obtained the Emperor's sword, she began to flourish it over his head, making passes at him. The Emperor retreated until at last she fairly pinned him up in the corner, telling him all the time that he had better say his prayers, inasmuch as she was going to kill him. From this position he was released by his grand chamberlain, whose parchment visage glowed with indignation at the insult offered to the Emperor. It is pleasing to hear that "Mademoiselle Betsee" had her ears pinched and her nose pulled heartily as her reward. The book contains other amusing stories. "Mademoiselle Betsee" appears to have made the imprisonment of Napoleon at times additionally unpleasing to him. She compelled him to play blindman's buff, she snatched away his private papers, and threatened to learn all

[1] "Recollections of the Emperor Napoleon on the Island of St. Helena." By Mrs. Abel. Third Edition. Revised, and added to, by her Daughter, Mrs. C. Johnstone. London: Sampson Low, Marston and Co.

his secrets, and she compelled him to show himself to ugly young ladies who wanted to view the Corsican ogre. Generally Napoleon seems to have treated her good naturedly; at other times he had his revenge. One day to annoy her he said that her countrywomen drank gin and brandy; and added in Imperial English, "You laike veree mosh dreenk, Mees, sometimes brandee, geen." After his removal to Longwood the family of the authoress frequently visited him. Naturally in a narrative of this kind events are chronicled which fall somewhat below the dignity of history. We are told of Napoleon's suffering severely when he had a tooth extracted; that the authoress cut an embroidered bugle from his coat; that he often slept in the day; that he once took some pills thinking them to be *bonbons*, and that he got drenched by the splashing of a Newfoundland dog. These incidents are related with amusing simplicity by Mrs. Abel. She does not deal much with more important subjects, but she clearly indicates the bitterness which existed between Napoleon and Sir Hudson Lowe. Mrs. Johnstone's Appendix to the Third Edition adds but little to the book. It consists chiefly of *her* recollections of Napoleon the Third. How that he was pleased to learn that his hair resembled that of his uncle; how he always came to her mother's house in a cabriolet, and finally how when he had become Emperor, he obtained for a *protégée* of her mother the post of Court milliner. It is therefore not unnatural that Mrs. Johnstone should confess to being an ardent Bonapartist, but we do not understand why she has added these details to her mother's narrative in the hope that they will be of any assistance to the "extraordinary position of France at the present moment."

Mr. Thackeray's "Four Georges,"* always readable, was never more so than in the present elegant and handy edition. It is unnecessary for us to speak of the book itself; it is known to all, yet perhaps no one will regret to have the following anecdote recalled. It is of George the Third.

> "One morning before anybody else was up, the king walked about Gloucester town, pushed over Molly the housemaid who was scrubbing the doorsteps with her pail, ran upstairs and woke all the equerries in their bedrooms; and then trotted down to the bridge, where by this time a dozen of louts were assembled. 'What! is this Gloucester New Bridge?' asked our gracious monarch; and the people answered him, 'Yes, your Majesty.' 'Why, then, my boys,' said he, 'let us have a huzzay!' After giving them which intellectual gratification he went home to breakfast."

How perfect is the picture.

The work† next before us introduces us into society very different from that with which Mr. Thackeray familiarizes us. Very few of the names which it contains are widely known, and yet they have had an influence which may or may not remain. Something without doubt has occurred to change the public opinion of all classes

---

* "The Four Georges." By W. M. Thackeray. A New Edition. London: Smith, Elder and Co.

† "The Early Heroes of the Temperance Reformation." By William Logan, Glasgow, Scottish Temperance League.

with regard to intemperate abuse of intoxicating liquors. The gross customs so graphically described by Mr. Thackeray no longer prevail in cultivated society, at least not openly, and meet in all society with a reprobation formerly unknown. How far this change has been brought about by the general increase of intelligence, and how far by individual enthusiasm and the contagion of example we are unable to decide. Mr. Logan and the Scottish Temperance League evidently suppose that much may be done by the united efforts of Temperance Societies, and the oratory and example of temperance advocates. They have now published short biographies of the chief Scotch temperance advocates. The present little book contains ten or a dozen of such biographies. They are written with great enthusiasm and without the slightest pretension to literary merit or interest. It seems that the first Temperance Society in Scotland was established in 1820, and it is surprising to notice how many of the temperance advocates have since passed away. Mr. Logan has, however, printed the epitaphs of most of them in large letters, which may add to the interest with which his book will be regarded by the members of his League.

A better book is the one by Mr. Halwin Campbell.[8] It is written in a very pleasant style for young readers, and contains excellent biographies of distinguished men. It includes those of Sir William Jones, Palissy, Tyndale, Flaxman, and Inigo Jones, which last, as being least known, is perhaps the best. The morals are not enforced with that reiteration of the intolerably obvious which characterizes many books of the same class.

For the students of the Public Records, and the national archives, Mr. Ewald's new hand-book[9] will be found extremely useful. A previous work of the same kind was compiled twenty years ago by Mr. Thomas, late secretary of the Public Record office. But the last twenty years have witnessed many important additions to the national archives, and no slight changes in the mode of their arrangement. Accordingly Mr. Ewald has drawn up a list of the most important documents, arranged in such a manner as to be easy of reference, and to readily catch the eye. The arrangement which he has finally deemed most desirable is the alphabetical. But besides this list, Mr. Ewald has several interesting chapters upon the custody of the Public Records, the Records themselves and the State Papers. Few students of history to whom is now accessible the magnificent series of volumes "published under the authority of the Master of the Rolls," can fully realize the difficulty with which permission was obtained until very recently to consult these national archives. The State Papers were always regarded as private and confidential. The keeper was bound by oath "to let no man see anything in the office of His Majesty's papers without a warrant from the king." This rule is still in force

[8] "The Art of doing our Best, as seen in the Life of Thorough Workers." Gall and Inglis.

[9] "Our Public Records; a Brief Handbook to the National Archives." By Alex. C. Ewald, F.S.A., one of the Senior Clerks of Her Majesty's Public Records. London: Basil Montagu Pickering.

for the examination of papers after a certain date, nor will any one be likely to question its propriety. The instances of permission conceded to search the papers were formerly extremely rare. In 1670 Evelyn, who was commanded by the king to write a history of the Dutch war, was allowed to have access to the papers. "I spent the whole afternoon," he says, Oct. 14th, "in private with the treasurer, who put into my hands those secret pieces and transactions concerning the Dutch war, and particularly the expedition of Bergen." In 1679 Dr. Burnett was permitted to have the use of certain papers which he thought might give him help in finishing his history of the Reformation of the Church of England. Roger Le Strange, Collier, and Strype were also granted this rare favour. Even so late as 1775 Lord North, then Prime Minister, had to beg "the king's approval to have free access to all correspondence in the Paper Office." Lord Romilly has changed all this, and students find now no difficulty in consulting the State Papers. The housing of the magnificent and unequalled documents which the nation possesses has been in strong contrast to the value of the muniments. The early Chancery records from the time of John, and the Admiralty Records were kept in the Tower of London. Part of them were in close proximity to a steam engine in daily operation; others were packed in the White Tower; others choked up Cæsar's chapel. Under the whole were stored several tons of gunpowder and inflammable stores. In 1842, within forty feet of this place a fire broke out, and fire engines deluged the Tower for a night. Other important records were in 1822, stored in a temporary shed at the end of Westminster Hall, but in 1830 they were removed to the King's Mews at Charing Cross. A select committee of the House of Commons in reporting upon the conditions of these records in 1836, stated that some of them were in the last stage of putrefaction. Six or seven perfect skeletons of rats were found embedded in the rolls, and bones of these vermin were generally distributed through the mass. Upon the demolition of the Mews the records were removed to the stables of Carlton House. Mr. Ewald says:—"These two repositories—the Tower and the Carlton shed—contained in those days by far the greatest bulk of our records." But other records were indifferently lodged. "Domesday Book" lay close to a wash-house and brewhouse, reported as dangerous, others lay in the Rolls Chapel, a place heated by hot air flues. Many did actually perish by fire at New Square, Lincoln's Inn. It was only in 1859 that the Records were rescued from their ignominious repositories and brought to their present secure lodgings in the Record Office. It is satisfactory to learn from Mr. Ewald that the accommodation now afforded to our invaluable archives would satisfy the most sensitive antiquary. The account of the records themselves deposited within the massive-walled, iron-bound building upon the Rolls Estate is no less interesting, and is excellently given by Mr. Ewald. The Close Rolls, the Patent Rolls, and the Pipe Roll are briefly but clearly dealt with, and their value to the lawyer, the historian, and the antiquarian pointed out. But the interest of ordinary Englishmen will centre chiefly round that which Mr. Ewald calls the Koh-i-noor of archives, "Domesday Book." This father of our record literature is now carefully preserved beneath a strong glass case in the room of the Curator of the Record Office. It consists of two volumes. Some of the capital letters and principal passages are touched with red ink, and the names of towns, manors, &c., have strokes of red ink run across them, the ancient mode of expressing italics. We have now almost said enough concerning Mr. Ewald's interesting book; it only remains for us to add that it contains an admirable glossary of words to be found in the Public Records. It has been compiled from the best sources, and will considerably facilitate the labours of those who consult the original documents of which Mr. Ewald has drawn up a list.

We shall now pass on to notice those record publications which have reached us this quarter. Sir Travers Twiss has issued the second volume of the work, the first of which we noticed two years ago, the "Black Book of the Admiralty."[10] The present volume is an appendix to the former, and not a continuation of it. It contains the "Domus Day of Gippeswiche;" the "Customs of Oleron and of the Judgments of the Sea;" the "Good Usages, and the Good Customs, and the Good Judgements of the Commune of Oleron." Also the "Constitution of the Commune of Royan." To these documents, which are in English and French, Dr. Twiss has prefixed a copious introduction which is characterized by his special learning and laborious research, and which deals with questions of the growth of modern maritime law. A good index completes the work.

Our next chronicle, "The Register of the Second Abbacy of John Whethamstede,"[11] is not without value as conveying the testimony of one or more contemporaries in reference to the political events of the times. The political history contained in the present work begins with the first battle of St. Albans, and ends soon after its second. Mr. Riley says in a very good introduction that those who wish at a glance to learn the nature and extent of the historical information which this register contains, will find facility in doing so by using the minute and copious index which he has supplied. He has added also a glossary wherein the curious may discover the meanings of such words as "*pandoxatórium*," "*sarabaita*," "*warderobarius*," and "*bobinantes*." The book appears to be of less value and interest than others of the record publications.

The record edited by Mr. Horwood[12] is a collection of early law reports which contain several points of interest. They contain among others constructions of the statutes *De Donis* and *Quia Emptores*. This

---

[10] "The Black Book of the Admiralty Appendix." Part II. Edited by Sir Travers Twiss. Published under the direction of the Master of the Rolls. Longman and Co. Trübner and Co.

[11] "Registra Johannis Whethamstede, Willelmi Albon et Willelmi Wallingforde abbatum monasterii Sancti Albani. Edited by H. T. Riley, M.A. Published under the direction, &c.

[12] "Year Books of the Reign of King Edward the First (years xxi. and xxii)." Edited and Translated by A. J. Horwood, of the Middle Temple, Barrister-at-law. Published under the direction, &c.

volume has no introduction, but a full index. A table of names also facilitates reference to the various cases. The next volume is to compr.se the years 33rd, 34th, and 35th Edw. I., being the last years of his reign.

This first part of the third volume of the "Spanish Calendar"[13] is a ponderous tome of more than eleven hundred pages. It is a continuation of the calendar which the late G. A. Bergenroth left unfinished at his death in 1870. The English portion of Bergenroth's collection was far from complete, his chief design being to write in his native tongue a general history of the Emperor and the religious troubles in Germany. He was, moreover, unaware of the mass of correspondence lying amidst the imperial archives of Vienna. The present editor learned their existence through the suggestions of Mr. Froude. Permission to see them was obtained through the agency of Lord Romilly, then Master of the Rolls, and transcripts of the portion relating to English history were made. In his introduction to this volume M. de Gayangos gives us a short notice of the various writers whose correspondence is registered in the present calendar, Praet, Le Sauch Sessa, Mendoza, and others. Of these papers and letters, in which England is only incidentally mentioned, the editor has abstracted only that portion having reference to the facts by which the politics of England were influenced. This huge volume has no index, the reader is therefore left for the present without compass upon an Atlantic of abstracts.

Another valuable collection of abstracts[14] written in the Latin language is edited by Herr Potthast. It contains the acts and decrees of Pope Innocent II. from February of the year 1203 to his death in 1216, "Cujus finis," says a chronicler herein quoted, "lætitiam potius quam tristitiam generavit subjectis." It contains, moreover, the annals of Honorius III. to the year 1227. The whole series, of which we have before us three numbers, extends from 1198 to 1304. The book appears to have been published at the expense of the Berlin Academy, from which society it received a prize.

The pleasant letters of Miss Betham-Edwards are a good specimen of a lady's literary work.[15] They are bright and sunny, and vividly bring before the reader the impressions which the foreign scenes described made upon a cultivated feminine mind. De Quincey, as every one knows, thought that the perfection of English style was to be found in the letters which ladies write. Ladies now-a-days do not write letters, they write books, and if De Quincey had lived in the days of Miss Braddon, Mrs. Wood, and Ouida, it is probable that his judgment would have been more guardedly expressed or altogether different. But Miss Betham-Edwards's letters go far to justify what

---

[13] "Calendar of Letters, Despatches, and State Papers, relating to the Negotiations between England and Spain, preserved in the Archives at Simancas and elsewhere." Vol. III., Part I. Edited by Pascual de Gayangos. Published under the direction, &c.

[14] "Regesta Pontificum Romanorum." Edidit Augustus Westfalus. Fasciculi II., III., IV. Berolini. Londini: D. Nutt.

[15] "Holiday Letters, from Athens, Cairo, and Weimar." By M. Betham-Edwards. London: Strahan and Co.

be said: they are simply and elegantly written. The following description of twilight at Cairo is pretty:—

"I think the loveliest sight to be seen at Cairo, or indeed anywhere else in the world, is the twilight. The vivid colours of sunset die out one by one, and are replaced by opaline hues, so vapoury, lucent, and etherial, that mosque and minaret, palace and fortress, appear part of cloudland. An extra sense of vision seems to be bestowed upon the gazer on those undreamed of and airy transformations. A few moments ago the Eastern city flashed resplendent in the light of the setting sun; now it is a structure of pearl floating in an amber-coloured mist."—p. 26.

Yet we confess we have a little suspicion of Miss Betham-Edwards's power of word-painting. Perhaps the colours are a little too ready to her brush, though she wave it never so gracefully. Thus (page 51) we have a light and delicate picture of the view from the Pyramid:—

"Looking down the river upon the Delta, with its patches of green and gold; its brown villages and palms; southward you look up the river; east upon the wonderful city of Cairo, with its domes and minarets innumerable; west upon the African Sahara, indefinable, illimitable, '*terra domibus negata.*'"

We said that we viewed Miss B.-Edwards's word-sketches with "suspicion;" perhaps "awe" would be the better word. For in fact Miss B.-Edwards confesses that she was never at the top of a pyramid. "I did not go to the top of the Pyramid," she says, "nor did I go to the bottom." But her description of the view from the top is very pretty. At Smyrna our authoress saw the dancing dervishes and then proceeded to Athens. Now with regard to Athens, we must say that Miss B.-Edwards brings it before us as it is, in a way that no other lady writer has done. The nightingales that sing during the May days, the little garden of the hotel full of familiar flowers, the ever-present shadow of the irrecoverable past which must hang over every visitor to Athens, are so vividly described that we quite forgive Miss B.-Edwards her fancy-picture of the Egyptian view. Having seen the ruins of Athens and recorded them with judicious and well-chosen references to Sophocles, Plato, Xerxes, &c., Miss B.-Edwards visited the Arsakion, a public school for girls, founded by M. Arsaki. Her account of this institution is charming. Then Miss B.-Edwards proceeds to the Acropolis, but we will not follow her, for the scenery is favourable to a dithyrambic fancy. From Athens our authoress went *viâ* Venice to Weimar. Here she spent two months, and made many reflections. Her notes upon music and art in Weimar are appreciative, and she was acquainted with the Frau Von Goethe. Her whole book may be read with interest, and her remarks on Athens are really good.

Mr. T. Hughes, in editing some lectures[16] of the late F. D. Maurice, has taken the opportunity of speaking upon the wider question of Mr. Maurice's position in theological matters. The present lectures or addresses are collected as illustrating how completely his theology underlay all his thoughts, and "how fresh and vigorous, and above all how intensely national and human" that theology was. Mr. Hughes,

---

[16] "The Friendship of Books and other Lectures." By the Rev. F. D. Maurice. Edited, with a Preface, by T. Hughes, M.P. London: Macmillan.

however, does not, as we have indicated, confine himself to the subject of the book which he has edited, but enters upon a general apology for Mr. Maurice's position. In this apology he meets the remarks which Mr. Matthew Arnold has made in his last work, "Literature and Dogma." There he has spoken of Mr. Maurice as "that pure and devout spirit—of whom, however, the truth must be at last said, that in theology he passed his life beating the bush with deep emotion, and never starting the hare." Mr. Hughes admits that it is as a theologian Mr. Maurice must be judged; he admits that in Mr. Maurice's system there was much "beating of the bush;" but he goes on to maintain that Mr. Arnold has also "much beating of the bush," and that his "definition of God" is not so good as that which Mr. Maurice taught. What Mr. Hughes says of Mr. Arnold is gently said, and every one will agree with Mr. Hughes in regretting that Mr. Arnold should so far forget his "sweet reasonableness," or, in plainer words, his good taste, as to talk as he has done of the three Lords Shaftesbury; but for all that we are left with the conviction that there is something in Mr. Arnold's view of Mr. Maurice which Mr. Hughes has not fully met. Mr. Hughes is less gentle in dealing with the other schools of thought. "We are asked by one clever school," says Mr. Hughes, "to write humanity with a big H, and then to fall down and worship it." This school is shortly dealt with; Mr. Hughes declines to worship the image which, by the way, he has himself set up. Mr. Morley has nearly a page of reprobation to himself. Mr. Frederic Harrison and Mr. Darwin are set up to be knocked down, and Professor Huxley is brought in to show how little he is at variance with the spirit of Mr. Maurice's teaching. By this judicious policy of extermination and reconciliation, we rapidly arrive at Mr. Hughes's conclusion, that it is the duty of every man to "take courage and make trial of the same guidance"—namely, that of Mr. Maurice. Mr. Hughes's preface is perhaps not altogether satisfactory; there is a tone of championship about it which Mr. Maurice does not at all need. The lectures which follow on literature, history, and language are excellent, they have a note of permanence which the preface is without. There is no fear that Mr. Maurice should be underrated, there *is* some fear lest the public should overrate his friends.

Another volume in the series of ancient classics for English readers, Lucian,[17] maintains the position which the previous volumes have deservedly won. The present author is the editor of the whole series, and some of the best volumes have come from his pen. Lucian is one of the most interesting writers of later Greece. He was born on the banks of the Euphrates, and lived, it is said, to be a century old. One question concerning him has long occupied the attention of students—the question namely, how far he was connected with Christianity. He has written, Mr. Collins says, the history of one Peregrinus who became a Christian, but being detected in some profanation of the Eucharist, threw off his profession, and returned to his

[17] "Ancient Classics for English Readers: Lucian." By the Rev. W. Lucas Collis, M.A. Edinburgh: W. Blackwood and Sons.

old profligate life. The self-immolation of Peregrinus described by Lucian bears a considerable resemblance to the martyrdoms often morbidly sought by the early Christians. But Mr. Collins is probably right in assuming that of the new kingdom which had arisen Lucian had in fact no conception. We quote Mr. Collins's words:—

"He did not care enough about the Christians to hate them much. Their refusal to sacrifice to the national idols—the great testing point of their martyrs under the reigning emperors—could have been no great crime in the eyes of the author of the 'Dialogues of the Gods.' Fanaticism in that direction was no worse than fanaticism in any other."

The whole series hitherto has been well done, this volume especially so.

Mr. Adams, who has sent us a translation of the first book of the Iliad,"[18] has before this made himself known to a section of the public. We learn from the advertisement which he has affixed to his present badly printed work, that he once wrote a tragedy which Mr. J. M. Bellew read in public. Thereupon appeared reviews in *Once a Week*, the *Examiner*, the *Era*, and the *Tablet*. All these reviews spoke favourably of the unknown poet whom Mr. Bellew had sprung upon the town. Fired by this praise Mr. Adams has determined to bring his scholarly mind to bear upon a translation of Homer. At present he has got no farther than the first book of the "Iliad," which is before us. It does not, we confess, strike us as a good translation. We will notice a few of the faults. The following bad grammar, for instance, is attributed to none other than Zeus himself:—

"Madam, *you* always are thinking and I by no means overlook *you*,
But to perform *thou* shalt not have power."

Of line 167 the following is no correct translation of the Greek:—

"Still do I take my share—my own, my dear little portion."

All the dignity of the original has evaporated.

The following line too (553) has not much epic grandeur:—

"Really I never before either searched or ventured a question."

Lines 393, 396, are incorrectly rendered. We take these lines at random, but as we turn over the pages we see several more, 158, 170, 171, 200, 205, 231, and others. Upon the whole we hope Mr. Adams will not go on with his translation of the "Iliad." Let him confine himself to writing tragedies for Mr. Bellew, he will then be sure of one reader.

Amongst the books which have reached us this quarter we find a volume of poems[19] by Mr. Brennan. Though the department of literature to which it belongs is usually treated elsewhere, we will

---

[18] "The First Book of the Iliad, Translated into English Hexameters." By W. Masham Adams, B.A., Author of "Zenobia," a Tragedy. London: Mead and Company.

[19] "The Witch of Nemi, and other Poems." By Edward Brennan. London: S. Tinsley.

endeavour here to mete it such justice as it deserves. It is an attractive work,—externally, we mean. It is strikingly got up. An Egyptian scarabæus in gold climbs up one corner, a golden butterfly flies down from another, a serpent is coiled in a third, and a comet flashes from a fourth. The appropriateness of these symbols we have failed to learn from a perusal of the volume. It consists of many lyrics and some dramatic pieces, but unity is preserved throughout by the pretentious poverty of all. The first poem, which gives its name to the book, is a somewhat long and confused story of the loves of Apollo and a Vestal. There is very little incident in it, and the author wanders into some incomprehensible vision of Jove and Hell and crimson worms seventy cubits long with bright teeth of an opal hue, which leads the poet to the conclusion that men hate light "like dogs who at the moon do bark." Farther on our poet proceeds to bark at the moon himself, and in a series of strophes extending over fifteen pages, addresses the moon in such stanzas as

"Thou monarch of the noctum gloom,
Thou fair and fruitful maid serene,
Over the slumbering world O shed
The tranquil glow of peace supreme,
And melancholy with thy light
Shroud in the magic of a dream."

Mr. Brennan is an authority on the subject of worms and serpents. The following facts will be interesting to naturalists:—

"The serpent hath eyes fascinating,
And kisses delicious and keen,
But treachery lives in its favours,
And death in its poisonous spleen."

With regard to kisses, we may mention that Mr. Brennan sprinkles them over his pages more profusely than Johannes Secundus ever used them. This is a fault of taste. Unfortunately there are worse faults in the book. The dramatic passage between Joseph and Potiphar's wife, as described by Mr. Brennan, we can only characterize as obscene, and the verses styled the "Dream of Cyborra" are repulsive to sight and hearing. None of the poems at all approach the world of art, most of them are nasty. We have read the book with surprise and repugnance, but the height of our surprise was reached when we found Mr. Brennan abusing Mr. Swinburne, whom he supposes to be the leader of a Communist band, in the following dismal imitation of the true poet's rhythm:—

"Justice—death crush such radical ravings,
They are prompted by maniac wit;
They'd have blood draughts to satiate their cravings.
Let them drink till they are drunk with it!

"Pour it forth till a new reign of terror
Shall succeed to the notes of such chaunts;
Whose reasonless rhymes do make error
Stand rampant in holier haunts!"

We think Mr. Brennan does better to bark at the moon than to yelp at Mr. Swinburne's heels.

Dr. Hildebrand has written in Swedish a very excellent account of Sweden,[50] its people, and the development of its civilization in pagan times. This has now been translated into German by Herr Mestorf. To this translation he has made certain additions of his own, with the approval of the author. The whole book is now a very clear and concise history of the early Scandinavian peoples, illustrated by the antiquarian remains which have been at various times discovered. A map and forty-four small woodcuts enable the reader to follow the author with increased interest.

Professor Whitney's German Grammar[51] has gone through several editions. It seems to us to be rather too diffuse for a young student, and not sufficiently complete for the student who would use it only as a book of reference. Its mode of dealing with the declensions of nouns, the *pons asinorum* of German students, is not a helpful one A learner would find it easier to acquire each plural by individual observation than to learn it from Professor Whitney's grammar. The chapters upon derivation and the construction of sentences are better, and the index is full and good.

Professor Whitney's German Reader[52] seems to be carefully compiled. There is a full vocabulary, which will enable the student to dispense with a dictionary until he has acquired a fair mastery over the language. The notes are grammatical and explanatory, but unnecessarily wordy. Professor Whitney is rather too addicted to variations of type. A certain variety may be useful, but a chase for a paragraph in Professor Whitney's book is like a ride across country. However, the two books of which we have spoken are two meritorious attempts to facilitate the acquirement of German, and we cordially wish them success. The Grammar has, indeed, already won it.

We cannot now do more than acknowledge the receipt of Mr. Howell's "Concise History of England,"[53] which seems an honest and symmetrical work; of Captain Bedford Pim's "War Chronicle,"[54] an energetic expression of sympathy with France in the late war, and of two more numbers of Mr. Black's translation of Guizot's "History of France."[55]

---

[50] "Das Heidnische Zeitalter in Schweden eine archäologisch-historische Studie." Von Dr. Hans Hildebrand, übersetzt von J. Mestorf. Hamburg: Otto Meisner.

[51] "A Compendious German Grammar."

[52] "A German Reader, with Notes and Vocabulary." By William D. Whitney, Professor of Sanskrit in Yale College. London: MacMillan and Co.

[53] "A Concise History of England to the Death of William IV." By E. J. Howell. W. Blackwood and Sons.

[54] "War Chronicle." By Captain Bedford Pim, R.N. London: Provost and Co.

[55] "The History of France." By M. Guizot. Translated by R. Black, M.A. London: Sampson Low, Marston, Low, and Searle.

BELLES LETTRES.

HAD Lord Lytton[1] lived to that age which classical poets are so fond of attributing to the crow and the stag, and had continued to improve, he would certainly have been the world's greatest novelist. There is no denying the fact that Thackeray, in his later works, never came to the level of "Vanity Fair," and that Dickens never rivalled "Martin Chuzzlewit." Both these great writers to a certain extent exhausted their peculiar vein of satire and humour. They did not, probably for very good reasons, change either their subject or their style. Lord Lytton's practice has been quite the reverse. Nothing can be more different from "Pelham" than "The Parisians." When Lord Lytton exhausted one theme he, without difficulty, turned to another, and succeeded equally well. Like Mr. Disraeli's recent speech to the Glasgow students, Lord Lytton's novels are an epitome of his life. They reveal the man in each stage. But as a man is never completely able to throw off his original nature, so in each tale we may detect the original Mr. Bulwer:—"Hans bleibt immer Hans." And in the Lord Lytton of "The Parisians," we may still see the Mr. Bulwer of "Pelham." In "The Parisians," which certainly appears to us, as far as we have read, the maturest and best of all the many works which Lord Lytton has written, we constantly come upon that false note of sentiment which so jarred upon us in his earliest and weakest writings. Every now and then, too, we come upon that same flashy style which the admirers of Lord Lytton mistake for epigram. Here for instance, is a good example of what we mean:—"She was one of those persons who play with fire in order to appear enlightened." (Vol. i. p. 234.) Now to a great number of people this will seem a very brilliant piece of wit. But in reality there is no connexion between playing with fire and intellectual power. It is simply a play upon the words "fire" and "enlightened." The whole of the wit lies in the words rather than in the sense. There is in fact a false intellectual ring about all Lord Lytton's writings. There is a false note. And though we see far less of this deep-rooted fault in "The Parisians" than in any other of Lord Lytton's writings, it is still there. Further we may detect the same thinness of thought, which, by the way, has in no small degree contributed to Lord Lytton's enormous popularity, in "The Parisians," as in "The Last Days of Pompei," which we believe passes for the author's greatest achievement. Here, for instance, is the opening of "The Parisians,"—a description of the last days of Paris before the German war:—

"It was a bright day in the early spring of 1869. All Paris seemed to have turned out to enjoy itself. The Tuileries, the Champs Elysées, the Bois de Boulogne, swarmed with idlers. A stranger might have wondered where

[1] "The Parisians." By Edward Bulwer, Lord Lytton, Author of "The Coming Race." With Illustrations by Sidney Hall. In Four Volumes. Vols. I, II. London: William Blackwood and Sons. 1873.

Toil was at work, and in what nook Poverty lurked concealed. A *millionnaire* from the London Exchange, as he looked round on the *magasins*, the equipages, the dresses of the women; as he inquired the prices in the shops, and the rent of apartments—might have asked himself, in envious wonder—How on earth do those gay Parisians live? What is their fortune? Where does it come from?" (Vol. i. p. 3.)

Now we do not think that a "*millionnaire* from the London Exchange" would have made any such remark. He would have known too well how, in that particular year 1869, much of the wealth in Paris had been accumulated, and by what frauds and villany. He, "a *millionnaire* from the London Exchange," not a country booby, we must remember, would have known too well what discount he must allow for all the flashy goods and tinselly jewellery in the shop-windows, and could have told at a glance to what sort of adventurers a great portion of the "equipages" belonged, and what sort of women wore the dresses. Had the "*millionnaire* from the London Exchange" been in the humour for moralizing upon the gay scene passing before him, he would most probably have said, as Lord Palmerston is reported to have said, "If France did not have a revolution every twenty years, it would be the richest country in the world." But the quotation which we have given from Lord Lytton contains precisely the whole sum of thought which arises in the minds of most commonplace people the first time that they ever visit Paris. We have heard the remark over and over again. The mistake which Lord Lytton makes is in putting an ordinary remark in the mouth of a man who would have said, or ought to have said, something very different. But as the majority of the world like to see their own commonplace opinions reflected, especially when set off with a capital T to toil, and a capital P to poverty, Lord Lytton's introduction to "The Parisians" will pass with his admirers for a profound piece of writing. We had marked a great number of other passages, where by a little judicious veneering and gilding of style, Lord Lytton makes a commonplace remark do duty for a bit of philosophy. But it is not worth the trouble to go through them. It is far pleasanter to be able to say, as we have already intimated, that "The Parisians" is, as far as we are able to judge by the first two volumes, one of the best of Lord Lytton's novels; that it often contains shrewd remarks upon men and women; and that the style, in spite of its grave defects, is lively, and full of what, for want of a better name, we may call dash.

With the great crowd of Lord Lytton's admirers we shall seem to be utterly unjust to him. We hasten, however, to make amends. If Lord Lytton does not, in our opinion, rise to the rank of a first-rate novelist, it is easy to see how much he is above the ordinary writer of tales. We have only to judge him by such a book as "Luna."[1] "Luna," let us at once say, is a most creditable performance. The writer possesses both knowledge of society, good powers of description, no little amount of humour, and a very great deal of cul-

[1] "Luna: a Mere Love Story." By Margaret C. Helmore. London: Smith, Elder and Co. 1873.

ture. It would be small praise to say that Mrs. Helmore in no way offends by any fast or vulgar writing, as is the fashion with our most popular lady-novelists. Every page is marked by delicacy and refinement; and yet, if we compare the scenes in "Luna" with those in "The Parisians," we find a want of substance. "Luna" is, in fact, thin. It may do very well for ladies, and we can conscientiously recommend it, but a novel to take any rank, to make, in short, any mark, requires a great deal more than mere refinement and good taste. There is, for example, an excellently conceived love scene in the first volume (pp. 143—149), but which fails in the execution. We doubt much if Lord Lytton could ever have imagined so pretty a scene, but we are quite sure that if he had done so, he would have thoroughly worked out the situation, and spared no pains to have made the dialogue between the three lovers as brilliant as possible. Here is where most novelists fail; they will not bestow sufficient labour. Again, it is very easy to see that Mrs. Helmore is a lady of no ordinary culture; yet the culture appears to us to be utterly thrown away. Lord Lytton would have economized every bit of learning, or brought it into play, as one may see he has done in the character of the young actress, and the criticisms upon the drama and literature in "The Parisians." We do not remember to have seen Mrs. Helmore's name before, and we take it that "Luna" is a first story. If this be the case, and Mrs. Helmore chooses to take to novel writing seriously as an art, she may achieve a success; but she has much to learn. We are not advising her by any means to take Lord Lytton as a pattern. Very far from that. We only mean to say, that if she determines to write any more novels of the stamp of "Luna," to draw any more pictures of fashionable life, she must put more substance into her writings. This is the secret of Thackeray's great success. There is more substance in a page of "Vanity Fair," than in a hundred volumes of the average Mudie novel.

Criticism often makes strange blunders. When "Adam Bede" first came out one of our best critics pooh-poohed the whole story, and declared that it was the work of a young country curate. We have fallen into an opposite error. When Miss Saunders published her "Haunted Crust," we imagined that we had found a second George Eliot. Miss Saunders has at all events in her present work[1] done her best to dispel our illusion. She has followed the paths of the Braddons and the Woods. Of course she will reap her reward with the publishers and the subscribers to Mudie's. "Margaret and Elizabeth" is a story worked out on principles of sensationalism. Violent contrasts and violent scenes form the staple of interest. They perform for Miss Saunders the same effects which the pans of red and blue fire do for a Surrey melodramatist. The story opens with a picture of a lovely quiet morning breaking on a seaside village. It is low-tide, and before us reaches "the most beautiful stretch of fair sand that the English coast can show. And on this sand are playing two fair-haired

---

[1] "Margaret and Elizabeth: a Story of the Sea." By Catherine Saunders, Author of "Gideon's Rock," &c. London: Henry S. King and Co. 1873.

children." Then Miss Saunders completes her picture by dwelling on "the sea and sands and shingle glittering in the sun's full light." Everything is made as pretty and as smooth as a scene in an opera. Then the mother comes down, and misses her children. She rushes to a dark pool. She feels, after the regular sensational pattern, "all sorts of fears, wild and vague at her heart." Her footsteps go "slow and wavering." She "glances fearfully," and in short performs all the stage antics of her type. But the children are not in the pool. Miss Saunders, so to speak, knows a trick worth two of this. The mother sees instead a female corpse, and her two children playing at sextons, burying it. Then Miss Saunders carefully rubs the reader's nose against the corpse, and so ends what we may call the first cadaverous chapter. Now, in this chapter we may see the principles upon which the sensational novelist works. The receipt is simple enough. It consists of violent contrasts. Contrast at any price is the sensational writer's motto. You take a beautiful scene in nature, put in whatever is fairest, and then side by side place whatever is most repulsive. Children playing at burying a corpse is the latest piece of sensationalism. We pass on to Miss Saunders's next chapter. Of course the corpse is not a corpse. It very soon comes to life, and of course says, "I wish I had died." One would have imagined that Miss Saunders would have been ashamed of repeating such an old and worn-out trick. But your sensational novelist and reader both come back like dogs to their vomit. We cannot pretend to follow Margaret, for that is the corpse's name, in her ravings. It is enough to say that she has "violent fits of shuddering, then incoherent ravings, floods of tears, and peals of laughter." All that we can suggest is, though the hint will probably be lost upon Miss Saunders, that such a creature is more fit to be described in the pages of some medical work on insanity than in a circulating library novel. We would, however, earnestly advise Miss Saunders, before she writes another novel, to ponder over Joubert's weighty words, "With the fever of the senses, the delirium of the passions, authors may as long as they like go on making novels, which shall harrow our hearts, but the soul says all the while 'you hurt me.'" But Miss Saunders's sensational scenes do not harrow us. They sink into utter bathos. No sensible person will ever be harrowed by two children playing at burying a corpse, though they may feel hurt and shocked. Perhaps the most offensive chapter in the whole story, we mean offensive of course from an artistic point of view, is "The Bittern's Cry." It is modelled upon Mr. Henry Kingsley's worst style, but is far more outrageous than anything which that spasmodic novelist has ever yet produced. Here again no sensible person will be harrowed by such violent scenes as Miss Saunders paints. They will be disgusted, and close the book. But unfortunately there are a vast number of people who are not sensible, and who delight in morbid and unwholesome reading. Once more we will quote Joubert's words for Miss Saunders's benefit. "Fiction has no business to exist unless it is more beautiful than reality. Once lose sight of that and you have the most frightful reality." Miss Saunders, however, instead of reality gives us monstrosity.

It is a perfect relief to turn from Miss Saunders's high-pressure story to the quietness and tenderness of "A Long Summer's Day."[1] We breathe another atmosphere. In one book we have nothing but terrific bursts of passion, in the other a representation of certain phases of life such as many of us know and recognise. It would be unjust to Miss Saunders to say that she is without any feeling for the beauty and tenderness of human life; but she recognises it much in the same way as sporting writers recognise the beauties of nature. After devoting whole chapters to the slaughter of beasts, birds, and fish, they incidentally mention the wood or the stream where their exploits have been performed. With Mrs. Simpson, on the other hand, a feeling for the sacredness of human nature pervades her writing. There is, too, an air of refinement in "A Long Summer's Day," which we miss in Miss Saunders's story. Mrs. Simpson is never sensational, but intellectual. These remarks will, we hope, show how highly we estimate "A Long Summer's Day." Much of the first volume is taken up with the old story of a young country girl's first season in London. But though all the scenes have been so often repeated, Mrs. Simpson contrives to invest them with novelty and freshness. Even the hackneyed subject of dress is treated from a new point of view. Dress, with Mrs. Simpson, becomes quite an art. And her artistic feeling is shown in other directions, more especially in her descriptions of nature. The little village of Allingham and the cathedral town of Minchester are so well done, that if we do not actually know them, we certainly think that we do. We could, we think, name the county in which they are situated, where the chalk downs are covered with the sweet-scented "down-flowers," throughout the spring. Again, Mrs. Simpson possesses a sense of humour, which is after all a greater gift for a novelist than is generally supposed. We have noticed that a sense of humour acts often as a controlling power over the novelist, preventing him from falling into the dangerous pit of sensationalism and fine writing. Aunt Charlotte is one of Mrs. Simpson's best studies in this line. But what we value far above the humour and the picturesque descriptions in "A Long Summer's Day" is the high moral tone. At a time when so many of our novelists, especially our lady-novelists, fill up their pages with descriptions of so-called sport, it is refreshing to find some one who dares to make her heroine use such language as the following:—

"'If you like country air, you may drive to Hurlingham, and see pigeons imprisoned, and mangled by the *jeunesse dorée*.'

"'What do you mean? Is there any such cruel, cowardly sport?'

"'Yes, indeed: it replaces the bull-fight and the tournament, and bright eyes look on and reward their deeds.'

"'I can only say,' said Rosamond, 'that if I heard of any one I knew doing anything so horrible, I would never speak to him again.'" (Vol. i. pp. 60, 81.)

If all young ladies would answer invitations to Hurlingham in the manner of Mrs. Simpson's Rosamond, we should not have our newspapers so often filled with brutalizing accounts of pigeon-shooting.

[1] "A Long Summer's Day." By M. C. M. Simpson. London: Smith Elder and Co. 1873.

On nearly the same level as Mrs. Simpson's "A Long Summer's Day" we must place Mrs. Parr's "The Prescotts of Pamphillon."[5] Mrs. Parr possesses that same sort of local knowledge which gives such a flavour to Mrs. Simpson's story. Only instead of being presented with scenes from the Hampshire Downs and pictures of Winchester, we have the still more beautiful scenery of Devonshire and the sea-views round Plymouth. Mrs. Parr, too, thoroughly knows the class of people whom she describes—retired admirals and half-pay naval officers, with their surroundings. In one respect she has an advantage over Mrs. Simpson, she knows the lower classes better, and describes them with great humour. Betsy, the Bunces, and Mr. Pethewick are all admirable.

For the last year *Macmillan's Magazine* has been looked forward to on the first of each month by many persons, who were not professed novel readers, on account of Mr. Black's story, "A Princess of Thule."[6] The reason of this is very obvious. Mr. Black, unlike the mass of novel-writers, has seen much, both of the world and of men. He has a large stock of information to draw upon. In "A Princess of Thule" he has broken completely new ground. The novel-reader is sated with the constantly repeated scenes of London or provincial life. Mr. Black takes us away to the far North, where life is lived in a fashion which some of us may envy. Now, there are very few novelists who dare venture on so bold an experiment. Most of them, too, would most certainly fail, especially on the very ground where Mr. Black has most emphatically asserted the triumph of his art. Here again the reason is obvious. Mr. Black is essentially a poet. We are not aware whether he has written any poetry. But the fact is certain that his genius is essentially at the bottom thoroughly poetic. He never loses an opportunity of describing the mountains, the sea, the woods, and the open moors. Hence the charm of his writings to the jaded professional man,—the statesman, the banker, or lawyer. Reading "A Princess of Thule" is almost as exhilarating as a walk by the sea-shore. We can only express a hope that Mr. Black may write many more such books. No one can read "A Princess of Thule" without benefit. It is without any doubt the best novel, whether regarded as a work of art or as a moral lesson, which Mr. Black has yet written.

The remaining novels on our list we must notice more briefly than we could wish. Mr. Wedmore[7] has already established a reputation as a novelist by his very graceful story of "A Snapt Gold Ring." His new story is quite as graceful and far more powerful. The scenes, however, which interest us most are those of literary life in London. These are excellently done. Mr. Wedmore tells the story of a struggling writer with great truth and insight.

---

[5] "The Prescotts of Pamphillon." By Mrs. Parr, Author of "Dorothy Fox." London: W. Isbister and Co. 1874.

[6] "A Princess of Thule." By William Black, Author of "The Strange Adventures of a Phaeton," &c., &c. London: Macmillan and Co. 1874.

[7] "Two Girls." By Frederick Wedmore, Author of "A Snapt Gold Ring." London: Henry S. King and Co. 1874.

Mr. Sydney Mostyn's new story[8] is a great deal above the average. His characters are at all events well-defined. Some of his sketches from nature are also good. But is he quite right as an artist in describing in his opening chapter nightingales singing in July in elm-trees? May and June are the two months for the nightingale's song, who generally prefer small brushwood, shrubs, and thickets to timber trees. Still we have no doubt that Mr. Mostyn describes what he has heard, but in novel writing he should remember in such scenes to give us not the exception, but the rule.

"Gabriel Denver"[9] is without doubt the most powerful novel which has appeared for a long time. But Mr. Madox-Brown must remember that sensational writing is very much like dram-drinking. Each time the dose must be stronger. We hope that in his next novel he will show his power without abusing it. Those, however, who love weird-like effects, strong situations, and a somewhat lurid style, may read "Gabriel Denver."

"Lady Bell"[10] we can most strongly recommend to all young people. We should think that it might be introduced as a text-book of history into all young ladies' schools, as such great pains have been taken to insure accuracy in describing the chief historical and literary characters. The style is as graceful as the matter is sound.

Mr. Dobson's "Vignettes in Rhyme"[11] is a dainty little book. The age has become so serious that Mr. Dobson runs the chance of being looked upon as a trifler. The art of Praed is forgotten. We have given up our albums with their Vers de Société. We have taken to photographic portfolios full of bishops or men of science according to the owner's taste. *Æs dabo pro nugis, et emam tua carmina sanus?* the learned world will say to Mr. Dobson. We can only answer, by all means. If there is any taste left in us for subtle wit, delicate humour, happy rhymes and well-turned expressions, "Vignettes in Rhymes" ought to be the most popular book of the day. Mr. Dobson is, we think, most at home with French subjects. We take at random some lines from a piece entitled "Une Marquise."

> "You are fair; oh yes, we know it
> Well, Marquise;
> For he swore it, your last poet,
> On his knees;
> And he called all heaven to witness
> Of his ballad and its fitness,
> "*Belle Marquise!*"
> You were everything in *ère*
> (With exception of *sévère*),—
> You were *cruelle* and *rebelle*,
> With the rest of rhymes as well.

---

[8] "Kitty's Rival: a Story." By Sydney Mostyn, Author of "The Surgeon's Secret." London: Samuel Tinsley. 1873.

[9] "Gabriel Denver." By Oliver Madox-Brown. London: Smith, Elder and Co. 1873.

[10] "Lady Bell: a Story of the Last Century." By the Author of "Citoyenne Jacqueline." London: Strahan and Co. 1873.

[11] "Vignettes in Rhyme, and Vers de Société." (Now first Collected.) By Austin Dobson. London: Henry S. King and Co. 1873.

But Mr. Dobson does not forget that his pet marquise was probably, as the Abbé Choisi said of the Duchesse de Fontanges, "as beautiful as an angel, and as silly as a goose." There is not a piece in the book which is not graceful. We would gladly linger over such a delightful volume, more especially as we know what tortures are awaiting us in the shape of the minor poets.

Minor poets are certainly extraordinary beings. They generally print their productions at the request of their friends and in spite of their critics. The friends laugh at them in private and the critics in public. In the first volume[12] which we take up, M. S. gives ill-health as his reason for publishing. M. S. also apologizes for the "many imperfections and shortcomings" of his poems, and attributes them to his want of leisure. All that we can say is, the poems had better have remained in MS.

Mr. Row[13] writes in a similar strain. He says that he has been "engaged in the darkest *cloaca* of society." By his account we must suppose that he is in some way connected with the Underground Railway, for that is the darkest *cloaca* which we know. He, too, "is all too conscious of numberless impotencies, of ungracefulness in the spoken thought." Then why inflict them on the public?

Mr. Owen dedicates his Lyrics[14] to a poet, Mr. Leicester Warren. Mr. Owen has decidedly a strong poetical feeling. He evidently loves nature, but these qualifications will not make a poet. His verses have not the beauty of art. They do not linger on the ear. They want perfect form. Mr. Owen, we cannot doubt, has felt much pleasure in their composition, and this after all is the highest reward which the greatest poet can have.

We are very glad to see a new edition of Mr. Richards's "Oliver Cromwell."[15] It is one of the few modern plays which is worth reading. We must pass nearly the same judgment on Mr. Austin's "Rome or Death,"[16] as we did on his Madonna's Child." We deeply regret that he should have abandoned the field of satire, in which he certainly would have been without a rival.

Mr. Emerson's poems[17] are of that well known stamp which the gods do not tolerate. "Early Blossoms"[18] do not belie their titles;

---

[12] "Progress, and other Poems. The latter including Poems on the Social Affections, and Poems on Life and Labour." By M. S. London: John R. Smith. 1873.

[13] "Maud Vivian: a Drama. And Poems." By Walter Row. London: E. Moxon and Son. 1873.

[14] "Lyrics from a Country Life: a Miscellany of Verse." By John L. Owen. London: Simpkin, Marshall and Co. 1873.

[15] "Oliver Cromwell: an Historical Tragedy. In a Prologue and Four Acts." By Alfred Bate Richards, Author of "So Very Human." London: Effingham Wilson. 1873.

[16] "Rome or Death." By Alfred Austin. London: William Blackwood and Sons. 1873.

[17] "Papers from my Desk: and other Poems." By William Emerson. London: Longmans, Green and Co. 1873.

[18] "Early Blossoms." By Thomas Gilbert. Bombay: Thacker, Vining and Co. 1873.

but then they are nothing else but early blossoms, which certainly will not stand the frosts of any severe criticism. Good taste and good feeling are the characteristics of "Lyrics of the Greenwood Tree." Mr. Fosbrooke has evidently been inspired by German influences, which have left a graceful mark upon his poetry. The writer of "Equality"[20] is a Platonist, and takes the poet's standpoint against the Utilitarian doctrines now in vogue. "Dreamland"[21] is, as far as we are concerned, Dreamland, and nothing more. At all events, we can recognise nothing in it belonging to daily life. It is of "such stuff as dreams are made of."

We have thus endeavoured to characterize as briefly as possible a few of the many volumes of poetry which cover our table. But there are still many left which deserve a longer notice. Mrs. Cowden Clarke's "The Trust and the Remittance"[22] is one of them. Both are love stories, idyls in fact, told with much delicacy and grace. Another volume, which shows much refinement and spiritual feeling, is "Resurgam."[23] If Mr. Carpenter is a young man, "Narcissus"[24] shows signs of promise. He possesses not only a deep feeling for Nature, but is able to translate that feeling into verses which are marked by beauty of form. The same praise, in a more modified shape, may be extended to the poems by Mr. Bridges.[25] Both he and Mr. Carpenter are artists in the same school. They have both studied our older poets not without effect.

We come now to two volumes which claim far greater attention than we can possibly give them. The lady first. Miss King[26] is a true follower of Shelley. She possesses not only Shelley's spirit of enthusiasm, but a great measure of his passion and lyrical power. We think, therefore, that it was a great mistake not to have taken full advantage of the lyrical power which she undoubtedly possesses, in one of the longer pieces in the present volume. Blank verse is an instrument requiring the most delicate skill in its management. Miss King possesses above all things fluency of style; but this very fluency of style is particularly dangerous in blank verse. It is particularly dangerous, too, because so many people mistake mere fluency of expression for thought. Here, in our opinion, lies Miss King's

---

19 "Erlinthula, King Ithol, and the Lyrics of the Greenwood Tree." By John Baldwin Fosbrooke, Author of "Rheingold;" "The Bridal of Fedlinbray." London: Provost and Co. 1873.

20 "Equality: a Satirical Poem. In which are sketched the Dreams, Triumphs, and Ambitions of Free Thought, Atheism, and Materialism." Liverpool: David Marples. 1873.

21 "Dreamland: and other Poems." By Richard Phillips. London: Longmans, Green and Co. 1873.

22 "The Trust and the Remittance." By Mary Cowden Clarke. London: Grant and Co. 1873.

23 "Resurgam." By the Author of "Ich Dien." London: E. Moxon, Son and Co. 1873.

24 "Narcissus: and other Poems." By E. Carpenter. London: Henry S. King and Co. 1873.

25 "Poems." By Robert Bridges, B.A. London: B. M. Pickering. 1873.

26 "The Disciples." By Harriet Eleanor Hamilton King. London: Henry S. King and Co. 1873.

great danger in the future. "The Disciples" will certainly increase the reputation which she gained by "Aspromonte." Many parts are very lovely.

The book which will excite most attention amongst poets and lovers of poetry is Mr. Gosse's "On Viol and Flute."[57] Since Rossetti's poems we have seen none so full of colour and melody. We most deeply regret that we cannot find room for a single quotation; but, as Fuller remarks, "there were never good ears wanting for good poetry." Mr. Gosse's poems are sure not to fall on rocky ground. He has by this one book alone won a high place amongst English poets, whether of to-day or yesterday.

And here, at the conclusion of our notices of poetry, let us call attention to two most excellent collections. Mr. Dennis's selection of "English Sonnets"[58] will be everywhere welcome. Mr. Davenport Adams has also shown equal taste and care in his "Lyrics of Love."[59] Both volumes, too, deserve high praise for the way in which the publisher has brought them out.

The Rev. C. Swainson has compiled a work on weather-lore[60] such as we have long desired to see. He has performed his work well. Like all good work, it has evidently been a labour of love. Mr. Swainson brings many qualifications for his task. He is a scholar, and possesses the tastes of a scholar. He does not confine himself to the weather-lore of England. He flings a wide net; he has gathered from the best sources. He has laid the principal European works on the subject under contribution. The result is a book which ought to find a place in every library. As we feel quite sure that the work will very soon go into a second edition we shall venture to make a few criticisms on the principle of the German proverb—that "a countryman and a philosopher know more than a philosopher alone." In looking down Mr. Swainson's long list of authorities we miss our old friend "The Shepherd of Banbury Plain;" and the new "Weather Book," by Admiral Fitzroy. We miss, too, many local glossaries, such as Miss Baker's "Glossary of Northamptonshire," where an immense amount of weather-lore may be found. In the book itself Mr. Swainson has left too many points without an explanation. Mr. Swainson must not suppose that the average reader is so good a linguist as himself. For instance, Mr. Swainson, at page 2, gives us, without a word of comment:—

> "A cherry year,
> A merry year;"

---

[57] "On Viol and Flute." By Edmund W. Gosse. London: Henry S. King and Co. 1873.

[58] "English Sonnets: a Selection." Edited by John Dennis. London: Henry S. King and Co. 1873.

[59] "Lyrics of Love. From Shakespeare to Tennyson. Selected and Arranged, with Notes." By W. Davenport Adams. London: Henry S. King and Co. 1874.

[60] "A Handbook of Weather Folk-Lore: being a Collection of Proverbial Sayings in Various Languages relating to the Weather; with Explanatory and Illustrative Notes." By the Rev. C. Swainson, M.A., Vicar of High Hurst Wood. London: William Blackwood and Sons. 1873.

which, we venture to say, will not convey much meaning to the generality of his readers. At page 4, Mr. Swainson further gives us:—

"A plum year,
A dumb year;"

adding between brackets, with a note of interrogation, as if he was doubtful of his own interpretation, "referring to the silence of death." Now if we turn to Ray (1737), to whom most modern dictionary makers and compilers of proverbs are under far greater obligations than they ever care to acknowlege, we shall find at page 40 these two proverbs packed into one:—

"A cherry year, a merry year;
A plum year, a dumb year."

And Ray adds, "this is a puerile and senseless rhyme, without reason, as far as I can see." But the riddle is easy enough to read. "Merry," connected with the French *merise*, is, like mazzard, a provincial word, as may be seen in Barnes' "Dorsetshire Glossary," for the bird-cherry (Prunus avium) in the South-west of England. On the other hand, "dumb" is nothing more than a corruption of damson. The meaning of the proverb at once becomes intelligible. A good year for cultivated cherries is a good year for wild ones, and a good year for plums is also a good one for damsons. We think, too, that Mr. Swainson would have done well to have explained the meaning of the Scotch word "findy," that is, substantial, solid, in the proverb, "A cold May and a windy, makes a fat barn and a findy" (p. 89). Those, too, who are not Devonshire bred and born will require some explanation of the Devonshire proverb "Wind west rains nest," unless this be a misprint for "mest," that is, most. But the book is a thoroughly good book, and, generally speaking, the most illiterate reader's wants are carefully attended to. Of course in a first edition of a collection of this kind we note many omissions. The weather-lore of England is practically inexhaustible. There is not a village which does not possess some peculiar proverb concerning the weather, the approach of storms, the shape of the clouds, or "the ride of the rack." Mr. Swainson should further give the localities of his proverbs, or else they are apt to be misleading. Thus, for instance, the rhyme—

"On the first of November, if the weather hold clear,
An end of wheat-sowing do make for the year," (p. 142)

is quite true when applied to the clays, but hardly to the sands. As it is we have to thank Mr. Swainson for a most enjoyable book, which, however, with a little more research, especially amongst our local glossaries, he may very easily make far more valuable. The weakest bits are those where he touches upon the peculiarities of the days of the week, proverbs concerning Candlemas and St. Martin's Summer, and the names of the clouds, especially amongst our sailors. Lastly, the book most urgently needs a very full index; without this it is mere chaos.

Great credit is due to the Glossary Committee of the Manchester

Literary Club."[a] Mr. Nodal's Report is most interesting from a great many points of view. To Lancashire belongs the honour of having first instituted a society for the express purpose of collecting the fast vanishing speech-lore of our land. Of the value of such an undertaking it is not necessary for us to say a word. Every philologist has fully recognised the importance of the provincial dialects of a country. In his great dictionary Littré has eloquently dwelt upon not only their value, if we may so speak, to the historian of language, but to the literary artist and the poet. Not on one but on many accounts our provincialisms have a special claim upon our attention. To the philologist, historian, antiquary, and man of letters they are in different ways of the greatest importance. We are glad to see from Mr. Nodal's report that the Lancashire Glossary Committee recognise this truth. The present report contains a short but clear summary of the labours of the society during the first year of its existence. It has had many difficulties to encounter. The first difficulty is, what ought a local glossary to include or exclude? Now upon this point many answers have been given. The *Saturday Review*, the value of whose opinion we should be the last to dispute, has answered the question in most decided terms. The *Saturday Review* would restrict a glossary to three classes of words (*Saturday Review*, April 20th, 1873, quoted in the report, pp. 7, 8, 9). We, on the other hand, as we have before stated in this Review (No. LXXXVII. p. 260), would most decidedly include every word, not now used in literary English, to be found in the district. We are glad that we have in this matter Mr. Skeat's able support. "All county glossaries," he says, "must be made on the inclusive system, otherwise the most characteristic and the most common words of all are actually omitted. County divisions have nothing to do with language. The rule is to record all your common and idiomatic words" (pp. 9, 10). With this we most thoroughly agree. And we rejoice to see that, with some additional classification, the Committee have adopted Mr. Skeat's plan. If words are omitted the result will be that, as Mr. Skeat says, we shall suppose that they are unknown in a particular district. The next difficulty is, should etymology be included? We answer at once most decidedly no. The business of a local glossarist is to register, not theorize. Every one can note down a word which he hears, but not every one is an etymologist. An etymologist is the reverse of a poet—he is made and not born. Most people think that they can derive, just as most people think that they can play chess. But knowing the moves and knowing half-a-dozen languages or so makes one neither a chess-player nor an etymologist. And here we are glad to find that we are supported by so great an authority as Mr. A. J. Ellis. "Glossaries," he most rightly says, "should rather be materials than results of materials, which require very special knowledge" (p. 12). This is precisely what we have urged in this Review (No. LXXXVII. pp. 266, 267). The

[a] "The Dialect and Archaisms of Lancashire: being the First Report of the Glossarial Committee of the Manchester Literary Club." By J. H. Nodal. Manchester: Ireland and Co.

business of the glossarist is to collect the raw material. In due time the Grimm and the Littré will be bord and reduce the chaos to order. Lastly, comes the most difficult question of all, what rules are to be adopted for the pronunciation? The Committee at first resolved to try Mr. Ellis's Glossic; but very great labour is required to understand Mr. Ellis's system; and we hardly feel surprised to learn that the Committee ultimately abandoned their intention. In the meanwhile the Committee have constructed a table of sounds and symbols for their own use. This we have not seen. But if a simple plan, which will give the peculiarities and intricacies of local pronunciation can be invented, a great difficulty will have been solved. There are many other points of great interest in Mr. Nodal's Report upon which we should have liked to have said something, but space prevents us. We have, however, to thank him for a most interesting account of what Lancashire men are doing for their mother-speech. We heartily rejoice that so good a start has been made, and feel sure that the results will form a most valuable contribution to our philological and historical knowledge. We trust that other counties will now follow the good example which Lancashire has set.

Mr. Heath's "Romance of Peasant Life"[m] is a well-meant but very badly written book on a most important subject. Perhaps most of the badness of the style arises from the fact that the greater portion of the work consisted originally of letters to the *Morning Advertiser*. This is not a paper in which we should expect to meet the graces of a refined style. The author, however, probably knows his audience. The first chapter is perhaps the worst written in the book. It is full of vulgar "cockney chatter." Here are a few specimens of our special correspondent's style: "The Great Western railway is one of the safest in England" (p. 2). "Buttercups add an inexpressible charm to the landscape" (p. 5). There is scarcely a page which has not some valuable remark of this sort. Mr. Heath, in fact, damages his own cause far more than his opponents can. Most people, after the first page or two, would be inclined to throw the book aside. Further, Mr. Heath adopts a sentimental lackadaisical tone which is totally out of keeping with the subject. If Mr. Heath will in the third edition, which he promises us, cut down all his fine writing about the Great Western railway and the buttercups, which takes up nearly a whole chapter, omit all his sentimental jargon, his threadbare poetical quotations, and his commonplace guide-book information, and not bespatter his friends with quite so much praise, he will greatly increase the value of his work. Canon Girdlestone's name can never be mentioned without respect for his noble endeavours to alleviate the condition of the agricultural labourer. We were, however, deeply grieved to find the following passage in Mr. Heath's book:—

"During the height of the cattle plague in 1866, the excellent canon

---

m "The 'Romance' of Peasant Life in the West of England." By Francis George Heath. Based, by permission, upon Letters contributed to the *Morning Advertiser*." Second Edition enlarged. London: Published for the Author by Cassell, Petter and Galpin. 1872.

(Girdlestone) preached a sermon in the Halberton Church from the text, 'Behold, the hand of the Lord is upon thy cattle;' and in this sermon he told the farmers present that they ought to regard the plague on their cattle as a punishment, because they treated their cattle better than their human labourers. This sermon raised a storm of indignation from the farmers in the district, and open war was at once declared against the minister who had dared in the pulpit to make so deep a homethrust." (p. 89.)

As Mr. Heath does not say a single word to the contrary, we must suppose that Canon Girdlestone's sermon meets with his thorough approval. We would, however, ask by what right does Canon Girdlestone claim authority to interpret the cattle-plague or any other epidemic? Such interpretations are apt to be double-edged. If the cattle-disease was sent as a judgment on the farmers for their treatment of the agricultural labourer, what was the potato disease sent for? But is it a fact that the farmer did suffer to such an enormous extent by the cattle disease? As Mill at the time rightly showed, the farmers and graziers were in a great measure compensated by the enhanced price of stock. All provisions and necessaries of life were, however, more or less affected by the cattle plague, and the man who most felt the consequences of the rinderpest was the agricultural labourer. According, then, to Canon Girdlestone's own showing, Providence has a very strange way of helping the labourer. But nothing can be more odious than this attempt to explain a natural phenomenon as a judgment of the Almighty upon those who happen to be opposed to our views. Such a claim to infallibility and inspiration may be left to the Roman Catholic priest. We repeat that we are deeply grieved to see a man of Canon Girdlestone's intellect led away by his zeal into such an unworthy and contemptible device.

"The Unprofessional Vagabond"[33] was apparently a special correspondent to the *Globe*. He writes, however, in a very much better style than Mr. Heath. What Mr. Heath attempted to do for the agricultural labourer the "Unprofessional Vagabond" has, in his way, done for the London beggar. If we understand the "Unprofessional Vagabond"—and we by no means feel sure that we do—he comes forward rather as an amateur than as a reformer. His book is by no means dull, and his descriptions are often very picturesque. The illustrations, too, are characteristic. But after all what is the practical lesson? In these days of indiscriminate charity—when charity is too often a curse instead of a blessing—it may be as well to remember a saying attributed to a well-known bishop—"I have done many wicked things in my life, but I have never given a penny to a beggar." This, however, we suppose, is not the conclusion which the "Unprofessional Vagabond" would wish us to draw.

"Master Spirits"[34] is a collection of Mr. Buchanan's lighter contributions to periodical literature. They are, however, the author says in a short preface, to be regarded as "mere desultory notes on literary

[33] "The Unprofessional Vagabond." By Thomas Carlisle (Haroun Alraschid). With Sketches from the Life. By John Carlisle. London: Sampson Low, Marston, Low and Searle. 1875.

[34] "Master Spirits." By Robert Buchanan. London: Henry S. King. 1873.

subjects of permanent interest, by one whose real work lies in another field." There was scarcely any need of this apology. All the papers possess considerable interest. We, however, disagree from a great many of Mr. Buchanan's views and opinions. The paper which will probably be read with most interest is the introductory one, "Criticism is one of the Fine Arts." The title is ironical. Mr. Buchanan is apparently of the same opinion as Mr. Disraeli, that critics are "those who have failed in literature and art." Mr. Buchanan's condemnation, although not so sweeping, is as severe as the ex-Premier's. Mr. Buchanan, instead of dealing in vague generalities, gives us two instances to show what manner of people critics are. He takes the case of Mr. Grote's "Plato." According to Mr. Buchanan, Grote's typical reviewer is a certain Tomkins, who "knows little of Greek beyond the alphabet." Now if Mr. Buchanan will turn to Grote's recently published life, he may find out from a letter of Mill's what kind of men Grote's reviewers were. Mill mentions one of them by name. Instead of being a person who "knows little of Greek beyond the alphabet," he turns out to be a man of European reputation, the Rector of Lincoln College, who is quite as capable of forming an opinion upon Plato as Grote. The other crucial case given by Mr. Buchanan might be as easily refuted. Generally speaking, however, as we have said, Mr. Buchanan's papers are full of interest. One of the most picturesque is "The Birds of the Hebrides." We have said nothing of Mr. Buchanan's attack on the editor of *The Fortnightly Review*. Mr. Morley is quite able to take care of himself.

Christmas books now crowd upon us. Of late years the Christmas Tree, instead of being hung with nick-nacks, has suddenly been transformed into the Tree of Knowledge. Christmas books are of all kinds: first come the poems, enshrined in caskets, as Alexander enshrined the Iliad: then come the Fairy Tales for girls, and those stories of terrible adventures for boys; and, last of all, the do-me-good books, for, we suppose, the old maids. In the first class comes "Arlon Grange,"[58] all radiant in enamel and gold. We hope Mr. Gibbs will take it not as an unmeaning compliment when we say that his poem fully deserves such a splendid binding. But *fœnum habet in cornu*. In addition to the "Grange" Mr. Gibbs gives us the farm-yard. He binds up with his poem a tract on harvesting corn and hay. Corydon and Thyrsis are all very well in poetry, but we object to them in plain prose, which is more fit for the Royal Agricultural Society's papers than any other place.

Next comes the Fairy Tales, and Semi-Fairy Tales. Mr. Haweis's "Pet"[59] is decidedly the most charming Christmas fairy whom we have yet met. She is, however, dressed a little bit too much like a

[58] "Arlon Grange: and a Christmas Legend." By William Alfred Gibbs, Author of "The Story of a Life;" "Harold Erle," &c. &c. Artist's Edition. London: Provost and Co. 1873.

[59] "Pet; or, Pastimes and Penalties." By the Rev. H. R. Haweis, M.A., Author of "Music and Morals," and "Thoughts for the Times." With Fifty Illustrations by M. E. Haweis. London: W. Isbister and Co. 1874.

ballet girl, and wears the fashionable frizzy hair, like a door-mat, on her head. But we suppose it is all right and proper. Then, as the showman would say, there are Fantastic Stories,[37] translated by Miss Granville, and illustrated by Miss Fraser-Tytler; and if this is not a recommendation we do not know what is. For boys there are some terrible stories. First comes Mr. Stanley's "Kalulu,"[38] who looks like a little Belzoni in his war paint and feathers. We have not read Kalulu's adventures, for the pictures are quite enough to satisfy us. "Adventures to the Adventurous"[39] is Mr. MacKenna's motto; and if the reading only keep pace with the illustrations it will be something very terrific. In fact, we have before us a whole library of bush-rangers, buffalo-hunters, Robinson Crusoes, and Men Fridays. After debating for some time we select two of them as especially worthy of notice: Mr. Sadler's "African Cruiser,"[40] and Mr. Bonwick's "Mike Howe, the Bushranger."[41] These, as the sporting prophets say, are our selection.

Lastly, there come a number of miscellaneous Christmas books. "Harry's Big Boots"[42] are full of fun. "Stories of Whitminster,"[43] like all Mr. Hope's books for boys, are marked by good sense. "Millicent Courteney's Diary"[44] may be recommended to all young girls. Below, too, will be found the titles of several[45] other books, all of which are much above mediocrity.

Our Christmas books have left us little room this quarter for noticing those from Germany. In England modern religious poetry is generally intolerable; and though Germany possesses a religious anthology such as scarcely any other nation can boast, yet even its

---

[37] "Fantastic Stories." By Richard Leander. Translated by Paulina B. Granville. Illustrated by M. Fraser-Tytler. London: Henry S. King and Co. 1873.

[38] "My Kalulu, Prince, King, and Slave." By Henry M. Stanley, Author of "How I Found Livingstone." With Illustrations. London: Sampson Low, Marston, Low and Searle. 1873.

[39] "At School with an Old Dragoon." By Stephen J. MacKenna, Author of "Plucky Fellows." Illustrated. London: Henry S. King and Co. 1874.

[40] "The African Cruiser: a Midshipman's Adventures on the West Coast." By S. Whitchurch Sadler, R.N., Author of "Marshall Vavasour." London: Henry S. King and Co. 1873.

[41] "Mike Howe, the Bushranger of Van Diemen's Land." By James Bonwick, F.R.G.S., Author of "The Early Days of Van Diemen's Land," &c. &c. London: Henry S. King and Co. 1873.

[42] "Harry's Big Boots: a Fairy Tale." With Illustrations by the Author. London: Samuel Tinsley. 1873.

[43] "Stories of Whitminster." By Ascott R. Hope, Author of "Stories of School Life;" "A Book About Boys," &c. &c. Edinburgh: William P. Nimmo. 1873.

[44] "Millicent Courteney's Diary; or, the Experiences of a Young Lady at Home and Abroad." By William H. G. Kingston. London: Gall and Inglis. 1873.

[45] I. "In His Name: a Story of the Dark Ages." By E. E. Hale. London: Sampson Low, Marston, Low and Searle. 1873. II. "Seeking His Fortune: and other Tales." A Book for Boys. London: Henry S. King and Co. 1873. III. "Miss Moore: a Tale for Girls." By Georgiana M. Craik. London: Sampson Low, Marston, Low and Searle. 1873. IV. "The King's Servants." By Hesba Stretton. London: Henry S. King and Co. 1873.

modern religious poetry is apt to become wearisome. Dr. Lüdemann[46] has increased the natural difficulties by weighing the subject with his philosophical reflections. We can simply say that he has succeeded as well as the circumstances will admit. To an intensely devotional spirit he has added the results of much culture and thought.

"Lieder aus Frankreich," with the date 1870, tells its own tale. No one who reads these poems and marks the patriotism which animated the writer and his fellow-soldiers, can be surprised at the victories of the Germans. We believe, however, that the high feeling which is embodied in these poems contributed far more to the successes of the Germans than even the tactics of their generals. Herr Jensen thoroughly deserves the honours of a second edition. And here let us take the opportunity of expressing our regret that by an inadvertence we stated (No. LXXXVI. p. 635) that Herr Krause considered the W. H. of Shakespeare's sonnets to have been Henry Wriothesley, Lord Southampton, instead of William Herbert, Earl of Pembroke. This, however, in no way affects our remarks.

ART.

IN the preface which introduces the reader to the contents of the handsome volume entitled "Leonardo da Vinci and his Works,"[1] Mrs. Heaton modestly tells us that it must not be supposed that the book is intended to rank as a history of the life, works, and discoveries of the great Italian whose name it bears. The materials are not yet collected which would enable a biographer to treat the subject exhaustively. The large folio volume in the Bibliothèque Nationale, which contains fourteen out of the sixteen MSS. left by Leonardo at his death, in the hands of his friend Francesco da Melzi, has never been thoroughly examined, nor described. Until this task has been accomplished, any biography of Leonardo must necessarily be incomplete. The main outlines of what we at present know concerning the life of this great artist, who was so richly and so equally endowed with the gifts both of the spirit and of sense, are carefully and intelligently traced by Mrs. Heaton, who has neglected no source of information and declined no labour involved by the effort to make her sketch as correct and trustworthy as possible. She has gleaned from works of the most opposite character. She has carefully mastered the laborious treatise on the "Trattato della Pintura," recently published

---

[46] "Die Heiligthümer der Menschheit." Ein Morgengruss an die bessere Zeit. Dr. C. Lüdemann. Professor der Theologie an der Universität Kiel. Kiel: Paul Toeche. 1873.

[47] "Lieder aus Frankreich." (Aus dem Jahre 1873.) Wilhelm Jensen. Zweite verhmehrte Auflage. Berlin: Gebrüder Paetel. 1873.

[1] "Leonardo da Vinci and his Works." Consisting of a "Life of Leonardo da Vinci," by Mrs. Charles W. Heaton; an "Essay on his Scientific and Literary Works," by Charles Christopher Black, M.A.; and an "Account of his most Important Paintings." London and New York: Macmillan and Co. 1874.

by Dr. Max Jordan, which is of such a scientific character as to be calculated to repel the general reader, but, at the same time, she has not neglected more popular authors. From the brilliant and careless pages of M. Arsène Houssaye we get one judicious extract, in which a lively picture is given of his expedition to Amboise in search of the buried and forgotten tomb of Leonardo, and of his active efforts for its discovery; efforts which he believes to have been crowned by undoubted success. The catalogue of paintings by Leonardo is also chiefly compiled from the appendix to M. Houssaye's book, taken in conjunction with an earlier catalogue of "works" published by Rigollot in 1849. But still further additions may have to be made; for instance, the Holy Family of the Hermitage obtains ample notice, but the Madonna of the same collection, which calls itself, we believe, the Litta Madonna, remains unmentioned. To Mr. Black has fallen the most arduous task of appreciating Leonardo in science and literature, a task for the apt performance of which no usual qualifications are required. As is remarked in the preface, the critic must bring to this work not only industry and acumen, and knowledge of science and literature, but knowledge of the state of science and literature at this precise moment of the Renaissance. Above all it is desirable that his mind should be of the same quality as the mind of the subject he attempts to study. Leonardo belonged to the small company of the wise—to the band of philosophers; hence the many complaints of the unintelligible character of his work. Such complaints arise because the purely practical instinct is at fault, when it tries its edge on the slippery surface of speculative genius. Given such a high standard as this of the endowments necessary to the accomplishment of perfect criticism of the personality of Leonardo da Vinci, it is no small praise to add that Mr. Black's essay, if not a distinguished success, is at least a highly respectable performance. The illustrations, which are so important in a work of this class, are excellently selected. All are rendered by the Woodbury permanent process; the paintings from the best engravings in each instance, whilst the drawings, many of which are now published for the first time, are reproduced straight from the originals. In point of handsome print, paper, and general get up, "Leonardo da Vinci" rivals the volume on "Raphael of Urbino," which we owed to the enterprise of the same publishers last year, whilst the design and colour of the binding shows a decided step in advance.

The most readable portion of "An Art Tour to Northern Capitals of Europe"* is that which does not treat of art. Mr. Beavington Atkinson describes scenery with a strong and appreciative sense of what Mr. Ruskin would call the forms of the "lower picturesque;" he has a laudable spirit of inquiry, an enduring anxiety to know all about anything he sees, and a persevering patience which leads him to master with interest even the minor details of processes of manufacture. Thus he gives us in chapter xi. a very intelligible account of the Imperial establishment for making mosaics at St. Petersburg;

* "An Art Tour to Northern Capitals of Europe." By J. Beavington Atkinson. London: Macmillan and Co. 1873.

he explains the mechanical procedures by which the tesseræ are produced, arranged, and permanently fixed. But, when obtaining a special appointment to see the melting of the enamel under the blowpipe, &c., Mr. Atkinson seems more at home than when he criticises the designs which these tesseræ are employed to produce. On this subject Mr. Atkinson speaks darkly; he says "painters (Russian) have sold themselves to France, and bartered their art to Italy." We should like to have the details of the arrangement. More shocking still, the mosaicists work from the designs of Professor Neff, who is known by three nude studies in the Hermitage. "Religious art," adds Mr. Atkinson, in solemn reproach, "is not to be made out of such meretricious stuff as this." We wonder whether Raphael unfitted himself for painting the Madonna because he designed the story of Cupid and Psyche. Further on we learn that "in small canvasses there is no room for the imagination." This is at least intelligible English; but what is meant by the mysterious statement that some "unaccredited pictures" (in the Hermitage) "are not dubious; on the contrary, some whose ubiquity over the period of two centuries is without published record I have specially marked for merit." What is the ubiquity of a picture? Is it something new which Mr. Atkinson has found in Russia? We ask with due diffidence, for Mr. Atkinson waves his wand with such an air of imposing authority as almost silences criticism. In the most instructive manner he puts all artists, living or dead, in their proper place. "I am sorry," he says, "that I cannot exalt Mr. Lagorio to quite a first-rate position amongst the artists of Europe." Poor Mr. Lagorio! And here are two sentences marked for admiration. This is the first—"The world is evidently much alike, especially when the conditions of altitude and of geologic structure are similar." How odd one never thought of that before! Then here is an exquisite euphuism for describing death from drunkenness. Mr. Atkinson has been told that artists in the north frequently drink themselves to death, and he kindly remarks, "I have been informed that in those northern climates the art temperament is singularly subject to catastrophe." The critical part of this book is not satisfactory; but the volume contains much careful description, the unknown names of northern artists, and many facts about northern art; and throughout Mr. Atkinson displays an exact memory and the most praiseworthy habits of patient inquiry.

Miss Tytler's book, "The Old Masters and their Pictures,"[3] is carefully written, and unusually free from blunders of any kind. The volume contains a simple account of the principal artists of the Italian, Spanish, French, Flemish, and German schools of art down to the beginning of the present century. The pictures selected for description are examples in the national collection whenever it is possible. But why has Miss Tytler omitted English artists in a book intended for the use of English schools? She gives a full account of Greuze; but his English contemporaries, Reynolds and Romney, are passed over in silence. The

[3] "The Old Masters and their Pictures, for the Use of Schools and Learners in Art." By Sarah Tytler. London: Strahan and Co. 1873.

excellent authoress is a little hard, too, on the Lelys hanging in the "Beauty Room" at Hampton Court. She says, "no good man or woman can look at them without holding such beauty detestable." Perhaps, however, the sentiment is intended, like the book, for the use of schools.

We learn from the preface of "Les Quatre Derniers Siècles,"[4] that the nineteenth century having made, both in science and industry, such progress as will command the gratitude and respect of posterity, now designs to prepare itself, by æsthetic studies, to crown the edifice by one of those intellectual inspirations of which we can count but one or two in the history of humanity. The pronounced taste for the beautiful augments the production of æsthetic books. France and England have already brought forth magnificent works, and now Holland follows the example; and, aided by the skill of the publisher, M. Schalekamp gives birth to "Les Quatre Derniers Siècles." To M. Schalekamp is due the conception embodied in its pages. He ordered M. Havard to write a letterpress agreeable to be read and accessible to every intelligence, neither too low, nor too elevated, above all not commonplace. M. Schalekamp thinks that M. Havard has successfully made up the draught prescribed, and anticipates that the book will charm the reader without fatiguing him by learning. A fit frame is thus formed to receive the illustrations of M. Madou, who is known to the entire art-public of Europe. The volume offers every mechanical excellence in perfection; the type, the printing, the quality and tone of the paper are superlatively good. As to the text, M. Havard has obeyed his orders, and does not fatigue the reader with too much learning. As to the illustrations, alas! we fear that the nineteenth century has not found in M. Madou the artist who is to give adequate expression to her æsthetic studies and intellectual inspiration.

---

[4] "Les Quatre Derniers Siècles." Etude artistique par Henry Havard. Illustrée par J. B. Madou. 1re et 2me livraison. Haarlem: J. M. Schalekamp. London: Kolckmann.

CONTENTS.

ERRATA.

Page 130, line 5 from bottom; *for* "1865" *read* "1855."
,, 139, line 23, *for* "agreement" *read* "argument."
,, 139, line 26, *for* "discourages" *read* "encourages."
142, line 12, *dele* "scientific."
,, 151, line 7 from bottom, *for* "rain" *read* "mine."

THE

WESTMINSTER

AND

FOREIGN QUARTERLY

REVIEW.

APRIL 1, 1874.

ART. I.—THE BIBLE AS INTERPRETED BY MR. ARNOLD.

Literature and Dogma: an Essay towards a Better Apprehension of the Bible. By MATTHEW ARNOLD. Smith, Elder and Co.

AMONG the many books which have appeared of late years, bearing directly or indirectly upon the subject of Religion, all shades of opinion have had their exponents—from what is called "Bible Religion" on the one hand, to the rejection of all supernaturalism on the other; but it remained for Mr. Matthew Arnold, in his recent work, to unite these two extremes. The object of the present Essay is to inquire how far he has been successful in this apparently impossible task.* But before we criticise Mr. Arnold's opinions, we must endeavour to define them. We must lay before our readers, as clearly and concisely as we can, what he affirms and what he rejects. To begin with the latter, as by far the more easy to grapple with, he rejects all Church Dogma; not alone the dogmas of any one Church, but the dogmas which all Christian Churches hold in common,—nay, more, he strikes at the root of "Natural Religion" also, for he rejects the idea of "a Personal God, the moral and intelligent Governor of the Universe," as an "unverifiable assumption."

Let us now turn to what Mr. Arnold affirms. His fundamental axiom is, "that there is a power, which is not ourselves, which makes for righteousness." For this he claims that it can be verified by experience, in the same way that we can verify that "Fire burns, or bread nourishes."

indispensable as the great inspirer of righteousness or conduct, which, Mr. Arnold tells us, is three-fourths of life. Besides the proof by argument above attempted, we are also recommended to make experimental proof of the superior power of the Bible to create in us an enthusiasm for righteousness, by taking a course of the Bible first, and then a course of Benjamin Franklin, Horace Greeley, Jeremy Bentham, and Mr. Herbert Spencer, and then seeing which has the most effect. Our readers may, if they feel disposed, try this experiment. For ourselves, our present concern is with the proof by argument. We will proceed to discuss Mr. Arnold's propositions, one by one. To the first, which we have called Mr. Arnold's fundamental axiom, we have nothing to object—that is, if the definition of it which we have given is correct,—viz., that there is, amongst the many laws of Nature, one which enforces morality. From the second (viz., that this power, which makes for righteousness, is what Israel worshipped, under the name of Jehovah), we dissent on two counts. First, we believe that Israel's God was no "law," or "power," or "principle," but a purely personal God. By a "person" we mean no metaphysical idea, such as Mr. Arnold attributes to the Archbishop of York, but the "magnified and non-natural man of popular theology," who, in fact, is, in one form or other, at the bottom of all Theology. Such a conception implies no acquaintance with metaphysics. Every savage fashions his God in his own image; but, on the other hand, such a negative abstraction as "the not ourselves" is a speciality of our own race, and our own time. It is, *a priori*, an improbability almost amounting to an impossibility, that a barbarous or semi-barbarous people should conceive the idea of an impersonal God—the embodiment of a law; for the idea of a law at all is beyond them. It is essentially an abstract thought, and abstract thought has no existence in the childhood of nations. Mr. Arnold tells us that Israel had no turn for metaphysics, that he had not the talent for abstract thought which belongs to the Aryan races. But Israel must have had a faculty for abstract thought quite unparalleled, if his conception of a God came to pass as Mr. Arnold describes it. (P. 32.) A people in a very early stage of civilization is so deeply absorbed in the study and practice of morality, that they discover that there is a law, which is not themselves, that makes for it, which law they proceed to worship! Can improbability go further? Surely such an argument needs only to be stated, to refute itself. Everything we know of the history of religions goes to prove that the conception of a God, of some sort, is the first stage in the process; while the conception of morality, as a part of his service, is one of the most advanced.

Having put forward at some length the *a priori* arguments against the opinion that Israel's God was not a person, but the deification of a natural law, we will next examine what Israel's own records tell us on the subject. If we there discover clear and unmistakeable evidence for Mr. Arnold's opinion, of course, objections founded on its improbability fall to the ground; but for such evidence we look in vain. The dealings of Jehovah, as there set forth, are characterized by none of the blind necessity, none of the remorseless impassibility of a law. On the the contrary, "The Lord repenteth him of the evil." He allows himself to be entreated. "He is long-suffering, abundant in goodness and mercy." Intercession, prayer, and sacrifice avail to change or modify his purposes. He loves his friends, and hates his enemies, after a thoroughly personal and human fashion. In short, one cannot help seeing in Israel's God, "the magnified and non-natural man in Heaven." Indeed, the text, "As for our God He is in Heaven: He hath done whatsoever hath pleased Him," seems to be the same conception in other words.

Our second ground of objection to the proposition that "the power not ourselves, which makes for righteousness," was what Israel worshipped, is that though righteousness entered largely into Israel's conception of the Eternal, still that conception contained much which conflicts with righteousness. But, to reproduce at all a faithful image of the God of Israel, we must consult the whole of the documents. We must not rely solely on selections from the Prophets, on the most spiritual utterances of the most spiritual writers, but must let the narrative portions, and those which treat of religious ceremonial, have their due weight.

In the narrative of the wars of Israel, we find much which forbids us to regard the Jewish ideal of God as one of pure, unalloyed righteousness. Jehovah is there held up to us as before all else the patriot God, who makes the enemies of Israel His own, and sanctions their extermination by any means, however immoral. The slaughter of captives is commanded and enforced by him. Nor are they simply slaughtered—they are "hewn in pieces before the Lord," like Agag; or they are made to go under barrows and axes of iron. Neither age nor sex is allowed to form a plea for mercy. Treachery and murder earned for Jael the praise of being "Blessed above women." In the same spirit of unscrupulous patriotism the Psalmist, apostrophizing one of Israel's enemies, says, "Blessed shall he be who taketh thy children and dasheth them against the stones." It is needless to multiply instances. Enough has been said to show that, in His dealings with other nations, the God of Israel was more patriotic than righteous.

Another part of the Scripture narrative from which we may

hope to gain some insight into the character of the Jewish God is that which gives us the histories or legends of His most favoured servants. No three men could be more different from each other than were Abraham, the friend of God, Jacob, who wrestled with God and prevailed, and David, the man after God's own heart.

Yet all three were, in the highest degree, pleasing in His sight. Now, if we can discover a common element in characters so dissimilar—any leading characteristic which, though diverse in all else, each of them possessed in a pre-eminent degree, we may conclude that in this characteristic we hold the key which gave them access to the Divine favour. That key was not righteousness—in the sense of morality—but intense devoutness—what is frequently called religiosity, including unhesitating belief and blind obedience. Hence we deduce that, either Jehovah did not love righteousness so much as worship, faith, and love; or else—the Jewish idea of righteousness was not wholly, nor mainly, made up of morality, but consisted largely, if not chiefly, of piety, enthusiastic devotion, and attention to religious ceremonial.

Whichever of these two deductions we may accept (and one of them, as it appears to us, we must accept) leads to the same conclusion, viz., that Jehovah was not the deification of the law of righteousness, as we understand the term—that is, rightness in conduct—for the law, or power, which makes for, or enjoins right conduct, can only be served by conducting one's self rightly. To fail in every social obligation could not, in the eyes of a moralist, be atoned for by a strong taste for devotional exercises, and a delight in the act of worship. Still less could such things avert the inevitable penalties which are inseparable from the violation of a natural law.

We have yet to consider what light is thrown upon the attributes of Jehovah by that elaborate and minute Ritual, which formed so large and important a part of the Jewish law. The first thing to be observed is, that this law of ceremonial was regarded as equally binding with the moral law. No doubt a Prophet from time to time arose, who, having more spiritual insight than the Priests, or the nation at large—more than the makers of the law—caught glimpses of a higher righteousness than that of the law, and exclaimed that "to obey was better than sacrifice, and to hearken than the fat of rams;" but these were the utterances of men who were at once reformers and poets. They in no way disprove that the original and current idea of righteousness in Israel, was largely made up of ceremonial observances; on the contrary, they prove it as the exception proves the rule; for no man strenuously asserts that which is generally admitted by all around him. Judaism was no more responsible for the saying that Jehovah would not eat bull's flesh nor drink the blood of goats, than is the Church of England, or Christianity, responsible for the saying of Mr. Tennyson, that—

> "Our little systems have their day,
> They have their day and cease to be."

Neither the one saying nor the other would be endorsed by the orthodoxy of the time in which they were written: both were innovations, expressions of Free Thought, opposed to, and subversive of, the religious system of their day.

Chief among Jewish rites was the sacrifice of victims. We find the practice fully established in the days of the Patriarchs; it was, therefore, not borrowed, like many of Israel's later religious ideas, from one or other of the Polytheistic nations around them, but was, on the contrary, the original nucleus round which all the later developments of their religion clustered. No trace remains in the Biblical records of the origin of sacrifice, nor of the state of feeling which first prompted its adoption; but the investigation of such mental phenomena, among races upon whom the religious idea is just dawning, has, of late years, engaged the attention of some of the most intelligent European travellers; and the result of their observation is to the effect, that the custom of sacrifice originates in terror acting on ignorance. The benignant aspect of Nature fails, from its familiarity, to impress the torpid mind of the savage with wonder or gratitude; but, when this beneficent routine is broken by calamities, such as sickness, or famine, he is struck with terror and amazement. His first idea is, that "an enemy hath done this"—either a known enemy, working by the occult agency of charms and incantations—whence the belief in witchcraft—or else an unknown enemy, too powerful and intangible to be resisted, but who, like his known enemies, can only be appeased by bloodshed. Hence the belief in the efficacy of sacrifices. That Israel's sacrifices to Jehovah had the same origin, we can hardly doubt; for no law is more certain than that similar effects are produced by similar causes. There are, moreover, indications that Israel had passed through the stage immediately preceding that in which the propitiation consists in the sacrifice of domestic animals. In Exodus xiii. we read that the first-born male of every animal was to be sacrificed to the Lord, but the first-born of man was to be redeemed. Now this claim of Jehovah to the first-born of man, though commuted, points as plainly to a time when it had been enforced as does a rent-charge on land, in lieu of tithes, point to a time when the tithes had been paid in kind. Other indications of the custom of human sacrifice having once existed but grown, as one may express it, rudimentary from disuse, may be seen in Abraham's all but consummated sacrifice of Isaac, and Jephthah's sacrifice of his daughter, in performance of his vow. No doubt, human sacrifice had ceased to be an institution in the days of Abraham, but the idea still clung to men's minds familiarly in the time of Jephthah, otherwise the consummation of his daughter's sacrifice would have been impossible. The argument to be deduced from the fact of sacrifices having formed an important part of the service of the God of Israel, is, that as sacrifices contain no element of morality, they would have been entirely without meaning if offered to a God who was conceived of as the Law, or Power, which enjoins morality; that, on the contrary, they mark a conception in which morality has no part; therefore, as we have shown that the custom existed in Israel, *ab origine*, Mr. Arnold's theory of Israel's original "intuition" falls to the ground, must be placed in the same category with such cherished illusions as "the good old times" and "the wisdom of our ancestors," which, at the touch of investigation, melt away "like the baseless fabric of a vision."

Of the four propositions which we extracted, as embodying the outline of Mr. Arnold's argument, two still remain to be considered, viz., that Religion is morality touched with emotion, and that this is pre-eminently the religion of the Bible. In support of the former proposition, Mr. Arnold tells us (page 20) that "Religion means either a binding to Righteousness, or else a serious attending to righteousness and dwelling upon it; which of these two it most nearly means, depends upon the view we take of the word's derivation, but it means one of them, and they are really much the same." Now we readily admit that, according to which derivation we prefer, religion means a "binding to" or a "dwelling on,"—but as to any allusion to righteousness, in either derivation, we "cannot find it, 'tis not in the bond." If we take the word in the sense in which it is generally used religion means a system of belief and worship, not necessarily including morality, for many religions have been, and some are, utterly immoral. But if we abandon the accepted meaning of the word, and frame definitions, each man according to his own fancy, many could be found, perhaps, not less true, though differing widely from Mr. Arnold's. Thus religion might be defined as the "Aberglaube" which has in all ages obscured and disguised morality, as mists enshroud a mountain, concealing its real outlines, and lending to it, at one time a glory and effulgence not its own, at another investing it with adventitious gloom and terrors. Or, religion might be defined as bearing the same relation to morality as alchemy to chemistry—astrology to astronomy. To the proposition, that "morality touched by emotion is the religion of the Bible," we have already had occasion to take exception when giving our reasons for rejecting Mr. Arnold's theory of the God of the Bible. We have endeavoured to prove that Israel's first conception of a God was that of an unseen but powerful foe, whose enmity might be turned aside and his wrath assuaged by the death of victims. But this first and lowest stage of religious thought belongs essentially to a pre-historic age. When Israel's history opens with the call of Abraham, already a higher phase had been reached. The custom of sacrifice was still in force, but the victims now offered were chosen from the flocks and herds. The spirit, too, in which the offering was made, was greatly changed: belief, obedience, and even love, were elements of worship, and had modified, though not cast out, the abject fear in which worship had its origin. From this point no substantial progress was ever made. The chasm which separates a religion chiefly consisting of worship, with an imperfect morality as a subsidiary element, from Mr. Arnold's ideal religion, in which morality is all in all—was never bridged over by Israel. We have already admitted that many utterances may be found in the Prophets exalting righteousness above ceremonial observances; but whether we regard these expressions of enthusiasm for righteousness, and of delight in the law of the Lord, as embodying the national sentiment, or as expressing the more spiritual thought of a chosen few, the truth which they illustrate, if read with the commentary afforded by Israel's history, is the same. It is that the connexion between lip-righteousness, and righteous living is small indeed, and that the praises of virtue, however ecstatically sung, are powerless to create in men's hearts an effectual love for it. Yet, Mr. Arnold thinks that the words which failed to turn the hearts of those to whom they were originally addressed, have an efficacy beyond all other words for the regeneration of our "masses." The formula which Mr. Arnold employs to bring the Bible into harmony with his theory is, that, "the language of the Bible is literary, not scientific;" and he tells us in his Preface, that the power to read it aright is only attained by culture. Only by help of the literary experience which culture implies, can we know what to insist upon, and what to pass over lightly. With this we entirely concur, but if we venture to take exception to Mr. Arnold's exegesis of the Hebrew Scriptures, it is not on the ground that he attaches less importance to some portions of them than to others, but because he imports into them his own ideas—ideas purely modern, and inconceivable as the product of the age and race to which Mr. Arnold attributes them. So powerfully does his theory possess him, that in some cases he refuses to see the obvious sense of a passage—preferring to find in it an esoteric meaning having reference to "The Eternal Power which makes for righteousness." We have a remarkable instance of this in his interpretation of the passage, "Hear O Israel! The Lord our God is one God." He says, "People think that in this unity of God—this monotheistic idea, as they call it—they have certainly got metaphysics at last. It is nothing of the kind. The monotheistic idea of Israel is simply *seriousness.* There are, indeed, many aspects of the *not ourselves;* but Israel regarded one aspect of it only—that by which it makes for righteousness." Now the meaning of the passage is so clear, that any paraphrase can but obscure it. Moses is supposed to announce solemnly to Israel that *their* God is one, in contradistinction to the Gods of the surrounding nations, who were many. The motive of the writer of Exodus for putting this solemn assertion of monotheism into the mouth of Moses, is not far to seek. It is to be found in the irresistible fascination which the surrounding polytheism exercised over Israel; the bulk of the nation having been probably polytheists down to the time of the Captivity.

We must now turn to Mr. Arnold's theory respecting the New Testament writings, which, though occupying by far the larger portion of the volume, may yet be summed up in comparatively few words. First—he asserts that Jesus was the Son of God, *i.e.*, of course, of "the Power, which is not ourselves, which makes for Righteousness;" "that he is the offspring of this power is verifiable from experience." Second, that the "Mission" of Jesus was to "renew the Intuition" formerly possessed by Israel, of the eternal power which makes for righteousness. Third, that Jesus fulfilled this mission by giving to mankind his "Method" (inwardness), and his "Secret" (self-renunciation). These are the cardinal points in Mr. Arnold's Theory of Christianity; but, in considering them, we shall have to notice many minor points, subsidiary to these. In the consideration of these points, we are stopped on the very threshold, by the difficulty of comprehending the assertion, that Jesus was the offspring of the Power which makes for Righteousness. When we are told that Jesus is the Son of a Personal God, we may dissent from the proposition,—it certainly, as Mr. Arnold observes, is unverifiable. But, at least, we know what it means. But, that Jesus was the offspring of an abstract Principle, conveys no meaning to our mind. However, Mr. Arnold tells us that it is not only true, but verifiable by experience.

"That there is an enduring power, not ourselves, which makes for Righteousness, is verifiable, as we have seen, by experience, and that Jesus *is* the offspring of this Power is verifiable from experience also.

For God is the author of righteousness; now Jesus is the Son of God because he gives the method and the secret by which alone is righteousness possible. And that he *does* give this, we can verify, again, from experience. It *is* so! try, and you will find it to be so."

Now so far as we can understand this argument, it is to the effect, that, because Jesus perceived and taught that, in order to act rightly we must feel rightly (the method of inwardness), and that self-denial (the secret) was a necessary element of morality; and further, because experience shows that his teaching on these points was true, therefore he is proved to have been the Son of that natural Law which enjoins morality. This reasoning is almost too intangible to be grappled with, but we will try to meet it, point by point. In the first place, the existence of "the power, not ourselves, which makes for righteousness" is utterly unverifiable, except in the sense we have assigned to it, viz.: a natural law, which enforces a certain line of conduct, by affixing good consequences to its performance, and bad consequences to its non-performance. But even this law is not an objective reality—all that we can predicate is, that certain consequences are found to follow upon certain courses of conduct. The law which we deduce from the observation of this external fact, is purely subjective—has no existence except in our minds; consequently, to say that any man is the son of a natural law is (with all deference to Mr. Arnold) absurd. Even waiving for the moment that a natural law is not an external reality, still, it can do nothing but perform its peculiar function. The law which makes oxygen and hydrogen unite in fixed proportions to form water, cannot send men into the world to teach its action; still less can any man be said to be the son of such a law. Yet this is precisely a parallel case. It follows that, though the teaching of Jesus may contain truths essential to morality, neither this, nor anything else, could prove him to be, in any real sense, the Son of "the Power which makes for righteousness." But, perhaps, in interpreting Mr. Arnold's words, as really meaning what they say, we are sinning in the same way as those who put a literal interpretation on biblical language. Perhaps Mr. Arnold's language, on this point, is, like that of the Bible, "not scientific, but literary;" "*thrown out* at a not fully grasped object of consciousness." We should, undoubtedly, have so taken it, from the sheer impossibility of giving it any scientific meaning, which should be, at the same time, reasonable, were it not that Mr. Arnold puts forward the statement that Jesus is the Son of the Power which makes for Righteousness, in the form of a logical demonstration, and claims for it an experimental basis; thereby taking it out of the province of literature into that of science. Nevertheless, considering Mr. Arnold's abandonment of supernaturalism, it is probable that he speaks of Jesus as the Son of God only by a violent metaphor, inspired by the hope of retaining the revered names ("familiar in his mouth as household words"), while changing the entire basis of religion, by new definitions of them.

A striking instance of this union in Mr. Arnold, of liberal thought and conservative feeling, is his new definition of Faith (p. 236). "Faith is the being able to cleave to a power of goodness appealing to our higher and real self, not to our lower and apparent self." The old watchword of Religion is retained with a meaning not its own indeed, but better calculated than its own to conciliate modern thought, which revolts from the idea that belief without evidence is to be regarded as a virtue. But if we are to follow Mr. Arnold's recommendation, and "use words as mankind generally use them" (page 21), we cannot perceive that the reconciliation of faith with science is one whit the nearer for his reformed definition; for, though it contains nothing repugnant to science, it does not touch upon faith, but describes a power of steadfast adherence to virtue, against which science has not a word to say. From these passages and another (p. 329) we gather that some scheme of revolutionizing the Spirit of Religion, while retaining its ancient Language, has recommended itself to Mr. Arnold; but we feel sure that such a scheme would have no success in actual working. A considerable proportion of mankind would never perceive that any change had been wrought, and, even among those who comprehended the change, it would soon be lost sight of; for two great forces would tend continually to reproduce the old order of things—the power of words to mould ideas, and man's inveterate tendency to anthropomorphism.

The idea of the "mission of Jesus" is open to the same objections that we have already advanced against the opinion that he was the offspring of the Power that makes for righteousness. Before a man can have a "mission," it must be entrusted to him by some one, and a law cannot, of course, communicate a mission. But neither can a man receive a mission from any but a human source: for this at once implies supernaturalism, or non-naturalism, as Mr. Arnold philosophically prefers to term it. As regards the object of the "mission," viz., "to restore the intuition," we have already endeavoured to prove that Israel never had this "intuition." Of the proposition that Jesus "fulfilled this mission by giving to mankind his method (inwardness, or change of heart), and his secret (self-renouncement)," we must treat at some length. Setting aside the idea of a "mission," which seems to us to be quite unnecessary to the main conception, we think that in singling out these two important principles of morality as the great gift of Jesus to mankind, Mr. Arnold has shown a fineness of perception, and power of generalization, of the highest order. No doubt these principles have always been recognised as characteristic precepts of Christianity, but Mr. Arnold has been the first, so far as we know, to assign to them their true relative value. There may perhaps be something of hyperbole, something more emotional than philosophic, in his way of regarding them; but then Mr. Arnold is the avowed advocate of "morality touched by emotion." In truth, in his treatment of the New Testament, and of Jesus its great central figure, as in his treatment of the Bible and Israel's God, Mr. Arnold is an advocate, and herein, in our opinion, lies his inferiority to Dr. Strauss, whose criticism derives added weight from its judicial character. Now, one cannot help feeling that Mr. Arnold, having once discovered the "method," and the "secret," desires to find them pervading every word ascribed to Jesus by the Evangelists, and, accordingly, he does find them in many passages where they are not visible to an ordinary observer, and in others concerning which the only certainty that we can reach is, that Jesus never uttered them. As an instance of the former we may cite the numerous passages in which Jesus contrasts life in this world with "life eternal;" as an instance of the latter, "Therefore doth my Father love me because I lay down my life that I may take it again." In passages like the former Mr. Arnold never seems to consider the possibility of the literal meaning being the true one, for it contains no allusion to the "secret;" yet it is hardly possible that Jesus should not have believed in the life everlasting after death, and, if he did, what more certain than that he should speak of it? As for the second passage we have quoted, it can but have been written after Jesus had laid down his life, and, as his disciples believed, taken it again.

Mr. Arnold tells us that, of the two great Gospel words, "Repentance" and "Peace," repentance belongs to the "method," peace to the "secret." And here, before we go further, we may as well confess that this word "secret," as applied to that self-denial inculcated by Jesus, seems to us the most infelicitous—the most jarring and inappropriate that could possibly have been picked out. The two leading principles in the teaching of Jesus—reformation from within, and self-denial—may, perhaps, together be the "secret" of His influence over men; but, in no sense can anything taught openly to all be fitly termed a "secret." Jesus offering His "secret" calls up, in our minds, at least, a train of associations derogatory to Him who said, "I spake openly to the world, and in secret have I said nothing."

To return. The word "repentance" does not seem merely to attach itself to "the method," but to be itself the "method." On the peace which attends the "secret," Mr. Arnold strongly insists as the proof of its truth. At page 211, he says, "This, we say, is of the very essence of his secret of self-renouncement as of his method of inwardness; that its truth will be found to commend itself by *happiness*, to prove itself by *happiness*, and of the secret more especially is this true." Now we cannot share Mr. Arnold's belief that the truth of a system of morality or of religion, proves itself by the happiness of those who obey its precepts. Happiness depends so much on health and temperament, that it forms a very fallacious test of the virtue of its possessors. Göthe, as quoted by Mr. Arnold, says, "Nothing after health and virtue, can give so much satisfaction as learning and knowing." Thus, wisely placing virtue second to health as a source of happiness. But even the happiness which we derive exclusively from virtue, by no means proves that our standard of virtue is correct, but merely that we are acting up to that standard. If we do but act in accordance with our ideal, let that ideal be never so imperfect or perverted, our conscience approves us and happiness is the result.

In attempting to define with any degree of precision, Mr. Arnold's views on the main topics of the New Testament writings, we are constantly baffled by what seems like an unwillingness to accept the necessary consequences of his own admissions. Thus, he admits that the record contained in our Gospels "passed through half a century or more of oral tradition, and through more than one written account" before reaching its present form; yet, he accepts from our Gospels, as really uttered by Jesus, many things which, on that view, are wholly inexplicable, but which on the supposition that they were ascribed to Him after the dogmas which they assert had come into existence, require no explanation. The most remarkable instance of this is to be found in Mr. Arnold's treatment of the passage (John ix. 58), "Jesus said unto them, before Abraham was, I am"—in which Jesus clearly asserts his identity with Jehovah, who revealed himself to Moses under the name, "I am that I am" (Exodus iii. 14). Mr. Arnold endeavours to explain away this obvious meaning, by a process which he has stigmatized elsewhere in the words of Bishop Butler, as one by which "anything may be made to mean anything," rather than reject the whole passage as an "effort to do something for the honour of our Lord's Godhead," of which dogma the author of the fourth Gospel was as zealous a champion as ever were Mr. Arnold's "twin bishops."

In the same spirit, though attempting no defence of miracles, and confessing that, if he could turn his pen into a penwiper, he should not, thereby, make what he wrote more true, or more convincing—by far the most humorous passage in the book—yet, Mr. Arnold would fain imagine in Jesus a power of healing, and, especially, of casting out unclean spirits, not granted to mere men. He pronounces, ex cathedrâ, that "the action of Jesus in these cases, however it may be amplified in the reports, was real;" but it "is not thaumaturgy." Mr. Arnold ascribes it to "moral therapeutics;" but this power was not supposed to be possessed exclusively by Jesus, witness the question, "If I by Beelzebub cast out devils, by whom do your sons cast them out?" Then, did the Jews, too, cast out devils by "moral therapeutics"?

Finally, though Mr. Arnold heaps scorn on the doctrine of "the Godhead of the Eternal Son," he yet invests Jesus with attributes which we can only characterize as Divine. As examples, we may adduce—first, Prescience, as shown in predictions of his death and the manner of it, as to the credibility of which predictions Mr. Arnold seems to have no misgivings; and second, an intuitive and unerring knowledge, little short of Omniscience, shown in his entire superiority to all error, Jewish or Christian, in the interpretation of the Scriptures—a superiority which Mr. Arnold is so bent on maintaining that, when Jesus, in argument with the Jews, uses the passage, "The Lord said unto my Lord," &c., in the sense in which it was understood by them and has been understood by all Christendom ever since, Mr. Arnold would rather believe that Jesus used an argument which he knew to be fallacious (which amounts, as we think, to imputing *mala fides*), than allow that he participated in an error of interpretation which was universal in his day, and was not discovered to be an error until more than eighteen centuries after his death.

Regarding this remarkable work as a whole, we think it a most ingenious and original attempt to place Religion on a scientific basis. Its great blemish, in our eyes, is its tone of uncompromising advocacy, which begets inconsistent and conflicting utterances. Of Jesus it reflects no clear mental image, for we are equally forbidden to think him human, or divine. The old proverb tells us that "we cannot eat our cake and have it;" but this seems to us to be exactly what Mr. Arnold attempts to do. He would gladly be rid of supernaturalism, yet he clings to the Bible, of which supernaturalism is the key-note.

At the commencement of this Essay we stated that its object was to inquire how far Mr. Arnold had succeeded in the apparently impossible task of reconciling Bible religion with the rejection of supernaturalism. We are now convinced that the impossibility of the task was not only apparent, but real; since Mr. Arnold, with all his known ability, has, in our judgment, failed to accomplish it.

Art. II.—Out-door Parish Relief.

1. *A History of the English Poor-law in connexion with the legislation and other circumstances affecting the Condition of the People.* By Sir George Nicholls, K.C.B. 2 vols. John Murray. 1854.
2. *The Book of the Bastilles; or the History of the working of the New Poor Law.* By G. R. Wythen Baxter. John Stephens. 1841.
3. *The Principles of Population and their Connexion with Human Happiness.* By Archibald Alison, F.R.S.E. 2 vols. Blackwood. 1840.
4. *Pauperism: its Causes and Remedies.* By Henry Fawcett, M.A., M.P. Macmillan. 1871.
5. *First and Second Annual Reports of the Local Government Board* 1871-2 *and* 1872-3. 2 vols. Eyre and Spottiswoode.
6. *Système des Contradictions Economiques; ou, Philosophie de la Misère.* Par P. J. Proudhon. Paris: Guillaumin et Cie. 1846.

ALTHOUGH many of the abuses connected with Out-door Relief have been abolished, the system still continues. It is our object to show that in its nature it is false and injurious and ought to be abolished.

The early history of the Poor-law is the early history of out-door relief. For centuries after relief of the poor in money and kind had commenced, we find no trace of house or in-door accommodation being provided. In the fourteenth century there was a general uprising against the serfdom in which the labouring classes had hitherto been held. As long as slavery had lasted there was clearly no room for a Poor-law, because each man could look for support to the master whose chattel he was. The 12 Richard II. (1388) is the statute which is, if not the origin of the English Poor-law, at least the first legislative enactment on the subject. In it the impotent poor are spoken of as a separate class. Both in this and in Acts passed in previous reigns, wandering labourers, capable of work, are dealt with and punished; but here for the first time paupers incapable of service are taken in hand, and forbidden to move from the place in which they were dwelling or from the place of their birth. No relief is provided for them, but the statute probably contemplated that their wants would be supplied by the casual charity of those to whom they were known, and by those religious foundations which attracted to themselves a large portion of the wealth of the country. This view is confirmed by a statute passed three years later, by which provision is made in certain cases that "the Diocesan shall ordain a convenient sum of money to be distributed yearly of the fruits and profits of the same to the poor parishioners, in aid of their living and sustenance for ever." The close of the 14th century saw a rapid advance in the progress of serfdom to freedom, and a corresponding increase of vagrancy. In 1414 (Henry V.) the Act above alluded to was confirmed, and wider power given to the Justices who were charged with its execution. Moreover, an inquiry was instituted into the abuses which had crept into the administration of those charities to which the impotent poor looked for relief. Two years later a fresh effort was made by the legislature (consisting, as Sir G. Nicholls points out, entirely of the employers of labour), to limit the rate of wages, whilst at the same time, those who refused to work at the fixed rates were punished with increasing severity. The same policy was pursued in a statute of Henry VI. (1427). The next statute which we need notice is that of 11 Henry VII. cap. 2 (1495), by which vagabonds able to work are no longer to be committed to gaol, but set in the stocks—a change recommended by the costliness of the former punishment; whilst those not able to work are forbidden to beg out of their own hundred. But in 1503 the severity of the prescribed punishment was diminished, and the impotent poor were ordered to remain in the place where they were born, or where they had last resided the space of three years, without begging out of that place.

In the reign of Henry VIII. a new era commences. Already before the suppression of the religious houses, two Acts were passed (1530-36) creating machinery for the relief and management of the poor. All impotent persons are to be registered, and are to receive letters authorizing them to beg within certain limits, and they are to be punished with the stocks, or by whipping if they beg without such letters, or beyond their assigned limits. Vagabonds, being whole and mighty in body and able to labour, when found begging are to be arrested and whipped "till the body be bloody," through a market-town or other convenient place, and this is to be repeated until the delinquents have betaken themselves to the places where they were born, or where they have last dwelt the space of three years, and there put themselves to honest labour. In the latter of the two above-named Acts, it is provided that the authorities of the places to which the "poor creatures," or "sturdy vagabonds," are enjoined to repair, shall succour them by way of voluntary charitable alms, so that the former shall not be compelled to beg openly, and the latter shall be set and kept to continual labour, in such wise as that they may get their own living. "Ruffelers," calling themselves serving-men, but having no masters, are not only to be treated as sturdy vagabonds, but in addition are to have their ears cropped, and on persistence in idleness to suffer death. The way in which the funds are to be raised for the relief of the poor, and the setting of sturdy vagabonds and valiant beggars to work is clearly set forth. The mayors and other head officers, and the churchwardens, or two others of every parish, are to gather the offerings of good Christian people, in boxes every Sunday and holiday. The parson is to exhort all people to give towards the fund, and an account is to be kept of the same. If the parson's exhortation fails in drawing a contribution from any obdurate individual, the bishop is to try his hand; mitred eloquence being presumably more efficacious than that of a common clerk. Moreover, no one is to give, under a penalty, any dole or alms otherwise than to the common boxes or gatherings; and persons or bodies corporate, that are bound to distribute food or money to the poor, are obliged to use the same channel.

Both Sir G. Nicholls and Mr. Fawcett omit to remark on the time when In-door relief of the poor commenced. Up to the time which we have now reached—and indeed up to a much later period—there is no law on the subject: yet it seems highly probable that about this time those persons who were charged with the execution of the Poor-law must have had recourse to something like In-door relief. It is improbable that the officials would in all cases be able to provide for the impotent poor without supplying some kind of public abode.

The abbeys and monasteries were suppressed in the period 1536-9. That this event had an important bearing upon the condition of the poor, by withdrawing from them the doles and alms which had been distributed at their gates, we do not deny; but, from the brief history which we have given, it is clear that it was not, what it has often been supposed to be, the cause of the establishment of the Poor-law.

In the first year of Edward I.'s reign some very severe punishments, such as branding and slavery were devised against vagabondage, but these were shortly after repealed, and the former acts were confirmed and strengthened. In the reign of Mary the collections for the poor were made weekly, but no other important change was made in the law. A most weighty event occurred when by 5 Eliz. cap. 3 it was enacted, that any obstinate person refusing to contribute to the support of the poor might be committed to prison until he paid the appointed sum. This is in fact the real commencement of a compulsory Poor Rate; but the Act of Elizabeth which has obtained far greater celebrity was not passed until the close of her reign.

By the 14 Elizabeth cap. 5 the penalties against beggars, if able to work, are made very severe. Mr. Fawcett places this event too early, although the expression he uses is capable of another interpretation. The delinquent was to be punished first by whipping and branding, and afterwards by death as a felon. The impotent poor are to be carefully sought for and registered, and they are to have convenient abiding places to settle themselves upon. It is difficult to avoid the conclusion that the system of in-door relief is now becoming an established fact. The same Act provides that persons, who are partially unable to work, shall yet perform such labour as the overseers appoint. Moreover, if there is any surplus remaining after the impotent poor are provided for, it may be employed in setting to work those of the sturdy poor who are disposed to labour.

The 18 Elizabeth cap. 3, marks another era. Houses of Correction are to be provided to the number of one or two in each county. Stocks of wool, hemp, flax, iron or other stuff are to be provided, and these materials are to be served out to the poor, who, if they neglect their work, shall be taken to the Houses of Correction and there "straitly kept as well in diet as in work." This Act remained in force about twenty years.

We have now briefly sketched the history of the English Poor Law, having noticed every Act of importance up to the passing of the statute which still remains in force, and is, in fact, the groundwork of the present system. Our apology for the length to which we have gone must lie in the obvious importance of the subject, and in the fact that the popular error has to be corrected—that legislation on the subject commenced with the Act known as 43 Elizabeth cap. 2 (1601).

That famous Act, which was an amplification of one which had been passed four years previously, in reality appears to have done little more than confirm and settle on a firmer foundation those principles which we have already noticed. Its chief effect was, however, to establish the right, which had been gradually growing up, of all persons to claim relief from the State. By this Act a compulsory rate is raised for the following purposes:—

Firstly, "For setting to work the children of all such whose parents shall not be thought able to keep and maintain them."

Secondly, "For setting to work all such persons, married and unmarried, having no means to maintain them, and who use no ordinary and daily trade of life to get their living by."

Thirdly, "For providing a convenient stock of flax, hemp, &c., to set the poor on work."

Fourthly, "For the necessary relief of the lame, impotent, old, blind, and such other among them being poor, and not able to work."

We shall now be able to confine our investigations almost entirely to the question of the relation between out-door and in-door relief. By this time, there can be no doubt that some important part of the money spent on the poor must have been expended on and in the Houses of Correction and other buildings which had been by this time, no doubt, erected. In the reign of James I. an Act was passed calling upon those counties which had bitherto neglected to do so, to proceed to the erection of such Houses of Correction, in which it was proposed to combine punishment and employment—the idle to be employed, the disorderly punished. Towards the end of the seventeenth century the name of House of Correction seems to have been changed into that of Workhouse. Many persons at this time—the most eminent being Sir Matthew Hale—appear to have regarded the Workhouse system with much favour. He recommended that one should be built for every two or three parishes, according to their size; but he did not take into account the difficulties which would inevitably arise when pauper labour should come into competition with the open market. At the close of the century this plan was put into operation by a special Act at Bristol, in which city a *Union* was formed with satisfactory results. Mr. John Carey, who had been mainly instrumental in its establishment, declares:—

"That it has had this good effect, that there is not a common beggar or disorderly vagrant seen in these streets, but charity is given in its proper place and manner; and the magistrates are freed from the daily trouble they had with the poor, and the parishes they lived in are discharged from the invidious fatigues of their settlements, when a great deal of what should have maintained them was spent in determining what parishes were to do it."

Other large towns shortly followed this example; for it was obvious that the only way to keep down the now rapidly increasing poor-rates, and to introduce something like order into the relief of the poor was to discover some better system than the mere distribution of money and food, for there is little doubt that this had hitherto been the method which had been mainly adopted. In 1722, by the 9 George I. cap. 7, the plan of permitting the union of parishes for the erection and maintenance of Workhouses was extended to the whole of England. Moreover, in case any poor persons should refuse maintenance in such house, or, to use the modern phrase, should decline the "offer of the house," they are to be "put out of the book in which the names of persons who ought to receive relief are registered."

Had this policy been adhered to, the advantage would have been great. It is in fact the policy which we desire to see established. But it could never have been carried out at that period, for the idea of the Workhouses was then, and until much later, based on the principle of the employment of the inmates with a view to profit. It needs very little argument to show that such a system must end in failure, because it would be impossible for an independent working-man to compete with rate-aided pauper labour. In the event it has been always found that this course not only fails to raise the pauper out of his pauperism, but actually drags down the independent labourer to the same level. The scheme failed; the legislature helping it to its failure by passing a law, the 7 George III. (1767), by which the poor were to be protected against the parsimony, as it was popularly called, of the officials, by the appointment of guardians of the poor. This opened the doors to the increase of out-door relief, and in 1782 an Act, known as Gilbert's Act, was passed, of which, and of a subsequent one, Mr. Fawcett says:—

> "By it most of the valuable safeguards in the old Poor-law were entirely swept away. The workhouse was no longer to be used as a test of voluntary pauperism, for by this Act the able-bodied were not obliged to enter it; the guardians were ordered to find work for all able-bodied applicants near their own homes, and to make up out of the rates any deficiency in wages. The same fatal policy was continued, and was brought to a climax in 1815, when by a statute known as East's Act, the workhouse test, imposed by 9 George I., was now altogether removed."

Justices were now made the sole judges, instead of the overseers, of the occasion or necessity of relief in any case, and out-door relief became more common than ever.

This was the condition of things which brought the country almost to the verge of ruin, for Poor-rates rose to such an extent that it became hardly worth while, in some instances, to retain the land in cultivation. An agitation then commenced which resulted in the New Poor-law Act of 1834. Counter-agitations went on for years, carried on by such men as the author of "The Book of the Bastilles," whose cry was to *Gilbertize* all parishes, that is, to give to the justices the autocratic power of ordering out-door relief, and to make the Workhouse system practically a nullity. During the period which had elapsed since the middle of the last century, the commercial idea of the Workhouse may be said to have died out; mainly, no doubt, because that system had itself, to a considerable extent, given way to out-door relief. It may be said that the main provisions of the Act of 1834 aimed at checking out-door relief, and introducing order and good government into the Workhouses, which were no longer expected to provide their expences by the labour of their inmates. The working of the Act was most satisfactory, and within very few years both rates and pauperism decreased to no small extent. We have no doubt that if the same principle were now carried out to its full extent, that is, to the point of the abolition of out-door relief, both pauperism and rates would be still further diminished in a very important degree.

But out-door relief still prevails to a very considerable extent. We extract the following statistics from the last report of the Local Government Board (1872-3):—

Ratio of Out-door to In-door Paupers.

In all England	5 to 1
In England (less the Metropolis)	6 to 1
In the Metropolis alone	2½ to 1.

There were in England on the 1st January, 1872 (the latest return), no fewer than 824,600 out-door paupers, or about one in twenty-eight of the whole population. The proportion of out-door to in-door paupers is highest in the South-Western and Welsh Divisions. In Dorset, for instance, the ratio is 11 to 1, whilst in some of the Unions of Wales the paupers appear to receive only out-door relief, and the ratio is found in certain instances to reach the high proportion of 32, of 70, and of 80 to 1. The ratio of 10 and 12 to 1 is common in many parts of England. The actual cost of in-door relief was (in the year ending Lady-day, 1872), 1,515,790*l.*, that of out-door relief 3,583,571*l.* The total amount expended on the poor was 8,007,403*l.*, being an increase of about tenpence per head on population since 1865. These figures show clearly that we are still engaged in the administration of a system which may be fairly called one of out-door rather than of in-door relief.

It will readily be conceded that the labourer has a right to receive the price of his labour without any deductions. Moreover, he may fairly expect that his wages should be paid to him in money; for all other forms of payment, by "privileges" or otherwise, are, in reality, relics of feudalism and tend to interfere with his freedom. In the last century and up to 1834, a period in which the remains of villeinage and serfdom were even more easily traced than now, out-door relief was deliberately regarded as a rate in aid of wages. Nor could any other view be justly taken. Wages were notoriously so low, that it was impossible for the labourer to exist on them. The farmers, the landowners, and even the manufacturers considered that they kept their labourers more under their control by paying them a fixed rate of wages, and supplementing these out of the poor-rate by an amount which would vary according to the season and the behaviour of the men. Nor were the employers wrong in their calculations, for they succeeded in obtaining labour at the lowest possible cost in money, although they reduced the labourer to the condition of a mere slave. At the present day, the idea that out-door relief is a rate in aid of wages would probably be scouted. We contend that the difference is one only of degree and not of kind. Much less out-relief is given now than before the passing of the New Poor-law, but it is now, what it was then, with an important exception, which we shall presently notice, nothing else than a clumsy expedient for making up the defect in the rate of wages.

Without attempting to define closely here the true relation between capital and labour, we shall assume that the labourer has the first claim upon the product of his toil. The farmer or manufacturer has no right to take his share, until the labourer has received sufficient to support himself in decency and comfort. If the industry in which capital and labour are embarked cannot pay the employer a remunerative rate of interest after the labourer has been paid, it can only be said that it should be abandoned. There is a general tendency among employers of labour to suppose that they have a right to make their profit by keeping down the rate of wages, as is shown by the fact that the landowners of the present day live much better, and the agricultural labourer much worse in proportion than the same classes did two centuries ago. In other words, employers see no wrong in taking for themselves luxuries before the necessaries of life are supplied to those associated with them in a common industry. These are the people who are the most eager in support of out-door relief. Wages being insufficient they must be supplemented, and this can be done in no other way than through the parish pay-table. Moreover, the circle is a vicious one, for high poor-rates deprive the employer of the means as well as of the will of paying full wages. Of course everything depends upon what may be deemed the necessaries of life for a labourer. Decent house accommodation and clothing, sufficient and wholesome food, and a margin of wages which shall enable him to provide against sickness and old age may be certainly claimed by every working-man in a flourishing community. Some persons may be inclined to think that the last requirement is excessive; but it must be remembered that a man is practically in a state of slavery, if he is unable, although he is a thrifty man, by any exertion however great of his own, to provide against the ordinary evils of life. Nor is the amount large which would be required for this purpose. The great benefit societies provide all that is absolutely necessary for less than one shilling per week. If the rate of wages in any branch of industry is not sufficient to supply these necessaries as we have stated them, it is clear that too many labourers are engaged in it, who are in fact underselling each other. Steps should be taken to give immediate relief by emigration and migration, and prospective relief by discouraging early and improvident marriages. Out-door relief, and indeed, the whole Poor-law system, tend to nullify the working of the law of supply and demand, by making it possible for labourers to accept lower wages than they can properly subsist upon. Moreover, a system of artificial support emasculates the powers of the labourer by rendering it not only unnecessary, but even foolish for him to be thrifty and industrious. All the provisions and contrivances which we observe to have been implanted in man are such as constantly spur him on to exertion. To deprive him of these incentives to diligence is to deprive him of his main support—a cruelty and not a kindness. A little reflection shows that a system by which a man is provided with money and food, if he needs them, must produce the effect of weakening his own efforts to obtain these necessaries for himself. Is it possible to conceive a greater cruelty or injustice than the deliberate breaking down of man's best safeguard against want and dependence? Those who desire to contemplate the full result of the system can study it in the Dorsetshire labourer of to-day.

There is, as we have said, one important exception to our assertion that out-door relief is an expedient for making up the defect in the rate of wages. The habit of looking to the parish pay-table has so completely taken hold of the wage-earning classes that it cannot be easily shaken off. Experience teaches us that those who earn high wages are not always the furthest removed from pauperism. One branch of industry—the coal trade—has recently received a great impetus, and a greatly increased rate of wage has been earned by the colliers. It is notorious that these men have launched out into almost every form of extravagance. The idea of thrift does not seem to have occurred to them. To what other influence than to that of the parish pay-table can this be ascribed? The French peasant or working man, whose earnings are probably far smaller, has before him the necessity of saving, and accordingly he saves. To the

English collier this is a new and strange idea; for during many generations he has been taught that the State charges itself with the duty of providing him with necessaries when he is in want of them, and that he may fairly spend his money in luxuries. Another instance of the vitiating influence of the knowledge that an allowance is waiting for every one who needs it, is found in that vast mass of persons who live by supplying the wants of the rich at the West End of London, as journeymen tailors and shoemakers, and in other trades. These classes earn wages in the season which are simply enormous. In the winter, when their patrons are far away in the country and trade is dull, they frequently pass weeks, and even months, in complete idleness. At such periods is seen the evil working of the out-door relief system. The very men who were revelling in most profuse abundance, and even luxuries, a few months before, are now clamorous for the parish relief, which they claim as a right, and obtain without difficulty. We do not indeed assert that every London journeyman tailor or shoemaker is unthrifty, but that of a not inconsiderable number the above statement is true. No effort of philanthropy, be it ever so wisely guided, is strong enough to undo, in such cases, the evil which is done by the noxious system of out-door relief. The working men of England are at this moment earning enormous wages. They ought to be saving money; no statistics will be demanded of us, if we state that they are not doing so. Yet the loss not only to themselves but to the country is very great. If, instead of spending their money as fast as it is earned, the wage-earners were to learn a lesson of thrift and economy, they would find in a few years that they had gained not one but many advantages. They would have become, as was recently shown in France on the occasion of the payment of the war indemnity, literally the backbone of the country. They would have gained thereby an influence in political life, such as no more reduction of the franchise can give them. They would have realized the necessity of not blindly and thoughtlessly introducing into the world a countless generation which should in less than a life-time eat up all their prosperity, and sink their class down once more into pauperism. Above all, they would feel that they were raised above the ordinary accidents of life. What is it that stands in the way of the realization of this state of things? We answer, mainly that system of Out-door Relief which paralyses their efforts by giving them a legal right to assistance.

Those persons who are in favour of giving the preponderance to out-door relief, are in the habit of pointing to the now famous Elberfeld method of administering a Poor-law. It must be acknowledged that they have a strong case; yet we believe that such a system will be seen on examination to be unsuited for general adoption. We extract the following account from the First Report of the Local Government Board (1871-1872):—

"The administration of out-door relief is entrusted to eighteen overseers (*Bezirksvorsteher*), or in case of unavoidable absence, substitutes elected from amongst the visitors or *Armenpfleger*, and to two hundred and fifty-two (252) visitors (*Armenpfleger*). The overseers and visitors are elected for three years, substitutes for one. One-third of the overseers and visitors retire every year and are eligible for re-election. Each visitor or *Armenpfleger* has under his charge a certain section of the town, and fourteen of these sections are under the general superintendence of one overseer or *Bezirksvorsteher*.

"The visitors of each district meet at least once a fortnight, the meeting being presided over by the overseer of the section.

"Every application for relief is made to the visitor of the section."

The superintendence of the whole rests with a Committee appointed by the Municipal Council. No visitor is allowed to have more than four cases in hand, and as the population of Elberfeld was 71,000 at the date of the report, there is a visitor to less than every 300 inhabitants. The offices of overseers and visitors are unpaid and compulsory. The general rules within which the administration of relief is restricted are as follows:—

"1. Every person who is destitute and unable to procure work shall, upon application by himself or by another on his behalf, be relieved from the town funds, except when other persons bound by law to relieve him possess the means of doing so, or except when he is in receipt of relief from private charity.

"2. Any able-bodied person being destitute and unrelieved by private charity may, by applying personally or through friends for relief, and upon proof that he has tried unsuccessfully to obtain work, be entitled to receive temporary relief until such time as he can earn a sufficient livelihood, he being bound in the meantime to perform such work as may be assigned to him.

"3. Single persons and heads of families whose income suffices to procure for themselves the absolute necessaries (*das unabweislich Nothwendige*) of life are not to be considered as destitute, that is, entitled to relief from the public funds.

"4. Poor relief in case of persons earning less than the means of subsistence may be administered as out-door relief by grants of money, soup, clothes and bedding, indispensable articles of furniture, free schooling, surgical, medical, and midwifery attendance; medicine, cost of funeral; or it may be administered indoor in the town poorhouse."

These rules are carried out with the greatest possible strictness, and have resulted in an important diminution of pauperism.

In criticising the Elberfeld system, our first remark must be that it would be practically impossible to introduce it in this country. The number of unpaid officials which would be needed to carry it out in London, with its population of between three and four millions, would be more than 11,000. The race of life is far more eager, and the conditions of success are far more stringent among the professional and commercial classes, from which these officials would be taken in England, than among the corresponding classes in Germany. Would the proposal to establish such a system be entertained for a moment in this country? We fancy not. Next, the system is founded upon the false principles which we have endeavoured to controvert in the present article. It is true, that by extreme strictness and by making relief exceedingly difficult to obtain, pauperism has been greatly checked, but the fact remains, that a considerable amount of out-door relief is still given, and must produce the same result in Elberfeld as it does elsewhere: it must weaken the natural resources of the recipient. Moreover, Elberfeld, we find, was formerly notorious for an extremely lax and indiscriminating system of public charity, the evil results arising from which aroused the authorities to the necessity of making a change; and the comparison of the two methods is heightened in favour of the new plan, from the extreme of pauperism which had arisen under the old.

It is difficult to see why the following argument should not hold good:—If, as in Elberfeld, where relief is almost wholly out-door, the imposition of strong restrictions on public assistance greatly reduces the Poor-law expenditure, and increases in a marked degree the thrift, and therefore the well-being, of the working-classes, why should not the complete abolition of out-door relief act still further in the same direction?

We return, for a moment, to statistics. Taking two Unions, Atcham in Shropshire, and Witney in Oxfordshire, in which the total amounts expended on the Relief of the Poor are nearly equal, being respectively 10,154*l.* and 10,918*l.*, we find, nevertheless, that the population of the former (45,561) is about double that of the latter (22,908). The numbers of the out-door and in-door paupers in the Atcham Union are nearly equal, whilst in the Witney Union there are eight out-door paupers to one in-door. The total number of paupers at Atcham are 719, or one in sixty-two of the population; at Witney 1582, or one in fourteen. We take these two Unions for no other reason than that the figures we quote admit of easy comparison. They are very striking, and clearly indicate the immediate financial and social results of even an approximation to the system which we uphold. The comparison is not, of course, complete, until we have learnt by observation what the condition of the labouring classes is in two such Unions as these: our own experience of similar cases is, that there is less misery in those places in which out-door relief is checked than in those in which it is lavishly given. We believe that no information of this kind, which would command attention, can be obtained save by means of a Royal Commission; and, in face of the figures put forward in the two Blue Books which we are reviewing, it is difficult to understand how a single session can be allowed to pass without its appointment.

To compel every applicant for relief to accept the "offer of the House" or to lose all assistance, may appear a harsh measure. At first many would suffer, however easy the period of transition might be made during the process of the abolition of out-door relief; but a great gain would be made if our arguments are reliable. At least, we may claim for them the merit of simplicity We have only striven to show that Logic suggests, and History proves, that in proportion as out-door relief is great or small, the thrift, and therefore the prosperity, of the wage-earning classes are increased or diminished.

Art. III.—Pangenesis.

1. *The Variation of Animals and Plants under Domestication.* By Charles Darwin, M.A., F.R.S., &c. Murray. 1868.
2. *On the Genesis of Species.* By St. George Mivart, F.R.S. London: 1871.

THE "Provisional Hypothesis of Pangenesis" has stirred up much discussion since it was first proposed by Mr. Darwin; but neither the propositions in which it consists, nor its merits, nor even its defects, have been correctly appreciated. The following remarks are intended to supply the omissions of its critics, and to point out a path by which the suggestions of the hypothesis may be carried a stage further towards elucidation and proof.

It is necessary first to state the propositions in which the hypothesis consists. They may conveniently be arranged under three heads, according to three principal divisions of the hypothesis itself, suggested by an obvious threefold division in the phenomena which it is designed to explain. The three heads are as follows:—(1) The doctrine of gemmules; (2) The laws of generative conception and orderly growth; (3) The laws of voluntary modification.

(I.) The doctrine of gemmules is suggested by the fact, that our physiological activities in the gross are generally admitted to have been traced to the activities of certain ultimate physiological molecules styled "cells;" so that the sum of the bodily activity is determined by the sum of the activities of the body's cells. If the cells be given, then also the body with its functions is given; whence it follows that a corporeal correspondence between descendants and ancestors suggests a connexion between the separate cells in their respective bodies. Such a postulated connexion between one cell (in the ancestor) and another cell (in the descendant) is supposed to be established by means of a minute physiological entity styled a "gemmule;" having somewhat the same relation to the cell which it represents as is borne by a seed to the parent plant. The conditions under which this connexion is supposed to be secured may be summed up in the following propositions:—

1. Gemmules are thrown off by every cell in the body; perhaps at every stage of the cell's growth, certainly at every stage of the body's growth;

2. Any one of which, when nourished under the fitting conditions, will reproduce the cell from which it sprang;

3. These circulate freely through the body itself;

4. And are so small,

5. And so numerous, that gemmules from every cell which has existed at any time in any part of the body during its whole life, not only may be, but almost certainly will be, collected together in every spermatozoon and in every ovule. Moreover, by reason of the ubiquity and number of the gemmules, this collection will not consist only of gemmules due to the actual *producer* of the spermatozoon or ovule: there will also be present gemmules derived from his or her parents, grandparents, and remoter ancestors; but the more remote the ancestor, the fewer, in general, are the gemmules directly derived from him.

Gemmules of all sorts are (probably) present everywhere in the body; but

6. They are specially determined to the generative organs, where they are perhaps modified, certainly arranged in definite and complex relations, by the operation of definite laws of the organic structure. This last statement covertly contains an indefinite number of propositions which, in the present state of our knowledge, cannot be reduced to exact terms. The same inevitable indefinitiveness is also conspicuous in the statement of the second head, the laws of generative conception and orderly growth; to which we proceed.

(II.) We are now to imagine the ovule to have been fertilized by the spermatozoon. The consequent processes are somewhat as follows. Only *ante-fetal* gemmules—gemmules, that is, thrown off by parents and ancestors when they themselves were in the same ante-fetal state—are available for the purpose. But there is present an immense number of these, derived from ancestors of various degrees in remoteness. Some process of selection is performed, either by the fecundated ovum, or by the enveloping organism, or by both together, whereby some of the ante-fetal gemmules are picked out and preferred as the material to form the fetal germ. This first act of selection is of incalculable importance; for its effects upon the offspring will extend (probably) to the last moment of life. The germ having been formed by the apt agglomeration of gemmules, these are developed into cells. Thereupon, more gemmules are required, taken from among those which date from the corresponding ancestral state;* of which, again, an immense number, from various ancestors, are present. The above described process of selection is performed again. The elected gemmules are attached to the fetal-germ, which grows by their being developed from gemmules into cells. More gemmules are then selected and attached; and so the process is continued, until we come to the time of birth.

Owing to the imperfection of the language at our command, we are forced to describe the above process, which is probably (or certainly) continuous, under the image of a series of discrete stages. The reader must make the same kind of correction as is made in mathematics, when the limiting polygon becomes a curve or the limiting polyhedron a surface. This process of selection from among gemmules seems to decrease in importance as it proceeds further; for then the power of selection is in great part (finally altogether) performed by the cells which have been previously selected; so that the results of the earlier acts of selection exercise a powerful influence upon the results of the later, and are therefore in some sense more important.

The laws of orderly growth will be only an extension of some of the laws by which the fetus grows before birth. The difference between the two cases lies in this, that in the infant a complete set of cells has been got together, which has now only to *grow*, whereas in the fetus two processes, *growth* and *formation*, go on together.

The growth and preservation of the body is known to be effected by the continual substitution of new cells in the place of those which are continually decomposed and excreted. This process is thus explained by the hypothesis. Each cell, before

* That is, which were thrown off by the ancestral cells, when these were only the germ of a fetus. The *date* of a gemmule is the same as the date of the cell from which it sprang; and the cells which the gemmules form are of the same date as themselves. For example, gemmules thrown off by an infant at the stage of dentition, can only be used to form cells in the infant's descendants at or about the time when they shall be cutting their teeth.

its decease and excretion, provides for itself a successor, selected from the attendant gemmules (1) of *the date next in order to its own date,* (2) springing from a corresponding cell in the body of some ancestor, whether near or remote. We are ignorant of the laws which govern that selection by which one gemmule is preferred to its competitors of the same date; but it is natural to speak of a *struggle for development* among the gemmules, analogous to the struggle for life among the members of a tribe or species.

Since gemmules can become candidates for development only at the same stage of the body's growth as that at which they were produced, it follows that when a gemmule has once been passed by, so that its appropriate stage has been left behind, it is condemned to organic torpor so long as it shall continue to inhabit the body of its present possessor. Torpid or dormant gemmules perhaps propagate themselves, by fission or otherwise, the *date* of their progeny remaining unaltered.

The facts to which the hypothesis appeals under this head, are briefly as follows:—

(1.) The various organs generally increase together by orderly development, each keeping its own form and function, and not suffering transmutation into any other.

(2.) Some organs, or characteristics, which regularly differ at different stages of life, may at a later stage exhibit an ancestral resemblance which was not apparent at an earlier stage.

(3.) Variations in organs, which are not regular but abnormal, exhibit the same phenomenon. As, for example, when there is hereditary tendency to disease which does not manifest itself in infancy. In short, we thus explain by the hypothesis all those phenomena which may be styled epochal or periodic, whether normal or abnormal. The beard sprouts at the age of puberty, because the beards of our ancestors during numberless generations have sprouted at that age; from the cells of whose chins, at that same age, were derived the gemmules which formed the cells of our chins at that age. This is an example of a normal epochal phenomenon. Examples of the other classes will easily suggest themselves.

(III.) There is another class of facts, peculiar to voluntary life, which the hypothesis is also to explain. These refer to the effect, upon descendants, of acquired habits in the ancestor. "How can the use or disuse of a particular limb or of the brain affect a small aggregate of reproductive cells, seated in a distant part of the body, in such a manner that the being developed from these cells inherits the characters of either one or both parents?" (*Animals and Plants under Domestication,* vol. ii.

p. 372.) The propositions hitherto stated will explain only the body's vegetable growth. In order to state the new propositions which are suggested by Mr. Darwin's question, we should need a much more accurate and particular knowledge of the organic effect of a confirmed habit upon the cerebral structure, than is at present within our reach. Some of the kinds of cerebral change which can be imagined as possible, would suit the hypothesis better than others. If, for example, the change should extend only to the number or arrangement of the cerebral cells, and not to the internal structure of the cells themselves, then the gemmules produced by the changed brain would differ only in number, not also in constitution, from those produced before the change. This merely numerical change would not fit in with the hypothesis so obviously as a structural change.

The defects of this hypothesis have been sharply canvassed under the stimulus of a theological bias. A preliminary bias of this sort does not always rob a man of candour; but it is incompatible with the simple desire to investigate the relevant facts, because it carries with it the duty of denying sundry statements before the truth has been investigated. Therefore, it is apt also to carry with it an attitude of hostility towards a novel hypothesis, no matter how cautiously its advocates may guard their advocacy: a hostile attitude which shows itself chiefly in the magnifying of defects, but partly also in the omission to credit the hypothesis with the philosophical merit, in this case very great, to which it is entitled.

Mr. Darwin was led to suggest the hypothesis, by the feeling that some hypothesis was needed to sum up and present in a small compass those relevant facts of which he has an unrivalled knowledge. That his attempt was a tentative effort, he has himself stated. But something less than justice has been done to the hypothesis by those who have found in it nothing more than may be found in Democritus, Hippocrates, Epicurus, or Lucretius. The sentences which have been, or (with the help of a little more learning in the critics) might be, quoted from the above-mentioned authors, are as much beside the point as if they had been written by the calculating machine in the Island of Laputa.

The defects of the hypothesis are divisible into two classes; namely, formal defect and material error. The former may be supplied by experiment and observation; the latter will need to be corrected, and will entail some modification of the hypothesis such as will bring it into harmony with those facts with which in its present shape it is at variance.

The formal defects of the hypothesis are summed up by saying, that it postulates not only hypothetical *facts*, such as the existence of gemmules which have not yet been observed, but also hypothetical *links of cause and effect*, such as the physiological properties of the gemmules; and that it postulates not only *some* of these links, but *all* of them. Without entering into the common verbal disputes about the meaning of the terms "hypothesis" and "explanation," we may safely say that a hypothesis of this kind is not to be called an explanation of the facts to which it appeals. It is a brief and most ingenious summing up of those facts; it probably is a necessary preliminary to the discovery of a true explanation; and it certainly is a most useful instrument to suggest lines of investigation which cannot fail to be fruitful of valuable results; but at present the hypothesis does not explain the facts: it only sums them up by an appropriate synthesis. Consider a parallel case, which is an example of a true explanation. The observed retardation of the exterior occultation of Jupiter's satellites was hypothetically explained, before the motion of light had been ascertained, by supposing that light travels with a finite velocity; but we had not also to *suppose* that, this being so, light would arrive the later at a given spot in proportion to the remoteness of its starting point. At present, the hypothesis of pangenesis both supposes that the gemmules exist, and also that they perform the functions assigned to them.

In order to supply the defect suggested by this criticism, we need either a microscopic observation of small bodies existing under such conditions that they may be plausibly identified with the gemmules; or else a chemistry and mechanology of gemmules analogous to the common chemistry and mechanics, such as might be plausibly deduced from a wide observation and comparison of physiological analogies. If these conditions should ever be fulfilled, the hypothesis would become a well grounded theory: if the deduction should be afterwards made not only plausible but scientifically rigorous, the theory would become a demonstrated truth. Mr. Darwin is well aware of the defect, and he himself has done something to supply it. At p. 380 of the volume quoted above, he assigns some deeply interesting analogies in support of "the assumed elective affinity [of a gemmule] for that particular cell which precedes it in the order o development." There is no need to wonder that so novel an inquiry has not yet been wholly exhausted.

The conspicuous candour of Mr. Darwin is shown by the prominence which he has given to a weak point, when he says, "Parthenogenesis is no longer wonderful; in fact, the wonder is, that it should not oftener occur." (*Ib.*, p. 383.) Its facile explanation of parthenogenesis is no advantage to the hypothesis. We should rather expect, if the hypothesis be true, that parthenogenesis would be the common rule, occurring every day and in all classes of animals, instead of being, as it is, the exception and wholly confined to organisms very low in the scale. This objection is by no means fatal to the hypothesis as a whole; but it is an objection, not a support; and it serves to mark the transition from the formal defect to the material error.

Material error in a hypothesis lies in its contradicting known matter of fact. The contradiction in the present case is summed up by Mr. St. George Mivart in the following passage:—

"The Jews are remarkably scrupulous as to marriage, and rarely contract such a union with individuals not of their own race. This practice has gone on for thousands of years, and similarly for thousands of years the rite of circumcision has been unfailingly and carefully performed. If then the hypothesis of pangenesis is well founded, that rite ought to be absolutely or nearly superfluous from the necessarily continuous absence of certain gemmules through so many centuries and so many generations."—*The Genesis of Species*, p. 212. "Yet," he adds, "it is not at all so, and this fact seems to amount almost to an experimental demonstration that the hypothesis of pangenesis is an insufficient explanation of individual evolution."

These remarks have undoubtedly great weight; but perhaps Mr. Mivart ought (both here and elsewhere) to have kept in view more closely the fact, that no one has asserted the perfect sufficiency of the hypothesis.

The same objection might easily be stated in a more general, not to say a better, form. Under the hypothesis in its present shape, the attainment of a given age, suppose a hundred years, by a given individual, would imply that at least one of his ancestors had attained to that age; and again, a still more remote ancestor would be needed to explain that one; and so on for ever, until we come to the origin of life. This is not easily compatible with the general hypothesis of evolution; for it is difficult and contrary to existing analogy, to assert the primitive type or types to have been immensely long-lived.

But these objections are not fatal. They might even in a certain sense be met at once by assigning further hypothetical powers or functions to the gemmules; but to do this would be, in the present state of our knowledge, only to employ our ingenuity in the dark. We rather hope to see the hypothesis at the same time interpreted, corrected, and established, by a course of fruitful investigation such as Mr. Darwin has already begun.

We trust that no disrespect is implied in thus freely criticising the work of a man who stands at the head of modern science:

᾿Ανδρὸς ὃν οὐδ᾿ αἰνεῖν τοῖσι κακοῖσι θέμις.

We submit the foregoing remarks to his judgment, for castigation or approval, if he shall think them worthy to be honoured by his attention.

Art. IV.—The Song of Songs.

Étude sur le Cantique des Cantiques. Par Ernest Renan. Paris: 1871.

THIS study of M. Renan's on what in our authorized version is called the Song of Solomon, is very interesting and very instructive. It does not indeed tend to alter the opinion of those who have long regarded the literature of ancient Israel as the necessary expression of the national character and position. It proves rather, so far as the poem in question is concerned, that such an opinion is the only one tenable. It may have rested, and probably did rest, on a plain common sense view of the question, rather than on deep archæological research. The present work, however, supplies the arguments by which it may be sustained, and proves once more the instructive judgment of free thought, to be in harmony with the results of scientific investigation. We hasten, however, to give some account of this very singular relic of a remote antiquity.

Israel it must be remembered did not always pursue its religious mission. There were periods of relaxation and indifference, when the national character alone was displayed, and but slight difference existed between the Hebrew and the Canaanite.* Now that Judea has become par excellence, "The Holy Land," it appears to us only as a country of priests and prophets; and all the monuments of Hebrew literature appear at first sight to be sacred books. But an attentive study of those writings which are supposed to be all of a religious nature, reveals numerous traces of a profane and worldly life; and this, not having been the most brilliant side of the Jewish people, has naturally been thrown into the shade. Now the Song of Songs is not the only profane work contained in the Bible. The book of Job is a philosophical speculation of the widest nature. The books of Ruth, Esther, and Judith are romances founded upon old traditions. Ecclesiastes† is the confession of an exhausted Sybarite—an Oriental Pococurante whom nothing can please. And in the same manner the Song of Solomon, written, as M. Renan proves, but a short time after the death of that monarch, is the expression of the unrestrained and natural genius of Israel, when untormented with the idea of a divine mission. The reign of

* The language was almost identical.

† Ewald and De Wette are of opinion this work was written at the close of the Persian period, or the beginning of the Macedonian: Hitzig, about 204 B.C.

Solomon is the Hebrew ideal of the profane or purely secular life. His alliances made without any regard for religious distinctions, his splendid harem, the order and magnificence of his palace, the industrial and commercial prosperity of his reign, the writings attributed to him, and above all the silence imposed on those formidable agitators, the "nabi" or prophets, all point to an interval of careless and joyous festivity. Whatever the influence of Moses once was, it was lost now. Ewald indeed has shown in the most conclusive manner, that the fame of Moses underwent a long eclipse after his death, that his name was almost unknown under the judges and during the early ages of the monarchy, and that it was not until within two centuries of the fall of the kingdom of Judah, that he attained his subsequent grandeur. Thus there was a kind of toleration of foreign cults, induced by intercourse with other nations, and supported by the influence of Egyptian, Phœnician, or Moabite women. It was an interval in the sacred career of Israel—a liberal and latitudinarian age, in which the consciousness of an all-absorbing destiny was as yet unfelt. Under such conditions as these the drama we are considering was produced.

For it is a drama. The widest opinions, it is true, have been held on this point. It has been regarded on the one hand as a poem properly so called, with both unity and progress of events, and on the other as a mere collection of love-songs, bound together only by the analogy of their nature. But M. Renan, by an exhaustive examination of the work itself, considered verse by verse, has shown in the clearest manner that it is a pastoral drama. The characters are distinct and well-defined, and it is sufficient to say that, whoever was its author, certainly Solomon was not. The part he plays is but a poor one, and indeed an ill-disguised hostility to his reign and his memory pervades the whole composition. The free tribes of the north preserved to the last more of the Semitic spirit and nomadic impatience of organized control, and, as we shall have occasion to show, the "Song" was undoubtedly a northern composition.

Briefly described, the dramatis personæ are as follows:—The Sulamite, a young girl of the tribe of Issachar, carried off from her native village of Sulem by the servants of Solomon, and brought into the harem at Jerusalem. Her lover, a young man of the same village, who follows her, and with whom, after several interviews she at last escapes. Solomon, who is displayed as the powerful but unsuccessful suitor, and various choruses of men and women of Jerusalem, odalisques and ladies of the seraglio, and at the close of the drama the brothers of the Sulamite. The concluding verses form a moral drawn from the events of the play, and were doubtless placed in the mouth of a sage or elder.*

The Song of Songs then is a composition occupying a middle position between the regular drama and the eclogue or pastoral dialogue. Regular drama, indeed, in our sense of the word, did not exist among the Jews. The idea as well as the practice was entirely opposed to their habits of thought, and in later times they regarded it with the strongest aversion. The High Priest, Jason, was execrated for having established a gymnasium at Jerusalem and celebrated the Greek Festivals.† Herod outraged this feeling still more deeply when he built a theatre in the holy city and encouraged dramatic representations.‡ The taste for this art, indeed, is still wanting in races of Semitic extraction. The Mussulman of our own day still retains his old antipathy towards it. It has never succeeded even in Algeria. When, therefore, we speak of this poem as a drama, we must entirely lay aside the idea of its being ever acted publicly and with what we consider the necessary decorations of a theatre. And yet undoubtedly it was acted. How are we to explain this apparent contradiction?

Now in an inquiry of this nature it would be singularly unjust to omit the names of those who have successfully preceded us. M. Renan, therefore, renders full justice to the perspicacity of Bossuet, and the good sense of Bishop Lowth. The former conjectured, and the latter accepted the theory, that this poem was intimately connected with the marriage rite as practised among the Jews; that it was divided into acts or scenes corresponding to the number of days during which the nuptial festivities lasted. Weddings in the East always took place in the evening. There was no religious ceremony. The rejoicing was entirely confined to the family or the village of the bride and bridegroom; lamps glitter everywhere like fireflies in the stillness of the evening; music adds to the enchantment, and the sound of sweet voices and of joyous revelry heighten the charm. Simple shows or charades are enacted, the object of which is to represent true

---

* The scene (ch. vi. 11, to vii. 11) is a very curious one, and presents more difficulties than any other. It takes place in the harem. The Sulamite describes the manner in which she was carried off, and then turns aside to hide her tears. The odalisques implore her to turn round so that they may look upon her. But the interest taken in the Sulamite awakens the jealousy of one among them, and she asks whether it is worth while to gaze on the Sulamite rather than on "a dance of Mahanaim" (cf. Gen. xxxii. 18. An ancient town, famous for its female dancers and orgiastic worship.) This dance she then performs, and its nature may be guessed from Solomon's enthusiastic approval of it. A species of Can-can apparently.

† Cf. Maccab. II. iv. 9 et seq.

‡ Josephus, Antig. XV. viii. i.; De Bello Jud. I. xxi. 8.

affection as triumphing over all obstacles; and in these "private theatricals," not only the newly married, but the guests also take a part. Here then we have the secret of this delightful poem. It is the Semitic counterpart of the Carmen Nuptiale of Catullus with its

Jam veniet virgo: jam dicetur Hymenæus.

Here as there we find the same "tale of true love," but in this case we find the overtures of an Oriental despot offered in vain to a simple shepherdess of Issachar. Solomon, in all his glory, cannot touch her heart. The free spirit of the northern mountains burns within her bosom. Better by far is the hillside, where the vines cluster, and the low notes of the turtle-dove are heard, and the voice of the well-beloved calls on his fair one to arise and come away, than all the splendour of Jerusalem. Other maidens may choose the degrading life of the seraglio, but the heroine of this poem would dwell among her own people, and is faithful to her northern lover.*

Such then, briefly described, is the nature and object of this poem—a simple village pastoral; in which, however great the dangers to which the heroine is exposed, we find, to use its own language, that "many waters cannot quench love, neither can the floods drown it." Others of the same nature, no doubt, existed. But this being associated with the name of Solomon, when Israel had reached the summit of its earthly glory, has alone been preserved.

The question that now arises is with regard to the date of this composition. This is a point on which critics have been greatly divided. A period of some 700 or 800 years intervenes between those who attribute it to Solomon, and those who, like Eichhorn and Gesenius, place it toward the close of Hebrew literature. But it may be laid down as matter beyond dispute, that Solomon was not the author of it; and, in fact, the mention of his name at the commencement no more proves it to have been written by him than the attribution of certain Psalms to David is evidence of their being written by that marauder. The insignificant and unsuccessful part that he plays, forcibly excludes the thought that he could have commemorated his own defeat.

---

* With regard to Jewish marriages, the following passages may be compared: Judges xiv. 10 et seq.; Ps. xliv.; 1 Maccab. ix. 37; 3 Maccab. (Apocr.) xiv. 6, and the familiar instances in the New Testament. The formula, "Awake not," &c. (ch. ii. 7, iii. 5, viii. 4), seems to indicate that the play was recited or performed in the evening. Nothing was more common in antiquity and throughout the Middle Ages than these bridal dramas. The "Jeu de Robin et Marion" is perfectly analogous to the Song of Songs. The practice still exists in Brittany. See also Mde. George Sand's "Les Noces de Campagne."

There is no mention or quotation of the Song of Songs in any other of the Hebrew books, though perhaps there may be an allusion to it in the book of Jeremiah. "Then will I cause to cease in the cities of Judah and from the streets of Jerusalem, the voice of mirth and the voice of gladness, *the voice of the bridegroom and the voice of the bride:* for the land shall be desolate."* The words italicised would be cold indeed if they simply meant the conversation of those newly married, and taken in connexion with the festivity just mentioned, certainly seem to indicate a kind of popular composition, of which the present was the best-known specimen. Jeremiah, it will be remembered, was the most erudite of the prophets, and almost all the earlier books are cited by him.

But it is by an examination of the poem itself that we shall best discover the date of its composition; and a strange discovery here awaits us. In ch. vi. 4, we find a compliment paid by Solomon to his youthful captive: "Thou art beautiful, O my love, as *Tirzah*, comely as Jerusalem," &c. She is here compared in beauty to the two capitals of Israel and Judah. Now Tirzah was the capital of the kingdom of Israel from the reign of Jeroboam to that of Omri, 974 B.C. Omri built Samaria in 973, which henceforth continued to be the capital, whilst Tirzah entirely disappeared. Its fall was so complete that its very situation has long been unknown. Now if this poem be of comparatively modern date, would the writer have selected the forgotten city of Tirzah to compare it in beauty and splendour with Jerusalem? And, on the other hand, how could Solomon contrast Tirzah—a town perhaps not then built, or at least of no importance—with his own stately capital? We are thus driven by force of these improbabilities to fix the date within narrow limits. On the one hand it must have been before the year 924 B.C., and on the other it is evidently later than the death of Solomon and the division which took place in 986. We are thus enabled in round language to assign the poem to the tenth century before the Christian era.

There is another feature which of itself would lead us to suppose that it is of very ancient date. If time destroys, time likewise renews and even exaggerates. What a cycle of legends, for example, has grown up around the real Arthur and the real Charlemagne. Napoleon himself has his own legend and romance among the Arabs of to-day. In the case of Solomon, all the East seems to have conspired to raise him to a pinnacle of fictitious glory, and we can even trace the myth in the process of creation. The books of "Kings," and still more those of "Chronicles," contain much of a fantastic nature with regard to

* Jer. vii. 34, xxv. 10.

his splendour and the extent of his power. Here, on the other hand, all appears natural and in reasonable proportions. His guard consists of sixty men. He has a thousand shields in his armoury, sixty queens and eighty concubines—a sufficient allowance one would suppose. But this is no doubt the truth. The fact is, the bands of thieves who made David's fortune were but few in number, and after the anarchy during the time of the Judges, in the century before, a thousand shields must have seemed a marvellous arsenal. In later years these modest figures increased to hundreds of thousands. In Kings and Chronicles, as we have just said, where legendary tales are mixed up with exact documents,* the numbers are very much larger. Forty thousand and twelve thousand are the numbers mentioned by the author, while the seraglio has increased to the portentous number of seven hundred queens and three hundred concubines.† The riches and the power of Solomon are described in glowing colours, to which the sobriety of the "Song" gives a singular relief. And beside this, there are many other traits which must be taken into consideration as affecting the probable date of it; such, for instance, is the mention of the two fishpools in Heshbon (which still existed and were seen by M. Seetzen in 1805); the familiar relations with the old Arab tribe of Kedar; the mention of "the chariots of Pharaoh" (and we know that Solomon procured both horses and chariots at great expense from Egypt); the lively impression of the reigns of David and of his son; the mention of the dances of Mahanaim, which are connected with the most ancient traditions of Israel‡—all these concur in the same result, and that is to render the opinion of those who would assign a late origin to the poem utterly indefensible. It was not, we repeat, written by Solomon, but it is a genuine record of ancient Israel during the happiest of its intervals of repose.

One argument, and one alone we have not adduced in evidence of its antiquity. It is the pervading and general animus of the poem. The Hebrews doubtless demanded a king like the nations around them. The majority were in favour of such a course. But a strong minority, led apparently by Samuel,

---

* Cf. 1 Kings i. 5, where Adonijah has fifty men to run before him, with id. iv. 26, &c., and chs. x. and xi.

† 1 Kings xi. 3. The revised Lectionary retains this edifying chapter. We are not much concerned with the Episcopal Bench, but it is odd it should be blind to the folly of wantonly offending common sense and propriety. The statement, if true, has no connexion with the Christian faith, and, if false, can form no portion of the (so-called) Inspired Word. In any case it seems deplorable to read such stuff to uneducated persons who may be misled by it.

‡ Gen. xxxii. 2. It is difficult to offer any explanation of this legend. Modern commentators merely repeat the worn-out hypothesis of divine interposition, &c.

took a different view.* Their chief objection seems to have been that the monarch, when throned and powerful, would take their sons and daughters and make servants of them. And even after the capricious reigns of Saul and David, the same sentiment still lingered in the north, and was intensified by the splendour and prodigality of Solomon. Hence the schism that arose after his death, when the formidable cry of "To your tents, O Israel!" was first raised. Now, humanly speaking, there is a very strong probability that our poem was written very shortly after that event. Solomon is depicted as he was; powerful indeed according to the idea of that age, but very far removed from the height of ideal glory which he subsequently attained. We observe, too, that we here find at every page the opposition which the luxury and the Egyptian and Phœnician practices excited among those who adhered to the ancient and simple cult of Israel. There is no mention either of priest or prophet. The former had not attained his subsequent importance, and the latter was entirely silenced. The air of freshness, of youth, and of vitality which pervades the poem, points to a time when the Hebrew mind was free and unembarrassed. It is impossible to believe that a purely profane composition such as this, or the book of Job, can ever have been produced in a narrow-minded age, such as that of Ezra or Nehemiah, or still earlier, of Josiah. After the triumph of the pietistic kings, Israel was absorbed by its religious idea, and became in consequence mean and trifling. All the great monuments of Hebrew genius—all the works which we may call Semitic rather than Jewish (since the neighbouring nations possessed a similar literature), were written before the religious vocation into which misfortune impelled the race. What a difference is there in the earlier and latter creations of Hebrew poetry! Ruth, Job, Deborah, the Sulamite, give place to pious heroines—to Judiths and Esthers—victims devoted to the faith preached to them. Compare for a moment Esther and the Sulamite. The first finds it quite a simple matter to make her fortune by winning the good graces of an eunuch, and makes no hesitation in prostituting herself in order to gain the favour of a Gentile. A religious motive excuses everything in her eyes: the interest and the vengeance of her co-religionists. The second obeys motives less refined: a sincere affection for the shepherd she has left at Sulem, a love of the mountains and the mountain air, a contempt for the artificial love of the seraglio, and the pure sentiment of freedom and vitality:—such is the sum and substance of her religion. The grandeur of Solomon's court, which after ages regarded with a kind of semi-

* 1 Sam. viii. 13.

sacred awe, calls forth only raillery and disdain. In a word, the Sulamite is the creation of nature, and Esther the formation of priestcraft and art.

We have no hesitation, therefore, in adopting the opinion of Herder, Ewald, De Wette, Hitzig and M. Renan, and in assigning the composition of the Song of Songs to the tenth century before the Christian era, and soon after the division between Israel and Judah. It was then that the Hebrew genius was most free and untrammelled. There was no great prophet to impose his own will on the popular conscience. Religious institutions had not the rigour and hardness they subsequently attained. Royalty, indeed, at Jerusalem feebly followed in the footsteps of Solomon, but the old republican spirit still existed in the north, and was soon to appear in the person of the demagogue Elijah—the most seditious of all the prophets. We have little doubt then that the poem was a northern composition. It is incredible that a Jew of Jerusalem would have placed the obscure town of Tirzah on the same level as his own stately capital. The antipathy too against the harem of Solomon, composed of "daughters of Jerusalem," is a trait which is suitable to the north alone. And lastly, the connexion which Hitzig* has established between the author of our poem and the prophet Hosea—himself a northern writer—if it does not prove the prophet to have been familiar with this composition, proves at least that the two authors lived in the same circle of images, and that the same expressions were common to them both. "Northern Palestine," says M. Revelle,† appears from Hebrew history to have been less accessible to religious spiritualism and less carried away by a feeling of antagonism against nature and natural life than Palestine of the south. It was there that popular poetry took its loftiest flight. It is from thence that we owe the song of Deborah, the apologue of Jotham, the histories of Gideon, of Jephthah and of Samson—so deeply tinged with the poetic spirit; the highly coloured prophecies of Hosea and the many prophets who left no writings, but whose lives, like those of Elijah and Elisha, were full of action. We may add too that the natural beauty of the district of Libanus, an agricultural country, and of marvellous fertility, abounding in woods, in fields and in clear and rapid streams, is far more fitted for the abode of pastoral poetry than the dusty and rocky terrain that environs Jerusalem. Lastly, and in confirmation of the view we have taken, it is to be observed that with the exception of Engaddi, Jerusalem, and Heshbon, all the localities mentioned in the poem—Sharon,

* "Das Hohe Lied," pp. 9, 10.
† "Revue de Théologie de M. Colani." Mai, 1857.

Gilead, Tirzah, Libanus, Amana, Hermon Sanir, Carmel, Baal-Lamon and Sulem, the village of the heroine—belong to the Kingdom of the North.

Two points, therefore, would seem to be ascertained from the foregoing inquiries: the date of the poem (the 10th century B.C.), and the place of its appearance, Northern Palestine, or Israel as distinguished from Judah. A third remains for our investigation connected with its preservation and interpretation, and to it we will briefly direct our attention. How, in the first place, did such a work find its way into the Canon of Holy Scripture? and when and how was it that a mystical meaning was attributed to it?

These questions are intimately connected.

There can be no dispute that the "Song of Songs" was from its origin a profane work—profane, that is, as distinguished from moral or devotional. There is not only no allegory or mystical afterthought involved in any way, but, in fact, the whole texture and plan of the poem absolutely exclude any such idea. The notion of religious symbolism never entered the mind of the writer. The mystical love-poems of India and Persia in which the love of the soul for God is described under the guise of earthly affections, were entirely unknown to the Jews, and indeed of comparatively recent date. It is evident, indeed, that there can be no connexion between the results of an advanced mysticism, and a mere pastoral drama destitute of religious physiognomy like the present. And to what improbabilities, to what contradictions are we not exposed if we talk of a great development of transcendental theology in Judea in the 10th century before Jesus Christ! Nothing was ever more remote from mysticism than the Hebrew mind, or Arab mind, and in general, the Semitic mind. The idea of bringing the Creator and the creature together, and supposing they can be amorous of each other, and a thousand refinements of a like nature in Hindoo and Christian mysticism, are the very antipodes to the severe conception of the Semitic God. Such ideas would have passed for blasphemies in Israel. Until the first or second century before the Christian era there was no secret doctrine in the bosom of Judaism. The old patriarchal religion was simple and natural and understood by all. No people, we repeat, were more chary of symbolism, of allegories and speculations on the Divine nature than the Jews. Tracing an absolute line of demarcation between God and man, it has rendered impossible all familiarity, every tender sentiment, all reciprocity between heaven and earth.

We are assured, therefore, that the author of the Song of Songs had no second and mystical object in writing his poem. How then was it that in course of time it became regarded as an allegorical work? and at what period did such an idea arise? The answer to this is, that a feeling of the necessity of an allegorical meaning was first shown when the Canon of Scripture was formed. Saved through its celebrity and almost daily use from the shipwreck of Hebrew literature, the Song ceased from an early date, probably from the time of Ezra and Nehemiah, to be thoroughly understood. But little by little the idea of inspiration spread. At the era of the Maccabees all the ancient books were highly valued, and in the days of Jesus had become sacred. The writers of the New Testament, it is true, never cite the Old as a collection of works: they refer merely to the Law, the Prophets, or the Psalms. But Josephus, their contemporary, gives us a canon of books "reputed divine," and among them we find the Song of Songs. But it was one of the first rules of a rigorous orthodoxy that the canonical books contained nothing but what was sacred and edifying. Hence an immense difficulty arose—a difficulty felt also with regard to other compositions, or at least passages. It was impossible to deny the antiquity of the Song. It was impossible also to deny its erotic character. They ingeniously escaped from the dilemma by discovering that it contained an allegorical meaning. What that character was they were not exactly agreed, and hence a torrent of interpretations of the most varied and often contradictory nature.

It is then to the first century before or the first century after Christ that we must attribute the commencement of this allegorical treatment. The taste for perverted and wrong meanings was never more strong than at that period; and, indeed, we see examples of it in Philo, in the Evangelists, in St. Paul, and in the Talmud. A father of the second century, well versed in such matters, Melito, Bishop of Sardis, composed a "key" of these allegories. If, however, the Jews first hit on the idea of mystical interpretation to save the honour of the old poem, the Christians who exaggerated the importance of canonicity and inspiration, made still more desperate efforts to shroud it under a veil of allegory. Theophilus of Antioch, in the second century, explains the wood of Libanon to typify Ruth, and says that Solomon's palanquin signifies in a mystical manner, "souls which carry God within themselves." Origen lastly, in the third century, gave the first complete allegorical explanation of the entire poem. Laying it down as a principle that everything in the Bible which appears unworthy of divine inspiration, and cannot consequently conduce to edification, must have a hidden meaning, he declares that divine love alone is here spoken of, and that the poem is nothing else but the Epithalamium of the Church with her celestial Bridegroom—Jesus Christ. And this view of Origen's has in the main been that of the Christian world for the last sixteen hundred years.

Thus we see how error is formed and perpetuated! how after the lapse of many generations the bridal drama of a rude Semitic tribe has become in the hands of theologians a fantastic and mystical allegory! "The whirligig of time brings about its revenges" of a truth. Strange indeed are the caprices of literary fortune, but one more strange than that which has converted the "*jeu d'esprit*" of a semi-barbarous race into a text-book of the Christian Church has surely never been witnessed.

Such, however, was the view formally propounded by Origen, and with the sole exception of Theodore of Mopsuestia in the fifth century, not a voice was raised to oppose it, and his presumption was of course condemned by the Church. Not a doubt occurred to the Middle Ages. New allegories even were invented, and a strange analogy between the Sulamite and the Virgin Mary was dexterously discovered. Nor did the first generation of Protestants refuse to accept the common opinion, with the sole exception of the noble and unfortunate Sebastian Castalio. This scholar—who in common with scores of other worthy and honest men had the honour of being persecuted by Calvin—took a novel and in many respects unfortunate view of the Song. In his opinion it was an obscene production, which had crept unobserved into the canon, and ought forthwith to be excluded from it.* The universal voice of modern criticism, however, has come to a very different conclusion, and our chief debt to Castalio is that he had the courage to break through the ignorance and superstition of the past. A century later Grotius and Leclerc followed in his footsteps, though in a more liberal spirit, and allowing, as was afterwards done by the famous Bossuet and our own Bishop Lowth, both a literal and a mystical meaning.

But the true movement and the real interpretation came later, and it came naturally enough from Germany. It is not within our limits to follow the various vicissitudes of the critical war that was then waged, nor to narrate the successive advances toward a fuller knowledge of the poem, from Jacobi (1771) to Hitzig (1855). It is sufficient to say, that the opinion thus educed is received among most educated persons who have studied the matter in Western Europe. The poem is not mystical, as the theologians tell us, nor sensual as Castalio thought, nor wholly erotic as Herder believed: it is moral in its nature, and its sum and substance is contained in the 7th verse of the 8th chapter:—"Many waters cannot quench love,

* Bayle, Dict. Art. Castalion.

neither can the floods drown it; the rich man who would buy love, he buyeth but shame." The object of the poem is not the voluptuous and degenerate life of the seraglio, but the course of true affection, the impotence of wealth to purchase it, and the final triumph of honest and innocent attachment. It would have been fortunate for humanity had there been nothing of a worse nature in the Hebrew writings. We could well spare a few books full of murder, massacre, and adultery for another such idyll, full as it is of youth, and joy, and nature.

The aim of the poem, therefore, is a sound one, and if its execution is somewhat wanting in delicacy of treatment, our own susceptibilities are perhaps more to blame than the coarseness of the poet. The Song of Songs indeed, considered in its natural sense, is far more a sacred book than others with which criticism is much less embarrassed—than the book of Esther, for example, hard, cold, vindictive, and supercilious, and in which the name of God is not even once mentioned. We have in this poem a relic of the ancient and free life of Israel in its happiest age, of Israel, the Arab tribe, before the wave of misfortune and fanaticism had swept over it, and environed it with the darkness and littleness of religious monomania.

But let us be just. Devoid of foundation in serious truth as is the mystical myth with which the Christian Church has involved the poem, no man of taste or poetic feeling can fail to appreciate its beauty. The Sulamite has taken the Christian veil. All the sweet remembrances of age and infancy are associated with that incomparable translation, that "well of English undefiled" in which the Church still expresses her longing for her absent Lord. How often in the still gloom of rich cathedrals, and when the dying day poured its last rays upon the blazoned windows, has the "*vulnerasti cor meum*" trembled from the organ and floated in waves of melody over faithful souls! And if the iron hand of criticism must sweep away the foundation of so much that is lovely and pleasant, even the sternest iconoclast will acknowledge that the Catholic tradition is full of spiritual truth and beauty. Encompassed as we are by the struggles of democracy, and stunned by the uproar of the most ignorant of mankind, it is with a pure and sacred delight that the soul takes refuge under these green leaves, and wanders at will beside these rivers of comfort. Men were far happier when the world was in its youth. The horrible state of tension in which modern society exists had no parallel in ancient times. Love was then free. The decrepitude of fashion was unknown, the ceaseless struggle for existence was unfelt. And yet in spite of it all, such is the element of truth in the human mind, true poetry always finds its level. The Sulamite, like

Ruth, like Deborah, like Antigone, like all really noble characters, will always find lovers and admirers. Seen even in her Christianized garb amid the lustrous gloom of Gothic arches, pale and veiled as a Madonna, and yet passionate as a Magdalen, she still represents an eternal truth—the fidelity of soul to soul. "*Casta est quam nemo rogavit*" was the verdict of the Roman Scoffer, but here love was weighed in the balances and not found wanting. No girl of Memphis or Babylon had before her preferred the hut of a shepherd to the harem of a king. She did so, or what comes to the same thing, she is described as having done so, and hence even as a creation of the fancy she is worthy of her long remembrance.

As to commentaries on this work, their name is absolutely Legion; but, with the exception of the recent German and French ones, they are without value, and curious only as examples of mental aberration. The worst with which we are acquainted in our own language are those by "Commentator" Scott and the present Bishop of Lincoln,—the efforts of both divines greatly resembling those of that illustrious Laputan who devoted his days to the extraction of sunbeams from cucumbers. It is to be hoped, however, that this fossil theology is becoming extinct, and that a more enlightened appreciation of Hebrew literature may be found amongst us. Patristic divinity, like the monastic orders, has done good work in its day, but it has now become an anachronism. The names of Jerome, Augustine, Athanasius, and Chrysostom have lost their power: the magicians are dead and their wands are without virtue. We have learned to smile at the credulity of the theologian, we deride his pretensions and tread his dogmas under our feet. Whether for good or evil, faith is becoming a thing of the past, and it would be wise in those concerned to set their house in order without delay.

To those who may be offended at the liberty we have taken in thus discussing this ancient work, we offer the following anecdote of the venerable historian Niebuhr, communicated to M. Renan by the late Chevalier de Bunsen. "As for me," said that illustrious writer, when consulted by a young Lutheran divine on the difficulty of accounting for its reception into the Canon: "As for me, I should feel that something was wanting in the Bible if I found in it no expression of the strongest and deepest passion which actuates the human heart."

Art. V.—Our Ocean Steamers.

ONE bright morning in April, five-and-thirty years ago, the Battery, New York, presented an animated and brilliant appearance. Thousands of men, women, and children—their eyes and faces bright with excitement—stood gazing at the distant horizon, the agitated crowd being continually swelled by fresh accessions of spectators, who kept thronging in from every part of the city. Yet the sea was calm, and except the usual white sails that dotted the bay, there was nothing to be seen that could call for so much excitement. Yet, hold—there was. Away in the purple distance, a grey streak against the horizon, arises a thin column of smoke, which tells the watchers of the approach of the first ship that had ever *steamed* from England to America. This was the plucky little steamship *Sirius*, 412 tons burthen, which had left Cork on the 5th April, 1838, and, in the teeth of strong gales and westerly winds, had succeeded in paddling its way across the Atlantic, and now, on the 23rd of the same month, her hull began to loom larger and larger on the view, until the gallant little craft sailed up the bay, and quietly dropped her anchor in the North River, amid tumultuous cheers, the ringing of bells, and the discharge of canon. Some hours later, the excitement was still further intensified by the arrival of another and larger steamship, the *Great Western*, which had left Bristol on the 8th, and after a splendid run of fourteen days and a half, drew up at the dock, while cheer after cheer rent the air, and the battery thundered a welcome through six-and-twenty guns. This was thirty-four years ago; and to-day steamships are crossing the ocean in such numbers as to make it one grand ferry, in which steamers almost jostle each other daily, and a broken voyage is a rare occurrence. To us, who live in an age when the Atlantic is annually crossed by more than a thousand steamers, it is hard to realize the difficulties which these early pioneers of oceanic steam navigation had to encounter. It was all but universally believed that the necessity under which steamers were of carrying sufficient coal for so long a journey, would effectually prevent the establishment of a regular line of steam-traders between Great Britain and America. So late as 1835, no less erudite an authority than Dr. Lardner affirmed, in the course of a lecture delivered by him in Liverpool, in the December of that year, that the project of running steamers direct between the two continents was perfectly chimerical, as they might as well try to establish a line between New York and the moon, as between New York and Liverpool.

Nor was Dr. Lardner alone in his scientific prophecies. Similar prognostications were indulged in by many other *savans*, and the nicest calculations, based on established principles and facts, were made to demonstrate the impracticabilities of the proposition.

"To accomplish a voyage of the same length as that across the Atlantic," they argued, "two tons of coal will be used for each horse-power of engines; that is to say, if the engines are of 300 horse-power, they will consume 600 tons of fuel before they reach the terminus of a 3000 miles voyage. But a spare supply must also be carried, to provide against accident or delay; so that the quantity must be raised to 700 tons. On the other hand, if the tonnage of the vessel be more than four times its horse-power, the latter will be inadequate to its propulsion at the ordinary rate of steamships. The tonnage of the vessel, therefore, could not exceed 1200; and, after making allowance for cabins, machinery, boilers, ship's stores, &c., the space left for fuel would not contain more than 500 tons, which would all be consumed before the vessel arrived within 500 miles of the Atlantic Coast."

We have just seen how these scientific predictions were falsified at the very moment they were being made. The success of the *Sirius* and *Great Western* demolished for ever the scientific objections of the learned, and within a few years a regular line of steam communication had been opened up between the two continents. Into the general history and growth of this great ocean traffic between America and England we propose briefly to enter, and although it will be impossible within the limits of one article to give minute details of the foundation and growth of each separate line of ocean steamships which knit the two countries together, we hope to overtake the general outlines, and give our readers a bird's eye view of the history of our Ocean Steamers. Most Englishmen have a vague sort of idea that to Henry Bell is due the honour of having constructed the first steamboat; but putting Fitch, Rumney, Miller, Symington, Stevens, Livingston, and Fulton, out of sight, we find that in 1543 a Spanish Captain, named Blasco de Garay exhibited, in the harbour of Barcelona, a steamboat of his own invention, of about 200 tons burthen. The motive power was supplied by a caldron of boiling water placed under a moveable wheel on each side of the ship. It was not, however, until James Watt patented his improved steam-engine, in 1769, that any progress was made towards the invention of a successful steamboat. Thirty-three years before, indeed, one Jonathan Hulls obtained in England a patent for a towboat, to be propelled by a paddle-wheel set in motion by a sort of steam-engine, but the project seems never to have been carried out. In 1756 the French mathematician Gautier, published a treatise on "Navigation by Fire," and in 1782 his theory was practically exemplified in the construction of a steamboat of considerable size, by the Marquis do Jouffrey, which navigated the Saone for some time, but was ultimately put aside as deficient in power. Partially successful attempts were also made from 1774 to 1790, by the Count d'Auxerion, the Brothers Pereire and others in France, and from 1783 to 1789, by Fitch and Rumsey in America. In 1785 Rumsey obtained from the Legislatures of Virginia and Maryland the exclusive right to run steamboats on the waters of those States, and in May of the same year he began building his first steamboat, which proved a failure. Nothing daunted, he tried again next year and succeeded in building a boat of nine tons that steamed against the current of the Potomac at the rate of four or five miles an hour. In the same year Fitch constructed his working model, and in 1787 built a boat of sixty tons, called the *Perseverance*, which made the trip from Philadelphia to Burlington at an average speed of six miles an hour. Three years later he placed another and a larger boat on the Delaware, which ran regularly during the season at an average rate of seven and a half miles an hour. The advertisement of this nameless ship, as it appeared in the *Federal Gazette and Philadelphia Daily Advertiser* is curious, as being the first steamboat advertisement ever published. It is as follows :—

"The STEAMBOAT

"Sets out to-morrow morning at ten o'clock, from Arch Street Ferry, in order to take passengers from Burlington, Bristol, Bordentown, and Trenton, and returns next day.

"Philadelphia, *July* 26, 1790."

Six years afterwards Fitch placed a small boat on the Collect Pond, New York City, which was moved by an engine and a worm-screw projecting from the stern ; but neither of these experiments led to the general introduction of boat propulsion by steam. Perhaps the most important experiment made, previous to the final successes of Fulton and Bell, was that of Miller and Taylor, in Scotland, in 1788, when they built a double boat, with a paddle-wheel in the interspace, which proved quite successful. Next year Miller fitted a vessel with larger engines, and tried it on the Forth and Clyde Canal, when it made seven miles an hour. In 1801 another Scotchman, Symington, took out a patent for the construction of steamboats, and in 1803 built the *Charlotte Dundas*, to tow vessels on the Forth and Clyde Canal. The success was complete, but the alarming wash caused by the paddles, which threatened to destroy the banks, led to the abandonment of the scheme. This ship it was which suggested to an American citizen the idea which ultimately grew into the first successful passenger steamboat. As early as 1793 Robert Fulton, a friend of Fitch and Rumsey, and the son of a Scotchman, *thought* of steam as a motive power for vessels, and in 1803 put in operation his first working model, at Plombières, in France. From France he proceeded to Scotland, where he visited the unfortunate *Charlotte Dundas*, and obtained drawings of her machinery, besides getting many hints from an ingenious young Glasgow inventor, Henry Bell, who accompanied him on his visit, and explained to him his own plans for the construction of a steamboat. Whether Fulton was a man of original inventive genius himself is not quite clear, but he possessed a gift almost as valuable and quite as rare—the power, namely, to make use of the crude ideas of another, to detect with prophetic eyes their infinite possibilities, and to develop them into success. And this Robert Fulton did. Returning to America, with the plans of Symington and Bell in his pocket and head, and one of Boulton and Watt's engines of eighteen horse-power, he formed a partnership with a countryman named Livingstone, and at New York, in 1807, built the *Clermont*, which made the first completely successful voyage by steam from New York to Albany, and is entitled to be called the first successful passenger steamboat ever built. Five years later, that is, in 1812, Henry Bell, of Glasgow, built and started the first European passenger steamship, the *Comet*.

But, although the practicability of navigation by steam was now completely and for ever established, it was not till 1819 that the attempt was made to steam across the Atlantic. In 1818 a Mr. Scarlborough, of Savannah, Ga., conceived the idea that the ocean could be navigated by steam. He went to New York and purchased a ship on the stocks, which out of compliment to his State and city he named the *Savannah*. Two brothers, Captains Moses and Steven Rogers, were selected to take charge of the new steamer—the one as engineer and the other as sailing-master. The *Savannah* was finished in February, 1819, was about 300 tons burthen, clipper built, full rigged, and propelled by one inclined, direct-acting, low-pressure engine, like those now in use. The cylinder was 40 inches in diameter, with six-feet stroke, and carried 20 lbs. steam. The paddles were of wrought-iron, with only one flange, and entirely uncovered. They were so attached to the shaft that their removal and shipment on deck could be effected in from fifteen to twenty minutes. She had two superb cabins, for ladies and gentlemen respectively. All her berths, 32 in number, were state-rooms, and provided with every comfort. Her speed, without sails, was about six knots, though vessels that passed her, under steam and sail, in her voyage across the Atlantic, reported her speed at from nine to ten knots. The *Savannah* sailed from New York for Savannah on the 28th of March, 1819, and reached the latter port, after a very successful trip, on April 6th. Thence she sailed to Charleston, where she took on board James Monroe, the President of the United States, and returned to Savannah. In the *Republican* of May 19th we find this advertisement :—

"For LIVERPOOL.

"The steamship 'Savannah,' Captain Rogers, will, without fail, proceed to Liverpool direct. to-morrow, 20th inst. Passengers, *if any offer*, can be well accommodated. Apply on board."

The italics are ours. No passengers "offered," and on the day advertised the *Savannah* set out on her voyage, direct for Liverpool, which port she reached on June 20th. Having all ready given the *Sirius* the credit of having been the first ship to steam from England to America, the voyage of the *Savannah* involves an apparent contradiction. But the *Savannah* did *not* steam all the way, having only worked her engines 18 days, and sailed the rest—it being found necessary to economize the fuel, which was pitch-pine, and did not last so long as coal. During the voyage several amusing incidents occurred. When first seen off Cape Clear the steamer was thought to be on fire, and the English Admiral, at Cork—for the more effectually to astonish the Britishers the wheels were restored to the shafts on nearing land and the fires rekindled—despatched a fast cutter to her relief; and great was the wonder of the crew at their inability to overtake a ship *under bare poles*. At Liverpool no little excitement and even apprehension were caused. It was suspected by some that the design of the *Savannah* was to rescue Napoleon Bonaparte from St. Helena, his brother Jerome having offered a large sum for that purpose. The steamer consequently was carefully watched by the British Government, and for a short time ships-of-war were stationed at certain points to prevent its departure from Liverpool. We have already referred to the *Sirius*, which sailed from Liverpool to New York in 1838, but the first ship that actually steamed across the Atlantic, though not to the United States, was the Canadian steamer *Royal William*, built at Three Rivers, in the Province of Quebec, in 1831. It was 160 feet long, 44 feet broad, 17 feet 9 inches deep, and registered 363 tons. The *Royal William* sailed from Quebec, August 5th, 1833, for London, put into Pictou, and arrived at Gravesend about 16th September. But neither the voyage of the *Royal William* nor of the *Savannah* was commercially successful, and led to no practical results. The carriage of a cargo, insuring remunerative freights, was impossible in the case of vessels which could hardly contain supplies sufficient for a single voyage, and it was not until 1838 that the splendid passages of the *Great Western* and *Sirius* fairly demonstrated the remunerative practicability of ocean steam-navigation. The *Sirius* was owned by the British and American Steam Navigation Company, which was therefore the pioneer and parent of our Ocean Ferries. The next ocean steamship built by this company was the *British Queen*, the size of which created as much astonishment in 1839 as did that of the *Great Eastern* thirty years later. The *British Queen* was built on the Thames, and engined on the Clyde by that most distinguished marine engineer, the late Robert Napier. From figure-head to taffrail she measured 275 feet, being 35 feet longer than her only rival, the *Great Western*. Her breadth of beam, excluding paddle-boxes, was 30 feet, and including them, 61; her depth of hold, 27 feet; her engines were of 500 horse-power; her burden 2016 tons; and her cost 60,000*l*. The *British Queen* started on her first trip from Portsmouth on July 12th, 1839, with a full complement of passengers, a crew of 100 men, 600 tons of coal, and freight valued at 1,500,000*l*. She reached New York after a good passage of 14 days 18 hours, and before the end of the year made five more voyages. In 1840 she made other five voyages to, and as many from New York, but did not pay, and was sold to the Belgian Government in 1841. The Company was now about to experience the truth of the old adage, "misfortunes never come singly." The consort of the *British Queen* was the *President*, which proved singularly unfortunate. She made three rough and protracted passages, and on March 10th, 1841, left New York for Liverpool with 23 passengers on board, and was never heard of more. The loss of the *President* ruined its owners, and brought the history of the pioneer line—the British and American Steam Navigation Company—to a tragic close. There were still left two other Companies, which had all been started in the same year, 1838. The earlier of these was the Great Western Steam Navigation Company, which built the *Great Western*, of which we have already spoken in connexion with the *Sirius*. The *Great Western* was 230 feet long; 58 feet 4 inches broad, including paddle-boxes; 23 feet deep; and drew, when laden, 16 feet of water. The paddle-wheels were 28 feet in diameter, each board being 10 feet long. There were two engines of 225 horse-power each, the tonnage was 1340, and the total cost 60,000*l*. The *Great Western*, with seven adventurous passengers, started from Bristol on April 8th, 1838, and reached New York on the afternoon of St. George's Day, having run the 3111 nautical miles in 15 days 10 hours. In 1839 this enterprising Company made another bold and doubtful experiment. Hitherto all steamers were built of wood and propelled by paddles: the GREAT WESTERN COMPANY now built a steamer of iron, and had her propelled by an Archimedean screw. This makes a great advance in our history. The ship was called the *Great Britain*, was launched on July 19th, 1843, and after being imprisoned for seven months in Cumberland Dock, Bristol, owing to the narrowness of the locks, she was released from durance vile on December 12th, 1844, and early in 1845 made a very rapid trip to London. Her dimensions were: length, 274·2 feet; breadth, 48·2 feet; and depth, 31·5 feet. She had 6 masts; engines of 1000 horse-power, driving a six-bladed iron propeller, 15 feet 6 inches in diameter; her gross tonnage was 2975, and she had berths for 360 cabin passengers. The *Great Britain* made but two passages across the Atlantic. Her last departure from Liverpool for New York took place on September 22nd, 1846, when she carried 185 passengers, and a large cargo. That same night she ran ashore in Dundrum Bay, where she lay for a year, and was finally sold for a small sum. This loss proved too much for the Company, which dissolved in 1848. The third of the three pioneer Companies established in 1838 was the TRANSATLANTIC STEAMSHIP COMPANY, which selected Liverpool as a starting-point, the two rival concerns having chosen respectively Portsmouth and Bristol. Their first ship, the *Royal William*, which they chartered from the City of Dublin Steam-Packet Company, was 617 tons burden and 276 horse-power. She was the first *purely passenger* steamboat that crossed the Atlantic, and sailed from Liverpool on her first run on July 5th, 1838, and reached New York on the 24th. She was not only the first purely passenger ocean steamer, but was also the first steamer to cross the Atlantic *from Liverpool*, and the first steamer built in water-tight sections. On July 25th, 1838, the New York papers contained the following advertisement:—

"BRITISH STEAMSHIP ROYAL WILLIAM,
617 Tons,
Captain SWAINSON, R.N., Commander.

"This fine Steamer, having lately arrived, will be dispatched again for Liverpool on Saturday, 4th August, at 4 p.m. She is only sixteen months old, and from her peculiar construction, being divided into five sections, each water-tight, she is considered one of the safest boats in England.

"Her accommodations are capacious, and well arranged for comfort. The price of passage is fixed at 140 dols., for which wines and stores of all kinds will be furnished. Letters will be taken at the rate of twenty-five cents for the single sheet, and in proportion for larger ones, or one dollar per ounce weight.

"For further particulars, apply to

ABRAHAM BELL & CO.; or, JACOB HARVEY, 28, Pine Street."

After making a few more passages the *Royal William* was returned to her owners, and replaced by the *Liverpool*—270 feet long, 1150 tons burthen, and 461 horse-power—which carried only first-cabin passengers (at 35 guineas each), had a surgeon on board, and was advertised to carry "light freight if applied for timely." She started on her first voyage from Liverpool to New York, October 20th, 1838, and, having accomplished about one-third of the route, put back to Cork on the 26th. On November 6th she again proceeded and reached New York on the 23rd, returning to Liverpool on the 21st of December, after a run of 14 days 10 hours. After making in all six voyages to and from New York, averaging 17 days out and 15 home, she was sold to the Peninsular and Oriental Company, and in 1846, her name having been changed to the *Great Liverpool*, she was totally wrecked off Cape Finisterre.

We have now briefly sketched the history of the three pioneer ocean steamship Companies. They were not successful commercially, but they proved beyond doubt the possibilities of success. During their short existence they were the means of conferring incalculable benefits on the mercantile classes of England and America. But, as we have said, they failed. Pioneers generally *do* fail, but their failures are valuable, if only because they furnish the stepping-stones which lead to success. The early steamships were irregular in their sailings, and were too few in number. But the quickness with which they crossed the ocean attracted the attention of the British Government and of large capitalists. The former saw a means of bringing their American colonies into close communication with the mother country, and proposed to establish a regular postal communication with Halifax and Boston. They advertised for contractors for the service. The Great Western Company applied, but without success, and the scheme was likely to fall through, when a few far-seeing capitalists in Liverpool and Glasgow resolved to form a Company, and undertake the execution of the contract with the Government. These capitalists were represented in their deed of agreement by three gentlemen, Samuel Cunard, of Halifax, George Burns, of Glasgow, and Charles MacIver, of Liverpool. This was in 1839, early in which year the preliminary arrangements were concluded; and, on July 4th, 1840, the mail service was commenced by the *Britannia* steamer, which, including the *détour* to, and a detention of 12 hours at Halifax, completed the voyage from Liverpool to Boston in 14½ days. Four steamers performed the service which at first was monthly, then fortnightly, between

Liverpool, Halifax, and Boston, and *vice versâ*, and for which 60,000*l.* were paid yearly by Government. Some years later this subsidy was increased to 100,000*l.*, New York being substituted every alternate voyage for Boston; in 1848 the allowance was further increased to 145,000*l.* per annum, the Company becoming bound to make weekly instead of fortnightly trips to Boston and New York alternately, constantly calling at Halifax. In 1850 permission was granted them to make fortnightly runs to New York direct, instead of as formerly by way of Halifax; which latter port was subsequently abandoned in favour of Boston; and at the present moment the Company receive 70,000*l.* a year from the British Government for the conveyance of two mails a week from Cork to New York. The Company have built, or bought and owned, 148 steamers, 111 of which have been engaged in the Transatlantic trade. Their Transatlantic fleet at present consists of 25 vessels, all except the paddle-wheeled *Scotia* being iron screw-propellers, with an aggregate tonnage of 66,000, and since the starting of the *Britannia* in 1834, the Cunard Company have not lost a single life nor letter through the carelessness of their employés, or misfortune to their ships. Yet this vast and prosperous concern, the very name of which is a synonym the wide-world over for speed, comfort, regularity, and safety, sprang from a very small beginning so far back as 1818, in which year two wealthy Glasgow burghers, James and George Burns, entered into partnership and engaged in shipping. In 1824 the firm was strengthened by the admission of a third partner, Hugh Matthie, of Liverpool. In that year they had 6 sailing craft trading between Liverpool and Glasgow, and 3 steamers between Glasgow and Belfast. Subsequently steam was substituted for canvas in the Glasgow and Liverpool trade; in 1830 the concern amalgamated with that of the Messrs. MacIver, of Liverpool; and in 1839 they concluded the first Transatlantic contract with the British Government, the old fleet of wooden paddle-steamer having all disappeared: the present fleet consists of 24 iron screw-propellers, and one paddle steamer, the year of build, name, and tonnage of which are:—

When built.	Name.	Net tonnage.	When built.	Name.	Net tonnage.
1857 ...	Calabria ...	1730	1865 ...	Malta ...	1450
1860 ...	Marathon ...	1213	,, ...	Zarifa ...	1400
,, ...	Olympus ...	1585	1866 ...	Palmyra ...	1390
,, ...	Atlas ...	1220	1867 ...	Siberia ...	1698
,, ...	Hecla ...	1214	,, ...	Russia ...	1710
,, ...	Kedar ...	1212	1868 ...	Samaria ...	1695
1861 ...	Morocco ...	1212	1870 ...	Abyssinia ...	2076
,, ...	Sidon ...	1212	,, ...	Algeria ...	2105
1862 ...	China ...	1540	,, ...	Batavia ...	1698
1864 ...	Cuba ...	1535	,, ...	Parthia ...	2214
1865 ...	Java ...	1701	1873 ...	Bothnia	
,, ...	Aleppo ...	1399	,, ...	Scythia	

During 1872 the Cunard steamers made 137 round voyages or 274 passages, the largest number of any line entering New York. The number of passengers carried during the same period was 72,611, divided as follows:—

From Liverpool:—Cabins, 9,770; Steerage, 46,655; Total, 56,425.
„ America:— „ 8,540; „ 7,610; „ 16,196.

The cargoes landed in America consisted principally of dry goods, machinery, iron, and tin, amounting in all to 210,000 tons. Those discharged in Liverpool were chiefly grain, provisions, and cotton, amounting in all to 274,000 tons. Notwithstanding the length of time the Cunard Company have been in existence, and the great number of ships employed by them, they have only lost two steamers—the *Columbia* and *Tripoli*—neither wreck being accompanied by loss of life.

The next stage in our history is marked by the project of a Liverpool gentleman, who proposed a scheme for freight-carrying boats, called "auxiliary screw-propellers," which differed from the principle of the *Great Britain* in this respect only, that the proportion of steam-power to tonnage was very much lower; the screw not being intended as the principal motive power, but as an incidental help to the wind and sails. An iron vessel of this kind was accordingly built in 1846, called the *Sarah Sands*, of 1020 tons and 180 horse-power, and in 1847-8 made nine voyages between Liverpool and New York—her average passage to New York being 18¼ days, and to Liverpool 16½. Up to this point all the ocean steamers were British built, and British owned. But in 1847 the Americans roused themselves to assert their equality in steam-navigation, and formed the Ocean Steam Navigation Company, which contracted with the United States Government to carry the United States' mails between New York and Bremen, twice a month, touching at Cowes, the compensation to be 40,000*l.* a year. So they built the *Washington* and *Hermann*, each 224 feet long, 39 feet broad, 29 feet deep, and 1700 tons. But the steamers proved too slow, and at the expiry of the contract the line was discontinued, and the ships were sold and transferred to the Pacific, where, in 1863, the *Hermann* was broken up, and, a few years later, the *Washington* was wrecked. In 1847, too, another American steamer, the *United States*, of 2000 tons burden, was built for the New York and Liverpool freight and passenger trade, by C. H. Marshall and Co., the owners of the famous Black Ball Line of Packetships. After making several trips the *United States* was withdrawn and sold to some parties in Bremen. The next company was the New York and Havre Steam Navigation Company, established in 1848, to ply between New York and Havre, stopping at Southampton, both going and coming, and carrying a fortnightly mail, for which they received 30,000*l.* per annum from the United States Government. Their pioneer ship, the *Franklin*, was launched in 1848, and in 1850 made her first voyage. She was 263 feet long, 52 wide, 26 deep, and measured 2183 tons. In July, 1854, she was wrecked, and totally lost on Long Island. Her consort, the *Humboldt*, made her first voyage in 1851, and was wrecked entering Halifax, October, 1853. To preserve the mail contract, the service was supplied by chartering unsuitable steamers at heavy cost, until in 1855-56 the Company built the *Arago* and *Fulton*. On the breaking out of the Civil War in 1861, the line was withdrawn, the *Arago* was sold to the Peruvian Government, and the *Fulton* had her engines removed and her hull broken up, the dry-rot rendering her useless as a sailing-ship. The strange fatality that had always attended American Transatlantic steamship Companies was again repeated in the rise and fall of the next ocean steam line, the United States Mail Line, which was organized in 1849, by Mr. E. K. Collins, with the aid of a few New York merchants. The Company began with a great flourish of trumpets, and of course with the aid of a mail subsidy from the American Government.

Their four pioneer ships, the *Atlantic, Pacific, Arctic*, and *Baltic* were to surpass anything afloat in size, speed, and splendour of fittings and accommodation. They were built, engined, equipped, and launched at New York in 1849, their dimensions being: length, 290 feet; breadth, within paddle-boxes, 45 feet; across paddle-boxes, 75 feet; depth of hold 31 feet 7 inches; and tonnage, 2860 tons. Machinery, 1000 horse-power. Each steamer cost not less than 100,000*l.*, and though built in and for America, the expense was paid with English capital, and all the steamers insured in Britain. The pioneer steamer, the *Atlantic*, left New York on the 27th April, 1849, and arrived in the Mersey on May 10th, thus making the passage in about 13 days, two of which were entirely lost in making repairs. The saloons and state rooms were fitted up with a splendour quite unprecedented in the annals of ship-building: there was a barber's store, a smoking room, bath rooms, &c., and nothing was omitted which the most luxurious might require. The *Atlantic* and her three consorts ran for one year, and not only did the *Arctic*, in February, 1852, make the passage from New York to Liverpool in 9 days 17 hours, but the average of 42 westward trips was 11 days 10 hours and 26 minutes, against the Cunarders' average of 12 days 19 hours 26 minutes. Their speed, therefore, was unequalled; the magnificence of their cabin appointments and the quality of their cuisine excelled those of any other line; and the original subsidy of 14,750 dols. a trip was afterwards increased to 33,000 dols. a trip, or 858,000 dols. a year. Yet in spite of all these advantages these steamers were run at a great loss, and in six years the Company was declared bankrupt. The *Arctic* was lost, with nearly all her passengers; the *Pacific* went on one of her home voyages and has never since been heard of; the *Atlantic* and *Baltic*, after rotting in their docks, were sold for old iron; and the *Adriatic*, a fifth steamer, built in 1851, was sold to the Galway Company, and for years has lain in an English dock, a warning of the evil results of lavish expenditure, reckless management, and Government subsidies.

The first Transatlantic steamer launched on the Clyde was also the pioneer ship of the next great Company—the Liverpool and Philadelphia Steamship Company, better known as the Inman Line. To William Inman, a Liverpool merchant, is due the credit of having founded the Company which still bears his name. Prior to 1850 Mr. Inman had been a partner in the firm of Richardson Brothers and Company, merchants and shipowners of Liverpool, which in that year became merged in the Liverpool and Philadelphia Steamship Company. In 1855 the brothers Richardson retired from the concern, leaving Mr. Inman sole representative of the Company. Active operations were commenced in November, 1850, by the purchase of the iron screw-steamer *City of Glasgow*, 1600 tons burthen and 350 horse-power, from her builders, Tod and Macgregor, of Glasgow, after it had made four successful runs between New York and Glasgow. Success attended Mr. Inman's efforts, and in 1851 the *City of Manchester*, 1296 tons register, also built by Tod and Macgregor, was added to the line, and soon after the *Kangaroo*, *City of Baltimore*, and *City of Washington*. In 1857 New York was included among the ports of call, and the firm became the Liverpool, New York, and Philadelphia Steamship Company. During the Crimean war they withdrew their ships from the ocean trade to employ them as Government transports; after which they made a futile attempt to establish a trade between the Clyde and New York, from which field they finally withdrew to dispute with the Cunard Line the honours and emoluments of the Government subsidy for carrying mails between Queenstown and Halifax, and the freight and passage trade between Liverpool and Boston. The Inman fleet at present consists of these ships:—

When launched.	Name.	Tonnage.	Horse-power.	When launched.	Name.	Tonnage.	Horse-power.
1850...	City of Baltimore...	1774...	350	1867...	City of Antwerp ...	1626...	350
1860...	„ Bristol ...	1805...	350	1869...	„ Brooklyn ...	1960...	450
1863...	„ Limerick ...	1724...	250	„ ...	„ Brussels ...	2323...	600
„ ...	„ London ...	1680...	450	1872...	„ Montreal ...	3027...	600
1865...	„ New York...	2350...	350	1873...	„ Chester ...	3000...	800
„ ...	„ Durham ...	538..	120	„ ...	„ Richmond...	3000...	800
1866...	„ Paris ...	1975...	650				

The following shows the number of passengers carried by the Inman ships from 1864 to 1873:—

1864	43,000	1869	61,000
1865	46,000	1870	58,000
1866	49,000	1871	60,000
1867	53,000	1872	61,000
1868	53,000		

Great as the prosperity of the Company now is, it was not attained without great loss of life and property. Altogether it has lost six passenger steamers. One of them sailed from New York for Liverpool in 1870 with 177 passengers, and has never since been heard of.

The *City of Glasgow* having proved the feasibility of profitable trade between Glasgow and New York, a Company was organized in the former city, under the title of the Glasgow and New York Steamship Company, to establish a line of steamers between these ports. It commenced in 1851 with the steamship *Glasgow*, followed by the *New York* in 1854, and the *Edinburgh* in 1855. The Company was fairly prosperous until 1856, when it lost the *New York*, and in 1859 it sold its fleet to the Inman line, and disbanded.

The next Company also had its birth in Glasgow, being the Clyde Screw Steam Packet Company started in 1854, by a firm that for ten years previously had been running a line of British sailing vessels between the Clyde and New York. The Company built the *Clyde*, and purchased the *Petrel*, both of which made a few trips, after which they were withdrawn during the Crimean War, and were subsequently lost. The Company dissolved in 1857.

The next attempt to establish a Transatlantic line was made in America, by the far-famed Commodore Vanderbilt. In 1855 the Commodore proposed to the American Government to run a semi-monthly line between New York and Liverpool, to alternate with the Collins' steamers, and asked 15,000 dols. a trip if he might confine his boats to the average speed of the Cunarders, and 19,250 dols. if they were to make as good time as the Collins' line. His proposition was refused, but nothing daunted, the Commodore placed the screw-steamship *Ariel* on the route to Southampton and Havre, and made another unsuccessful attempt to extract a subsidy from Government. Next year he put the *North Star* on the Bremen route, followed in a year or two by the *Ariel*, *Vanderbilt*, and *Ocean Queen*. The New York and Bremen Ocean Steam Navigation Companies being unwilling, on expiry of their contracts in 1858, to attempt the performance of the service on the small pay of the gross ocean and inland postages, Vanderbilt determined to undertake it, but gave it up after three years' trial, and sold his entire steam-fleet to the Pacific Mail Steamship Company.

Twelve attempts had now been made to establish regular steam communication between England and America, only two of which had proved permanently successful. But as yet every effort to knit together Glasgow and New York by similar bonds had failed, and in 1856 this great and important field was absolutely unoccupied. A Glasgow firm, Handyside and Henderson, saw their opportunity and lost no time in taking advantage of it. The Company was not then one of great importance. They owned some ten or twelve sailing ships which traded to South America and to India, one of which, the *Tempest*, they converted into a screw-steamer, and despatched across the ocean to New York. If in that year, 1856, any one had said to these Glasgow merchants, "seventeen years hence you will be running more than a score of steamers across the Atlantic, and yours will be the largest steamship line in the world," he would have been laughed at as a madman. Yet at the present moment, this Anchor Line comprises a fleet of ocean steamers, which, in respect to number, tonnage, and extent of operations, surpasses that of any other Company. Its growth has been so extraordinarily rapid that its history reads like a chapter in romance. Although the Transatlantic service of the Anchor Line was formally opened in 1856, by the small and converted *Tempest*, it was not till 1863 that the Company, which had till then been chiefly engaged in trading to and from the Mediterranean and between Glasgow and Canada, finally resolved to throw their chief energy and strength into the development and prosecution of the New York and Glasgow trade. In that year, accordingly, were built, in addition to their other existing fleet, the *Caledonia* and *Britannia*, which are fairly entitled to be called the parents of the present magnificent Transatlantic Anchor Line Ferry. From the outset the adventure was a success. The enormous and rapidly growing commerce of Lanarkshire and the West of Scotland had long wanted a local outlet for its American interests, and every year saw two or more new steamers added to the Anchor Line. A glance at the following table will show the progress of the trade between New York and Great Britain:—

Year.	Sailing ships.	Steam-ships.	Tonnage.	Year.	Sailing ships.	Steam-ships.	Tonnage.
1865	8	24	30,260	1869	24	60	80,842
1866	18	38	55,120	1870	24	93	114,400
1867	10	52	72,900	1871	31	93	141,690
1868	11	53	78,060				

Within comparatively a few months from the launching of

the two parent vessels, the necessity of having a weekly service became evident; and in a short time even this was found to be insufficient. The upshot was the establishment of the present system, by which two steamers are despatched regularly week by week—one each from New York and Glasgow to Glasgow and New York, on Wednesday and Saturday respectively. In addition to this service, which is carried on summer and winter, one or more steamers arrive at New York every week or ten days from the Mediterranean ports, so that there are often as many as six ocean steamers belonging to the Anchor Line lying at the Company's wharf at New York at one time. Its last two steamers are models of symmetry and beauty internally and externally, each being fitted up with every imaginable improvement and convenience, an organ and piano, an elevated promenade running round an immense skylight situated immediately above the saloon, a barber's shop, gas, baths, and electric communication between each state-room and the steward's room, &c. The year of building, names, and gross tonnage of the Company's fleet are :—

Year built.	Name.	Gross tons.	Year built.	Name.	Gross tons.
1863	Caledonia	2390	1870	Dispatch, steam-tender	
1864	Iowa	2114	„	Sidonian	1235
1865	Roma	657	1871	Assyria	1632
„	Scandinavia	1230	„	Olympia	2051
„	Valetta	656	„	Trinacria	2247
„	Venezia	656	1872	Caledonia (lengthened and re-engined).	
1866	Arcadia	749	„	California	3287
„	Columbia	1608	„	Italia	2450
„	Scotia	632	„	Victoria	3213
1867	Europa	1701	1873	Bolivia	4250
„	Trojan	744	„	Carsalia	2700
1868	Dorian	1036	„	Elysia	
1869	Anglia	2142	„	Ethiopia	4250
„	India	2222	„	Utopia	3700
„	Shamrock	2000	„	Macedonia	
„	Tyrian	1039			
1870	Alexandria	1630			
„	Australia	2140			

But the New York trade is only one branch of the Anchor Line service. Their ships sail regularly to Halifax and St. John's; Lisbon, Genoa, and Leghorn; Naples, Messina, Palermo; Trieste, Venice, and Algiers; Tunis, Malta, and Alexandria, and the Grecian Archipelago. At Alexandria they connect with the Peninsular and Oriental and British India Steam Navigation Companies, so that passengers and merchandize can be forwarded to all parts of India. It is scarcely hyperbole to say that the Anchor flag streams in every harbour of mercantile importance; its steamers traverse every sea; so to whatever country or clime one wants to be transported, he can find a cheap and comfortable means of conveyance by one of its hundred ships. In Glasgow alone the Messrs. Henderson Brothers give support to over 30,000 persons, being owners of the largest ship-building and engineering establishment on the Clyde, and of the only graving dock at present in Glasgow. They are their own managers, engineers, builders, and riggers; having their own foundaries and workshops, where every one of their steamers is built, engined, and fitted out. A Company employing upwards of one hundred ships must expect accidents, and the Anchor Line have lost altogether five ships—the *United Kingdom*, which left New York in 1868, and has never since been heard of; the *Hibernia*, which foundered in 1869; the *Cambria*, lost off the Irish coast in 1870; the *Britannia*, which went ashore on Arran a few months ago; and the *Ismailia*, which left New York on the 29th of last September, with one saloon and five steerage passengers, and after being once spoken in a disabled condition, has never since been heard of. Besides these a small steamer was lost off Nova Scotia in 1872, commanded by Captain Laird. The only consolation the Company had in the first three and the last of these calamities was the fact that all of them, so far as could be ascertained, were due to causes quite beyond human control, and no blame attached to officers or owners.*

The next line to start was The National Steam Navigation Company, Limited, afterwards altered to its present title, The National Steamship Company, Limited, which was founded on a joint-stock basis in 1864, by some Liverpool merchants. They began with four large-sized freight steamers in 1865, in 1867 they had six, and now the number is twelve, with an aggregate carrying capacity of 51,190 tons.

Year built.	Name.	Net tons.	Year built.	Name.	Net tons.
1864 ...	Canada, formerly Pennsylvania ...	3286	1866 ...	Helvetia	2769
„ ...	Erin	2766	„ ...	Holland, formerly Louisiana	2162
„ ...	Greece, formerly Virginia	2524	1866 ...	The Queen	3324
1865 ...	Denmark, formerly Chilian	2421	1867 ...	France	2429
„ ...	England	2249	1870 ...	Egypt	2960
			„ ...	Italy...	2437
			„ ...	Spain	2876

* These losses have more than been made good by recent splendid additions to the Anchor Line, and the Messrs. Henderson have now in process of construction at Barrow-in-Furness, Lancashire, six Leviathan steamers for their Atlantic trade which will surpass everything afloat.

This great increase of steamers accurately reflects a proportionate increase in trade, as the following table abundantly shows:—

Year.	Round trips.	Passengers.	Year.	Round trips.	Passengers.
1866 ...	52 ...	34,912	1870 ...	64 ...	43,101
1867 ...	49 ...	29,035	1871 ...	66 ...	46,935
1868 ...	51 ...	32,000	1872 ...	73 ...	52,605
1869 ...	60 ...	41,662			

A further analysis of the returns for 1872 shows that these ships, in addition to their enormous passenger business, carried nearly 470,000 tons of freight, nearly 275,000 of which were transported between Liverpool and New York, an average of 2778 tons per ship, a marked increase on the business of any previous year. The National Line have lost two steamships, the *Georgia* and the *Scotland*, the latter off Sandy Hook. Their steamers are the largest in the trade.

In 1866 Messrs. Ruger Brothers, of New York, started the North American Lloyds, which purchased the steamers *Atlantic*, *Baltic*, and *Western Metropolis*, and chartered the *Ericsson*, *Merrimack*, *Mississippi*, and *Northern Light*, running them between New York and Bremen, touching at Southampton both ways. The scheme proved a failure, and in 1867 the Company was reorganized as the New York and Bremen Steamship Company. The *Atlantic*, *Baltic*, and *Western Metropolis* were taken over, and with the *Northern Light*, which was re-chartered, plied between New York and Bremen, but with no better success. Still a third attempt was made by the Rugers, in 1868, to establish a line on the same route with similar results, which ended in their abandoning the field to the North-German Lloyds.

A last attempt was made in 1869, by the same enterprising but ill-fated firm, to run American steamers to and from New York, Stettin, Copenhagen, and Christiansand, but with so little success that the scheme was abandoned after a brief trial.

From 1864 to 1866 the New York agency of the National Company was managed by the old and much respected shipping-house of Williams and Guion, and on the withdrawal of the agency from the latter, that firm, in connexion with the Liverpool house of Guion and Co., established the Liverpool and Great Western Steamship Company, Limited, better known as the Williams and Guion. This line started with two steamers, the *Manhattan* and the *Chicago*, and was successful from the outset. In 1870 when Cunard and Inman refused to carry the United States mails, unless at what were deemed exorbitant prices, the Postmaster-

General contracted with the Guion Line to carry the United States mails to Queenstown on Wednesdays, for two years, at the expiration of which time the contract was renewed for a similar term. Although the Guion steamers are large and strong, and great favourites as goods carriers, they are the slowest afloat, and only strong political influence, backed up by representations that the Company was largely composed of Americans, could have got for them a contract which they have never once been able to carry out with satisfaction to either the English or American public. The Guion Line have lost two steamers, the *Chicago*, in January, 1868, which ran ashore near Queenstown, and became a total wreck, though all lives were saved, and the *Colorado*, which was run into in the Mersey, when six passengers jumped overboard and were drowned.

The Guion fleet is now as follows:—

Year.		Name.	Net tons.	Year.		Name.	Net tons.
1866	...	Manhattan...	1951	1870	...	Wisconsin ...	2060
1867	...	Minnesota ...	1904	,,	...	Wyoming ...	2081
1868	...	Nevada ...	2020	1873	...	Dakota ...	
1869	...	Idaho ...	2025	,,	...	Montana ...	

During the seven years this line has been in existence, each of its ships has made eight round trips each year, carrying on an average 600 passengers to, and 100 from, New York, giving a total per year of 33,600, and a grand total of fully 250,000 passengers.

The next great ocean line was the Oceanic Steam Navigation Company, more generally known as the White Star Line, which was projected by Messrs. Ismay, Imrie, and Company in 1869-70. The White Star Line began in 1871 with the *Ocean* and *Atlantic;* which were followed during the next two years by the *Baltic, Adriatic, Celtic, Republic, Germania*, and *Britannia*. The number of steamers engaged during 1872 was 6, tonnage 21,000, trips 72, total passengers 17,226, total freight 163,000 tons. Owing to the magnificent fitting-up of these vessels, their great size, and unrivalled speed, the White Star Line shot into immediate popularity, and in spite of several mishaps and one terrible disaster, it has fought its way to a brilliant success. The disaster referred to is, of course, the loss of the *Atlantic* off Mar's Head, Nova Scotia, on the first of April last, when 546 persons perished.

The average speed of this line over the aggregate passages of competing lines is 2 days 3 hours and 37 minutes; and since the 1st of October, 1871, they have carried the Saturday United States Mails from New York, which had formerly been carried by the Inman Line. The boats are of great length, with narrow beam, averaging 440 feet, being nearly eleven times their breadth, which is 41 feet. The White Star Fleet now consists of:—

Year.		Name.		Tonnage.	Year.		Name.	Tonnage.
1870	...	Oceanic	...	2350	1872	...	Celtic	—
1871	...	Baltic	...	2350	1873	...	Germanic	—
"	...	Republic	...	2167	"	...	Britannic	—
"	...	Adriatic	...	2458				

The trips made and passengers carried by this line in 1872 were as follows:—

Name.	Trips.	Average Passengers.	Total.
Atlantic	19 ...	900 ...	17,100
Oceanic	18 ...	800 ...	14,400
Baltic	18 ...	800 ...	14,400
Republic	9 ...	800 ...	7,200
Adriatic	10 ...	800 ...	8,000
Celtic	6 ...	800 ...	4,800
			Total 61,900

The last line to start was the State Line, which trades between Glasgow and New York, but having only four steamers, and no history, it calls for no further remark.

The extent of ground covered, and the number of lines engaged in inter-ocean traffic, have compelled us to limit our remarks almost exclusively to Companies trading between New York and Liverpool. Besides the lines already mentioned there are many others, including the Rotterdam, Eagle, Baltic, Lloyd, Hamburg, American, Transatlantic, and North German Lloyd, all between New York and the continent; the Cardiff, Bristol, between those ports and New York; and the new American line lately started between Philadelphia and Liverpool. The following table gives a bird's-eye view of the routes, character, and relative strength of all these lines, which comprise no fewer than 138 steamers, with an aggregate registered capacity in round numbers of 375,000 tons, all engaged in the Atlantic carrying trade.

The following table shows how literally enormous has been the growth of this traffic. During the past decade the average annual number of steam-ships added to the Atlantic fleet was twelve, being at the rate of one steamer per month, and it is within the bounds of probability than in a few months more the Anchor and Cunard lines will be running a steamer daily from each side. In the foregoing sketch we have been compelled, by the limited space allowed us, to confine ourselves to a bare narrative of facts, and have hardly once touched on principles. But at least one fact stands out broadly from the history of ocean steamship navigation—namely, the suicidal nature of the system of legislation pursued at Washington in reference to American shipping in-

1.	Cunard	22	60,000	274	16,186	56,495	274,000	210,000	72,611	484,000	Liverpool.
2.	Anchor	29	63,000	220	8,935	30,243	179,500	150,000	39,178	329,500	Glasgow, London, and the Mediterranean.
3.	National, Liverpool	7	31,132	109	5,393	33,698	274,076	141,829	54,012	416,805	Liverpool.
4.	National, London	6	20,058	41	1,121	13,800					London.
5.	North German Lloyd	14	42,000	150	10,350	40,420	90,000	67,500	56,770	157,500	Southampton and Bremen.
6.	Inman	14	36,852	172	9,170	64,500	185,000	91,900	63,670	260,300	Liverpool.
7.	Hamburg American	10	30,000	114	9,025	42,758	65,000	60,000	51,813	145,000	Plymouth, Cherbourg and Hamburg.
8.	Guion	7	23,737	110	3,880	24,092	111,600	96,500	28,872	208,000	Liverpool.
9.	White Star	6	21,000	72	5,458	11,769	83,000	80,000	17,225	163,000	Liverpool.
10.	Transatlantic	6	18,000	72	5,243	5,243	20,000	24,200	10,356	44,200	Brest and Havre.
11.	Baltic Lloyd	5	11,800	23	740	6,003	13,200	9,750	6,743	22,950	Stettin, Copenhagen, Havre.
12.	Bristol*	2	3,500	...	......	......	......	......	......	......	Bristol.
13.	Cardiff†	3	8,000	...	......	......	......	......	......	......	Cardiff.
14.	State	6	15,000	2	32	84	2,000	1,800	116	3,500	Glasgow.
15.	Eagle‡	...	......	...	......	......	......	......	......	......	Hamburg.
16.	Rotterdam	9	4,000	14	300	2,600	12,000	11,600	2,800	24,600	Rotterdam.

* The Bristol line is composed of two steamers, the *Great Western* and the *Arragon*. Messrs. Morgan & Sons, 70, South Street, are the agents.

† This is known as the "South Wales Atlantic Steamship Company," and the agents are Archibald Baxter & Co., 17, Broadway. It consists of three steamers, the *Glamorgan*, *Pembroke*, and *Carmarthen*.

‡ The German Transatlantic Steam Navigation Company of the City of Hamburg are now building eight first-class steamers on the Clyde, one or more of which will open the line this summer. Messrs. Knauth, Nachod & Kuhne, 113, Broadway, are the agents.

terest, and the operation of the absurd and ruinous Registry law, under both of which the North Atlantic trade has passed almost wholly out of the hands of Americans. Attempts, more or less vigorous, have been made from time to time to revive the once cherished hope of American builders and shippers, of possessing an American steam service on the Atlantic worthy the name, and of thus securing a fair share of its rich and promising commerce. But the mismanagement of the "Collins" line, and the melancholy fate of a majority of its steamers, gave the death-blow to American mercantile prestige on the Atlantic, and since the three successive failures of the Ruger Brothers there has been little to record in this branch of navigation, calculated either to gratify the American national pride or revive their hopes of future maritime supremacy. One-third of all the sailing-vessels, and two-thirds of all the steamships of the civilized world carry the British flag; after which comes the United States, but at a very long distance. Against 19,182 British sailing vessels engaged in commerce, the United States possess only 7097; with a tonnage of 2,272,120 against a British tonnage of 5,366,927.

The steamships of Britain number 2538, with a tonnage of 2,382,145; and those of the United States only 420, with 401,043 tons. The Americans themselves are keenly conscious of their own inferiority in this respect, and the following extract from an article on "Our Ocean Ferries," in the New York *Evening Post*, one of the most respectable and influential daily journals in the country, only reflects the public sentiment:—

"A few of the once famous and still splendid American 'clipper' ships are yet engaged in the Liverpool trade, but the vast bulk of merchandize of every description now passes between the two countries by steam, and the ships transporting it, as we before stated, are built and owned by foreign capital. European gold builds the steamers; European seamen officer and man them; they sail under and are controlled by European law, and over them float the flags of the different European nationalities. Except for the utterly insignificant sums received from the steamship companies in the way of landing fees and taxes, neither the general or state or city government have an interest in their welfare. For all practical purposes, therefore, they are simply so many means of communication—floating bridges, so to speak—established between rival territories for the joint use of the people inhabiting them, but the sole profits or tolls of which accrue to one and only one of the parties to the transaction. In other words, if our readers will imagine the East and North River ferries, on a somewhat extended scale, in the hands of British or any other foreign capitalists, owning their own franchises, occupying their own docks and wharfs, collecting their own tolls, and regulating their own domestic affairs in their own way, sovereign and independent of any existing international law, they will be able to realize the exact status of the several Atlantic steamship companies as they exist among us to-day."

The only other point which we shall dwell upon is the comparative safety, comfort, and speed of ocean passages. Indeed, the number of accidents accompanied by loss of life, that occur in land-travel greatly outnumbered those which mark steam travel by sea. During the last thirty-three years the number of steamships which were lost while plying between the United States and Europe was 53, being a little over 1·50 a year, and the vast majority of these wrecks were unaccompanied by loss of life. It is impossible to say definitely how many lives were lost, but making a liberal allowance, the number can hardly exceed 5000, being at the rate of about 150 a year. Now, if we bear in mind that during 1872 the number of passengers carried across the Atlantic in steamships alone, exceeded 360,000, we shall see how remarkably small is the proportion of the drowned.

These ocean steamers too, are models of elegance and comfort, in the sumptuously furnished saloons of which one can enjoy every luxury, from the daintiest viand and the choicest wine, to shampoos, porridge, pianos, and organs. With such precision and speed are the best of them driven, that in moderately good weather their arrival in port can be calculated on almost to an hour, and the vast expanse of the Atlantic is spanned in little over a week. On board of the *Scotia, Adriatic, Victoria,* or *City of Chester,* one can live, passage paid, more cheaply than in a Broadway hotel, and calculate on arriving safely and on a certain day at his destination with more certainty than if he travelled from New York to Oyster Bay by a south-side steam car.

Art. VI.—The Development of Psychology.

1. *Divi Thomæ Aquinatis Opera.* Venetiis. 1787.
2. *The English Works of Thomas Hobbes.* London. 1839-46.
3. *An Essay concerning the Human Understanding.* By John Locke, Gent. London. 1817.
4. *Observations on Man.* By David Hartley. London. 1749.
5. *Analysis of the Phenomena of the Human Mind.* By James Mill. New Edition. London. 1869.
6. *The Senses and the Intellect.* By Alexander Bain. Third Edition. London. 1868.
7. *The Emotions and the Will.* By the Same. Second Edition. 1865.
8. *The Principles of Psychology.* By Herbert Spencer. Stereotyped (second) Edition. London. 1870-2.

THE progress of Psychology has been determined by agencies which may, with much precision, be discriminated as two sets of conflicting yet co-operating forces—those maintaining equilibrium, and those producing motion. This language would be justly condemned as mechanical if it in any degree pre-supposed the vulgar notion of force, as acting on visible masses of matter and causing sensible motion. But since vital, mental, and even social phenomena, as well as the oscillations of molecules and the ethereal undulations, are now alike interpreted in terms of mechanism, we may reasonably claim that the phraseology shall receive the greatest latitude of interpretation consistent with the admission of no mechanical assumptions. If, with more propriety, it be censured as scholastic, as raising mere observed uniformities into self-acting entities, it may be replied that the term force is scholastic only when used scholastically, that it has a true and unmistakeable meaning as a generalization simply, and that progress of all kinds can be best described in the language of the science which has clothed the laws of the action of force with the greatest possible precision and certainty. Under these reservations, we use no mere metaphor in describing the development of Psychology as due to two sets of forces, which may be styled kinetical and statical respectively, according as their function has been to produce external change or to effect those internal readjustments which previous changes had rendered necessary.

The statical factor in psychological history is Theology. The mother of all the sciences, it gives birth to Psychology first of the sciences of mind; all the great problems, the discussion of which carries the science through its subsequent revolutions, are raised by it; and we may find that its perpetual function, of which it can never be discharged, is to recall attention from temporary physical solutions to the insoluble problems themselves.

The kinetical factor is constituted by the whole series of the physical sciences, though at any particular epoch it takes the character of the dominant science. Each stage in the development of Psychology corresponds to some stage in the evolution of the natural sciences; by each such transition has each psychological development been caused and conditioned; and the progress of Psychology in fundamental truth, and its more complete emancipation from Theology and Metaphysics, are to be measured by the degree in which physical methods, physical conceptions, and even physical metaphors have been applied to the interpretation of the facts of mind.

The primitive savage, looking out upon the world, finds no God; gazing inwards upon himself, perceives no Soul; and thinking of the origin of things, can conceive no Creation. His gods are parts of the world, not makers of it; such soul as he ascribes to himself is merely his own double, which perishes with him or soon after, or he has several souls; and the earth, as he sees it, was not made but hooked up from the bottom of the original sea.* To the undiscriminating mind of the savage the Cosmos is accordingly all but homogeneous, with just the beginnings of "differentiation," and God, Man, and Nature have yet to acquire an independent existence. There is still, therefore, no room for Psychology.

Plato gets several stages further than this. With him the Cosmos is a divine immortal being or animal, composed of a spherical rotatory body and a rational soul. The gods dwell in the peripheral or celestial regions, and men and the animals inhabit the lower or more central regions. The cranium of man is a little Cosmos, with an immortal rational soul, composed of the same materials as the cosmical soul, and moving with the like rotations. Within the body on which this cranium is placed are two inferior and mortal souls; one, the seat of courage, &c., in the chest, the other, the seat of appetite in the abdomen; both of them being rooted in the spinal marrow,

* Lubbock, "Origin of Civilization," pp. 246-50.

which is continuous with the brain, and is the medium of the unity or communication of the three souls.* In this semi-barbaric Cosmology we may note that the gods are still mixed up with the Cosmos, though the beginnings of separation are shown by their lodgment in a specific place; that they still want unity; and that there is yet no conception of nature. But we are here more concerned to observe that though the human soul is never actually separated from the body, *i.e.*, is not yet detached from the Cosmos, and though it has the corporeal properties of extension and motion, body and soul, microcosmical and macrocosmical, are set sharply over against one another, and the first decided step towards their absolute separation is taken.

The metaphysical advance of Aristotle is immense. The three Platonic souls are merged in one, though the remains of the old idea are visible in the different attributes and distinct origin of the Nutritive, the Nutritive-sentient, and the Noëtic principles. But the Nutrient principle is the indispensable basis, without which neither of the others can exist, and the next higher principle, the Sentient, implies and contains the lower. In the investigations of the properties of these we have the beginnings of Psychology. It is not yet indeed an independent science, for the soul is still imperfectly extricated from the Cosmos—the Noëtic principle having its proper abode in the concave of heaven, and being only temporarily localized in the human body. The soul is still, as regards man, mortal, though as regards the Cosmos it is imperishable.†

Between Aristotle and the thirteenth century the metaphysical evolution was slow, and the stages few and short. The idea of God as an independent existence received its first elaboration in the controversies of the Greek Fathers about the Trinity; was perhaps first sharply discriminated by Anselm; and was raised to the highest pitch of sublimation by the Deistic debates of the seventeenth century, with which the "return of the curve" begins. The idea of Nature, isolated alike from God and Man, emerged from the Italian pantheistic schools of the fifteenth century, to be decisively established with the foundation of Natural Philosophy. The idea of the Soul, with which we are here concerned, was the first of the three elements latent in the primitive homogeneous Cosmos to be completely "differentiated." Whether there was any intrinsic necessity in its earlier evolution; whether it was earlier developed because

---

* Grote, "Psychology of Aristotle," in Bain's "Senses and Intellect," pp. 613-14. † Ibid.

humanity itself and not merely the metaphysicians contributed to it;* or whether it was solely the result of the working of the statical factor in the history of Psychology—the necessities of Theology; its first clear, though not complete, extrication may plausibly be placed as high up as the thirteenth century. As with the other two constitutive ideas, its emergence was the issue of a prolonged debate. No mediæval controversy made more noise while it lasted than the fierce war between the Averroists and the Schoolmen *de unitate intellectus*. Averroës himself, the Arabian Hobbes, had been dead for half a century, but his doctrines had excited an extraordinary ferment among the younger and more speculative minds, and they reached the climax of their popularity just when the Scholastic Philosophy attained in Thomas Aquinas the culminating point in its history. East and West, Semitism and Aryanism, pantheistic absorption and political individualism, in the guise of Aristotle Arabized and Aristotle Christianized, met in final conflict, and the overthrow was, for the time at least, decisive. The theory of Averroës about the Soul was an imposing and picturesque development of the cosmical Psychology of Aristotle. The Nous of Aristotle was only temporarily localized in the body, and after the death of the matter which it *informed*, returned to the grand region of Form, the Celestial Body. Averroës first severed the Nous from the Cosmos, unified it in humanity which it actualized, and made it eternal there. But it was only the common possession of the race through all time, and not particular to the individual; there were no souls, but only a single vast Soul, of which each generation was the perishable embodiment, but itself imperishable. Simple-minded, undoubting Thomas, with his eternal "Aristoteles dicit," "Aristoteles respondet," "Aristoteles habuit," as if the question were to be thus settled, had no difficulty in showing that this was not, what the Averroists felt obliged to maintain, the doctrine of Aristotle.† But it was an advance upon that doctrine without which Aquinas's own unquestionable advance upon Averroës might never, or not so soon, have been made. While, however, Thomas successfully asserted against the Arabians the individuality of the soul,‡ and against the older Aristotelians its substantial unity,§ there was still another step to be taken before its independence on all sides could be regarded as established, and the ground cleared for the science of Psychology.

* See Michelet, "Histoire de France," b. iv. ch. vi.

† "De Unitate Intellectûs," passim.

‡ "Quæstiones Disputatæ." De Spiritualibus Creaturis, artt. ix.—x., and De Anima, artt. ii., iii., v.

§ Bain, "Mind and Body," p. 131.

That step was taken by Descartes, in whom mankind may be said to have come to a consciousness of itself. His "*Cogito, ergo sum*" was not logical but genetic. The force of the *ergo*, as Ferrier long ago pointed out, lay in the fact that the existence of Descartes as a self-conscious being—*sum*—was resultant upon the process described by the word *cogito*—the turning of the light of self-consciousness upon the thinking principle itself. We have but extended Ferrier's interpretation from the development of self-consciousness in the individual to the metaphysical evolution of the *ego* in human history. Not till this had been accomplished, and the Mind made a separate individual existence as against God and Nature, was any independent science of Psychology possible. Observations and reasonings on Man, as on the Deity and the Creation, formed part of the "undifferentiated" mass of speculation on things in general called Cosmology or Theology, and latterly, in a mutilated condition, Metaphysica. Any mediæval cyclopædia will furnish illustrations.

Thomas Aquinas, a faithful representative of the frightened orthodoxy of the Middle Ages, unsuspectingly follows the course of Creation, well known to have happened as laid down in the Book of Genesis. After forty-four *Quæstiones* on God (under whom he discusses the nature of ideas and the metaphysics of truth) and the Trinity, and thirty on the Angels, the Devils (here arises, naturally, a discussion on the nature of evil), and the seven days of creation and rest, Thomas arrives, by an obvious logical sequence, at the psychology of man. One *quæstio* settles the essence of the soul, another the union of soul and body; three exhaust the powers of mind in general and special, and the intellectual powers; four expound appetite, sensuality, the will, and free will; and having in seven more disposed of the remaining faculties of the soul, including such small subjects as "the mode and order of intellection," Thomas is prepared to deal with the production of man's body, and then, evidently, with the production of woman's body.* A witty journalist is reported to have said of an eminent living thinker: "God made the world in six days, and So-and-so wrote it down on the seventh;" but the entire Synthetic Philosophy might fall out of a corner of the "*Summa Theologiæ*" and hardly be missed. Yet arrogant as this encyclopædic comprehensiveness now seems, there was really nothing else to be done. Mathematics was the only one of the natural sciences which had succeeded in disengaging itself from theology; there was no social science, no independent science even of politics; there

* "Summa Theologiæ," prima pars, qu. ii.—xcii.

was no history other than ecclesiastical; and (what concerns us here) there was no science of man. Man was not yet a unit in the creation, and inquiries concerning him were properly included in Cosmology, which is pagan for Theology. "*Naturam autem*," says Thomas, "*hominis considerare pertinet* ad Theologum *ex parte animæ*."* The theologus kept hold of the nature of man till Descartes had emancipated him from his serfdom; but to him and his theological science—our statical factor—we may justly ascribe that first successful raising of the problem of human individuality which made possible, as we shall see, its establishment and utilization under the influence of the dynamical factor—physical science.

The fostering aid of Theology to Psychology does not, however, end when the latter is able to walk alone. All great questions subsequently raised, the settlement of which by physical methods marks each fresh stage, issue from the theological *incunabula* where the science was reared. A history of the embryogeny of ideas would demonstrate that ideas which were afterwards properly philosophical were at first purely theological. The idea of the infinite, at first negative, was made positive, through being made theological, by the Greek Fathers. Professor Jevons believes that his "Law of Simplicity," though almost unnoticed in modern times, was known to Boëthius, and he adds:—

"Ancient discussions concerning the doctrine of the Trinity drew more attention to subtle questions concerning the nature of unity and plurality than has ever since been given to them."†

With greater emphasis, which, however, only exaggerates an important truth, it has been said that the doctrine of the Trinity is the "foundation of all the metaphysical thought and speculation of the ages after Gregory the Great."‡ This will be sufficiently near the mark if the honour is shared with the dogma of Transubstantiation after, say, the "captivity" at Avignon. In more recent times, especially in Germany in the first half of the present century, the doctrine of the Incarnation has been the "motive" of various metaphysical developments.

In Psychology the final cause of Locke was theological; for the rise of an *à priori* philosophy in Herbert of Cherbury was theological, and it was to overthrow apriorism that Locke undertook his examination of the "original, certainty, and extent of human knowledge." Berkeley avowed that his motive, in investigating the nature of perception, was to provide a bulwark

---

* "Summa Theologiæ," prima pars, qu. lxxv.
† "The Principles of Science," i. 40.
‡ Quoted in Mullinger, "History of Camb. Univ.," p. 55.

against the atheists. Hume is essentially theological, and in his "Inquiry concerning the Human Understanding," a section on Miracles stands side by side with one on the Idea of Necessary Connexion. Reid wrote his "Essays on the Powers of the Human Mind" to refute Hume, and became, with this theological motive, the founder of Scotch psychology. Kant undertook his "criticism of pure reason," and thus established *à priori* psychology, to show against Hume that the ideas of God, freedom, and immortality, could not be disproved by mere empirical reasoning. And the impulse which Hamilton, through Mansel, communicated to Psychology by the new face he gave to the old problem of the Infinite, was a theological movement in its origin.

Under whatever name we give to it, under whatever form it may hereafter assume, Theology, the science of causes, essences, and origins, will play, as it has hitherto played, an important part in the development of the mental sciences, and especially of Psychology. When physical science is driving its ploughshare into untrodden regions till now only gazed down upon by the metaphysician in his balloon; when the speed of thought itself is measured; when the most complex effort of quantitative reasoning is proved to be fundamentally identical with the simplest perception of relation; when the nature of intelligence is tracked upwards in graduated sequence from the Radiata and Articulata to Newton and Shakspeare; and when the physical sides of all but the most subtle mental phenomena are being identified; the temptation is great to suppose that we are nearing the goal—that as so many laws of mind have been explained by physical laws, and so many facts interpreted in physical terms, the time is at hand, or at least will come, when the nature of causation, and of the substance of mind, and of the relation of phenomena to their source, and of that inscrutable source itself, will yield their secrets to the analysis of the inquirer armed with the weapons of physical science. Whatever power stands in the old place of Theology, which is dead—whether Metaphysics, if that be not dead also, or some "Unknowable" section of our compendiums of first principles—will show all such Comtist dreams to be vain, by eternally asking the unanswerable questions which it has been asking since the beginning of speculation. And each old question newly asked after each fresh advance of physical science tends to restore the equilibrium deranged by the operation of that dynamical factor, the history of the effects of which we will now briefly sketch.

The application of physical methods to the phenomena of mind, we believe to have originated in the fact that outside the territory which (as we saw by the quotation from St. Thomas), was sacred to the *theologus*, there was a sort of no-Man's land, which profane persons might enter into and possess. For Aquinas goes on :—"non autem ex parte corporis, nisi secundum habitudinem quam habet corpus ad animam."* That is to say, while the *anima intellectiva*, which issues directly from the hand of God, is the exclusive province of the theologian, the *anima sensitiva*, which is propagated in a physical manner,† the passions, and the appetites, may be left to the uncowled cultivator of science as not requiring the help of divine inspiration. It was at any rate in this field that the foundations of inductive psychology were laid, and it was to the explanation of the simpler phenomena of sensibility that physical conceptions were first applied. The two greatest thinkers of the seventeenth century were almost simultaneously on the ground.

Descartes is not now remembered by his "Treatise on the Passions," (which was published within a year of Hobbes' work on "Human Nature,") and we only note it here as an early example of experimentalism in Psychology. We are more concerned to observe that his vindication of the immateriality of the thinking principle, and his clear perception of the unity of the mental aggregate, were almost contemporaneous with the "new geometry." We are not, indeed, solicitous with regard to Descartes to justify our thesis—that each advance in Psychology has been caused and conditioned by a corresponding and previous advance in physical science; for the enunciation of the Cartesian principle was less a fact in Psychology than the accomplishment of a stadium in the metaphysical evolution, which made Psychology possible. But, perhaps, it may not seem fanciful to mention that Cavalieri, "the generally reputed father of the new geometry," published in 1635, his Method of Indivisibles (which had been largely anticipated by Kepler), or to connect his leading principle—that a solid is generated out of an infinite number of surfaces placed one above another as their indivisible elements—with the effort to unite into a single substance, itself localized, the endless multiplicity of the mental manifestations. It is, at least, clear that the application of physics to mind will follow the development of physics; and as physics had not yet advanced beyond the geometrical stage, as the period immediately preceding "Descartes' Meditations" was the epoch of a great geometrical advance, as we now know that in virtue of the *consensus* which governs all social phenomena, all the conceptions of any age are moulded in the same matrix, it seems not wholly imaginary to adduce the psychology of Descartes, who

* "Sum. Theol.," pt. i. qu. lxxv. † Ibid, qu. cxviii. art. 1.

was himself an eminent geometer, as in some degree the result of the dominance of the earliest developed of the sciences.

Emerging from this doubtful region, we pass on to the *terra firma* of demonstrable fact. Hobbes was rather older than Descartes, but he had the advantage of delaying at least the publication of his speculations until another great scientific advance had been accomplished. We cannot state his antecedents better than in his own words:—

"The beginning of astronomy, except observations, I think is not to be derived from farther time than from Nicolaus Copernicus, who in the age next preceding the present revived the opinion of Pythagoras, Aristarchus, and Philolaus. After him, the doctrine of the motion of the earth being now received, and a difficult question thereupon arising concerning the descent of heavy bodies, Galileus in our time, striving with that difficulty, was the first that opened to us the gate of natural philosophy universal, which is the knowledge of the nature of *motion*. So that neither can the age of natural philosophy be reckoned higher than to him. Lastly, the science of *man's body*, the most profitable part of natural science, was first discovered with admirable sagacity by our countryman Doctor Harvey, principal physician to King James and King Charles, in his books of the 'Motion of the Blood' and of the 'Generation of Living Creatures;' who is the only man I know that, conquering envy, hath established a new doctrine in his lifetime. Before these, there was nothing certain in natural philosophy, but every man's experiments to himself, and the natural histories, if they may be called certain, that are no certainer than civil histories. But since these, astronomy and natural philosophy have, for so little time, been extraordinarily advanced by Joannes Keplerus, Petrus Gassendus, and Marinus Mersennus; and the science of human bodies in special by the wit and industry of physicians, the only true natural philosophers, especially of our most learned men of the College of Physicians in London. Natural Philosophy is therefore but young; but Civil Philosophy yet much younger, as being no older (I say it provoked, and that my detractors may know how little they have wrought upon me) than my own book, '*De Cive*.'"*

The application of all this to the psychological philosophy of Hobbes is so patent, as hardly to need elucidation in detail. Like his contemporary Descartes, Hobbes was extremely jealous of his independence, and what was of less consequence, his originality; and one may even now hear, not without surprise and otherwise, the unlucky epigram which makes him say, that if he had read as many books as other people he would have been as ignorant as they. Hobbes had read a great deal more than he deemed it prudent to admit, and if he had read more still the good effect of it would not have been doubtful. But like the Greeks of the time of Sophocles, he had an advantage which

* "Elements of Philosophy," Epistle Dedicatory, pp. 8-9.

would have made up for any deficiency of literary acquisition. He lived in an atmosphere heavy with ideas, and at a time when epistolary communication performed the functions very much which scientific journals now fulfil. Hobbes does not appear to have corresponded with Descartes, but he was in constant intercourse, by letter, with Mersenne, who acted as the intermediary between the two philosophers. And as philosophers then concerned themselves with the whole range of the sciences, there was hardly a speculation stirring the European mind that need have escaped the notice of even a thinker somewhat out of the main lines of communication. Hobbes was moreover a traveller, had lived much on the Continent, and had possibly met Galileo at Pisa. It was under the influence of these two men, or rather of the methods they represented—Descartes and mathematics, Galileo and the laws of motion—that Hobbes proceeded to work out his philosophy. In the language of a distinguished professor, to whom we look for an exhaustive account of Hobbes's relations to the science of his time, "he set about reducing all his thoughts into the unity of a system, whose central idea was this of motion, and whose guiding principles were those of mathematical deduction."* "His great postulate," says the same writer, "is motion or mutation,"† and he makes copious use of it within the sphere to which Aquinas banished the experimental psychologist, and a little beyond. His explanation of sensation is wholly mechanical. The crass materialism with which he set out may have had something to do with his trenchant rejection of the audible, visible, and intelligible species of the Schoolmen, but the hypothesis which replaced them betrays its own origin. "The apparition of light," he says, "is really nothing but motion within."‡ This thesis is more elaborately developed in a passage which we quote at length, as it appears to contain an anticipation of the undulatory theory of light and heat:—

"From all lucid, shining, and illuminate bodies, there is a motion produced to the eye, and, through the eye, to the optic nerve, and so into the brain, by which that apparition of light and colour is effected. . . . First, it is evident that the fire . . . worketh by motion equally every way. . . . And further, that that motion, whereby the fire worketh, is dilation, and contraction of itself alternately . . . is manifest also by experience. From such motion in the fire must needs arise a rejection or casting from itself of that part of the medium which is contiguous to it, whereby that part also rejecteth the next, and so successively one part beateth back another to the

* *Westminster Review*, April, 1867. † Ibid.
‡ "Human Nature," p. 6.

very eye," and so from the eye to the optic nerve, and from that to the brain.*

This postulate of motion, applied in this thorough-going manner, led Hobbes to a great discovery in the psychology of sensation. He clearly demonstrated that the secondary qualities of body are purely subjective, and his language is almost strong enough to lead us to believe that he would have gone a long way with Berkeley. For he claims to have proved that "as in vision, so also in *conceptions* that arise from the other senses, the subject of their inherence is not the object but the sentient." If the word "conceptions" be interpreted according to a definition previously laid down in the same treatise, in which the "images produced by things" are described as conceptions, imaginations, ideas, knowledge, it should seem that he might have applied the analysis to the primary qualities as well, had the two sets of properties been as sharply contrasted as now, instead of being first discriminated by Descartes and Hobbes. The same conception (motion) is used to explain the feelings, which when pleasurable, are the result of the vital motion being "helped" by the motions which, having produced conceptions in the head, afterwards proceed to the heart.† But external objects not only "cause conceptions, and conceptions appetite, and fear;" as the latter are "the first unperceived beginnings of our actions," and as in a state of doubt, appetite and fear rapidly succeed one another, "this alternate succession of appetite and fear . . . . is that we call deliberation."‡ As all Hobbes's successors of the same school have followed him in thus ignoring the *ego*, it may be inferred that every system of experimental psychology is self-condemned to incompleteness, and that no system can cover the whole of the ground which does not make what can only be called metaphysical assumptions.

The psychological advances made by Hobbes were then—that he helped to banish the imaginary entities of the Schoolmen, and substituted for them hypotheses that implied at least *veræ causæ*; that he replaced the method of deduction from assumed principles by that of observation (which was not yet, however, that of introspection), and thus founded the inductive philosophy of the mind; and that by his summary rejection of the common metaphysical assumptions, and his patient building up on an independent foundation, he decisively separated psychology from the metaphysics in which it was enmeshed.

If the psychology of Hobbes bears evident marks of the daring speculative character of contemporary physical science, that of Locke witnesses to the change in the tone and spirit of inquiry.

---

* "Human Nature," pp. 6-7. † Ibid, p. 31. ‡ Ibid, pp. 67-8.

If the key-word to Hobbes is Galileo, that to Locke is Sydenham. Locke and Sydenham were both surgeons, were friends, and were of kindred cautious temperament; and the pacific revolution which Sydenham wrought in medicine has been described in language that, with the necessary change of terms, might word for word be applied to the great psychological advance initiated by Locke. A competent writer describes Sydenham as being—

"most careful to exclude the prevailing theories from affecting his study of the facts of disease: he followed the inductive method which his countryman, Bacon, had just completed, and under the guidance of his friend, John Locke, himself a surgeon, he applied it to the investigation of disease with splendid success. The laws ruling the prevalence of epidemics were elucidated, and new and old diseases described with an accuracy and graphic colouring which have ever since remained unrivalled. The treatment of disease Sydenham found lamentably uncertain from want of any fixed principle, and from the countless remedies prescribed mainly in accordance with a capricious fashion. In place of this, he left therapeutics an art ordered by the principle of aiding nature, and observing the indications afforded by morbid processes themselves. . . . Bacon had justly reproached the physicians of his time for their neglect to make records of the cases of their patients. . . . Sydenham . . . by his bedside study again brought it into favour." And finally, "he found English medicine reduced to the lowest state of empiricism—he raised it once more to the dignity of a science of observation."*

The disposition in which Locke entered on his inquiry was certainly "to exclude prevailing theories," for he has himself recorded that his Essay originated in a conviction that before advancing to abstruse problems, "it was necessary to examine our own abilities, and see what objects our understandings were or were not fitted to deal with." His method of induction was truly Baconian: he approached the subject without any clear design, proceeded without a plan, and attained such results as can be so reached. But the "laws ruling the" formation of ideas were elucidated, and mixed and simple modes "described with an accuracy" and in one or two cases with "a graphic colouring" which have not been greatly surpassed. The philosophy of the mind he found an untrodden jungle, with a few bridle-paths in the directions marked "Sense" "Appetite," &c.; he cut a highway through the part where the bush was thickest—the region of ideas. The *à priori* method was in favour, and "bedside study" of the human patient out of fashion; the *à priori* method he did not indeed kill, but he left it to die a lingering death; and though to Hobbes belongs the

* Mr. Balthazar W. Foster, in "Essays of Birmingham Speculative Club," pp. 277-8.

honour of introducing the experimental method into Psychology, it may be truly said of Locke that he "raised it to the dignity of a science of observation." And just as Sydenham, follower of Hippocrates as he was, attributed a number of diseases to morbid fermentation in the humours, so Locke, in spite of his anti-scholasticism, could still assign the motion of the "animal spirits" as a "natural cause" of certain ideas.* The defects and the merits, in truth, of Locke's procedure were equally those of the physical science of the age. The patient observation of which Sydenham set the example gave rise to the first discriminative account—we can hardly call it analysis—of the proximate origin and more obvious constituents of our ideas. To the same causes and doubtless also to the impulse of conquest in unexplored regions which the post-mediæval world owed to Bacon, we may ascribe it that Locke's "Essay," as he named it, "inquiry," as he described it, was the first comprehensive survey of mental phenomena; while the small part which hypothesis and theory play in his investigation, his incomplete statement of mental causation of all kinds, his bare discovery of association as producing a few obvious compounds, were clearly due to the unspeculative character of the contemporary science to the influence of which he was most exposed.

Berkeley's most notable contribution to philosophy belongs rather to the metaphysics, than to the psychology, of sensation; and his less disputed discovery of the acquired nature of our perceptions of distance we may pass over with the remark, that if the genesis of it could be traced, it would probably be found to have derived its impulse from that "century of inventions" which witnessed Snell's discovery of the law of refraction in 1624, Newton's discoveries in the composition of light in 1674, Huyghens' proof of the polarization of light about 1692, and the explanation of the structure of the eye by Petit in 1700. The conjunction will seem more than a coincidence if it is added that Berkeley's "Theory of Vision," which appeared in 1709, was preceded by "Newton's Opticks," in 1705.

The next great advance of Psychology combined, in principle, the advances made by both Hobbes and Locke. As Hobbes had incorporated the conceptions of physical science, and Locke had adopted its methods, we find Hartley professing to follow the "method of analysis and synthesis recommended and followed by Sir Isaac Newton,"† and appropriating from the "Principia" the hypothesis of vibrations by which he explained sensation:—

"My chief design in the following chapter is, briefly, to explain, establish, and apply the doctrines of *vibrations* and association. The

* "Essay," b. ii. ch. xxxiii. † "Observations," ch. i.

first of these doctrines is taken from the hints concerning the performance of sensation and motion, which Sir Isaac Newton has given at the end of his 'Principia,' and in the *questions* annexed to his 'Optics;' the last, from what Mr. Locke, and other ingenious persons since his time have delivered concerning the influence of *association* over our opinions and affections, and its use in explaining those things in an accurate and precise way, which are commonly referred to the power of habit and custom, in a general and indeterminate one. . . . One may expect that *vibrations* should infer *associations* as their effect, and association point to vibrations as its cause."*

It may seem somewhat bold in Hartley, whose name has almost passed into a by-word as that of an hypothesis-maker, to shelter himself under the ægis of Newton, who declared—"hypotheses non fingo." But, as is observed by Professor Stanley Jevons, "the greater part of the 'Principia' is purely hypothetical, endless varieties of causes and laws being imagined which have no counterpart in nature."† Psychology had reached in Hartley's time, as Natural Philosophy in Newton's time, the stage when the mere generalization of observed uniformities is no longer sufficient to cope with the accumulated multitude of ascertained facts, and when some comprehensive hypothesis is required which shall connect the empirical generalizations of one science with the ultimate laws of nature and the principles of all the sciences. Newton's force of gravity, and Hartley's theory of vibrations, were such hypotheses. But besides the intrinsic difference between them residing in the fact that the one could be proved and the other, at best, only made probable, there was the further contrariety, which explains their very different success, that the Newtonian conception was the complement of a slow development. The first natural philosophers, down even to Kepler and Galileo, had contented themselves with studying *effects*, *e.g.*, the orbits described by the heavenly bodies, and the period of their revolutions. But with the decay of the scholastic metaphysics, which was also physics, a new idea began to stir the minds of men—that of force. It is said to have been conceived by Nicolas of Cusa;‡ it found tortuous expression in Descartes' Vortices;§ and, specialized as governing gravitation, it was perhaps first dimly seen by Gilbert little less than a century before Newton, was asserted by Kepler nine years later (1609), and in 1674 was stated by Hooke with remarkable clearness and accuracy—all before Newton had thrown out any hint of his sublime discovery.‖ Hartley's hypothesis, on the other hand, was a chance

* "Observations," ch. i. † "Principles of Science," ii. 228.
‡ Morin, in Migne's "Encyclopédie, Théologie Scholastique," sub. nom.
§ Hallam, "Literature of Europe," iii. (ed. 1872) p. 415.
‖ Grant, "History of Physical Astronomy," pp. 16, 17, and 29.

shot, a private guess, and was no matured result of previous theorizing. It accordingly passed into the limbo to which Nature consigns her mistakes; but the gain to Psychology was, though not equally great, of fundamentally the same kind as the gain to Natural Philosophy from the establishment of the law of gravitation. The idea of force subsumed that of law, the conception of causation superseded those of sequence and conjunction; and the basis for an explanation of the phenomena of mind was for the first time sought outside the limits of these phenomena. Hartley was unsuccessful, but the mere attempt has been as a light on high to guide the uncertain steps of later inquirers, and has at last led to the physical syntheses of our own day.

Even a false, or at least a partially true, theory has the advantage of making possible a reasoned arrangement of the facts, as well as the acquisition of more. To Hartley this hypothesis of vibrations gave strength of wing to sweep the entire field of Psychology, and we accordingly find that his was the first systematic effort to explain the phenomena of mind by the law of association.*

A very great advance in Psychology was made by James Mill, and it was initiated by Chemistry. During the first ten years of the nineteenth century Chemistry was revolutionized. In 1800 Nicholson and Carlisle decomposed water by means of the Voltaic pile, and enabled Davy in 1806 to make the generalizations which founded electro-chemistry. The decomposition of potassa, soda, and other bodies of the same kind soon followed. Beginning with hydrochloric acid in 1809, the discovery of the various hydracids was made. And in 1803–4 a great synthetic addition was made to the analytic gains: Dalton's law of chemical combination was established.† The influence of these brilliant discoveries upon the thought of the age was not doubtful. The literature of the day was drenched with metaphors taken from the dominant science. Fashion, after a long interval, once more patronized nature, and the "bottle-and-squirt mania" spread. Experimentalism in Psychology was still under a cloud, from the discredit which had attached to the premature theorizing of Hartley. But in the early part of the century, Dr. Thomas Brown had gained a hearing, under cover of the respectable orthodoxy of the Scotch Universities, for speculations thickly sown with revolutionary germs. One of his pupils was James Mill, and in 1829 that resolute and thoroughgoing, if narrow and aggressive, thinker published the treatise which marked the turn of the tide. Deriving his inspiration from the neglected work of Hartley, gathering up the hints freely scattered in

---

* Bain, "Mental and Moral Science," p. 633.

† Whewell, "History of the Inductive Sciences," iii. pp. 167-9, 141 9, 145.

Brown's lectures, and imbued with the spirit of the prevailing chemistry, he set about constructing a new science of mind, of which the physics should not be obsolete, and which should push the analysis of the accepted metaphysical mysteries to the furthest possible limit. He obeyed the double analytic and synthetic movement in contemporary chemical investigation. As specimens of his analytical advance, we may point to his further resolution of the apparently simple ideas of hardness and extension, which had been begun by Hartley and continued by Darwin.* But, as better illustrating the dynamical influence of physical science, we prefer to lay emphasis on what may, as it appears to us, be justly styled his synthetical contribution to Psychology. This was his conception, applied to the whole range of mental phenomena, of the chemical nature of association. Quite to realize the new shape which the welding mental power took in his hands, we must glance back at its history. It is comparatively young. Hobbes knew nothing of it: his "synthesis," by which things are "constructed or generated," is purely geometrical,† and with him association is mere sequence.‡ Locke's advance on this is clear, though inconsiderable: he speaks of the "tying together of ideas," and describes certain ideas as appearing in "gangs, always inseparable,"§ but he regards "mixed modes" as made by men voluntarily with a view to communication.‖ Hartley, according to Mr. J. S. Mill, had reached the stage we have above stated as only attained by James Mill:—

"It was reserved for Hartley to show that mental phenomena, joined together by association, may form a still more intimate, and as it were chemical union; . . . the compound having all the appearance of a phenomenon *sui generis*, as simple and elementary as the ingredients, and with properties different from any of them."¶

This is far too strongly stated. That the union of the associated mental elements as conceived by Hartley was more intimate than their mode of conjunction as conceived by Locke, or their rigidity of sequence as imagined by Hobbes, is unquestionable; but how Mr. Mill could describe that union as chemical, and as analogous to the compound formed like water, by hydrogen and oxygen, is inexplicable if it be remembered that the composition of water was not discovered by Cavendish till 1784—thirty-five years after the appearance of the "Observations"—and that Chemistry only passed from the metaphysical to the positive stage with the deposition of phlogiston by

* "Analysis," i. 92.

† "Elem. Phil.," i. pp. 312-13.

‡ "Hum. Nat.," ch. iv.

§ "Essay," b. ii. ch. xxxiii.

‖ *Ibid.*, ch. xxii.

¶ "Dissertations," iii. 108.

Priestley and Lavoisier in the last quarter of the century. The following quotations from Hartley himself will confirm this *à priori* argument by showing the real nature of association as figured by him:—

"Upon the whole, it may appear to the Reader, that the simple Ideas of Sensation must run into Clusters and Combinations, by Association; and that each of these will, at last, coalesce into one Complex Idea, by the Approach and Commixture of the several compounding Parts."*

No chemist would describe chemical union as "coalescence," or speak of the new substance produced by the operation of affinity as made up of "clusters and combinations" by the "approach and commixture" of parts. As appears still more clearly when Hartley proceeds to explain and illustrate this "coalescence," he had in his mind, as the physical type of his conception, no more "intimate union" than that combination of different kinds of matter called *solution*: †—

"If the Number of simple Ideas which compose the complex one be very great, it may happen that the complex Idea shall not appear to bear any relation to these its compounding Parts, nor to the external Senses upon which the original Sensations, which gave Birth to the compounding Ideas, were impressed. The Reason of this is, that each single Idea is overpowered by the Sum of all the rest, as soon as they are all intimately united together. Thus, in very compound Medicines, the several Tastes and Flavours of the separate Ingredients are lost and overpowered by the complex one of the whole Mass: so that this has a Taste and Flavour of its own, which appears to be simple and original, and like that of a natural Body."‡

We should be disposed to describe Hartley's view of mental composition as bearing a similar relation to James Mill's synthesis as Newton's composition of light to Goethe's theory of colours—as implying some species of union closer than the mechanical and less binding than the chemical. Thomas Brown clearly stated the law, as chemically conceived, in one of his introductory lectures. In mere statement James Mill's exposition is no advance upon Brown's, but the law took enormous extensions in his hands, and was applied to the senses, the feelings, memory, classification, language, ratiocination, the will, belief, &c. Something has been added to his synthesis, and a little has been taken from it, but he appears to have made as much as could be made out of the bare laws of association, unextended to the rest of the animal kingdom, and confined to the existing generation. His conception of the indissolubleness of certain associations, in

* "Observations," p. 74.

† Youmans, "New Chemistry," p. 55. ‡ "Observations," p. 75.

particular, preluded the elucidation of their organic character as resulting from the intercourse of the mind with its environment.

Great as were the services of Mr. John Stuart Mill to Philosophy in general, and Psychology in particular, we cannot ascribe to him any notable advance in psychological doctrine, or in the conception or application of psychological method. In doctrine, his chief contributions were the re-statement, in a form adapted to the changed conditions of the controversies, of Berkeley's theory of material, and Hume's theory of mental, existence. But neither the psychological theory of mind nor the psychological theory of matter contains any new principle, or exhibits any new way of applying old principles. In constructive method, he could get no further than Brown's half-century-old "chemistry of the mind," and though he earnestly recommended the St. Andrew's students to make the acquaintance of Physiology, as supplying to Psychology the principles of predisposition, habit, and development,* he never made the smallest use of these principles himself, and had not a single word to say in favour of Mr. Spencer's use of them.† That he still traded on the old conceptions is evident from his metaphors: the "thread of consciousness" is a decided advance on Locke's "gang of ideas," but he shies at Professor Masson's "organic union" of states, and prefers to connect them by an "inexplicable tie."‡ Mill, in fact, was above all things a logician, and whatever he accomplished in the sciences was in virtue of his clear perception of the extent of a principle, the limitations to which it was subject, and the conditions under which it could be most fruitfully applied. His services to psychological method were of this order, and therefore belong rather to the logic of science than to the history of Psychology. But as his luminous exposition of the logical *status* of the "laws of mind"§ had an unquestionable influence on the most systematic application of these laws yet made, in the comprehensive work of Professor Bain, it will be proper to inquire whether this advance too had its antecedents in the physical sciences.

Mill's logic of psychology is characteristic. Like all his doctrines, it has a positive and a hypothetical part—the hypothetical admitting almost all that his opponents of every school would assert, and the positive so stated as if those admissions had not been made. The positive aspect of it may be embodied in three propositions. Psychology is a *science*, because the facts of mind present certain uniformities of succession, which we call laws. It is an *independent* science, because its laws are ultimate, and cannot be deduced from the physiological laws of our nervous

* "Inaugural Address," pp. 61-2. † "Dissertations," iii. 99, note.
‡ "Examination" (third ed.), pp. 256-7. § "Logic" (sixth ed.), ii. pp. 431-42.

organization. Finally, this science has certain *limits*, which are stated, however, with a vacillation and obscurity very far from usual with so clear and resolute a thinker, but which appear to be: that sensations of one sense cannot be resolved into those of another; that "the other constituents of the mind, its beliefs, its abstruser conceptions, its sentiments, emotions, and volitions," have probably not been generated from simple ideas of sensation; and that even if this can be proved, "we should not be the more enabled to resolve the laws of the more complex feelings into those of the simpler ones." In the hypothetical part (which has been much more strongly expressed in the later editions of the "Logic," though without any corresponding alteration of the positive part), Mill is quite prepared to admit that "the laws of mind may be derivative laws resulting from laws of animal life, and that their truth, therefore, may ultimately depend on physical conditions." But the probability of this genesis being shown, he apparently regards as so remote that it is not worth while to take the antecedent physical conditions into account except as disturbing agencies.* He refuses to see that if the evolution of the higher forms of life from the lower can be made out, we do not say as an induction, but even as a good working hypothesis, the foundations of Psychology will be subverted, and it will be changed from what we may call a statical into a dynamical science.

Mill belonged, less by age than by precocious mental development, to a generation which found in him its perfect scientific, and in Mr. Carlyle its most consummate literary, expression. In literature, it turned with reverted eyes to an ever-receding golden age, and wrote histories; in science, the impulse was rather to widen, clear, and connect the old paths, than to strike out in new directions—to get round obstacles, than to tunnel them. "Reaction" is so ready a spell to conjure meaning out of facts by pretending to put an explanation upon them, that we will not ascribe the critical mood of the last generation to mere revulsion from the profuse hypotheses of the period when Chemistry promised to reveal the secret constitution of nature; but clearly after a time of discovery and accumulation of facts, there comes the necessity for arrangement, classification, method, and the logician takes the place of the discoverer. To this work the generation of 1820—1850 set itself in no scholastic spirit, and one of its first achievements in the new field was Herschel's picturesque and elevated "Discourse."† Ardent and imaginative as is that fine essay, it

---

* "Logic," ii. 433.

† "Preliminary Discourse on the Study of Natural Philosophy." 1830.

is nevertheless essentially logical. Four of his nine "rules of philosophizing" were converted by Mill into the experimental methods, and thus made a part of the logic of proof; his conception of a law is predominantly that of a generalization which seems to imply no inductive leap; and he appears to look for the openings to future discovery in the purely analytic direction of finding some more general laws of which the laws already discovered are cases. So faithfully did the work embody the tendencies of the period that its phraseology at once became classic, and its ideas of cause and law the commonplaces of science. They certainly formed a large portion of the mental pabulum of Mill, and are reflected, though with infinite widening and clarification, in the "System of Logic." We have already said that his four "methods" were but four of Herschel's "rules;" Herschel's "presumed permanence of the great laws of nature" appears in Mill as the statement that "the uniformity of the course of nature is the ultimate major premise in all cases of induction," and the relations of induction and deduction, the value and test of hypotheses, the nature of empirical laws, and the analysis of cause—are all striking *aperçus* which Mill pursued to their limits on every side, and thus was able to give to the exposition of them systematic completeness. All these conceptions, as being important parts of the logic of science, belong equally to the logic of psychology, and if their statement in reference to mental science is due to Mill, the statement of them in reference to science generally is due to Herschel. But we are here more concerned to point out that the scientific conditions laid down by Mill as defining the logical *status* of psychology, belong to the type of physical investigations of which Herschel was an early representative. The definition of science as having for its subject "uniformities," the description of the independence of a science as arising out of the irreducibility of its laws to other laws, and the exposition of the limits of scientific inquiry; all find their prototypes in the "Discourse." Here again, therefore, the advance in Psychology, though only logical, had its initiative in the physical sciences.

The rate of change quickens as the type of social structure rises, and the progress made by Psychology within the present generation is not only far greater than has been before made in any period of equal length, but greater than has been made since the foundation of the science. The large acquisitions of new facts, the faithful description of phenomena, the reduction of them to law, and the investigation of the physical "sides" of mental products, which we owe to Professor Bain; and the application to mind of the revolutionary principle of development, and the inclusion of it within the larger philosophy of evolution, which we owe to Mr. Herbert Spencer; have changed not only the aspect but the constitution of Psychology. Like all the previous advances we have recorded, the developments due to both of these distinguished psychologists have had their dynamic in the subsidiary sciences.

Mr. Bain describes his work as being "the first attempt to construct a Natural History of the Feelings, upon the basis of a uniform descriptive method," and the characterization is just. All preceding surveys of the mind had been undertaken to establish a doctrine, as by Hobbes; to refute a theory, as by Locke; to prove an hypothesis, as by Hartley; or to furnish analytical justification of a foregone conclusion, as by the elder Mill. Mechanics, Natural Philosophy, and Chemistry having exhausted their constructive impulses on Psychology, it was reserved for Mr. Bain to adopt a method which makes no presuppositions, rests on no hypothesis, and conducts to no necessary conclusions—the method employed in the organic sciences in their undeveloped state. The natural history "method" is very old. The first full-blown specimen of a naturalist, whose reputation has reached posterity, appears to have been Solomon, and of him it is said that "he spake of trees, from the cedar tree that *is* in Lebanon even unto the hyssop that springeth out of the wall: he spake also of beasts, and of fowl, and of creeping things, and of fishes."* Linnæus was even more comprehensive, and added minerals to plants and animals; but with him the differentiation of science and accompanying specialization of method begin. The first great classifier himself constituted Botany a separate science; Haüy followed with Mineralogy; the discovery of Oken (or Goethe) and the theories of St. Hilaire founded Comparative Anatomy; Comparative Physiology issued out of its sister science; and morphological and functional divisions of all these sciences were successively established. With such advances in classification, the natural history method becomes immensely more complex, but its character is fundamentally the same—that of description. We cannot better exemplify this than by quoting the words of Dr. Carpenter. Contrasting him with the "enterprising discoverer," the horticulturist, and the breeder, he says that:—

"The philosophic naturalist. . . . aims to reduce the number of species, by investigating the degree of variation which each is liable to undergo, the forms it assumes at different periods of its existence, the permanent characters by which it may be distinguished during its whole life, the habits which are natural to it, the degree in which these may be changed by the influence of circumstances; and, in fine, he endeavours to become acquainted with the *whole* Natural History of a reputed species, before separating it from another to which it may be closely allied."†

* "First Book of the Kings," iv. 33.

† "Comparative Physiology" (fourth ed.), p. 032.

The "philosophic naturalist" plainly requires just so much philosophy as is implied in keeping his eyes open, and indeed so long as species were believed to be separately created, and organic characters could be only correlatively and not genetically explained, there was nothing else for him to do. Natural History before Darwin was like Natural Philosophy before Newton; its inductions were incomplete, and the deductive procedure which could alone raise its constituent groups into sciences was impossible. It was at this stage in the development of Natural History that Mr. Bain took up its method, and set about applying it to the "Feelings." Its power in the hands of a keen and dispassionate observer is indisputable, and the two instructive volumes which contain Mr. Bain's systematic exposition are at once a treasure-house of observations of priceless value, and such a compendious generalization of mental facts of all orders into laws as doubtless marks the climax of the method. But it is fundamentally unscientific. If it be true that the higher forms of life and mind have been evolved out of the lower, then the most resolute introspection, and the most cutting analysis, with the help of stray observations of children, and some patient experimenting on animals, will go no appreciable distance in discovering mental constituents which may have had their origin in an indefinitely remote past. That this is not only a necessary result of the "natural history method," but that it has in point of fact resulted in Mr. Bain's treatise, it may be well to make clear. To keep the analogy in view, we again quote from Dr. Carpenter. The naturalist, he says—

"Endeavours to simplify the pursuit of his science, by the adoption of easily-recognised external characters, as the basis of his classification of the multitudinous forms which he brings together; but such can only be safely employed when indicative of peculiarities in internal structure, which are found to be little subject to variation, and which are not liable to be affected by the influence of physical causes."*

Now such an endeavour to simplify, by the adoption of easily recognised external characters as the basis of his classification, is a feature prominent in the forefront of Mr. Bain's work. The mode of diffusion of an emotion, the institutions it generates, and its peculiarities as a state of consciousness—all of them the most manifest characters of the emotions—are avowedly adopted as bases of classification.† That easily recognised external characters are not always "indicative of peculiarities in internal structure," has been shown by Mr. Spencer, and is indeed a corollary from the theory of development.‡ Mr. Bain's method is there-

* *Op. cit.*, p. 633. † "Emotions and Will," *first* edition.
‡ "Essays" (sec. ser.), p. 125.

fore misleading from its contracted range, but we must here record, as part of our history, its very great advance on the still more incomplete methods of the older psychologists.

Mr. Bain's other contributions to Psychology are connected with the recent development of one of the sciences whose general method he appropriated. The physiology of the nervous system was of late foundation. Vesalius, Fallopius, Vieussens, Boerhaave and Willis, had indeed assigned the special functions of certain organs (as those of the senses) to their appropriate nerves, but even in the middle of the eighteenth century the great Haller could deny the existence of any nerve which did not possess the double function of sensation and motion. Whytt and Prochaska, in 1768 and 1800, made observations on reflex and spontaneous movements, and decisively raised the question of the mode of action of the nervous system. In the first quarter of this century Sir Charles Bell established the existence of two great systems of nerves, with different functions, and thus revealed a definite mental mechanism. A few years later Dr. Marshall Hall (or some one else) discovered the independent action of the spinal cord, and helped further to determine the organic conditions of mental activity. His contemporary, Müller, went so far as to assert that the spinal cord was the centre or source of *all* motor power. At this point Mr. Bain came into the field. Appropriating the discovery of Hall, he was the first among psychologists to attempt systematically to elucidate the spontaneous movements, as no less a part of the phenomena of mind than those of consciousness. Combining Bell's discovery with a hint of Müller, he introduced the first organic modification into the association psychology by his theory of the brain as a fountain of force and not merely the passive instrument of impressions. This theory has led him, not only to take into account the secondary mental states generated by the bodily organs, but to trace genetically the origin and growth of voluntary power, and thus to constitute a separate department of Psychology by the analysis of volition, which had previously been the victim of introspection. It has also led him to devote a section to "constructive association," which could have no place so long as there was recognised in the mind no power of original construction. The tendency to materialize the mental agencies—the assumptions that nerve force is of the nature of a current, that it moves in diffused waves, that associations are generated by shocks—are consequences partly of the introduction of the same new element. They are consequences also of that assumed correlation of the mental and nervous with the physical forces which Mr. Bain has, in his later editions, done much to prove and illustrate.

If Mr. Herbert Spencer had no other titles to fame, he

would still be the greatest of psychologists. The vast constructions of his "First Principles" will ever be a monument of his extraordinary powers of generalization. His designed organization of the Social Science opens up the prospect of intellectual acquisitions in the future to which the past may furnish few parallels. But the "Principles of Psychology" will still remain, in its symmetrical completeness and perfect adequacy to the subject, at once the most remarkable of his achievements and the most scientific treatise on the Mind which has yet seen the light. Its publication in 1855 did not make a sensation. The persistent efforts of Mill had not yet succeeded in stemming the muddy tide of the prevailing scholasticism. The bastard Kantism of Hamilton did duty for metaphysics, and the Common Sense philosophy of Reid, with the common sense left out, usurped the place of Experimental Psychology. Experimental Psychology was, as usual, busy with analysis, and had no eye for the merit of an imposing synthetical effort. Mr. Spencer's work had accordingly a chill reception. Greeted by the aristocratic metaphysicians with a few words of courtly compliment, but treated practically with supercilious disregard, it was received by psychologists of the Association school with hardly more favour than the snarling approval with which a Constitutional Whig views the entry into the Cabinet of a Birmingham Radical. Mr. Spencer was ahead of his generation, and paid the penalty of his prescience in twenty years of neglect. But now the wheel is coming round. The bovine British public, constitutionally disposed indeed to apathy, but drugged into a leaden slumber by its medicine-men, is at last awakening to the fact that the peer of Bacon and Newton is here. Writers of all schools are hastening to define their position with reference to the Synthetic Philosophy. A younger generation has grown up, with minds unhardened by the limitations of obsolete Sensationalism, and inclined rather to a somewhat undisciplined acquiescence in what the Germans call "world-shattering," that are also world-constructing, theories. But whatever part of his philosophy may be transitory, Mr. Spencer's present influence is indisputable; and since the lamented death of Mill, no one can now contest his claims to the philosophic supremacy in these islands.

That supremacy rests mainly on his Psychology. Cosmological speculation has been so long out of date that we are hardly yet able to incorporate his "first principles" as a vital and vitalizing part of our mental acquisitions. Sociological inquiries are just coming into fashion under the dusky auspices of the "savage races;" but the Social Science, though undoubtedly destined to play a great part in the immediate future, still wants an audience, except for sanitary discussions in autumn among peripatetic philanthropists in provincial towns. But Psychology, at least the kind of thing found in Reid with an infusion of Hamilton, has long formed part of the higher education in Scotland; and at one of the English universities the hash of cosmology, metaphysics, logic, and ethics, named Aristotelianism, yields under pressure some small psychology. Besides being, therefore, in whatever rudimentary forms, a pet academical study, much encouraged by philosophically-minded Heads, the science itself is vastly further advanced than any of the mental sciences, its province is tolerably well defined, in the statement, at least, of its main problems the most opposite schools agree, and both likewise agree in the tests to be applied to their solutions. A pretender to psychological discoveries has accordingly a decided advantage over his brother discoverer in the more embryonic mental sciences in so far that, if he is not out of sight ahead of his generation, he can secure a competently instructed audience, eager and, on the whole, capable to decide on his pretensions. The extreme fascination of Mr. Spencer's theories, and doubtless their fundamental truth, have obtained for him a large *clientèle;* and the position of the philosophy of mind as the foundation of all other philosophies, social, ethical, æsthetic, and political, has created channels through which his characteristic ideas have percolated in all directions. Such a supremacy as this could only have been gained, if our history of the parallel development of the physical and mental sciences be exact, by a substantial identity of the method and unity of the principles of the synthetic psychology with those of the last-developed organic and inorganic sciences. We shall see that this is the case.

Mr. Spencer's numerous psychological advances may be grouped in two divisions: the application to mind of the theory of development, and the connexion of psychological evolution with evolution in general. The last edition of his work also incorporates Mr. Darwin's law of natural selection in the explanation of the emotions, but this may be regarded as simply an extension of the development theory. In the working out of both principles, Mr. Spencer has followed the lead of the physical sciences.

Before it could be discovered that species were evolved from one another, it had to be discovered that there were among them fundamental kinships. The foundation of the comparative sciences was the beginning of the movement, and we suppose that Goethe's *Sketch of a Universal Introduction into Comparative Anatomy,* may be regarded as striking the first note. Thirty years further research reduced the skull of all vertebrate animals to a uniform structure, and determined the laws of its variation. In 1820 Audouin partially succeeded in filling up the chasm between insects and other animals. In 1830 Laurencet and Meyraux assimilated the structure of molluscs to that of vertebrates. Out of these discoveries an internecine war arose between the schools of Cuvier and Geoffrey St. Hilaire, the former contending that the structure and functions of animals should be studied in the light of final causes, the latter setting up their analogies as the only safe guide. And out of the struggle came the new philosophy. "*The principle of connexions*," says Whewell, "*the elective affinities of organic elements, the equilibrization of organs*;—such are the designations of the leading doctrines which are unfolded in the preliminary discourse of his [St. Hilaire's] Anatomical Philosophy. Elective affinities of organic elements are the forces by which the vital structures and varied forms of living things are produced; and the principles of connexion and equilibrium of the forces of the various parts of the organization, prescribe limits and conditions to the variety and development of such forms."* Now for the first time we hear such phrases as "unity of plan," and (more significant still), "unity of composition." Then came Von Baer's law of progression of structural development from the general to the special, afterwards extended to functional development, and giving rise to the conception of the specialization of functions. Out of this, too, arose the term "evolution," and though confined to organic development, implied an advance in generalization. The mere mention of such further advances as are implied in the establishment of the functional identity between the contractile tissues of plants and those of the higher animals; in the use of the phrase "psychical powers" to designate the sensorial and mental endowments of animals; in the proof of the absence of specialized sensibility among the lower tribes of animals, and of the hereditary transmission of certain characters required under the influence of *external* circumstances; in the parallel traced between the progressive complication of the psychical manifestations during the early life of a human being, and the gradual increase in mental endowment to be observed in ascending the animal scale†—may serve to indicate the conceptions forming the matrix in which a philosophically constructed Psychology was to be moulded. How great a revolution had taken place in biology, and how far we have now got from the natural history method, may appear from Professor Huxley's definition of "zoological physiology," which,

* "History of Inductive Sciences," iii. 504.

† See Carpenter, "Comp. Physiology," passim.

though made some years after the first publication of the "Principles of Psychology," at least points out the direction in which thought had been moving. He says:—

"It regards animal bodies as machines impelled by certain forces, and performing an amount of work, which can be expressed in terms of the ordinary forces of nature. The final object of physiology is to deduce the facts of morphology, on the one hand, and those of distribution on the other, from the laws of the molecular forces of matter."*

With a prescient insight into the future of science which has probably few parallels, Mr. Spencer founded his Psychology on the hypothesis of development. To all but a few deep-thinking observers there can have seemed few signs in 1855 that that hotly disputed theory was ever likely to be in the ascendant. The exposition of none of the organic sciences that we know of, had yet been based on it, and its application to mind was undreamt of. But with a confidence in the intuitions of reason which is one of the clearest attributes of speculative genius, and which may have its analogue in the statesman in the nerve to take the vessel of the State over a bar, Mr. Spencer assumed the provisional truth of the theory, and it might be difficult to exaggerate the extent to which his exhibition of it in Psychology has contributed to its establishment.

It was first requisite to find a generalization on which to base a synthetic Psychology. The assumption being made that mind and bodily life are but subdivisions of life in general, it was required to seek out some characteristic common to both—some characteristic of vital actions in general, and distinguishing them from non-vital actions. Applying a method which Professor Stanley Jevons has omitted to note in his "Character of the Experimentalist," Mr. Spencer arrives at a definition of life of which the essential point is that it implies a correspondence between life and its circumstances. Here is the first notable advance—the inclusion of the environing world in the definition of the science of mind; and in this is contained the germ of Mr. Spencer's later differentiation of Psychology and circumscription of its province.† If correspondence with the environment is the *differentia* of life, it is almost an identical proposition to assert that the *degree* of life will vary with the completeness of the correspondence and the complexity of the environment. An ascending

* "Lay Sermons," pp. 106-7.

† "Psychology," sec. ed. (1870) vol. i. § 53. Swedenborg's "Law of Correspondences" is not without analogy to Mr. Spencer's original generalization.

synthesis accordingly finds the correspondence at first direct and homogeneous, then direct but heterogeneous, as extending in space and in time, and as increasing in speciality, in generality, and in complexity. Along with the all-sided development thus going on in the correspondences, there goes on a development in the degree in which the organs and functions of the individual are so correlated and united as to respond promptly and effectually to the answering changes in the environment. Contemplating now the correspondences in their totality, it is found that the generalization on which it was proposed to base a synthetic Psychology is established, that manifestations of intelligence are found to consist in the establishment of correspondences between relations in the organism and relations in the environment, and the preliminary assumption that life and mind are fundamentally identical is proved.

Nevertheless, though these two kinds of life are primordially the same, they are in their general aspects widely unlike, and we must inquire whence the differences arise. Instinct, Memory, Reason, Feeling, and Will have specific differences; a science of Psychology which is based on the theory of development must determine whence these arise, and if mind is merely a higher manifestation of life, they must be interpretable as life was interpreted.

Intelligence in general is differenced from life in general by the fact that the order of changes of which it consists are successive. The science of intelligence having thus for its subject-matter a continued series of changes, it is the business of Psychology to determine the law of their succession. Bringing up the "law of correspondences" left in the rear, it is found that one mental state tends to follow another with a strength proportionate to the intimate union between the external things they represent. Here is a "law of association" of Hegelian depth, cutting down to the adamantine pillars of the universe, and compared with which the so-called laws of association are mere empiricism. The law is also of Hegelian content—rivalling that cocoon *das Werden*, and out of it shall be woven all the phenomena of unfolding intelligence. Reflex action we have already seen Mr. Bain incorporate in Psychology; Mr. Spencer shows how it necessarily arises out of developing life. Instinct, too, Mr. Bain prefixes to his analysis of ideas; Mr. Spencer evolves it out of reflex action. With the increasing complexity of experience Memory arises, and Mill's "insoluble problem" is solved. The chapter on Reason is, perhaps, the finest synthetic exposition in the literature of Psychology. Reason, like Memory, is shown to be developed by an insensible transition out of instinct; and Locke is reconciled with Kant by the intervention of that theory of the secular transmission of mental acquisitions which has become so familiar that it is now difficult to appreciate its daring originality. Feeling, like Reason, arises out of instinct; and emotions of the greatest complexity, power, and abstractness are formed out of the simple aggregation of large groups of emotional states into still larger groups through endless past ages. Thus out of the feeble beginnings of life have been woven all the manifestations of mind, up to the highest abstractions of a Hegel and the infinitely complex and voluminous emotions of a Beethoven. Well may a French writer say:—"Si on la rapproche par la pensée des tentatives de Locke et de Condillac sur ce sujet, la genèse sensualiste paraîtra d'une simplicité enfantine."*

Hitherto the psychologist, proceeding objectively, has made no use of consciousness; and it is now necessary, in order to justify the findings of the synthetic method, to examine consciousness in the only possible way—by analysis. Setting out with the highest conceivable display of mind, compound quantitative reasoning, he tracks all the mental phenomena down to that which is *only* a change in consciousness, the establishment of the relation of sequence, and proves that the genesis of intelligence has advanced in the same way as was shown in the synthesis—by the establishment and consolidation of relations of increasing complexity. Thus throughout all the phenomena of mind there exists a unity of composition; and the doctrines of innate ideas, intuitions by gift of God, supernatural revelations, mysticism of all kinds, have the ground cut from under them.

The very great extension of plan which Mr. Spencer's work received between 1855 and 1870-2 was due solely to the creation of his own philosophy of evolution. That in its turn had its initiative in the theory of the correlation of forces advanced by Grove in 1842. As the new philosophy conceived all existence to result from evolution through differentiation and integration, it was incumbent on Mr. Spencer to show that mental phenomena, or at least the physical correlatives of them, can be interpreted in terms of the redistribution of matter and motion, and explained by a series of deductions from the persistence of force. This is the task of a Physical Synthesis, which shows the structure and functions of the nervous system to have resulted from intercourse between the organism and its environment. And thus is laid the coping-stone of a treatise which has definitively constituted Psychology a science.

With the definitive constitution of the science our inquiry, which began with the differentiation of its subject-matter, comes to an end. We have seen mind slowly emancipating itself from

* Ribot, "La Psychologie Anglaise," p. 215.

the barbaric Cosmos, and raised into an independent object of speculation. Once "differentiated' it begins itself to unfold, and at the same time to gather round it the at first alien facts of sensation, appetite, and bodily feeling generally. These are increasingly matter of inquiry, and theories respecting them take the hue and shape of the sciences which relate to the material world. The science of motion evolves, and the idea of orderly sequence enters into Psychology. Natural Philosophy rises from motion to force, and Psychology passes from conjunction to causation. Chemistry tears aside a corner of nature's veil, and a shaft is sunk in a mysterious field of mind. The sciences of organic nature receive a forward impulse, and mind and life are joined in inextricable union. A philosophy of the universe, incorporating all the sciences, is created, and Psychology, while attaining increased independence as regards the adjacent sciences, is merged in that deductive science of the Knowable which has more widely divorced, and yet more intimately united, the laws of matter and of mind.

ART. VII.—THE GREATEST OF THE MINNESINGERS.

1. *Deutsche Classiker des Mittelalters, Mit Wort und Sacher-klärungen.* Begründet von FRANZ PFEIFFER. Erster Band, Walther von der Vogelweide. Leipzig: F. A. Brockhaus. 1870.
2. *Das Leben Walthers von der Vogelweide.* Leipzig: B. G. Trübner. 1865.

IN the history of German literature no period is more interesting, than that short classical epoch at the end of the twelfth century and the beginning of the thirteenth, which gave rise to the literature written in Middle High German. More especially does it attract attention, because within very narrow limits it comprises many and great names, but above all it is remarkable because within these limits it saw the birth and death of a new kind of poetry, a poetry of an entirely different character from that of the old epic poems. They were grand, massive, and objective; the new style was light, airy, plaintive, and subjective. To this style belongs the German Minnesong. The songs of three hundred Minnesingers are preserved all belonging to this short period. In their themes there is not much variety. The changes of the seasons, and the changes of a lover's mood do not in fact present a wide range of subjects to the lyric poet. And most of the Minnesongs are confined to these. But the following simile seems true. If any one enters a wood in summer time, and listens to the voices of innumerable birds, he hears at first only a confused mixture of strains. In time, however, he distinguishes now a petulant cry, now a deep bell-like reiterated note, and now the unbroken song of some joyous chorister. Finally he recognises the individual character of each strain, the music runs clearly in ordered threads,

> "E come in voce voce si discerne
> Quando una e ferme e l'altra va e riede."

And the Minnesong of this period exhibits a phenomenon not dissimilar from that described. The subjects and the songs themselves are likely at first to seem monotonous. Lamentations at winter, the russet woodlands, and ashen grey landscapes, no less than the joyous welcomes to spring, are repeated over and over again. But notwithstanding this, the German Minnesong, as the rich and peculiar growth of an extraordinary literature, is worthy of attention. As in the former instance so now in this forest of song, the listener soon discovers that some notes are clearer and more solemn than others, and that in them he may follow a music well worthy the hearing.

The Minnesong is entirely distinct from the lyrics of the Provençal Troubadours. A feminine character has been attributed to it, and a masculine character to the songs of the South. To a certain extent this description expresses the difference between them, but it does so only partially. The Minnesong is certainly more reticent and coy. It sighs deeply, it smiles and blushes; it seldom laughs aloud. It is pervaded by an innocent shame. But it is bold and brave too. It has a scornful contempt for danger, a profound belief in honour and virtue, and an unutterable longing for love and beauty.

This is how the Minnesong came to be born. When Conrad III. led his people to the Holy Land, Louis VII. of France brought to the same place his French hosts. There, amidst the magnificence of the East, the German knights and soldiers listened to the songs of the troubadours who accompanied the French armies. The "gay science," as the troubadours named their art, was then in its bloom. The soldiers of Conrad were enchanted with the soft melodies and musical rhymes; they could not forget the rich colours and gallant romances of the Southern singers when they went back to the North. They felt indeed that such poetry was not for them. It had not the deep sentiment, and that inner soul of song which their sterner natures required. But the Minnesong sprang from this contact of Teuton and Celt under Eastern skies.

The greatest of the Minnesingers was Walther von der Vogelweide, with whose life and poems it is proposed to deal briefly in this paper. And as his works cannot be understood without reference to the events of his life, and as those events were controlled by the wider movements of political affairs, it will be necessary to speak in some detail of the circumstances which mark the decadence and follow the fall of the illustrious Hohenstaufen dynasty.*

The place and date of Walther's birth have been matters of dispute. The former may now be considered as settled, the second difficulty can only be approximately solved. For while we are thrown back to Walther's poems for most of our information in reference to the events of his life, those poems are by no means autobiographical, and it is only partially that we can construct a connected history of the poet's life.

Quite as many countries have contended for the honour of being Walther's birthplace as strove to enrol Homer amongst their citizens. Switzerland, Suabia, the Rhineland, Bavaria, Bohemia, Austria, the Tyrol and others have claimed him. There is scarcely a district of Germany that has not sought the honour of being connected with him. All this, however, is a point of minor interest in the face of his own words—*Ze Osterriche lernt ich singen und sagen.* But as a matter of fact the question has been recently set at rest by the discovery, in the Royal Library at Vienna, of a MS., which shows the revenue of the Count of Tyrol towards the end of the 13th century. Amongst the returns therein recorded is found the yearly sum paid by the Vogelweide estate, namely, three pounds. This entry is between those of Mittelwald and Schellenberch,

* The first edition of Walther's poems, founded upon the Paris MS., was that by Bodmer and Breitinger, published at Zürich in 1758. In 1838 Von der Hagen sent out a second edition. It was of little value. The first really critical edition was that of Carl Lachman. Wackernagel's edition of 1862 was also good. Pfeiffer's edition of 1864 is perhaps, upon the whole, the best. Its speciality is the excellent commentary which accompanies it, but it is admirable from every point of view. It is the first edition which has laid the treasures of Walther's poetry open to the ordinary German reader. The introduction is good, and the prefatory remarks to each poem are well and judiciously written. It is provided with explanatory notes, and the glossaries and index are models of arrangement. Middle High German has been so long the monopoly of a few students that it is desirable it should be known that, with a fair knowledge of German, a moderate acquaintance with some good Middle High German grammar, and Herr Pfeiffer's book, Walther von der Vogelweide is easily accessible to all who are interested in Minne song. There has sprung up rapidly in the last few years a whole body of literature around the name of Walther von der Vogelweide. Uhland's book is perhaps the most widely known: Pfeiffer uses it freely. The best and completest life of the poet is that by Dr. Menzel. The book is complete and instructive, but fails to be popularly interesting through abundance of minute historical details. Where Menzel and Pfeiffer differ, the preference has been given in this paper to Pfeiffer's theories. All the references are to Pfeiffer's edition.

places ten miles apart upon the Eisach. The exact site of the poet's house cannot be pointed out, but a wood divided into two parts still bears, according to investigations made in the winter of 1863, the double name of Upper and Lower Vogelweide. Of all the places previously suggested, this alone corresponds with the indications which the poet gives of his early home.

There is nothing to fix the exact date of his birth; a consideration of his poems leads Dr. Menzel to place it earlier than 1168 by, perhaps, ten or twelve years. His life thus comprises the period of at least sixty years, for we find him in 1228 a bowed and venerable pilgrim from the Holy Land, ready to lay his head in its last resting-place. These sixty years were filled by important events not uninfluenced by the poet.

It is probable that he belonged to the lower ranks of the nobility. The name of his family and the land-tax which they paid prevent us from ranking them with the great families of the time. Probably, too, his childhood was passed amongst the bowery solitudes of the Tyrol, where a free and happy boyhood, which he never forgot, grew amid the songs of birds and the music of waters into a manhood no less musical and free.

Somewhere between the years 1171 and 1183 Walther left his home for the ducal Court at Vienna. It was then a general practice for the younger sons of noble families to seek education by such means as this, and the renown which the Court of Vienna acquired for the splendour of its pageants and the patronage which it bestowed upon music and poetry, made it peculiarly attractive to a youth whose imagination had already been awakened. And no eager dreams which Walther had dreamed in the woods of Tyrol were to be rudely banished when he reached the ducal Court. The star of the German empire never shone brighter than it did at that time. Then it was that the old Barbarossa finished his Italian wars. The Church was developing her powers. Chivalry had reached its highest point and had not begun to decline, and over all Europe swept that inspiring breeze which hurried away warriors and priests to do pious duty in the Holy Land. Everywhere there was a keen atmosphere of new and large ideas. The contact with the East, even at that time, lent more of magnificence to the national pomp, and the great festival which Frederick celebrated in Mayence, at Whitsuntide of the year 1184, stands out still as the greatest national festival which Germany has celebrated. All the spiritual and temporal lords of Germany were present. Princes from far lands, from Italy, France, Illyria, and Sclavonia assembled with innumerable followers. And it is no wonder if the centre figure of such an assembly kindled then an enthusiasm over all the Empire which has never since been extinguished, however hidden the sparks have lain. For, as a contemporary averred, "The flower of chivalry, the strength of dominion, the greatness of the nation, and the glory of the empire were united in his single majestic person." With these great events the Court of Vienna was closely connected. The Duke Leopold VI. took the most active interest in the policy of the Hohenstaufen dynasty, and was a conspicuous sharer in the Mayence pageant. Nor was his own Court behind any other of that time in such knightly display. With Leopold's two sons, the young and promising princes, Frederick and Leopold, Walther was, as we may divine from later poems, upon terms of intimacy and affection, which, at least in the case of Frederick, never suffered change.

But if the stirring spirit of the times did much to give the poet a love for magnificent energy, the Court at which he resided furnished him with modes of culture which scarcely another could. Whatever was graceful and chivalric in life flourished here, and here the Minnesong was oftenest sung. The master poet of this early time was Reinmar, the "nightingale of Hagenau," as they delighted to call him, and in him Walther found the best model for his poems. But it was only for the lighter poems that Reinmar could serve as a model. Walther's earnest political lays belong to the sphere of poetry, which Reinmar's flight never reached. Yet the education which Walther derived from his residence at the Court was gained by no system of learned instruction, nor at that time (any more than at present) did courtly culture deem learning requisite. Life, action, the free circulation of ideas, and a readiness to receive them were the means of instruction, by using which Walther acquired the deep knowledge of mankind, and the perfect command over artistic material which are exhibited in his poems.

Leopold died in 1194, and was succeeded in Austria by his son Frederick the Catholic, a youth twenty years of age. For four years Walther enjoyed under his patronage all that a poet and a patriot could desire, for the Empire was yet in its splendour, which seemed to wax rather than to wane. But this splendour was to meet with a speedy and long-lasting eclipse; and never again do we find in the poems of Walther the bright and careless happiness with which they open. Henry VI. the successor to Barbarossa, succeeded likewise to that idea of the Empire, which filled the mind of Frederick. He swayed an Empire greater than any since the time of Charlemagne, and possessed qualities which rendered him likely to sway one yet greater. Regarding himself as the heir of the old Cæsars, he deemed his Empire incomplete until all that belonged to them should own him as its liege lord. Once more the East should be won back to the West and far-away kings hold their power only as vassals to the Kaiser. To follow out this idea, and advance his power in the East he announced a crusade. All preparations had been made, part of the Eastern countries had acknowledged his authority, and much more was about to yield, when suddenly, on the 25th of September, 1197, at Messina, Henry died. With him died too the splendour of the German Empire; but it was to this, as it sank lower and lower, that Walther continually turned his gaze, and it is this which colours his political poems, and gives them their significance in the eyes of his countrymen. Yet it was not only the destruction of so much glory that caused the change in the tone of Walther's song. With the national catastrophe his own fall at the Court of Vienna was nearly contemporaneous. The exact cause of the Prince's disfavour is uncertain, but with the departure of Frederick the Catholic, on Henry's crusade, Leopold, who was Regent, began to withdraw the Court patronage from Walther, and at Frederick's death in 1198, Walther found himself compelled to leave Vienna.

And here it will be well, before we follow him out into the dark and troublous times which follow, to refer to those poems which are associated with this period of his life—associated with it, though it is impossible to assert with certainty that all the songs of "*Minnedienst*" which we still have were composed before he left Vienna.

Walther's poems fall into two divisions. They are either Minnesongs, such as court-singers of the time were wont to sing, differing only in degree of excellence from contemporary lays, or they are poems of an earnest, religious, and political tendency. Of these latter we shall presently see something. But certainly the greater part of the former class belong to the Vienna period. All the fairest and freshest of these were written before the trouble came, and possess that charm of conscious happiness which does not recur. And although, from the nature of the poems, it is not possible to refer them to a fixed date, a process of growth and development is to be traced in them. In Walther's youth court-poetry had not as yet crystallized into those rigid forms in which development ceases. Nor was the first inspiration of a young poet's fancy likely to exhibit itself in the mould of artificial excellence, at least as long as that freedom from care, which external circumstances guaranteed, favoured a spontaneous and happy production of works of art. For this reason Menzel, unlike Pfeiffer, is inclined to place many of the "Lieder" in a later period. He is inclined to think that Walther did not submit to conventional trammels until the necessity of finding an audience and patrons became dominant. Be this as it may, the songs of the early period are undoubtedly pleasing, and amongst them may be reckoned the exquisite lyrics :—

"Under der linden, an der heide,"

and

"Sô die bluomen ûz dem grase dringent."

We have altogether about eighty of Walther's "*Lieder*," but probably many of the earliest are lost. With those that remain, some German critics (as was to be expected) have endeavoured to build up a consistent history of Walther's youth. Little success, however, has attended the attempt, and the best critics dismiss the autobiographical theory altogether. Nor is it necessary to literary enjoyment that the theory should be established; it is better to regard these exquisite poems as blossoms of a happy period. If indeed we think of him as the laureate of a dazzling and polite Court, the friend and favourite of a prince only a little younger than himself, amidst the circumstances of an Empire whose highest glory did not yet seem to have been reached, in enjoyment of a reputation that was ever growing, we shall be more prepared to understand the change that came over the spirit of his verse when the Empire was racked by internal dissension, and he himself was sent from the light and kindliness of a Court into the uncertainty of a wandering life.

The condition of the Empire was now such that it might well leave him in doubt where he should find a home. The rightful heir to the Imperial throne, Frederich the Second, was a child three years of age. Besides him Henry had left two brothers, Otto of Burgundy and Philip of Suabia. Henry's death set free all those elements of disorder which his iron hand had kept in subjection. The Pope would not recognise the claims of Frederick, and Otto and Philip became competitors for the crown. Philip was indeed willing to act as regent for the child, but the partisans of the Hohenstaufen dynasty were cold in their interest for Frederick, and desired to see Philip himself Emperor. Meanwhile confusion was universal, the Empire was wasted in a destructive war, its wealth squandered, and its power broken. The Court of Vienna took the side of Philip, and Walther became his poet-champion. It was now that he commenced those poems or "*Sprüche*" which were the first of their kind, and which, repeated from mouth to mouth, exercised considerable influence upon events. In the Paris manuscript of his works there is a picture of the poet musing upon the disorder of the times. He is represented as a bearded man in the prime of life; a cap covers his curly hair; he wears a rich blue cloak and a red coat, and looks pensively to the ground, whilst in his right hand he holds a scroll of his poems, which winds upwards between the escutcheon and crested helm of Vogelweide. And in somewhat similar attitude the first "*Spruch*" represents him.

"I sat upon a stone and mused, one leg thrown over the other; my elbow rested upon my knee, and upon my hand I leant my head, cheek, and chin. There I mused with much despair what profit it were to live now in the world. I saw no way by which a man might win three things that are good. Two of them are Honour and Wealth, which often injure each other. The third is God's Favour, which is more excellent than the two. Would that I might bring these into one life. But, alas! it may not be that Wealth and Honour and God's Favour should ever come to one heart again; the ways and paths are closed against them. Untruth lies in ambush; Might rules in the highways, and Peace and Justice are wounded sore. So the Three can come no more till the Two are healed" (p. 81).

To Walther, the only method of healing the wounds of Peace and Justice seemed to be in electing Philip king. In him he recognised a man strong enough and good enough to stay the disorders of Germany. And his song gave no uncertain sound. He says:—

"The wild beast and the reptile, these fight many a deadly fight. Likewise, too, the birds amongst themselves. Yet these would hold themselves of no esteem had they not one common rule. They make strong laws, they choose a king and a code, they appoint lords and lieges. So woe to you, ye of the German tongue; how fares order in your land? when now the very flies have their queen, and your honour perishes! Turn ye, turn ye. The Coronets grow your masters, the petty kings oppress you. Let Philip wear the Orphan-diadem, and bid the princes begone" (pp. 81-2).

The "petty kings" are the other competitors for the crown. The "orphan" is a jewel in the crown of the Roman emperors. Albertus Magnus, according to Menzel, says of it:—"Orphanus est lapis, qui in corona Romani imperatoris est, neque unquam alibi visus; propter quod etiam orphanus vocatur." Philip's chief competitor seemed to be Berthold, of Zuringen, and he had on his side Adolphus, the Archbishop of Cologne; but as Berthold did not prove an open-handed candidate, Adolphus entered into negotiations with Richard of England, and (after being well paid for his trouble), consented to crown Richard's nephew, Otto of Poitou, on the 12th of July, 1198. Previously to this, Otto had taken Aix-la-Chapelle, which had refused to recognise him, and Philip seeing that there was now no time to be lost, was crowned in the following September, at Mayence, by the Archbishop of Treves. This coronation, subsequently deemed insufficient, was performed with great splendour, and gave hopes to the Hohenstaufen dynasty of once more beholding an united empire.

The diadem of Charlemagne wherein glittered the peerless "orphan" was placed upon Philip's head, and amongst those who swelled the train of the young King and his wife Irene was Walther. The crown, said Walther, seemed made for him.

"Older though it be than the king, yet never smith wrought crown to fit so well. And his imperial head no less becomes the diadem, and none may part the twain. Each lights the other. The crown is brighter by its sweet young wearer, for the jewels gladly shine upon the true prince. Ah! if any one doubts now to whom the Empire belongs of right, let him but see if the 'Orphan' so shines upon another brow. This jewel is a star that finds the true prince."

Walther's enthusiasm for the "sweet young" king seems justified by contemporary evidence. An old chronicle says with quaint Latinity :—"Erat Phillippus animo lenis, mente mitis, erga homines benignus, debilis quidem corpore, sed satis virilis in quantum confidere poterat de viribus suorum, facie venusta et decora, capillo flavo, statura mediocri, magis tenui quam grossa."

We have, however, now two emperors on the stage. The Chronicle has described Philip: Otto presented a complete contrast to the gentle brother of Henry. Nearly the same age as his rival, he was a man of lofty and commanding stature and resembled both in person and character his uncle Richard. His bravery was rash and impetuous, and his unyielding severity alienated more hearts than his courage could retain. The literary tastes of the two Emperors exhibited a contrast no less striking than that presented by their persons. Otto listened with pleasure to the masculine strains of the Troubadours. Philip heard with delight the soft complaining rhymes of the Minnesingers. It was by these rhymes that Walther won the favour of Philip and found admission to his court. But there was need of something else to be done than to listen to the strains of troubadour or minnesinger, before either of the rival Emperors could deem his empire safe. Philip had the wider support, and Otto, perhaps, the more valuable foreign assistance. Philip had on his side all South Germany, Bohemia, and Saxony. He was supported, moreover, by many Episcopal princes both in the south and in the north. Abroad France was his ally. The centre of Otto's power was Cologne, then the chief town of Germany, and though his kingdom was more contracted than that of Philip, the inequality was rendered less dangerous by the efficient help which his uncle Richard of England was ready to supply. Thus all Europe was divided into two parts awaiting the decision of its destiny. This seemed to hang upon the word a power which had not yet spoken—the Papacy.

Now Walther saw clearly enough, nor yet more clearly than the Pope himself, that whatever dissensions arose between native princes, the real antagonistic power to the German Empire was the papal supremacy. For a man now sat upon the papal chair whose ambition was even more imperial than that of Henry VI., and who possessed an energy of character and a subtle power of statecraft that seemed likely to bring his designs into effect. Innocent III. had inherited the ambition and the ideas of Gregory VII. With him he looked upon the Pope as the rightful source of all power, as above all kings, emperors and princes, who received from him their unction and their virtue, and who held their possessions as vassals of the Bishop of Rome. This notion he caused to prevail in Italy, and there the papal power regained all it had lost. The two candidates for the Empire he contrived for some time to keep without a decisive answer, by means of evasions and deceptions as unscrupulous as they were diplomatic. Yet he left no doubt in the minds of Otto's friends that he preferred the candidature of their monarch, though it may have escaped their notice that his chief object was the dissolution of the Empire, which had stood so firmly under the dynasty to which Philip belonged. It did not escape the notice of Walther, and he set himself to work against the papal machinations with that patriotic and impassioned enthusiasm with which his love for the German Empire had inspired him. The Pope seemed to him the incarnation of the anti-national spirit, and only that king to be worthy of the name who strove once more to realize the imperial ideal which had animated Germany under Barbarossa and Henry. Such a monarch he thought at this time he recognised in Philip. And since Philip, after his coronation, had met with some successes in the field, and his rival had been deprived of his chief support by the death of Richard, it was not unnatural that he should look upon the festival which Philip held, Christmas, 1199, as the dawn of a better era. The dawn of a better era, however, it was not, in spite of Walther's joyous song. The war which Philip was now waging did not advance his cause, and once more we find Walther at Vienna, reconciled to Leopold, perhaps, through the intervention of Philip, or, perhaps, with some political commission to the Duke. Meanwhile (1201) Otto advanced as far as Alsace, and Philip invaded the district of Cologne, when the long delayed decision of the Pope fell like a thunderbolt. Otto was declared Emperor by the title of Otto IV., and Philip, with his followers, was excommunicated. But though this bull caused more anger than terror amongst the partisans of Philip, its practical consequences were serious. Many supporters fell away, and Walther gave utterance to his grief in a poem which deprecates the use of religious weapons for political purposes.

"I saw," he says, "with mine eyes the secrets of the hearts of men and women. I heard and saw what each one says and does. At Rome I found a Pope lying, and two kings (Philip and Frederick) deceived. Then arose the greatest strife that has been or shall be. The priests and the people began to take opposite sides, a grief beyond all griefs. The priests laid down their swords and fought with their stoles. They laid the bann on whom they would and not on whom they should, and the Houses of God were desolate" (pp. 61-3).

In March, of this year, those of Philip's party who were faithful, renewed their oath of allegiance, and a formal protest against the Pope's decision was sent to Rome. The Pope received it with consideration but firmness, and fresh successes followed the arms of Otto. Philip sought to strengthen his connexion with France, by an embassy, to which Walther was attached. As we are at present more interested in Walther than in the history of events, it will be well to mention a conjecture of some critics, that it was upon his return from this journey that he wrote his celebrated song (39) in praise of German ladies:—

I.

"Ye should bid me welcome, ladies,
He who brings a message, that am I.

All that ye have heard before this,
Is an empty wind, now ask of me.

But ye must reward me.
If my wage is kindly,
Something I can tell you that will please;
See now what reward ye offer.

II.

"I will tell to German maidens
Such a message that they all the more

Shall delight the universe,
And will take no great payment therefor.

What would I for payment?
They are all so dear,
That my prayer is lowly, and I ask no more
Than that they greet me kindly.

III.

"I have seen many lands,
And saw the best with interest.

Ill must it befall me
  Could I ever bring my heart

To take pleasure
In foreign manners.
Now what avails me if I strive for falsehood?
German truth surpasses all.

IV.

"From the Elbe to the Rhine,
  And back again to Hungary,

These are the best lands
  Which I have seen in the world.

This I can truly swear,
That, for fair mien and person,
So help me heaven, to look upon,
Our ladies are fairer than other ladies."

Philip's supporters continued to fall away and to swell the ranks of Otto; his ecclesiastical adherents, terrified by the fulminations of the Pope, were amongst the earliest deserters. Indeed, at one time it seemed likely that the whole party would be broken up, but the judicious concessions which Philip made to the Pope turned the current, and Philip's cause was strengthened by the accession of the Bishop of Cologne, who, perhaps, found Otto ungenerous. At any rate he was now willing (upon the receipt of pecuniary remuneration) to crown Philip and his wife. This second coronation took place in 1205. We have no poem by Walther in reference to it. In fact, he was losing faith in Philip. The Emperor of Germany should have been a man firm in will and ready in deed. Philip was not realizing this ideal. A second coronation was in itself a confession of weakness. Lachmann imagines that there had even been a personal quarrel between the king and the poet, but the ground for such a belief seems hard to find. In 1208 Philip was assassinated, and Otto was now universally recognised as Emperor.

Without doubt Walther had been much disappointed in Philip. He had grown up under Barbarossa and Henry, and the magnificent ideas of the Empire had grown strong with his growth. Those brilliant anticipations of supreme dominion in German hands he expected to see fulfilled by Philip, and they had not been fulfilled. On the contrary, the papal power, which he detested, was leaving everywhere a contracted sphere for another Empire, and, when a year before his death Philip became, as a matter of political necessity, reconciled to Innocent,

Walther, whose ideal monarch was no king, but an emperor, saw with a despair which is reflected in his poems, the dissolution of his hopes.

From 1204 to 1207 Walther resided at the Thuringian Court. This is to be gathered from certain indications in his poems, and from a consideration of the history of events. Until 1204 Hermann the Landgrave had been on Otto's, and Walther upon Philip's side. The poet's residence at the Landgrave's Court could not, therefore, have belonged to an earlier period. The exact length of its duration is uncertain: it was probably three years. And had Walther been able to see the Empire in a prosperous state, his days might have been as bright under the "gentle Landgrave" as they had been at the Court of Vienna. The Landgrave was not only gentle but generous. His Court was a regular caravansary of warriors and minstrels. "Day and night," says Walther, "there is ever one troop coming in, and another going out. Let no one who has an earache come hither, for the din will assuredly drive him wild." The Landgrave's hospitality was, indeed, unbounded. "If a measure of good wine cost a thousand pounds no knight's beaker would be empty" (p. 99). And later too, upon another occasion, Walther sings of his host, that he does not change like the moon, but that his generosity is continuous. When trouble comes, he remains still a support. "The flower of the Thuringians blossoms through the snow" (p. 109).

About the year 1207 Walther found it necessary to leave the Court. He had not been without enemies there, especially amongst those of his own craft. Hermann was not to blame for this, nor did Walther lose his favour; for later on we find him again at the Thuringian Court. There seems to have been two parties amongst the Minnesingers, and Walther was in the minority. For the next two years Vienna was again his home, and Leopold forgot or forgave the old quarrel that had been between them. But he did not long remain here, and his life until 1211 was unsettled, and was spent at various Courts. But it will be necessary to bring down the history of the nation to this period, for several great and important events had occurred.

The death of Philip was followed by an interval, in which lawlessness and crime prevailed throughout the country. Pillage and incendiarism desolated the inheritance of the Hohenstaufens, and recalled to the recollection of the superstitious the comets and eclipses which had appalled them during the previous year. Many persons thought that the last day was approaching, and Walther found the signs in the heavens corroborated by the unnatural wickedness of man. "The sun," he says, "has withheld his light. Falsehood has everywhere scattered her seeds along the way. The father finds treachery in his child; brother lies to brother. The hooded priest, who should lead us to heaven, has turned traitor." It was indeed a dark time for Germany, nor did it at first appear from what quarter amendment should come. The real representative of the Hohenstaufen line was the young Frederick, who was now fourteen years old, but this was no time for a boy-emperor. Many of those who might have protected his interests had already joined the party of Otto, a party that openly took the supremacy when Otto declared his intention of espousing Beatrice, the daughter of Philip, and the storm of party passion for awhile abated. The interests of the Empire, too, clearly pointed to Otto as Emperor. Walther saw this, for Otto was by no means a man who would not follow up the advantages which his position gave him. Personally the poet could feel little cordiality towards the new monarch, whose patronage of song would little benefit the Minnesingers. And when Otto received the imperial crown from the hands of the Pope, in Rome, it was accompanied by no strain of triumph from Walther. This coronation was in the autumn of 1209. But Otto, instead of leaving Italy to its ghostly monarch, remained there for a year, in which time he restored the imperial authority in Northern and Central Italy, and then marched into Southern Italy. One result of this policy was inevitable. He was excommunicated by the Pope, who now put forward the young Frederick, as king in his stead. Then first, when Otto was under the Papal bann, did Walther step forward as his fellow combatant for the idea of the Empire. As reconciliation with the Pope had estranged him from Philip, so now it was a variance from the same authority that was to place him upon close terms of sympathy with Otto. And for the next two years we find Walther at the height of his political influence.

The Pope, not contented with the declaration of excommunication, set in motion other measures for Otto's destruction. Once more he fanned the subsiding embers of civil discord in Germany. At the Pope's call the Archbishops of Mayence and Magdeburg, the King of Bohemia, the Margrave of Meissen, and the Landgrave of Thuringia, formed a confederation, whose object was the deposition of Otto, and the elevation of Frederick to the throne. This confederation was accomplished in the autumn of 1211, and was joined by the Archbishop of Treves, and the Dukes of Bavaria and Austria. In February of the following year Otto returned from his victorious campaign in Italy once more to German soil, and held a parliament at Frankfort.

In the political complications which followed these circumstances, we find Walther an influential diplomatist, for it was undoubtedly through his influence that the two princes of

Meissen and Bavaria returned to their allegiance to Otto; and the princes themselves thanked him for his services upon that occasion. Further: through his negotiations the crown of Bohemia was given to the Margrave's nephew, and to the Duke's son as consort the daughter of the Count Palatine, by which union the Palatinate afterwards passed into the ducal family. These important negotiations, and the results which attended them, give us an adequate notion of Walther's position at this crisis. The time came when he found the Margrave forgetful (as even monarchs may be) of former services, but he could still refer with conscious dignity to the benefits he had conferred upon the Margrave's family: "Why should I spare the truth?" he asks, "for had I crowned the Margrave himself the crown had even yet been his" (p. 157).

But Otto had still important enemies. Amongst them was the Landgrave of Thuringia. Whilst engaged in operations against him he heard of the approach of Frederick, who with a gathering retinue of supporters was gradually winning the whole of the Rhineland and North Germany. In 1213 Frederick ratified his submission to the Pope, and resigned all German pretensions to the disputed territory in Italy. Thus for awhile we have the curious spectacle of a Guelph fighting for that Imperial idea which should have been the heirloom of the Hohenstaufens, and a Hohenstaufen carrying the banner of the Papacy.

Whilst thus the power of Frederick was increasing, and the followers of Otto were falling away, Walther struggled both as poet and politician against the Pope, and the corrupt use of ecclesiastical power for political purposes. That he himself respected the office of the clergy, and that his own religious convictions were deep-seated, is certain. He viewed, however, with aversion the struggle of the Papacy for temporal power, and the humiliation of the German national spirit. In a struggle of this kind he seemed to see the decay of faith, and the imminent ruin of the Church herself, and his language to the Pope was outspoken from the first. He bade him remember that he himself had crowned and blessed the Emperor (p. 131); he reminded the people that the same mouth which had pronounced the bann had declared the blessing (p. 132); and he referred the Pope to the scriptural command, that he should render unto Cæsar the things that are Cæsar's (p. 133). The corruption of the clergy he rebuked almost with the fire which afterwards was to belong to Luther.

"Christendom," he says, "never lived so carelessly as now. Those who should teach are evil-minded. Even silly laymen would not commit their crimes. They sin without fear, and are at enmity with

God. They point us to heaven and themselves go down to hell. They bid us follow their advice, and not their example."

Again :—

"The Pope our father goes before us, and we wander not at all from his way. Is he avaricious? So are we all with him. Does he lie? We all lie, too. Is he a traitor? We all follow the example of his treachery."

And then he calls him a modern Judas. He accuses him of simony, and hints at his collusion with infernal powers. Against the Pope's attempt to collect tithes in Germany he spoke out strongly, and not without effect, for his poem on this subject (116) aroused much bitterness.

Yet even in Otto, the Pope's enemy, Walther did not find an Emperor like those whose names he loved. His star waned before that of Frederick. His manners were marred by an unroyal boorishness; his Court was the scene of drunken and disorderly revels, and the flower of poetry no longer blossomed in its ungracious precincts. In 1214 Walther joined the party of Frederick. With this new allegiance closes the dependent period of Walther's life, for Frederick presented him with a small estate, which he enjoyed until his death. His first feeling was one of intense delight, and he celebrated the event in a strain of fervent gratitude (150). However, in the interval stretching from 1217 to 1220 he does not appear to have resided there. Probably he did not find it so valuable as he at first imagined it to be, when he sang his pæan as a landholder. There were ecclesiastical claims upon it, and he was in no mood to satisfy them with equanimity. At any rate he determined, after the residence of a year or two, to betake himself to the Court of Vienna. It was no longer that brilliant home of poets and fair women which it had once been. The Duke Leopold was absent in the Holy Land: his two youthful sons were in need of an instructor and guardian, and it is probable that until the return of their father Walther undertook their instruction. In 1219 Walther greeted the Duke with an ode of welcome (152), and this is followed by a sarcastic poem (120) directed against the miserly habits of the Austrian nobility. This poem may perhaps indicate the reason why Walther left the Court of Vienna, but all reasoning here rests upon conjecture. A quarrel between himself and Leopold has been surmised, but upon insufficient grounds. Then, in 1220, we find him at the Court of Frederick II. His political muse had been silent since his adoption of Frederick's cause: his vehement protestations against the papal influence were hushed: he aided in no agitation for the imperial cause. This silence was probably in accordance with Frederick's wishes. Honorius III. was now upon the Papal throne, a man of a different disposition from that of Innocent.

Four important subjects were still matters of consideration between the Papal and Imperial Courts:—Firstly, the separation of the Italian and German crowns; secondly, the supremacy of Lombardy; thirdly, the succession to Matilda; and fourthly, the fulfilment of Frederick's promise to enter upon a crusade. And so long as no open breach had been made in the friendship of Pope and Emperor, and whilst Frederick was furthering his views more by policy than war, there was no room for the efforts of Walther. From this time, however, till 1228 we find several political odes dictated by his sympathy with Frederick. After this period he returned to his own estate, and henceforth his mind seems to have been occupied with religious ideas and the support of the Crusaders. He did not cease to urge the German princes to that holy undertaking. Frederick had, long before, promised Innocent that he himself would lead an army to the East; he had delayed to do so during the life of Honorius; he was punished for his delay with excommunication by Gregory IX., and set out upon the crusade in 1228. Amongst his followers was Walther the Minnesinger.

For it is clear that the bright dream of a restored Empire, which once filled the poet's mind, had now given place to another feeling. Fainter and fainter the hope had grown which inspired so many of his songs. Barbarossa could not come again, at least not now, and there was no comfort remaining, except in religion. An overwhelming longing for the Holy Land seized him. The last winter a terrible storm had swept over the country. What else could it denote than the anger of God at the negligence of Christians who left the Infidel in undisturbed possession of his Holy City? The bands of pilgrims who passed through town and village did not fail to warn those who lingered that they were incurring the divine wrath. Terror and enthusiasm took possession of all, and Walther, old and worn as he was, left once more his home and his repose. His steps were turned towards the Alps. He travelled through the Bavarian Oberland, and the Inn Valley, until he came to the Brenner Pass. There at the foot of the hills lay the place of his birth, a place which he had not visited since his boyhood. And here he wrote the renowned poem (188) which touchingly and truthfully depicts his feelings:—

"Ay me! Whither are vanished all my years? Has my life been indeed a dream, or is it all true? Was that aught whereof I believed it was something? Nay, I have slept and knew it not.

"Now I have awakened, and no longer know that which of old was as familiar to me as mine own hand. People and land where I grew up from a child, these are become strange to me, as though what is past had never been.

"They who were playmates of mine are feeble and old; that which was wild land is planted and trained; the woods are felled. Only the rivulet flows as it flowed of old; otherwise my sorrow were fulfilled.

"I scarce win a greeting from those who once knew me well; the World has become ungracious. Of old I had here many a happy day; all has fallen away like the print of a stone on the waters, alas! for evermore.

"Ay me! there is a poison in all sweetness. I see the gall above the honey. Outwardly the World is fair hued, white and green, inwardly she is black and dark, and coloured with the colour of death.

"Yet if she has misled any one, let him take this to heart, for he may with slight service be free from great sin. Look to it, knights; this touches you. Bear the light helm and the ring-linked panoply of arms;

"Also the strong shield, and consecrated sword. Would God that I, too, were worthy to join in the Crusade. Then should I, for all my poverty, become most rich, though not in land nor lordly gold;

"But I should wear that eternal crown, which the simple soldier may win by his own spear. Could I but fare that happy journey oversea, then would my song be 'Joy!' and never more 'Ay me!' nor ever more 'Alas!'"

If Walther sang joyous songs after his return from the Crusade, these songs are no longer to be found. We cannot doubt, as has been doubted, that he accompanied the expedition to the Holy City. Two devotional poems (78, 79) remain, which were probably written later, but they are not songs of triumph. His voice does not reach us any more; only the grave at Würzburg gives further indications of his fate. For he died, as they say, in 1229, at the age of seventy-two.

Yet another pleasing memorial. In his will the poet left a sum of money to provide seed which the birds might gather every day upon his grave. And four holes for water (still to be seen) were scooped in the stone that covered him. The birds no longer derive any benefit from his legacy, it is commuted into a dole which upon his birthday is given to the choristers of the Church.

It has already been indicated that Walther's poems fall into two divisions, "Lieder" (*songs*) and "Sprüche" (*poems.*) These are different both in form and purpose. A *Lied* was intended to be sung to a musical accompaniment; a *Spruch* was to be read or recited. The form of a *Lied* was artistic and severe, that of a *Spruch* admitted of anomalies. Their subjects were also different. The *Lied* chanted a lover's hopes and fears, welcomed the Spring and Summer, bemoaned the Winter, or a lady's coldness; the *Spruch* dealt with ethical situations, or, as is mostly the case in Walther's poems, expressed strong political convictions. A *Minnelied* was a complex work of art. It comprised three elements, which may be named, after the German analysis, the tone, the time, and the text. The tone was the rhythmical form or metre into which it was thrown; the tune was the melody to which it was sung; the text was the verbal wording of the poem. A Minnesinger must, therefore, be artist, musician, and poet. Of the three elements the tone was almost the most important, for it was no traditional lyric form, but in each case the invention of the individual poet. No poet could creditably appropriate another's metre, nor could any poet repeat without danger to his reputation the same tone upon several occasions. Hence the infinite variety of tones which characterize the poems of Walther. But in all this variety one rule prevails—the rule that each stanza should have three parts (two *Stollen* and an *Abgesang*). Each stanza begins with corresponding portions, and concludes with a third, differing metrically from the others. To some of Walther's poems this triple character is wanting. We may unhesitatingly assign them to a very early period of the writer's life. The following simple little Minnelied is an example:—

"Winter has injured us every way:
Copseland and woodland are russet and grey,
Where many voices rang merry and gay.
Ah, would that the maidens could come forth to play,
And the birds again carol their roundelay.

"Would I could slumber the winter through;
Now, when I waken my heart is low,
In winter's kingdom of ice and snow.
God knows that at last the winter must go;
Where the ice lingers now flowers will grow."

To an early period also belongs the poem already referred to, "Under der Linden." It is, perhaps, impossible to reproduce in English verse the delicate music of this airy lyric. The following is a literal translation. It preserves the triple division of the tone:—

I.

"Under the lindens,
On the heather,
Where the couch of us two was,

You may discover,
Both beautiful
Broken flowerbells and grass,

By the woodside in the vale.
Tandaradei,
Sweetly sang the nightingale.

II.

"I went, I hastened
To the meadow;
Thither my love had gone before.

There was I welcomed
Lady Mary!
That I am happy evermore.

Did he kiss me? A thousand times,
(Tandaradei),
See how red my lips are yet.

III.

"There he had fashioned
A beautiful
Flowercouch and bed of flowers;

And laughter arises
In inmost heart,
If any one passes that way;

By the roses he may well
(Tandaradei)
See yet where my head was laid.

IV.

"That he lay beside me,
Should any know,
(O God forbid!) I were ashamed.

And what he did with me,
No one—never—
Shall know but he and I alone,

And one dear little bird that sang
Tandaradei,
And he will ever be true."

In reference to this poem, Simrock has remarked that the folksong also is not without instances of lyrics, whose simplicity throws the magic light of innocence upon situations which would be intolerable in any other. But in reality to raise a moral question upon this artless song is wholly inappropriate: the difficulty for a modern reader is to appreciate the subtle delicacy and infinite reserve which characterize Minne poetry. To name his lady's name was deemed a shameless breach of good taste in a lover; and Walther has one indignant poem addressed to those who sought with some importunity to win such a secret from him (19). In another graceful little poem (21), he speaks of his eyes as ambassadors to his lady, ambassadors that return always with a kindly message. But these eyes are not those of his corporal vision, for they have long been unblessed by beholding her; they are the eyes of his mind.

"Es sint die gedanke des herzen min."

"Shall I," asks the poet, "ever be so happy a man as that *she* shall gaze upon *me* with eyes like mine?"

It was not much, indeed, that the Minnesinger asked from his lady. That she should smile upon him when he greeted her, or that, if others were by, she should at least look toward the place where he stood. A glance threw him into an ecstacy of delight, yet if his lady endured the presence of other admirers he sank into the depths of despair. Thence again he rose buoyantly with the slightest straw of hope. Here is the immemorial love-oracle (24):

I.

"In a despairing mood,
I sat me down and pondered.

I thought I would leave her service,
Had not a certain solace restored me.

Solace it may not rightly be called. Alas, no,
It is indeed scarcely a tiny comfort,
So tiny that if I tell you you will mock me,
Yet one is comforted by a little, he knows not why.

II.

"Me a blade of grass has made happy,
It tells me that I shall find favour.

I measured this selfsame little blade,
As of old I have seen children do.

Now listen and mark if it does so again.
'She loves me, she loves me not, she loves me, she does not, she does.'
As oft as I have done it, the result is good,
That comforts me; *but one must have faith, too.*"

Who the lady was whom Walther wooed is unknown now, if it was known in his time. It has been conjectured that she was of low birth, and the following poem (14) gives some ground for the conjecture. Walther's treatment of the subject is different from the way in which Horace handled a subject of similar nature.

I.

"Maiden, heart beloved of me,
God give thee ever help and aid;

And were there any dearer name,
That would I gladly call thee.

What can I dearer say than this,
That thou art well beloved of me? Alas! 'tis this that pains me.

II.

"They taunt me oft that I
Turn to a lowly maid my song.

That they can never know
What love is, is their punishment.

Love never came to those
Who woo for wealth or beauty. O what love is theirs?

III.

"Hate often follows beauty;
Be none too eager for it.

Love is the heart's best tenant,
Beauty stands after love.

'Tis love makes lady fair,
Beauty can not do this, it never made lady fair.

IV.

"I bear it as I have borne
And as I shall ever bear it.

Thou art fair and wealthy enough,
What can they tell me of this?

Say what they will, I love thee.
The crystal ring that thou givest is better than royal gold.*

V.

"If thou art faithful and true,
Then I am thine without fear;

Thine—that no sorrow of heart
Can come against me by thy will.

If thou art neither of these,
Then thou canst never be mine. Ah me, should this happen to be!"

In another poem (17), however, he praises his lady's beauty with much enthusiasm. The following stanza runs more lightly into the mould of English verse :—

"God formed with care her cheeks so bright
And laid such lovely colours there,

Such perfect red, such perfect white,
Here tinted rose, there lily fair,

That I will almost dare to say
On her with greater joy I gaze
Than on the sky and starry way.
Alas! what would my foolish praise?
For if her pride should grow,
My lip's light word might work my heart some bitter woe."

But in fact it is useless arguing from these poems to the actual circumstances of the poet's life. The *Minne* of this period was after all rather a subject of the imagination than a passion of the heart. The nameless lady whose praise a poet sang, belonged to the ideal portion of his life. We find nowhere among the poems of the Minnesingers songs which celebrate what we call "domestic happiness," or which look forward to nuptial union. The ideal and the real were kept widely sundered by the knights and poets of *Minne*. In actual life the poet composed and sang these *Lieder* at the court of some noble patron, whose approval was his reward. Often he sang, too, with the hope of receiving a more substantial recognition, the gift, perhaps, of a small estate where he might settle, and marry the daughter of a neighbouring vassal landholder. For her, however, there were certainly neither *Stollen* nor *Abgesang*. She reared his children, and directed his frugal household. She managed the estate in sum-

* A glass ring for pledging a lover's faith was not unfrequently used in the Middle Ages by the poorer classes.

mer whilst he visited his patrons, gave orders to his servants and herself set arrow to bow, if any burglarious miscreant attacked the house. Possibly the poet appreciated what she did, and was a good husband and father. But the domestic life lacked poetical utterance; it was not within the region of the art of the time. Hence there is an artificial atmosphere about the whole circle of Minnesong. It does not come into close contact with real life. It is, if not in opposition, at least in contrast with the masculine and adult energy by which the German character of the Middle Ages was marked. Minnesong was of the court, courtly. It sprang, it is true, from the same source as the great folk-epic of Siegfried and Brunhild, but the waters of that fertilizing stream were diverted now to rise in the private fountains and tinkling cascades of royal gardens. If Walther's muse had been confined to this line of poetry alone, the poems which he has left us would amply have justified the title which has been assigned him in this paper. But his large and earnest nature is inadequately commemorated in such a title. He was the greatest of the Minnesingers, and he was much more. He was a politician penetrated with the idea of the necessity of German union. In his maturer years he applied himself more and more rarely to the composition of *Lieder*, and in the later works there is breathed a very different spirit from that which animates the lyrics of the Court of Vienna. We find in them the real life of the poet, as we should expect to find it, when a poet is possessed by an idea which is neither selfish nor small. The idea which possessed Walther was a great one, and has never been absent from the best minds of Germany, the idea of national union. What suffering, what immense power run to waste would have been spared that noble country, if the dream of our Minnesinger had been realized five centuries ago. This was not to be. Perhaps even now the full attainment is distant. But it is well for his countrymen to look back upon his pensive figure seated, as shown in the Paris manuscript, in the attitude of deep thought.

"Ich saz ûf eime steine
Und dahte bein mit beine,
Dar ûf sast' ich den ellenbogen;
Ich hete in mine hant gesmogen
Min kinne und ein mîn wange.
Do dahte ich mir vil ange,
Wes man zer werlte solte leben."

For strangely enough, the ecclesiastical and political contest of the present day, has much resemblance to that which was fought in the times of Walther. To-day, as then, Rome and the

Empire dispute the point of supremacy. The question at issue may be disguised and deceive even the wise and far-sighted. But the present is not the first time that Rome has learnt to throw an appearance of right over audacious and transcendant injustice. Five hundred years ago she failed to blind to her designs the vision of our Minnesinger, and now-a-days, happily there are men numerous enough and strong enough to be true to the spirit of these poems of Walther, and to insist upon wresting from the hands of Rome, at least the national education of their children.

"Tiuschiu zuht gât vor in allen."

Art. VIII.—Moral Philosophy at Cambridge.

First Principles of Moral Science. A Course of Lectures delivered in the University of Cambridge. By Thomas Rawson Birks, Knightsbridge, Professor of Moral Philosophy. London: Macmillan and Co. 1873.

NEARLY forty years have passed since Mr. Mill, in his review of Professor Sedgwick's celebrated Discourse, declared that "the end, above all others, for which endowed universities exist, or ought to exist, is to keep alive philosophy." The "studies of the University of Cambridge" in 1835 were not the studies of the present year. In every department there has been progress. Great reforms have been instituted from without: those which have proceeded from within have still been greater. Unattached students have received recognition. Dissenters, at first admitted within college precincts for study and then allowed to graduate, after many years of probation have been placed on a footing of equality in the competition for college fellowships. The badge of creed has been abolished: the stigma of sex is passing away. Lectures and Examinations for Women have been inaugurated, and there is a fair prospect of the entire removal, at no distant time, of the intellectual disabilities under which they still labour. University influence has been extended far beyond the boundaries of Cambridge by the institution of Local Examinations; and more recently still, by the official establishment of Courses of Lectures by university men in provincial towns. New professorships have been founded. Degrees are conferred for proficiency in Moral and in Natural Science. The course of study for the

Classical and Mathematical Triposes has been reformed. The proceedings for the ordinary degree have been revolutionized.

How far may the university of Cambridge be considered to fulfil the supreme function for which, with Mr. Mill, we regard it as existing—the promotion of philosophy? Amidst the various marks of progress just enumerated, has all been accomplished that may be fairly expected for the advancement of that study? By what causes is the growth of the philosophic spirit in the university still retarded? Such are the questions which we propose to discuss in the following pages, while we shall endeavour to exemplify the truth of our criticisms by a brief reference at the close of this article to the volume, the title of which we have placed at its head. A fairer illustration of our argument than the work before us it would be difficult to obtain. It is the latest product, not only of Cambridge philosophy, but of the Cambridge Professor of Philosophy. Coming thus before us with the stamp of university authority upon it, it shows us the kind of pabulum on which the university thinks it well that its race of rising thinkers should be fed.

Whatever opinion we may form as to the sincerity of the university in its efforts to promote philosophy, there can be no doubt as to their inadequacy. Scotland can show a succession of metaphysicians and psychologists almost apostolical, from Dr. Reid to Professor Bain. Seldom during the last century have her universities been destitute of a thinker, not merely of British but of European celebrity. Far otherwise has it fared with Cambridge. Nor is this because speculative minds have been driven away by the restraints of dulness on the eccentricities of genius: they have not been produced. To what extent, then, is the university responsible for this?

Circumstances, though they cannot create a great mind, can materially assist or retard its development. The universities cannot manufacture a philosopher, but they can make it nearly impossible for a philosopher to arise. They can encourage individuality or they can repress it. They can facilitate the pursuit of truth or they can obstruct it, by inflicting pains and penalties on those whom it leads away from the narrow track of orthodoxy. They can prescribe such studies as shall foster, or such as shall check, habits of free inquiry and independent thought in their students. According as they adopt one course or the other, there is some reason in saying that their students have become profound thinkers in consequence, or in spite of the training they received at college. Still, the causes which cooperate in the formation of a great mind are so enormously complex that a comparative estimate of the merits of rival universities, based on the number of philosophers which they have respectively reared, is likely to be erroneous. Taken in connexion with other facts, however, such an estimate is not without value as a means of verifying conclusions to which an examination of their courses of study may lead us. Weighed in this balance the university of Cambridge must be pronounced wanting. Of the contributors to mental philosophy, since the beginning of this century, Oxford may claim to have furnished Hamilton, Ferrier, Whately, and Mansel—men whose joint renown certainly far exceeds all that Cambridge can set up in comparison with it. But then are Hamilton and Ferrier in any true sense the production of Oxford teaching? If this question means, Did Oxford training in any important measure lead them to the systematic study of philosophy, we imagine that the correct answer would be No; but if it means, Did Oxford training tend to develop in them the philosophic spirit, we are inclined to think that to some slight extent it did.

It is not only in the higher regions of speculation, however, that the dearth of Cambridge thinkers is apparent. The great practical results of the intellectual energy of our age had their origin at Oxford. The Tractarian movement and the Positivist movement displayed no great liberality or breadth of thought indeed, but a high degree of its activity. The former, originating with a few men of profound earnestness and commanding influence, has had its logical outcome in a return to the garish upholstery and priestly assumption of mediævalism. Courts are occupied, newspapers filled, γυναικάρια engrossed, with controversies about baldacchinos, genuflexions, elevation of the host, confessionals, and the other adjuncts of superstition. This is what everybody sees. What everybody does not see is the theory of ecclesiastical supremacy which underlies the whole masquerade: yet the theory is the only element which need disturb those who have the welfare of the race at heart. Pleasure for pleasure, Bentham would have said, the antics of a priest may be as good as the antics of a harlequin: and they would be as harmless if they implied nothing more. The Positivist movement was a rebellion from what was considered the despotism of one creed, and, in the case of those who followed M. Comte into the arcana of the religion of Humanity, a re-enlistment under a creed no whit less despotic. The thorough-going religious Comtists have made few proselytes, have scarcely indeed maintained their position. But the Positivist spirit took hold of many of the foremost men of the Young Oxford school, in whom, if they cannot be called philosophers, renouncing as they do psychological and metaphysical inquiries altogether, we may at any rate find some of the ablest writers and the most zealous reformers of the day.

Why, it may be asked, has Oxford enjoyed this monopoly of practical activity? Granting that neither the High-Church nor the Positivist movement was exactly what might be wished—granting, if you please, that they were quite remote from what might be wished, still they were movements, though erratic: they showed vitality, not intellectual torpor. Cambridge thought, on the contrary, has continued on a dead-level of lifeless orthodoxy. Is this accidental? or specially-providential? Could Tractarianism or Comtism have germinated on the Cam? If so, how is it that they were never even transplanted thither? They were due, it has been said, to the personal influence of a few master-minds. But how were the master-minds formed? and how is it that the little society in which they worked was so well fitted for their propagandist enterprise? Were these things the result of causes? and if so, can the causes be assigned?

These facts, and the fact that the study of philosophy flourishes more at the Scotch than it does at the English universities, are certainly not ultimate coexistences of nature; there must be an explanation of them though we may fail to discover it. A comparison between the universities of Oxford and Cambridge is an easier task in many respects than that between the universities of England and Scotland. The subjects of the comparison are small, single, and homogeneous. Considerations as to the effect of differences of climate, of scenery, of race, or of national character may be eliminated at once. We have, then, two universities, drawing their students from the same society and from the same classes in it, receiving them indifferently from the same schools, and rewarding those of them who are the most successful in the same manner, but with widely different results as regards their moral and intellectual character. The only possible inference concerning the cause is this, that there must be a difference of moral or of intellectual training, or of both. The moral training is not appreciably different. The same apparatus of college chapels and university sermons, the same enthusiasm for athletics combined with a passionate love of luxury, exist in both seats of learning. The explanation must be sought, therefore, in some difference between the courses of study which they respectively enjoin.

The popular distinction between Oxford and Cambridge, which assigns supremacy in classics to the former and supremacy in mathematics to the latter, has the charm of simplicity but not of truth. If thought necessary, the reply may be made that Cambridge too confers an honours degree in classics: that the senior classic is esteemed quite as highly by those competent to form an opinion as the senior wrangler: that to obtain a place in the first class in classics at Cambridge involves as much study as a similar distinction at Oxford: and that Bentley and Porson, who in times past represented the climax of Latin and Greek scholarship reached by Englishmen, were Cambridge men, as are Professor Munro and Mr. Jebb who occupy the same position at the present day. The real distinction, which is something much more subtle than this, lies, we conceive, in the different character of classical pursuits at the two universities. At Cambridge the chief stress has been laid on accuracy of scholarship: at Oxford greater weight has been allowed to knowledge of the subject-matter of classical authors: familiarity with Greek thought, especially in the case of Aristotle, is valued higher than an exact acquaintance with the niceties of the language in which the thought is expressed. We do not pretend that this course is adequate for the due study of philosophy. It is far inferior to the system of the Scotch and German universities, where a certain portion of each student's career must be devoted to attendance at the lectures on philosophy, and where an examination in philosophy forms an integral part of the proceedings for his degree. At Oxford, philosophy is recognised in only a left-handed fashion, but in the classical tripos at Cambridge it has not been recognised at all.*

In assigning as the effect of this difference in the courses of classical study the widely different intellectual temperament of the two universities, we do not really exaggerate its potency. The outcome of Oxford teaching has not been a large amount of philosophy but a general disposition to philosophize. It has shown men that there are great problems which have occupied reflective minds from early ages. It has encouraged them to regard the knowledge of the results of Greek speculation in ethics, or logic, or forms of government, as of more worth than an acute faculty of discrimination in the use of particles and a memory well-stored with various readings and conjectural emendations. What is requisite to complete this teaching is the systematic instruction in philosophy of those so well prepared for its reception, but for anything of the kind we may search Oxford, as we may search Cambridge, in vain.

We conclude, then, that while there has hitherto been an

---

* The new regulations for proceedings in classics were put in force in 1872. In these some prominence is given to Ancient Philosophy, as well as to History and Philology. The university has done its best to effect an entire change in the character of Cambridge classical learning, and we wish it all success in the attempt. In considering the nature of the studies, however, by which the minds of university men have been moulded during the last forty years, we cannot take into account a revised scheme of reading which has been in operation but two years, and the results of which must be sought in future generations of Cambridge graduates.

absence from the course of classical study pursued at Cambridge of any element which would tend to "keep alive philosophy," the presence of this element, though only to a small extent, at Oxford, has led to a marked divergence in the influence of the two universities on modern social action.

The next question to be decided is, whether the very general study of mathematics at Cambridge exerts a tendency, though indirect, in this direction. We have no intention of working an exhausted mine of controversy as to the effect of mathematical training on the mind, but refer the reader to the combat between Sir W. Hamilton, and Dr. Whewell and Mr. Mill, for some brilliant dialectical efforts on the subject. No doubt a certain grounding in algebra and geometry is almost indispensable, and the practice of solving puzzles in these subjects excellent discipline. But in the revolt from the old system of instruction, under which the pupil was in a great measure passively receptive of facts compendiously arranged by skilful bookmakers in question-and-answer form, our modern education-mongers are apt to dwell too exclusively on studies as mere exercises of intellectual gymnastics. The mind, according to them, is to be for ever forming and never furnishing.* Supposing, however, that we concede everything that is claimed for mathematics by its warmest advocates, as a means of mental discipline, and admit the supreme importance of a study which calls so continuously for the exercise of the pupil's powers in solving difficult conundrums, we are not afraid of contradiction when we add that all this has no bearing on philosophy. Any book on Logic or Psychology may probably contain a discussion whether the axioms of mathematics are generalizations from experience, or derived from a source beyond experience; whether its definitions involve a hypothesis when employed in demonstration; why a theorem proved true respecting one circle may legitimately be held true concerning all circles; and similar questions. These points belong to the logic of mathematics, and are interesting to the metaphysician. The mathematician treats of his subject under quite another aspect, and is no

* Even Mr. Spencer seems to us to fall into an analogous error when, towards the close of his "Sociology," he describes the discipline necessary for one who will successfully pursue inquiries into Social Science, and prescribes preparation in the Abstract, Abstract-Concrete, and Concrete sciences. We are quite ready to admit that the appropriate method of sociological research might not have been adequately conceived, unless considerable progress had previously been made in Physical Science; but now that the true method has been discovered we submit that a tyro may adequately appreciate it by seeing it employed in sociological speculation. There is surely exaggeration in representing a man as unable to appreciate the difference between the various methods of inquiry and proof without seeing them practically exemplified in laboratories and dissecting-rooms.

more obliged, or expected, to pay attention to this one, than a physicist or biologist is bound to study the logic of his particular science.

Thus far we have dealt with those university agencies which might possibly be supposed indirectly to furnish some teaching in philosophy. We pass now to a consideration of the encouragement directly given to the study. This is twofold: we have, first, a Professorship of Moral Philosophy; secondly, a Moral Sciences Tripos. Supposing both of these instruments to be fully efficient, there is thus provision already existing for teaching students, and for examining and appropriately rewarding them with degrees,—the two functions which a university ought to combine, if Mr. Lowe will allow us to say so; two functions at any rate which we may expect to find combined by the university of Cambridge. Now if the agencies are considered adequate we must confess that the results are lamentably deficient. It behoves us, therefore, to inquire how far the agencies are themselves at fault, and how far their operation is obstructed by the circumstances in which they work. What has to be said respecting the Professorship will come most naturally when we speak of the Professor: accordingly we shall deal first with the tripos.

The moral sciences tripos must be considered on the whole a failure. It does not secure the same respect for itself that the old-established mathematical and classical triposes enjoy. A degree in philosophy ranks, perhaps, with a degree in natural science. To some extent it legitimately occupies a lower position than its older rivals. In conferring an honours' degree the university may be considered to bestow the stamp of its approbation on the whole of the previous education, both at school and college, extending over many years. The classical or mathematical teaching which a pupil has received, possibly from the age of eight, till he presents himself for his degree, is subjected to a searching test. His success is usually the result of ten or twelve years steady work. An examination in moral science, on the contrary, can take cognisance of a man's industry during a much shorter period only, generally comprising but three or four years. Except a little school teaching perhaps in Formal Logic or Political Economy, rarely given, the student comes to subjects entirely fresh to him when his preparation for the moral sciences tripos begins. Previous work can count for very little here. All competitors start on a level at eighteen.

Yet while giving the fullest recognition to this fact, we feel that the examination in moral science might deservedly occupy a position of greater dignity, were it not for other disadvantages against which it has to contend. The scheme of subjects is judicious: the list of treatises of which a knowledge is required is extensive. We sometimes hear that the contempt in which the tripos is held arises from the fact that the subject-matter is so easy. Proficiency in moral science, we are told, cannot enter into comparison with proficiency in classics or mathematics. It is one thing to do a stiff bit of a Greek chorus or to solve an awkward equation, and a very different thing to cram enough philosophical terminology to write with seeming profundity about matter *per se* and the *ego*.* The assertion is really too absurd for deliberate refutation, seeing that philosophy demands the very highest intellectual ability, not only for original speculation, but sometimes even for the correct reproduction of the opinions of others. To obtain a firm grasp of Kant's Transcendental Analytic, or even of Mill's Theory of International Values, probably requires as great powers of mental concentration and as special an aptitude, as to master Laplace's Coefficients.

It is quite true that the language of moral science is unfortunately in large measure the language of common life, and this circumstance, while it is a continual source of difficulty to the scientific inquirer who would have preferred a technical terminology free from ambiguities, enables any shallow-brained but fluent-tongued pretender to discourse with a show of depth that may occasionally mislead. Hence examiners are required of thorough ability, prompt in discerning an impostor who strives to conceal his philosophical nakedness in a panoply of scientific phraseology, and no less prompt in recognising the merit of strokes of talent whenever they occur. Unfortunately the importance of a strong examining staff is not appreciated by the university authorities in the case of the moral sciences tripos. For the examination in natural science men of eminence are called in from without if they are not forthcoming in Cambridge. Of late years it has been thought absurd for an examination, let us say, in geology, to be entrusted to an individual merely because he happens to be a distinguished botanist, and a competent geologist has been sought elsewhere. But it is not thought at all absurd for a youth who has obtained some distinction in classics or mathematics, and has subsequently spent six months in reading for a place in the moral sciences tripos, which shall serve as a makeweight towards a fellowship, to be forthwith appointed examiner in philosophy. A critical survey of exami-

* A friend of ours, who would have easily secured a fellowship for his mathematical attainments had he been willing to devote himself to three years' preparation for the tripos, informed his college tutor of his intention to renounce mathematics and read philosophy, on account of its higher interest and utility. His tutor, finding him proof against all appeals on the pecuniary ground of loss of fellowship, exclaimed, "Well, but you can't read moral science three years, you know: more than half your time will be idle on your hands."

nation-papers is quite foreign to our purpose, but the reader who will take the trouble to scrutinize them carefully for himself, will find the foolish questions of incompetent examiners jumbled up with the judicious questions of those who are fit for their work. What, for instance, can be a sign of greater feebleness in an examiner than to isolate from its context an antithetical sentence from some German transcendentalist and to ask a candidate to discuss its truth? The first question which meets our eye, as we glance over a copy of old papers, is the following :—"Trendelenburg describes the fundamental controversy of philosophy as waged between the efficient cause and the final cause. Explain this representation, and point out in what the strength of each position lies." All that a problem of this sort can disclose is the unsuitability for his office of the man who set it.

No doubt the examination would improve in character if its reputation rose, and a larger number of candidates drew upon it increased attention. Why, then, is the number of candidates so small?

This question admits of a very sufficient reply. It is a merely pecuniary matter. Moral science is not studied at Cambridge because it does not pay. Undergraduate studies are guided by the commercial principle, and so, if exhibitions, scholarships, and fellowships are to be picked up for classical and mathematical attainments, and nothing of the kind is to be had for philosophy, classics and mathematics will be toiled at with ardour and philosophy will be left in the cold. And this is precisely what has happened. The great mass of youthful talent is all forced into two channels by a gigantic system of bribery. Supposing money rewards to be a good means of promoting learning and culture, let us have a fair field for intellectual energy, in which it may follow its natural bias, whether literary, scientific, or philosophical.* That the natural sciences will ultimately get their

* The overwhelming influence of fellowships and similar bribes in concentrating the attention of the most promising undergraduates on classics or mathematics, to the exclusion of every other study, would probably frustrate the expectations of those who look for great results from the mere nomination of professors of first-rate ability to university chairs. At Cambridge there are, of course, professors and professors, and we heartily sympathize with those who lament the narrowness of the area from which the old universities select their teachers,—a narrowness which frequently involves a poverty of choice and consequent unsuitability of appointment. Still it would be absurd, and worse than absurd, to deny that there are some amongst their number whose scholarship would be an ornament to any seat of learning. Generally speaking, it is the system rather than the professor which is at fault. It is deadening work to lecture to empty benches, and the best professor in the world would get no class at all, or a class that was utterly unworthy of his energies, if his subject was one which did not pay in the competition for college emoluments. We may cite

fair share of endowments is highly probable: the danger, not very great, indeed, at present, is that in the general grumble of the anti-literary agitators, they should engross too much. It is to be hoped that the comparative silence of the noisy band of zealots during the last year or two, shows that scientific education has passed from the stage of talk to the stage of action. But the most reasonable fear for philosophy is that she will receive no encouragement at all.

Not that we regard the forcing system of university education by means of lavish pecuniary inducements to study as a good one: far from it. It continues to flourish, partly because of its inertia, being a vast institution to overthrow, and partly for the same reason which has given such vitality to slavery, standing armies, state-churches, and other abuses—the number of persons interested in its maintenance. Oxford and Cambridge colleges are in fact oppressed with their wealth, and the mental vigour of their students is overlaid with rich prizes. There was a reason for this once. In the Middle Ages the nation was poor: now the classes from which the universities draw their alumni are extremely well-to-do. Then the students begged from house to house under the protection of a certificate of mendicancy: now they live in a state of luxury never dreamt of by their grandfathers. Then the universities were centres of learning in the midst of great darkness: now there is more wisdom outside their walls than within them, as anybody but a college Don would admit. When students were many and teachers poor and few, the gift of funds to supply the best instruction which the age could afford was a noble act, and the creation of fellowships a wise mode of securing the object. But with the multiplication of these prizes the scholar's ideal has deteriorated. Knowledge as an end in itself has given place to knowledge for what it will fetch. A good degree at two or three-and-twenty means *σίτησις ἐν πρυτανείῳ* for the next seven years of one's life, perhaps for

---

the case of Professor Fawcett as especially appropriate to our present topic. Mr. Fawcett is not only an excellent lecturer, but is probably, after Mr. Cairnes, one of the first of living British economists. His audience, however, is composed of poll-men, and to poll-men his discourses have to be adapted: indeed, we are inclined to believe that the Professor would be the first to dissuade a student who had already mastered the elements of economic science from attending his lectures, as it would be a sheer waste of time to do so. Now we regard the presence of so many pass-men as a matter for congratulation, and acknowledge the wisdom of the Senate in making their attendance at a course of professorial lectures compulsory. It is the absence of candidates for Honours that we regret. On the one hand, a university professor ought to have a class for whom he can do something more than expound the elements of his subject, and, on the other hand, poll-men should not enjoy a monopoly of the means of general culture.

the whole of it. As a man is thus rewarded for doing what it was his highest interest to do for himself without any reward at all, it is not surprising to find that he is contented with doing very little more when once his independence is secured. Had the system reared a race of profound classical or mathematical students, the costliness of the agency might be forgiven. But the results are grievously disproportionate to the means. Whether Cambridge thinkers have contributed their fair share, or more than their fair share, to mathematical progress, we must leave to mathematicians to decide, but in classical literature one may say without any suspicion of an "anti-patriotic bias" that, in spite of our time-honoured jibes at German editing, English annotations seldom exhibit scholarship that is not derived from German sources. Contrasting the threadbare German professor with his sleek, over-fed British rival, we may learn that to lead men to study a subject is a good thing, but to provide for them so that they need never study it further is a very bad one.

Look down the lists of college fellows and ask yourself in what way they have aided in the diffusion of learning? Assuming that you have kept yourself pretty well *au courant* with university matters, we will suppose that it is only of nine men out of every ten that you have never heard. And what of these? We will grant that four out of the nine are usefully or ornamentally engaged in the office of steward or bursar, master or dean, and charitably imagine that the remaining five are lecturing to the generations of freshmen successively appearing, their lectures being appreciated so highly that the greatest boon which a tutor can ordinarily bestow upon a pupil of talent is the permission to "cut" them, and considered so efficacious that the most characteristic figure of university society is the "coach." But the tenth man is known to you by repute: and how? Perhaps he published an elementary treatise on Trigonometry the same year that he took his degree, and has retired on his laurels and the profits from the publisher: or it may have been a synoptical view of Paley's Evidences in one sheet imperial folio, to be pinned up by poll-men over their washing-stands, that first brought him to your notice. Or again, he may have taken a loftier flight, and become an unrivalled specialist for beetles, or coins, or the literature of the Fathers; in which case we gratefully acknowledge the value of an entomologist, numismatist, or Patristic scholar in the world's economy, though probably at the sacrifice of general culture in himself. On one point no doubt you might obtain some serviceable testimony if you happened to visit high-table at hall-time—the opinion of college fellows as to the place of Gastronomy among the Fine Arts. But take your Diogenes'-lamp and scan the Electoral Roll to find the names of those "writ large" on the Temple of Fame. We will make no parsimonious estimate of the possibilities of the situation, but fear that if we leave you to look till you find a score whose reputation has reached the metropolis, and half a dozen who are known over Europe, you will have to look a long time.

These splendid emoluments might be devoted to the maintenance of an educational staff, consisting of original thinkers whose fame should make the renown of all other universities pale before it. Instead of this, they are handed over to those whose sole claim to consideration is that they have learnt what has been done by other people. Learning is debased by the keen struggle for rewards, just as old boating-men tell us that rowing is demoralized by the rage for "pot-hunting." A careful study of an author or a literary period as a whole would not pay, so the classical man must content himself with "tips." The better sort of university men confess this. A candidate sees an examiner in every bush, says Professor Seeley, somewhere: his object is not to master Aristotle, but to "floor" papers on Aristotle. "What do you think of Blank's coaching?" we once asked a friend who went up to Cambridge with a reputation which he justified by becoming senior wrangler. "Well," he replied, "it is splendid cram."

Not only are the truest interests of learning thus directly injured, but a spirit of extravagance is fostered by these endowments which is directly bad for learning and for morals alike. It is a rare thing, now-a-days, for the award of a scholarship to decide whether a boy shall go to the university or not, though it swells the pocket-money which he spends there if he wins it. We are as heartily glad as any one can be that the invidious badges of poverty which sizars were once obliged to bear have disappeared; but we are far from glad to find men receiving an education from charity, when they are as well able to pay the price for it as their more conscientious neighbours, and spending the surplus on those secondaries which are the legitimate enjoyments of affluence. Not long since we expressed our surprise at hearing that the son of a member of Parliament, in comfortable circumstances, had gone to the university on this footing. "Horatio is a noble fellow," exclaimed an admiring relative. "He cared nothing for the degradation provided he could spare his father the expense." The nobility displayed by a man of property in sending for his dinner to a soup-kitchen would probably be disputed by most men.

We are far from attributing to the lavish distribution of these bounties at every stage of a student's career the whole of the spirit of luxurious extravagance which pervades the old universities. This is but the youthful mimicry of the great characteristic of the classes from whom the undergraduates are drawn. But it is a spirit which the university authorities should check, not indeed by the sumptuary laws of a Cato, but by presenting in their own persons examples of the simple life of a Kant. Unhappily in this matter they trouble themselves very little about their precepts or their practice. A man who goes to the university, like a traveller who takes a trip on the Rhine, must submit to be cheated, unless he has a liking for worry and brawls. An occasional Joseph Hume may be found among undergraduates with a taste for tracking items of expenditure, but we never heard of his efforts being crowned with anything of Joseph Hume's success. We have duly received and paid in our time weekly steward's bills, the details of which it was as impossible to decipher as to determine the secret meaning of the numerical square in Albert Dürer's Melancholy, or the application of the mystic number of the Beast. But we are unreasonable to expect serious endeavours to be made by masters and fellows for cutting down the authorized impositions to which students are subjected for the support of porters and bed-makers, when they must know very well that their own maintenance is frequently no whit more defensible. What rational argument was ever constructed for the existence of Heads of colleges—"corruptors general," as Bentham used to say of kings—beyond the assertion of the fact that they exist already? What course could be more beneficial than the disestablishment and disendowment of Masters, and the appropriation of the revenues to the erection of college laboratories, under competent directors? Yet which is the expedient that the colleges will most probably adopt, when public opinion compels them to provide suitable scientific instruction—the one indicated here, or the more congenial application *in formâ pauperis* to old students for contributions to carry out the work? "But if the work of reformation once begins, where are you going to stop?" is the cry of a safe conservatism, and accordingly hitherto it has never in real earnest been begun.

Passing from these abuses, "gross as a mountain, open, palpable," which are the staple of University Reformers' discourses, observe again how, in the regulations affecting the larger part of the undergraduates, pecuniary considerations dictate a low standard of scholarship, and, by so doing, encourage the presence of men whose habits are idle and luxurious. It is hardly too much to say that at least one-third of the undergraduates have no business to be at the university at all. A university may be a place at which young men shall jostle one another and rub off their awkward angles of rusticity and prejudice. It may be a place where they shall cultivate their muscular powers by every kind of athletic exercise. But pre-eminently it is a place where men are to be taught, and for this end it is useless that they should go to it unless they carry with them the disposition and the ability to learn. Their ability can be tested by an examination at entrance, and this will also, to some extent, determine what has been their disposition to study in the past. Not only is there no uniform examination at entrance at the different colleges, but hardly at any college is there an examination even in form. A college which made a laudable effort to raise its standard of scholarship would only be rewarded by diminished numbers and diminished fees, while its less ambitious sisters reaped a pecuniary benefit. The university is the only organization really fitted to perform the task of judiciously weeding freshmen, and it might easily effect this by substituting a genuine examination at matriculation for the formal procedure of inscribing one's name in the register.* As things are, the colleges receive incapable students, and the university must adapt its pass examinations to its materials. However incompetent a man may be, he must be let through at last, though repeated attempts may be requisite.† These are the men who give the tone to the worse half of the students: men of exquisite dress, riding the finest horses and petting the ugliest dogs; the better ones amongst them possibly maintaining the honour of their college on the river or in the cricket-field, though not in the Senate House. But they are not the men for whom a university is designed, and it will be a happy day for the university when she definitely says she will have no more of them.

Briefly to recapitulate the hindrances which prevent philosophical studies from receiving a due amount of attention at Cambridge, we have, first, the absence of any tendencies indirectly exerted by the course of classical or mathematical reading to foster the growth of the philosophic spirit; secondly, an artificial inducement for the rising university talent to occupy itself exclusively with classics or mathematics; thirdly, the comparatively

---

* We understand that this is one of the things which they order better at Oxford, where the colleges do impose a real, and, in a few cases, a severe, examination on candidates for admission. If it is so, the difference between Oxford and Cambridge pass-men as a class must be very marked.

† There used to be a singer in one of the college choirs who had laudably won his degree, after a series of failures which might have tried the proverbial patience of Bruce's spider. Instead of regarding his misfortunes as discreditable, however, he prided himself on the circumstance that he was accompanied in them by a noble viscount, since summoned to the House of Lords. "Me and Broadacres was plucked together," was a statement which he loved to reiterate; implying, though in a remote degree, an aristocratic connexion. There was a slight advantage after all in Broadacres' favour, as his lordship is reported to have undergone no less than eight "post-mortems" before his perseverance was crowned with success.

slight estimation in which the honours degree in moral science is held; fourthly, the low tone of the greater part of university society respecting the value of intellectual activity for its own sake, a want of moral earnestness, and an excessive regard for a luxurious standard of living, promoted, though not originated, by the existing system of lavish money-prizes for the very immature results of mental power. We have now to deal with the fifth and, perhaps, the chief impediment, the prevalence of a spirit of theological dogmatism.

Whether theology has any inherent sentiment of antagonism towards science and philosophy, it is not our present business to discuss. That theology and philosophy, as they have generally been pursued, are antagonistic; that the theologian and the philosopher have regarded each other with feelings of mutual enmity, is a truism that needs no support. Without appealing to the history of the past, in which the interferences of religious authority in matters beyond its proper cognizance are amply related—interferences invariably on the wrong side—we shall merely notice those general grounds on which the spirit of ecclesiasticism is inimical to the spirit of philosophy.

In the first place, the theologian is tied down to a set of doctrines more or less narrow, with which all other truth must be reconciled or rejected. With him, therefore, the question is—whether a doctrine is safe, and not whether it is sound; thus violating that fundamental canon expressed or implied by every scientific inquirer from the time of Bacon, which demands the reception of all truths, irrespective of their consequences. Take the first of the four precepts by which Descartes proposed to found his method:—"Never to accept anything for true which I did not clearly know to be such; that is to say, carefully to avoid precipitancy and prejudice."* . . . . . Descartes' maxim, revised according to our national theology, must become—"Never to accept anything as true which I do not clearly know to be reconcilable with the Thirty-Nine Articles and the Prayer-Book."

We have been told that the burgesses of Bradford, during a siege in the Civil War, surrounded their handsome steeple with bags of wool. The enemy, hopeless of doing damage through the resisting mass, fired a few ineffectual shots, and gave up the attempt. The clergy are our great modern wool-bags. Alike in practical reforms, and in the spread of new truths, abuse and error, the objects of attack, have their bulwark of this dense material. Not that we object to an ordeal of strong opposition through which every fresh principle must pass, provided the

* "Discours de la Méthode," part ii.

means employed tend only to refute and not to repress it. Those pleas which Mr. Mill has stated so nobly in favour of the freest discussion of received opinions are equally valid in the case of new ones. The doctrines may not be true, or they may combine truth and error: or, even if entirely true, their force will never be fully realized if the liberty to question them is withheld. The Athenian habit of always running after some new thing is in no circumstances indeed likely to become an English characteristic, but a party of conservation is, nevertheless, important in the field of thought, just as it is in the arena of political action. But it is something very different from this, not only to subject the advancement of scientific knowledge to the supervision of an organized body of spiritual police, but to place the members of the force in such situations at our seats of learning that progress must be made by them, if it is made at all.

It is little more than a restatement of the same fact to say that the philosophic spirit is checked according to the extent to which there is a recognition of authority. No doubt, there is more speculative ability outside the sects than within them, but how many of our foremost thinkers, if nominally Churchmen, are really Nothingarians? *Cæteris paribus*, we should look, on *à priori* grounds, for more hostility to scientific progress at the hands of the ministers of an established church than from the sects. And we should expect a greater liberality of tone on the part of the dissenters for these reasons, contrary though such a view is to currently-adopted opinion on the subject. To begin with: many of the sects are without a written creed at all; or, if they have one, it is expressed in the most general terms, assent to which is a widely different matter from subscription to thirty-nine categorical propositions, assent to everything contained in the Prayer-Book, and a vague recognition to boot of the validity of the decrees of a metaphysical creation, the Church. Again, the various sects, founding upon the exercise of private judgment, consequently admit the possibility that other denominations may contain the truth almost equally with themselves. There is nothing to familiarize them with the injurious idea that orthodoxy is a monopoly of their own. The fact of dissidence from prevailing opinion meets them at every point: they are themselves dissenters. A zealous national churchman has a horror of anything like schism in religion, and it is only natural that he should extend the feeling to other subjects. It is churchmen who commit dissenters, not dissenters each other, to the "uncovenanted mercies of God." And further, wherever a connexion of Church and State is maintained, the established clergy will, by the law of their existence, be conservative, not only in the narrow field of politics, but in thought and belief, too; while equally by the law of their existence, a nonconformist ministry will be reforming and progressive. Lastly, the pugnacity of the sects will in large measure be spent upon the Establishment and each other; they are many and heterogeneous, incapable of combined action. A State Church is normally one and homogeneous, admirably adapted for a campaign against obnoxious doctrines, whether in politics, science, or religion. The present capabilities of the English Church in this direction are, indeed, vastly impaired, owing to the numerical importance of the denominations and her want of that homogeneity, which is essential. Internal dissension is immediately followed by loss of influence, and, if not healed, is a sure harbinger of rapidly approaching dissolution.*

Thus the spirit of theological dogmatism is hostile to philosophy because it adopts a body of doctrine to which fresh truths must be accommodated if they are to meet with acceptance. It is hostile also because it familiarizes those who cultivate it with modes of thought injurious alike to their intellectual and moral character. The logomachies of our modern theology are often as frivolous as the quibbles of the schoolmen, though we can rarely congratulate the combatants upon exhibiting the dialectical skill of scholasticism. Theologians have not been wanting in most religions to maintain, not only that two contradictory propositions can be believed together, but that those who do not so believe them will, without doubt, perish everlastingly.

The "reconciliation of antagonisms" between science and religion in their widest sense, is one of the profoundest problems with which the philosophy of the future will have to deal. The history of scientific progress is the history of their perpetual warfare. It exhibits the man of science engaged in continually

---

* If the reader who doubts the alleged breadth of view of sectarianism, respecting questions not closely connected with its own specific difference, will compare the tone of some of the church and the dissenting periodicals in commenting on the death of Mr. Mill, he will see some reason to question the axiom which identifies bigotry with denominationalism. The *Nonconformist*, the *English Independent*, and the *Freeman*, "a Baptist Record," contained notices of the event in perfect taste and of considerable power. Not that the writers were ignorant, as might perhaps be asserted, of the character of Mr. Mill's teaching or of his rejection of the commonly received creed. These facts were alluded to and lamented, but the nobility of his character, his moral courage, and freedom from conventionality, were singled out for a tribute of admiration. Contrast with these the foul outpouring of the writer in the *Church Herald*, who rivalled in malignity, though inferior in power to defame, the now notorious biographer of the *Times*. If this case is considered accidental, we may instance the fact that in two recent numbers of the *Congregationalist*, a translation is given of copious extracts from a work by Professor Bois of Montauban, entitled "Evangile et Liberté," advocating the most absolute freedom of religious opinion and inquiry. The topic is hardly one which would recommend itself to purveyors of literature for the clergy.

annexing portions of the territory where the jurisdiction of his theological rival was once undisputed; while, as the latter falls back upon successive strongholds, the tenacity increases with which he clings to the relics of an empire once universal. Still, there must be an evolution of harmony by an ultimate consilience of their principles, when in the clearer light of fuller knowledge the combatants cease to raise false issues. By the laity the problem is ignored. Ordinarily they are ready to give a sleepy adherence to two conflicting aggregates of beliefs: the scientific they realize vividly and act upon it; the religious they hold in a nebulous form, allowing it to interfere as little as possible with the progress of their speculations. By the clergy the problem is misunderstood, and its real difficulties are never faced. In lieu of any unimpassioned, deliberative effort, they engage in victorious though bloodless conflicts with straw personifications of obnoxious *isms*, set up to be torn to pieces. The position will never be carried with blank cartridges like theirs. When a difficulty has to be met our modern divines have recourse to threats familiar to political obstructives. "Accept this doctrine and Christianity is swept away!" is only an echo of the cry of Toryism in despair, "Pass the Bill and you destroy the British Constitution." Yet they might have learnt from the records of biblical criticism how fresh theories, when once established, are reconciled with Scripture by expedients of interpretation, just as lawyers bring new cases under old principles by legal fictions. They might have observed that the words indeed are fixed but that the theologian has repeatedly involved himself in errors through failing to perceive that the sense to be attached to them may vary widely at different stages of moral or intellectual advancement. And they might have appreciated the depth of the aphorism of Agassiz, himself a religious philosopher, that at first men say of a new doctrine that it is not true, then that it is contrary to religion, and at last that everybody always believed it.*

It has sometimes been urged that the clergy of the universities are such only professionally, and that hence their sympathies are not with the cause of obscurantism. To our thinking, their sympathies are for this reason all the more likely to be identified with it. An ecclesiastic in full parochial work, probably has too much to do in preserving his flock from religious schism, to leave him opportunities for combating scientific heresies. Engaged

* "There is hardly a single nascent science," says the Rev. Dr. Farrar, a Chaplain to the Queen and Master of Marlborough School, "against which theological dogmatism has not injuriously paraded its menacing array of misinterpreted or inapplicable texts."—"Chapters on Language," pp. 6, 7, note.

in rescuing souls from dissent, dispensing patronage in soup and blankets, organizing Dorcas societies, and diffusing the inestimable blessings of culture in agricultural parishes, he is not likely to have much leisure for denunciation of physicists. What can be the *raison d'être* of a clergyman who abandons these functions of his office we cannot conceive, but there can be no doubt that in a hive where many such clerical drones swarm the class-bias will be strong and the bigotry intense. No barrister in active practice can equal the country squire who has merely eaten his dinners at the Temple, in the vigour of his opinions on Law Reform. No veteran general of division can approach the colonel of the county militia in his indignation at abolition of purchase, and the consequent deterioration of the service. And no examining chaplain is likely to surpass in abhorrence of heterodoxy, and the readiness to "magnify his office," the parsons unattached, whose coterie is held together solely by the bonds of the same cloth. University sentiment is lenient towards moral laxity of conduct, but severely rigorous in dealing with delinquency of belief.

George Grote was no bigot, as his whole life showed, but he made it a condition of the legacy with which he endowed the Professorship of Philosophy at University College, London, that no minister of religion should ever occupy the chair. This conduct has been censured for its narrow exclusiveness, but Mr. Grote may have agreed with the Frenchman who divided humanity into men, women and priests, and might have justified his seeming intolerance by such considerations as we have just enumerated.

We pass now to the means by which the branches of moral science are taught at Cambridge, so far as the university supplies any teaching in them at all. Interpreting the term in its widest sense we may mention Professorships of Modern History, of Law, of the Laws of England, of International Law, of Political Economy, and of Moral Theology or Casuistry. The last two are all that would generally be regarded as dealing with departments of moral science; thus, if we consider Moral Theology to comprise Ethics, or what is commonly called Moral Philosophy, the important branches of Logic, Psychology or the Philosophy of Mind, and Metaphysics (supposing that Ontology is important) are altogether unprovided for. The chair of Moral Theology was founded by one Dr. Knightbridge in 1683, but when Dr. Whewell was appointed to it in 1838, it had long been held as a sinecure. Dr. Whewell was a zealous reformer of abuses, and in this case he speedily reformed two. He showed that his tenure of office was to be no sham, by throwing himself into his work with characteristic energy; and he boldly changed the subject-matter of the professorship from Casuistical Divinity to a topic of greater terrestrial interest, Moral Philosophy. With this alteration the university subsequently signified their approval.

This provision strikes us, of course, as remarkably inadequate for the teaching of philosophy, whether we consider the extent to which a university ought to supply the means for its prosecution, or merely compare it with the provision actually made by the universities of Scotland and Germany. In these a professor may be fairly expected to touch on all the departments of mental science, though he may not find it expedient to treat them all at equal length. At Cambridge, on the contrary, not even would Dr. Whewell have felt justified in digressing into Logic or Psychology. And while these branches are tacitly ignored as a part of education, Ethics, a subdivision usually the most unsatisfactorily treated of all, because of the peculiar difficulties it presents, has to be expounded to students who have had no previous discipline in kindred subjects where progress is easier. Ethics is the hardest part of moral science, because of the bias given to the inquirer by the prevailing theology and by the mass of inherited sentiment, against which he rarely strives successfully. And hence it would not be easy to name many thinkers whose ethical writings are not the weakest part of their contributions to philosophy. Conspicuously is this the case with Kant, with Brown, and, we may add, with John Stuart Mill.

Of Dr. Whewell we would speak with profound respect. His is the prominent figure in Cambridge university society during the time which we are passing under review. He was an intellectual gladiator whose immense reading gave birth to a currently received mythology during his lifetime, and whose vast knowledge of facts suggested the epigram of Sydney Smith—"Science is his forte, omniscience his foible;" though, as De Morgan retorted, he knew more of half-a-dozen sciences than Sydney Smith knew of theology. But whatever value we may attach to his works on scientific method—and it is possible to estimate them very highly, though dissenting from the leading doctrines which they enunciate—his warmest admirers would probably hesitate to put forward his ethical writings as constituting any claim for his philosophical renown. The Lectures on other moralists contain many felicitous observations, even where they fail as general attacks; but the "Elements of Morality," in which he appears as the constructor of an ethical system, largely original, has by most readers, we imagine, been considered as a tedious and voluminous amplification of a vicious circle.

In 1855 Dr. Whewell resigned the chair, and was succeeded by Prof. Grote. Of Grote's merits as a lecturer we cannot speak from personal knowledge, but his "Exploratio Philoso published a few months before his death, and his "Exam of the Utilitarian Philosophy," posthumously edited,* lead us to think that he was far more admirably fitted for the post he occupied than either Dr. Whewell or his own successor, Mr. Maurice. In these two volumes the reader will find, not many hints for the construction of a system of philosophy, nor even original efforts of great profundity on isolated parts of philosophy, but the continual exercise of a faculty of great critical acuteness, ever striving after an exact appreciation of the meaning of terms in any matter under discussion, though not perhaps invariably employing them with the precision that might be looked for. Add to this that the critical tendency—his chief characteristic as a philosopher—was exercised with extraordinary freedom from polemical personality, and found expression in a style which, though tedious in print, was probably not without a certain charm in conversation, and we have three qualifications of a professor whose merits, we imagine, are not easily over-estimated.

Mr. Maurice has been lost to us so recently, and the notices of his life and writings are probably so fresh in the minds of our readers, that it is unnecessary to add to the many conflicting estimates of the value of his work in philosophy even a brief criticism of our own. In view of a reputation for heterodoxy which had led to his expulsion from a college in the Strand, more remarkable, indeed, for bigotry than for intellectual brilliance, his appointment was in many respects highly creditable to the six electors—at that time all clergymen; and even if it is doubtful whether he was the ablest candidate for the post, there can be no question that his reputation was the widest.

When the newspapers stated that a successor to Mr. Maurice had been found in the Rev. Mr. Birks, we imagine that the common opinion was that the grave and reverend electors had been the victims of a dismal *jeu d'esprit*, perpetrated by some Cambridge correspondent of the London press. Time brought no contradiction of the statement, however, but the announcement of a course of lectures by the new professor; on which we concluded that, so far from being the victims of a hoax, these gentlemen had themselves practised a *mauvaise plaisanterie* on the university—whether with an ulterior motive of showing the estimation in which they held the study of philosophy, or with

---

* By the Rev. J. B. Mayor, late Fellow of St. John's College. We hope that the success of this work will be sufficient to encourage Mr. Mayor to give us another selection from Grote's philosophical writings. Whether Mr. Mayor has as much to do for his late friend as Dumont did for Bentham we have no means of knowing, but we are quite sure that what passes through Mr. Mayor's hands is eminently more readable than what the Professor saw through the press for himself.

the object of keeping somebody else out, we have never been able to divine. Mr. Maurice's nomination had made us too sanguine, no doubt, for the future. Not that we ever expected an attempt on the part of the university to obtain a profound thinker from without, such as Mr Bain or Mr. Spencer, who might adorn the professorship of Philosophy. The conspicuous absence of the names of our chief British philosophers from the annual lists of distinguished men whom the universities invest with honorary degrees, would preclude our anticipating so wise and liberal a policy as this. These decorations are reserved for continental thinkers, whose religious belief is of no particular consequence in England, and for the superfluous clergy who are shipped off to colonial bishoprics.* But are there not, we asked, Cambridge men who might fill the chair with respectable efficiency? Is there not Mr. Mayor, or Mr. Venn,† clergymen both, if orders are essential? or better still, if a layman be admissible, is there not Mr. Henry Sidgwick, than whom it would be difficult to find an abler candidate?

We entertained no feeling of hostility to Mr. Birks. His antecedents indeed were entirely creditable to him, but we were at a loss to know in what respect they qualified him for a chair of philosophy. He was a second wrangler; a fluent preacher with a crowded church; and had brought out for the Religious Tract Society an edition of Paley's Evidences, containing a translation of the Latin quotations, and an occasional declamatory foot-note against his author's "cold and cautious" expressions, or "a theory of morals as superficial and illogical as it is cold and heartless,"—criticisms with which we have not the least intention of quarrelling, but which can scarcely be accepted as evidence of profound speculative ability.

It was not unnatural to suppose that this job having been accomplished, it would be long before we heard of the Professor of Casuistry again. A professor who exerts no influence on the undergraduates because they never attend his lectures, or on the nation because he never publishes his researches, is unfortunately no rarity at our English universities. But as Mr. Birks has hastened, with perhaps more candour than discretion, to publish

* Though Halle and Bonn singled out J. S. Mill for such an award, Oxford and Cambridge understood their responsibilities as bulwarks of the faith too well to do honour to themselves by attempting to do honour to a man who held their articles in light esteem.

† We speak of Mr. Venn's merits as a moralist in these guarded terms, because we have had no experience of his powers in this department of philosophy, but we feel little doubt that the author of the "Logic of Chance," who has discussed so acutely the foundations of the Theory of Probability, would display the same acuteness in dealing with the controversies of Ethics.

his first course of lectures, adding a plain hint that the rest will follow, it appears to us desirable to offer some criticism on the introductory volume. And, indeed, we came to our task with the best hopes of deriving some advantage from the perusal, in spite of a style which a short experience has shown to be intensely rhetorical. Almost any work on ethics, which is the result of persistent thought by an intelligent student, will be found to contain the qualified or improved statement of some doctrine, by which the way is opened up for reconciliation with a doctrine of the opposite school, and progress towards a compromise of rival systems effected. We regret to say that for anything of this kind we have read the "First Principles" in vain. When we have said that the last lecture, on the Doctrine of Utility, is the best in the volume, because the freest from rhetorical exaggeration, we have satisfied our own instincts of clemency, and have enabled the reader, by the perusal of twenty pages, to decide whether he will read the previous two hundred and fifty. Not indeed that it contains a single point which would strike a student, who has read any elementary work on ethics, as new, but in it Mr. Birks's besetting sins of tumid grandiloquence and boisterous caricature of other schools are less prominent, while in his remarks (in which, however, we do not agree) on the impossibility of making the required calculation of consequences, we are willing to regard his employment of mathematical language as apposite and felicitous. The remarks again on over-legislation and Mill's "Liberty," though occupying only a page, show that the professor can write effectively when he throws off his rhodomontade, and the few lines of criticism on the episcopal antithesis in which England free was preferred to England sober have our entire concurrence (pp. 180-1).

Having thus eased our conscience by doing justice to the professor's merits, we proceed to the performance of our duty towards the public by indicating a few of his defects. On the whole we may deliberately record our conviction that this is the worst book on a philosophical subject that we have ever read, and that nothing short of solitary confinement will ever induce us to read such another.

The first objection that we have to make to Mr. Birks is his style, of which the reader must judge from the extracts which we have inserted, for other purposes than for that of exhibiting it, in the following pages. Eloquence in a philosopher we invariably regard with great suspicion. In spite of Mr. Mill's admiration of this quality in Cousin's lectures on the Philosophy of Locke, we have never been able to regard it as anything better than misplaced rant. "Philosophy," says Ferrier, "is a body of reasoned truth," and as such it requires reasoned, not impassioned expression. If we carry with us the reader's sympathy in favour of an asceticism, which banishes eloquence from a scientific treatise, we are sure of his approval in describing the tawdry rhetoric of our author as simply detestable. The end of the preacher is to stir men's feelings, and for this all the aids of oratory are rightly invoked. The end of the philosopher is to convince their reason, and here appeals to the emotions are irrelevant, or worse. But Mr. Birks is professional throughout. He is always in the atmosphere of the Trinity vicarage. The rostrum may be placed in the Law Schools, but the manner is the manner of the pulpit. Occasionally the lectures rise to the level of a Sunday morning's sermon; more frequently they seem adapted to the week-night service; while now and then they sink to the bathos of the female bible-class. The only deficiency that must have struck the audience is the absence of a hymn at the beginning and a doxology at the end. With these additions one lecture might fairly be accepted in lieu of a week's attendance at college chapel.

Mr. Birks is probably quite unconscious of any tendency towards fine writing. There seems, indeed, an irony quite unsuspected in his quotation of Aristotle's remark that it is an error "to require demonstration from the rhetorician" (p. 51). Nor do we think that his clerical functions have formed (or shall we say deformed?) his expression. He seems to the manner born. "A college essay or declamation" is appended to the lectures, delivered over forty years ago, with a slight depreciation of its style; but so far as we can discover, the style of 1833 is undistinguishable from that of the present year. The object of the republication, we may add, is to show that the "views held in the present volume . . . . . are no hasty product of recent study, but convictions early formed." Probably few men would care to claim such complete consistency as is implied in holding at sixty the raw theories of their boyhood.

We understand that Mr. Birks belongs to the Evangelical section of the Church; nevertheless, this volume marks him as an adherent of the still larger school of preachers, the Platitudinarian. He surrounds a platitude with an amount of tinsel that might well conceal a paradox. His thoughts lie hidden beneath flowers of rhetoric, and obscured by inappropriate illustrations. Or, if for a moment we may adopt the language we deprecate, we should say, that the barrenness of his reflections is disguised by a luxuriance of imitation flowers, like the tinted gewgaws with which modest housewives hide the nakedness of their stoves in summer months. The reader moves through a jungle of tropes, similes, and metaphors, from which he must continually extricate himself for a clear point of view and a firm footing; while he finds that the effort required to grasp the thought when once reached is quite incommensurate with the effort required to reach it.

Our author reveals with great frankness his contempt for modern scientific inquirers and their hypotheses. Speaking of moral truths, he says:—

"It is quite conceivable that the mode of operation of such truths, and the amount of influence they exercise, may wholly elude the notice of keen-eyed, worldly men, or even of clever essayists and philosophers, intent on physical research, or buried in the strife of parties in the political world" (p. 25.)

Again:—

"The tendency of the homogeneous to become heterogeneous and the persistency of force, where force is made to mean half a dozen different things, are signal examples of vague, unscientific, deceptive substitutes for the certainties of science" (p. 59).

"The modern theory," he remarks elsewhere, "which would isolate Physical Science from moral truth, and form the visible universe into a gigantic preserve, sacred from all intrusion of direct spiritual agency, where blind destiny alone is to rule, undisturbed by any subordination to a moral purpose, and condemned to roll for ever the stone of Sisyphus, without ministering to the moral government of responsible creatures—like the old hypothesis of Cartesian vortices—'is pressed with many difficulties'" (p. 139).

But perhaps the professor's highest flight is in the peroration of the introductory discourse, where he describes "the parting words of Milton in Comus," as "no mere utterance of a sportive fancy, but the veiled expression of the deepest philosophy, and of the highest lesson of Christian faith—a faith and a philosophy far more profound than modern theories for manufacturing some miserable semblance of a conscience out of the transmuted instincts of the ape or baboon"* (pp. 26-7).

The fact is that our author has but an indifferent idea of the value of evidence and of the methods of proof. Inquiries into the phenomena of mind conducted from the physiological side possess little charm for him. Read this:—

"Certain changes in the nervous tissues, let us grant for a moment, accompany the moral emotions of love or hatred, sympathy or envy, hope or fear. How can this *prove*† that the physical change is the cause of the emotion and not its effect? How can it *prove* that the connexion is not wholly arbitrary, and capable of being entirely different for other races, or for men themselves in the life to come?" (p. 90).

But though exacting enough in his demands for rigid demon-

* Observe the bitter alliteration.

† The italics are our own throughout.

stration from his opponents, he exhibits marvellous credulity in cases where a moral bias is strong. We find him deprecating the "cautious, defensive line of thought, which Butler and other writers have employed in their advocacy of revealed religion" as tending "to canonize doubt and uncertainty, and consecrate dimness of moral vision," whatever that means (p. 33). The professor, however, is not one of the "owls and bats of the moral world, who find it easy and natural to rest content with the dim twilight alone." He has penetrated within the veil, and not only brought word back that the angels have freewill and responsibility, but discovered something of the political constitution of the heavenly host. The practical result of these transcendental experiences is that Mr. Birks does not adopt the Woman's Rights platform, but goes in for "the subordination, in loving union, of woman to man" (p. 175).

A natural accompaniment of our author's contempt for "cautious, defensive lines of thought," is his fluctuating and unscientific employment of ethical terms requiring the most precise definition. The want of a clear perception of the meaning of the words he uses, continually leads to redundancies of language which merely offend the reader's taste; but when we find that the habit is not thrown off in dealing with the conceptions of freedom, law, responsibility, &c., we are prepared for disastrous consequences. Pleonasms like the following only show that Mr. Birks cannot write English:—"It" (Ethics) "must be from its very nature of *high and inestimable* worth. *Spurious counterfeits*, indeed, may be not only *unprofitable* but most mischievous" (p. 24). We find him alluding to "the *disputes and controversies* among moralists" (p. 35), to "a world of *actual realities*" (p. 56), to "*worthless and almost unprofitable* (!) truisms" (p. 120); "the great laws of duty" are said to "open a *wide and immense* field for the attainment of certain truth" (p. 262), while of the divorce of moral theory from practice, we are told that "it *aggravates and redoubles* guilt" (p. 46). But we have no wish to be hypercritical, and should be quite ready to explain these blemishes as due to a hysterical endeavour to be persuasive rather than to an obscurity of thought, were there no more serious failings below the surface.

The word law and the correlative terms freedom and necessity, have probably given birth to a larger family of metaphysical absurdities, than all the other names in the philosophical vocabulary together. Yet we fancied that its double meaning of command and uniformity had been sufficiently expounded of late years to prevent any one but an amateur from talking nonsense about law. The following extract shows the professor on very dangerous ground:—

"Why, then, should Moral Axioms be less fertile than the Laws of Physics in the results to which they lead? The field is higher and nobler, and the capability of large development, on every ground of reason, is just the same. If mankind at large were half as zealous in the pursuit of moral excellence as astronomers have been, since the days of Newton, in their calculation of attractive forces, and their practical study of the heavens, a thousand years would not suffice to exhaust the various development of the great laws of social duty, or bring to a close their progress in moral insight, and their successful labours of thought, and practical endeavours in this higher field" (p. 24).

Twenty pages further on we find him plunged head and ears in the ambiguity:—

"Astronomy has attained a comprehensive simplicity in its primary law, and fountain truth, such as ethics, with the aid of a Divine message, had attained long years ago. For what is the second great commandment? *It is a higher law than that of universal gravitation*, binding together the whole universe of moral agents. And it has been revealed, more dimly by natural conscience, but in plain and express terms by the great and divine Author of man's moral being" (p. 44).

What ground for comparison there can be between the extent to which a uniformity exists and the extent to which a precept is obeyed, the professor does not attempt to explain, and we find ourselves reduced to this painful dilemma: either Mr. Birks is not aware of the distinction between Laws Proper of jurisprudence and Laws metaphorically so-called (*i.e.*, scientific generalizations), in which case he is unfit for his chair; or, he is aware of the distinction, but presumes upon the ignorance of his class, in which case we can only describe his conduct (in his own words) as "immoral trifling."

Let us see how the professor fares with the venerable problem of Free-will and Necessity.

"The vexed question of the freedom of the human will," he remarks, "enters into the very foundations of Moral Science." To those who are not very sanguine of seeing the solution of this and of sundry other metaphysical puzzles, it is reassuring to read on the same page, that "we do not need fully to resolve a deep problem which loses itself in mystery, how far the will is determined by motives, or itself fixes the weight and decides the relative order of the motives themselves." The question being thus insoluble is relegated to a niche in a sort of Theory of the Conditioned. "All we need to know is that there is an extreme on either side, which is fatal to moral obligation." Responsibility disappears if we "suppose that choice is an illusion, that human acts are decided . . . simply by the concurrence and resulting effect of many external impulses and physical sensations" [the reader will observe the caricature of the necessarian doctrine that human acts are decided by motives]. "Men would then have no more claim to be moral agents than the falling apple or the flashing meteor, than stocks or stones, or the waves of the sea." Responsibility disappears equally if the will acts "without any motive, by a blind caprice." Such an agent becomes "an embodied chance, a capricious and senseless atom" (pp. 78-9).

So far Mr. Birks, in dealing with the terms freedom and necessity, has kept to the old controversy as to the existence of uniformity of sequence in the mental, as in the physical world, and has put an end to the puzzle by reducing it to a paralogism. Let us turn now to what he says in his preceding lecture on the same point. He is professing to meet the objection "to the doctrine of fixedness and certainty of Moral Science, that it is opposed to the freedom of the human will, and would tend to mechanize and freeze down to a cold, bare and heartless uniformity, the whole course of personal and social life" (p. 62). And he does so by stating the true lessons of Moral Science.

> "It lays down principles and motives, which ought to be the living fountains and sources whence our actions are to flow. It discloses, also, limits on the right hand and on the left, which they are bound not to transgress, and within which they ought to move. But when these conditions are fulfilled, it still leaves a wide and various range for the exercise of voluntary choice and human freedom. . . . . It is a law, but in the truest sense a law of liberty. It is firmly rooted in the soil below. But above it drinks in the free sunlight, ramifies into a thousand branches and branchlets, and effloresces freely amidst the play of the breeze, and under the light of heaven" (p. 64).

Now, if Mr. Birks were framing philosophical language for posterity, he might do good service by restricting the use of the word freedom to the absence of external compulsion, as he does in the last paragraph, and by keeping the obnoxious metaphor out of the theory of volition altogether. But how his present argument, with its unprecedented display of fireworks in the last line, has any connexion with the question of freewill as ordinarily understood, and as he has himself understood it in the previous extract, we are quite at a loss to discover. The readiness with which our author employs as a weapon against an adversary, a word or a doctrine picked up in the metaphysician's armoury without knowing its use, is continually reminding us of those tragical accidents in which a clumsy sportsman discharges his fowling-piece into his own body instead of bringing down his game. We are far too humane to find it, "sport to see the engineer hoist with his own petard," but the most sanguinary reader must think the repetition of the amusement dreary before he reaches the end of the volume.

Having dealt with these collateral points, we must touch slightly on the professor's treatment of what are more strictly ethical questions. Ethics he defines as "the science of Ideal Humanity" (p. 28). His object is, therefore, not Morality as it has been, but Morality as it ought to be—Deontology not History. He begins by discussing certain "difficulties which seem to beset its approaches." The first, we are told, "is grounded on the low standards of moral feeling and practice in savage tribes" (p. 33). We cannot help suspecting that the professor has introduced us to the familiar face of the savage in the wrong place. In any dispute as to the immediacy, certainty, universality and therefore intuitive character of moral judgments, our old friend is always welcome; but if any one has maintained that the existence of a low standard among barbarians prevents us from forming a high one, we wonder that Mr. Birks has wasted ammunition upon him.

Passing over a second objection drawn from the disputes between different schools of moralists, we come to the third objection to the scientific claims of ethics—"the supposed barrenness and entire want of real progress" of its truths. Before meeting this difficulty the professor decides what is meant by scientific progress.

> "Scientific progress," we are told, "may be of four different kinds. These may be styled briefly, ascensive, expansive, descensive, and diffusive. A science may climb higher towards those simple laws which rule over all its complex phenomena. It may range over a wider landscape, by unfolding those laws into a rich and large variety of secondary axioms. It may stoop down, to apply its discoveries more frequently and largely to the uses of daily life. It may gather around it a wider and wider circle of disciples, and may thus spread its light further and further in successive generations" (p. 39).

This passage is a fair sample of our author's acuteness for scientific classification. The subdivision of Ecumenology, in the first lecture, into three departments dealing respectively with "lifeless matter, *plants* and *animals or living things*," may be due to a mere *lapsus calami*, which might have befallen anybody. But the present is a more ambitious effort, in which we imagine the author takes some pride. Yet, surely, it is a very lame and illogical performance. We will not say that, in the language of everyday life, the expression might never be used in each of these senses, and more besides, but a philosopher is expected to use common language with due attention to what is properly its meaning. If for the professor's terms ascensive and expansive we substitute the old ones, inductive and deductive; if we reject his descensive kind of progress as being progress in art, not in science; and if we get rid of his diffusive order, on the ground that it denotes progress, not in science but in society, his scheme will be reduced to much humbler proportions, but will have a better basis on which to rest. Fancy a chemist replying as follows to our inquiries respecting the progress of his science since the beginning of the century: "The progress of chemistry has been ascensive; Dalton's law is a good example. It has been expansive; take for instance Andrews' identification of the ozone of the air with the ozone obtained by electrolysis and by the electrical machine. It has been descensive, for we can make our own selzer-water. It has been diffusive, as is proved by the large number of ladies who attend the British Association."—"What progress are you making?" asks a professor of his former pupil. "My progress, sir," replies the youth, "is ascensive, since I am growing tall: it is expansive, for my tailor tells me I am getting stout. It is also radical, for I intend to vote for Odger; and equatorial, because I am on my way to winter at the Cape." We imagine that a suspicion would cross the professor's mind that his quondam charge was making game of him, and in much the same fashion does Mr. Birks make game of the principles of logical division.

The replies to objections derived from the want of progress of the third and fourth kinds being thus irrelevant, we notice next how the professor meets the objection urged against Ethics on the ground of a want of progress in ascent. Mr. Buckle is quoted to the effect that there is nothing which has changed so little as the great dogmas of morality. Our author's reply to this seems somewhat of an *ignoratio elenchi*. Instead of showing that there has been progress towards higher generalizations, he tells us that moral truths are of importance.

"If the Divine wisdom," he says, "has secured to all men, whether by the voice of conscience, or by supernatural revelation, direct access to the vital elements of moral truth, and has left the answering laws or principles of the outward world to reward the study of the philosopher, and to be explored by human toil, ought the free gift, on this account, to be despised, or consigned with contempt to the list of useless and barren truisms?" (p. 42).

The reader may suppose, after reading this passage, that the professor agrees with Ockham, Dr. Johnson, Soame Jenyns and others, in regarding morality as dependent on the will of God; or that with Shaftesbury, Hutcheson, and the majority of ethical theorizers, he supports the doctrine of a Moral Sense; or that he combines the two, making the Bible the standard and Conscience an ultimate, underivable faculty, the decisions of both being identical through some pre-established harmony not specified; but the professor does nothing of the kind. On p. 229

he repudiates the first doctrine as one "which makes the Divine goodness a fiction without meaning;" and on p. 230 he repudiates the second as a mere reappearance of the former "under a thin disguise." He adopts in their stead Cudworth's theory of a certain eternal and immutable *fitness* in our actions, determined by the reason. Whenever this system is set aside, "Moral Philosophy expires, and nothing but a lifeless corpse or a shadowy phantom is left in its stead." By utilitarianism, for instance, "the fountains of thought are poisoned, and a moral palsy must quickly seize on all the springs of national and social life" (p. 238). We have no wish to underrate the value of scientific research, and the importance of truth merely because it is truth, but we should be better pleased if Mr. Birks would occasionally err in this direction, and, instead of picturing the horrible consequences which may ensue from rearing a system of ethics on a wrong basis, be willing to regard philosophy as a highly refined sport. Since the "middle or secondary principles" of utilitarians are scarcely distinguishable from those of intuitive moralists, and since, in practice, the fundamental principles of the professor have to be qualified "by a wise expediency," a little less terrorism would be the better for us all.

To return from this digression. It remains to be shown that, as regards expansion and development, the laws of ethics are free from the charge of barrenness, and this our author does by a practical illustration: *solvitur ambulando.*

"Let us consider the great maxim of the Divine Law—Thou shalt love thy neighbour as thyself. The simplicity is extreme. But the law of gravitation is also very simple. . . . And still the most profound geometers and analysts, for more than two hundred years, have tasked their powers to the utmost in tracing out and exploring its necessary consequences. . . . . Why should the Divine rule of duty revealed in the Law and the Gospel, and confirmed by the voice of natural conscience, be less fertile and various in the deductions that flow from it, and the results to which it leads? It resolves itself at once into the double inquiry—Who is my neighbour?—How ought I to love myself?" (p. 07).

In a subsequent chapter (on the Divisions of Moral Science) the problem is discussed, with an amount of subtlety which, to the unsophisticated man, may seem to border rather closely on sophistry. We are not to love our neighbour with exactly the same kind of love, which may be excessive, diseased and impure: nor exactly in the same degree, for that is hardly possible in itself (though how this makes any difference, seeing that ethics is the science of Ideal Humanity, we cannot understand). But further, the word *neighbour* excludes such a notion, for this shows that nearness helps to determine the moral obligation. "We are nearer to ourselves than to others, and have thus fuller opportunities to seek our own good, and to act for it, than theirs." All we have to say is, that this new interpretation of an old precept brings it into dangerous proximity with the maxims of the gospel of selfishness—Take care of Number One; and, Every man for himself and God for us all.

We shall make a hasty reference to but one more chapter, and then conclude. It is that in which the professor discusses the relation of ethics to political economy. After quoting an admirable passage from Senior, to the effect that the business of the economist is neither to recommend nor to dissuade—that political economy is a science, not an art—and that it deals not with virtue or happiness but with wealth, our author cracks a cumbrous joke at the economists for transgressing the rule which forbids them to offer "a single syllable of advice." He says:—

"There are few articles of general commerce of which the production has been more copious and abundant. Whatever the demand for it, either on the part of statesmen or of the general public, it has usually been far exceeded by the supply. The consequences in agreement with the maxims of their favourite science, has been a frequent depreciation in the market value of the counsels they have offered."

No doubt Mr. Birks would have but little difficulty in showing that his proviso has not always been fully acted on, but we do not think that it has been systematically ignored. Such considerations as these may go some way towards defending economists for their apparent disregard of it:—(1) We have no standard work on Political Philosophy in the language, so their occasional transgression of the strict boundaries of their own science is excusable. (2) If we lose in scientific exactness we gain immensely in interest. (3) Some writers have announced their intention to overstep the narrow limits; thus, Mr. Mill describes his work as dealing with the principles and "some of their applications to social philosophy." (4) Questions of policy, *e.g.*, forms of taxation, if discussed at all, are discussed expressly as to their economic or commercial effects. (5) In many cases, even of practice, ethical considerations are not involved at all, or are involved only in the slightest degree, so that if legislators acted on political maxims framed in accordance purely with the economical conclusions, no harm would be done. Such are the questions as to adopting gold or silver as the standard; making the sovereign conform to the napoleon in value, &c.

The Professor then gives us "the true and just view" of the science. It discusses "the laws regulating the relations between men, and all those outward objects which minister to their life, health, comfort, intellectual progress and moral welfare." The wealth about which it reasons must not be divorced from the aim of promoting the true good and welfare of man, otherwise it breeds worms and turns to corruption. "The food becomes first husks and then poison. The gold and silver rust and are cankered, and when the mischief proceeds further, eat the flesh as a consuming fire" (pp. 147-8).

Having thus sketched out a tolerably comprehensive science, our author proceeds to misrepresent the economists. Their reasonings, he says, "often rest on a secret assumption that men, in all relations of worldly business, are actually guided *and may lawfully be guided* by self-interest alone. Now, even as a statement of facts, the simplification is excessive and untrue," and we can only say the same of Mr. Birks's representation of the reasonings. The assumption of economists is that men prefer a greater gain to a smaller, in all cases, except so far as habitual aversion to labour and desire of the present enjoyment of costly indulgences operate as counter-motives. "Not that any political economist," to quote Mr. Mill, "was ever so absurd as to suppose that mankind are really thus constituted, but because this is the mode in which science must necessarily proceed." As for any assumption that mankind may be lawfully so guided, we challenge the Professor to make good his assertion by pointing to a single passage to that effect in any author of repute. His protestations on such a doctrine as "an outrage on the simplest lessons of true morality" are therefore simply superfluous.

Our author is not satisfied, however, with declamation at economists for having done the things they ought not to have done and left undone those things which they ought to have done, but descends into the arena and gives them battle with their own weapons. Remarking, with truth, on the supreme importance of the idea of value in political economy, he exhibits its analysis in the following extraordinary passage:—

"The whole of economical science may be said to depend on two or three fundamental equations, which are the moving forces in the whole system of trade. Cost, increased by a first profit, is the market value. Market value, increased by a second or third profit, is the worth, or value in use. But cost may be either real or imaginary. There is the same contrast of true and imaginary worth. The mechanism of trade depends on the cost and worth, as defined by the mere fancy, often the erring fancy, of the producer and consumer. But the benefits of trade depend on a comparison of the real cost and the real worth, and of these alone. The great and all-important contrast between a cost and a worth which are real, and one which rests on erring and mistaken impressions only, is the principle on the recognition of which it depends whether Political Economy shall be a moral or an immoral science" (p. 150).

We used to think that Mr. Ruskin had reached the climax of

economic infatuation; but as Mr. Ruskin's meaning is generally clear, we gratefully recognised the service of his writings in furnishing young students with abundant fallacies for examination, just as the Spartans used to make the intoxication of their Helots a moral lesson to their own children. Unfortunately such utterances as this of Mr. Birks are too absurd to be intelligible, and refutation is therefore impossible. It is true that the Professor considers his views of "vast importance," and tells us that "one main duty is plain,"—"to moralize Economical Science." We can only state our conviction that, had economists hampered themselves as Mr. Birks proposes, not only should we have been without a theory of value at the present time, but we should have never had one at all.

The facility with which the professor forgets on one page what he has written on the page before, is curiously illustrated ere we reach the end of the chapter. After transcribing extracts from Senior and Mill about the scope of the science, a remark of the latter that "the use of a thing in political economy means its capacity to satisfy a desire or serve a purpose," leads to the following extravagant outburst:—

"The *object* of Political Economy, as thus defined, is to multiply the production of things desired, however vicious, hurtful, and even ruinous the indulgence of those desires may be. If men are swine, its object is to provide more husks and refuse for the troughs in which they feed. If they degenerate into devils in malice and hatred, it is to multiply the desired engines of mutual destruction" (p. 160).

The object of political economy, we retort, is not to multiply the production of anything, but to expound the laws which regulate production, and the investigation is one worthy of a philosopher who values truth, even though men are swine or devils, producing nothing better than husks or engines of destruction.

But our space is filled, and we must close the book. We lay it aside with profound sadness. There have been times, it is true, when a sense of the ludicrous has been strong, but our prevailing feeling is one of regret. That Mr. Birks is a most estimable man we have no reason to doubt, but in a chair of philosophy he is in the wrong place. During his tenure of office we have no hope of seeing philosophy raised to due eminence among university studies—small hope indeed, so far as depends on his labours, of philosophy being kept alive: an increasing contempt for speculation seems a more likely result. It may be said that few attend the lectures; we reply that a university course on such a subject ought to draw crowds. It may be said that they are poll-men who go; but a poll-man, as Corporal Trim said of the negro, has a soul, and deserves to be treated as an intelligent being till something is proved to the contrary. In conclusion we venture, in all sincerity, to offer the Professor two small items of advice respecting his future publications. He tells us in the preface that this volume is offered as "a small sheaf of first fruits." We recommend, then, that to the next volume he add a marginal analysis of the contents of each paragraph, free from the meretricious embellishments of rhetoric. And secondly, that since the present crop seems to have been got up before it was ripe, he forbear for a time to invite the public to share the festivities of the harvest-home.

Art. IX.—Medical Charity: Methods of Administering it.

1. *Hospital Patients, Doctors, and Nurses.* A Lecture by Lionel S. Beale, M.B., F.R.S. London: 1874.
2. *St. John's House and Sisterhood for the Training and Employment of Nurses for Hospitals, the Poor, and Private Families.* Twenty-fifth Report of the Council. London: 1873.
3. *Report of Sub-Committee upon an Inquiry made into the Circumstances of Patients attending the Queen's Hospital, Birmingham, July,* 1873.
4. *First Report of the Medical Committee of the Charity Organization Society and Rules for Provident Dispensaries adopted by the Council, October 30th,* 1871. Second Edition. *With a Report of a Conference held at the House of the Society of Arts, December 12th,* 1871. London: 1872.
5. *The Provident System of Medical Relief Impartially Considered.* London: 1872.
6. *Report of the Committee appointed by the Medical Charities of Manchester and Salford, February,* 1874.
7. *An Act to provide for the better Distribution, Support, and Management of Medical Charities in Ireland; and to Amend an Act of the Eleventh Year of Her Majesty, to Provide for the Execution of the Laws for the Relief of the Poor in Ireland.* 7th August, 1851.
8. *Report to the Right Honourable Gathorne Hardy, M.P., President of the Poor Law Board, on the System of Medical*

Relief to the Out-door Poor in Ireland, under "The Dispensaries Act," 1851. By JOHN LAMBERT, Esq., Poor Law Inspector. Presented to the House of Commons, 8th Feb., 1867.

9. *Annual Report of the Local Government Board for Ireland, being the First Report under "The Local Government Board (Ireland) Act,"* 35 & 36 Vict. c. 109. *With Appendices.* Presented to both Houses of Parliament by command of Her Majesty. Dublin: 1873.

10. *An Act for the Establishment in the Metropolis of Asylums for the Sick, Insane, and other Classes of the Poor, and of Dispensaries; and for the Distribution over the Metropolis of portions of the Charge for Poor Relief; and for other purposes relating to Poor Relief in the Metropolis* (29 March, 1867).

IN our last number we exposed several grave abuses of medical charity as now generally administered: in the present article we intend to describe and discuss different plans which have been proposed as remedies of those abuses, and to consider whether it be possible to organize a comprehensive system for the administration of medical relief of the destitute poor, and for the lower classes generally, which shall be dissociated from the evils we have dwelt upon, which shall comprise different methods worked harmoniously with each other, and adapted to the different classes of persons needing relief, and which shall prove itself that which has long been anxiously sought for—an agency for the distribution of medical charity at once thoroughly efficient and wholly beneficent.

The evils or abuses of medical charity which we exposed in a former article may be summed up as follows:—

1. That, exclusive of paupers, the number of inhabitants of this metropolis who are recipients of medical charity is upwards of 1,200,000, or 3 in every 10 of the whole population.

2. That a large portion of these recipients are not really and truly proper objects of such charity in any rational sense of that term.

3. That the rate of increase in the number of persons receiving medical charity during the last forty years has been astonishingly rapid—nearly five times faster, in fact, than has been the rate of increase of the general population during the same period.

4. That persons whose incomes enable them to command many luxuries are in the habit of obtaining all the medical aid they require from an hospital or dispensary.

5. That as time advances the administration of medical charity

is being extended, step by step, to persons occupying successively higher positions in the social scale.

6. That the special form of pauperism consisting in the receipt of medical and surgical aid without paying for it, tends to induce general pauperism.

7. That the extensive dispensation of medical charity now prevalent has the effect of supplementing, or, in other words, lowering, the wages of the working classes, and thus of benefiting their employers to a corresponding extent.

8. That the benefits thus obtained directly by the employed, and indirectly by their employers, are conferred chiefly by the members of the unpaid professional staffs of the different medical charities—men who are confessedly among the hardest worked of the community.

9. That, owing to the enormous magnitude which medical charity has attained, the hospital waiting-rooms are excessively over-crowded, it being customary to see patients, to listen to their complaints, and to prescribe for them at the rate of about one per minute, and often much more rapidly.

10. That though an indefinable proportion of the recipients of medical charity are benefited by it, "very much of the assistance given is merely nominal," and "is both a deception on the public and a fraud upon the poor."

11. That voluntary medical charity, as now administered in the metropolis, costs at least 600,000*l.* a year, exclusive of the annual value of the lands and buildings occupied by the several hospitals and dispensaries; and that even if it were expedient to administer such charity to the extent now practised, its present cost is extravagantly great—quite double, in fact, what it might and ought to be.

12. That as a general rule, the so-called "advertising hospitals," those—namely, which are mainly supported by voluntary donations and subscriptions, are in the habit of so stating their respective claims for help by the charitable public as to imply that they are on the verge of bankruptcy, whereas, in fact, the majority of them receive almost every year more than they expend, accumulate capital the interest of which yields them a permanent income, and thus become enabled in proportion to the magnitude of that income to act independently and, not seldom, in defiance of the salutary influence of public opinion.

The proposals for the reform of the system of which the grave abuses here summarized form a large part are many: some of them are intended to deal with special evils, and others are designed to effect constitutional changes; but, so far as we are acquainted with them, none of them seem to us satisfactory. A reformation, to be thorough, must recognise and grapple with all the evils of the system in question, and must so deal with them that while effecting their abolition, the origination of other evils of equal if not of greater magnitude consequent on their destruction must be rendered impossible. How far these conditions have been fulfilled by the reformers whose plans have been already proposed or carried out in practice, our readers can judge for themselves in the sequel.

Some persons who interest themselves in the subject of medical charity are chiefly impressed with one only of its numerous evils—namely, that of the wonderfully rapid and unsatisfactory manner in which the treatment of out-patients is conducted. Concerning themselves less with the question whether any proportion, and if so what proportion, of these patients are really fit objects of medical charity than with the question are these patients properly treated, such persons speedily conclude that existing arrangements absolutely preclude them from being properly treated; that no physician or surgeon, whatever may be his natural ability and professional skill, performs his hospital duties efficiently if he sees, listens to, and prescribes for patients at rates varying from, say 40 to 90 per hour; and that the obvious remedy for this great and glaring evil consists in increasing the number of the Medical and Surgical staff of each medical charity to such an extent as may suffice to insure adequate examination and treatment of each patient. A preliminary and cogent objection to this remedy consists in the fact that in a large proportion of cases it is impracticable. The number of consulting-rooms at each institution is, of course, limited, and, as a part of the present system of administration, each of these rooms is occupied each day alternately by the physicians and surgeons who see the out-patients, and to provide additional rooms as well as additional hospital-porters or attendants in these would necessitate either a greatly increased expenditure or a radical change in the management of the expenditure now incurred. The probability that either of these expedients will be resorted to is very small indeed. But a much stronger and more fundamental objection to the plan in question is that, in reality, it would greatly increase and perpetuate the very evil which it is proposed to remedy. We have, we believe, demonstrated that the provision of gratuitous medical aid as now obtainable in the metropolis creates a demand for it in classes of persons who, before it was thus obtainable, were in the habit of maintaining their independence in respect to medical men, and that just in proportion as that aid is to be had without being paid for, are the spirit and habit of independence undermined, and the practice of requesting medical charity becomes wider and wider spread, so that, in effect, if arrangements were made insuring satisfactory treatment of all out-patients who now apply for it, the demands for it would rapidly increase until the evil which had been temporarily got rid of had re-established itself on a scale many times larger than before. Until a radical cure of the evil in question has been effected it may be expedient to attempt to palliate it by appointing additional physicians and surgeons to those hospitals or dispensaries which are most especially over-crowded, and in which it may be possible to provide an extra set of consulting rooms; moreover, in some cases the rooms which are used in one part of the day by one physician and surgeon might be used by another physician and surgeon during another part of the day. But, for the reason just given, such measures should be regarded as at best only palliatives, and palliatives which, while capable of smoothing the difficulties attending the transition from one system to another, would most assuredly, if long persisted in, augment and intensify enormously the very malady they were intended to lessen.

It has been suggested that a sufficient length of time for an adequate examination and treatment of each patient might easily be given without any change of, or addition to, existing arrangements, if only the physicians and surgeons of each hospital or dispensary would attend during a longer period on each occasion when they are there to see their patients. This suggestion has been especially insisted on by those courageous conservators of acknowledged abuses—viz., the gentlemen forming that minority of the professional staff of the Metropolitan Free Hospital, which made itself the instrument used by the General Committee of that hospital when demanding the resignation of Dr. Chapman, because he had adverted in a public journal to the excessive over-crowding of the waiting-rooms of that institution. Those Gentlemen pointed out to the General Committee that if he thought the number of patients attending at the Hospital were greater than could be treated satisfactorily within the time customarily allotted to them, it was quite competent for him on the days of his attendance there to remain the whole afternoon, in order to give to each patient as much time as he might think desirable. But this suggestion if it were good for anything, applied not only to Dr. Chapman but to each member of the professional staff of every hospital and dispensary in which the evil in question obtains. No doubt some members of those staffs can afford to give nearly the whole of two days a week to the treatment of hospital patients; but such persons occupy exceptional positions in respect both to professional practice and private fortune. Much the larger number of the professional officials of medical charities have so many, and such imperative claims on their time, and the greater part of the remainder are so engaged in the struggle for existence, that the suggestion that they should give without any remuneration, nearly two-thirds of their working hours to attendance on hospital patients is not merely unreasonable—it is simply absurd. And herein lies in fact one of the most essential, and perhaps insuperable, difficulties in the way of organizing a thoroughly efficient system of medical charity the professional officials of which shall be wholly or in great part honorary.

The evil now adverted to has been encountered in some hospitals, but certainly not destroyed, by limiting the number of out-patients admitted each day for treatment. Some time ago the Committee of St. George's Hospital adopted a rule of this kind and applied it very stringently. Accordingly, no medical officer attending out-patients was allowed to see more than twenty fresh cases on any given day; and in that number all in-patients who afterwards became out-patients, and all out-patients whose tickets of admission had been renewed, were not only counted but took precedence of other applicants and thus greatly diminished the number of really new cases. Moreover, the circumstances of applicants for admission were, we believe, inquired into by, or at the suggestion of, the Charity Organization Society. But while writing, we learn that the authorities of this hospital have modified these rules: now in-patients who have become out-patients, and out-patients whose tickets have been renewed, will not be counted as fresh cases, and therefore twenty *bonâ-fide* new applicants will be admitted each day. The patients, excepting those in the Ophthalmic department, will still be subject, we understand, to inquiries conducted by the Charity Organization Society. We learn that the Westminster Hospital has also adopted restrictive regulations of a kind similar to those just described.

A still more decisive step in the same direction has been taken by the Committee of the Great Northern Hospital, which has closed its out-patient department. Insufficiency of funds has partly operated, we are told, in conducing to this end; but we understand that a consideration of the abuses associated with the out-patient system as now conducted, has also had a large share in originating the resolve just mentioned; and it is not improbable that this hospital may reopen its out-patient department, subject to restrictions like to those of St. George's, or reorganized in such manner as the managers of the hospital may, after due deliberation, deem expedient.

We heartily congratulate these three institutions on the possession and practice of the moral courage which they have exhibited in attempting at least to grapple with the difficulties now adverted to; but though they have fairly set themselves to do so, they have certainly not overcome them: instead of untying the knot, they have simply cut through it. Of the large number of persons who are in the habit of applying at St. George's and at Westminster Hospital, a portion of them are no doubt fit objects of medical charity, and a portion of them are not; now the admission of twenty fresh patients, by any process of selection, before the claims of the whole of the applicants have been examined, even although the twenty admitted may be subsequently subject to adequate scrutiny by the Charity Organization Society, is liable to leave, and in fact must leave each day medically destitute a considerable number of persons whose claims are as great as, and often greater than, the claims of those who have been fortunate enough to obtain admission. We say *fortunate enough* advisedly; for such a method may be fairly likened to a system of gambling—the favoured recipients of the medical charity sought for obtaining it, not by any merit of their own, or by possessing any special claim to exceptional consideration, but by happening to be those who reach the hospital first on the morning when they present themselves for admission. Such a system as this, by affording, as it does, ample time to physicians, surgeons, and students, thoroughly to examine and study the limited number of fresh cases admitted each day, may be eminently conducive to the efficiency and success of the medical schools attached to those hospitals; but as an agency for the dispensation of medical charity, in so far as out-patients are concerned, it is all but an abandonment of the work which those institutions are supposed to be peculiarly fitted for; and the need still remains as great as before of an organization capable of selecting rightly from the crowds of applicants for medical charity those who are really deserving objects of it, and of affording them real relief, while sending "empty away" the herd of impostors of various kinds who swell the daily crowds which now fill the out-patient waiting-room of the metropolitan hospitals. There is no medical school attached to the Great Northern Hospital, but in so far as the closure of its out-patient department is due to an appreciation of the inherent difficulties of working it satisfactorily, even if sufficient funds for the purpose were forthcoming, that closure is an especially impressive intimation that the Committee of the hospital are of opinion that a radical reform of the present system of hospital-administration is necessary in order to justify them in undertaking the treatment of out-patients.

It has often been urged, and with considerable justice, that if those who in great measure maintain hospitals by their donations and subscriptions, and who are generally called governors —we presume on the *lucus à non lucendo* principle, because they never govern—would really exercise a thorough supervision and control of them the evil in question, as well as many others, might be easily and speedily remedied. We are confident that a great improvement in the general administration of hospitals might thus be effected, but we doubt if the special abuse we are now considering will be eradicated, or even much lessened by the "resolutions" of governors

The primal necessity of self-preservation is felt quite as keenly by hospital-officials as by other living things: even if the managers of a hospital are intent only on discharging their duties in the best possible manner, the organization, consisting of the hospital and its paid officials, of whom its secretary is chief, needs a considerable income for its support; and in the case of most hospitals—viz., those mainly dependent on donations and subscriptions, that income is uncertain and precarious—its fluctuations being, to a large extent, the expression of the fluctuating opinions and feelings of its donors. As we have already explained, many of these consider their contributions as a kind of investment, to be drawn upon at any time when they desire to obtain medical or surgical assistance for their employés, dependents or other persons, free of cost. It is not to be supposed that in such cases governors whose inducements to subscribe are wholly or in part of the kind just indicated would continue to do so if their recommendations of persons for admission into or treatment at the hospital should fail to accomplish the object intended in the majority of cases in which such recommendations are given. It is well known that there is an implied understanding that they shall, as a general rule, be acted upon; and, indeed, as we have previously pointed out, an inducement is held out by hospital committees to the charitable public to subscribe, by assuring it that its power of recommending persons for admission as in- or out-patients is in proportion to the amount subscribed—a definite statement of the privileges obtainable in this respect in proportion to the amount of subscriptions, being published by different hospitals. Considering these facts, our readers will readily understand that the managers of subscription-supported hospitals must find it extremely difficult—indeed, almost impossible—to exercise any really selective power when admitting patients for treatment. No doubt, in really glaring cases of abuse of the charity, the Secretary does venture occasionally to disregard a governor's letter of recommendation; but he knows that were he frequently to do so, the income of the hospital would decline; and as he, together with the whole staff of permanent officials, whether lay or professional, are deeply interested in the maintenance and growth of the institution, the force of temptation to admit patients indiscriminately is almost irresistibly great. Moreover, benevolent motives ally themselves with selfish ones in working to one and the same end: a hospital Committee, including the permanent Secretary, inspired with a strong desire to alleviate human suffering may easily, and indeed is very likely to assure itself that in the present state of society at all events, it is impossible to minister to the wants of those who are really deserving medical charity, without at the same time affording aid to a large number of those who have no rightful claim to it, and hence it is easily intelligible that a man in the position of Secretary of any of the hospitals in question feels that the growth of his personal importance, influence, and income, which is generally proportionate to the growth of the hospital, is a satisfactory indication of the amount of benefit which it confers. Assuming this view of the operation of the causes at work in the organization and growth of subscription-supported hospitals to be approximatively correct, we think that there is in their very constitution an obstacle to the selection of patients who are alone deserving of charitable assistance—an obstacle which seems to us insuperable.

It is manifest from the tenor of the immediately foregoing remarks that in proportion as hospitals are supported by permanent endowments they disembarrass themselves of the obstacle just indicated, and therefore, that hospitals deriving their income wholly or nearly so from real property, possess the power of instituting a thorough scrutiny into the character and condition of every applicant for medical or surgical assistance before granting it. Accordingly, the great metropolitan hospitals, St. Bartholomew's, St. Thomas's, and Guy's, being in a position to exercise such a scrutiny—or in other words, being lifted above the temptation prevailing in subscription-supported hospitals to avoid such a scrutiny—they ought systematically to practise it. As a matter of fact, however, they do not. Were we to attempt to explain why they do not, we should be led into a discussion beyond the limits assigned to this article, we must now content ourselves therefore with pointing out that so long as their constitutions and legal powers are what they are, their administration is beyond the reforming influence of public opinion, unless through the agency of Parliament.

It appears, then, that as matters now stand, a thoroughly efficient system of selecting from the daily crowds of applicants for medical charity those only who are fit objects of it, and of restricting it to them, is not likely to be spontaneously adopted, either by the hospitals supported by subscriptions or by those supported by the endowments: the former dare not adopt such a system, and the latter will not. Under these circumstances it remains for us to inquire whether extraneous influences can be brought to bear upon them, in order to enable the former and to constrain the latter to do so.

The real controlling power over the hospitals supported by donations and subscriptions lies, of course, in the supporters of those hospitals—the governors; but, as a general rule, they refuse to give themselves the trouble of exercising it, and in the majority of those exceptional cases in which they do use it, personal interests intervene to cause it to be misused. Thousands of persons willingly give money in aid of the medical charities, but how few there are who are also willing to give their time, in order to supervise and insure the rational expenditure of the money they contribute! It may be urged, and with a considerable show of reason, that the very question, What constitutes a thoroughly judicious administration of medical charity, especially with respect to out-patients, is of recent origin; that persons who have given much attention to the subject are far from unanimous in answering that question; and that therefore we have no right to expect that hospital governors, whose average mental calibre is probably neither more nor less than that of the majority of people constituting the society in which they move, should be animated with sociological and politico-economical ideas in advance of those held by their acquaintances, and should come forward as energetic reformers in a department of our social system which they are by no means sure needs any change at all, and which, in fact, they have always supposed to be precisely the one least liable to abuse of any kind. But indeed, we have formed no extravagant expectations of what the average hospital governor is likely to do, although we have a very decided opinion of what he ought to do, so long as he is a governor at all; we judge of him by his works, and those are almost wholly of a negative character. In his capacity of governor he is called upon to work for a short time during one day only in the year; he ought, in fact, to attend the annual meeting of the subscribers to the hospital, and to aid in securing a free expression of opinion concerning the administration of the hospital affairs during the preceding year. Were he only to do so much, he would in fact do a great deal, and a reasonable hope might then be entertained that, although the Managing Committee would scarcely be likely to enter on a vigorous war with the chief evil of the out-patient system by adopting the system of selection just mentioned, it would probably inquire into and cause the destruction of many other evils of lesser magnitude; and in doing so, would really work a great change for the better.

A Committee called upon to give an account of its administration during the preceding year to a meeting of a considerable proportion of the subscribers to the hospital, would not dare to confess that it had rigorously excluded from the Committee-room every member of its professional staff, as the Managing Committee of the Metropolitan Free Hospital, for example, persists in doing. It is manifest to any one who thinks at all, that inasmuch as the physicians and surgeons of a hospital are the only persons connected with it who, besides possessing a general education presumably equal at least to that of any lay member of the Committee, possess professional knowledge and experience, and special acquaintance with the character, condition, and needs of the applicants for medical charity, derived from intimate and confidential intercourse with them, which is alone practicable by the professional members of the hospital staff, they are pre-eminently qualified to take an active part in the government of the hospital with which they are connected. They know best the class of medicines most needed, and the nature and quantity of the various and special luxuries likely to be required for particular classes of patients; they are the most competent to determine the arrangements of the respective wards, and how many beds may be placed in each; they can best judge what surgical and other professional instruments and appliances are necessary; and, in brief, they are best qualified generally to declare what are the several constituents of an efficient hospital organization. Being so, they are also of course the most able to discern and point out any abuses which may grow up in it. Such being their qualifications for membership, prudent governors—in fact, governors intent merely on "getting their money's worth for their money"—would not dream of stultifying themselves by sanctioning, or even permitting, the exclusion of the professional staff from the Managing Committee.

Moreover, if the "secretary and house governor," or any lay member of the Managing Committee, should advocate or suggest such an exclusion at a meeting of a considerable number of independent governors, he would expose himself to grave suspicion of being animated by some very questionable motive. If the secretary did this it would probably—and, indeed, reasonably—be surmised that he was anxious to avoid the scrutiny of those who could see and appreciate most clearly both his conduct and accounts; indeed, any member of the Committee favouring such a scheme might be supposed anxious to promote the secretary's virtual despotism and personal advancement at the expense of the hospital as an agency for the distribution of efficient medical relief. Lay members of the Managing Committee who should propose or aid in the exclusion from it of the professional staff, but who could not be suspected of abetting the usurping designs of the secretary himself, would certainly by such conduct invite an inquisition into their own doings and objects; for it is scarcely conceivable that such attempts are ever made except in order to secure personal advantages of some kind, if not in the shape of money in the shape of power more or less irresponsible, and it is well known that money and power of this sort are to a great extent at least mutually convertible elements. If, after such an inquisition, it should appear that the member in question could not be suspected of acting from either of the motives just mentioned, the governors would probably and reasonably conclude that he was a dupe of the secretary, and that the sooner he was relieved of his functions as a member of the Committee the better for the hospital.

We cannot here enter into a detailed examination of the facts, a knowledge of which is necessary in order to enable us to judge rightly on the question of authority which has recently arisen between the Committee of King's College Hospital and the nursing staff supplied by the Sisterhood of St. John's House; but we are of opinion that if the governors of that hospital had been careful to perform conscientiously the duties implied in their name, the ladies of the nursing staff would not have found it necessary to bring their grievance before the public. Indeed, it is difficult to avoid regarding with grave suspicion the motives of the attempt of the Hospital Committee to obtain for itself formally, but practically for its secretary, the power hitherto exercised by the chief of the Sisterhood at the Hospital. Such a procedure would obviously disintegrate the organization of the Sisterhood employed there, and would therefore render all efficient discipline and control of its members by the Lady Superior impossible. It appears that, step by step, and much to the detriment of the nursing arrangements, her authority has been seriously undermined. All the female domestics within the Hospital were under her control, but recently those waiting on the resident officers and those serving in the Hospital kitchen and having charge of the linen (except in the wards) have been withdrawn from her charge and placed under that of the Secretary or, in his absence, under that of his subordinate, the Steward. Moreover, the Committee have established a laundry within the basement of the Hospital (the fumes from which do not improve the air breathed by the patients in the wards above), and have placed the housekeeper and laundry-women also under the same authority. Our readers will not be surprised that—

"As a natural consequence the Sister in charge has been compelled to complain again and again of neglect of duty in relation to the wards on the part of these domestic officers and servants, almost entirely without remedy; her complaints and those of the Sisters having been too often simply negatived, and therefore dismissed as undeserving of attention. A spirit of resistance and opposition has been presented in those countless details of administration which, though individually trivial, have in the aggregate a most important bearing upon the nursing of a Hospital, which so largely depends upon exact and careful attention to orders given; and thus the performance of the duties of the Sisters and Nurses has become not only irksome, but extremely difficult."

We learn that when the Sisterhood of St. John's House undertook the nursing at King's College it was understood by those who framed the agreement on behalf of the Hospital and the Sisters "that St. John's House brought with it into the Hospital its own internal government and its control over its nurses, with which the Hospital Committee was not to interfere so long as the work of nursing was well done." St. John's House supplies to the hospital, at a cost to the Hospital of 2000*l.* per annum, a nursing staff of forty-two persons, besides the Sisters and lady pupils who conduct the work, and whose services are given freely and without charge. Eight Sisters, as well as from eight to twelve lady pupils, some of whom are nearly as efficient as the Sisters themselves, are always resident in the hospital. It is only reasonable to suppose that such a body of educated women thoroughly disciplined and skilful, as well as zealous in the performance of their honorary duties, must be a great acquisition to any hospital; and when it is considered that the nurses under their direction are educated by them to do their work in the best possible manner, and are thoroughly superintended in the doing of it, it is difficult to avoid the conclusion that the nursing arrangements of King's College Hospital are of a thoroughly superior kind; and indeed the duties of the Sisters there have been regarded by them as so much the most important part of their work that in order to discharge them the more efficiently "St. John's House was removed from Westminster to Norfolk Street, Strand, in order to be near its new field in the Hospital." In proof of the efficiency of the organization in question as a nursing agency we may mention that it is employed to conduct the nursing of Charing Cross Hospital, of the Hospital for Sick Children at Nottingham, and of the Galignani Hospital in Paris. In February, 1873, the Governors of Charing Cross Hospital at their annual meeting "thanked the Lady Superior and Sisters of St. John's House for their valuable services as nurses in the Hospital;" and also in the same month the Governors of King's College Hospital "in annual court renewed their grateful acknowledgment for zeal, kindness, and devotion which have been evinced in the conduct of the nursing department of the Hospital by the Lady Superior and Sisters of St. John's House." In February last a protest, signed by six members of the professional staff of the Hospital, was addressed to its President and

Governors. The first paragraph of that protest contains the following passage:—

"When we first knew that differences existed between the Committee of Management and the ladies who, for seventeen years, have nursed our Hospital so much to our satisfaction, we, as members of the In-patient Medical Staff of King's College Hospital, felt it to be our duty to address the Committee of Management, and to assure them that, in our opinion, any change which would remove the nursing from the care of the Sisters of St. John's House, is greatly to be deprecated, and would be calamitous to the Hospital and to the interests of the patients."

In presence of the evidence here adduced, it would be difficult to maintain that the work of nursing in King's College Hospital is not "well done," and therefore that the Hospital Committee can either justify its interference with the Management of the Lady Superior, or its resolution to determine the connexion which has subsisted upwards of seventeen years between the Hospital and St. John's House.

We have, we believe, carefully read every document and letter which has been published in consequence of the resolution just mentioned, as well as the report of the meeting of Governors of the Hospital, which recently took place, and we have been unable to find any substantial charge against the management of the nursing department, or any valid reason why the Sisters should be dismissed from the Hospital. Considering judicially the whole facts of the case, and aiding ourselves in estimating their significance by the light shed upon them from the history of the administration of other hospitals, we are constrained to conclude that the resolution of the Committee to get rid of the Sisters of St. John's House, and to replace them by a body of nurses each of whom shall be under the immediate direction and control of the Committee or its representatives, is a resolution which has originated in a desire of the Committee to obtain for itself and to exercise a greater share of power than it has hitherto possessed, and especially that that power may be mainly vested in the hands of the Secretary, who will thus become—as nearly all hospital secretaries do—virtually despotic. But whether this conclusion be right or wrong, it is manifest that the case in question is one for the decision of the Governors, and we are glad that in this instance the aggrieved party brought their case before the public with such resolute energy as to excite a considerable interest in it, and thus to assemble an unusually large and important annual meeting of those in whom the power over the hospital is vested. Fortunately for the Sisters, their cause excites interest in and is espoused by many important and influential persons, owing to the fact that they are a religious body; but for this reason it is to be noted that the energy of the Governors cannot be taken as a sample of that which they would display in ordinary cases, in which the subject to be investigated is devoid of the charm attaching to the redress of the grievances of distressed ladies, who moreover are surrounded with a religious halo.

The Soho Hospital for Women is also presenting a case claiming the especial intervention of its governors or supporters. It appears that its medical staff, with one distinguished exception—viz., Dr. Protheroe Smith—has hitherto been deplorably subordinate to the General Committee of this charity, in accordance with the following bye-law:—"On 31st day of December, 1854, and on the 31st day of December in every alternate year from that date, all acting honorary medical officers (excepting officers appointed before the year 1850) shall go out of office." But this bye-law not being sufficiently humiliating to the professional staff, the General Committee has enacted that each member of that staff shall resign his office, and then, if he please, offer himself for re-election. From all that we have previously said, our readers will readily appreciate the significance of this remarkable bye-law, by virtue of which the physicians and surgeons of the hospital, while denied any voice in its management, are held in a position of helpless and pitiable subjection to the General Committee.

We presume that if these gentlemen choose to unite in laying their case before the whole of the subscribers to the hospital, and in appealing to them so to recast its organization as to insure to its medical staff an adequate share in its government, its subscribers might be induced to meet together in order to revise and amend the laws of the hospital, and to found its government on reason and justice. Here, again, therefore, is a case affording ample scope for the common sense and energetic action of the subscribers—a sphere in which they might work great good; but whether they can be so far roused from the apathy in which they usually slumber as to be induced to take part in the reform urgently needed in this hospital, remains to be seen. Certain it is that—

"the form of government established and sought to be strengthened at the Hospital for Women is," as observed by the *British Medical Journal*, "one of unmixed and irresponsible despotism. A self-elected committee at a special hospital propose to assume the absolute right of annually dismissing their medical staff, *en bloc* or individually, without question asked, without appeal to the governors, or without notice given. Such pretensions are absurd, irrational, and go to the root of all good government. The committee will undoubtedly consult the interests of the hospital by revising such rules. No medical staff of repute will, we are satisfied, be found willing to submit to them. If they did, they would certainly incur a loss of self-respect and of the respect of the profession."

We agree with our contemporary in thinking that the committee *would* "undoubtedly consult the interests of the hospital by revising such rules," but we are far from thinking that it "*will*" spontaneously do so. Moreover, experience does not justify the assertion that "no medical staff will be found willing to submit to them;" but, on the contrary, experience teaches that every day in several of the London hospitals medical men "of repute" do submit themselves to an amount of humiliating treatment from the committees of the several hospitals with which they are connected, which can only be accounted for by supposing that there are few avenues to professional success in the metropolis, except those involving exposure to the disgraceful ordeal here indicated. How far those who expose themselves to it incur a loss of self-respect and of the respect of the profession, we leave the profession itself to determine. We rejoice, however, in observing that the professional journals thoroughly concur in the views we have advocated on this subject. The one just quoted deserves great credit for the courage and outspokenness with which it has treated the question, and we observe that the *Medical Times and Gazette* assumes a like attitude. In its issue of February 21st last it says:—

"Arrogance, ignorance, disregard of the views and interests of the actual workers, and a most extraordinary exaggeration of their own consequence, characterize many of the bodies entrusted by the charitable with the duty of disbursing what they give for the benefit of the poor. . . . Will the public never discover that the medical staff of our public charities ought to work *with*, instead of being at the mercy of, the committee? In some few hospitals every physician and surgeon is a member of committee by virtue of his office; but this wholesome rule we believe to be still the exception, while in many institutions there is not a single member of the staff on the Committee of Management. In several hospitals we are acquainted with the physicians and surgeons, like the domestics and porters, are looked upon as the 'servants' of the committee, and in some instances treated accordingly. . . . The secretary often possesses more real power than the entire medical staff; and, in many instances, all that members of committee know of the staff is 'reported' to them by this individual, who, as their officer and representative, exercises absolute power in a manner certain to earn their confidence and support."

The writer of the article just quoted concludes it by expressing the opinion that "the great interests of the medical charities would be more fully considered and better provided for if the public would insist that the responsibility of administering the funds and managing the paid officials were shared by the medical staff," with, we presume he means, a certain number of lay members of the executive committee of each hospital. We do not know whether by "the public" he means the general public, and if so we do not understand how he thinks the general public should insist on the reform he suggests. The only way, as far as we can see, in which the general public could do so would be by an Act of Parliament, which is certainly not likely to be passed. That part of the charity-giving public which supports the unendowed hospitals, might and ought to insist on such a reform, and as we have shown, if they would only do what they have the power of doing a very large measure of improvement would be effected. There are three ways in which they might be influenced and induced thus to do their duty:—

(1) The professional staff of any given hospital finding itself excluded from exercising any governmental control over it might appeal to the subscribers, setting forth the abuses which they desire to remedy as well as the reforms they advocate, and urging the subscribers to meet and pass such resolutions as might be necessary to effect the changes desired. For such an attempt to have a chance of success it would be indispensable that the whole or nearly the whole of the staff should be convinced of the desirableness of the change proposed, that they should have the courage to act out their convictions, and that they should co-operate unanimously to achieve the end proposed. We confess that our knowledge of hospital staffs does not encourage us to hope that such unanimity and co-operation for such a purpose is at all probable; and even if it were it is by no means certain that the deplorable apathy of hospital subscribers or Governors could be so far overcome by an appeal of the kind suggested as to induce them to meet together in numbers sufficient to prevail over "the powers that be."

(2) The several professional staffs of the subscription-supported hospitals might constitute themselves an association for the reform of hospital abuses, for the assertion and maintenance of their own rights as hospital officials, and especially, therefore, for the acquisition of a due share in the Government of the hospitals, with which they are severally connected. Such an association would be able to exercise considerable power, and would achieve indirectly all that the Hospital Out-patient Reform Association will ever be able to achieve directly, and very much more besides. We have given reasons why it is unlikely that the out-patient reform, to effect which that association was established, can be thoroughly accomplished by the unendowed hospitals, with or without the stimulus of that association, or of any other extraneous influence. But while a considerable improvement in that direction may no doubt be effected, the sphere for hospital reform in other directions is so ample, and by obtaining the reforms required in various directions the out-patient system itself could be so beneficially acted upon, that we commend to the consideration of the Committee of the Out-patient Reform Association the expediency of enlarging their scope, and so modifying their programme as to

enable themselves to comprise, in the object of their endeavours, the achievement of the several kinds of hospital reform which would be easily and certainly accomplished, if the professional staffs of the various hospitals possessed that ascendancy in their government which is indispensable for their good management and maximum degree of usefulness. We fear that so long as the Out-patient Reform Association continues simply as such, and limits its efforts to achieving the reform which its name indicates, it will fail to produce any effects proportionate to its efforts, and will continue to have a mere lingering existence.

(3) The Committee of the Hospital Sunday Fund in the exercise of its discretion as distributor of that fund, may exert, we believe, a large amount of controlling influence over the conduct and administration of the numerous hospitals and dispensaries among which the money is divided. Of course the sum of Thirty, Forty, or even Fifty Thousand pounds, is small in comparison with the aggregate income of those numerous institutions, yet inasmuch as any hospital or dispensary which refuses to comply with the conditions which the Committee chooses to prescribe may be debarred from participating in that fund, the Committee is thus, to a certain extent, virtually master of the situation, and can exert a controlling influence over most of the medical charities of the metropolis. If this Committee were fully informed of the abuses obtaining in any given hospital, and especially of the exclusion of the medical staff from its governing body, the Committee might probably exert so much pressure upon it as to induce it to reconstitute itself on a rational and just basis, and, as far as practicable, to put an end to the abuses complained of. The Chairman of the Committee for the apportionment of the Hospital Sunday Fund, like a Chancellor of the Exchequer in a still wider sphere, will probably find his favour eagerly sought by most of the numerous bodies, whose interests he will have the power of promoting; and in order to insure that favour they will, we suppose, be willing, as a general rule, to give such ample information, statistical and otherwise, about themselves, and adopt such various reforms as he may think the interests of the public require. We say "*various* reforms," because we do not think that even he will be able to induce the subscription-supported hospitals to make a *radical* change for the better, in their out-patient departments, unless their supporters should in yearly increasing numbers send their subscriptions direct to him to be appropriated as he and the Committee over which he presides may think best. It seems, indeed, that to a certain extent they are already doing so: the aggregate amount of subscriptions sent direct to the dispensaries last year was 1000*l.* less than previously; and it is reasonable to suppose that the more the nature of the office of the Committee and of its relations to the several Medical Charities is understood

by the most enlightened and most truly disinterested members of the charity-giving public, the more they will become inclined either to entrust their gifts directly to the chairman of that Committee, or only to those charities which freely submit themselves to its supervision. In this way that element of responsibility which hitherto has been in great measure wanting in our voluntary medical charities might be gradually and to a great extent, if not completely developed.

Governors of even the most thoroughly self-regarding sort—men, for example, who subscribe to a hospital in order to secure for their workmen and their families medical aid free of cost—would be interested in insuring for such persons better treatment than they can possibly receive, when the average length of time of their interviews with the "Doctor" does not exceed one minute. If such governors, who may be supposed to be practical common-sense men, were to sit down before the problem—how to lengthen the interview of each patient with the doctor from one minute to two or even to three, they would at once be brought face to face with the main difficulty and opprobrium of the present out-patient system; and then we imagine they would do one of three things: they would insist on an increase of the professional staff and of consulting-rooms for its efficient working; or they would restrict the number of patients admitted for treatment; or, if neither of these plans were found practicable, they being as we have supposed common-sense men, and therefore intolerant of absurdities, would withdraw their support from an institution which they had discovered to be, in respect to its out-patient department, little better than a sham. But we are not sanguine that by any effort, however energetic, or any device however ingenious, the governors of subscription-supported hospitals in London will be systematically convened sufficiently often, and in numbers sufficiently considerable, to effect and sustain any great reform of the hospital abuses prevailing in the metropolis.

In provincial towns the difficulty of dealing with the abuses in question is probably less than it is in London, each inhabitant of which most usually lives as a stranger even to his next door neighbour. Those abuses have already assumed such magnitude in several of the provincial towns as to have attracted a good deal of attention, and to become, in fact, objects of grave public concern.

At Birmingham a considerable effort has been made to reform the existing hospital system. In February, 1873, the General Committee of the Queen's Hospital requested the Charity Organization and Mendicity Society (Birmingham) to inquire into the circumstances of patients attending that hospital. The inquiry extended over seven weeks and was of a searching character, the results being generally confirmatory of the view expressed in our last number concerning the extent and abuses of medical charity. A sub-committee which was then appointed, considered and reported on the evidence obtained; and subsequently the General Committee invited a conference of representatives from all the medical charities of the town (ten in number). The conference was attended by representatives from each of them, and from one hospital in a neighbouring town. It met twice and passed the following "Recommendations:"—

1. "That a Central Committee be formed for the purpose of inquiring into the fitness of applicants for Hospital Relief.

2. "That this Committee consist of Representatives of each Medical Charity.

3. "That all applications for Hospital Relief be reported to the Central Committee for registration (forms being supplied for the purpose); and that the Central Committee make inquiries into such cases as it may deem necessary.

4. "That pending inquiry, all cases be treated as at present.

5A. "That in all cases, which from information obtained, appear unfit to be treated, a form, with details of such information, be returned to the Hospital (within a week where possible); and that all hospitals should consent to receive the decisions of the Central Committee as final upon the evidence, *other than Medical*, of the cases investigated by them.

5B. "That in all cases, which from information obtained, appear unfit to be treated, a form, with details of such information, be returned to the Hospital (within a week where possible); and that each Hospital be left to decide for itself upon the continuance of the relief.

6. "That the cost, estimated at about 600*l*. per annum, be borne, *pro rata*, by each Institution."

These recommendations were sent to the authorities of each hospital, enclosed in an admirable circular-letter by the Chairman of the Conference, the Rev. J. C. Blissard, M.A., dated 3rd February, 1874, and containing several cogent arguments in favour of the adoption of the scheme. Several of the hospitals have not yet replied, but the authorities of the General Hospital, the largest and longest established medical charity in the town, have declined to join in the scheme, on the ground that they do not believe that the abuses alleged are sufficiently extensive to warrant the expenditure proposed; and also on the ground that they can themselves most *effectually* and *properly* investigate their own cases.

The refusal of this important hospital to co-operate in carrying out the proposed scheme will long delay, if it does not prevent, any efficient reform of the medical charities of Birmingham. Moreover, another formidable and wholly unexpected obstacle to the scheme is presenting itself: it is rumoured that the advocates of reform are anxious to adopt a "wages" test of fitness for receiving gratuitous medical relief—persons earning 20*s.* not being considered eligible; and this rumour has provoked the opposition to the scheme of the working men *en masse*, though the more intelligent of them support the reformers. Substantially, the rumour is erroneous, for though a wages test may be regarded by them as a good preliminary indication of the circumstances of the applicants for medical relief, it was not intended to regard it as more than such; but, on the contrary, it was proposed in determining on the fitness or unfitness of such applicants to consider their circumstances as a whole. But however erroneous may be the rumour in question, the opposition it has excited is none the less real and powerful.

Apart from this special kind of difficulty, the scheme was from the first unlikely to receive the general support of the hospitals invited to join in working it. The want of accord at the Conference in respect to resolution 5A, and the recommendation of resolution 5B as an alternative one, would, in our opinion, invalidate the whole scheme. This consideration, and the inherent difficulty already pointed out, which must be encountered by subscription-supported hospitals in rejecting as unfit objects of medical charity persons recommended by subscribers, lead us to anticipate that the plan of reform proposed by the Birmingham Conference will have to be indefinitely postponed, or at least shelved not only until hospital authorities become more fully alive to the extent and gravity of the abuse, and more ready than they are now to consult the welfare of the poor instead of the fancies of subscribers, but also until the latter will consent to surrender their present privilege of giving a "governor's letter" to whom they please, regardless of the question—"Is the receiver of it really entitled to it?"

The main current of opinion and feeling in the minds of men who are interesting themselves in the subject of medical charity is at present setting strongly in favour of the establishment of Provident Dispensaries, and their affiliation, when practicable, to hospitals to which severe cases requiring treatment of a kind not practicable at a dispensary may be sent.

Most of the Provident Dispensaries now at work are supported partly by the periodical contributions of the patients who receive medical and surgical aid from them, and partly by the donations and subscriptions of honorary members. Generally speaking the whole or nearly the whole of the amount contributed by the patients themselves is paid to the professional staff of the institution by way of remuneration for the professional services rendered; and the donations and subscriptions of the honorary members constitute a fund for defraying the ordinary expenses of the Dispensary. Its management is usually vested in the hands of the subscribers or honorary members, and a certain number of the ordinary members who have been connected with the dispensary a certain time and who are supposed to represent the main body of members. This body selects from itself a Committee of Management, the members of which are partly honorary subscribers, and partly representative members; and, as a general rule, we believe, the Treasurer, Honorary Secretary, and members of the Professional Staff are *ex-officio* members of the Managing Committee. Of course the different dispensaries differ more or less in respect to the character of their several constitutions; but the differences chiefly relate to matters of secondary importance: fundamentally they are all of one and the same type.

The St. Marylebone Provident Dispensary, now about thirty-nine years old, was the first of the kind established in London. Two years after it began another was started at Paddington—the Paddington Provident Dispensary, which also still exists. But the existence of each of these institutions is little better, we understand, than a severe struggle: though the St. Marylebone Dispensary is "worked most economically and carefully," the medical officers receive "only 40*l.* gratuity per annum from all sources!" In other cases, however, the medical officers are paid considerably better. Seeing how long these two Dispensaries have exemplified the experiment of the "Provident" system, our readers will perhaps conclude that if that system is a good one it must have been greatly extended in the metropolis since they were founded. As a matter of fact, however, there are now only eleven Provident Dispensaries in the metropolis. It is manifest that the Charity Organization Society does not regard the smallness of their number and the slowness of their growth as evidences of their intrinsic defectiveness or want of adaptation to the conditions which they are intended to meet, for that Society has adopted and published a report of its Medical Committee which recommends that the public should be advised "to support the existing Provident Dispensaries in preference to those which stand on a purely eleemosynary footing . . . . . that wherever it is possible the Local Provident Dispensaries should be affiliated to the Hospital of the district, so that members might be entitled to the advantages of hospital treatment if it were deemed necessary;" that the Society should endeavour, through the agency of its district committees to "induce the Governors of existing free Dispensaries to consider whether they might not with advantage convert their institutions into Provident Dispensaries," and that "in some districts where there is an urgent want of a Provident Dispensary, the local committee should perhaps take the initiative in the formation of such an institution."

Notwithstanding the strong opinions thus expressed in favour of Provident Dispensaries, opinions which, as we have said, are shared by a large proportion of the whole of those persons who are anxious to remedy existing abuses of medical charity, it must be admitted that the process of conversion of existing Metropolitan Free Dispensaries into Provident Dispensaries, is so slow as to be scarcely appreciable, and that in London the fresh origination and continuous growth of such Dispensaries cannot be said to occur. In short, the project of substituting them for the present methods of administering medical relief to out-patients in London is generally confessed to be a failure. In various parts of the country, on the contrary, Provident Dispensaries certainly flourish. Whether London is too vast to admit of that vigorous and thoroughly efficient organization under the control of a central authority, which is indispensable for the successful working of the Provident system, or whether its failure is due merely to the fact that such an organization, though possible, has not yet been attempted, are questions which, indirectly, will be answered in the sequel.

If the Provident system is capable of effecting all, or any large part even of that which its zealous advocates expect of it, it is probable that its first great achievements will be displayed in the large provincial towns of England, and that the collective medical charities of London will be the last to come under its sway. Obviously, Provident Dispensaries cannot compete successfully with Free Dispensaries and the out-patient departments of hospitals in one and the same neighbourhood, so long as the conditions and feelings of the poor are what they are; therefore, unless the authorities of the Free Dispensaries and of the Hospitals in London can and will effectually combine to close the former and the out-patient department of the latter, we see little chance of the establishment of Provident Dispensaries here on a scale sufficiently large to enable them to operate as a remedy of the abuses of medical charity now prevailing. We doubt if any force less than that of an Act of Parliament will suffice to effect the combination; and during the present century at least, Parliament will, we imagine, be scarcely likely to pass such an Act.

Manchester is sufficiently large to favour the growth on an extensive scale of the ordinary abuses of medical charity, and yet sufficiently small to facilitate the co-operation of the authorities of the several hospitals and dispensaries within the town and its suburbs, in order to carry out any concerted plan of action which collectively they may determine on. We are very glad, therefore, that in Manchester an effort is being made to introduce Provident Dispensaries as reforming agencies, under conditions as favourable as can fairly be hoped for by their promoters; and the result of the experiment, if it really be tried sufficiently to afford adequate data for a correct judgment of it, cannot fail to be especially instructive. A Committee representing all the Medical Charities of Manchester and Salford was appointed in July, 1873, "to inquire and report as to the best method of establishing Provident Sick Societies in Manchester and Salford, which will, as far as possible, relieve the charities of improper applicants, and be likely to be acceptable to the working classes and the medical profession." The chief conclusions of the Committee are embodied in the following paragraphs:—

1. "The Committee are decidedly of opinion that Provident Dispensaries ought ultimately to be self-supporting, but after careful consideration have come to the conclusion that until they become generally known and accepted by the working classes, it will be necessary to include Honorary as well as Ordinary members in their constitution.

2. "That it is desirable to divide Manchester and Salford into districts, and to establish a Provident Dispensary in each district, so as to place Medical Relief upon the Provident principle within the reach of each member of the class eligible for membership.

3. "That no Provident Dispensary shall accept as members persons residing outside its own district.

4. "That a member of a Provident Dispensary who shall remove from one district to another, shall have the privilege of being transferred, free of charge, to the Provident Dispensary of the district to which he has removed.

5. "That no Medical Charity shall receive as an out or home patient any person residing in a district in which a Provident Dispensary has been established, except upon the recommendation of such Provident Dispensary. But during the two years following the adoption of this scheme by the Committee of the Medical Charities of Manchester and Salford, any person suffering under disease *showing urgency* shall be at once prescribed for on the statement that he is unable to pay for medical aid.

6. "That any member of a Provident Dispensary who may, in the opinion of his medical attendant, require a consultation or treatment at a hospital, shall be entitled to a recommendation to the hospital most suited to his case.

7. "That it is desirable that the scheme, as approved by the Committee of the Medical Charities of Manchester and Salford, should be laid before the Managers of the Medical Charities by their respective representatives on that Committee. A Council shall then be immediately formed, and each Medical Charity concurring in the scheme shall be requested to send representatives thereto."

The Committee also defined in detail the constitution and procedure of the proposed Council, and supplied a set of elaborate rules for the formation and government of each of the several "District Provident Dispensaries," to be worked under the general control of the Central Council. These rules are substantially the same as those governing most provident dispensaries; we shall therefore only mention those which have been especially important, bearing on the scope and management of the institutions, and on the interests of the medical men immediately connected with them. It is proposed that "the members shall be artisans and others in receipt of weekly wages, whose average earnings do not exceed thirty shillings per week, and who are not in receipt of poor-law relief;"* that "any sick person unable to pay the dispensary charges shall be referred to the poor-law officers, or be recommended to one of the medical charities, as circumstances may require;" that "the honorary subscriptions to any provident dispensary shall be paid to the Council either directly or through the dispensary, and any annual subscriber of one guinea to such fund shall be considered as a subscriber to the Council;" that "one-half of the payments of the ordinary members (with the exception of midwifery fees) shall be divided amongst the medical officers, in proportion to the amount received from the members who have selected them;" that "the midwifery fees shall be paid to the medical officers or midwives attending the cases, in respect of which they were received;" and that "each dispensary shall be managed by a Committee composed of four ordinary members, four honorary members, and four members of its medical staff."

The Committee which framed the recommendations and rules in question is thoroughly alive to the fact that the efficient working of its proposed network of "District Provident Dispensaries" is mainly dependent on the hearty co-operation of the pre-existing medical charities of Manchester and Salford; and hence the recommendations contain a proposal to effect a federation of them by means of the "Council," which has been already mentioned, and which is designed to "consist of (*a*) two representatives from each medical charity joining in the scheme, (*b*) two representatives from each provident dispensary, and (*c*) of additional members elected by these representatives." If this federal scheme could be thoroughly realized by obtaining the assent to it of the authorities of each of the existing medical charities, and could therefore be carried out as designed, it would probably put an end to the abuses of medical charity in Manchester. All patients in that city who are not attended by private practitioners would be divided into three classes: (*a*) those who are received as in-patients by the hospitals, (*b*) those who become members of provident dispensaries, (*c*) and those who,

* But the Committee may admit any applicant for membership if they think the case a suitable one.

being too poor to do so, are to be referred to the poor-law medical officer for such medical aid as they may require. A portion of the in-patients of the hospitals would of course consist of persons who had sustained mechanical injuries, and were therefore needing immediate surgical attention, and also of persons suffering from various other maladies of a character so severe as to justify their immediate admission into hospital without the intervention or recommendation of a district provident dispensary. Under all circumstances the number of in-patients of the hospitals would remain *comparatively* small, and therefore the pecuniary resources of such patients and their claims to receive medical relief could as a general rule be easily investigated and ascertained, and hence it is manifest that the abuse of medical charity, in so far as the in-patients already mentioned are concerned, would be very slight indeed. Such other persons as would become in-patients would be admitted only on recommendation of one of the district provident dispensaries, and as each patient of this class would be thoroughly known in the district from which he was recommended, and would indeed be a contributor to the funds of the provident dispensary of which he was a member, the element of abuse of medical charity would in his case—and in all other cases like to his—be eliminated. The adoption of the scheme in question by the whole of the medical charities in Manchester presupposes, of course, one of two things in respect to the out-patient departments of the hospitals there: either those departments would have to be converted into provident dispensaries in immediate connexion with the several hospitals; or they would have to be abolished—the patients who had previously been in the habit of obtaining medical relief being relegated to the district dispensaries nearest to their several homes. The hospitals would thus be to a considerable extent dependent for the supply of their in-patients on the provident dispensaries, and would be bound to receive such patients so long as there might be room for them, and, as well as the provident dispensaries themselves, would, as members of the proposed federation, be subject to the control of the federal council already mentioned, in the same manner as the several States of the United States of North America are subordinate to the supreme power of Congress.

The system of administering medical relief to the lower classes just sketched would certainly be an enormous improvement on the methods of indiscriminate Medical Charity now practised in London and the provincial towns; for that system introduces, at least, the principle of self provision—a principle which, when once habitually practised, becomes more and more appreciated and valued. The constitution of the Provident Dispensary, as it includes honorary members, that is, persons who contribute to its support without deriving any benefit from it, is a compromise between the principle of dependence and that of independence, and is at least a great step onwards. It is certainly calculated to originate and foster self-help and self-respect; it is likely to generate aspirations for complete independence and social advancement; and it is to be hoped that in the course of no long period the element of charity now forming a large part of the institution will be gradually eliminated. In fact, the ordinary members should be encouraged to keep this object constantly in view, and should be tempted to strive for its accomplishment by the prospect of sharing the government of the Dispensary only with its professional staff. The fact that as a general rule the physicians and surgeons of existing Medical Charities give their time and labour to them without remuneration is a great evil, and has long been deplored. The practice of paying all the Medical Officers, which forms a part of the Provident Dispensary system, seems at first sight at all events a great improvement upon the existing usage, and will probably commend itself strongly to those members of the profession who are likely to connect themselves officially with Provident Medical institutions.

There is no doubt another side to this picture—a side which will present itself in different aspects to different observers according to the point of view from which they regard it. According to the rules drawn out by the Sub-committee already mentioned, persons receiving medical aid must receive it from one of the medical officers of the Dispensary in the district in which he resides, and though he may select any one of the medical officers of that Dispensary whom he prefers to treat him, he is not permitted to change his medical attendant, without the consent of the Committee, during his illness. Now we have good authority for stating that a considerable number of the out-patients of the London Medical Charities are in the habit of migrating from one to another, occasionally to several in succession—trying first one physician or surgeon and then another, until they are cured either of their malady or their changeableness. There is nothing surprising in this, the classes above them do essentially the same thing: every physician who listens to a fresh patient's story is accustomed to hear the names of half a dozen, and sometimes half a score, medical men whom he had previously consulted, and it is highly probable that many of the members of Provident Dispensaries feel the restriction to one medical man during the illness on account of which he is consulted as decidedly irksome. This may be one cause why Provident Dispensaries are so unpopular as they appear to be in the metropolis.

Those philanthropists who are especially possessed with the idea of the supreme importance of developing the spirit and practice of independence in the lower classes object to the partially charitable character of Provident Dispensaries. "It appears to me," says a recent writer concerning them, "that not only the object to be achieved, but the very spirit of the Provident Dispensary system shows that it should be, when once fairly started, entirely self-supporting. I fail to see any material difference from a moral point of view, between a Provident Dispensary dependent on charity for existence, and preaching independence, but unable to pay its medical officers; and a Free Dispensary entirely dependent on charity, with its medical officers gladly offering their gratuitous services." We fail to see much force in this objection, because it may be fairly said that people who have already been induced to exchange the habit of receiving gratuitous medical relief for the habit of receiving that which is only partly gratuitous, may be expected in the course of no long time to make a further advance by proposing to pay for the whole of the medical aid they require, and therefore the objectors just mentioned, in order to be consistent and faithful to their own principles, ought to be precisely those to welcome most heartily that first endeavour towards independence represented by the Provident Dispensary as now constituted.

We have heard of complaints of existing Provident Dispensaries by medical men who have had experience of them, that there is a disposition in many of their ordinary members to treat their medical officers *de haut en bas*, as though they were servants duly paid for work done, and whose services might be claimed in a tone at once so commanding and humiliating that no honorary Medical Officer of the free Medical Charities would submit to it for a moment. If this be so now that Provident Dispensaries are partly supported by charity, it will, *à fortiori*, be much more so when they are wholly supported by their ordinary members. Perhaps, however, this objectionable feature is not generally characteristic of these institutions, and that means may be found to counteract the evil whenever it presents itself; still it must be admitted that in some degree it is probably inherent in the very nature of the institutions in question when ministering to the wants of, and partly managed by, uneducated men.

If, notwithstanding the difficulties which beset the development and working of Provident Dispensaries, experience should teach those who concern themselves with them how to avoid these difficulties, and to make these institutions yield their maximum amount of good associated with the minimum amount of evil, great progress will have been made in solving the problem how to remedy the very great abuses now attendant on the administration of Medical Charity.

It is, we think, worthy of note that if Provident Dispensaries become successfully and extensively worked, and finally become wholly self-supporting, their benefits will probably cease to be confined to the classes the chief members of which do not earn more than thirty or forty shillings a week, and we may anticipate that individuals of successively higher strata of society will organize themselves into co-operative medical associations, engaging their medical officers either at fixed salaries or to be paid in proportion to the number of patients treated, so that cheap medicine and the absence of doctors' bills may be among the allurements of the future. What may be the effects on the medical profession of that good time coming cannot, perhaps, be wholly foreseen: we incline to think that the medical profession of to-day would view with grave apprehension the prospects of such a change; but, as we shall hereafter show, it is not probable that there would be substantial reasons for doing so; and, at all events, as the social transformations which time elaborates are to a great extent inevitable, if Provident Medical Institutions become generally established, medical men will evince their wisdom in adapting themselves to the new conditions in question.

Before we can form any definite opinion of the chances of success of the Manchester scheme above described, we need to know to what extent it will be assented to by the Medical Charities already existing. We understand that the Committee which has adopted the recommendations and rules laid before it by the Sub-committee appointed to prepare them, consists for the most part of Medical Officers of the various Medical Charities of Manchester, and of gentlemen who have given largely of their time and money in promoting the well-being of those institutions. We do not learn, however, that the managing authorities of them have become members of that Committee, and have therefore given their sanction to the scheme in question. They may have done so, but until assured that they have, we hesitate to believe in their co-operation. We greatly doubt whether even the authorities of the subscription-supported Hospitals will consent to surrender a large part of their independence, and whether the subscribers to them or their governors will consent to relinquish their privilege of recommending patients for treatment. Unless they will do these things the scheme of reform must, we fear, prove abortive; and, judging from all we know of men's motives, and especially of the conduct of the managers of Medical Charities, we confess that we are not sanguine of the success of the Manchester reformers. If the

Manchester scheme fails, it seems to us that any similar scheme would have no shadow of a chance in London, where the materials and the difficulties to be dealt with are of a magnitude so much greater than those in Manchester, and especially where there are three immense Hospitals, the resources of which consist of endowments, and which therefore are so thoroughly independent that there is little hope of inducing them to join in carrying out any scheme like to that attempted at Manchester, and without their co-operation no such scheme would be at all practicable in the metropolis.

The authors of the Manchester scheme are thoroughly aware of the great difficulties to be contended with, and evidently do not expect to accomplish the federation of all the Medical Charities speedily: for we observe that in the body of rules which have been adopted, one of the duties of the Council is stated to be—"To admit into the federation, from time to time, any Provident Dispensary or Medical Charity deciding to adopt these principles." Probably the existing Free Dispensaries and the out-patient department of any hospital "deciding to adopt these principles," will be converted into provident institutions, and thus the principles will in the first instance become realized in one district, and if experience shows them to work well will gradually spread into others. It has been found, we believe, that of the few Provident Dispensaries in the metropolis, those which are most in the outskirts succeed best, and for the obvious reason that the patients in the neighbourhood of it find it much more convenient, and more to their advantage to obtain treatment there, even if they pay a small weekly sum for it, than to go to a Hospital or Free Dispensary at a considerable distance from their homes. This indeed is only another method of stating that Medical Institutions ministering to the lower classes, if sustained by payments from those who avail themselves of them, cannot compete successfully with Medical Institutions ministering to the wants of the same classes, and receiving from those under treatment no payment for it. Both reason and experience thus point out that the best chance of developing Provident Medical Institutions in London can only be secured by starting them in neighbourhoods as remote as possible from the Hospitals and Free Dispensaries—in the close proximity of which they are either unable to live at all, or if when started they do survive, they merely continue a lingering and all but useless existence.

Having demonstrated that the various reforming agencies now passed in review are unlikely to remedy in a radical manner the chief evil arising out of the existing system of Medical

Charity, we proceed to direct the attention of our readers to a system which has been continued during more than twenty years, which has been conducted on an extensive scale, and which while not inimical to the growth and wide spread of Provident Medical Institutions would, we believe, if associated with them achieve all which is needful in order to insure that every person really and truly medically destitute shall receive adequate relief, and that at the same time the abuses which have grown up as evils inseparably associated with the practice of Medical Charity hitherto shall be brought to an end. We refer to the system of medical relief given to the out-door poor in Ireland, by authority of "an Act to provide for the better distribution, support, and management of Medical Charities in Ireland," passed in 1851.

Until the date of that Act, the provision for the Medical relief of the poor in Ireland consisted of the voluntarily supported Hospitals, of the Dispensaries, about six hundred in number (which were supported partly by voluntary subscriptions, and partly by contributions from the county cess), and of the Workhouse Hospitals. All the Workhouses have a very large amount of Hospital accommodation, and most of them have detached Fever Hospitals. The average number of patients in the whole of the Workhouse Hospitals of Ireland on the 1st of January of each year, from 1869 to 1873—both inclusive—was 16,837. But in January, 1851, *i.e.*, immediately before the Medical Charities Act was passed, the number in hospital was 28,922; and it is not unreasonable to suppose the largeness of the number at that time was due in great measure to the fact, that the provision for out-door medical relief was at that time very insufficient. "The Irish Poor Relief Act of 1838 contained no provision for the medical relief of the out-door poor; but by section 5 of the 10 Vict. c. 31, the Poor Law Commissioners were authorized to require the Guardians to appoint Medical Officers, for the purpose of affording medical relief out of the Workhouse, in those cases in which it should appear necessary and expedient that such appointment should be made." But little use, however, was made of this authority: only nineteen orders were issued. These were "addressed to the Guardians of sixteen unions, and applied to twenty-nine districts, for which twenty-nine Medical Officers were authorized to be appointed." But though so little was done under the powers conferred by the section just mentioned, that little seems to have been the nucleus or beginning of the system formally embodied, and thoroughly set in motion by the Dispensaries Act of 1851.

The chief administrators of that Act are two Commissioners, one of whom is a physician or surgeon of not less than ten years' standing, and who has the title of Medical Commissioner; these, together with the Commissioners appointed under the "Act to provide for the Execution of the Laws for the Relief of the Poor in Ireland," now administer that Act and the Dispensaries Act of 1851. The two Commissioners just mentioned, "may from time to time appoint so many fit persons as the Commissioners of their Majesty's Treasury shall sanction, being practising physicians or surgeons of not less than seven years' standing, to be Inspectors to assist in carrying out the provisions of this Act, and may remove all or any of the said Inspectors, and appoint others in their place." The two Commissioners and Inspectors whom they appoint constitute the Governmental part of the organization for working the Act in question.

For the purpose of the Act each Irish Poor-law Union is subject to the approval of the Commissioners, divided by its Guardians "into so many Dispensary Districts, having regard to the extent and population of such districts as may to them appear necessary," and care being taken always that no electoral division "formed under the Acts for the more effectual Relief of the destitute Poor be divided." In September, 1872, the number of such districts was 719.

In each district there is a Dispensary Committee which is elected annually, each Committee holding office until the appointment of a new Committee after the next annual election of Guardians in the Union of which the district forms a part. The Committee consists of the *ex-officio* and elected Guardians resident, or being the owners or occupiers of property in the district, together with so many resident ratepayers rated on a value of not less than 30*l*., as may be necessary to make up a Committee of the prescribed number. The latter are elected by the Guardians.

There is at least one medical officer for each district, and there may be two or more if required. Each medical officer is appointed by the Dispensary Committee, at a salary determined by the Guardians, and subject to the approval of the Poor-law Commissioners.

A dispensary or office for the Medical Officer of each district, and for the meetings of the Committee is provided by the Guardians. This comprises a waiting-room, a room in which the medicines are kept and dispensed, a consulting-room (in some cases there are two or more consulting-rooms), apartments for the dispenser or dispensers, and at one of the dispensaries of each district a room for the meetings of the Dispensary Committee.

The staff of each dispensary consists of the medical officer (in some cases there are two or three medical officers), a dispenser, and a porter, the dispenser being in every case a duly certified apothecary, and as a general rule resident on the premises.

The salaries of the medical officers rarely exceed 100*l.* per annum, exclusive of vaccination fees, and no extra fees are allowed for difficult operations. The salaries of the resident apothecaries vary from 70*l.* to 100*l.* a year, besides which they are provided with suitable apartments for residence at the several dispensaries.

Every member of the Dispensary Committee, every Relieving Officer, and every Warden* acting for an electoral division, included in a dispensary district, has power to afford Medical relief by the issue of a ticket for medicine and advice.

The tickets, the possession of which insure to their holders Medical relief, are of two kinds, the one printed in black entitles the applicant to advice at the dispensary, the other printed in red entitles him to attendance at his own residence.

After the applicants who are able to come to the dispensary have been prescribed for, the Medical officers usually proceed to visit the poor persons who may have to be attended at their own homes, taking with them a supply of prescription forms. These forms are filled up on the spot, and left with the patients, who send them to the dispensary and obtain their medicines. It is the duty of the dispensers to compound these prescriptions at any hour of the day or night.

Though every person supplied with a ticket is entitled to immediate Medical relief, he is only entitled to continue receiving such relief if the Committee do not declare him an unfit object of it: according to section 9 of the Act, "if any person who shall obtain a ticket for Medical Attendance from any Relieving Officer or Warden, or from any Member of the Committee, shall, at the next or any subsequent Meeting of the Committee after the issue of the ticket, be declared by a majority of the members then present, not to be a fit object for Dispensary relief, the ticket shall be cancelled and the holder thereof disentitled to further relief."

The total number of cases of Medical relief afforded under the Medical Charities Act, during the year ended September 30th, 1872, was 724,020, of these 513,170 were attended at the dispensaries, and 210,850 were attended at their own houses. During the last ten years the greatest total number of cases attended was 790,716 (during the year 1863), and the smallest total number was 760,797 (during the year 1866).

The following table exhibits under the six usual heads the

* The Wardens are unpaid officers appointed by the Guardians, and their chief duties are to provide for the conveyance of sick and infirm paupers, to receive applications for admission into the workhouse, and to report to the Guardians relative to the residence of the applicants.

general expenditure under the Medical Charities and Vaccination Acts for the two years ended September 29th, 1872.

Medical Charities Expenditure.

		1871.	1872.
1. Medicines and medical appliances . . .		23,420*l*. ...	23,570*l*.
2. Rent of Dispensary buildings		7,503 ...	7,844
3. Books, forms, stationery, printing, and advertising		1,106 ...	1,275
4. Salaries of { Medical officers		80,725 ...	81,771
Apothecaries		2,509 ...	2,620
5. Fuel, porters, and incidental expenses .		10,001 ...	10,364
Expenses under Vaccination Act:—			
6. Vaccination fees and other expenses:			
Fees to medical officers . . .	8,720*l*.		...13,354*l*.
Other expenses	907		... 932
		9,627 ...	14,286
Total		135,005*l*.	141,648*l*.

If the expenses under the Vaccination Act, amounting in 1872 to 14,286*l*., be deducted from the total amount of Medical Charities expended for that year, we find that the expenditure by authority of the Dispensaries Act of 1851, exclusive of Vaccination Expenses, was 127,362*l*. This sum divided by the total number of cases attended in 1872, gives the cost of treatment of each case as very nearly three shillings and sixpence farthing. In order to meet the total expenditure, *i.e.*, including Vaccination expenses, an average poundage on the Poor Land Valuation of Ireland, now amounting to 13,320,354*l*., of 2·55*d*., was required.

Such in outline is the District Dispensary system of Ireland. Of course many details would have to be filled in in order to present a correct picture of it in every particular. We believe, however, that for the purpose of this article the above sketch will amply suffice. Mr. John Lambert, whose Report on the system contains a good account of it, sums up its advantages as follows:—

1. "It ensures for the destitute sick poor a sufficient supply of all necessary and proper medicines and medical appliances.

2. "It enables those who are not confined within doors to obtain medical advice at fixed hours, and within a convenient distance from their homes.

3. "It ensures for those who are unable to go out medical attendance, and enables them to obtain their medicines promptly.

4. "It affords facilities for vaccination, as well as for medical relief generally, by establishing fixed places at which it is well known that the medical officers must attend at stated hours.

5. "It provides an organization always ready, and capable of expansion, if necessary, to meet any outbreak of epidemic disease with promptness; whilst, at the same time, it is calculated to prevent disease becoming epidemic by early treatment, and by procuring the adoption of precautionary measures in any locality which may be threatened. These benefits have recently been largely realized in reference to cholera.

6. "By preserving a record of the medical treatment in every case, it furnishes a test of both the skill and attention of the medical officer.

7. "It prevents that conflict between interest and duty which must so often arise in the mind of the medical officer when he himself is required to provide medicines out of his salary."

We will add to this list another advantage, which in the eyes of the Medical Profession will, perhaps, seem the greatest of all, and which in our opinion is extremely important. The Act in question secures to every one of the Medical officers engaged in working it *payment for his labour*. As we have already stated the total cost, exclusive of vaccination expenses, was during 1872 127,362*l.*, and of this amount 81,771*l.* was paid to the Medical Officers, in other words they received nearly two-thirds of the total amount expended under the Act. It has been calculated that if the number of those who are merely qualified and who practice as apothecaries, of those who do not practice owing to old age, of those holding appointments which preclude them from practice, and of those who devote their whole time to special scientific pursuits, together with the number of the retired Army and Navy officers and young men whose names appear on the Irish Register for a few months merely till they enter the Army or Navy or go to England or elsewhere, be deducted from the total number of physicians, surgeons, and apothecaries in Ireland, the number remaining as physicians and surgeons in actual practice is about 2000. Now the total number of Medical Officers engaged during 1872 in administering the district Dispensaries Act was 801. If to these be added the number of Medical Officers of the 163 Workhouses in Ireland, the total number engaged as Poor Law Medical Officers amounts to close upon 1000, or the half of the whole of the Medical men in actual practice in Ireland. Now, by means of the salaries which this large proportion of the whole of the Medical practitioners actually practising in Ireland receive as Medical Officers under the District Dispensaries Act, the young medical men of Ireland obtain an important start in life, and are enabled to support themselves in modest comfort during the period of struggle which most medical men have to pass through before they succeed in establishing themselves in fairly remunerative practice.

An argument often advanced in favour of the Out-patient Departments of English, and especially of London Hospitals, is that they afford an invaluable sphere in which the rising generation of medical men obtain practice and experience of a most important kind, which otherwise would not be within their reach. The practice offered by the Irish District Dispensaries supplies all that which the Hospital Out-patient Departments supply in this respect and much more besides, for the experience obtained by visiting patients at their own homes—an experience presented by nearly a third of the whole of the District Dispensary cases—is in our opinion far more valuable than that of merely seeing and prescribing for patients in the out-patient consulting-room of a hospital or at an ordinary dispensary.

But even this admirable Act—admirable in its design, and to a great extent in its working—is grossly misapplied, and by a reckless perversion of its agency that cardinal abuse of medical charity—viz., its bestowal on persons who are not entitled to it, presents itself as the chief, if not sole evil of the system. According to the last Annual Report of the Local Government Board for Ireland "the returns of the Dispensary Medical Officers for the year ending September 30, 1872, give 257 cases in which tickets were cancelled in Ulster, 88 in Munster, 89 in Leinster, and 54 in Connaught." Now knowing as we do how large is the number of persons who apply for gratuitous Medical relief although they are not entitled to it, we are compelled to regard the smallness of the number of cancelled tickets just named—even the comparatively large number cancelled in Ulster—as evidence of one of two things: either the Act is administered with such wise discrimination and conscientiousness that as a general rule people who have no rightful claim on gratuitous Medical Charity know that it would be useless to apply for it, or of the many tickets which are probably granted to such people very few are cancelled. We fear that there is little room to doubt which of these two conclusions is the right one. Mr. Lambert says:—"I was assured at one place that retail tradesmen have been known to sign a book of tickets, and leave them to be distributed by their shopmen amongst any customers willing to accept them; and in another the Medical officer informed me that a member of the Committee had sent one of his children with a ticket, under a fictitious name, and obtained cod-liver oil for a period of three months. The dispenser at Limerick, who is also the House Surgeon to the Barrington Hospital, stated that the right conferred upon so many persons to give Medical orders is open to great abuse." Indeed, private practitioners complain of it as ruining their practice, just as private practitioners in London complain of the injury they sustain from the abuses of the out-patient system. It is alleged that in Ireland the abuse in question is partly "attributable to the professional etiquette which prohibits even a Surgeon from attending a patient for a less sum than a guinea; so that the question upon which the granting of medical relief is supposed to hinge is whether or not the applicant is provided with that sum." There is probably some truth in this statement, but we doubt if there is much: it may be that the prohibitions of professional etiquette are proclaimed more emphatically, and are heeded more deferentially in Ireland than they are in England, but we venture to affirm that a large proportion of Irish physicians and surgeons see many of their patients more than once, and in many cases several times for one guinea fee, and that in the experience of many general practitioners fees represented by some fraction of a pound form the rule—guinea-fees being rare and memorable exceptions. The fact is, the framers of the District Dispensaries Act were not impressed with the evils associated with the administration of Medical Charity and intent on remedying them: their object was to provide more general and effective relief of the medically destitute than was possible before the passing of that Act, and hence their attention was not specially directed to guard against the abuse which has grown up in connexion with its administration.

The one defect of the Act consists in the absence of a clause making a thorough scrutiny of the claims of each applicant for relief stringently obligatory, insuring the refusal of relief to all found to be disentitled to it, and providing for the appointment of officers, or the organization of a system by which those two objects would be accomplished. In sparsely populated districts probably the best method of effecting them would be by the appointment of an officer in connexion with each Dispensary, whose chief if not sole duty should be that of rigorously investigating every fresh case, and who should be entrusted with the power of cancelling the ticket of every patient whom he might judge disentitled to gratuitous medical relief. He, like the medical officer, should hold his appointment from the Dispensary Committee, to which he should furnish periodical reports of his proceedings, and which, while exercising a general supervision and control over them, should form a sort of court of appeal in cases in which patients whose tickets he has cancelled complain that they are not justly treated. In those Dispensary districts most sparsely populated of all, and in which therefore the salary of such an officer would prove unduly burthensome, an arrangement might be made with the apothecary, or even the medical officer, to discharge the duties of investigator just described: in such cases a moderate addition to the salary of the one or the other undertaking those duties would, we doubt not, insure their efficient performance, seeing that precisely in the districts in question the professional duties of both the medical officer and apothecary are comparatively light. In the metropolis, and in all the largest provincial towns, an inquiry office in intimate relation with all the District Dispensaries of the town should be established, so that persons disentitled to relief, and who could not bear inquiry in their own district, should not be able, by baffling investigation, to obtain such relief elsewhere. In very populous districts a central office, with subordinate district officers for the purposes in question, would, we believe, achieve those purposes far more completely and far more economically than would be possible by the appointment of a special officer exclusively connected with each separate Dispensary.

It has been suggested that the right of giving orders for medical relief should be limited to relieving officers and *ex-officio* guardians, and though such a limitation might be inconvenient in thinly populated districts, it would probably prove very useful in towns. That by means of some plan well thought out in the first instance, and corrected by increasing experience, the evil in question may be got rid of we feel quite certain, because, unlike the out-patient system of the voluntarily supported Hospitals now prevalent in England, the Irish District Dispensary system has no constitutional taint or inherent evil inseparable from it.

As an organization for administering medical relief to the poor, we believe this system to be the best which has yet been devised, that without serious difficulty it may be freed from the one fault attaching to it, and that thus freed it will accomplish all that the most enlightened philanthropist can reasonably expect from any method designed to fulfil the purpose in question. Freed as we have pointed out from the fault in question, and subject to certain restrictions to be presently mentioned, this organization is in our opinion especially well adapted to overcome the difficulties and to root out the abuses now characteristic of the English method of administering Medical Charity, so far as out-patients are concerned, and we should therefore rejoice to see it applied to the whole of England. Mr. Lambert, whom we have already quoted, and whose Report to Mr. Gathorne Hardy mainly contributed, we presume, to induce him to apply a somewhat similar measure to London, says respecting the Irish Act, "I think it right to add, that, after giving my best consideration to the system of Dispensary relief, I am of opinion that it is admirably adapted to the exigences of large and densely populated communities; and I do not hesitate, therefore, to recommend that it should form an element in any scheme for the improvement of Poor Law administration in this metropolis, subject, however, to a restriction, such as I have indicated, with respect to the issuing of tickets for relief."

The clauses of "The Metropolitan Poor Act, 1867," viz., those from 38 to 46 inclusive, which are headed "Medical Outdoor Relief," and which enable, but do not compel, the Poor-Law Board to order the formation in the metropolis of District Dispensaries similar to those in Ireland, are much less definite than are those of the Irish Medical Charities Act, and seem to be framed so as to give to the Poor-Law Board a large discretionary or controlling power in the matter, rather than to define and direct with a master's hand how the guardians of the several Unions or Parishes shall so carry out in detail the principles of the system in question as to insure the best possible administration of it. In the English Act there is no provision whatever for restricting the application of Out-door Medical Relief to those only who are rightfully entitled to it. There is no definition of what constitutes a just claim to such relief—no one is empowered to grant tickets or letters of recommendation insuring it, and there is no provision by which any person receiving it, but found to be disentitled to it, shall cease to receive it. Moreover, in this Act there is no provision for insuring that the Medical Officers shall visit patients at their own homes, and our readers will remember that this is a most important feature of the Irish Act—nearly a third of the whole of the patients being, as we have already said, relieved by authority of that Act at their own homes.

Another and most vitally important difference between the effects of the two Acts consists in the fact that whereas in England a recipient of out-door medical relief is *ipso facto* disfranchised, the political status of a person receiving like relief in Ireland, by authority of the District Dispensaries Act, is in no way affected thereby. We are quite certain that so long as disfranchisement attaches to the fact of receiving merely medical relief, any Act for the introduction of the District Dispensary system into England on a scale commensurate with the needs of the case, will virtually remain a dead letter; and we see no sufficient reason why such a penalty should attach to the acceptance of temporary out-door medical relief by the poor. Experience has decisively demonstrated that one of the most effective methods of keeping down the poor-rates consists in affording *thorough* and *prompt medical* relief to the sick poor, who, being restored to health, soon support themselves again; but who, if allowed to linger in suffering until their diseases assume chronic forms, become permanent invalids, and therefore more or less permanent burdens on their respective parishes. Wise administrators of the Parish or Union funds would best consult the interests of those who are compelled to provide those funds by facilitating to the utmost possible degree the discovery and treatment of the diseases of the poor in the first stages of their development; and of all contrivances for inducing those who are at once poor and suffering from disease to go on bearing their maladies until the time for curing them is past, we know none so admirably calculated to effect that purpose as that of affixing to every person who applies for medical relief the "scarlet-letter" of disfranchisement.

If Hospital reform were to be limited to the out-patient system, we should say what is wanted is a repeal of that part of "The Metropolitan Poor Act, 1867," which relates to "Medical Out-door Relief," and the application to all England, by a special Act of Parliament, of the Irish District Dispensaries Act, after it has been modified in the direction already indicated. The administration of relief by virtue of it should not entail disfranchisement on the recipient of such relief. The Act should not only give power to certain persons to grant tickets insuring medical treatment to their holders, but should, as far as possible, surround the exercise of that power with safeguards against its abuse. It should be the duty of some person in official communication with the District Dispensary to investigate every case of doubtful title to relief, and to cause the ticket of any person who, though receiving relief, may be found to be disentitled to it, to be cancelled. Moreover, the Act should define the condition of persons entitled to relief; and in our opinion such a definition would be absolutely essential to the successful working of the Act. Considering that all persons above the class of the very poor may, in the event of an extensive development of the Provident Dispensary system, secure all needful medical assistance from Provident Dispensaries, that such dispensaries would be generally established were it not that they cannot compete with the system of gratuitous medical relief now given by the Hospital Out-patient departments and Free Dispensaries, and that it is desirable to encourage and foster provident habits to the uttermost, we are strongly of opinion that the District Dispensaries ought, so soon as Provident Dispensaries are generally established, to afford medical relief only to such persons as are incapable of contributing to a Provident Dispensary the small weekly sum which would entitle them to efficient medical assistance during illness.

In order to foster as much as possible the spirit and practice of the provident system it would, we think, be extremely desirable that every prescription paper issued by the District Dispensaries should have on the back of it (1) a concise description of the conditions of those persons who are alone entitled to gratuitous relief; (2) a statement that though such relief is granted at once to every applicant presenting a ticket entitling him to it, his position will be forthwith investigated, and if found such as to prove him an unfit object of such relief his ticket will be immediately cancelled; and (3) a description of the character and object of, and of the terms of admission to the provident dispensaries. Such information so conveyed would, we believe, greatly aid the officers of the district dispensaries in restricting the benefits of those institutions to those for whom they are intended, would be of great use to, and would be duly appreciated by, many of the recipients of gratuitous relief, and would be the means of diverting a continuous stream of persons accepting such relief from the district to the provident dispensaries. If such an Act were passed, an Act ably and clearly drawn, and appointing special officers to carry it into operation as the Irish Act, 1851, does, but which the Metropolitan Act, 1867, does not, we believe it would be productive of an incalculable amount of good.

When once such an Act had come into full operation there would no longer be any reason for keeping open the out-patient departments of hospitals, or for continuing the free dispensaries, and it is to be hoped that the authorities of most of the hospitals and many of the dispensaries would spontaneously close them as agencies for the administration of *gratuitous* out-door medical relief. If they should not, probably the supporters of those institutions seeing that as such agencies they were no longer required, and were, in fact, doing more harm than good, would gradually cease to subscribe to them. It might be necessary, in order to hasten this consummation, that some organized body of hospital reformers—the Medical Committee of the Charity Organization Society, for example—should make it one of their duties to inform the charity-giving public of the change which had been introduced, and that it was undesirable to continue supporting those voluntary medical charities which were endeavouring to prolong the present vicious system. The greatest difficulty which would have to be encountered in bringing that system to a close would probably present itself in the shape of the endowed hospitals. Those in London, having immense out-patient departments, being very powerful, and so constituted and privileged legally that it is very difficult to influence them, would most likely offer serious opposition to the proposed abolition of their out-patient departments. But any Home Secretary who should have the courage and determination to deal with this subject, in the comprehensive manner here indicated, would not allow the execution of his scheme to be marred by the resistance of the governing bodies of those institutions. After their opposition had been withdrawn, or overcome, and the out-patient departments of both endowed and subscription-supported hospitals, together with the free dispensaries, had been closed, the gross abuses of medical charity, notoriously characteristic of those institutions would, of course, be brought to an end, and the funds now devoted to them could be diverted to other, and perhaps less questionable purposes.

Those agencies being abolished, and the out-door medical relief afforded by the new district dispensaries being limited to persons belonging to the classes above indicated, an ample sphere would exist for the operation and usefulness of provident dispensaries, on a scale sufficiently large to provide for the medical necessities of that majority of the lower classes who, though unable when ill to pay the ordinary fees of medical practitioners, can easily pay the small sum demanded weekly by the provident dispensaries from each of their members. When the working classes have been rescued from their present habits of relying upon gratuitous medical assistance during every illness, and have thoroughly adopted the provident system, they themselves, in many cases, will probably suggest to the medical men whom they know, and whose professional attendance they would prefer, that they should be allowed to pay them instead of a provident institution, a small weekly or monthly sum, in order to insure their professional help in times of need: we believe that a large number of the general practitioners would cheerfully accede to such a proposal, and would set aside a certain part of each day for seeing such provident patients. In this way the development of the individuality, self-respect, and spirit of independence of the lower classes would receive additional impetus; they would come in contact with professional men on a footing far more satisfactory than that on which they now consult them; and those members of the medical profession who should enter into the arrangement here indicated would, like those officially connected with provident dispensaries, derive a portion of their income from a source which has not hitherto been utilized for the remuneration of the medical assistance given to the lower classes.

It remains for us to explain what in our opinion ought to be the arrangements for the accommodation of in-patients, or in other words, how our hospitals ought to be constituted, supported, and governed. Unfortunately we have left ourselves so little space in which to deal with this part of our subject that we shall be unable to discuss it with the fulness which its importance deserves, and which the difficulties besetting it demand.

We consider that the persons now receiving medical and surgical treatment in hospitals are divisible, and should be divided into three classes: (*a*) those inmates of workhouses who under existing arrangements are received into Workhouse Infirmaries; (*b*) those members of the working-classes who are suffering from maladies of such gravity as to need treatment in a hospital, and who, when suffering from lighter ailments, would be entitled to medical relief at one of the District Dispensaries; (*c*) all persons applying for admission as hospital in-patients, who are not members of either class *a* or of class *b*.

The whole of the patients forming class *a* should be provided for much in the same manner as they are now in the workhouse or poorhouse (we prefer the term poorhouse) infirmaries. The whole of the patients forming class *b* should be received into hospitals, the existence and support of which should be insured by Act of Parliament in the same way as the creation and support of the Irish District Dispensaries were insured by that authority. Class *c* should be admissible, and only admissible into hospitals, the inmates of which pay certain weekly sums for their support and treatment. There would thus be three kinds of hospitals—viz., the Poorhouse Infirmaries; the Public Hospitals; and the Provident Hospitals. The Poorhouse Infirmary would, as now, receive those members of the poorhouse community who were too ill to take part in the ordinary life of that community, and to be treated merely by being supplied with medicines from the house-dispensary; the Public Hospitals would receive from the District Dispensaries patients whose maladies had become so grave as to need treatment in a hospital; and the Provident Hospitals would, in like manner, receive from the Provident Dispensaries patients whose maladies had also become so grave as to need treatment in a hospital. But the Provident Hospitals would not only receive such patients: they would also receive persons of any class above the three just described, who might be at once able and willing to pay for the medical or surgical assistance rendered to them.

Patients suffering from severe accidents, or sudden attacks of grave disease, apoplexy for example, whose circumstances may be unknown, would of course be taken to the Public Hospital, it being understood that of such patients who recover, those able to pay for their treatment will be bound to do so according to a scale to be determined on and announced in each Public Hospital.

According to the arrangements here proposed the House-dispensary and the Infirmary of the Poorhouse would, as now, be two parts of one whole system adequate to administer medical relief to all the sick members of the pauper community; the District Dispensary and the Public Hospital would be two parts, also intimately connected, of one system insuring adequate medical relief to the sick portion of those strata of society the members of which, except during illness, claim no extraneous upport; and the Provident Dispensaries and Provident Hospitals also closely correlated, would minister to the medical and surgical needs of all persons who were above the classes previously mentioned, who were thoroughly self-supporting, and who, though being so, were intent on securing for themselves when needed the best possible professional assistance at the least possible cost.

The Poorhouse Infirmaries and Public Hospitals being charitable institutions would, of course, restrict their benefits to the classes *a* and *b* respectively—classes which, though more or less definitely separate from each other, have each a recognised claim on public compassion and beneficence, and which by virtue of receiving the latter, are distinctly marked off from the other classes of society. But the Provident Hospitals, on the contrary, would, in the course of time, extend their benefits to every person choosing to subscribe to them the minimum amount which, according to their rules, would insure admission into them. All classes above classes *a* and *b* being self-supporting and independent classes, are classes to which provident, or self-supporting hospitals are capable of being adapted. Obviously, the relative advantage derivable from them by any given class will be proportionate to the intensity of the struggle for life, and the need for the practice of stringent economy by that class. It is probable, therefore, that the class immediately above class *b* will make by far the greatest use of Provident Hospitals—at least in the first period of their extensive formation. We believe, however, that it is likely that the time will come when Provident Hospitals will be made use of by a large number of persons of almost every social grade except the two lowest already indicated, that many such hospitals will be fitted up with wards and apartments of various degrees of comfort and luxury as, if we are not mistaken, is already the case in the *Maison Municipale* of Paris, and that as the great usefulness and value of such hospitals become increasingly recognised some will be built, furnished, and have the whole of their appointments and management on a scale and in a style adapting them for the exclusive use of special classes of society. Of course such a differentiation of the invalid parts of the community into hospitals representative of several different social grades could only occur in large cities; but as a like differentiation can be effected to a considerable extent even within the limits of one medium-sized hospital, the feeling of caste may thus be amply ministered to in any town sufficiently large to support only one hospital on the Provident principle. We feel sure that many thousands of persons of the fairly affluent classes would avail themselves even now of such hospitals if they already existed, and, to put an extreme case, in order fully to exemplify our meaning, we see nothing extravagant in the supposition that if the Duke of Westminster, or one of our Merchant-princes, were convinced, as he might be, that were he dangerously ill he would probably fare better on the whole in such a hospital, and that the cost of his treatment and nursing would be very much less than in his own home, he would decide to enter the hospital.

The professional staff of each Public Hospital should consist not only of the resident medical officers, but of physicians and surgeons in general practice, and each member of the staff ought to be appointed, as in Paris, after he has proved himself by competition with rival candidates for the office, the best man applying for it.*

The Poorhouse Infirmaries as now conducted are considered, and we believe for good reasons, unsuitable places for clinical instruction: a large proportion of the cases to be seen in those infirmaries are of a chronic type, and therefore, comparatively speaking, are but slightly instructive. Moreover, many of the patients are so old and so infirm, that it would be cruel to submit them to the frequent examinations of a number of medical students. There is, no doubt, a certain number of patients in each of these infirmaries who are not old, and whose maladies are not of the chronic type; still we incline to think, that as the prevailing features of the majority of the Infirmary cases are of the kind just stated, Poorhouse Infirmaries are far from being the most appropriate places for clinical study. On the other hand, we do not think that the patients in each of those Infirmaries ought to be left under the sole charge of one resident medical officer, whose salary is such as to be unlikely to command a man above the grade of mediocrity; and we are strongly of opinion, that a consulting physician and a consulting surgeon in general practice, ought to be attached to each of these institutions.

The Provident Hospitals could not be made available for teaching purposes, except to a very limited extent, because persons who pay—and patients in the Provident Hospitals would pay for their medical or surgical assistance—would be unwilling to allow themselves to be examined over and over again, first by one student and then by another, as they must be if they are to serve as profitable illustrations of clinical lectures.

The Public Hospitals considered as places for clinical teaching are, however, free from the difficulties and objections which present themselves both in the Poorhouse Infirmaries and in the

* The appointments of all medical men constituting the several professional staffs of the Paris hospitals are competed for before a body of hospital medical men, who are bound to appoint the best men. The successful competitors once appointed, and thus placed on the list of *Médecins des Hopitaux de Paris*, take their turn in getting other and higher places by seniority.

Provident Hospitals: the patients would present the greatest possible variety of disease, and under conditions most favourable for a thorough study of them; and being treated without any cost to themselves, such patients would consent to submit themselves to the examination, clinical study, and discussion necessary for the medical education of the young men attending these hospitals. Moreover, only in hospitals of this class could professional teachers at once sufficiently eminent, and sufficiently numerous to conduct thoroughly superior medical schools, and to maintain them in high repute, be *insured:* the Poorhouse Infirmaries are not, and are not likely to be, attended by such teachers; the members of the Medical staff of the several Provident Hospitals would be appointed by persons responsible only to the supporters of those hospitals, and though many such members might be first-class men, the only guarantee that they would be so, would consist in the gradual increase of knowledge and common sense in the supporters of those institutions; but the appointments of the professional officers of the Public Hospitals, made as already suggested, would be made by men who would be selected on account of their special fitness for the duty, who would be directly responsible to the public authorities selecting them for the faithful discharge of their duty, and who only after a rigorous competitive examination would choose the ablest and most accomplished candidates.

In order to secure to the medical students attached to any given hospital the greatest possible facilities for that kind of practice which is now presented in the out-patient departments of Hospitals and in the free dispensaries, every public Hospital should have a District Dispensary attached to it; and such a direct connexion of the two which in all cases would be already connected by their oneness of principle, by their mutual co-operation, by the restriction of their beneficence to one and the same class of persons, and by the fact of their support from one common source, would always be easily accomplished—generally, indeed, by the simple conversion of a pre-existing out-patient department into a District Dispensary.

Such, thus briefly sketched, is the method of administering Medical Charity which we should organize and establish, if we were called upon to design and apply a system capable of insuring adequate Medical relief gratuitously to all persons—whether as out-patients or as in-patients—who are really fit objects of it, capable of restricting such relief to such persons, capable of aiding and strengthening the endeavours of those who are struggling either to achieve or to maintain their independence of gratuitous medical assistance, and capable of so developing and fostering provident habits in the people at large as, without straining their resources, to insure ample and efficient professional assistance in times of sickness, and thus to cause the number of those who depend on receiving gratuitous medical relief, to become in proportion to the whole population gradually less as time advances.

But here the question arises—Is such a system practicable? We believe it is. Certainly no part of it is practicable without the assistance of Parliament; but if Parliament interferes at all, it would be quite possible as well as extremely desirable that it should do its work thoroughly. The medical relief of the poorhouse communities is already provided for. The establishment of the District Dispensaries and their correlatives the Public Hospitals, and the provision necessary for their permanent maintenance would constitute the chief need for Parliamentary action. The nature and force of the opposition from "vested interests" which that action would encounter, would be determined by the nature of the plan for dealing with existing hospitals, which would have to form a part of the measure proposed for enactment. Happily Parliament has already affirmed, we believe, in no doubtful terms, its complete competency to deal as may seem to it best with existing endowments—ecclesiastical and educational endowments for example. In our opinion, all endowed hospitals in the kingdom ought to be reconstituted so as to become "Public Hospitals," in the sense in which we have defined and used this term, and ought then be placed under the responsible control of the parochial or municipal authorities of the place in which they are situated, subject to the supervision, and if need be, the order of a Commissioner especially appointed by Parliament, to superintend the working of the District Dispensaries and Public Hospitals, and responsible to the chief of the Poor-law department, who in his turn is responsible to Parliament. Were this plan adopted, and were the endowed hospitals, thus reconstituted as Public Hospitals, to extend their benefits only to those persons comprised in class *a* as above defined, the funds derived from their endowments would not only suffice for maintaining and conducting them in an efficient manner, but would, in many cases, yield a surplus amply sufficient for the support of the District Dispensaries of the district or districts contiguous to them. Of the metropolitan hospitals, St. Bartholomew's, St. Thomas's, and Guy's would certainly have to be subject to the change just described. Others which are only partially endowed, and which have medical schools attached to them, would have to adopt one of two courses: either they would have to submit themselves to be changed into "Public Hospitals" and to all the conditions attaching to them, and could thus retain their medical schools; or they could convert themselves into Provident Hospitals, and thus insure their independent existence as hospitals only. They would be obliged to adopt one of these two courses for the following reasons :—they would be unable to maintain their *status quo* in the presence of "Public Hospitals" sufficiently extensive or numerous to minister to the medical need of all persons constituting class *a*, because when the charity-giving public becomes assured that the needs of that class are adequately provided for, it will discontinue its support of hospitals of the kind in question; and, therefore, unless they become transformed into "Public Hospitals," and thus obtain support by order of Parliament, or into "Provident Hospitals," and thus obtain support from the provident, they would no longer have a *raison d'être*, and would probably, after suffering a lingering decline, become extinct.

We think the great multiplication of Medical Schools which has taken place in the metropolis is a great evil, that in this respect we should do well to approximate to the system exemplified in Paris, and that in any case three distinct schools, connected respectively with St. Bartholomew's, St. Thomas's, and Guy's, would more than suffice for all the medical students likely to assemble in the metropolis. We believe that were there only one large school, the students of which would be admissible to each of the Metropolitan Public Hospitals, it would be possible to insure that its professional chairs should be filled by men of the very highest eminence, and that, therefore, the whole of the students might have the inestimable advantage of being taught by such men instead of as now, in the majority of cases, by a large number of respectable mediocrities who lecture to all but empty benches. Moreover, by the concentration of force and appliances here suggested, the total cost of educating the whole of the students assembled in London at any one period would be wonderfully lessened, to the great advantage alike of the students and the public, which must ultimately re-imburse that cost.

In those cases in which entirely new Public Hospitals would have to be established, the funds would have to be raised as are those which are appropriated for the establishment and support of District Dispensaries. Calls on the parochial or union authorities for such funds, would probably be met in the first instance by vehement protests and efforts of resistance. But if Guardians and Ratepayers can be convinced that by providing such hospitals to the full extent required they will really lessen the total amount which will have to be levied for the support of the poor, they will soon learn the wisdom of co-operating cheerfully in establishing them; and we affirm that they can be thus convinced by being thoroughly informed of the financial results of the working of the system of District Dispensaries throughout Ireland—results which have been carefully analysed and described by Dr. Rogers, President of the Poor Law Medical Officers' Association.

Experience has proved—that in the initiation of Provident Dispensaries, honorary subscriptions are required; and in like manner the Provident Hospitals which are first established, will probably also need some extraneous aid at starting. It is, therefore, with peculiar satisfaction that we contemplate the prospect of a transformation of subscription-supported hospitals and free-dispensaries into Provident Hospitals and Provident Dispensaries respectively, because the majority of such subscription-supported hospitals and dispensaries possess endowments or invested funds to some extent, which might be rendered available for assisting them after their transformation. We presume, of course, that the funds belonging to every hospital and dispensary so reconstructed by its Managing Committee, with the consent of its subscribers, would be appropriated to aid in carrying it on. Such aid would, as we have said, be needed in the first instance, and would continue to be necessary until the competition for patients, forming part of the present vicious hospital and dispensary system, and impeding the establishment of provident medical institutions, shall have wholly ceased, and until the beneficence of the provident principle should have become so thoroughly, generally, and practically recognised as to insure that the difficulty of establishing and successfully carrying on wholly self-supporting Provident Dispensaries and Provident Hospitals, to an extent commensurate with the needs of those strata of society immediately above class *b*, would be no longer experienced.

Our readers will observe, that the preceding sketch of the reform we think desirable consists of two parts—the one proposing a remedy for the abuses of Medical Charity associated with our method of giving relief to out-patients only, the other proposing along with that remedy a scheme for the thorough reformation of our whole hospital system.

If only the first part of our programme of reform were adopted and enforced, there would, we doubt not, be an end to the grossly tyrannical conduct of hospital committees and hospital autocrats towards medical men who expose and protest against existing abuses; there would possibly, if not probably, be an end to the despotic reign of hospital secretaries; impostors, hypocrites, and other persons demanding gratuitous medical relief, but having no rightful claim to it, would be speedily detected, and summarily dismissed by officers especially appointed on account of their peculiar aptitude to investigate and judge of the character of doubtful cases, and responsible for the efficient discharge of their duties either primarily to the District Dispensary Committees, and secondarily to the District Dispensary Inspectors, or to the chiefs of offices especially established to conduct inquiries over areas, the extent of which would differ in different cases, and would be so determined in each case as most likely to conduce to the accomplishment of the end in view; the really fit objects of out-door medical relief would, as a general rule, liable of course to occasional, but we believe rare, exceptions, become the exclusive recipients of it; the development of Provident Dispensaries would receive a powerful impetus; the whole of the medical men engaged in the administration of out-door medical relief, whether through the agency of the District Dispensaries, or that of the Provident Dispensaries, would be paid, as they certainly ought to be, for their professional labour; and there would be an end to the present prodigal expenditure of hundreds of thousands of pounds on a kind of medical charity a large part of which is productive of much more harm than good.

But if the larger measure of reform which we think needful, and which would consist in the establishment, *directly* in the manner described not only of a number of District Dispensaries but of Public Hospitals—a number sufficiently great to meet the requirements of the class for which they are designed, and *indirectly* of Provident Hospitals in numbers corresponding to the demand for them, were carried out, the provision of medical help for the lower classes of the United Kingdom would then, in our opinion, be complete. The nature of that provision would be various, the different kinds corresponding to the differing conditions and needs of the sufferers. The organization of medical charity insuring those results would be expansible, and capable of orderly growth in accordance with the growth of the population. It would especially favour the relatively rapid development of self-supporting institutions for the supply of medical relief, and would, therefore, tend to lessen the need of the purely charitable element more and more. It would provide for the payment of all medical men concerned in its administration. It would insure that the posts of official honour and responsibility in the Public Hospitals should be awarded only to those physicians and surgeons who were proved by a rigorous competitive examination to be most truly worthy of them. While providing the most ample opportunities for clinical study, it would foster the development of a really great and thoroughly national school of medicine in the metropolis. And finally, it would facilitate the gradual transformation of existing medical institutions, so that they might mould themselves in accord with the changing conditions of the present and of the future, and thus while effecting a thoroughly radical reform, would do so in a wise and truly conservative spirit.

As these results cannot be achieved without the agency of

Parliament, we are confronted with the question—Will the present Government be likely to undertake the task of effecting a reform of the existing system of Medical Charity, of a kind and of the magnitude we have described? We confess we are not without hope that it may. Those of our readers who belong to the medical profession will probably remember that the first long period of struggle for reform of the constitution and working of the numerous medical and surgical diploma-granting bodies of the United Kingdom, and for causing them to co-operate in increasing the quantity and improving the quality of medical education, was closed by the Medical Act, 1858, which owes its existence to the fact that the Conservative Home Secretary of that time, Mr. Walpole, recognised the expediency of making Medical Reform a Government measure, and worked at it indefatigably, as we can testify from personal knowledge, until that measure became law. He was pleased to express his indebtedness to articles* which were published in this *Review* at that time, and which he intimated had been of essential service to him in enabling him to deal with the complex subject in question; and we venture to hope that the present Home Secretary, after duly considering the gross abuses of Medical Charity now prevailing, and the measures we have proposed for their eradication, may resolve, with the concurrence of his colleagues, to grapple with the evils which we have endeavoured to expose in language free from exaggeration, and which is now attracting a large share of public attention. We encourage this hope because, paradoxical as the fact may appear, experience teaches that "Conservative" statesmen, while slow to make changes in the distribution of political power, or to introduce what are usually understood as "political" reforms of any kind, not seldom surpass their "Liberal" opponents in appreciating the necessity of so-called "social" reforms, in willingness to undertake them, and in the broad and comprehensive spirit in which they effect them. We therefore earnestly commend the subject we have been discussing to Mr. Secretary Cross's serious attention, and confidently prophesy that if he should deal with it as becomes a Minister of the Crown duly solicitous to free existing institutions intended to lessen or assuage the sufferings of the sick poor from their notorious abuses, and so to supplement and perfect them that they may fully accomplish the objects of their founders, he will achieve a pre-eminently beneficial work, and will earn the gratitude of millions of British subjects.

---

* Articles on "Medical Reform" and "Medical Education," which, with additions, have since been republished under the title of "Medical Institutions of the United Kingdom."

Contemporary Literature.

The Foreign Books noticed in the following sections are chiefly supplied by Messrs. Williams & Norgate, *Henrietta Street, Covent Garden*, and Mr. Nutt, 270, *Strand.*

THEOLOGY AND PHILOSOPHY.

A MELANCHOLY interest attaches to the "Literary Remains"[1] of Mr Emanuel Deutsch. The author belonged to a class of Jews more rare in this country than on the Continent, who are at once deeply versed in Hebraic lore, and have assimilated the highest results of a cosmopolitan culture. But that he was much more than this, the passages quoted from his letters in the memoir touchingly show. He was a man of intense and poetic nature, and inspired a singular degree of personal attachment. It is therefore not to be wondered at that some of our contemporaries have indulged in expressions of admiration which the memorials here published altogether fail to justify. It is of course possible, though there is no intimation of it in the memoir, that the present volume is but the forerunner of specimens of Mr. Deutsch's work as a philologist or historical critic. But so far as the book before us goes, we can only say that the author's remarkable literary gifts entirely obscure his abilities as an independent scholar. Sparkling with wit, and glowing with imagination, his articles contribute absolutely nothing to our stock of scientific materials. The one, for instance, with which he sprang into celebrity—we mean the *Quarterly Review* article on the Talmud—is a fine specimen of poetic prose, and beyond measure wonderful as the achievement of a foreigner. But it is disfigured in the eyes of a critic by two great blots: an unfounded assumption of originality, and a provoking reticence on the date of its Talmudic authorities. We are not ourselves disposed to be hard upon Mr. Deutsch for this. He knew his public but too well, and the horror with which drawing-room readers regard a page bristling with references. And if he is reticent, it is not necessarily from ignorance or carelessness. At the very opening of his article he points out the need of an answer to the question, What is the date of the Talmud? And in his review of "Les Apôtres" (pages 199, 200), after reproaching M. Renan with adducing a few proverbial parallels out of old collections, and verifying them with foreign aid, he continues—"What was wanted now, and what we looked forward to in this book, was the proof of the existence within the Jewish community of such notions as the Logos, the Trinity, the working of the Holy Ghost, the

[1] "Literary Remains of the late Emanuel Deutsch." With a Brief Memoir. London: John Murray.

suffering and redeeming Messiah." It is also only fair to recollect that the article in the *Quarterly* was intended to be supplemented by a comprehensive work on the Talmud, in which the subject would doubtless have been treated from a more critical point of view. Writing, however, as we presume we do, for a more exacting public than Mr. Deutsch, we are bound to say that his statements on the relation of the New Testament to the Talmud must be received with caution. He puts merely one side of the question, and is not always exact in his quotations. That Christianity borrowed something from contemporary Judaism, is, we believe, an axiom among historical critics; but a rigorous examination of evidence will be necessary before a Judaistic influence can be admitted of such weight and importance as Mr. Deutsch asserts. He ought at any rate to have mentioned the possibility that the Jewish religion was modified in the direction of Christianity, just as one section of the Christian community was swept over by a distinctly Hebrew wave of Unitarianism. His loose way of treating evidence may be strikingly shown from his use of a well-known saying of Hillel—"That grand dictum, 'Do unto others as thou wouldst be done by,' against which Kant declared himself energetically from a philosophical point of view, is quoted by Hillel, the President, at whose death Jesus was ten years of age, not as anything new, but as an old and well-known dictum 'that comprised the whole law'" (page 27). What Hillel really quoted to the foreigner who wished to become a proselyte easily was this, "That which is unpleasing to thee thou shalt not do to thy fellow." A truly noble saying, whoever may have been its author, but differing both in what it affirms and omits to affirm from the creative combination of the active love of God and man expressed in the evangelical saying (Mark xii. 28, 34; Matt. xxii. 35—40). And what a contrast between the casuistical subtleties to which Hillel and his companions devoted their lives, and the free spiritual religion both taught and practised by Jesus! We pass on to Mr. Deutsch's next *Quarterly Review* article, that on Islam, which is less brilliant, but, we believe, more original than its predecessor. Its object is to show that Islam is not merely full of reminiscences and echoes of Judaism, but "neither more nor less than Judaism as adapted to Arabia—plus the apostleship of Jesus and Mohammed." But most readers will agree that there is too much of the Talmudic element in the essay, and too little of the Islamic. Considered as a popular article, great praise is due to a paper, reprinted from the *Saturday Review*, on M. Renan's "Les Apôtres," to the picturesque and poetical merits of which Mr. Deutsch does full justice, while sharply criticising its want of scientific precision and logical consistency. The articles on the Targums and on the Samaritan Pentateuch are well executed compilations, which filled a discreditable gap in learned literature, but have no other claims on our attention. The remainder of the volume is taken up with essays, collected from various periodicals, on the Talmud, Semitic Culture, the Book of Jasher, Arabic Poetry; Egypt, Ancient and Modern, &c., and Five Letters "on the Ecumenical Council;" all of which display a remarkable talent for investing dry subjects with the interest of poetic associations.

Mr. Moncure Conway's beautifully got-up "Sacred Anthology"[1] professes to be a collection of choice passages from the Scriptures of various nations, from the Chinese to the Scandinavians. It would be captious to take exception to the title, yet the poems of Sadi and Hafiz have surely never been recognized as "Ethnic Scriptures." The object of the book is defined by the Editor as being "simply moral," *i.e.*, to promote the gradual approximation of the votaries of different religions, by showing the large spiritual element common to all. The specimens are well selected, though Mr. Max Müller will miss some of his chief favourites in the Veda, and Buddhist literature is far from adequately represented. They are 740 in number, and are arranged under twenty headings, such as Laws, Religion, Theism, Ethics of Intellect, Charity, Humility, Action, &c., while each specimen has a separate title of its own, which is often a useful guide to the sense. Thus a very long extract is given from the Book of Job, under the title of "Problems of Life," and another from the 8th of Romans, under that of "Spiritual Evolution." It is certainly instructive to see the essential agreement of so many venerated religious writings, though for depth of meaning and classicality of form none of them approaches the Hebrew and Christian Scriptures. Mr. Conway has gone to the best available sources for translations—the list of authorities at the end will be most helpful to the student—but we fear that he has, with the best intentions, diminished the value of his book by the numerous omissions and amalgamations. There is also a realistic tone in some of the Oriental apologues which cannot be genuine, and considerably interferes with the literary enjoyment of the reader. Still, the idea of the work is an excellent one, and Mr. Conway deserves great credit for being the first to realize it. Whether the mass of his readers will adequately appreciate it may, perhaps, be doubted. Religious utterances are vague and obscure till we know something of the time and place of their origin. We still seem to want, as was remarked in our last number, a popular sketch of the growth of the principal religions, with an account of their sacred books, to which a collection of extracts like the one before us would form a fitting supplement. The Chronological Notes at the end of the volume cannot be held to supply this want, especially as they are not uniformly trustworthy. For instance, the Book of Job is assigned to the latter part of the 6th century, B.C., and described as "a version probably of a Persian form of a Brahminical story of similar character." But the date here given (after Bunsen) is against the balance of argument, and the resemblance between the Book of Job and the touching Indian story of Harischandra, as given by Dr. Muir in vol. i. of his "Sanskrit Texts," is both slight and superficial. We have also the authority of Dr. Birch for saying that something like the Book of Job exists in Egyptian literature, and other parallels might doubtless be found.

---

[1] "The Sacred Anthology." A Book of Ethnical Scriptures. Collected and Edited by Moncure Daniel Conway, Author of "The Earthward Pilgrimage." London: Trübner & Co.

The character and object of Mr. Butler's "The Fair Haven"[3] have been discussed to satiety elsewhere. Its apparent object is to defend the cause of supernaturalism, by proving the Resurrection of Christ on purely rational grounds, thus fighting the rationalists with their own weapons. But it is not difficult to see on which side the sympathies of the author are engaged. Never was there such tedious reading as the parody of the orthodox argument, while two of the chapters which most repay perusal are statements of the rival hypotheses to account for the Resurrection story known as those of "Hallucination" and "Apparent Death." The former is ably resumed in the second chapter, and refuted on grounds about as solid and satisfactory as those of the lower order of "Christian Evidences." Chapter iii. is headed "The Character and Conversion of St. Paul." The author accepts Strauss's view of the mode in which Paul's conversion was affected, in preference to the threefold account in the Acts of the Apostles, but (to the confusion of the orthodox) converts it into an argument for the Resurrection. Chapter iv., on "Paul's Testimony Considered," contains an additional argument, not without plausibility, against the Hallucination-theory. We are then treated to a "consideration of certain ill-judged methods of defence." The unfair procedure of orthodox commentators, represented by Dean Alford, is exposed with considerable flourish of trumpets. Then follow the "difficulties felt by our opponents," especially those which have led to the Apparent-death theory. "I consider this position," says the writer, "to be only second in importance to the one taken by Strauss, and as perhaps, in some respects, capable of being supported with an even greater appearance of probability." Judging from the extreme crudity of the refutation supposed to be given in the "Conclusion," we may probably regard this as Mr. Butler's private opinion, but it may be doubted whether many critics of religious history will agree with him. Chapter iv., headed "The Christ-Ideal," is the most ingenious and interesting in the whole book. It contains a severe satire on the orthodox opponents of free inquiry. The object of the doctrine of the Divinity of Christ is to give a sanction to the Christ-ideal which would place it above the reach of criticism, and the misfortunes which have happened to the Gospels, considered as historical records, have been permitted with a view to the enhancement of that ideal! With too bitter irony it is observed that "the apparently contradictory portraits of our Lord, which we find in the Gospels—so long a stumbling-block to unbelievers—are now seen to be the very means which enable men of all ranks, and all shades of opinion, to accept Christ as their ideal" (p. 218).

A third series of "Essays on Religion and Literature,"[4] edited by

---

[3] "The Fair Haven." A work in Defence of the Miraculous Element in our Lord's Ministry upon Earth, both as against the Rationalistic Influences and certain Orthodox Defenders, &c. Second Edition. By Samuel Butler, Author of "Erewhon." London: Trübner & Co.

[4] "Essays on Religion and Literature." By Various Writers. Edited by Henry Edward, Archbishop of Westminster. Third Series. London: Henry S. King & Co.

Archbishop Manning, contains little or nothing that can be called either critical or literary. We need, therefore, only remark that those who wish for the Ultramontane view on such subjects as Church and State, the Philosophy of Christianity, Ancient and Modern Spiritism, Mr. Mill's essay on Liberty, Darwinism brought to book, and the Controversy with the Agnostics, will find a clear and emphatic statement of it in the present volume.

Mr. Fowle's courageous "Essays on the Reconciliation of Religion and Science,"* are among the ripest and most attractive productions of Broad Church theology, though they seem to possess a higher value from a practical or educational than from a critical point of view. They contain, that is, many thoughts which, if received into a candid mind, will probably germinate into something very different from the theological opinions of the author. We do not mean to assume that the mind of the author himself has done growing, or that he has anything like a scholastic and immutable system of beliefs, but he seems to us to be too much under the influence of imagination, and too little familiar with the methods of historical criticism, to be able to carry out his own principles consistently. "The methods, the assumptions, the opinions, the dogmas, the creeds of Christendom, will pass under the yoke of scientific inquiry, and will continue to exist only so far as science permits and approves. And with the death of the old theology will begin the new religion" (preface, p. xvi.). In other words, Science is, and Religion claims to be, based upon facts. The foundation of the one has been, and that of the other is to be, experimentally verified. As soon as this is done, the feud between Science and Religion will be at an end. This is no doubt the only tenable position. The question is whether Mr. Fowle's analysis of the facts, especially the historical facts, and doctrines of Christianity is scientific. So far as that of the historical facts are concerned, we must reply in the negative. The author is too much the creature of moods, sometimes imaginative, sometimes crudely rationalistic, but never calmly critical. "As a safe test of the reality and meaning of these ancient narratives," he says, "let us put the question, Can they be told in modern prose so as to give a natural explanation of every fact?" And to prove that they can be, he proceeds to modernize the story of Balaam, to which he appends a note on the date, only less uncritical than that of an orthodox commentator. Again, he ventures on these two "simple" but surprising questions with regard to the fine semi-mythical passage in Exod. xxiv. 9—11:

"1. Will any reasonable man deny that this is a faithful tradition of some real event? Not unless we are to apply totally different tests to the Bible from those by which historical criticism judges other books.

"2. Will any reasonable man assert that the words are to be understood

* "The Reconciliation of Religion and Science; being Essays on Immortality, Inspiration, Miracles, and the Being of Christ." By the Rev. T. W. Fowle, M.A., Vicar of St. Luke's, Nutford Place, London. London: Henry S. King & Co.

literally? Not unless he is prepared to assert that man can see God and live." (p. 219.)

It is hardly possible to show a greater misapprehension of the canons of historical criticism, on the one hand, and of the phenomena of mythology, on the other, than is shown in this passage. He seems to think that Ewald's "History of the People of Israel" is the latest utterance of Biblical criticism, and naïvely remarks (p. 157), "It is too soon to predict with any certainty the fate of this attempt" (to reconstruct the History of Israel); whereas the book has long been judged by severer critics than him of Göttingen, who has no doubt rendered invaluable services to the literary criticism of the Bible, but is notoriously deficient in the sense of historical perspective. But into this and cognate matters we have no space here to enter. Suffice it to add that Mr. Fowle is more at home in discussing the religious elements of a doctrine than its historical setting. His essays on Immortality in relation to Science, Morality, and Christianity are therefore more permanently valuable than those on Miracles and Inspiration; in the former of which he even states his opinion that the existence of three great ages of miracles, those of Moses, Elijah, and Christ, can be proved by the ordinary tests of historical evidence. A deeply interesting essay is added on the Church and the Working Classes, to show the urgent practical need for such a scientific reform of theology as Mr. Fowle has advocated. He indicates as one of the sources of the indifference of the Working Classes to religious teaching "doctrines either false, or so perverted and petrified as to become false to the people at large," and instances the doctrine of eternal or endless punishment. Another fruitful source, he thinks, is the temptation to divide religion from morality in the supposed interests, and to meet the pressing wants of the former, instancing popular theories as to the Atonement, the defence of the characters of the Old Testament heroes, and "much of the ordinary views of religious graces and virtues." But how unlikely that a scientific reform of theology should stop short, as Mr. Fowle seems to suppose, at the Apostles' Creed!

Mr. George St. Clair's "Darwinism and Design"[6] is distinguished from other contributions to Evolution-literature by its calm scientific tone. His object is to show that the Design argument is unaffected by the doctrine of Evolution.

Mr. Alfred Plummer[7] has translated another of the minor works of Dr. Döllinger, with several interesting appendices from his own pen. His task has evidently been a labour of love, and must have been greatly facilitated by the simplicity of his author's style, so uncommon a virtue in German theologians. The fact is, that Dr. Döllinger is something more than a theologian. "By a privilege," says M. Rio, "of which it would be difficult to cite another example, he [has] the

[6] "Darwinism and Design; or, Creation by Evolution." By George St. Clair, F.G.S., M.A.I., &c. London: Hodder & Stoughton.

[7] "Prophecies and the Prophetic Spirit in the Christian Era." An Historical Essay by J. J. I. von Döllinger. Translated, with Introduction, &c., by Alfred Plummer, Fellow and Tutor of Trinity College, Oxford. London: Rivingtons.

passion of theological studies as if he had only been a priest, and the passion of literary studies as if he had only been a *littérateur*." It is the "passion of literature" which has mainly impelled him to the present work, which is a purely objective historical sketch of the prophecies of the first fifteen centuries after Christ. It is obvious, however, that the subject has a profound theological bearing, and we think the author would not disown the opinion expressed from this point of view by the translator.

"To start with a ready-made axiom that the supernatural (*i.e.*, what seems to be such to us) is *à priori* inadmissible, is to beg the whole question at the outset. What we have to inquire in each case is, whether the amount of evidence in favour of the prediction is such as to outweigh the antecedent improbability. We must inquire, to quote the well-known canon laid down by Davison, whether the prediction be known to have been promulgated before the event; whether the event be such as could not have been foreseen, when it was predicted, by any effort of human reason; whether the event and the prediction correspond together in a clear accomplishment. There are prophecies in Scripture which can stand this threefold test. The early promulgation, the supernatural foreknowledge, the manifest fulfilment, have been fully ascertained. Can as much be said for any of the prophetic utterances in the Middle Ages?" (Intro., p. xii.)

Mr. Plummer adds:—

"That the Prophets, and Christ Himself, predicted His passion, and death, and resurrection; and that he actually suffered, and died, and rose again, are facts attested by contemporary witnesses, and can only be impugned at the peril of invalidating all historical evidence, and involving our whole knowledge of the past in doubt." (p. xiii.)

Now, it is, no doubt, essential to the historical critic to bear in mind the limited extent of our present knowledge of nature, and we are grateful to Mr. Plummer for the admission that "the supernatural" may turn out to be only another name for "the unknown." But how does this agree with his subsequent statement that the supernatural foreknowledge of at least some of the Hebrew prophets has been fully ascertained? He has gone out of his way to acknowledge that supernatural may be a misnomer; how, then, can he accept as a canon of true prophecy that the event be such as could not have been foreseen by human reason? Surely we have got beyond the stage of the lower rationalism, when anything above the common intelligence was set down as enthusiasm or trickery. And then what a stupendous statement about the life of Christ having been circumstantially predicted in Hebrew prophecy! Circumstantial predictions may, indeed, have been uttered, just as thaumaturgy was almost certainly practised by the religious leaders of the Israelites (see Isaiah vii. 2, and 14-16), though it is often difficult to prove this, owing to the modifications introduced into their prophecies by the authors subsequent to their oral delivery. But circumstantial predictions of the distant future are completely abandoned even by so orthodox a writer as Tholuck ("Die Propheten," Gotha, 1861). Passing to the body of the work, we may observe that, though the limits of the periodical in which the Essay first appeared (Raumer's "Historisches Taschenbuch") precluded an exhaustive treatment, a fuller account of some prophecies, and a brief reference to others, might fairly have been expected. Among the former we may specify those of Roger Bacon and those ascribed to Archbishop Malachi; and among the latter the traditional prediction of the conquest of Constantinople by the Moslems, exhaustively discussed by Dr. Pusey, in "Daniel the Prophet" (second edition, pp. 639-641); with which compare the prediction of the conquest of Hindostan by the English, and their subsequent expulsion, quoted by Lord Stanley of Alderley, from a Persian ode of the twelfth century, in the Hakluyt Society's edition of Vasco de Gama. The Abbot Joachim's theory of the three ages of the Church (p. 116) should have suggested a reference to Lessing's prophetic anticipations of the Everlasting Gospel. A tantalizingly brief allusion is made to Dante as a prophet. This subject would, doubtless, have been more fully treated but for the author's intention to write a monograph on the subject. We learn with regret that it is only too doubtful whether this intention will ever be realized. But even in its incomplete state, Dr. Döllinger's Essay deserves to be welcomed by students of all shades of opinion.

Mr. George Williams gives to the world a posthumous fragment of Dr. Neale's "History of the Holy Eastern Church,"* descriptive of the Church of Antioch during the first four centuries of its existence. If a life-like style, deep learning, and profound convictions could make a historian, Dr. Neale would be among the greatest ornaments of historical literature. Unfortunately, he is utterly destitute of critical faculty; fails to perceive the motive power of ideas, and neglects Protestant—and especially German researches in the same field. He believes, for instance, in the miracle of the "Invention of the Cross," though he admits that the details are uncertain, and regrets that Eusebius was not more willing to allow the supernatural assistance of evil spirits in the production of the heathen oracles. Mr. Williams has prefixed an interesting Introduction, containing an account of the ruined towns between Homs and Antioch (the central district of the Antiochene diocese), especially of the churches and Christian inscriptions. He has also inserted a complete list of the Patriarchs of Antioch, by Constantius, a late learned Patriarch of Constantinople, and three appendices, of which the first contains authentic records relating to the Patriarchal Throne of Antioch during the latter half of the 18th century, mostly extracted from the Patriarchal archives at Constantinople; the second, a historical account of the Patriarchate of Antioch, translated from a Russian pamphlet; and the third, a sketch of the state of the Patriarchate in 1650, also translated from the Russ.

---

* "A History of the Holy Eastern Church." The Patriarchate of Antioch. By the Rev. John Mason Neale, D.D. (A Posthumous Fragment); together with Memoirs of the Patriarchs of Antioch. By Constantius, Patriarch of Constantinople. Translated from the Greek; and three Appendices. Edited, with an Introduction, by the Rev. George Williams, B.D., Vicar of Ringwood. London: Rivingtons.

Dr. Dorner,[9] the younger, may be congratulated on his first appearance in the field of theological authorship. His sketch of the opinions and belief of Augustine is accurate and well arranged, and superior in impartiality to the only English work which can enter into competition with it, Dr. Mozley's learned work noticed in this *Review* in 1855. There are two great difficulties which the describer of Augustinianism has to surmount. First, the temptation of using Augustine as an authority for some modern sect or party. Secondly, the absence of anything like a severely logical system in Augustine's works. The first can only be overcome by viewing this great Father in the light of his time; the second, by discovering the central points from which all his opinions flow. And this is what Dr. Dorner has tried to do. The two subjects by which, from his youth up, Augustine was fascinated, are God and sin. But as he regards sin mainly as an interruption of the relation between man and God, we may say that the central point of his doctrinal system is God. Hence even his Anthropology must be treated as a subdivision of his Theology. Dr. Dorner divides his book into two parts—first, the doctrine of God, and the doctrines connected with it; such as Creation, Providence, the Origin of Souls, Miracles, Revelation: and secondly, those which concern the relation of man to God, especially sin, grace, and the Church. In conclusion, he surveys the work of Augustine as a whole, his services to Christianity, and his relation to the Reformation.

The new edition of Dr. Liddon's sermons on Religion[10] derives its claim to attention from the preface, which contains a reply to a friendly criticism in the *Spectator*. The gist of the latter was, that Dr. Liddon had missed the point of the scientific argument against prayer, drawn from the idea of Law, which is "that to pray for anything which involves a violation of that [physical] order is to pray for what it is unreasonable, arrogant, and even irreverent to ask." Dr. Liddon replies, first, that this objection to prayer is rather theological than "scientific;" secondly, that "real answers to prayer are no more inconsistent with God's Wisdom and Sovereignty than any other real consequences of human free-will." He thinks, too, that "if the presence of law is an objection to prayer anywhere, it is an objection to it everywhere," and that answers to prayers for spiritual blessings are as miraculous as answers to prayers for temporal ones. Here he is, of course, at issue with divines of the ordinary Broad Church type. But so thinking, he is able to look calmly forward to the recognition of law in psychology as well as in physics.

Criticism would be wasted on the gross and unblushing partiality displayed in the "Dictionary of Sects and Heresies."[11] There is not the least attempt to comprehend the principles which lie at the root of the

---

[9] "Augustinus. Sein theologisches System und sein religionsphilosophische Anschauung dargestellt." Von Lic. Dr. A. Dorner. Berlin: Hertz.

[10] "Some Elements of Religion." By H. P. Liddon, D.D., Canon of St. Paul's. Second Edition. London: Rivingtons.

[11] "Dictionary of Sects, Heresies, Ecclesiastical Parties, and Schools of Religious Thought." Edited by the Rev. J. H. Blunt, M.A., F.S.A. London: Rivingtons.

English religious communities. Still it must be admitted that facts are, for the most part, given with sufficient fulness; we do not pretend to vouch for their accuracy. The articles on non-Christian religions and philosophies are less objectionable, and may, at any rate, lay claim to the merit of being judicious compilations. We may mention in particular those on Buddhism, Mohammedanism, and Spinoza. That on Atheism is every way inferior to the lucid and accurate essay in the "Dictionary of Historical Theology."

Little or nothing of importance has appeared lately on the interpretation of the Christian Scriptures. Mr. Sharpe[12] has brought out a little volume of notes on the Old Testament, acute and original as ever, but with insufficient discrimination between the domains of fact and conjecture. Mr. Pelham Dale[13] deserves great credit for the pains he has bestowed on his Commentary on Ecclesiastes. In his own sphere—that of philology—he is much more independent than the contributors to that perfunctory compilation, the "Speaker's Commentary." But he is evidently a self-taught man; modern grammarians have left no traces on his labours; nor has he even a comprehensive knowledge of the Hebrew Bible, for he modestly confesses *homo unius libri*. And we cannot say that he has thrown any new light on the interpretation of this obscure book, though he is on the right track in comparing the LXX. The translation aims at expressing too much; a false emphasis is the result.

Messrs. Rivingtons[14] have brought out a new edition of Mr. Isaac Williams' Commentary on the Apocalypse, the exquisite style of which might with advantage be imitated by other than Catholic commentators. Mr. Rust, a Cambridge prizeman,[15] has given us a careful comparison of the same book with other Apocalyptic writings, arranged under topics, such as Messiah, Angels, Satan, &c. He makes no affectation of criticism.

A new series of papers, edited by Mr. Charles Anderson,[16] will be heartily welcomed. A healthy moral earnestness is conspicuous in every one of them. Perhaps the best papers are those on Almsgiving, Sermons, Lay Influences, Liturgical Reform, and the Education of the Clergy.

The "Authorized Report of the Church Congress"[17] is chiefly taken up with subjects of a purely practical kind. But there are two papers

---

[12] "Short Notes to accompany a Revised Translation of the Hebrew Scriptures." By Samuel Sharpe. London: J. Russell Smith.

[13] "A Commentary on Ecclesiastes." By the Rev. T. P. Dale, M.A., late Fellow of Trinity College, Cambridge, and Rector of St. Vedast with St. Michael Le Querne. London: Rivingtons.

[14] "The Apocalypse, with Notes and Reflections." By the Rev. Isaac Williams, B.D. London: Rivingtons.

[15] "The Revelation of St. John, compared with other Apocalyptic Writings." By the Rev. J. C. Rust, M.A., Fellow of Pembroke College, Cambridge. Cambridge: Deighton, Bell, & Co. London: Bell & Daldy.

[16] "Church Thought and Church Work." Edited by the Rev. Charles Anderson, M.A. London: Henry S. King & Co.

[17] "Authorised Report of the Church Congress held at Bath, October 7th, 8th, 9th, and 10th, 1873." London: Rivingtons.

on the means of quickening an interest in Theology which deserve a special notice; the one by Canon Lightfoot, the other (which is rather an oration) by Dr. Farrar, of Marlborough. We cannot, however, see much force in the suggestion of Canon Lightfoot, that our relations towards physical science on the one hand, and non-Christian races on the other, would be improved by a proper use of the doctrine of the Logos. Recollecting that this very doctrine was once the fertile mother of heresies, we are curious to see how Canon Lightfoot will avoid the fate of his great predecessor, Origen. Dr. Farrar gives us a noble but rather vague plea for a liberal and progressive Theology. He tells us, that "so far from being the badges of intellectual servitude, we look upon the Orders we have taken as the highest pledge of honesty, and the strongest incentive to the fearless search for truth." Noble words, but could they be carried into practice by any beneficed clergyman?

The Anglo-Continental Society has printed a very interesting report of the Old-Catholic Congress held last summer at Constance; the two Pastoral Letters of the Old-Catholic Bishop Reinkens, and a striking speech by Prof. Messmer at Constance, on the degrading practices of Pilgrimages, Image-worship, &c.[18]

Mr. Frederic Myers,[19] of Keswick, a retiring but highly gifted Theologian of the Coleridgean school, left behind him a work called "Catholic Thoughts," consisting of four books, two of which are contained in the present volume. It was in many respects in advance of its age, and was originally printed for private circulation only. One of the last acts of the late Bishop of Argyll was to obtain the permission of Mr. Myers' representatives to publish it in the "Present-Day Papers." The portion here published is a luminous exposition of the principles of Coleridge's "Church and State."

The extreme "High Church" party have started a new series of tracts under the taking title, "Studies in Modern Problems."[20] Of the two mentioned below, the second may be especially recommended for its collection of facts in proof of the Zwinglian—not Lutheran—origin of the 39 Articles. It also contains a high testimony to the merits of Mr. H. B. Wilson, the Zwingli of English Rationalists.

Mr. Scott's tracts[21] have always the merit of insight and point.

---

[18] "Report of the Congress of Constance." By the Rev. J. E. B. Mayor, M.A. London: Rivingtons. "Bishop Reinkens' First and Second Pastoral Letters." London: Rivingtons. "Speech of Professor Messmer at the Congress of Constance, September 13th, 1873, on the Substitution of Pilgrimages, Image-Worship, &c., for Inward Spiritual Religion." London: Rivingtons.

[19] "Present Day Papers on Prominent Questions in Theology. Catholic Thoughts on the Church of Christ and the Church of England." By the late Frederic Myers, M.A., Perpetual Curate of St. John's, Keswick. London: Isbister & Co.

[20] "Studies in Modern Problems." By Various Writers. Edited by the Rev. Orby Shipley, M.A. No. 1. Sacramental Confession. By A. H. Ward, B.A. No. 2. Abolition of the 39 Articles, Part I. By Nicholas Pocock, M.A. London: Henry S. King & Co.

[21] "Three Notices of the *Speaker's Commentary.*" From the Dutch of Dr. A. Kuenen. Revised by the Author and Translated by J. Muir, Esq., D.C.L. Thomas Scott, No. 11, The Terrace, Farquhar Road, Upper Norwood, London.

With a little more literary finish they might become a valuable instrument of religious reform. We mention three of the best below.

No record of contemporary theology would be complete without some reference to homiletic literature. Mr. Artom's[72] eloquent addresses are recommended by their deep sense of the poetry of the Jewish religion; Dr. Vaughan's[73] by an ease of manner and a purity of tone (we wish we could add by a liberality of theology) which have seldom been equalled. Dr. Farrar's[74] striking sermons are full of genuine eloquence, but avoid the religious difficulties of the age. This is not exactly the fault of Dr. Perowne,[75] but though his manner is conciliatory, his matter (see sermon on Prayer, and essay on Abraham's Sacrifice) is reactionary. Hebraists, however, will appreciate his valuable paper on Isaiah viii., ix. Mr. Body's[76] discourses differ comparatively little from those of earnest Evangelicals; Mr. Oxenham's[77] are the condensed extract of dogmatic theology. Those of a well-known Scotch preacher[78] have nothing distinctive about them but their polished style. How far is the ideal of the religious speaker, so eloquently sketched by Professor Seeley, from being realized!

A few miscellaneous books may be fitly grouped at the end of this summary. Mr. J. B. Waring sends us a chaotic but truly liberal "Record of Thoughts"[79] of the last thirty years. Miss Hennell, the second part of "Present Religion,"[80] in a style which we do not profess to have mastered; Mrs. Heckford, a sketch[81] of the life, or rather character, of Christ as the highest embodiment of Communism, *i.e.*, Altruism. Mr. Finch, a discourse[82] "On the pursuit of

---

"Orthodoxy from the Hebrew Point of View." By the Rev. T. P. Kirkman, M.A., F.R.S. Thomas Scott. "The *Edinburgh Review* and Dr. Strauss." By G. Wheelwright. Thomas Scott.

[72] "Sermons Preached in Several Synagogues." By the Rev. B. Artom, Chief Rabbi of the Spanish and Portuguese Congregations of England. London: Trübner & Co.

[73] "Words of Hope from the Pulpit of the Temple Church." By C. J. Vaughan, D.D., Master of the Temple. London: Henry S. King & Co.

[74] "The Silence and the Voices of God; with other Sermons." By F. W. Farrar, D.D., F.R.S., late Fellow of Trinity College, Cambridge, Master of Marlborough College. London: Macmillan & Co.

[75] "Sermons Preached Chiefly in the Chapel of St. David's College, Lampeter, and in Llandaff Cathedral." By J. J. Stewart Perowne, D.D., Canon of Llandaff, and Fellow of Trinity College, Cambridge. London: W. Isbister & Co.

[76] "The Life of Temptation." A Course of Lectures. By the Rev. G. Body, M.A., Rector of Kirkby Misperton, Yorkshire. London: Rivingtons.

[77] The Soul in its Probation." Sermons Preached at the Church of St. Alban the Martyr, Holborn. By F. N. Oxenham, M.A. London: Rivingtons.

[78] "A Scotch Communion Sunday." To which are added Certain Discourses from a University City. By the Author of "Recreations of a Country Parson." London: Henry S. King & Co.

[79] "A Record of Thoughts." By J. B. Waring, Architect. Two Vols. London: Trübner & Co.

[80] "Present Religion: as a Faith owning Fellowship with Thought. By Sara S. Hennell. Part II. "First Division: Intellectual Effort." London: Trübner & Co.

[81] "The Life of Christ, and its Bearing on the Doctrines of Communism." By Sara Heckford. London: Field & Tuer.

[82] "On the Pursuit of Truth, as Exemplified in the Principles of Evidence, Theological, Scientific, and Judicial." A Discourse delivered before the Sunday Lecture Society. By A. Elley Finch. London: Longmans.

Truth," clear, and well thought out, but singularly arriéré in its views of theology; Mr. Baynes, a collection of religious poems,[33] which suffers by comparison with "Lyra Anglicana;" Dr. Ryder, an Irish clergyman, a pamphlet[34] with a number of second-hand facts relative to Jewish Baptism, and supposed by him to confirm the Baptismal Regeneration of Infants; Mr. Moore,[35] a book of prayers sufficiently described in the title; Mr. Jukes,[36] a third edition of his Scriptural argument against Eternal Punishment; and an anonymous writer a quaint parallel[37] between the outer and inner man of various classes of religionists.

No work of Mr. Herbert Spencer's is likely to attract a wider circle of readers than his lately published volume on "The Study of Sociology;"[38] a work of which it is difficult to exaggerate the interest or the importance. The essays of which the volume is composed have previously appeared in a separate form both in England and America, and the volume itself has already reached a second edition, so that it is now unnecessary to give an account of its contents; probably all who take any interest in social speculations have read the book for themselves. It is, we fear, too late now to regret that Mr. Spencer has adopted the barbarous hybrid name "Sociology," from Comte and his followers, for a science which he has done so much to create and extend; indeed, he makes so ostentatious a parade of his unfamiliarity with the two great languages of antiquity, that it is possible his taste has never been disturbed by a word which steals an element from each, in defiance of all philological propriety. As, however, he is a purist in regard to his own language, perhaps he will excuse a word of protest on behalf of another. But apart from its title, which no familiarity can redeem from barbarism, the work is admirable. What Bacon did, or helped to do, for natural knowledge, Mr. Spencer is endeavouring to do for the knowledge of social phenomena; and just as one of Bacon's chief tasks was to sweep away the Idola which beset his path, so Mr. Spencer's main endeavour is to indicate the hindrances in the way of social knowledge, and as a true pioneer to cut a track through the jungle which future explorers can expand into a highway. So insurmountable, indeed, do the impediments seem, that one is at times disposed to despair of progress, and to fear that man-

---

[33] "Home Songs for Quiet Hours." Edited by the Rev. R. H. Baynes, M.A. London: Henry S. King & Co

[34] The Baptismal Regeneration of Infants." A Scriptural Study, by the Rev. A. G. Ryder, D.D. Dublin: Hodges, Foster, & Co.

[35] "Daily Devotion; or, Prayers founded on the successive portions of the New Testament as appointed in the New Lectionary," &c. By Daniel Moore, M.A. London: Kirby & Endean.

[36] The Second Death and the Restitution of all Things." By Andrew Jukes. Third Edition. London: Longmans.

[37] "The Physiology of Sects." London: Tinsley Brothers.

[38] "The Study of Sociology." By Herbert Spencer. Second Edition. London: Henry S. King & Co. 1874.

kind must, after all, wait till the struggle for existence and the survival of the fittest shall have developed a new organ for the unbiassed perception of social phenomena. As well might a man try to see white light through a prism, as to envisage such phenomena in their due relations with the unpurified intelligence of ordinary life; and Mr. Spencer would almost have us believe that for the study of Sociology mankind are at present hoodwinked with prismatic spectacles which cannot be set aside, and that each man's prism is different to that of the rest. Still, to see the difficulties clearly, is one step towards removing them, and in this respect Mr. Spencer has done yeoman's service. In a notice of another work, published under Mr. Spencer's auspices, the "Sociological Tables," we ventured to express some distrust of the close analogy frequently insisted on by Mr. Spencer between Biology and Sociology; the analogy is enforced and illustrated with much vigour and ingenuity in the present volume, but we cannot say that our scruples are entirely removed by the discussion. Such an analogy is, of course, not new, nor peculiar to Mr. Spencer; it is at least as old as Plato, and has always been a great favourite with constructors of social theories; but a metaphor may be so often used that it at last comes to be mistaken for a fact, and we cannot help suspecting that something of the kind has happened in the present case. "The Human Intellect," says Bacon, "from its peculiar nature, easily supposes a greater uniformity and equality in things than it really finds; and though there are many things in nature unique and full of disparity, yet it feigns parallels, correspondences, and relations which do not exist." "Nov. Org." i. 45; we give a translation, as Mr. Spencer affects to despise Latin. Of course, the theory of Evolution, of which Mr. Spencer is the acknowledged exponent, inclines him rather to individualism in politics, and to a distrust of what may be called constructive legislation; indeed, but for his own disclaimer, we should be inclined to describe him as an apostle of "*laisser-faire*." Perhaps in this respect he has fallen somewhat under one of those "biases," the influence of which he has in other cases so mercilessly traced. Constructive legislation is often premature, and sometimes pernicious; but the evolutionist must surely regard it as an effort to meet new circumstances with new adaptations; and even if it fails in nine cases out of ten, yet the success is a step in advance; and it is, perhaps, only by such tentative efforts that progress can be won at all. We regret that pressure on our space compels us to give so meagre a notice of a work of such sterling worth. We can only make amends by earnestly commending its study to all who are interested in questions of social philosophy. Politicians of all parties will find in it much food for reflection, though its range is far above the level of party politics, the crude antagonisms of which it ruthlessly dissects and exposes. It needs only be added that, in literary form, the book exhibits a notable advance on Mr. Spencer's other writings; it teems with felicitous illustration, and is a model of lucid arrangement; and though, perhaps, occasionally wanting in the higher elements of refinement and grace, it maintains with unflagging vigour a style which is at once stimulating, lively, persuasive, and direct.

The second title of Serjeant Cox's now completed work, "What am I?"[*] is "A Popular Introduction to Mental Philosophy and Psychology." In reality, the book is a temperate, but still one-sided, statement of the so-called Psychic theory of the phenomena which commonly go by the name of Spiritualism. It is needless to say that the author discards with much emphasis the Spiritualist hypothesis, though he pleads with the skill of a practised advocate for the admission of the phenomena to scientific inquiry. For tone, temper, and moderation there is no fault to be found with his argument, but it may be questioned how far it is fair or prudent to introduce into a work avowedly popular a discussion of phenomena which have never yet been admitted without question, either into Physics or Psychology. "Let me earnestly recommend to the reader," says Serjeant Cox in his preface, "not to waste time in witnessing any of the Psychic phenomena, unless he has resolved to undertake a long and laborious course of experimental inquiry." The caution is excellent, but it seems to us to apply with even greater force to a book which relates the phenomena at secondhand, than to the direct observation of the phenomena themselves. Serjeant Cox maintains that the evidence collected by the Dialectical Society would satisfy any court of justice; but the plea is somewhat misleading, as of course no court would accept the evidence at all without rigid cross-examination; nor would any jury return a verdict on a mass of unsworn and unattested affidavits. Scientific proof is one thing, and of that Serjeant Cox does not profess to constitute the tribunal to which he appeals a judge. Judicial proof is no doubt different, and it is apparently on this that he relies; but here he seeks a verdict on hearsay evidence alone, a procedure we believe totally unknown to any recognised system of law. Moreover, Psychology is not a science whose primary data can be placed beyond the reach of dispute, and we venture to think a popular audience is the very worst judge of psychological proof. A Psychic force, analogous to that of Magnetism, directed to definite and intelligible purposes in total unconsciousness by the intelligence of a child in arms, points to a hypothesis which is not perhaps scientifically inadmissible, as it at least professes to appeal to a *vera causa*, but it is beset with such gigantic difficulties, physical, psychological, and evidential, that we may well hesitate before we accept it. While giving Serjeant Cox every credit for his candour, courage, and fairness, we sincerely regret that he should have attempted, as it were, to snatch a verdict by a *provocatio ad populum*, an appeal to a tribunal totally unfit to estimate the evidence, or to draw a trustworthy conclusion from it.

The promoters of the Theological and Philosophical Library have rendered a great service to the study of Philosophy, by giving as their first publication an excellent translation of the late Prof. Ueberweg's very valuable "History of Philosophy,"[**] the second volume of which

---

[*] "What am I? A Popular Introduction to Mental Philosophy and Psychology." By Edward W. Cox, Serjeant-at-Law. Vol. ii. The Mechanism in Action. London: Longmans. 1874.

[**] "History of Philosophy from Thales to the Present Time." By Dr.

has lately appeared. The original work is too well known to all students of Philosophy to need description here; it is pretty generally recognised as one of the best handbooks which the erudition of modern Germany has produced. The translation, so far as we have been able to test it, is carefully and accurately executed; and the notes, references, and bibliographical information (a most valuable and important feature in the original work), have been transferred to the English edition with commendable diligence and precision. One point of typographical detail calls for passing notice. The original German edition is printed in type of two sizes, and this is sufficiently embarrassing, but the translation presents us with three sizes, which is almost distracting. If the German smaller type had been put in notes separate from the text, and the remainder printed uniformly, the book would have been far easier to read. Dr. Porter's appendix on English and American Philosophy is interesting, and fairly adequate, but is scarcely up to the level of Ueberweg's own work; and Prof. Botta's appendix on Italian Philosophy throws considerable light on a subject which has been treated by most historians of Philosophy with unaccountable neglect. On the whole, the work deserves, and will probably secure, a considerable success; the only drawback is its bulk and its expense. It is strange that translations in England should generally be more ponderous and expensive than the original works; France and Germany are both considerably ahead of us in this respect.

The translation which has lately appeared of M. Ribot's "Psychologie Anglaise Contemporaine,"[41] is another illustration of the same remark; the volume is about twice the bulk of the original work. The work deserves translation if only as an acknowledgment of the homage offered to English philosophy, by the careful study M. Ribot has devoted to it; but we cannot commend the execution; the translation is not minutely literal, yet it has an unmistakeably foreign air about it, and it contains not a few positive blunders and innumerable inaccuracies. Either it has been executed with unnecessary haste, or the corrections for the press have been very carelessly and inaccurately made, for it contains errors and oversights which a decent revision could not have failed to detect. This is the more inexcusable as the work consists largely of extracts from English writers, which might have been exactly given with ordinary care and attention. We should recommend all who can read French with tolerable ease to go to the original work.

The author of "The Science of Sensibility (Intelligence)"[42] displays in his work neither science, sense, sensibility, nor intelligence, to say nothing of grammar and spelling. It is a pity he cannot find a better

---

Friedrich Ueberweg. Translated from the Fourth German Edition. By Geo. S. Morris, A.M. With Additions. Vol. ii. "History of Modern Philosophy." London: Hodder & Stoughton. 1874.

[41] "English Psychology." Translated from the French of H. Ribot. Hartley, James Mill, Herbert Spencer, A. Bain, G. H. Lewes, Samuel Bailey, John Stuart Mill. London: Henry S. King & Co. 1873.

[42] "On the Science of Sensibility (Intelligence)," &c. By John Nelson Smith. London: Published for the Author, by Trübner & Co. 1873.

use for his money than spending it in paying respectable publishers to print books of nonsense. The most charitable supposition is that the whole thing is a joke; but if so, it is a very tiresome and bad joke.

In "The Psychology of Scepticism and Phenomenalism,"[*] Mr. Andrews makes some minor points against the psychological theories of Hume and Berkeley. Mr. Andrews is apparently a physiologist by training with a turn for psychology, but without much practice in psychological analysis. His physiology is very dogmatic, but it is not, we suspect, beyond the reach of criticism. There is, however, ingenuity and, we believe, novelty in the suggestion, that the tactile or quasi-tactile sensations of the muscles associated with the organs of special sense, contribute to the growth of acquired perceptions; but their function in this respect is, we imagine, exaggerated by Mr. Andrews.

Dr. Cunningham's "New Theory of Knowing and Known,"[*] may not be unfamiliar to some readers of the *Westminster Review*, for an outline of it appeared in an article in July, 1862, on "Sir W. Hamilton's Doctrines of Perception and Judgment." It is bold enough to take away the breath of any but a Scotch metaphysician, though we imagine that the last title Dr. Cunningham would think of claiming is that of "metaphysician." We give the theory in his own words, for we dare not try to paraphrase it: "Through the senses we get our knowledge, and by memory we recall it. Our intellectual states, therefore, are either sensations or recollections. There is no other. What we call ideas are simply recollections, but perhaps in that form which we call imagination. To have ideas, is, therefore, simply to be remembering or imagining; and the mind remembering something, imagining something, needs not be conscious of the operation, but in the operation is conscious of the thing. . . . Hamilton held that we are conscious only of our perceptions, and that in the perception there is involved a knowledge of the thing perceived. I, on the other hand, maintain that we are conscious only of the thing perceived, but that in the perception of it there is involved the conscious existence of the perceiver," pp. 180 and 102. This is simple enough at any rate; mind is conscious of matter and of nought else, and there is nothing more to be said. That with such a theory Dr. Cunningham contradicts himself at every step is a slight matter, for of course he will maintain, as Mill did in a similar case, that philosophical language is based on the theory which he discards, and, therefore, cannot be accommodated to his view without readjustment. It is easy to simplify philosophy by ignoring the difficulties it presents, but the process is scarcely satisfactory. Dr. Cunningham's book reads like a treatise on colour, written by a blind man. It is surprising to find a writer so conversant with philosophical literature, and with such a keen interest in his subject, complacently adopting so inadequate a theory.

---

[*] "The Psychology of Scepticism and Phenomenalism." By James Andrews. Glasgow: Maclehose. 1874.

[*] "A New Theory of Knowing and Known, with some Speculations on the Borderland of Psychology and Physiology." By John Cunningham, D.D. Edinburgh: Black. 1874.

In his "Philosophie des Bewusstseins,"[45] Dr. Hicking attempts a solution of the old problems in an incoherent series of axiomatic sentences rather obscure than profound. The work is apparently posthumous. It was, perhaps, not very judicious of the author's friends to give it to the world.

Dr. Alfred Hölder's "Darstellung der Kantischen Erkenntnisstheorie,"[46] gives a lucid exposition of one of the most difficult portions of the Critical Philosophy. The "Transcendental Deduction of the Categories" is the well-known *crux* of Kant's system. Our own acquaintance with the controversy to which it has given rise is so limited, that we cannot venture to determine whether Dr. Hölder has succeeded in unravelling the mystery which has baffled so many of his predecessors. We must leave the question to professed students of Kant. But Dr. Hölder's exposition is so clear and painstaking, that, in default of a systematic study of Kant's own writings, it may fairly be commended to the attention of ordinary students of philosophy.

Dr. Hoppe, in "Die Analogie,"[47] makes a fierce onslaught on the logical process called Analogy, and proposes to banish it entirely from the logic of the future. He is also very angry with the logicians, German and foreign, who have given it a place in their system. Dr. Hoppe has little difficulty in showing, what any English logician could have told him, that analogical reasoning is not necessarily conclusive, and that many processes are commonly included under the head of Analogy, which might with advantage be disengaged and ranged in more appropriate fashion; but this is a very different thing from discarding Analogy altogether. As well might he propose to discard Hypothesis because it is not a complete Induction. However, Dr. Hoppe's general theory of Induction and its relation to Deduction is so startling, and, to our thinking, so unsound, that we are not surprised to find him at sea on the comparatively minor question of Analogy. "Every complete chain of inference," says he (p. 24), "consists of the three Inductive and the three Deductive propositions, and these six propositions should ever stand clear before the mind: *e.g.*, A. 1. Caius is mortal. 2. Caius is a man. 3. Men are mortal. B. 4. Men are mortal. 5. Cæsar is a man. 6. Cæsar is mortal." It is, indeed, surprising that this mode of stating the matter should appear satisfactory to any one who has ever read, not to say written, a work on Logic. If we were to argue that Kant was a sound reasoner, Kant was a German, and therefore Germans are sound reasoners, and hence proceed to infer that Dr. Hoppe is a sound reasoner, we should, for all we can see, be reasoning in a fashion which Dr. Hoppe would sanction; but the conclusion would be so manifestly unsound that we

[45] "Philosophie des Bewusstseins in Bezug auf das Böse und das Uebel." Von Dr. med. Franz Hicking. Hinterlassenes Manuscript. Berlin: Denicke's Verlag. 1873.

[46] "Darstellung der Kantischen Erkenntnisstheorie mit besonderer Berücksichtigung der verschiedenen Fassungen der transcendentalen Deduction der Kategorien." Von Dr. Alfred Hölder. Tübingen: Laupp. 1874.

[47] "Die Analogie." Eine Allgemeine verständliche Darstellung aus dem Gebiete der Logik. Von Prof. Dr. L. Hoppe. Berlin: Denicke's Verlag. 1873.

should be forced to suspect that either the premises were false or the process illicit. It is worthy of notice, that in criticising Mill, Dr. Hoppe has very seriously misrepresented the meaning, and even the words, of that writer. The fault may lie with Mill's German translator, but in that case we are surprised that the translation has had such a wide circulation in Germany. Dr. Hoppe is apparently very angry that this should be the case, and he assures us, on the authority of Herr von Grauvogl (a philosopher whose fame, so far as we know, has not yet passed the Rhine), that Mill has written an Inductive Logic without in the least knowing what Induction is. If Dr. Hoppe's book should be translated into English, we cannot promise it a very wide circulation, but, perhaps, such readers as it might find would be disposed, but for politeness, to return the compliment.

Dr. Hermann Siebeck's "Untersuchungen zur Philosophie der Griechen,"* is a valuable example of that specialization of study for which modern Germany is so remarkable. It consists of four essays, illustrating with greater minuteness and completeness of detail than is possible in a general history of philosophy, isolated but interesting points connected with Greek Philosophy. The first Essay, on "Socrates' relation to Sophistic," deals with one of the most vexed questions of modern criticism. It is, perhaps, strange that Dr. Siebeck should pay so little attention to the labours of English scholars on a question which they have almost made their own. Grote is, we think, only once mentioned, and Professor Jowett not at all. The second Essay, on "Plato's Theory of Matter," is full of interest, and furnishes in a convenient form a mass of information which it would be difficult to find elsewhere. The same may be said of the remaining Essays on "Aristotle's Doctrine of the Eternity of the World," and on "The Connection of Aristotle's Philosophy of Nature with that of the Stoics." Students of Greek philosophy will find the work both instructive and interesting.

We have received several numbers of "La Critique Philosophique,"** a weekly journal of Philosophy, Literature, and General Criticism, published under the direction of M. Renouvier. It consists of original articles, bibliographical notices, and notes of general interest. It does not confine its survey to the literature of France, but deals extensively with that of England and of Germany. M. Pillon is the responsible Editor; his name and that of M. Renouvier are sufficient to secure the attention of all students of philosophy. The philosophical principles espoused by the journal are those of the French developments of Kant. We gladly call the attention of our readers to this interesting publication, and cordially recommend it to their notice.

---

* "Untersuchungen zur Philosophie der Griechen." Von Dr. Hermann Siebeck. Halle: Barthel. 1873.

** "La Critique Philosophique, Politique, Scientifique, Littéraire." Publiée sous la direction de M. Renouvier: Paris.

POLITICS, SOCIOLOGY, VOYAGES AND TRAVELS.

THOUGH the students of Mr. Mill's "Principles of Political Economy" in its successive editions, will have little to learn as to the author's most matured opinions on that subject, yet it is probable that it is those who are best acquainted with that work, and with all Mr. Mill's other works, who will be most rejoiced to find any stray papers of Mr. Mill rescued from oblivion, and will be most inquisitive as to their contents. Not, indeed, that the "Essays on some Unsettled Questions on Political Economy"[1]—the second edition of which is now published—was at all an unknown treatise, or inaccessible to persevering students; but curiosity was whetted, and not easily appeased through the sort of obstruction which is offered by the fact of a book having been long out of print. The essays themselves will be found to be full of interest, both biographical and scientific; and the conscientious thoroughness with which Mr. Mill performed every piece of work he undertook, is of itself a sufficient security for the permanent value of what might have been, in the hands of another, mere desultory decompositions. The essays were written in 1829 and 1830, and were, all but one, long kept in manuscript "because, during the temporary suspension of public interest in the species of discussion to which they belong, there was no inducement to their publication." The first essay on the "Laws of Interchange between Nations," discusses a subject which, at the time of its first publication, was becoming matter of debate in Parliament, that is, the exact mode in which the advantages flowing from free trade between two countries is reaped by both of them. Mr. Mill explains and illustrates the doctrine of Ricardo, to the effect that "it is not a difference in the *absolute* cost of production which determines the interchange, but a difference in the *comparative* cost. Towards the close of the essay Mr. Mill illustrates the whole subject by applying the principles which underlie it to answer a question of great practical moment,—Which of the countries of the world gains most by foreign commerce? Mr. Mill makes the answer the more interesting, as he selects for purposes of comparison the case of France and England, and investigates the consequences of free trade between them in a way which subsequent policy has developed into a prophesy. He first says that if by *gain* be meant advantage, that country will generally gain the most which stands the most in need of foreign commodities. But if by *gain* be meant saving of labour and capital in obtaining the commodities which the country desires to have, whatever they may be, the country will gain, not in proportion to its own need of foreign articles, but to the need which foreigners have of the articles which itself produces. Mr. Mill then imagines the case of the restrictions being removed "which have loaded the commercial intercourse of

[1] "Essays on some Unsettled Questions of Political Economy." By John Stuart Mill. Second Edition. London: Longmans. 1874.

France and England to such an extent that, regard being had to the wealth and population of the two countries," the trade carried on between them is so little that it may be called none at all. England, thought Mr. Mill, would be the greatest gainer. "There would instantly arise in France an immense demand for the cottons, woollens, and iron of England; while wines, brandies, and silks, the staple articles of France, are less likely to come into general demand here; nor would the consumption of such productions, it is probable, be so rapidly increased by the fall of price." Mr. Mill traces various detailed consequences which would flow from opening this trade, and which he thinks are such as would not be expected by the friends or by the opponents of the restrictive system.

"The wine-growers of France, who imagine that free-trade would relieve their distress by raising the price of their wine, might not improbably find that price actually lowered. On the other hand, our silk manufacturers would be surprised if they were told that the free admission of our cotton and hardware into the French market would endanger *their* branch of manufactory; yet such might possibly be the effect. France it is likely could most advantageously pay us in silks for a portion of the cottons and hardware which we should sell to her; and though all our manufacturers may now be able to compete advantageously in some branches of the manufacture with their French rivals, it by no means follows that they could do so when the efflux of money from France, and its influx into England, had lowered the price of silk goods in the French market, and increased the expenses of production here."

The essay on the "Definition and Method of Political Economy," is one which might advantageously be put in the hands of every one commencing a study of the subject, and is a valuable contribution to the study of the moral sciences generally. The essay on the words *productive* and *unproductive* will also richly repay perusal.

An interesting discussion on a subject which, in some of its aspects, may shortly become of practical concern in England, is contained in a pamphlet by Dr. Theodor Schütze.[1] The subject is the desirability of admitting persons other than professional lawyers to take part in the conduct of criminal trials. The writer distinguishes the different modes in which this participation may take place, and points out the distinct aspects in which the question is presented, according as the "laymen" merely find a verdict of fact, or expound the law, or perform either of these functions with or without the help of a professional assessor or assessors. In dealing with the subject, the author recognises the value of giving publicity, or rather popularity, to the proceedings, and also considers how far the kind of law to be administered (that is, whether of home or foreign growth, traditional or statute, unwritten or codified) affects the question. The author's own conclusions are rather unfavourable to the undue extension of unprofessional co-operation, and he will allow no other test to prevail but that of the proved superiority of the judicial decision. The like question is presented in England in the case of the unpaid magistracy, and (in

[1] "Laien in den Strafgerichten!" Rechtliches Bedenken von Dr. Theodor Reinhold Schütze. Leipzig. 1873.

civil cases) in discussing the expediency of introducing commercial tribunals.

Herr Nicolaus Schüren has published a second and much improved edition of his work on "A Solution of the Social Question,"[3] and added to it an historical introduction which much increases the whole value of the work. The subject of the work is not exactly co-extensive with what in England is meant by political economy, but covers a good deal of what is sometimes called in England "social philosophy." The new portion of the work will be found interesting, as describing the political aspirations of some sections of foreign democracy which are little understood or appreciated in this country. For instance, we are told that the "social-democratic" party holds it to be the essential problem before a State how to "introduce a new organization into labour;" or how, in other words, to apply its own power in such a way as to enable the non-possessing classes to put themselves on a par with the possessing. It is only in matters of very occasional legislation that the English House of Commons is brought face to face with these questions, or that the most enlightened democrats desire it to interfere with them. A similar lesson on the sort of instruction by means of which continental democrats are reared, is given in the people's edition of Bastiat's "Political Economy,"[4] especially in the section on "The Law."

A curious and original mode of argument adopted by Mr. James Harvey, of Liverpool, in assaulting the monopoly of the Bank of England and the policy of the Bank Charter Act, is to make copious extracts from Bishop Berkeley's "Querist,"[5] and to supplement them by queries of his own in something the same style, and touching upon the money problems of this day.

Some interesting and somewhat curious documents, throwing light upon the most advanced socialistic organizations on the Continent, have been published by the International Association of Workmen by way of justification of their own conduct in refusing to associate themselves with socialists of all types.[6] At the congress held at the Hague, the Council General demanded an inquiry into the nature of the organization entitled the Alliance of Socialist Democracy, and a commission of five members was appointed for the purpose of conducting the inquiry. The result of the inquiry was among other things to exclude Michel Bakounine from the International, on the ground of his having founded the Alliance, and for some more personal reasons. It appears that Bakounine prepared the statutes of the Alliance; and in fact they were produced partly in his handwriting. Two of the first clauses in these statutes are that the "International brethren have

---

[3] "Zur lösung der Socialen Frage." Von Nicolaus Schüren. Zweite mit einer historischen Einleitung und vermehrte Auflage. Leipzig.

[4] "Essays on Political Economy." By the late M. Frederic Bastiat. London: Provost and Co.

[5] "Bishop Berkeley on Money." Being Extracts from his celebrated "Querist." By James Harvey. London: Provost and Co.

[6] "L'Alliance de la Démocratie Socialiste et l'Association Internationale des Travailleurs." Londres: A. Dawson.

no other country than that of universal revolution, and know no foreign country or enemy but reaction." "They renounce all compromise or concession, and treat every movement as reactionary which has any other end but the immediate and direct triumph of their principles." In other clauses the "passion of revolution" is treated as the sole qualification, and a supreme consecration to the service of revolution the paramount and absorbing duty of a brother.

The public have had such copious and various information of late on the subject of Ashanti that they can hardly be expected to be voracious after fresh facts, especially as the Parliamentary Blue Books have yet to be read. However, a little work on "Fanti and Ashanti,"[7] by Captains Brackenbury and Huysche, the latter of whom was unhappily killed in the war, will command attention from the historical circumstances under which the materials it contains were prepared. Major-General Sir Garnet Wolseley, with thirty-six officers, volunteers for service in the Ashanti expedition, was on board the *Ambriz*, bound for Cape Coast Castle. An order had been issued requesting officers to make themselves acquainted, as far as possible, with everything relating to the country and the war. It is said that the Head-quarter Staff so much used the books of reference that the rest of the party could seldom get a chance of reading them. Sir Garnet Wolseley requested the members of his staff to put into shape and read to their colleagues the results of their long daily studies. "The time given was less than a week, and we had to work under the most unfavourable conditions of tropical heat, a rolling ship, and the sickening smell of bilge water." The work is full of important matter, and affords the readiest and safest mode of studying all the facts of the case.

It is not uninstructive to read occasionally the language and reasonings of those who take an extreme view in any political question, and are not hampered in their thought or expression by so much as a sidelong glance at views of truths which rival, or excel in importance their own. In the "Modern Avernus"[8] Junius Junior travels over every one of the topics of what may be called the "Catholic Question," and does his utmost to awaken his countrymen to a due sense of the danger they incur from the various measures of toleration towards Roman Catholics which have successively been adopted. The author endeavours to prove from the history of the chief countries of Europe, and from the testimony of the ablest writers in those countries, that the source of all evil, political and personal, is the Papacy and its representatives in different places. In successive chapters the modern Junius combats what he calls the "Popular Illusions" to the effect that Popery is changed, "that Popery is not advancing," "that there is nothing to fear from Popery." He discusses, in the light of his main thesis, the several "Pressing Questions" of the day, such as the "Convent

---

[7] "Fanti and Ashanti." Three Papers read on board the S.S. *Ambriz*, on the voyage to the Gold Coast. By Capt. H. Brackenbury and Capt. G. L. Huysche. London: Blackwood. 1873.

[8] "The Modern Avernus. The Descent of England: How far? A Question for Parliament and the Constituencies." By Junius Junior. London: Hatchards. 1874.

Question," the "Chaplains' Question," the "Education Question," and the "Irish Question." In discussing some of these questions, the author propounds views of fact which have all the charm of novelty or at least of courage. The general upshot is that the "Catholic Emancipation Act must be repealed;" that "the first duty of Government is to repel Papal encroachment; and the English Minister who wantonly permits that encroachment deserves to be impeached as a traitor to the State."

In a clear and well-reasoned pamphlet[9] Mr. Calvert, Q.C., endeavours to dispose of the arguments for reconstructing the Inns of Court on the basis of making them institutions for the education of both branches of the legal profession. The main strength of Mr. Calvert's arguments lies in his assertions that the two branches need different kinds of training, and can best get it apart, and that the present training given to the students for the Bar by the Inns of Court is the best attainable. No doubt on both these heads Mr. Calvert makes out a tolerable case, though his reasoning is not novel. But Mr. Calvert fails to apprehend the real gist of the attack on the present state of things. It is complained that it is impossible for any body, or assemblages of bodies, like the Inns of Court, to give a really efficient system of education. In the mode by which the governing members of those bodies are appointed, and in the nature of their occupations, there is nothing to secure their competency for a very hard and special task—that of education; and there is still less to animate them to give sustained attention to the task when once undertaken. Again, it is complained that, even if barristers and attorneys have each much to learn that is special, they have, or ought to have, still more to learn that is in common; and if once a truly national system of education is devised for teaching of this common part, it would be so much pure waste (to say the least) to teach the same matter twice over in two different places with two different staffs of teachers.

Professor Blackie's[10] works are always worth reading, and always mark the presence of an original, sensitive, thoughtful, and accomplished mind. He belongs to the Conservative order of spirits, but his very Conservatism is of that generous and spiritualized type which attracts rather than repels his natural antagonists. He is at once gentle and searching, discontented with what is, and yet cautious in his selection of remedies. He loves democracy, not because he hates tyrants, but because he loves and reveres man. Professor Blackie's essays on "Self-culture" reveal him at his best, as the inspirer of worthy and elevating thoughts, the friend of the young, and the believer in the possibilities of the steady march of society towards perfection. These essays are on the culture of the intellect, physical culture, and moral culture. The Professor gives some useful warnings to young

---

[9] "Remarks upon the Jurisdiction of the Inns of Court." By Frederick Calvert, Q.C. London: Ridgway. 1874.

[10] "On Self-Culture: Intellectual, Physical, and Moral. A Vade Mecum for Young Men and Students." By John Stuart Blackie. Edinburgh: Edmonston and Douglas. 1874.

would-be critics. "There is no good to be looked for from a youth who, having done no substantial work of his own, sets up a business of finding faults in other people's work, and calls this practice of finding fault criticism. Young men of course may and ought to have opinions on many subjects, but there is no reason why they should print them.

Sir C. Adderley has published "A Few Thoughts on National Education and Punishments."[11] The two main topics are not kept enough apart. Indeed, they run into one another, the link being that of the education of pauper children. With a good many of Sir C. Adderley's remarks on education we should be disposed to agree; as for instance, that the State has within the last forty years gone somewhat wide of the strict limits it had first in view—the education of children of the working classes. He is in favour of more effectually concentrating the whole Governmental functions of education in a single department, and of getting rid of all special pauper schools. In speaking of punishments we are at one with him in his criticisms of some of the arguments used at the late International Prison Congress to the effect that the sole or main purpose of criminal punishment is moral reformation, though his addiction to corporal punishments proceeds, we think, on an insufficient estimate of the indirect effect of such punishments on national character. It would have been well if the pamphlet had been better arranged and expanded into a larger treatise.

Probably there could be no better way for a foreigner to acquaint himself with some of the most important characteristics of English social and political life, than that of studying the life and institutions at one of the great manufacturing towns in the country. Such an opportunity is afforded by Dr. Langford in his interesting work on "Modern Birmingham and its Institutions."[12] The work professes to be a chronicle of local events from 1841 to 1871; but these thirty years have proved so important in the development of English municipal life that the work presents, in fact, a vivid image of the modern growth of much that is most significant generally in modern life and institutions. Thus the history of the "Birmingham and Midland Institute" describes the first practical step taken to found it in 1840, by presenting a memorial to Lord John Russell requesting the government to extend the Act for encouraging the establishment of Museums in large towns. All the details of the mode in which the movement was carried out are described, and (what must be very interesting to the people of Birmingham), the names are given of all the persons who took part in the different proceedings. So with the Birmingham Free Libraries and Free Art Gallery. The provision made of late years for education and literature, and even for amusement, are described with the most scrupulous precision.

---

[11] "A Few Thoughts on National Education and Punishments." By the Rt. Hon. Sir C. Adderley, K.C.M.G., M.P. London: Longmans. 1874.

[12] "Modern Birmingham and its Institutions: a Chronicle of Local Events from 1841 to 1871." Compiled and Edited by John Alfred Langford, LL.D. Vol. I. Birmingham: Osborne. 1871.

The author of Williams's "Working Man and his Representative"[13] professes to have done his utmost to put himself in the actual situation of a true "working-man," and to taste all the experiences of his life. With the help of a "dialect and bodily disguise," he says that he contrived to pass as a workman. The result was that, to quote his own words, "I found the work far more trying than I had expected; it was weary work, painful work, but I hope my labour has not been in vain. I have a greater love for the working classes, and far greater pity." The work contains, no doubt, a great number of true and useful observations, and many of them may supply valuable correctives to the superficial sophisms and rhetoric, by help of which the character and situation of the "working-man," as a construction of the fancy, is sometimes idealized. But the mode of generalizing adopted by the writer, leads to just as misleading conclusions as the vague declamation in use among a certain class of politicians. Probably no general idea whatever is, or can be, true about the "working-man" as such; till education has had more to do with him, he can be called with little precision even a man. He is rather an assemblage of possibilities and incoherences or inconsistencies. He certainly, as the writer indicates, belongs as yet to no political party, and the first party he will belong to is the narrow one that promises most for his own interests as he understands them. But all this comes to very little, because it is one of the main objects of a good public system to raise the "working-men," that is, the bulk of the population, out of their embryonic condition, and to make them men and citizens.

Miss Lees' "Handbook for Hospital Sisters,"[14] might have won for itself a wider, and therefore a worthier welcome, if its title had more plainly denoted that it is a book as useful to women who have to nurse at home and wofully feel their lack of training and knowledge, as it could be to the class for whom it has been specially intended. Miss Lees brings to her task of authorship a very unusual and rarely valuable amount of capability and preparation. She may speak with authority who has been trained at St. Thomas's Hospital; has studied and nursed in Berlin, Dresden, and Kaiserswerth; was a "surgical sister" at King's College Hospital; examined the Dutch and Danish Hospitals; was further trained in the French Hospitals of the Hôtel Dieu, Lariboisière, Enfant Jésus, Val de Grâce, Vincennes; served under the Sœurs de Charité de St. Vincent de Paul, and was allowed thoroughly to inspect, not only these, but other great Parisian Hospitals; had sole charge of the typhus station of one Army Corps before Metz; and finally took the superintendency of the ambulance for wounded of the Crown Princess of Germany. The danger besetting so experienced a person is that into which the writers of most directions for nurses have fallen, that of forgetting what ignorance means. But with the true spirit of humble genius, Miss Lees is a learner still, and a learner

---

[13] "Williams's Working Man and his Representative." Being an Account of the Experiences of an "Amateur Working Man, and their Results." London: Longmans. 1874.

[14] "Handbook for Hospital Sisters." By Florence S. Lees. Edited by H. W. Acland, M.D., F.R.S. Isbister and Co. London: 1874.

of beginnings, and the most inexperienced will find their wants supplied by her. The book contains directions for the training of nurses and of superintendents throughout their course of training and examinations, together with wise advice as to the relation of "sisters," or matrons, and probationers, as well as of all of them to the patients. The comparison of English with the French and German hospitals and training systems is very interesting; while the detailed directions given for the management of rooms, linen, attendance on various sorts of illness are of great practical use. An appendix containing papers for the guidance of hospital nurses by Dr. Acland and Mr. Whitfield is also valuable. In fine, it is a book which "no lady's library should be without."

There is not much leisure in the present day for reading works that are neither wholly amusing nor wholly instructive, but are in some measure both at once. Indeed, the writing of such books implies an absence of pressure on the author's time and spirits which the weight of literary labour in modern times renders somewhat uncommon. People who are not professional authors do not write, and those who are, usually write too hastily and too much. An elegantly printed work on "Business,"[15] by a "Merchant," well illustrates these observations. It is a book written for people who want something to read, and have plenty of time to read it in. It is quaint in its style and materials, and recalls the manner of Sir Thomas Browne. It is full of short poetical quotations, classical and mythological allusions, and fanciful images and metaphors. The following is a specimen of the sort of thing.

"As with Adam in the Garden of Eden, it is not good for the business man to be alone. He has therefore servants, clerks, agents, partners, that is, co-operative powers, *climacida* as the classic would call them. Astutely remarks our scientific essayist: 'One of the great arts of all persons placed in authority is to multiply themselves, as it were, by a judicious and trustful employment of other men's intelligence and abilities.'"

There was no department of Roman law which was more thoroughly worked out with logical precision, and with due regard to the exigences of practical life, than that which concerned the constitution, duties and right of corporate bodies of all sorts. In a most interesting and erudite treatise, Dr. Max Cohn[16] of Berlin investigates the history and character of some of these corporations, especially those which were not what may be called constitutional or political bodies, such as municipal corporations, the senate, and organized bodies of priests. The corporations, or rather "collegia" whose history and position form the subject of Dr. Max Cohn's inquiries, are rather those bodies which occupy an intermediate position between that of a private partnership or *societas*, and that of an integral element in the constitution of the state. These bodies are rather of the nature of guilds, or perhaps "joint-stock companies," though neither of these institutions exactly recalls the class of *collegia* here referred to. The history of them is

---

[15] "Business." By a Merchant. Edinburgh: Edmonston and Douglas. 1873.

[16] "Zum Römischen Vereinsrecht." Abhandlungen aus der Rechtsgeschichte, von Dr. Max Cohn. Berlin. 1873.

difficult to investigate, extending as it does from times previous to Augustus, through the reign of Augustus, and through that of the Emperors. The sources of information are of course numerous and scattered, and the present author deserves thanks for his painstaking laboriousness in bringing together and sifting the authorities.

In the course of discussing the question as to the best mode of reconstructing the English army, a treatise by Dr. Carl Walcker, on the "Necessity from a Military, National, Social and Ecclesiastical Point of View, of an Effective and Universal Military Training for the Young,"[17] will be found of great service. The work gives an account of the actual constitution and recent history of the armies of the chief European States, and examines (among other matters) the financial and political aspects of what the author calls the "military question." His view would receive some sympathy in this country so far as he resists the exemption from forced service accorded to the clergy, but rather less when he recommends military training for the young as an eminent *conservative* measure.

An instructive work for the increasing number of military students is supplied by an account of the operations of the First Bavarian Army Corps, under General Von der Tann, in the late Franco-German war.[18] The work is compiled from the Bavarian Official Records by Captain Hugo Helvig, of the Royal Bavarian General Staff. A special feature of the work is a volume exclusively devoted to five very large and clear maps.

Among the valuable group of works on the military tactics of the chief States of Europe which Messrs. King are publishing, a small treatise on "Austrian Cavalry Exercise,"[19] will hold a good and useful place. The translator says he was present in the autumn of 1872, at the exercises of the Austrian Cavalry, at the great camp of instruction at Bruck, on the Leitha, some twenty miles distant from Vienna. A previous study of the cavalry drill-book had convinced him of the excellence of the system employed, owing to its extreme simplicity and the absence of all superfluous details, and that conviction was thoroughly confirmed when he witnessed it in practice.

The Registrar-General of Victoria publishes the Indexes to the Patents and Patentees for the year 1871.[20] The work is very complete, containing as it does, in three separate departments, a "subject matter" index, a "descriptive" index, and (what is the most interesting feature of the whole) a collection of very elegant drawings.

---

[17] "Die militärische, nationale, social-und-kirchenpolitische Nothwendigkeit der militärischen Jugenderziehung und wirklich allgemeinen Wehrplicht." Von Dr. Carl Walcker. Leipzig. 1873.

[18] "Operations of the Bavarian Army, 1870–1." Official War Documents. By Captain Hugo Helvig. Translated by Captain George Salis Schwabe. In two vols. Text and Maps. London: Henry S. King. 1874.

[19] "Austrian Cavalry Exercise." Translated from the Abridged Edition of Captain Illia Woinovitts of the General Staff. By Captain W. S. Cooke. Henry S. King. 1874.

[20] "Patents and Patentees." Indices for the Year 1871. By William Henry Archer, Registrar-General of Victoria. Melbourne. 1873.

The general efforts in the direction of national education are making themselves felt in the character of the elementary school books. Nothing could be better or more readable than the "Public School Series," commencing from the simplest materials, and proceeding gradually to the more complex, published by Messrs. Strahan.[11] Messrs. Johnston's "Educational Atlas of Modern Geography,"[12] is also a valuable supplement to their other public-spirited efforts to make geographical knowledge increasingly popular. We would especially desire to notice "Philips's Handy General Atlas, illustrating Modern, Historical, and Physical Geography."[13] It is really a most valuable work, and contains much matter which has not been set out in the same form, for the geography of the English colonies is especially attended to, and the changes effected in the map of Europe by the wars of Napoleon illustrated by successive maps.

It seems strange that until our own day it never seems to have occurred to any inquirer to investigate the question of the existence or non-existence of a mythology in Italy more purely popular than the mythology which centuries have identified with the very name of Rome and Italy. It is an instance of knowledge darkening counsel. For, far apart from Jove and all his train, there has been handed down a quantity of Folk-lore among the peasantry, as little dreamt of in the philosophy of the learned, as has been the lovely poetic fountain, of whose existence in the Tiberine district Mr. Hemans has lately disclosed the existence. To Mr. Busk[14] is due the honour of believing, and of confirming his belief by discovery, that our ancestors fell into the vulgar error of despising the common life around them and ignoring its existence, while they fixed their eyes upon a lore which was far less moralizing and elevating to folks in general than that which Mr. Busk has now discovered, and which needs no deep research before it can be made out to be a fresh sign of the common mental needs and tendencies of, at least, all the Aryan nations. It is refreshing to find Cinderella, the man with twelve feet of nose, and other old friends getting disinterred on classic soil. At the same time it is observable, as Mr. Busk says, that while witchcraft was never much practised or persecuted at Rome, few witches appear in their stories, and few animals as prominent actors; while the religious turn given to myths, and generally the reverent tone of all the folk-lore make the temper of the people stand out in strange contrast to that of the wild and profane tone of many of the Russian tales told by Mr. Ralston.

"Albums," "Gems," and "Souvenirs" are out of fashion, and it has long become a problem in what shape the world should be presented

---

[11] "Public School Series. First, Fourth, and Fifth Readers." London: Strahan. 1873.

[12] "The Edinburgh Educational Atlas of Modern Geography." With Complete Index. Edinburgh and London: W. and A. K. Johnston. 1874.

[13] "Philips's Handy General Atlas of the World." A Comprehensive Series of Maps, illustrating Modern, Historical, and Physical Geography. By John Bartholomew, F.R.G.S. London: George Philips and Sons. 1874.

[14] "The Folk-lore of Rome." By R. H. Busk. London: Longmans. 1874.

with the perennial supply of such papers as used to find their home in those volumes. This seems to be almost a pity; for it places much pretty writing at an unfair disadvantage. "From January to December,"[33] for instance, is not at all a book for children, but it is a collection of gracefully written accounts of facts and fancies never couched in language suited to children—not even to the "advanced" children of our day—but sufficiently pleasant to read in odd minutes, and some of them invaluable as materials for stories or small lectures to children. To the latter class belong a few pages about Tree-frogs; the habits of Storks; an account of the Children's Hospital, with hints as to what toys are useful presents there; a descriptive saunter through the Zoological Gardens, and the Museums at Kew and Hampton Court. The first paper, called "Marguerite; The Precious Jewel," a history devised to illustrate the superiority of mental over physical beauty; and several descriptions of natural scenery, are tasteful trifles. The whole collection would have been improved, and the likeness to an "Amulet" diminished, had the authoress's attempts in verse been excluded. But it is a disappointment to find a book "for children" so like most of its modern companions. Long words, complex ideas, subjects which do not concern children in the least and about which the spurious familiarity they get makes them priggish in childhood and unteachable in maturer life, have only too much taken the place of the simple stories of an earlier generation, even when the object of the writers has genuinely been the pleasure and instruction of children; while the race of books which profess to be written for children, but of which every sentence is a pun for the benefit of the older audience, are a mere phase of mocking at the little ones and must tend to raise a generation of mockers.

On every hand there is a constant buzz of announcements of newly discovered utilities of old and new substances, but to most people these announcements remain an empty sound, because they are either too fleeting in their publicity, or are made with too little detail. Mr. Simmonds[34] takes upon himself with great industry and success the task of making the requisite detailed knowledge as to a large mass of these inventions permanently accessible. Machines he leaves on one side, unless they be incidentally mentioned, and he devotes his present volume to the illustration of the leading processes and industries which have arisen of late years out of the utilization of substances usually and heretofore considered as wholly unprofitable. The information collected by him in the course of long and extensive reading on the subject is systematically arranged and is rendered more practically attainable by a good index—always a high recommendation to any book. Extracts from, or a synopsis of, such a book were impossible; but it may safely be recommended either to the merely curious reader, or to the economically inclined who have to dispose of either small or large "scraps" of any sort.

---

[33] "From January to December." A Book for Children. London: Longmans. 1873.

[34] "Waste Products and Undeveloped Substances." By P. L. Simmonds. London: Robert Hardwicke. 1873.

Among the "Wonders of the Yellowstone Region," most vividly described in the papers from which Mr. Richardson has made a compilation, few will seem more striking than the fact that, as soon as the Legislature of the United States ascertained what a marvel-bearing tract belonged to them in the Rocky Mountains, they set it apart from all settlement, occupancy, or sale, to be a great national park or pleasure ground. Of the strange things to be found in this gigantic park of fifty-five by sixty-five miles, a complete and very inviting picture is given, and the volume may be recommended to all lovers of the romantic or the picturesque.

Mr. T. T. Cooper undertook a journey at his own risk in order to test the possibility of making a trade route from Assam into Thibet. The Lama priesthood, who have the monoply of the tea trade between China and Thibet, are quite determined to prevent any introduction of tea from Assam, and Mr. Cooper has been foiled in a previous attempt to enter Assam from Thibet; but he was resolved to try his fortune again on a reverse route. He penetrated for some distance on the road he had marked out for himself, and has probably done good service by getting on friendly terms with chieftains who look with jealous fear on the British power on their borders; but when he had again to deal with the Lamas his plans were entirely frustrated, and he had to return by the way he went. The volume in which he recounts his adventures is as full of "sport" and sportsman's English as most of our modern books of travel are; but it is bright and vivacious, and the reader's mind is not harrowed by any very dreadful narratives of peril, unless it be in stories of hunts where a man deserves anything that he may get in the way of risk and suffering.

During the last Franco-German war the tendency of the Catholic Rhine Provinces of Germany was, to a strange degree, towards sympathy with the French arms because they belonged to a Catholic Power; and a similar passion for French, or at least Parisian, manners and customs as they were under the Second Empire absorbs the writer of "Sketches of Modern Paris." But for the author's statement of his German origin, too, it would be impossible to figure to the imagination a son of that grave and studious and unsensational nation portraying, as this writer does, with enthusiasm the late emperor's coat and smile. Long a resident in Paris and a diligent frequenter of sights and shows, he takes us to many scenes which are quite pathetic in the light which so short a time has cast upon them. The Court at Fontainebleau, the well known story of "the small house in the Elysée," a Tuileries Ball, the origin of the adoption of violets as the Bonapartists' emblem, an imaginative narrative of the late ex-emperor's daily life, all are so redolent of imperialism that it becomes sufficiently obvious that even this frivolous book is published, so much out of

---

"Wonders of the Yellowstone Region." Edited by James Richardson. London: Blackie and Sons. 1874.

"The Mishmee Hills." By T. T. Cooper, F.R.G.S. London: H. S. King and Co. 1873.

"Sketches of Modern Paris." Translated from the German. By Francis Loocock. London: Provost and Co. 1874.

date, as a sort of tract for the conversion of English public opinion in preparation for any possible future attempt at the restoration to power of the Bonaparte family. The translator's work must, however, be spoken of with great praise. It is rare to find any translation, especially from the German language, with its seductive similarity to a cumbrous English style, so light, easy, and graceful. Is it, however, that small and unimportant remarks are easy to transfer to another tongue; while true thought, having in its outward expression all the essential national peculiarities of mental temperament, must everywhere bear that same stamp, and can only be made intelligible in, though not translated into, another tongue.

It is to be regretted that works upon the Holy Land and upon Egypt should be published by gentlemen who do not even flatter themselves that they have anything of more than personal interest to add to the forces on any side in the long-waged war as to the true Sinai, nor that they can do more than enable "the Bible student perchance to distinguish a very few fitful gleams cast upon the boundless ocean of truth contained in the inspired volume of Scripture." Mr. Maughan cannot be credited with originality, research, special adventures, or unusual power of brilliant description; and his book on "The Alps of Arabia"[30] might well have made way for the many books of merit which publishers have not time to consider, or whose authors dare not publish at their own risk, because the world is getting as full as it can contain of books good, bad, and indifferent, with a large majority of the last class, as is instanced by the one now noticed. One grudges it the nice print, and the firm paper, and the colouring matter that makes the paper so restful to look at, and the fair brown and gold of the outside. But, for those readers who are never weary of reading oft-repeated descriptions of Arab Sheikhs, the first view of Jerusalem, Ains, Wadys, Hebron, the entrance to Petra, the convent on Mount Sinai, the Cairene donkey boys, and so on, it may be mentioned that Mr. Maughan went from Brindisi to Alexandria and Cairo, and up by steamer to Assouan; then from Cairo by Suez to Mount Serbel, Mount Sinai (begging Dr. Beke's forbearance!), Akabah, Petra, Jerusalem, Jericho, Nazareth, Damascus, and Baalbec, to Beyrout. They will find that, though Mr. Maughan had the opportunity to make this tour in consequence of illness, he was enabled to make the entire journey in perfect safety and without the smallest injury to his health, and such readers may be induced to follow his example, and the end may conceivably be that all will feel it to be too familiar ground to make a fuss or a book about.

The change of government and the consequent possibility of a change of policy in foreign affairs, together with the fact that even out of the tragedy of famine good may come to India through the aroused attention of England to Indian politics, render Mr. Vambéry's reprint of papers on the Anglo-Russian Frontier[31] doubly useful. His name,

---

[30] "The Alps of Arabia." Travels in Egypt, Sinai, Arabia, and the Holy Land. By William Charles Maughan. London: H. S. King and Co. 1873.

[31] "Central Asia, and the Anglo-Russian Frontier Question." By Arminius Vambéry. Translated by F. E. Bunnett. London: Smith, Elder, and Co. 1874.

too, though identified with what many believe to be very exaggerated —if not fanatical—views, carries great weight in England. He himself is induced to republish his political papers by the belief that information on the subject is now eagerly sought, and by the fact that, having been written at intervals during the last seven years, they are in themselves a history of the question during the last nine years. They are valuable for the further reason that Mr. Vambéry's opinions have been proved to be "nowise bold or fanciful, as my adversaries asserted, but just the contrary." The nine years have convinced him that Russia has designs upon India, because the prevailing feeling, of which proof has again and again been adduced, among Mahommedans in the East, the ambition of the reigning dynasty of Russia, the traditional policy of Russia in enlarging her boundaries, and the practical difficulty which would surround her if she attempt to stop short in her career of Asiatic conquest; all combine to make it hard to see how the collision between Russia and England is to be avoided. For some minds this apprehension is dispelled by the reply that it will be better to have one civilized neighbour in Asia than the numerous wild tribes which now lie on our frontier. But Mr. Vambéry would have all such considerations compared first with the fact that Asiatic Russians are considered by all their Asiatic neighbours as wild, lawless, rough, and degraded almost to the same degree as the hordes of Kirghis, and that thus we should gain little by having as neighbours such a rabble supported by the strength of the civilized European Russia, which would avail to keep them there, but not to control them. Secondly, Mr. Vambéry advises that the comfortable doctrine should be looked at in the light of the readiness of our Mahommedan subjects in India, not to change masters, but to avail themselves of any help or excuse which might free them from the yoke of unbelievers, especially since an independent Mahommedan power has arisen among the forty millions of Mahommedans in China. And, thirdly, Mr. Vambéry declares plainly that "Russia, though she may be animated by the best intentions, is not able to fix the bounds of an 'Hitherto shalt thou come and no further.'" "It is not only unrestrained thirst for conquest which impels the Russian eagle towards the south, but there are local, ethnological, and political reasons which prevent it from standing still." Mr. Vambéry's sentence last quoted is only applied to the advance of Russia up to the boundaries of English rule, but enough has been already indicated to make it probable that he has the same opinion as to a yet further advance southward should elements of discord appear among our subjected peoples in India. It may be a somewhat alarmist position to take up: but Mr. Vambéry warns England to remember the false security of other great commercial states, and to make all things safe by prevention. The remedy he advises again, as he advised six years ago, is that Afghanistan should be "neutralized;" and this object is to be attained by the adoption of such a vigorous policy towards Afghanistan as shall secure respect for English travellers and traders; by the definition of a northern and north-western boundary of Afghanistan, if necessary, with the help of a mixed commission of English and Russian officers; by securing that Russia shall as carefully define the territory which she must hold as the result of her wars with the Khanates; and finally, by strengthening Persia so as to secure her from even so much Russian dictation as she now has to submit to. Whatever view may be taken of Mr. Vambéry's facts, theories, or remedies, it must be admitted that in contrast with the care which the Russian government takes to inform itself as to Central Asian affairs even beyond the boundaries of its established authority, the ignorance of Englishmen of all classes respecting not only the passing events, but even respecting the unchanging facts of geography, religion, race, numbers, habits, and resources of their fellow-subjects in India is so dense as to be scarcely adequately illustrated by the difficulties which surround our present efforts to relieve the distress of a portion of India. Mr. Vambéry says:—

> "Any one who knows the great ignorance of public opinion in England respecting events in India, respecting the relations of the neighbouring states to these vast possessions—any one who during the course of a year, has registered the absurd and ridiculous reports and telegraphic despatches of the English press, which are sent through Bombay and Calcutta to Europe and England—any one who knows the limited number of the English statesmen who, accurately informed on Asiatic matters, can pronounce a sound judgment on the questions of Eastern policy—must truly be astonished how Great Britain established her foreign possessions, to say nothing of how she has retained them up to the present day."

As to this there is little doubt that the common ignorance has, at all events in past days, been one reason why Great Britain has acquired much of her Indian territory. Knowledge of the modes of that acquirement and of the small title we have to consider as ours much which is so considered would probably have greatly diminished our responsibilities in India; and it behoves us now that those steps are irretraceable to bestir ourselves to gain all the knowledge that is requisite to protect and cherish what we have won.

Mr. Neil B. E. Baillie[30] has prepared for the second edition of his work on the "Land Tax of India," an introductory essay which discusses with much erudition the ancient and modern history of that tax. The work opens with an explanation of distinction between the *Ooshr*, or tithe, and the *Khiraj*, or tribute. The former is more appropriate to Moslems, and falls on the actual produce. The latter is more appropriate to infidels, and is due on productive land whether it yield any produce or not. The writer gives an account of the modes in which these two heads of taxes became originally levied, and were subsequently regulated. He also describes towards the close of the essay how the different interests in the land or its produce were affected by the perpetual settlement of the revenue under Lord Cornwallis in 1793.

A work of the greatest popular interest and importance on Peru, is published by Mr. Thomas Hutchinson,[31] a traveller who evidently

---

[30] "Introductory Essay to the Second Edition of the Land Tax of India, according to the Mohammedan Law." By Neil B. E. Baillie. London: Smith, Elder, and Co. 1873.

[31] "Two Years in Peru with Explorations of its Antiquities." By Thomas J. Hutchinson, F.R.G.S. In Two Vols. London: Sampson Low and Co. 1873.

combines in himself a variety of tastes and faculties usually held to be opposed or even inconsistent. The description of the country contained in this work reaches from a precise account of the antiquarian curiosities in which the country abounds to an exact calculation of the amount of the most important products and existing economical resources. A complete account is also given of the recent political movements in the country, and part of the second volume is mainly a poem in praise of the President of the Republic, Don Manuel Pardo, to whom the work is dedicated, as the "advocate of progress, scientific, industrial, and commercial, as well as the inaugurator of a new era in the government of the country." Mr. Hutchinson gives a very stirring account of the circumstances attending the accession to power of Don Manuel Pardo. At the time of the yellow fever in Callao, in 1868, Don Manuel Pardo was President of the Beneficencia, or Benevolent Society in Lima, and was especially distinguished by his great humanity and philanthropy in trying to alleviate the scourge. The people of Lima presented him with a gold medal on the 1st of January, 1869, as a proof of their appreciation of his services. "The result was the earnest conviction that made the people believe he was the best man to be a President. For, in spite of the extensive influence of the old spirit of Spanish Hidalgoism that is engrafted with the military rule, the people at Peru are now opening their eyes to the fact of their having been for centuries suffering from such tyranny." Mr. Hutchinson reports some of the early addresses of the President, and they certainly show a width of view, a balance of judgment, and a strength of purpose which go far to justify Mr. Hutchinson's enthusiasm. Mr. Hutchinson does not speak very favourably of Peru at present, as a field for the emigration of agricultural labourers. "The fiscal lands available for cultivation are nearly all in the Amazon valley, and therefore out of reach of the ordinary emigrant." Carpenters and other mechanics, however, are now freed from the necessity of obtaining a government licence to work, or what is called a "matriculation paper." The fullest liberty for all industrial, commercial, and professional purposes is afforded to foreigners as well as to citizens. Mr. Hutchinson did all he could to ascertain the state of the case as regards future supplies of guano. On the whole he believes that the exportable guano which Peru possesses to-day, may be safely estimated as under 8,000,000 tons. He thinks that the large number of seals and sea-lions which frequent the localities where guano is found, makes it extremely probable that some of their deposit is left by these animals as well as by birds. Mr. Hutchinson is of opinion that many of the most interesting antiquities (of which he gives a particular account accompanied with excellent illustrations) date back to a period long before that of the Incas, to which they are usually attributed. He gives pictures of a stone idol (not so very unshapely) and of water-pots found sixty-two feet under guano.

The frequently reappearing controversy as to the fitness of the Brazils for European colonization may receive some fresh light upon it from a beautiful volume just published by Herr Keller-Leuzinger.[a]

[a] "Vom Amazonas und Madeira." Skizzen und Beschreibungen. Von Franz Keller-Leuzinger. Stuttgart. 1874.

who, after a long residence in Brazil, was employed as an engineer by the Brazilian Government to survey the valleys of the Amazon and the Madeira, with a view to the construction of a railway there. The report they made was so favourable that an American contractor has obtained a concession from the Governments of Brazil and Bolivia, and has raised money in England for a railway which will, ere long, open the very centre of the South American tropical world to travellers and to commerce. Thirty-one days from Liverpool will bring the traveller to the first rapids of the Saint Antonio, and thence the new railway will carry him to the place for trade in indin-rubber, rare woods, cocoa, dyestuffs, and all other tropical products. Herr Keller-Leuzinger is quite convinced by his seventeen years' experience of South America that prosperity and complete development can only come, and can easily, and must finally, come to South America, through an extensive colonization by the Germanic races. It is very possible that English emigrants may be less fitted for the life yonder than the patient, sober, and self-denying German; and it is in his native language that Herr Keller-Leuzinger writes; but his book is well worthy the attention of those who care for the question of Brazilian colonization, as well as those who are attracted by scientific and thorough descriptions of interesting countries, and also who appreciate artistic pictures of tropical scenery.

Even in these days of grotesque and terrible bindings, Mr. Simpson[*] has succeeded in making his book of travels outwardly remarkable. In "good red and yellow" he comes forth to seek the sunshine of popular favour, and will, in many quarters, find it, without doubt. He was sent out as a special correspondent to report on the marriage of the Emperor of China for the benefit of the readers of the *Illustrated London News* and the *Daily News*, and being so far away was engaged to go further, and returned by way of Japan and California. The principal object of his journey appears to have been a most dreary ceremonial. At midnight, a small procession passed through the streets of Pekin, the whole population being forbidden, under the strictest penalties, to look at it, the windows being papered up to prevent any infringement of this command, and the author of this account having to peep at it on the sly through a little hole in order to fulfil his contract. It was an awkward position to be in, to have been sent to China to look at a thing which the national feeling of propriety held to be sacredly private, and so Mr. Simpson must be acquitted of any descent from "Peeping Tom." There are some vivid sketches of life in China and in Japan, and some very useful information put in readable shape. The illustrations of the volume, which are numerous, are guaranteed by the fact that they are reproduced from the *Illustrated London News*.

It is not known for how many centuries the emblem of Japan has been the Rising Sun, and to foreigners, whatever may have been the case with themselves, it has not seemed a singularly descriptive one

[*] "Meeting the Sun: a Journey all Round the World." By William Simpson, F.R.G.S. London: Longmans. 1874.

for a land that would neither lift up the light of its countenance upon others nor suffer a similar kindness to be shown to itself. But in these days it is in both ways a land of the Rising Sun: it is grown suddenly wise and cordial in a day; and Mr. Mossman[26] details with the utmost minuteness the steps of its progress during the twenty years that have elapsed since the first treaty for intercourse, properly so called, with foreigners was wrung from Japanese authorities by the American Admiral Perry. It is a very interesting story, and even the too great minuteness and the absence of English in Mr. Mossman's writing cannot spoil it; but its interest culminates in the last three years, which have seen the unique spectacle of a class of military nobles voluntarily resigning rank, wealth, and power into the hands of the Sovereign in order to bring about the better government and education of the whole people. This self-renunciation is so incomprehensible to Europeans that the smallest tumult among the people is telegraphed as a serious revolt, and wise people shake their heads and say that it is vain to try to progress so quickly as Japan is trying to do. And certainly it does seem a very great experiment: one which none can watch with perfect confidence except those who do truly and thoroughly believe that freedom of thought, religious equality, education, freedom of trade, and the most advanced applications of scientific knowledge, are invariably better for a people than protection, privileged classes and creeds, ignorance, and adherence for its own sake to the modes of thought and action of our ancestors. To those, however, who have this faith, Mr. Mossman's book will be full of hope and interest.

Mr. Ranken[27] has written a book the title of which is somewhat misleading. He is not concerned with any large question as to the possibility, probability, or desirability of a confederation of the Australian colonies. It is a subject which he only touches upon in the most cursory manner, as a result certain to come "in time," but which—at least as involving any severance from Great Britain—if it were mooted at home, "would be taken as a slight by every colonist." The aim of the book is to give an exhaustive survey of the past and present condition of Australia in its different divisions; of the climate, and consequent productive powers of the soils of each colony, together with the history of the various uses, wise or unwise, to which it has been attempted to put each section of the country, and including the vicissitudes of trade and of land laws since the earliest settlements were made; of the mineral resources already ascertained and those which are believed to be yet discoverable, together with the history of Australian mining and mineral trade; of the labour question; of the political history of each colony; of the state of roads and other means of communication. The work also contains an elaborated theory of the reasons which produce the peculiar climatic conditions of Australia. Mr. Ranken is

---

[26] "New Japan, the Land of the Rising Sun." By Samuel Mossman. London: Murray. 1873.

[27] "The Dominion of Australia." By W. H. L. Ranken. London: Chapman and Hall. 1874.

a decided conservative and aristocrat. He attributes all sorts of evil results to the use of the ballot in elections and to democratic government; he mentions with some displeasure the allegations brought, for instance, against the Government of Queensland as to the importation of coloured labourers; and he objects to small holders of land; at the same time he prefers free trade to protection as it exists in Australia, and is desirous to see education general in the colonies. For information the book, though apt to repeat itself rather too much, is most valuable.

SCIENCE.

IT happens very often that a particular physical investigation is carried out or a scientific principle studied by independent observers and inquirers at wide distances from one another. A proof of this is given by two works before us, which are devoted to a study of oceanic phenomena and certain mechanical effects which depend on them. One of these books is by Mr. William Leighton Jordan,[1] who designates his work as being, to a great extent, a third edition of a formerly published treatise on the action of *vis inertiæ* in the ocean, although in each of the three editions the subject is, according to the author, treated in a different manner. To judge from the author's admissions, the three editions appear to form a history of his own progressive reasoning on the subject; for while in a former edition the question of existence or non-existence of any action of the *vis inertiæ* in the ocean is treated as a question to be solved, the author accepts in this work the oblate spheroidal form of the earth as a sufficient demonstration of its action in the ocean and on the surface of the earth, leaving only the amount of that action to be ascertained. The author has impressed us as a man gifted with great power of observing and classifying facts, but possessing at the same time too prone a tendency to generalization. He does not agree with Newton's definition of inertia as an innate force of matter, or power of resisting, by which every body, as much as in it lies, endeavours to persevere in its present state, whether it be of rest, or of moving uniformly forwards in a right line; and he declares this innate tendency to move uniformly forwards in a right line a mere assumption. It has been all along assumed that a ball projected along the ground would move continuously, but for the friction of the air and of the ground. This the author declares to be an error. According to him, it is not *vis inertiæ* that keeps the ball going after it once left the hand which projected it, but it is the *vis inertiæ* of the particles which resist the motion that stops the motion. So at least have we understood the meaning, and our opinion is that nothing whatever is lost or gained by such a form of explaining the cessation of the motion; but the denial of Newton's first law, which

---

[1] "The Ocean: its Tides and Currents, and their Causes." By William Leighton Jordan. London: Longmans, Green, and Co. 1873.

explains the continuation of the motion, appears to us extremely crude. No evidence can clearly be brought for the support of Newton but the undoubted occurrence of phenomena calculated upon it; and to reason with the author on the truth of the assumption must appear superfluous at a time when all physics is founded on the very conception which the author declares to be an error. As usual in such cases, where clear notions are wanting, a new word is made for the obscure ideas. Thus the author speaks of an astral gravitation, and believes that the force of gravitation which draws the earth onwards in its orbit is that of solar gravitation, and "that the force of *vis inertiæ* which acts in the opposite direction to that of the motion of the earth, is the force of astral gravitation, which opposes that of solar gravitation." There are, as we have indicated, a great many valuable facts and incidental truths scattered through the work, but we do not think that Mr. Jordan's conclusions from, or interpretations of, them will be applauded by the best scientific judges.

The second work[1] which bears on the same range of natural knowledge, investigates the tidal phenomena in its connexion with the secular periodic fluctuations of the sea level. The author proceeds precisely on the assumption of the truth of Newton's theory of gravitation, and shows that the periodic secular changes of the sea level, and the simultaneous displacements of the climatic zones are not only proved to be in perfect accordance with the results of all modern inquiries in geography, natural history, geology, and geognosy, but are also capable of a scientific explanation and irrefragable proof by an inquiry into the cosmical relations of the earth, in so far as these have an ever changing influence on oceanic distribution. The theory rests on a circumstance hitherto neglected in the study of tidal phenomena—viz., the extension of the circles of greater attraction to hemispheres of which they properly do not form any portion. Every part of the inquiry is illustrated by most recent facts, and the whole is undoubtedly a solid foundation for further inquiry into a subject of the highest importance.

The treatise on the Mechanics of Physics, by Professor Buff,[2] differs from the usually purely mathematical treatment to be found in most text-books, in this respect especially, that greater weight and extension is assigned to the clear exposition of the fundamental principles which underlie mechanical philosophy—viz., rest and motion, mass and force, action and reaction, inertia, work, &c. These principles are never demonstrable by mere mathematical reasoning, but are really derived from the experience of the physical inquirer. As a consequence of a more careful study of these fundamental notions, there results at once as an important consequence, that great simplicity is gained, and that the real technical applications of mechanics are so many results of simple but wide-bearing facts. This is the more important when the con-

[1] "Das Flutphänomen, und sein Zusammenhang mit den säcularen Schwankungen des Seespiegels." Von Dr. Heinrich Schmick. Leipzig: Scholtze. 1874.

[2] "Lehrbuch der Physikalischen Mechanik." Von Dr. Heinrich Buff. Erster Theil und Zweiter Theil; Erste Abtheilung. Braunschweig: Vieweg und Sohn. 1873.

tinually growing connexions of mechanical science with the various industrial branches is taken into consideration, which renders it in our times almost imperative for every educated man to gain some sure insight into theoretical mechanics. Professor Buff has a most attractive mode of stating what in most other works on the same subject is always dry and sometimes even repelling; his secret lies in the great variety of facts, which he, however, not simply adduces as illustrations, but rather presents to the reader as subjects of thought, of observation, and of independent working. Hence at every page his interest is growing, and his knowledge expands. The mathematical portion is in most cases simple and elementary; only in some parts differential equations are used which for each case are developed and proved, without however further discussing the resulting integrals. Students unacquainted with the higher calculus should not be deterred by the formulæ and demonstrations which are interspersed; the results are in all cases stated in clear language, and may be easily checked by the given numerical examples.

Of Professor Mousson's excellent treatise on physics[4] some of the former parts have already been noticed in these pages. The work has proceeded to the third volume, Part I., which treats of magnetism and frictional electricity. The author has been somewhat too brief in many portions, and his otherwise very clear manner of stating facts has suffered; thus the totality of errors to which a dip observation is liable, the author comprises (page 102) in the following statement:—"By turning the axes, by reversing the needle so that the axes change their supports, by turning the apparatus through 180° upon the horizontal circle, and finally by changing the magnetism of both poles by means of a new magnetisation, a mean determination is obtained which is free from the errors depending on the form of the axis, the non-horizontality of the supports, the position of the magnetic axis, and the position of the centre of gravity." No one who is not already well acquainted with the subject would learn anything from such a brief instruction. The same objection must be made to many other similar statements. Otherwise the work has the immense advantage of great completeness.

Of the more popular books before us we must mention a new volume of short treatises by Mr. Proctor,[5] which are brought together under a very sounding title. They are light and agreeable reading, like Mr. Proctor's writings generally. To several of these articles the objection raised on previous occasions in these pages must again be made—viz., that no class of readers anxious to learn anything about scientific subjects can really gain anything from a style of writing which is only to be found in books for little children. In the present book this objection applies especially to the article, "A dream that was not all a dream."

---

[4] "Die Physik auf Grundlage der Erfahrung." Von Dr. Alb. Mousson. Zürich: Schulthess. 1874.

[5] "The Expanse of Heaven." By R. A. Proctor, B.A. London: H. S. King and Co. 1873.

To the same class belongs a little German book[6] called "Rambles in Natural Science," which, indeed, ranges over a vast area of knowledge, and treats each subject very briefly, but by no means superficially. The author has, with clever tact, eliminated those oratorical embellishments which are the bane of popular science writings. Indeed, his articles are so many sentences, so many independent facts. The facts are valuable. They are arranged logically, and every reader must learn something. Thus, spectrum analysis is treated on four pages; but they are a mine of experimental facts and results. We wish that only one of these little treatises could be translated into an English scientific periodical, to show to the 'popular' writers in this country that scientific facts may be made very pleasant reading without literary artifices and poetical quotations.

A German book for young students anxious to make physical and chemical experiments[7] is somewhat incongruously planned, and the experiments are not described with sufficient detail. The experiments begin with frictional electricity: then follow in order, magnetism, contact-electricity, optics, acoustics, mechanics, heat. This arrangement, or rather absence of arrangement, is simply inexplicable. After physics comes chemistry, and here the order is more sensible. Again, the difficulty for young students to perform by themselves any experiments correctly is well known to every teacher, and the question whether such domestic experimentation in science does not in the end more harm than good, has frequently been raised, and men of experience have decided that a few selected physical and chemical operations under the eye of a teacher bring more lasting advantage to the student than any number of superficial flighty 'experiments' performed at home from a book. The only legitimate substitute for a teacher's instruction is a book which gives the most accurate directions for the various experiments to be performed, which the present work fails to do, at any rate in the portion devoted to physics, where precisely the greatest difficulties present themselves to the beginner.

Of all geological questions, none have given rise to so much discussion, since geology became a science, as those connected with the glacial epoch. We have had endless disputes upon its date and cause, upon the climatal conditions which prevailed during its existence, upon the effects produced by the vast masses of ice which then covered this country and the greater part of the northern hemisphere, and upon the relations of man to the glacial epoch. In his "Great Ice Age," lately published, Mr. James Geikie,[8] who is already well known as the writer of some excellent papers on these matters, sums up the arguments, *pro* and *con.*, in a most admirable fashion. His

---

[6] "Naturwissenschaftliche Streifzüge." Von Philipp Spiller. Berlin: Denicke's Verlag. 1873.

[7] "Des deutschen Knaben Experimentirbuch." Von Emsmann und Dammer. Bielefeld und Leipzig: Velhagen und Klasing. 1874.

[8] "The Great Ice Age, and its Relation to the Antiquity of Man." 8vo. London: Isbister and Co. 1874.

work is by far the most important contribution to this chapter of geological inquiry that has yet appeared. In his investigation of the phenomena which testify to the occurrence of a great glacial epoch in later geological times, Mr. Geikie very judiciously confines himself to Scotland, not only because it is the country in which his own personal researches have been chiefly carried on, but also because it exhibits on a grand scale those deposits and traces of abrading action which are now generally ascribed to the action of ice. Having explained the nature and mode of occurrence of the boulder clay and its associated deposits, and shown to what extent they must be ascribed to glacial action, and having further elucidated by descriptions of existing glacial phenomena, especially in Greenland, what is the mode of action of ice, he proceeds to discuss the various hypotheses which have been put forward to account for the occurrence of a period of intense cold in the northern hemisphere. The most prevalent of these ascribe the production of wide-spread glacial conditions to a change in the distribution of land and sea, or to cosmical causes. Mr. Geikie regards the former as untenable, not only because we have no positive evidence of the occurrence of the hypothetical changes in the arrangement of land and water at the surface of the globe, but because he considers that such changes, if they actually took place, would not produce the effects ascribed to them. With the cosmical causes of change of climate the case is different. Their reality can be proved mathematically, and the only question remaining relates to their power of giving rise to the required phenomena. These cosmical causes consist in the varying eccentricity of the earth's orbit, combined with the precession of the equinoxes, and, to a certain extent, nutation. The effects of these are discussed in great detail by our author, and shown, we think, satisfactorily, to be adequate to the production of glacial conditions on a grand scale. The period of greatest cold is placed by astronomical calculations about 210,000 years ago. At this time, as Mr. Geikie tells us, all the north of Europe and of America were covered by a thick coat of ice and snow, the glaciers of mountain regions assumed gigantic proportions, and the valleys were everywhere filled up by a sheet of ice, which, being really formed by confluent glaciers, moved constantly downwards from the mountains in the direction of the principal valleys, and pushed far out to sea, where it terminated after the fashion of the icy covering of Greenland, or of the great Antarctic land. The shallow basin now occupied by the North Sea proved no obstacle to the Scandinavian ice, which swept across it to coalesce with the Scotch glaciers; and in the same way the glaciers born in the mountains of Wales and Cumberland crept out to unite with the Scotch and Irish ice upon what is now the bed of the Irish sea. On the other side the Scandinavian mountains sent down a vast ice-sheet, which swept through the basin of the Baltic and over Finland, on to the plains of northern Germany. This period of intense cold was succeeded by a warmer one, in which the ice and snow gradually retreated to the mountains, and plants and animals were able to live in the lower grounds. This was the period of the woolly rhinoceros, the mammoth, and the great Cave bear. The seasons were strongly marked, and the action of floods caused by the annual melting of the snows on the high grounds was very powerful. The warmth of the climate continuing to increase, the mammals above mentioned retired to more northern and congenial localities, and our island was inhabited by elephants, hippopotami, lions, and hyænas. Another change gradually brought back the old icy covering, and these alternations of cold and warm periods seem to have occurred more than once, although the evidence does not enable us to say how often. It was during one of these warm interglacial periods that palæolithic man made his way into Britain, where he was certainly the contemporary of the mammoth and the hippopotamus. Later still, the land, both in these islands and over a great part of northern Europe, gradually sank down into the sea, the submergence reaching to about 2000 feet in North Wales. Then came on the last great period of cold, when the projecting mountain-tops of Britain and Scandinavia became converted into a frozen archipelago, the ice floated from the shores of which carried away angular stones and rubbish, and dropped them on the bottom of the sea. Then came the last act in this great drama, the elevation of the land once more above the sea, and its reoccupation by animals which indicate that arctic conditions still prevailed, such as the reindeer, the moose, the Arctic fox, the lemming, and the marmot. Man followed or accompanied these animals in their migration, having probably lived with them, under arctic conditions, in the south of Europe during the preceding period of depression. But the new human inhabitants of these regions exhibit a considerable advance upon their predecessors: their weapons were still made of stone, but they present the more highly finished character of what is known as the neolithic type. There is evidence of the occurrence of a similar series of climatal changes in North America. Such is a general sketch of the results arrived at in this most interesting volume. To the facts adduced and to the detailed arguments founded upon them, it is of course impossible for us to refer, but we can assure our readers that they will find in Mr. Geikie's book an admirable and satisfactory summary of the present condition of opinion on some of the most interesting of geological questions, which are here discussed in a most agreeable and readable manner. The book is illustrated with several maps and charts, and with numerous wood engravings.

We have heard so much about coal and colliers of late that most of us are nearly sick of those subjects, but the question of the amount of our available supplies of fossil fuel is of so much national importance that we must still welcome all sound contributions to our knowledge in this direction. Mr. Anstie's account of the "coal-fields of Gloucestershire and Somersetshire"* is of this kind. The author gives us a sketch of the geology of the district, which includes rocks of all ages from the Silurian to the Oolitic period, but, of course, dwells especially upon the Coal Measures, which are really the subject of his book. The importance of this coal-field is shown by its extent, which has been

* "The Coal Fields of Gloucestershire and Somersetshire, and their Resources." By John Anstie. 8vo. London: Stanford. 1873.

estimated by the Coal Commission at 240 square miles. Of this area 48 square miles are exposed at the surface and 102 concealed beneath later deposits, but 40 square miles of the latter have been proved for coal. The total amount of coal worked up to the date of the inquiries of the commission was 114,024,685 tons, and the remainder was estimated at 6,104,310,982 tons. If these numbers are correct, "about one fifty-fifth of the total supply has been exhausted during workings which have extended over probably two hundred years." Nearly half this quantity, however, is below 3000 feet, so that there may be some difficulty in working it. Of the future importance of this coal-field, Mr. Anstie speaks confidently. The coal is of excellent quality, especially for steam and manufacturing purposes, and the small extent to which it has hitherto been worked is attributed by him to the want of the means of conveyance, which renders it possible for consumers who ought naturally to draw their supplies of fuel from this locality, to procure it from other districts more cheaply by sea. Mr. Anstie's book, which contains much important information on the geology of the coal-measures in the Somersetshire and Gloucestershire district, is illustrated with several elaborate sections and tables which will prove valuable in the future development of the collieries in this part of the country.

Mr. Belt's "Naturalist in Nicaragua"[10] is an exceedingly interesting book, not on account of any stirring incidents of travel described in it, for these are few enough, but as giving a good description of many curious natural phenomena. The author describes what he saw in the out-of-the-way country in which he resided for four years and a half, and he does this in a pleasant manner, which, however, does not prevent him from discussing some of those higher questions of natural history which have for the last few years engaged so much general attention. Birds and reptiles, insects, the vegetation of the country, its geology, and its human inhabitants all come in for a share of Mr. Belt's notice, but the last we may dismiss with a passing remark that they seem to be one of the idlest sets of people on the face of the earth. Of all the animals of Nicaragua, if we may judge from Mr. Belt's narrative, the ants seem to occupy the most prominent position. Ants turn up in half the pages of his book, and considering the account he gives of their obtrusive habits we cannot much wonder at it. We have the foraging ants, which do not make regular nests of their own, but frequently attack those of other species, and prey upon every suitable living thing that comes in their way; the leaf-cutting ants, whose attacks upon the trees in a small garden which our author tried to establish, appear to have driven him to the verge of despair; standing armies of ants apparently maintained by certain trees for their protection; and many other kinds, some of which seem to have kept his attention constantly on the stretch. Of the wonderful actions of these insects, which seem to indicate their possession of reasoning faculties, Mr. Belt gives us

[10] "The Naturalist in Nicaragua: a Narrative of a Residence at the Gold Mines of Chontales. Journeys in the Savannahs and Forests, &c." By Thomas Belt. Small 8vo. London: John Murray. 1874.

many accounts. With regard to the leaf-cutting species, he puts forward a very curious notion. The use to which these insects put the portions of leaves carried off by them in such large quantities has always been a mystery; the author tells us that on digging into their subterranean dwellings he always found their chambers, which are about as large as a man's head, "about three parts filled with a speckled brown, flocculent, spongy-looking mass of a light and loosely connected substance," which "proved on examination to be composed of minutely subdivided pieces of leaves, withered to a brown colour, and overgrown and lightly connected together by a minute white fungus that ramified in every direction through it." The author believes that the ants carry in and store the fragments of leaves in this curious manner for the express purpose of growing the fungus, upon which he supposes them to feed. This interpretation seems to us rather far-fetched and not in accordance with the general habits of ants. As larvæ and pupæ, with numerous small mature ants, whose duty appears to be that of nurses, are found scattered through the mass of vegetable material, we should be inclined to regard the latter merely as furnishing a suitable bed for the young, in which certain necessary conditions for their development are realized. Upon mimetic species of animals, and especially of insects, Mr. Belt has some exceedingly interesting remarks, upon which, however, we cannot dwell here. His notices of birds are not so numerous as might have been expected, but some of them are of considerable interest. On the geological structure of the country we find remarks scattered in various parts of the book, but the most important statements relating to this department of the subject, are the author's notices of the occurrence of gold, and connected with this his discussion of the modes of formation of mineral veins, and his description of a genuine boulder-clay, due, as he believes, to the action of glaciers. One can hardly imagine the occurrence of a glacial epoch within fourteen degrees of the equator, but the evidence here adduced by Mr. Belt seems to place it almost beyond a doubt. Into his archæological discussions and his remarks upon the present and former inhabitants of Nicaragua we shall not attempt to follow our author, but the anthropologist will find much valuable information in his pages.

The first volume of Dr. Brown's "Races of Mankind"[11] contains an account of the American tribes. Of scientific ethnology it contains no traces. Commencing with the Eskimo, the author notices successively the Indians of north-western America, of California and the central plains, of the north-eastern States and Canada, of Central America, and of the southern continent, describing less their physical peculiarities than their manners and customs, and leaving all questions of language entirely untouched. The work is in fact what is commonly called a popular book, full of sensational incidents, and will doubtless be read with great interest by those for whose perusal it is intended.

---

11 "The Races of Mankind: being a Popular Description of the Characteristics, Manners, and Customs of the Principal Varieties of the Human Family." By Robert Brown, M.A., &c. 8vo. London: Cassells. 1873.

Of the Eskimo and several of the western tribes the author has some personal knowledge. The woodcuts are numerous and generally effective, but the sensational element is strongly displayed in them.

Messrs. Adams have brought out an exceedingly pretty book on our smaller British birds,[12] which cannot but prove most acceptable to the young folks for whose especial behoof it is intended. It gives a popular account of the natural history of the different species, which is of course a compilation from various well-known sources of information, interspersed with some not very profound remarks by the authors themselves, and with numerous fragments of poetry. The subjects are treated of in small groups, such as the Tits, the Pipits, the Larks, &c., and to the account of each group is appended a short appendix, describing the behaviour and mode of management of the different species in confinement. The plates, which are printed in colours, represent the species of the different groups arranged in small landscapes, and figures of the eggs are given in another series of plates. The plates of birds are exceedingly pretty at the first glance, but many of the figures are by no means satisfactory when closely examined.

Mr. Coultas's little book on "Animals and their Young"[13] is intended for a still more juvenile circle of readers. It consists of twenty-four rather spirited full page wood engravings showing various Mammalia with their young, accompanied by a short general account of the natural history of the species figured. The volume forms one of a series entitled "Our Dumb Companions."

Of the series of "Treasuries" projected by the late Samuel Maunder and published by Messrs. Longman, two were devoted to natural history subjects, and these seem still to retain their popularity. Of the "Treasury of Botany"[14] a new edition has just been issued under the care of Mr. Thomas Moore. It consists of a dictionary of botanical names and terms alphabetically arranged, with longer or shorter articles explanatory of each; and as these bear the initials of some of the best botanists in this country, the little book takes a more authoritative position than most of its class. The introduction of many French and other foreign names of plants will also greatly increase its usefulness. The illustrations consist of numerous small, but nicely executed, wood engravings, and of about twenty plates, the latter containing scenes in various localities, to illustrate the character of vegetation as governed by geographical distribution. The new matter in this edition is contained in a supplement.

The art of preparing and mounting objects for microscopic examination has made great progress of late years; it is now so compli-

---

[12] "The Smaller British Birds, with Descriptions of their Nests, Eggs, Habits, &c." By H. G. and H. B. Adams. 8vo. London: Bell and Sons. 1874.

[13] "Animals and their Young." By Harland Coultas. Small 4to. London: Partridge. 1874.

[14] "The Treasury of Botany: a Popular Dictionary of the Vegetable Kingdom. With which is Incorporated a Glossary of Botanical Terms." Edited by John Lindley and Thomas Moore. New and Revised Edition with Supplement. 12mo. London: Longmans. 1874.

cated a business as to require long and careful study before the practitioner can claim to be anything of an adept. We have many books treating of the microscope and of all appliances thereto belonging; but very few in English which are devoted exclusively to the business of preparation unconnected with any account of the characters or history of the objects to be examined. One of them is a little volume by Mr. Thomas Davies, a second edition of which[15] prepared by Dr. Matthews has just been published. So far as we can pretend to judge it seems to be an admirable treatise on the subject, giving a very clear and distinct description of the various processes adopted in microscopic research, whether for the purpose of discriminating the structure of objects, or for that of preserving them for future examination.

The publication of Dr. Ferrier's remarkable investigations into the functions of the higher brain has given a vigorous impulse to the study of the psychical and higher motor centres in the hemispheres. Before, however, any common understanding can exist among students of the brain, it is clear that its topographical anatomy should be established on a firm basis and its minutest parts strictly named. Dr. Ecker's little treatise[16] fulfils this end, and Mr. Galton has done well to place in the hands of the English physiologists a descriptive survey of the surface of the hemispheres which will promote accuracy in work and prevent misunderstandings among the workers. Nor does Mr. Galton place the physiologists alone in his debt; no less have physicians to thank him for a volume which will enable them to register with accuracy their all-important observations upon the pathological changes in the cortex of the cerebrum. Mr. Galton, indeed, has done more than this; himself a diligent student of development and nomenclature in cerebrology, he has prefixed to the present edition an exhaustive bibliography, founded, no doubt, upon a list of Ecker's, but far exceeding it in extent. We trust that Mr. Galton, who shows so high an appreciation of the instruments of learning, will ere long give us some results of his own.

Dr. Klein's reputation as an investigator of the anatomy of the lymphatic system was made before the appearance of the first part of his formal treatise. The present instalment[17] contains one hundred pages of letterpress and ten plates, each plate consisting of numerous figures. The volume is well brought out by the publishers, but we are sorry to see that the reproduction of the author's admirable drawings had to be entrusted to a Leipzig firm. The discovery of the true relations of the serous cavities and of their connexion with the lymphatics by Recklinghausen, and the process of staining with nitrate of silver, which Recklinghausen was the first to use, has been

---

15 "The Preparation and Mounting of Microscopic Objects." By Thomas Davies. Second Edition. Greatly Enlarged. By John Matthews, M.D. 12mo. London: Hardwicke. 1873.

16 "The Convolutions of the Human Brain." By Dr. Ecker. Translated by J. C. Galton, M.A. Oxon. London. 1873.

17 "The Anatomy of the Lymphatic System." By E. Klein, M.D. London. 1873.

the starting-point of a new investigation which has yielded great results in a short time. The part before us deals with the minute structure of the omentum, the centrum tendineum of the diaphragm, and the pleura-mediastini. In dealing with these membranes, the author arrives at conclusions of a more general kind, for which we must refer the reader to the book itself. It is a great gain to English anatomy to have secured the services of so patient, methodical and successful an inquirer as Dr. Klein, who is Dr. Burdon Sanderson's assistant at the Brown Institution.

There are some books which are very welcome, and which even a jaded reviewer takes up with a fresh sense of pleasure and satisfaction. Dr. West's well-known volume[11] is one of these, for it is not only full of good teaching, but the spirit of it is so kindly, the style so finished, and the author himself is so pleasantly revealed to us in his pages, that we are tempted to call him the Sir Thomas Watson of children's diseases. It is a very instructive study to take up a work like Dr. West's, which has reached its sixth edition during a time of great progress, both in medicine and in pathology. The first edition was published in 1848, and the last quarter of a century is perhaps the most successful time in the history of the art. How has Dr. West borne himself during this period, and what judgment has he passed upon its work? The judgment of a man so candid so learned, and so ripe in experience is inestimable. It were impossible in this place, and it were also inappropriate, to enter into every disputed question which Dr. West has handled, or even to deal in much detail with single points. We may say, on the whole, that Dr. West shows a conservative spirit, and, in some matters, a degree of belief in discredited remedies which deserves attention. For instance, he believes still that mercury possesses a peculiar specific power in controlling acute inflammation of the serous membranes of the chest and abdomen, and of the mucous membrane of the large intestine. On the other hand, he is strongly opposed to its use in tubercular meningitis, and blisters he has "almost entirely abandoned" in infancy and early childhood. Of new drugs Dr. West finds both bromide of potassium and chloral of great value, and his testimony concerning the former is of especial interest at the present time, when our estimate of its value has been attacked by Professor Binz. We ourselves are strongly convinced of the great therapeutical importance of the drug, and we are glad to notice that Dr. West has found it valuable, and chloral likewise, in overcoming the persistent sleeplessness of delicate children. Indeed, we have found the prescription of bromide of potassium in many cases to be the starting-point of an amelioration of the whole state, both mental and physical, of sick children. Of new instruments of research the ophthalmoscope is the chief, and we think Dr. West estimates the value of that instrument in meningitis correctly when he says that although it undoubtedly reveals the presence of changes in the eye which have great diagnostic

[11] "The Diseases of Infancy and Childhood." By Charles West, M.D. London. 1874.

weight, yet that the late appearance of these changes, or the difficulties of examination in the earlier periods, defer our knowledge of them to a stage in the disease when diagnosis is no longer in doubt. But Dr. West, in combating Dr. Clifford Allbutt's higher estimate of the chance of recovery from meningitis of the base rather misses the point at issue, and with this issue the ophthalmoscope is much concerned. Dr. West says he does not regard the cases adduced by Dr. Clifford Allbutt as cases of meningitis at all. Surely this is the very issue. The question raised is whether cases of this kind to which the name of meningitis is now denied are not often attended with optic congestion or neuritis, and whether this fact ought not to lead us to suspect their meningitic nature. Among other points of interest is that of paracentesis thoracis; we agree with Dr. West in preferring a simple canula with india-rubber tube to the aspirator, and on the whole the author's remarks in this section seem to us eminently wise and suggestive. We are surprised that he makes no reference to paracentesis pericardii. The chapter on croup is one of great importance. Dr. West contends for the existence of a membranaceous croup, as opposed to diphtheria (though in one or two places he seems less confident), and what is more important still, he is disposed in acute sthenic cases to prefer antimony, emetics, mercurials and depletion to stimulants and perchloride of iron. In discussing valvular diseases of the heart Dr. West makes some acute comments upon their peculiarities in childhood. In one sense they are more hopeful, on account of the special power of repair and self-adjustment in early life; but in another sense less hopeful, on account of the easy yielding of the walls of the cavities under the strain. We have said enough to assure the reader that there is not a page in this book which is superfluous or unworthy of the author's great reputation, and that, as a whole, it is a fine example of that clinical insight and careful treatment which distinguish the English school of medicine.

In Dr. Dickson's death the profession and the public have to regret the loss of an earnest, industrious and intelligent worker in the field of mental diseases, and it is well that these lectures[19] were prepared for the press before the night came upon him. To the duties of lecturer on mental diseases at Guy's Hospital the author brought not only adequate instruction, but also a considerable personal experience obtained as medical superintendent in St. Luke's Hospital, and subsequently in private practice and in other official positions. The volume is illustrated by a few excellent and characteristic photographs of insane persons, and by some good and faithful chromo-lithographs taken from sections of morbid nervous tissue prepared by the author himself. The various chapters in the book deal with insanity in each of its forms, and, if we do not find anything very novel in the book, nor that exceptional kind of handling which makes new thoughts out of old materials, yet we discover no inadequacy and no oversights. With a quick ap-

---

[19] "Medicine in Relation to Mind." By J. Thompson Dickson, M.B. London: 1874.

preciation of the chief features of each inquiry, and of the practical bearings of each, the author has given us a very useful, handy volume which may be set beside almost any contemporary books of the kind and above most of them. More immediately practical in aim than Maudsley's works, and smaller and less expensive than the standard treatise of Bucknill and Tuke, Dr. Dickson's volume will fill a useful place in alienist literature, and will deserve and find, no doubt, many purchasers.

Dr. James would apparently claim for himself not only the merit of an early worker in the field of laryngeal diseases, but also of an original discoverer.[10] He tells us that his impulse to investigate diseases of the throat and larynx came from himself and not from without; that when others invented laryngoscopes he was likewise perfecting an instrument, and was in the field as soon as they. Without following Dr. James into any question of priority, which we will leave to those who care for their own laurels, we need only point out that the author has for many years devoted himself to an inquiry too long postponed, and which stands in need of all the good work which can be given to it. The writers on laryngoscopy are but too few, and we should welcome Dr. James' book, even were its merits less than they are. Moreover, the author's purpose is distinctly practical, and he wishes to encourage all medical men to learn the use of an instrument which is indispensable for the proper diagnosis of no small number of cases. Most of the matter contained in Dr. James' small volume has been published before in the journals, and its re-issue is now made especially valuable to learners by plates which are faithful pictures of actual examples of disease. Examination of the posterior nares is also plainly taught, and the various modes of treatment both operative and medicinal receive a full consideration in the respective chapters.

The strength of this volume[11] lies in the chapters on emphysema, which at the time of their first appearance were both fresh and useful in their mode of handling, and contained evidence of patient personal research. Nor are they now less welcome as containing the maturer experience of a physician who so long and with so much intelligence has watched this form of disease. There is a great deal of practical matter also in other sections which treat of pulmonary affections, nor indeed can any part of the treatise be objected to, but much of it seems to partake too nearly of the nature of padding. The chapters on heart diseases are none of them more than any well-read and experienced physician might have written off without preparation. We should be sorry indeed to think that they far exceed the average of clinical lectures given by the physicians of our leading schools of medicine. Good practical teaching founded upon the reading of a case or cases with much irrelevant or trivial detail which need not have been reprinted, is scarcely work which calls for presentation in so goodly a form and under so goodly a title. We regret that Dr.

---

[10] "Lessons in Laryngoscopy." By Prosser James, M.D. London. 1873.
[11] "Diseases of the Chest." By A. T. H. Waters, M.D. London. 1873.

Waters allowed himself to be carried away by the ambition of writing a complete treatise. A smaller book would have been better filled. It is curious to notice that in opposition to Dr. West, whose work we previously notice, Dr. Waters disapproves of mercury in serous inflammations, and cannot see that it has any power whatever to remove the products of inflammation in pleurisy or pericarditis. That two men of so much clinical ability and experience should differ thus extremely, proves how difficult it is to arrive at any firm principles of therapeutics. Dr. Waters does not notice tapping of the pericardium, though we think one of his fatal cases might have been saved by it. Like Dr. Walshe, the author fails to estimate duly the rôle of physical strain in the causation of heart disease, which disappoints us, for we had hoped his post as physician to the Liverpool Hospitals would have brought much material of this kind before him. Chronic aortitis, however, is an affection not as yet fully realized by either writer. Besides the clinical matter we find chapters on anatomy and physiology, both healthy and morbid, which bear the marks of genuine research and are not copied at secondhand from other sources. Taking the volume as a whole its practical and unpretending pages make it pleasant reading, and it would be ungracious therefore to regret their publication.

This standard work on diseases of the heart[m] has in the present edition been carefully revised, much new matter has been added, and the entire volume in a measure remodelled. The chief additions have been made throughout the clinical portions of the book, and the author has endeavoured to render clearer the essential nature of functional disorders of the heart by an analysis of their dynamic elements. We have found much both of pleasure and of profit in consulting again this admirable treatise, which is so full of accurate knowledge and withal so quiet and unassuming in style. Indeed, in his desire to avoid display and prolixity, the author seems to us to have fallen into the opposite extreme and to have pushed concentration to dryness, if not to baldness, both of style and matter. Nor would he have done ill to have given the rein a little more to his imagination. Dr. Walshe will never forget what is due to sobriety and caution, and we think that over-timidity in his case has in many places prevented a fair use of hypothesis and has weakened his conceptions of the wider relations of his facts. At the same time we have too many verbose and windy writers nowadays not to welcome a book which can be thoroughly trusted. Among the many passages which we have noted for reference we may take that which expresses the author's estimate of the sphygmograph, an estimate in which we fully agree. He says (p. 129) "it has certainly disappointed the expectation of those who expected it to furnish a special tracing for every form of cardiac disease . . . . its mission appears to be rather to indicate general conditions of the circulation than to detect specific organic changes. . . . . and thus to aid prognosis rather than diagnosis."

[m] "Diseases of the Heart and Great Vessels." By W. H. Walshe, M.D. Fourth Edition. London. 1873.

It is under the head of Causation that we seem to be conscious of some sterility of thought in the book; a like want also is noticeable in the treatment of the several morbid changes to which the heart and its valves are subject. Nothing can be more satisfactory than the respective sections, but there is no adequate survey of their relations of interdependence and coexistence. As regards causation much more has been made probable than would appear from Dr. Walshe's pages, and he seems scarcely himself aware how large a part muscular efforts are now known to take in the causation of disease both of valves and chambers. Of galvano-puncture in aortic aneurism Dr. Walshe speaks very doubtfully, and he would limit its use to superficial aneurisms tending to thin out their coverings. He does not speak from personal experience, but his opinion is certainly in agreement with our own. As we have stated, the sections on functional affections have the newest kind of interest, and as an instance of this we may refer the reader especially to the chapter on dynamic aortic pulsation.

Dr. Robert Liveing has done well to reprint his Gulstonian lectures on leprosy, containing, as they do, both a record of personal observation and a historical sketch of leprosy from mediæval sources. Dr. Liveing gives us also an account of leprosy in its geographical distribution. His own observations were made in Norway in 1871. It is a very curious fact that the laws now in force in China closely resemble the very stringent laws of the Middle Ages in Europe. Dr. Liveing does not say whether this is an instance of a like result arising independently from like social conditions, or whether these customs were introduced into China by the Jesuits or other early travellers. With respect to the Jews, the author points out that much confusion has arisen from the indiscriminate use of terms either by the old writers themselves or their translators or both. In Europe it would seem that leprosy passed like a wave across the Continent from south to north in the twelfth century and subsided in the same order. This, he adds, was an epidemic accession to a disease already more or less endemic. Its contagious properties were probably falsely attributed to it by contemporary writers, and Dr. Liveing suggests that its increase was rather due to hereditary transmission from the crusaders, who acquired it in the East. Of its primary and secondary causation the author speaks clearly and judiciously, but he adds nothing to our knowledge. We, who have seen but two cases of leprosy in our life, can only say that neither heredity nor bad food are essential factors in the causation. One case arose in an English youth of ten or twelve years of age, in good circumstances, whose parents, both English and healthy, resided for a time in a leprous district in the New World, I think in the West Indies. In him it presented the anæsthetic form. The second case, which presented the tuberculated form, appeared in a gentleman's gardener who had lived all his life in Yorkshire, and who had never heard of leprosy otherwise than in his Bible. This man died, and we are still in possession of the microscopic

---

[a] "Elephantiasis Græcorum: or True Leprosy." By R. Liveing, M.D. London: 1873.

sections of his tubercles, which correspond with the anatomical description given by the author on p. 134, and resemble those taken from lupus or syphilis.

The author of this treatise[84] tells us in his preface that he has studied the mercury question with eager industry for nearly twenty years, that he has constantly sought the true teaching of facts and has avoided any deductions based upon hypothesis. He feels himself therefore to be now armed not only with the more vulgar weapon of knowledge but also with a moral force which will inspire him in the interests of the happiness of mankind to withstand the blunders and delusions which oppose themselves to scientific truth as exemplified in his own person. This being the outset of the book, we were tempted irresistibly, after the fashion of lady readers, to turn stealthily to the end in order to assure ourselves that the good hero will find his reward, and that the champions of error and delusion will be covered with confusion. We scarcely obtained, however, the assurance we required; on the contrary, the powers of light seem to hanker after the support of the secular arm, as if no longer confident in their own endurance. Dr. Hermann concludes with this eloquent appeal: "It would indeed be an exalted idea of the wise Government of my fatherland if it would take the initiative in this direction, and would upon the unanimous vote of the representative body publish an edict against the use of quicksilver as a medicine." "Such a noble determination would not only secure," Dr. Hermann goes on to say, "the thanks of mankind, but also the gratitude of pure Science herself, and would present a brilliant example for the imitation of other nations." Here is the ill consequence of peeping at the end. Fired as we were by the vision thus presented to us, and seeing in our mind's eye Dr. Hermann, Prince Bismarck, and Count Andrassy dropping a unanimous tear as they foresaw the new salvation in store for their people, we could not command ourselves so far as to read with any coolness the arguments which are to prevail with the coming generation. We felt more able to enjoy four stirring chromo-lithographs which presumably depict the ravages of mercury. We certainly thought at first sight that we recognised in them the familiar characters of a disease we will forbear to name. Thinking, however, that these suspicions were unworthy of the author, we turned to the histories of the cases, where we find that two out of the four assured Dr. Hermann that no such complication was possible, and that they had been subjected to mercurial treatment by a censorious administration in spite of all disclaimers. The other two did in some measure admit the possibility of another morbid influence, but assured Dr. Hermann that the terrible consequences were all due to the mercury. Like the servant girl and her baby, they admitted a syphilis, "but it was a very small one." Fortunately, hideous as are the ravages of mercury as depicted by Dr. Hermann, we need not despair. A remedy exists which, when combined with a healthy house, cold bathing, &c., is singularly effi-

---

[84] "Ueber die Wirkung des Quecksilbers auf den Menschlichen Organismus." Von Dr. Josef Hermann. 4to. Teschen. 1873.

cacious, especially when given in full doses. The drug is known to many physicians and is called iodide of potassium. In conclusion, we can only urge upon all persons, whether English or German, who are unfortunate enough to be suffering from mercurial poisoning, to hasten to Dr. Hermann at once.

This useful little book[55] is intended for the elementary teaching either of children or of adults to whom the conditions of health are unknown. It contains chapters on food, cookery, clothing, exercise, sleep, cleanliness, housing, atmosphere and mental work. There are also sections on physiology and on sick nursing, both of course being sketchy. Such a popular treatise cannot fail to do good, and Dr. Smith, who has himself worked out many physiological problems with great labour, was a fit person to be entrusted with the authorship. We do not profess to subject the book to any careful criticism; it would perhaps be scarcely fair to do so. Otherwise we might find more than one kind of fault with it—faults of knowledge and faults of manner. There are many incorrect or inadequate statements, like that on p. 5, where it is said dogmatically that "Sugar and fat and starch make heat only." Now it is highly probable, if not certain, that starch and sugar when converted into glycerine and lactic acid give out energy which appears not only as heat but also as mechanical work. The faults of style consist in a tendency to a feeble kind of sermonizing, which disfigures the sections on the use of alcohol, of smoking, and other subjects. We trust these paragraphs may in future editions be revised in a more manly and intelligent spirit.

Now that the public attention has been thoroughly roused on the subject of adulteration of food, and numerous analysts, good or indifferent, are at work, this little book[56] comes at least opportunely. By its aid also the dealer or purchaser may find himself enabled in some measure to assure himself of the quality of his goods. Of the technical merits of the book we are incompetent to speak in any thorough manner, but it is certainly well put together, and seems to contain that information which is most likely to be required. Its alphabetical arrangement we think especially to be commended. We turned somewhat curiously to the chapter on bread, and we notice that no doubt of his own ability to detect aluminous adulterations is present to the author.

The title of this book[57] is very inaccurate, to say the least of it. Its contents are extracts from Fletcher's physiology, and from certain other writings of his, compiled by Dr. Richardson. By whomsoever written it is one of those endless scholastic discussions, so dear to our friends ayont the border, which never do lead to anything, never have led to anything, and probably never will. But the disputants are as voluble and as acrimonious as such disputants were three centuries ago and always will be, and thus they justify their claims to the name of philosophers κατ' ἐξοχήν. We have but glanced through the present treatise,

---

[55] "Health." A Handbook. By Edward Smith, M.D. London. 1874.
[56] "Adulterations of Food." By R. J. Atcherley, F.C.S. London. 1874.
[57] "The Simplicity of Life." By R. Richardson, M.D. London. 1873.

so we have no right to review it; of one thing only we are sure, that it was scarcely kind to poor Fletcher to prove his want of "vitality" by calling him again into "action," only again to die and be forgotten.

HISTORY AND BIOGRAPHY.

A NEW work by the historian of the Netherlands must be received at least with general interest. The present work[1] will indeed be regarded with something more than interest by students of the period to which it refers. That period, well known in its commencement through the early works of Mr. Motley, is only partially dealt with in those works, and the present volumes form as it were the centre portion of a triptych, the last wing of which is to present to the public the history of the Thiry Years' War. In this centre portion the interest lies chiefly round a single individual, the great Advocate of Holland, whose name is prefixed to the book. In previous works by the same author, "John of Barneveld" had occupied a conspicuous position. During the War of Independence he was a marked and prominent figure, and in reality the volumes before us can only be said to deal with the concluding years of his life, for they start from the year 1609, and in 1610 Barneveld was executed. A few pages, however, contain a resumé of his previous life. He was born in 1549, and from his earliest years exhibited a sincere enthusiasm for the independence of the States which had just thrown off the Spanish yoke. At the age of twenty-nine he was Chief Pensionary of Rotterdam, and ten years later he was created Advocate of the Province of Holland. In 1590 he was sent Ambassador to England with the view of gaining Elizabeth's assistance for the Provinces, and by his eloquence he succeeded in gaining at least the promise of her aid. "I will assist you," she said, "even if you were up to the neck in water. Jusque-là," she added, pointing to her chin. Barneveld's reputation was, however, established before the great work of his life, the truce with Spain, was achieved. Long before this time he had seen through the secret designs of Prince Maurice of Nassau, who had been raised to the dignity of Stadtholder, and he himself became the head of the Republican party. Spain then entered into peace negotiations, and Barneveld exhibited during the whole course of these negotiations the talent of a statesman and the firmness of a republican. Maurice, who saw in war alone a chance of personal aggrandizement, was opposed to the peace, and it was only after long and complicated events that Barneveld was able to conclude the twelve years' truce with Spain. Theological controversies embittered the relationship of the Advocate and Stadtholder. To obviate a civil war Barneveld proposed a general measure of

---

[1] "The Life and Death of John of Barneveld, Advocate of Holland; with a View of the Primary Causes and Movements of the Thirty Years' War." By J. L. Motley, D.C.L., LL.D. London: Murray.

tolerance. At first the States seemed to agree with him, but the intrigues of the party of Nassau, who represented the Arminians as secret friends of Spain, changed their views. Gradually Maurice became the idol of the people, and Barneveld tasted the bitterness of unpopularity. Although inclined to resign his office he was prevented from taking this step by his sense of duty. The whole course of events resembles a "sacred war." When in 1618 Maurice assembled the synod at Dordrecht almost all the Calvinistic churches of Europe had sent their deputies to oppose the Armenians. These were treated with unmitigated severity. Amongst other chiefs of the party Barneveld was taken and sentenced to death. The representations and entreaties of the Princess of Orange and the French Ambassador were alike disregarded. He was executed on the 13th of May, 1619, at the age of seventy-two. The execution is thus recorded by Mr. Motley:—

"The statesman then came forward, and said in a loud, firm voice to the people:—

"'Men, do not believe that I am a traitor to the country. I have ever acted uprightly and loyally as a good patriot, and as such I shall die.'

"The crowd was perfectly silent.

"He then took his cap from John Franken, drew it over his eyes, and went forward towards the sand, saying:—

"'Christ shall be my guide. O Lord, my heavenly Father, receive my spirit.'

"As he was about to kneel with his face to the south, the provost said:—

"'My lord will be pleased to move to the other side, not where the sun is in his face.'

"He knelt accordingly with his face towards his own house. The servant took farewell of him, and Barneveld said to the executioner:—

"'Be quick about it. Be quick.'

"The executioner then struck his head off at a single blow."

Around Barneveld Mr. Motley has grouped all the sovereigns of Europe. The religious point of view is that from which he chiefly looks out, and intolerant of intolerance he has not always been quite just. He is no doubt justified in his view of Henry, the ridiculous lover of the Princess of Condé, but he is certainly unfair to James. He recognises his superficial shrewdness and social aptitude for repartee, but he does not do justice to the common sense which underlay the disagreeable personality of the king. James certainly had a greater part at the siege of Jülich than Mr. Motley admits. But it is the religious struggle between Calvinism and Arminianism that claims the chief attention of Mr. Motley. Readers of Mr. Motley's earlier works will not need to be told which way his sympathies lie, and all students of history who are at all concerned with this special section of history will know at once that it is imperatively necessary for them to make themselves acquainted with these last works of the writer to whom this section has been unanimously assigned.

Sir Joseph Arnould's life of Lord Denman[1] is pleasant reading, and

---

[1] "Memoir of Thomas, First Lord Denman, formerly Lord Chief Justice of England." By Sir Joseph Arnould. Two Vols. London: Longmans, Green, and Co.

the biography was one which could not escape being written. Luckily it has fallen into good hands. It is the doom of biographers that they have to deal not only with their heroes, but with the grandfathers and great-grandfathers of their heroes. Sir Joseph Arnould begins with the Denman line in the reign of the third Edward, but he is not prolix, and a page and a half brings us to the father of Lord Denman, Dr. Thomas Denman, who went to London in the year 1733 with his patrimony (amounting to 75*l.*) in his pocket. Lord Denman was born in 1779, at which time his father was a fairly prosperous professional man. At a very early age Thomas was sent to Mrs. Barbauld's school, where he was the schoolfellow of Sir William Gell, and entered Eton in 1788. At that school the notices of his progress appear to be very scanty. He was an excellent extemporary speaker as a boy, and it was the delight of his companions to insist upon the unpremeditated exercise of this talent. On one occasion he was roused from sleep and ordered to "make a speech," and on his obstinate refusal to comply was burned on the leg with a red-hot poker, the scar of which branding he carried with him to his grave. He took but an ordinary degree at Cambridge, a fact which was some disappointment to his father, and commenced his legal studies in London in the first year of this century. In 1804 he married Theodosia Vevers, and began his professional life, but it was not until 1810 that he emerged from the comparative obscurity of mere provincial reputation. In this year he defended the Luddite prisoners charged with machine breaking and rioting. It was a gloomy time in the history of the country. No Factory Laws had interposed their humane regulations between the avarice of Capital and the sufferings of Labour, and the Poor Laws were destroying the independence and sapping the honour of the peasantry. Denman's defence was not of much avail, the unfortunate prisoners were sentenced to be hanged, beheaded, and quartered. This was only fifty-seven years ago. Owing to royal clemency they were not quartered, but they were drawn on a hurdle to the county gaol of Derby, where they were hung and beheaded. In 1819 Denman took his seat as member for Wareham. The trial of Queen Caroline was one of the most important events in Lord Denman's life. It is unnecessary now to trace the part which he took in it. He was always enthusiastic for his royal client, and earned her husband's undying hatred. It was only in the year 1828, and by the special efforts of the Duke of Wellington, that he obtained the tardy honour of a silk gown. The first Reform Administration was formed by Earl Grey in 1830, and Denman was appointed Attorney-General. The first Reform Bill, as drawn up by him still exists, but does not throw much light upon the secret history of that measure. In the year of its passing Denman was raised to the Judicial bench and was sworn in as Lord Chief Justice of England. We will not follow Sir Joseph Arnould through the remainder of Lord Denman's life. It does not indeed lie so far from our own times. Lord Denman died in 1854, being aged nearly seventy-six. Of Sir Joseph Arnould's book we have given but a faint idea in this outline sketch of Lord Denman's life. It is written with an easy fluency, and is an admirable picture of the best society of the time. Lord Denman was intimate with so many of the great names of the early part of this century, that his social life alone is of interest. A better and more genial biographer than the present could not have been found, and all who care to read the life of Lord Chief Justice Denman will be grateful for the work which in two interesting and gracefully written volumes is now offered them.

Sir Gilbert Elliot, the first Earl of Minto, was the son of the third Sir Gilbert, and his wife Agnes Kynynmound. His biography has been written by his descendant and representative the Countess of Minto.[1] Gilbert with his brother was sent at an early age to France. Amongst their schoolfellows were the Chevalier de Mirabeau and the Comte de Lamarck. After completing his education at Oxford, he married in 1770 Miss Amyand. In the same year he was returned to Parliament for Morpeth, and by the death of his father became the head of the family. At this time the great American War of Independence was going on. Generally he supported the royal policy, but in 1782 he with great candour admitted that his opinions had undergone a change. In 1786 Sir Gilbert was returned to Parliament for Berwick, having several years previously lost his seat for Morpeth. He was now the close ally and coadjutor of Burke during the trial of Warren Hastings. Then followed the French Revolution. Sir Gilbert never held a cabinet office. His ability was rather for diplomacy, and in 1793 he was sent as minister to Toulon. From this place, which indeed after a month he was obliged to evacuate to the French republicans, he proceeded to Corsica, and was received with voluble enthusiasm. At the end of 1794 Sir Gilbert had established British authority in Corsica, but he appears to have been entirely neglected by the Cabinet, his despatches even remaining unopened. At last, however, he received orders to abandon Corsica. Then followed the battle of Cape St. Vincent, of which Sir Gilbert was a witness from the deck of the *Lively* frigate. In 1797 he was raised to the peerage. Subsequently he was ambassador at the Court of Vienna, and afterwards Governor-General of India. He died in 1814. The real interest of these three volumes lies in the vivid manner which the letters enable us to realize the foreign situation in the Georgian era. Sir Gilbert was an able letter writer, and an accurate observer. It was the age of letter-writing. Most of the letters in these volumes are good and vigorous. Lady Malmesbury writing to her sister Lady Elliot in 1792 of the September massacres at Paris, in speaking of the murder of Madame de Lamballe relates the following particulars. The mob had killed their victim with atrocities too revolting to be detailed, and had cut off her head.

"They then carried the head on a pike to the Palais Royal, where Lindsay was dining with the Duke of Orleans, and of course started back with horror seeing it under the windows. The Duke said only, "Je sais ce que c'est;" and then walked into the next room, and sat down to dinner with complete coolness. You are to observe she was his sister-in-law."

---

[1] "Life and Letters of Sir Gilbert Elliot, First Earl of Minto." Edited by his great niece the Countess of Minto. Longmans, Green, and Co. Three Vols.

The letters from Italy and Corsica are interesting. On his second visit to Florence, Sir Gilbert met two old friends with their children. Amongst the latter he mentions especially, "Harry, now nine years old. He speaks French and Italian very well, and has probably secured a knowledge of those languages, but has not yet began Latin." "Harry" is known to a later generation as Lord Palmerston. But it is useless quoting these letters, they are full of social anecdotes of a period which is separated from us by a short interval. The book is well edited.

Our next work[4] is one which refers to the same era. Mr. Rae has written three monographs upon the most distinguished members of the opposition under George III. These members were Wilkes, Sheridan, and Fox, and the monographs are worthy of praise both for their style and matter. Mr. Rae does not succeed in making Wilkes appear an amiable character, but he shows with sufficient clearness that Wilkes was much more than the sly, diabolical character he is generally considered to have been, an unenviable reputation, owing in great measure to Hogarth's spiteful caricature. It may well be that he had, as Dr. Carlyle, his fellow student at Leyden, asserts, an "ugly countenance," but he was also on the same authority "a sprightly and entertaining fellow," and was able for several years to fill the vapid head of King George the Third with a very wholesome and uncomfortable disquiet. This is good hearing of a time when the general spirit of adulation inspired the House of Lords with the following peculiarly elegant and happy piece of sycophancy to the king who "gloried in the name of Briton." "What a lustre does it cast upon the name of Briton, when you, sire, are pleased to esteem it among your glories." Wilkes struck the key-note of his policy in the first number of the *North Briton.* "The *liberty of the press* is the birthright of a Briton, and is justly esteemed the firmest bulwark of the liberties of this country." The liberty of the press John Wilkes claimed with a vengeance; his sarcasm was virulent and unsparing. Nor was his sarcasm veiled and wavering; it went straight to the mark. Other journalists had used initials and stars; he spoke openly —*ἔπος τ' ἔφατ, ἔκ τ' ὀνόμαζεν.* In an incredibly short time the Government was a laughing-stock, and the circulation of the paper was increasing week by week. In the twenty-seventh number he told his readers that he was threatened with an action for libel, and at the forty-fourth he himself suspended the publication. We will not follow the obscure and discreditable measures of the Government to crush their enemy. The whole story is well told by Mr. Rae. But who can refrain from laughter on learning that less than a hundred years ago an obnoxious paper, No. 45 of the revived *North Briton*, was solemnly condemned by a ministerial majority in Parliament to be burned by the common hangman. The common sense of the country gave the matter another turn. Mr. Rae says:—

"When the common hangman was about to execute the order of the House

---

[4] "Wilkes, Sheridan, Fox, the Opposition under George the Third." By W. F. Rae. W. Isbister and Co.

of Commons, he was forcibly prevented from committing a copy of No. 45 to the flames; a petticoat and a jack boot, symbolizing the King's mother and Lord Bute being burned in its stead. Williams, one of the journeyman printers employed to reprint the *North Briton*, having been sentenced to the pillory, went to the place of punishment in a coach marked No. 45. The spectators treated him as a martyr; cheered, instead of pelting him with missiles; made a collection for him, which produced 200*l*., and suspended from a temporary gallows a boot and a Scotch bonnet in derision of the supposed instigator of the proceedings. Whenever Wilkes appeared in public and was recognised, he was hailed with loud huzzas. At great city banquets it became the custom to give as a toast, 'Wit, Beauty, Virtue, Honour,' these being as Walpole records, 'ironic designations of the King, Queen, Princess Dowager, and Lord Bute.'"

Wilkes's later days were less turbulent. In 1779 he became Chamberlain of the City, a lucrative and coveted post. It has been said of him in this capacity:—"Perhaps a more punctual, patient, and penetrating chamberlain has not filled the office during the century. As a magistrate also he was equally able, assiduous, candid, and just." He died at the age of seventy in 1797. Mr. Rae's chapter upon his character and services is good, he tells many anecdotes of him, which even if known one is not sorry to have recalled. One anecdote on page 137 Mr. Rae might have omitted without injuring his work, but his remarks on the verdict of posterity in reference to Wilkes are just and discriminating. Mr. Rae's second monograph is on Sheridan. A brief but able narrative of the chief incidents of Sheridan's life, of his marriage with Miss Linley, his first attempts in play writing, his managership of Drury Lane Theatre, and his Parliamentary career, are followed by a critical examination of his characteristics as a writer, and as an orator. There is truth and insight in the following remarks:—

"Sheridan wrote and spoke as he lived, with a persistent view to effect. His whole life abounded in surprises; all his writings and speeches are filled with unexpected points. He was perpetually occupied in preparing and letting off literary fireworks. To be thought the sayer and writer of good things was with him an object of ambition, second only to that of getting credit for uttering and writing the ordinary products of his mind. He wished the world to think that epigrams were as natural to him as commonplaces are to other men. During his lifetime, his success in these respects was complete. But since his biographer has disclosed the mechanism of his art, the world while still retaining admiration for his ability, has ceased to regard him as a wonder. A conjuror's tricks are none the less clever after we have shown how they are done; but they cease to startle when they are no longer mysterious and incomprehensible."

What Mr. Rae has here said of Sheridan is true indeed of all wits, whose renown rests chiefly upon their being wits. It is true of Theodore Hook, and it is certainly true of Sydney Smith. It is especially true of Sheridan. Mr. Rae attributes much of Sheridan's peculiarity to the Celtic cast of his mind and temperament. He had, he says, a love for Ireland amounting to a passion. In speaking of Sheridan's premeditated oratory Mr. Rae recalls an anecdote preserved by Lord Eldon, which will bear repeating:—

"During the debate on the India Bill, at which period John Robinson was Secretary to the Treasury, Sheridan on one evening, when Mr. Fox's majorities were decreasing, said: 'Mr. Speaker, this is not at all to be wondered at, when a member is employed to corrupt everybody in order to obtain votes.' Upon this there was a general outcry made by almost everybody in the House: 'Who is it? Name him, name him!' 'Sir,' said Sheridan to the Speaker, 'I shall not name the person. It is an unpleasant and invidious thing to do so, and therefore I shall not name him. But don't suppose, sir, that I abstain because there is any difficulty in naming him; I could do that, sir, as soon as you could say Jack Robinson."

Mr. Rae's third and last monograph is on Charles James Fox. Our author after noting the bright promise of his early life speaks of his passion for gaming. He was remarkable for his addiction to play, and whilst Junior Lord of the Admiralty, founded a club at Almack's where the stakes were rouleaus of 50*l.* each, and where as much as 10,000*l.* were on the table at one time. After a very full and close account of Fox's political career, Mr. Rae, in two admirable chapters, estimates and weighs him as an orator and a statesman. Mr. Rae is fond of comparisons and his comparisons are good. He has already compared Sheridan to Mr. Disraeli, and certainly succeeds in deducing resemblances. He now draws a parallel between two of the greatest Parliamentary orators in the reign of George the Third, and two of the greatest in the reign of Victoria:—

"The resemblance is notable even in its broad and superficial aspect. The store of rounded and rhetorical sentences which Pitt had ready for instant use was not more copious than that on which Mr. Gladstone can draw at pleasure and with equal effect. Consciousness of intellectual superiority and austerity of demeanour distinguish both. . . . .

"Fox differed from Pitt as Mr. Bright differs from Mr. Gladstone, while the oratorical likeness between Mr. Bright and Fox is as close as that between Mr. Gladstone and Pitt. The 'Man of the People' of the reign of George III. is represented by the 'Tribune of the People' in the reign of Victoria. In warmth of feeling; in hatred of tyrants; in reverence for the Constitution, coupled with a readiness to remove from it all excrescences and defects; in devotion to peace as the one thing needful for a great and self-respecting nation, combined with the purest and most ardent patriotism; in poetic imagination and humorous sallies united to the strongest common sense; in love and reverence for their noble mother tongue, which they have shown to be grandest when least adorned, most effective when spoken in homely simplicity, Fox and Mr. Bright display an identity which is almost unprecedented."

Mr. Rae has studied his subject thoroughly, and has written *con amore*. He has a vigorous outspoken style, which is not unpleasing, and he is gifted with a clear literary insight.

Mrs. Somerville's biography[1] is not a continuous biography in the ordinary sense of the word. It is rather a series of detached recollections, written partly in the words of Mrs. Somerville herself, and partly in those of her daughter. To this some of her letters are annexed. The main outlines of her life are there. She was born in 1780, at Jedburgh, the daughter of a naval officer, Sir William Fairfax.

[1] "Personal Recollections, from Early Life to Old Age of Mary Somerville. With Selections from her Correspondence." By her daughter Martha Somerville. London: John Murray.

Her mother was a connexion of the Minto family, of which we have already spoken. Mary Fairfax's first introduction to the great study of her life took place when she was very young, and is thus told:—

"I became acquainted with a Miss Ogilvie, who asked me to go and see fancy works she was doing, and at which she was very clever. I went next day, and after admiring her work, and being told how it was done, she showed me a monthly magazine with coloured plates of ladies' dresses, charades and puzzles. At the end of a page I read what appeared to me to be simply an arithmetical question; but on turning the page, I was surprised to see strange looking lines mixed with letters, chiefly X's and Y's, and asked: 'What is that?' 'Oh,' said Miss Ogilvie, 'it is a kind of arithmetic; they call it Algebra, but I can tell you nothing about it.' And we talked about other things; but on going home, I thought I would look if any of our books could tell me what was meant by Algebra."

In 1804 she married her cousin, Samuel Greig, commissioner of the Russian navy, and was left a widow with two sons after three years of married life. The next few years were spent in abstruse mathematical studies, but in 1812 she married another cousin, William Somerville. There can be no doubt that this union was the greatest happiness of her life. In the year 1832 appeared her "Mechanism of the Heavens," a book which at once raised its author to a position of eminence in the scientific world. She received letters of homage from Herschel, Whewell, Peacock, Biot, Sir R. Peel, Sedgwick, and La Place. Other works followed this first great work, but the remainder of her life contains no stirring events. She settled in Italy, and lost her husband in 1860. Twelve years later she herself passed away. Whatever Mrs. Somerville has taught, there is one thing she has proved,—that a lady may hold the highest intellectual honours, and lose nothing of the delicate feminine charm which is her peculiar atmosphere. Not by the loud assertion of admitted rights, nor noisy pretensions to unearned regard, can the freedom of intellectual citizenship be gained, but by actual work done. Mrs. Somerville has done more to establish the claims of woman that even Mr. Mill could do. She wrote the "Mechanism of the Heavens," and, retaining her feminine sensitiveness to the last, she wept, in 1869, at the death of a little bird who used to sleep upon her arm while she was writing. Her love for animals was so great that she could not deny them immortality. Up to the day of her death she was engaged in the study of Quaternions, and almost her last utterances were against cruelty to animals. We shall quote the final entry in the biography of this dear and kindly lady, unequalled since Sappho for intellectual power, and never surpassed in womanly tenderness; a lady who illustrates, under unusual circumstances, the words of Goethe:—

"Das Ewig-Weibliche
Zieht uns hinan."

"The Blue Peter has been long flying at my foremast, and now that I am in my ninety-second year I must soon expect the signal for sailing. It is a solemn voyage, but it does not disturb my tranquillity. Deeply sensible of my utter unworthiness, and profoundly grateful for the innumerable blessings I have received, I trust in the infinite mercy of my Almighty Creator. I have every reason to be thankful that my intellect is still unimpaired, and, although my strength is weakness, my daughters support my tottering steps, and by incessant care and help make the infirmities of age so light to me that I am perfectly happy."

The character of Dr. T. Guthrie, as exhibited in the pages of this readable volume,* is one that is strongly defined. Vigorous, protestant, Scotch, it was one that has much that is admirable, but it was one that was wanting in much. It was fearless, open, and honest. It lacked subtlety, culture, and breadth. The present volume contains the autobiography, an imperfect work, and a portion of the memoir. The autobiography is written in a pleasant style, and was the last work of its author. It goes no further in his life than the period of the disruption conflict between the Scotch churches. Dr. Guthrie was one of those of whom it is customary to say that they have "large" natures. He was "large" physically, and he was hard and strong. As a child he was subject to severe punishments from his tutors and his father, and as a man he was proud of their severity. "Blows," he said, "had no more effect on me that on an iron pillar." When beaten on the head by his schoolmaster with a ruler till he was black and blue, he refused to yield the point which that gentle discipline was intended to carry. He adds of the schoolmaster, "Seeing me return next day with a brow and face all marred and swollen, he regretted, I believe, his violence, and was very gracious." Home discipline seconded scholastic rule. When the "marred and swollen" lad sought his mother, and asked if he had not better tell his father, that lady replied, "You had better not; he will lick you next." Well may Dr. Guthrie add, "We were brought up hardier louns than the present generation." It must, indeed, be admitted that Dr. Guthrie was a "hardy loun." He is also an outspoken "loun." He stoutly pleads for the Scotch Sabbaths, with their absence of interest, and he is against Sabbath walks. He says (p. 23):

"As to the plea set up for Sabbath walks and excursions for the sake of health by the working classes, there is no truth in it. If women would spend less on finery, and men on whisky and tobacco, they could spare an hour or two every day for more than all the relaxation which health requires. Besides, I feel certain that statistics which have no bias to either side, would show that the good old Scottish way of hallowing the Lord's day is most favourable to morals and health and length of days—that Sabbath-keepers have happier houses and longer lives than Sabbath-breakers—and that in this as in other things, 'godliness is profitable unto all things, having promise of the life that now is, and of that which is to come.'"

Now, no doubt, if men and women will stint themselves in finery, whisky and tobacco, they may be enabled to spend their Sabbaths like Dr. Guthrie's aunt in the perusal of Boston's "Fourfold State," or Ambrose's "Looking to Jesus," but there certainly is a fallacy in Dr. Guthrie's appeal to statistics. The "sabbath-keepers," to whom he triumphantly refers, these readers of the "Fourfold State," are evidently a picked and select class, the prize specimens of the system. It is of

---

* "Autobiography of Thomas Guthrie, D.D., and Memoir." By his sons Rev D. K. Guthrie and C. J. Guthrie, M.A. Isbister and Co. Vol. I.

course unfair to pit them against the whole body of "Sabbath-breakers," for some of these are (if we may venture to say so) men of culture and intelligence and perhaps even rudimentary morality. He should have taken the best of each, if he wished really to apply statistics to this question, and he should have stated his thesis in some some such way as this:

"Men who adopt the Scotch method of keeping the Sabbath, who do not whistle, walk, or read novels upon that day, have happier houses, and longer lives than an equal number of men of the same position and intelligence who do whistle, walk, and read amusing literature upon the first day of the week, which we Scotch call the Sabbath."

And if statistics proved the truth of this thesis, then, by all means let its truth be widely known. But if we remember rightly the proposal to apply statistics as a religious test of the efficacy of prayer was so indignantly scouted by the Scots that even a minister who in relation to this subject ventured to define somewhat closely the character of prayer was severely dealt with by the body of which he was a member. With this in our mind it is pleasing to hear a Scotch clergyman jauntily appealing to statistics in support of the "Sabbath-keepers" *versus* the "Sabbath-breakers." We will only add of this autobiography that it contains many pleasant pulpit anecdotes and clerical gossip.

There could be no more complete contrast to the life of Dr. Guthrie than that which is afforded by the life of Thomas Grant,[7] first Bishop of Southwark. Dr. Grant has been fortunate in his biographer, for she has command of a fervent and engaging style which is calculated to win the reader. Her book narrates the difficulties with which the first Roman Catholic Bishop of Southwark had to contend. He was the son of an Irish soldier, and was born in France in 1816. His education was conducted by a priest who took an interest in him, and he was sent to Rome, where he became secretary to Cardinal Acton. He was then appointed Rector of the English College (1844). In 1850, when a Romish hierarchy was established in England, he was appointed Bishop of Southwark, a position which he occupied until his death in 1870. It is a strange world into which this book introduces us. Strange words and mediæval sentiment meet us continually. Dr. Grant was learned, subtle, and ascetic as any ecclesiastic of the dark ages. Minute self-observation was the atmosphere that surrounded him, and we seem to move in it as we turn these pages. The gloom of monastic twilight hangs about them; there is a sound of midnight bells, and an odour of incense. Many pages are concerned with "scrupulosity;" "self-mortification" is much glorified. Of the Bishop himself we are told that while hospitable to others he was abstemious in his own person.

"Sometimes, indeed," his biographer adds, "he was caught *en flagrant délit* of an act of mortification, as when a nun came upon him unawares, and found him shaking the pepper-castor over an orange that had been carefully sugared for him, and on another occasion when he was caught emptying

---

[7] "Thomas Grant, First Bishop of Southwark." By Grace Ramsay. London: Smith, Elder, and Co.

the salt-cellar into his tea-cup at breakfast. A slight start would show his embarrassment for a moment, but as the intruder ventured on no indiscreet remark, the Bishop probably flattered himself his little trick had not been observed."

Now it is clearly obvious that to judge a great and noble character upon an instance of this kind would be wrong. Doubtless, too, it is wrong to give prominence to such isolated acts, but from our point of view what are we to say of them? Can we, with the morning-star of the twentieth century upon the horizon, regard such things with any other feeling than that of pity? Dr. Grant had a wiser, sweeter, more loving, more learned, and more attractive personality than had Dr. Guthrie; yet, happily, for all that Dr. Guthrie has been and will continue to be better known and more admired than the Bishop of Southwark amongst the people of this country. We are pleased to record two incidents referred to in this biography. One is an anecdote.

"On one occasion a person was being rallied too pointedly on the carelessness of his dress, and showed signs of not liking it; Dr. Grant suddenly enquired of the company: 'How many neckties had Job, and what became of them.' Everybody having given it up, he replied, 'Three wretched comforters, and they were all worsted!'"

The other we commend to those ritualistic clergymen who endeavour to establish the formalities of Roman Catholicism within the Church of England. A Bruges merchant had written to the bishop informing him that he (the merchant) was supplying vestments to the English Ritualists at the rate of 800*l*. to 1000*l*. a year, and asked if he could conscientiously continue to do so. The result of the bishop's reply was that the merchant refused to supply the vestments any longer. Upon this the bishop remarks: "It is sad to think that these Ritualists, *having no orders and no consecration*, are keeping up the material idolatry of exposing to adoration bread and wine."

A brief life of St. Vincent de Paul[1] may be well placed with the preceding work, since, although emanating from the English church, it delights in recalling the spirit of mediævalism. The story of St. Vincent's life, as told by Mr. Wilson, is as follows. St. Vincent was born in the year 1576, at the village of Pouz, near Dax, not far from the base of the Pyrenees. He studied at Toulouse, and after various fortunes accepted the Cure of Clichy, and by the aid of the Countess of Joigny founded the Congregation of the Mission, designed for the conversion of poor country people. This was St. Vincent's great work. The chief seat of the institution was at St. Lazarus in Paris. After the death of the founder, the principles which he had inaugurated spread widely, and he himself was canonized. Mr. Wilson thinks that St. Vincent is worthy of the attention of English churchmen, because he believes that the four institutions to which he devoted himself have been recently revived and organized—missions, retreats, the employment of religious women amongst the poor, and the better training of candidates for Holy Orders. It is with the last institution, as

[1] "The Life of S. Vincent de Paul." With an Appendix containing some of his Letters. By the Rev. R. F. Wilson, M.A. Rivingtons.

examining chaplain to a bishop, that Mr. Wilson is evidently most interested. His wish is that candidates for Holy Orders should be tested as to their attainments early in their course, so that Ember Week, now ordinarily spent in examination, should be left free to be devoted to prayer, meditation, and spiritual exercises to which the ordinands might come with tranquil minds. This appears to be Mr. Wilson's chief desire. His book will interest those who sympathize with his views. It has no literary interest. As a historical work it is compiled from previous authorities, especially Collett, and the Abbé Maynard. In the Abbé's work there are many references to the National Archives at Paris, and to the Archives belonging to the community of St. Lazarus. These Mr. Wilson has, he tells us, taken on trust, "without any attempt to verify them, which would have been beyond the writer's power."

It is pleasant to pass from the theological to the literary atmosphere once more. Professor Masson has published a life of Drummond of Hawthornden.[9] Whether Drummond's life was worthy the pen of Professor Masson we will not assert, but the book is an interesting one. William Drummond was born in 1585, and was educated at the High School and University of Edinburgh. At the age of twenty-four he was left a man of property with literary tastes, and every means of gratifying them. That which makes him chiefly noteworthy to us is that he was a student and admirer of Shakspeare while Shakspeare was yet alive. In his library at Hawthornden, when he came into possession of it, there were copies of "Romeo and Juliet," "Love's Labour's Lost," "Midsummer Night's Dream," "Lucrece," and the "Passionate Pilgrim." Professor Masson conjectures that he was the only Scotchman of that time who had read Shakspeare. Drummond was a poet also. Certain poems of his attracted the notice of Michael Drayton; and what is more worthy of our attention he was a friend of Ben Jonson. Jonson visited him at Hawthornden, and the *noctes cœnæque* are well imagined by Professor Masson. Yet alas! of all the gossip preserved from those banquets one scrap alone tells of Shakspeare, or rather gives Jonson's opinion (not worth much in this case), of one of his plays. Drummond is not a character which can interest many to-day. He wrote some poetry, but it is worth very little; he took some part in historical events, and his biographer not wisely, though well, has woven round that little part a great deal of history. To the general reader the life of Drummond will only occasion the feeling of regret that one who had lived so near the rose should bear away so little of its perfume. Even Mr. Masson feels this. "Why," he asks in speaking of Ben Jonson, "why, when Drummond had beside him the man who could have told more of Shakspeare personally than any other living, did he not tap this particular fountain of gossip and keep it flowing for several hours?" Ah, why indeed?

Colonel Chesney's essays,[10] though most of them are reprints, will

---

[9] "Drummond of Hawthornden." By David Masson, M.A., LL.D. London: Macmillan and Co.

[10] "Essays in Modern Military Biography." By Colonel Chesney. Reprinted chiefly from the *Edinburgh Review*. London: Longmans, Green, and Co.

meet with many readers in their collected form. Their range is wide: Cornwallis and the Indian service, Gordon and the Taeping Rebellion, Von Brandt, a German soldier of the First Empire, De Fezensac and the Grand Army, are subjects of some of these essays. But the most important, as they are the most characteristic of these papers, are the four last which deal with the military excellence of American Generals in the late national struggle. Colonel Chesney successfully endeavours to disabuse the reader's mind of the prevailing belief that these generals and the troops they led were inferior to regular soldiers. He thinks, and his readers will think so also, that the conditions of war on a grand scale were as much illustrated in the American contest as they were in the late Continental war. And, perhaps, no portion of these essays is better written or fuller of suppressed feeling than the pages in which Colonel Chesney pays tribute to the genius of the unfortunate but amiable American General, Robert Edward Lee.

Sir Hope Grant's account of the Sepoy war[11] is drawn chiefly from the private journals which he kept during the revolt. It was written day after day within twenty-four hours of the recorded events, and the vivacity and freshness of the book are results of this method of composition. The modest volume is accompanied by two excellent maps, one of the disaffected provinces, and the other of the neighbourhood of Lucknow. The latter is intended to illustrate the operations for the relief of that town.

Mr. Hayward has published the third series of his essays.[12] Like all that he writes, these essays are eminently readable, they are full of anecdotes, and they have a tone of society about them. Perhaps there is too much of the tone of society about them. Pleasant gossip they are, polite, and cultured,—but if they are to be characterized by one word, that word is—frivolous. Anecdotes of parliament, anecdotes of foreign courts, anecdotes of the aristocracy abound. Some of them are old, but all of them are amusing. Here one may find the "good story" of society in perfection, and here one may learn how little it is worth. Years ago, if we are not mistaken, Mr. Hayward translated, with a commentary, Goethe's "Faust." That was a noteworthy book. It was the work of a man who could do much more. Now he gives us a series of anecdotes, dining-room chit-chat, club gossip, and such trifles, and wraps the whole in a *blasé* envelope of commonplace, so that we regret to find a man equally familiar with the three great European languages, and yet the mere retailer of good stories. What a writer may be in that line of literature which Mr. Hayward has chosen, has been shown by Lord Houghton; and if Mr. Hayward can measure the superiority of Lord Houghton's "Monographs" to his "Essays," he will know how far inferior his own works are to the promise of his "Faust."

---

[11] "Incidents of the Sepoy War, 1857-58." Compiled from the Private Journals of Sir H. Grant. With Explanatory Chapters. By H. Knollys. Edinburgh and London: W. Blackwood and Sons.

[12] "Biographical and Critical Essays." Reprinted from Reviews. Third Series. By A. Hayward, Esq., Q.C. London: Longmans, Green, and Co.

Our next volume[13] appears to owe its existence to a quarrel. There is a proverb that when "knaves fall out, honest folk come by their rights." This is as it may be; but it is certain that when honest and clever people dispute, the world is the better for their argument. Mr. Hazlitt and Messrs. Moxon appear to have differed on certain particulars in reference to the publication of Charles Lamb's works and letters. The result is that Mr. W. C. Hazlitt has published a very pretty and interesting little volume of his own. It has many pictorial illustrations which were supplied by Mr. Camden Hotten, and above all it contains a *fac simile* of the first page of *Elia* on "Roast Pig." It is well got up and has a good portrait of Elia. There are also some letters and poems of Mary Lamb which are not easily accessible elsewhere.

The present volume[14] completes the Calendar of the Carew Papers, now remaining at Lambeth. It contains all that Sir George Carew thought fit to collect respecting the "plantation" of Ulster and the events of Ireland during the reign of James I. It contains moreover a good and impartial introduction by Mr. Brewer, who fairly analyses James's relation to Ireland, and a thoroughly good index. Indirectly Mr. Brewer shows that the English poet Spenser could not, at least in his later years, have suffered from want.

Our next volume[15] in the State Paper Series refers only to those six months of the year 1639 which are concerned with the campaigns against the Covenanters. The whole story of the abortive enterprise which ended in the Pacification of Dunse Law, is told with a minuteness of detail that makes the reader capable of taking the part of a contemporary. The book has a full preface of thirty-seven pages and a good index. The work of this Calendar appears particularly well done.

The letters of Lord Cockburn[16] to the Right Hon. T. F. Kennedy relate to an important period in the modern history of Scotland, the period, namely, 1818—1841. But the book is an unsatisfactory one. "Each reader," says the introduction, "can correct them (the letters) with the information he may himself possess, or acquire from other sources, and thus they become contributions to the true history of the country." With so much at hand, more might have been done for the editing of a book like the present. Very little has been done; but the letters will be interesting to legal students.

We can only notice the second volume of Mr. Van Laun's transla-

---

[13] "Mary and Charles Lamb: Poems, Letters, and Remains." Now first collected, with Reminiscences and Notes. By W. C. Hazlitt. London: Chatto and Windus.

[14] "Calendar of the Carew Manuscripts." Edited by J. S. Brewer, M.A., and W. Bullen, Esq. Published under the direction of the Master of the Rolls. London: Longman and Co.; Trübner and Co., &c.

[15] "Calendar of State Papers. Domestic Series of the Reign of Charles I., 1639." Edited by W. D. Hamilton, Esq., F.S.A. Published under the direction, &c. Longman and Co.

[16] "Letters chiefly connected with the Affairs of Scotland, from Henry Cockburn to T. F. Kennedy, M.P." 1818–52. London: W. Ridgway.

tion of Taine's History of English Literature." We have already expressed at length our good opinion of this work.

Books *d'occasion* are not generally very good, and Mr. Markham's History of Persia[18] is not a brilliant exception to the rule. It is good, as anything Mr. Markham writes would be likely to be, but it is not very good, as it ought to be. The book has been called forth by the visit to our country of a Barbarian potentate, and if that monarch were to buy up all the copies of Mr. Markham's work the loss to our literature would not be overwhelming. For the early history of Persia, our author has taken the authority of Ferdosi. He makes a distinction between the "history" of Persia, and the "actual historical facts." We do not follow him in this, and we care little for his book. If there is any valuable information in the work at all it is the geographical information. There are appendices which give abstracts of treaties between England and Persia, a list of English envoys to Persia, and a list of Persian titles.

"The Child's History of Jerusalem"[19] is one of the prettiest children's books we have seen. It is a general outline of the history of Palestine for four thousand years down to the most recent times. It is written in a light and charming style, well calculated to engage the attention of every reader, and is illustrated by a few well chosen engravings of gems, coins, and views. The book is in large type and is unpretentious. It is tolerably free from superstition and gives a brief and unbroken account of the city whose name it puts forward.

Mr. Hunt's History of Italy[20] forms part of the historical course for schools. We dislike the course, and we believe that the general scholastic verdict is against it. Mr. Hunt's book is dull reading, and would be, we imagine, dull teaching. History is a difficulty for the schoolmaster which has not yet found its solution.

Mrs. Sewell's "Catechism of the History of Greece"[21] is simple, and we think, good. The fault of her books is, as we have had occasion to say before, that the parts to be learnt by heart are too long. Children who would use this book *cannot* learn half a page of prose by heart to advantage. Let her break up pp. 19, 22, 29, 32, 72, 73, 91, 95, 100, 130.

For pure unmixed nonsense we have seen few books which can compete with "Veritas,"[22] by Messrs. H. Melville, F. Tennyson, and A. Tuder. The book has been, we are told, "forty years in embryo." It is a pity it ever reached that stage of existence, and a still greater

---

17 "History of English Literature." By H. A. Taine, D.C.L. Translated by H. Van Laun. Edmonston and Douglas.

18 "A General Sketch of the History of Persia." By C. R. Markham, C.B., F.R.S. London: Longmans, Green, and Co.

19 "The Child's History of Jerusalem." By Francis Roubiliac Conder. With 15 Illustrations. W. Isbister and Co.

20 "History of Italy." By W. Hunt, M.A. London: Macmillan.

21 "Catechism of the History of Greece." By E. M. Sewell. London: Longmans, Green, and Co.

22 "Veritas." Revelation of Mysteries, Biblical, Historical and Social, by Means of the Median Laws. H. Melville. Published for the Author. A. Hall and Co.

pity that it should make its present abortive appearance. It is a mixture of astrology and freemasonry. We imagine it would be offensive to astrologers, and we learn from the preface that it is offensive to freemasons. As it certainly must be offensive to every man of sense, we will refer to it no further.

We can deal but briefly with the German literature which has reached us in this quarter. The first work we should notice is Dr. Eberty's "History of the Prussian State."[53] It is in seven small volumes, and ranges over the period from 1411 to 1871. The history is told in clear and popular language. The completest and most satisfactory part of the work is that which deals with the last half century included in its programme. It has an index.

We have received also the fourth and last part of Dr. H. Reuchlin's "History of Italy,"[54] from the establishment of the reigning dynasty to the present time. It deals with the revolution of 1860, and the relation of Cavour to Garibaldi, and brings events down to the year 1800. Most of our readers will know that last year Reuchlin died. Suddenly, and in the fever of his work upon this volume, his death occurred. Happily the book was in such a condition that it could appear as a perfect conclusion to the chief labour of his life. He lived to send it to the press—he did not see it reappear therefrom. But his work was done, and it is now a year since he has gone.

Herr Julian Schmidt's "History of French Literature, since Louis XVI."[55] is a great work, and one to which we cannot do justice in the short space at our disposal. It is written of course from a German point of view, and not without a shadow of the national feeling induced by recent events. "Am fernsten liegt mir, den Hass, den uns die Franzosen zeigen, erwidern zu wollen," says the author, and truly he does his best to keep himself free therefrom. No one will read the book without finding his knowledge of French literature widened and enriched.

In view of the late terrible loss by fire at the Pantechnicon, Herr Fiedler's "History of the German Institutions for the Saving of Life and Property during Conflagrations"[56] will claim marked attention. It contains a history of the different engines used in various periods for extinguishing fires, and for rescuing persons from burning buildings, and is illustrated with explanatory cuts and engravings. The book has cost its author much trouble and research.

We must content ourselves with acknowledging the receipt of J. Marquard's "Römische Staatsverwaltung,"[57] which forms part of

---

[53] "Geschichte des preussischen Staats." Von Dr. Felix Eberty. Breslau: Verlag von Eduard Trewendt.

[54] "Geschichte Italiens." Von Dr. Hermann Reuchlin. Vierter Theil. Leipzig: Verlag von S. Hirzel.

[55] "Geschichte der Französischen Literatur seit Ludwig XVI." Von Julian Schmidt. Zweite Auflage. Leipzig: Grunow.

[56] "Geschichte der deutschen Feuerlösch-und-Rettungsanstalten." Ein Beitrag zur deutschen Kulturgeschichte. Von Ottomar Fiedler, Stadtrath in Zwickau. Berlin: Verlag von J. Springer.

[57] "Römische Staatsverwaltung." Von J. Marquard. Leipzig: S. Herzel.

the "Handbuch der Römischen Alterthumes," published by himself and Th. Mommsen; of Wickede's "Ein vielbewegtes Leben,"[illegible] the history of a German soldier from 1700 to 1827; and Dr. Phillips' "History of the Relations between Church and State in France."[illegible]

PHILOLOGY AND CLASSICS.

ONE of the most interesting difficulties still awaiting solution is the mystery which surrounds Etruscan inscriptions.[1] Whether the language of Etruria was an Aryan or non-Aryan language may be considered an open question until the publication of Corssen's work upon the subject, a publication which is soon to take place. Perhaps it will be an open question even after Professor Corssen has made his views known. At any rate, that philologists are looking forward to the great work of Professor Corssen is evident from the fact that each person who has formed opinions upon the subject is anxious not to be forestalled and is giving his theory to the world. Some time ago we noticed the brochure of Dr. Maack, who claimed to have translated the inscriptions through Erse. In his opinion Etruscan was an Aryan language. Tarquini in Italy, Stickel in Germany, Chavée in France, have endeavoured to prove Etruscan Semitic. Dr. Donaldson believed it to have affinity with Low-German. Mr. Taylor boldly opposes all these authorities and explains it through the Turanian and Finnic languages. The key to the secret is supposed to lie in a pair of dice discovered at Toscanelli, and marked with words instead of pips. It was therefore at once supposed that these words might represent Etruscan numerals. If this be the case, and if the order of the numerals can be definitely ascertained, then considerable progress has been made, for it becomes possible to ascertain the family or group to which Etruscan belongs, and further deciphering is henceforth only a matter of time. All readers will agree that Mr. Taylor has brought both learning and ingenuity to bear upon the subject. His philological as well as his ethnical arguments must be seriously and thoroughly met before any opposing theory can be considered successful. But until Corssen's work has appeared the proper attitude of every student must be that of tempered and respectfully sceptical attention.

The work whose title we give below[2] endeavours to prove the onomatopœic origin of language. It adduces all the authorities from Zoroaster to Max Müller who have by any utterance given support to

---

[illegible] "Ein vielbewegtes Leben." Von Julius von Wickedes. Hanover: Karl Rümpler.

[illegible] "Das Regalienrecht in Frankreich." Von Dr. G. J. Phillips. Halle: Verlag des Waisenhauses.

1 "Etruscan Researches." By Isaac Taylor, M.A. London: Macmillan and Co.

2 "Primitive and Universal Laws of the Formation and Development of Language." By the Count de Godiles-Liancourt and Frederic Pincott. London: W. H. Allen and Co.

this theory. The last named authority is, the author admits, opposed to it, but this does not save him from being forced into the hostile ranks. When Count de G.-Lisncourt uses such violence towards a living philologist, one is not surprised at the most unusual *tours de force* upon unresisting words. There is a curious index of "onomatops." We will leave our readers to meditate over the following passage:—

"'L onomatop of tongue, and the tongue's operations, licking, smearing, shining, brightening, liking, attaching, binding:—*lai*, 'tongue,' Cochin-Chinese; *lih* 'lick,' Sans.; *lap*, 'speak,' Sans.; *lu'âb*, 'viscosity,' Arab.; *likh*, 'write,' Sans.; *lip*, Eng.; *light*, Eng.; *relish*, Eng.; *leash*, Eng.; *link*, Eng.; *lo*, 'law,' Cochin-Chinese; *lex*, Lat.; *loi*, Fr., &c."

If the reader will carefully read through this passage, he will probably not desire further acquaintance with the book.

The "Treasury of Languages"[3] is a book sent us with a request for a "favourable consideration." If this means a favourable notice, we regret to say that we are unable to comply with the request of Messrs. Hull and Co. The book is poor. We are told that it is the work of a literary amateur, and liable to error. The one fact does not recommend it, and the other we might have discovered for ourselves. At the end there is affixed a list of contributors, but what share they have taken in promoting the work we do not know. Occasionally their initials appear in the body of the work. Thus, Mr. Skeat of Cambridge is marked as the author of the information under the word *Cornish*—"an extinct dialect of Celtic, closely allied to Welsh and Breton, formerly vernacular in Cornwall." We imagine Mr. Skeat will not be particularly rejoiced at finding his initials attached to this recondite article. We turn to the article "Etruscan." The "literary amateur" tells us that it is "classed by some as 'Thraco-Pelasgic,'" and refers us to the article on "Palæo-Georgian." We find this to consist of two lines with the initials of Hyde Clarke, Esq., and we find that it is the "class name" for Caucasian languages. Satisfied with this information we have no more to say about the work.

At length the "Public School Latin Grammar"[4] has appeared with the honoured name of Dr. Kennedy upon the title page. It was indeed well known that the deep-searching scholarship of the Primer, and the first edition of this work was due to no other than the first of English scholars: but those books were conventionally anonymous, and the attacks which were made upon them gained such advantage as was allowed them from the obscuration of that royal name in the world of English scholarship. In this second edition Dr. Kennedy has defended himself against the charges recklessly made. The Primer was too abstract it was declared, it bristled with new names, and with hard and uninviting terms. How Dr. Kennedy meets these charges we

---

[3] "The Treasury of Languages. A Rudimentary Dictionary of Universal Philology." Hull and Co.

[4] "The Public School Latin Grammar." By Benjamin Hall Kennedy, D.D., Regius Professor of Greek in the University of Cambridge. Second Enlarged Edition. London: Longmans, Green, and Co.

leave the reader to learn from his preface. But we will quote one passage in reference to the use of "new" terms, which seems to us to contain the essence of the defence, and to be perfectly unanswerable.

"A new term proposed in grammar is not to be condemned because it is new; but if at all, for one of three reasons: that it is superfluous; or that it is inadequate; or because a better term is suggested. And as respects myself, I repeat that I have not the least disposition to use hard terms; and I affirm that those which I have introduced are unjustly so described. But I cannot adopt the poor pedantry, which refuses to abridge discourse by the use of proper terms, any more than I would imitate the Negro and the Red Indian in discarding pronouns, or when going to 'London,' say that I am going to the chief city of the land in which we live."

We need only add that the book appears with an enlargement of its type, and opening out of its textual matter, and that it has a complete index of subjects and of words.

The specimen number[3] which Herr Bockemüller has forwarded of his edition of the Georgics contains little more than an introduction. The introduction gives a clear analysis of the various books, and numerous specimens of (German) translations. We should have liked to have seen more of the text and commentary.

Doctor Ljunberg's edition of Horace is a fearful and wonderful work. Upon opening it the reader must be seized with a feeling resembling vertigo, so strangely do the familiar yet unknown lines present themselves to his sight.

"Jam satis terrorum abiit. Deorum
Non dies miscet pater hac rubente
Dextera, sacras jaculans qua in arce
Terruit urbem."

In vain he turns the page:

"Cui fluxam relavas comam
Supplens munditias?"

"Dulce ridentem ad Lalagen redibo,
Dulce loquentem.

"Ne sit ancillæ tibi amor pudori,
Xanthia, posco."

But it is superfluous to quote throughout this curious edition, the ancient landmarks are removed, the solid ground is shaken, no ode stands as we know it; a depraved and licentious text runs riot where we expect the words of Horace. The preface does not supply an elucidation. The editor does not state upon what principles his prodigious changes are based. He believes in them himself, and thinks that finally they will be universally adopted; "post decem, opinor, aut

[3] "Virgils Georgica, Nach Plan und Motiven erklärt." Von F. Bockemüller, Stade. Verlag von F. Steudel.

[4] "Q. Horatii Flacci Carmina Lyrica, ex intimæ artis criticæ præceptis emendata." Edidit Nicol. Guil. Ljunberg, Doct. Phil. Carolstadii. Ex officina typographica Caroli Kjellin.

summum viginti annos" is his modest computation. A few lines further on in his preface is suggested that which we think the explanation of his work. "Me gravi morbo jam diu laborantem usque eo superstitem fore non est credibile." He died in July, 1872, and the second volume which was to have enunciated his principles has not appeared. Meanwhile there are few who will not regard these melancholy pages with a feeling which is best described in the lines of Horace :—

> "Credite, Pisones, isti tabulæ fore librum
> Persimilem, cujus, *velut ægri somnia* vanæ
> Fingentur species : ut nec pes, nec caput uni
> Reddatur formæ."

Mr. L. Campbell has published two more plays in his version of the works of Sophocles.[7] We may say unhesitatingly that we prefer this translation to any preceding rendering. The choruses run easily and well, and the verse of the speeches is good. Particularly admirable and true to Greek spirit is the stickomuthia.

To compass the essence of Plato within 197 short pages is a bold undertaking, if not an impracticable one. Still within that space Mr. Collins has given the English reader a fair bird's-eye view of the life and works of his author.[8] The extracts are well chosen, and he who has read this book will feel that he has breathed something of the divine Hellenic air which surrounds the greatest of the Athenians. Professor Jowett's work has been freely and advantageously used, but we must record our conviction that no author can be so little revealed to the merely "English reader" as Plato.

Mr. Sedgwick's brief editions of the Greek tragedians are now well known, and this last work[9] does not fall short of the others in merit. Nothing can be better adapted for boys in the forms of our public schools below the highest than his scenes from the Greek dramatists. In some respects we think the "Alcestes" superior to its predecessors. The preface is good, and does not ignore the merits of Mrs. Browning's translation. Mr. Sedgwick says of it : "It is a greater help to the true understanding of the drama than all the commentaries put together." But the whole selection is worthy of Mr. Sedgwick.

The Early English Text Society continues its good work of re-issuing those memorials of ancient language and literature which it guards and preserves.[10] Mr. Skeat's edition of the "Vision of Piers Plowman" is an admirable work, with a learned preface and good

---

[7] "The King Œdipus and Philoctetes of Sophocles." Translated into English Verse by Lewis Campbell, M.A., LL.D., Professor of Greek in the University of St. Andrews. W. Blackwood and Sons.

[8] "Ancient Classics for English Readers. Plato." By C. W. Collins, M.A., H.M. Inspector of Schools. Edinburgh : W. Blackwood and Sons.

[9] "Scenes from Euripides." Rugby Edition. By A. Sedgwick. "The Alcestes." Rivingtons.

[10] Publications of the Early English Text Society:
"Vision of William concerning Piers the Plowman." By William Langland.

critical notes. The first part of Mr. Wright's "Generydes" contains only a portion of the text. Mr. Blunt's "Myroure of Oure Ladye" has a good introduction, some quaint pictures, and a glossarial index.

BELLES LETTRES.

THE following quotation explains the title of "Jupiter's Daughters:"[1]—"The Prayers are daughters of the Great Jupiter. Tottering, and with a wrinkled brow, scarcely lifting their heads, they hasten anxiously after the steps of wrong." And the meaning of the title is made still more plain to us, when the authoress on the last page says in reference to the heroine:—"She had undertaken to bring her feelings into subjection to duty. Who can doubt her ultimate triumph, when her war-cry is—*God will, I shall.*" And yet the book is not "goody-goody." It is, on the contrary, a bright, crisp story of French life in the provinces and Paris. It is full of characters carefully individualized, and scenes which have been skilfully worked up to give effect to the characters. The story opens with a sketch of the little town of St. Eloi. The rich man of the place has suddenly died without any near relative. The heir appears, however, in the person of M. de Saye, unmarried and under thirty. The little town, of course, soon selects for him a wife in Mdlle. Pauline Rendu. But with M. de Saye comes his friend M. Vilpont, who, without the aid of the town, takes a fancy for the same young lady. The whole of the love-scenes are most tenderly and delicately sketched. M. Vilpont is witty and amusing. Mdlle. Rendu is innocent and charming. But who is this M. Vilpont, who, with his wit, and his jokes and poetry, has dropped from the clouds upon St. Eloi? He turns out to be a Bohemian, a writer of newspaper articles, and, still worse, of plays. After this we need not say that Mdlle. Pauline Rendu marries a certain M. Leon Subar, a rich stock-broker, or something of the sort, for we do not feel quite sure about his calling. But he is rich, and that is the main thing, and very good-looking, which also counts for something. At this point the interest of the story begins. "Dans l'opinion du monde, le mariage, comme dans la comédie finit tout. C'est précisement le contraire qui est vrai; il commence tout." So writes Madame Sevetchine, and upon this principle Mrs. Jenkin constructs her story. She begins where the generality of novelists

---

"Richard the Redeles." By the same Author. "The Crowned King." By another hand. Edited by the Rev. W. Skeat, M.A.

"Generydes." A Romance in seven-line stanzas. Edited from the unique MS. in Trinity College, Cambridge, by W. Aldis Wright, M.A. Part I.

"The Myroure of Oure Ladye." A devotional treatise on Divine service. Edited by John H. Blunt, M.A., F.S.A., Rector of Beverstone, Gloucester. London: Trübner & Co.

[1] "Jupiter's Daughters." By Mrs. Charles Jenkin, Author of "Two French Marriages," "Cousin Stella," "Who breaks Pays," &c. London: Smith, Elder, and Co. 1874.

end. And no one can for one moment doubt but that she is perfectly right. With marriage life in reality commences. Then comes the real test of character on both sides. Then the temper of the metal is proved. It is in analysis of character that Mrs. Jenkin shines. She probes, too, the social sores of the day. Here is a happy bit of satire:—"Her husband had been to her a species of necessary disease, somewhat analogous to vaccination" (p. 177). Here again is a truth neatly expressed,—"I have, *ma très chère*, but a poor opinion of men. How can I, when I see what fools we can make of them?" (p. 200): and here again,—"You men! pretty examples you set us, with your oscillations—now at the shrine of virtue, and piff-paff bowing the knee to some ugly Dalilah" (p. 202). But we might quote pages of such sayings. The whole of the third chapter in the second part, entitled "A French Play," is well worth a careful study. It gives in a few pages, in language which is as much marked by its reticence as by its passionate eloquence, some of the chief vices of modern life, especially married life. We cannot follow the fortunes of M. Leon Subar and his wife. It is enough to say that he is ruined in the crash of 1870, and flies from Paris and his creditors. Pauline becomes a Sister of Mercy under the Geneva Cross, and nurses her former lover, who is brought in frightfully wounded. The whole of the concluding scenes, during the siege, are most pathetically told, apparently by an eye-witness. Every portion of the book, however, is most carefully and conscientiously written, and we can recommend it as the best tale of French life which we have for a very long time read.

"Thorpe Regis"[1] is, we should suppose, written either by a clever, well-read, amiable woman, or clergyman. It is one of those novels which must give the author great pleasure to write, and the publisher to print. It is pre-eminently safe. Its tone disarms criticism. Such a book is sure of success. Yet we think that the writer might do far better things. Now and then she or he strikes a note, which shows that the meanness and frivolity of ordinary life are fully apprehended. Here is a passage in which the cynicism is not unpleasant:—

"'There goes Sir Peter, on his way to patronize the Association, I'll be bound. He'll walk up to the front, and believe they know all about him, how many pheasants he has in his coverts, and what a big man he is in his own little particular valley. Why shouldn't he?—we're all alike. I caught myself thinking that Parker would be astonished if he could only see my Farleyense; and there's Charles as proud as a peacock over his Homer that he's going to display, and Mrs. Jones thinking all the world will be struck with the frilling in which she'll dress up her ham, and so we go on,—one fool very much like another fool. And as the least we can do is to humour one another, and as to judge from the shops, the Association has in it a largely devouring element, I'll go and look after Mrs. Jones' lobster" (vol. ii. p. 80).

That the majority of the world are fools, and that most men and women are merely "one couple more" has been said over and over again by philosophers, but has hardly been sufficiently dwelt upon by

---

[1] "Thorpe Regis." By the Author of "The Rose Garden," "Unawares," &c. London: Smith, Elder, and Co. 1874.

our novelists. The writer, we think, might with profit indulge a little oftener in this vein of sarcasm. The touch about the Association and the lobster is also good, and reminds us of Lord Dudley's comment on the death of a friend,—"He was a good man—an excellent man; he had the best melted butter I ever tasted in my life." But not only does the author perceive this meanness of English conventional life, but constantly dwells upon its only true corrective—the beauties of Nature. His painting of scenery is quite pre-Raphaelite. The writer has evidently made a study of the fields, and woods, and lanes at every season of the year. He delights, too, in colour. Here is a delicious little bit:—

"It was a spring afternoon, one of those days in which sudden surprises of shade and brightness alternate with each other. Now and then an intensity of light flashed out from a break in the grey hurrying clouds, and the young green of the larches and the tender pink blossoms of the elms grew vivid and sparkling under its touch; now and then it all faded into sober tints. A line of heavy blue marked the distant moorland; between a thinly-clothed network of branches might be traced a crowd of small fields, patches of red soil crossed by sombre lines of hedges, brown nests in the rookery swaying in the wind, a pear tree standing up in ghostly whiteness before the rent clouds" (vol. i. p. 192).

Again, too, take the following description of meadows seen after a heavy rain, just when the sky is clear and blue:—

"The meadow was transfigured with a depth of colours; there were rich patches of indigo and russet, poplars lighting up the sober background with streaks of brown light, breadths of freshly turned earth, infinite traceries springing from dark stems, a delicate sky broken by soft shadows and round masses of living light, little pools of shining beautiful water left by the rains, hedges ruddy with crimson berries, a white horse, an old man leaning on his stick—the picture was full of simple, homely grace" (vol. i. 251).

This is very different to the slap-dash style of most novelists. A writer who can do so well, can do a great deal better. Lastly, the author possesses no little humour. The story of the Sky-terrier, whose delight was to roll a newly washed Spitz in the mud is excellently told.

Sir James Kay-Shuttleworth[3] is somewhat too ambitious. We are perfectly overwhelmed with the number of his characters and the intricacy of his plot. We are whirled about to all quarters of the globe. We are treated to Italian and the purest Ribblesdale. We are instructed in law and investments, we have detailed descriptions of places such as would befit Murray's Handbook of Yorkshire. Now half or a quarter of all these good things would have been sufficient. A true artist beats out his gold. He does not give it to us in lumps. In spite of Sir James Kay-Shuttleworth's ingenious glosses, the Ribblesdale dialect becomes very fatiguing to the ordinary novel-reader. It would be doubtless intensely interesting to Prince Louis Lucien Bonaparte or Mr. Skeat. But novels unfortunately cannot be

---

[3] "Ribblesdale; or, Lancashire Sixty Years Ago." By Sir James Kay-Shuttleworth, Bart. London: Smith, Elder, and Co. 1874.

judged from a philological point of view. In a novel a little dialect goes a very long way. One quince in an apple-tart is all very well, but too many spoil it. So, too, of the descriptions of Ribblesdale scenery. They are very good, but they weary from repetition. Of course we are aware that a true Yorkshireman cannot have too much of Yorkshire. Now if we might venture to give a hint, we think that Sir James Kay-Shuttleworth might write a most interesting and valuable account of Ribblesdale. He would bring to the task many very rare and special accomplishments, such as are seldom combined in the local topographer. As it is we do not think that he possesses on the one hand the dramatic power, nor on the other hand, that light touch which are both required to enable any one to take a place in the first rank of novelists. Sir James Kay-Shuttleworth is a painstaking and exact writer, with a hundred times the knowledge of most novelists. But this knowledge is a hindrance to him as a novelist. It loads his pages. In a topographical work his learning would be seen to advantage.

"Too Late"[1] has many attractions. Soft grey-toned paper and large clear-cut type make it quite luxurious reading. A pleasant atmosphere of cultivated people, tastefully furnished rooms, well-appointed dinners, and all the belongings of well-to-do country life, have also without doubt a certain charm upon us. Still there is a less pleasant side of society, which the writer can paint with great force. We do not ever remember reading a more painful chapter than "Husband and Wife," in the last volume. The husband, a hard-worked, badly-paid literary man reproaches his wife for the expensive dress in which she is going to the opera. "Glad, you notice it at all; generally you notice nothing," is the substance of the reply. The husband again remonstrates about the expense,—"You do not expect my friends to give me a dress as well as a box at the opera," is the retort. What such a lady as this turns out may easily be guessed. We must give Mrs. Newman, too, credit for a good deal of dramatic power. The hackneyed subject, "Caught by the Tide," is treated with a great deal of freshness and originality. The concluding pages are finished in too much hurry. Laudanum and Steeplechases do their work a little too close together. But the writer was probably, as reviewers so constantly are, prevented by want of space from saying more.

"Ivan De Biron"[2] must not be confounded with ordinary novels. The ordinary novel plays its part in modern society, and a very useful part. Like a leading article in a paper, it is read one day and forgotten the next. The generality, too, of novel readers are not very critical. Any story does as long as there is plenty of love and excitement. Critics, too, are not very exacting. They are only too happy if they can, without recommending a positively harmful book, say a word of praise. They are aware, in spite of all the loud boasts to the contrary, that as a rule novel-writing is a poorly paid profession.

---

[1] "Too Late." By Mrs. Newman. London: Henry S. King and Co. 1874.

[2] "Ivan De Biron; or, The Russian Court in the Middle of Last Century." By the Author of "Friends in Council." London: W. Isbister and Co. 1874.

Hence we find so many an ephemeral tale praised in terms which might be applicable to *Hamlet*. But this custom has its disadvantages. When a book like "Ivan De Biron" appears, the critic is obliged to apply the same stereotyped praise, which he has just applied to some Minerva-press novel. The experienced reader, who has been so often deceived, passes the criticism by with a smile of incredulity. A really good novel is too good a thing for belief. Yet "Ivan De Biron" is this or nothing. It fulfils all the conditions of a good novel. The plot is good, the characters are interesting, the incidents natural, and the language, we need scarcely say, as in all of Sir Arthur Helps's writings, marked by beauty and dignity. But this is not all. The book is a full book. Every page abounds with knowledge of character, of the world, and of those men and women who play the most important parts in its destinies. We find ourselves in a different atmosphere to that of the ordinary novel. Both the late Lord Lytton and the present Premier have attempted the same themes. They have, as we have so frequently had occasion to say in these pages, signally failed. They have both of them mistaken the tinsel of sentiment and fine language for thought, and smart epigrammatic sayings for wisdom. Sir Arthur Helps has made no such mistake. There is no flashy writing in "Ivan De Biron." There are no epigrams for the sake of epigrams. The interest is derived from a much higher source. We watch with admiration, or sorrow how human beings play their parts in a world where there is so much misery and so much mystery, and where the little happiness which we enjoy is so largely dependent on our own conduct, and of those with whom we associate. We watch, too, with keen interest the growth of mind in the Queen, the conflict of wit, and plot and counterplot between rival politicians, the progress of a pure love between the two lovers, and last and most powerful of all the love for art—that highest love—in the actress Azra. These themes must possess an enduring interest for us all, as long as the world lasts. Character, in the largest sense of the word; art, too, in its largest sense, friendship, love, ambition—these things make up life. And with this, "Ivan De Biron" deals. The book is cramful of observations. Here is one on love:—"A man is seldom more respectful to all women than when he is very much in love with any one" (vol. ii. p. 34). To this we may add, that a woman is seldom more loving to all women, than when she is very much beloved by a man. Here is a subtle account of an artist's love, especially an actress's. "Their love, if love it may be called, is apt to be of a universal character, and appeals not to any one person, but to humanity in general" (vol. ii. p. 190). The same may be said, though of course the manner of showing it will be different, of the painter, the poet, and the philosopher. We find the same thought, or rather an extension of it, expressed by the Empress when speaking of Azra:—"All the time that soft-looking velvety-cheeked girl, to the outward eye so rich in woman's charms, was telling a story, I thought how like she was to a man, who would sacrifice anything to an idea—but very little for a person" (vol. iii. p. 62). And is not this love the very highest love possible? And have not the greatest pictures, the greatest poems, the greatest movements, the greatest reformations been achieved by this love? Here again is a comment worthy of a kind-hearted Rochefoucauld :—"When men talk about their hatred for all women, it merely means that there is some one woman whom they love very much, but who does not seem fully to appreciate their special merit" (vol. iii. p. 128). The next might have been written by Rochefoucauld in his ordinary mood :—"It certainly is a great merit in women that they do not mind the bloom being taken off the peach, especially when they have had some hand in removing it" (vol. iii. p. 177). In a somewhat similar strain of cynicism, a satirist has observed, that rakes take wives, as they do soda-water—after a debauch. Here, however, is an observation which we think far truer :—"A certain kind of familiarity (the familiarity, for instance, which must exist in a sick-room), endears men to women, but has not a similar effect or, at anyrate, not so great an effect upon men with regard to women" (vol. ii. p. 91). The explanation lies, perhaps, in the fact that much of woman's love proceeds from pity, pity for even downright helplessness, whereas a man's pity is oftener not akin to love but contempt. Now we have made all these extracts upon one single subject—love, and have not nearly exhausted Sir Arthur Helps's treatment of it. But there is scarcely a single passion which he does not treat with equal fulness, shrewdness, and versatility. Statecraft, operas, exile, joys of private and public life are all dwelt upon by one who has long and deeply thought on all their manifold bearings. The stamp of thought is impressed upon every page. Even in places where descriptions of scenery, and where word-painting might have been indulged in, Sir Arthur Helps instead gives us a graceful, sparkling little essay. A noticeable instance of this may be seen in his account of a batch of exiles reaching Siberia. Instead of giving us, as most novelists would certainly have done, a picture of a Siberian pine forest, Sir Arthur Helps analyses for us its peculiar charms. He shows in what its beauties consist. He dwells on the fact how each of our senses, hearing, sight, and smell are delighted in a Siberian forest. He recounts the variety of colours, diversity of odours, and "that low murmuring noise,"—the *ψιθύρισμοι* of the fir-wood in Theocritus,—"which prevents solitude and scarcely hinders silence." And then he goes on to show in a somewhat Dantean strain, how much a forest resembles human life,—the individual tree dwarfed and stunted like the individual human being in the crowded city. His landscapes are, like everything else in his book, informed with thought. We cannot bestow higher praise on any work.

"Lady Moretoun's Daughter"* opens capitally. The picture of the poor Oxford "coach," who has thrown up all his chances of preferment at the University by marrying a pretty face, is evidently taken from life. The surroundings, too, are all in keeping. The fire is out and there are no coals. The "slavey" is only to be seen at such places. She dirties everything except what she breaks. The

* "Lady Moretoun's Daughter." By Mrs. Eiloart, Author of "The Curate's Discipline," "St. Bede's," "Woman's Wrong," &c. London: Henry S. King and Co. 1873.

young men, too, are well done, and their conversation is characteristic. But we think that Mrs. Eiloart is more at home in the country. Her descriptions of Helsdon Green and Helsdon House are full of poetry. Helsdon Green was close to London, and yet to all appearances miles away from it. It was one of those "Greens" such as you may see in Devonshire or Warwickshire. All the houses upon it had been built a hundred or two hundred years ago. Each stood in its own grounds. Here the old fashioned roses bloomed in abundance, and thick ivy clothed the walls. And everybody knew each other on the "Green." There was Miss Beauville, the great lady of the place, who owned most of the land, and then, of course—there always is—a half-pay Captain in such a village. Then there was the half-pay Captain's sister, "a widow lady of great family and very small income," and Mr. Burton, the microscopist and naturalist, and his daughter Euphemia, a devourer of novels. Each of these people, and there are a vast number more aunts and cousins, have a distinct individuality of their own. Their peculiarities are carefully preserved. Mrs. Eiloart has a very quick eye for characteristics. The love scenes are prettily touched in between Maurice and Phemie. Mrs. Eiloart is always at her best in short sketches. In the third volume the interest is quickened, and the scenes are more exciting. But we hardly like Mrs. Eiloart so well in them as in the first volume. Her strength lies in depicting quiet character, old maids, old servants, and in drawing scenes of homely life. Her book may with confidence be recommended to members of circulating libraries in the country, who will probably remember many similar scenes to those which take place in "Lady Moretoun's Daughter."

Mrs. Macdonald's "Nathaniel Vaughan"[7] is a novel quite above the average, both because it is written in remarkably good English—no slight merit in these days of slipshod work—and because, a matter that is much more important, it is a really artistic composition, with a sound moral expressed, though not obtruded, on the canvas. Readers who like only Miss Braddon's sort of novels, or Mr. Anthony Trollope's, will not care for it; but admirers of George Eliot will be glad to find, not at all a servile imitation of her style of work, but an independent and respectable study of character in the law of circumstance such as even George Eliot might not have been ashamed to own as her first novel. The theme is almost too painful, but life is often painful, and the book is only true to life. Nathaniel Vaughan, its hero, is a well-meaning priest of the Church of England, who thinks it his duty to purge out of himself the world, the flesh, and the devil by rigid asceticism, and to enjoin on others at least as much self-mortification as he deems necessary for his own spiritual advantage. A more vigorous presentment of the mischievous nature of modern Christianity in its most honest and consistent form need not be desired. The priest tries his hardest to be a devout Christian and to Christianize his flock. On most of his flock he produces no

[7] "Nathaniel Vaughan: Priest and Man." By Frederika Macdonald, Author of "The Iliad of the East," "Xavier and I," &c. In Three Volumes. London: Hurst and Blackett.

effect at all, and of the few members of it who come under his influence all turn against him and break away from his teaching without being able to shake off all its pernicious effects. The most notable of these is a Faith Daintree, whom he carefully wins from the world, only to turn her into a hypocrite and very nearly into a harlot. But the two heroines, if we may call them so, never come fairly under his influence. One is a little girl, Winifred, whom the priest adopts in the hope of fashioning her from infancy according to his ideal, and who, after a year or so of miserable oppression, is saved from further ruin by an early death. The other, Missy Fay, is the Undine-like daughter of a sceptic, who resists his teaching from the first, and is at last married happily to his favourite disciple, whom she has been the main instrument in converting from a devout Christian into as thorough a sceptic as herself or her father. We do not think Mrs. Macdonald improves her novel by filling Nathaniel Vaughan with an infatuated passion for Missy Fay, but this helps her to show how utterly worthless is his faith, and to furnish a dramatic, if not a melodramatic, climax to the story. The story is certainly a very bold and trenchant attack on Orthodoxy, and the earnestness with which it is made throughout is not marred by the grace and humour with which its lighter passages are told. Altogether this novel is one to be grateful for, and we shall be disappointed if it is not followed by better ones from the same skilful hand.

A short time since there appeared in the *Cornhill Magazine* a poem, "The Swallows," by Mrs. Webster, which excited by its feeling and beauty general attention. There was nothing to be surprised at in this, for the poem thoroughly deserved the admiration which it received, but in the fact that the public did not seem even to know Mrs. Webster's name. Habent sua fata libelli. A flashy novel sells by thousands on the railway book-stalls, whilst a genuine poem, like Mrs. Webster's "Auspicious Day," is treasured up only by one or two students of poetry. Yet the explanation is easy enough. A true poet must make his audience. He must in fact educate the public up to his level. Only here and there will he at first find a few sympathetic minds. This was the case with Keats, with Wordsworth, with Browning. Each struck a new note, to which the public was not accustomed. The same is the case with Mrs. Webster. She has just put forth a new volume "Yu-Pe-Ya's Lute, a Chinese Tale." * Of course an objection will be raised to the title. But a public which daily at dinner admires the Chinese willow plate, need not assume airs on this matter. The story is very simple. Yu-Pe-Ya having left his native land when young, and having made his fortune, and being in honour with the Emperor, returns to see it. But his stay must be short, as he is required at Court. He begs as a favour to be allowed to go back down the great river which flows through the land. The beaten road will take him away too quickly, but the

* "Yu-Pe-Ya's Lute: a Chinese Tale." In English Verse. By Augusta Webster, Author of "The Auspicious Day," "Portraits," &c. London: Macmillan and Co. 1874.

great river will lead from town to town, and wind about the meadows, and pass underneath the mountains, traversing the whole land. And the boon which he craves is granted. So Yu-Pe-Ya embarks, and the river bears him away, and with him he takes his lute, his "second heart." Wordsworth first taught us how nature ever sympathizes with man, and how she ever puts on the colours of the spirit. Mrs. Webster has extended the lesson. She has set the old myths of Amphion and Orpheus to modern music. Yu-Pe-Ya's lute sympathizes with every passing mood of its master. It interprets himself to himself, as all those who have felt the spell of music know. To him it is—

"The nearest love he had, nearer and more
Than wife or babes, for ever to him it bore
The sweet and subtle echoes of his thought,
And sudden answers to the things he sought,
Like soul to equal soul when each one shares
The other's fulness" (p. 6).

So the solitary man embarks with his lute. We wish that we had space to give some of Mrs. Webster's descriptions not merely of the scenery, but Yu-Pe-Ya's feelings as he pours them forth in song, which the lute helps him to interpret. But a storm suddenly comes on, and the ship is run into a creek. Yu-Pe-Ya finds his consolation in his lute. Suddenly the strain broke. A chord had snapped. Yu-Pe-Ya knew the sign. He had been overheard. The listener is only a simple woodman. Will this boor judge my lute? asks Yu-Pe-Ya.

"Ill said, my lord; unworthy words I hear
For such as thou to speak. And art thou then
A master minstrel, yet will measure men
By only rich and low?" (p. 13).

With these words the woodman leaves him. But Yu-Pe-Ya sends after him, and finds him not the boor he thought, but

"One who knows
The answering rhythms, the complex harmonies,
The difficult skill, knows the deep mysteries
And far traditions of the lute; *who hears*
As lovers see, to whom each look appears
Familiar long and yet a fresh surprise,
Teaching new beauty to accustomed eyes" (p. 13).

The lines, which we have italicized, appear to us for delicacy of sentiment to be unrivalled in modern poetry. We must go back to Shakspeare and Milton to hear the praises of music sung in higher strains. Space warns us to be brief, and we must, most unfairly condense the story. Yu-Pe-Ya and the woodman become, not friends but brothers—

"Both seemed to teach,
And both to learn the things they most had known,
As though 'twere not to know to know alone
And each had missed the other heretofore" (p. 25).

At last they part. Yu-Pe-Ya returns to the Court, with a promise, however, that he will come back next year to see his brother, as he calls him. As he departs he leaves two ingots of gold in the woodman's hands. The year goes, and Yu-Pe-Ya keeps his word and returns. But the gold has brought a curse. The woodman is dead. How he dies we will not reveal. We have already done the story great injustice. This is the most beautiful part, and should be given as a whole or not at all. The story is from beginning to end full of beauties. We have already in this *Review* expressed an opinion that Mrs. Webster's strength is in song-writing. The songs in Yu-Pe-Ya's Lute possess all the sweetness of an Elizabethan lyric. Here is one which might have been written by Beaumont and Fletcher—

"Waiting, waiting. 'Tis so far
To the day that is to come:
One by one the days that are
All to tell their countless sum;
Each to dawn and each to die—
What so far as by-and-by?

"Waiting, waiting. 'Tis not ours
This to-day that flies so fast:
Let them go, the shadowy hours
Floating, floated into Past.
Our day wears to-morrow's sky—
What so near as by-and-by?" (p. 33).

But undoubtedly the most powerful song in the volume is the dirge which Yu-Pe-Ya sings over his brother's grave. There is passion about it, which at last subsides into tones of noble resignation. We close the book with a renewed conviction that in Mrs. Webster we have a profound and original poet. Yu-Pe-Ya's Lute is marked not by mere sweetness of melody—rare as that gift is—but by the infinitely rarer gifts of dramatic power, of passion, and sympathetic insight.

Does the public read plays? Is Shakspeare read by any one but a few students? The man who ventures on a closet play in these days and expects an audience, expects that which Shakspeare certainly has not. Of course Professor Nichol does not at this hour hope for any revival of the tragic drama. The course of the stage is downward. Farce, burlesque, melodrama, spectacle, and ballet are the amusements of the public. Some two thousand years separate Professor Nichol from the Victorian playwright. He is more akin to Sophocles than to Mr. Tom Taylor. Professor Nichol has thrown his fine poem of "Hannibal"* into a dramatic form, simply because his whole tone is dramatic. He throws himself into each of his characters. He speaks through them. There is a curious mixture, however, of the antique and modern in some of the speeches. We need not now go into the character of Hannibal. He may at least, and Professor Nichol seems to admit the resemblance, have been in one moral trait like our own Nelson.

* "Hannibal: a Historical Drama." By John Nichol, B.A. Oxon., Regius Professor of English Language and Literature in the University of Glasgow. London: Macmillan and Co. 1873.

This is not what we are thinking of. Professor Nichol seems now and then to be lecturing us moderns through his heroic republicans. When Hasdrubal speaks, we can fancy that he is rebuking our own peace-at-any-price party. The *εἷς οἰωνὸς ἄριστος* has seldom been translated into nobler English—

"Of our power
We owe to valiant ventures half the sum.
Caution's a virtue that o'ercharged is vice,
And dull content is poverty of soul.
Who shuns offence and holds with neither side,
Who dreads the deep and never dares to swim,
Who fears to trip and never tries to run,
May yet in walking stumble. By this peace
We are allowed to live, to crouch at home,
To render thanks to Rome for Africa.
Go, plume you on your policy, which pays
Best service by worse faith."

But this high strain is the note of Hannibal. The drama is pitched throughout in a high key. In Myra's speeches we have the ring of antique valour. She speaks about her son as some noble Spartan matron might have done in Lacedæmon's noblest days. In the same high spirit is conceived the conversation between Hamilcar and Hasdrubal concerning the nature and attributes of the gods—

"The gods who rule the earth are far removed,
Their dwelling place is all the round of Heaven.
The stars, the moon, the hill-tops and the sea,
The sun himself, are but their sentinels.
Their temples are the oracles that stand
Nigh to the gates of their serene abodes;
They come there, when we meet them with a heart
That has a single aim, and with a voice
That speaks their language."

Throughout the poem there is this solemnity of tone. The play is religious in the highest sense of the word. There is an elevation about it very different to the mere hedonism of the newest school of modern poetry. Death is celebrated in strains which Harmodius and Aristogeiton might have sung—

"'Tis well to live for glory, home, and land;
And when these fail us, it is well to die.
The latest freedom never fails our band,
From scornful Earth, on wings of scorn, to fly."

And here we may remark upon the beauty of the lyrics which are scattered with so lavish a hand throughout "Hannibal." They resemble the odes in a Greek play rather than the songs in our own dramatists. The latter too often are only put in to fill up the stage business. But the former are always bound up with the play, and interest us not only from their beauty, but the light which they throw on the whole drama. Nor must we omit to notice the moral apophthegms, which Professor Nichol so skilfully introduces also in the manner of the Greek dramatists. Here is one, "who cannot hate need never hope to love," and here is another, "dregs and scum, twin plagues of patriots." But they should be read with the context in order that their full meaning may be brought out. We have only touched upon a few points in this very remarkable poem. It stands out alone by itself from all other modern poems. Its charm rests upon its lofty ideas, and its solemn sense of the nobleness of a high and unselfish life.

"Poems and Sonnets"[10] are evidently the production of a young man. Sonnets, unless they have some special "note," like Wordsworth's and Milton's, are seldom read. The "sugared" sonnets of Shakspeare are not popular. Stevens used to declare that not even an Act of Parliament could make them popular. Now, Mr. Barlow's poems and sonnets are, if he will pardon us the expression, sometimes of the "sugared" order. He has probably, without knowing it, been influenced by the feeling of the day. And a man may resemble another in his style without having read him. Influences are, as it were, in the air. The series of poems "Under the Gaslight," appears to us to represent much of the spirit of the rising generation of poets. Mr. Barlow writes not merely fluently, but with a command of both language and thought. His ideas are thoroughly under his control. Again, the series of poems "Christ is not Risen," well represent much of the spiritual unrest—for we have no better title—of the day. It would be utterly impossible, judging by the present volume, to say what Mr. Barlow may do. His verse is full of promise. But to say this is little. We should advise him to wait several years before he again publishes. He will by that time be a far better judge of his own powers than any of his critics.

The four friends who contribute "Songs for Music,"[11] are Juliana H. Ewing, Greville I. Chester, Stephen H. Gatty, and Reginald A. Gatty. The songs are all very pretty, but somewhat thin in thought. We have no doubt, however, that they admirably suit the purpose for which they are intended.

"Metrical Translations"[12] is an unassuming pleasant volume, which may be recommended, not so much perhaps to scholars as to those who wish to know what it is that scholars find so beautiful in the Greek and Latin poets. They will here become acquainted with some of the most famous passages from Homer, Æschylus, and Sophocles not unworthily rendered, and some dainty bits from Catullus, for whose beauties Mr. Boswell seems to have a special liking.

"Fretwork"[13] and "Waves and Caves"[14] are of the ordinary stamp.

---

[10] "Poems and Sonnets." By George Barlow, Ex. Coll. Oxon. Part III. London: John Camden Hotten. 1871.

[11] "Songs for Music." By Four Friends. London: Henry S. King and Co. 1874.

[12] "Metrical Translations, from Greek and Latin Poets: and other Poems." By R. B. Boswell, M.A. Oxon. London: Henry S. King and Co. 1874.

[13] "Fretwork: a Book of Poems." By C. E. Bourne. London: Simpkin, Marshall, and Co. 1874.

[14] "Waves and Caves: and other Poems." By Cave Winscom. London: Basil Montagu Pickering. 1873.

"Versicles,"[15] on the other hand, deserve high praise if only for this one epigram—

> "Classic Querno in the size
> Of his works is very wise;
> For he prints to sell, and so
> Prints them all in folio—
> Knowing that the biggest books
> Are preferred by pastrycooks."

We once heard a grocer say he liked the *Saturday Review* best of all newspapers, because a page of it held exactly a pound of sugar.

Sir Vincent Eyre's "Lays of a Knight-Errant in many Lands"[16] can hardly be called poetry. When we look at its bulk and size, we are tempted to repeat the epigram on "Classic Querno." We give a hearty welcome to new editions of Buchanan's "Ballads and Romances,"[17] and Bryant's "Poems,"[18] but can hardly do the same to Mr. Fosbroke's "Rheingold"[19] or Mr. Bickersteth's "Yesterday, To-day and for Ever."[20]

"Cupid and Chow-Chow"[21] is an amusing collection of stories which may suit old as well as young. The first tale, from which the volume takes its name, is as good as any. Cupid is a little five-year old, so called from his resemblance to the god, especially in his blindness in love matters. He has, however, neither wings, nor arrow, nor dart. He is the most inoffensive, dimpled, golden-haired lover conceivable. He falls desperately in love with his little cousin, Chow-Chow, who resembles the preserve of that name, and has as much sour as sweet in her composition. The course of such love runs very unsmoothly. Chow-Chow is an ardent disciplinarian, an advocate of the Rights of Women, probably a supporter of "Women's Whisky War," and, if we may just hint a defect in such a character, somewhat of a tomboy. Poor Cupid is no match for such a Yankee Amazon. "Free speech, free love, free soil, free everything; and Woman's Puckerage for ever!" cries the little lady. She soon puts her theories into action. She cuts off poor Cupid's golden locks, covers his dimples with sticking-plaster, and nearly chops off his fingers to test his bravery. After Cupid has successfully passed through all these ordeals, he is allowed to play at husband. This is decidedly the cleverest part of the story. The satire is here keener and better

---

[15] "Versicles: from the Portfolio of a Sexagenarian." London: Longmans, Green, Reader, and Dyer. 1873.

[16] "Lays of a Knight-Errant in many Lands." By Sir Vincent Eyre, K.C.S.I., C.B., Major-General, &c. London: Henry S. King and Co. 1874.

[17] "The Poetical Works of Robert Buchanan." Vol. I.: Ballads and Romances; Ballads and Poems of Life. London: Henry S. King and Co. 1874.

[18] "Poems." By William Cullen Bryant. Collected and Arranged by Himself. Author's Edition. London: Henry S. King and Co. 1874.

[19] "Rheingold: a Romantic Legend." Second Edition. And "The Bridal of Fortinbras." By John Baldwin Fosbroke. London: Provost and Co. 1873.

[20] "Yesterday, To-day, and for Ever." A Poem in Twelve Books. New Edition. By Edward Henry Bickersteth, M.A. London: Rivingtons. 1874.

[21] "Cupid and Chow-Chow. And other Stories." By Louisa M. Alcott. London: Sampson Low, Marston, Low, and Searle. 1873.

directed. The two little people remind us, and in no way to Miss Alcott's disparagement, of one of Dickens's most beautiful Christmas stories, where two little things run away to some child's Gretna Green. To draw children is by no means the easy matter commonly supposed. Authors generally succeed in making them childish instead of childlike. One or two great names, both in literature and art, stand supreme in painting infancy, when, as Coleridge says, "body and spirit are in unity." We hope Miss Alcott may draw many more such Twoshoes, such as Reynolds might have painted.

"You may tell a carpenter," says the proverb, "not by the quantity but the shape of his chips." We may say the same of Miss Thackeray's miscellaneous writings.[8] These are the chips from her workshop, not quite entitled to the German title Gedankenspäne, but still good serviceable chips. The book takes its name from the first essay. Who the "Toilers and Spinsters" are we need not say. With tender pathos Miss Thackeray writes, "it demands a degree of public sympathy for this particular class, which would be insulting almost in individual cases." And there is the greatest difficulty to find out those who do need relief. Many a well-educated and refined gentlewomen has, when brought to poverty by some reverse of fortune, died literally of starvation rather than reveal her distress. It is easy enough to call this spirit false pride. We will not pretend to judge. But we do say that it is a monstrous thing in a rich country like England, where riches are to many people a perfect burden and curse, not knowing what to do with them, that such a state of things should exist as Miss Thackeray's pages disclose. What is the cure for this great evil of the day it would be out of our place to discuss in this portion of the *Westminster Review*. Much has lately been done, but very much more remains. Not until women have obtained the so-much ridiculed "Rights of Women," not until they are brought up very differently to what they are now, will this terrible distress even partially be cured. We say partially, because we are by no means so hopeful as many are. As long as the world is constituted as it is, as long as life has to be lived by competition, so long will the weakest, and women are undoubtedly the weakest, suffer. But it is our duty to see that the inequality between the sexes is not made greater than Nature has already made it. Miss Thackeray's next essay is on a less painful subject. She deals with that most delightful of novelists, Jane Austen. Every word of her criticism is worth weighing. Perhaps one of the most important points she touches upon is the difference between the higher class of novel of the present day and that of the last generation. It is difficult, as Miss Thackeray observes, to determine how much each novel "reflects of the times of which it was written; how much of its character depends upon the mind and the mood of the writer." And Miss Thackeray goes on to say, "the living writers of the day," pointing, we should suppose, to one novelist in particular, "lead us into

---

[8] "Toilers and Spinsters: and other Essays." By Miss Thackeray, Author of "Old Kensington," "The Village on the Cliff," &c. London: Smith, Elder, and Co. 1874.

distant realms and worlds undreamt of in the placid and easily contented gigot age." Again, in another very clever and amusing essay, "Heroines and their Grandmothers," she reverts to the subject. No answer, perhaps, can be given, or rather no answer to which a dozen people would agree. But such considerations as Miss Thackeray puts before us, help us to estimate Jane Austen's weaknesses and shortcomings. Of passion, such as in all ages has formed the novelist's and dramatist's chief theme—for the novel and drama only essentially differ in form—we have not a trace. Love, with Miss Austen, is a very prosaic feeling. Of religion she seems to know little, except that it is a form established by the State, and that some clergymen, like Mr. Collins, make very amusing characters. To philosophy there is no pretence in her pages. But these blanks, great as they are, are not the only ones. We meet no sympathy with anything, except with what is fashionable and respectable. Music and painting are mere accomplishments. Not one of her characters ever betrays any enthusiasm. She herself, never steps out of the way to describe the beauties of a sunset, or a landscape. The seasons go by in her pages without a remark on their loveliness. Winter is known only by its balls, and summer by its picnics. But we have already sufficiently played the devil's advocate. Those who wish to know in what Jane Austen's great merits really consist should, by all means, study Miss Thackeray's most sympathizing and intelligent paper. The other articles in the volume are all equally good. Many of them consist of letters to our contemporary *The Pall Mall Gazette*, which attracted attention on their appearance, and will again be read with pleasure. In "Five o'Clock Tea" there are some curious speculations on literary work. In spite of the high authority quoted we cannot say that the statement that "the eighth hour is often worth all the others put together," agrees with our own experience. It reminds us rather of an old definition of eloquence, "speaking nonsense till sense comes." It is not, we suppose, necessary to formally recommend Miss Thackeray's book to our readers.

Mr. Bardsley's volume on "English Surnames"[22] is a very good specimen of the work which the nineteenth century can turn out in such abundance. Every year the Universities send out a number of men, highly trained and educated, who are capable of writing well upon any subject to which they may give their attention. And Mr. Bardsley has evidently bestowed a great deal of attention not only upon surnames, but upon philology in general. The great fault of his book is a tendency to flippancy and weak jokes. His jokes, too, are not always new. His derivation of "ostler," as if "oat-stealer," has, to our knowledge, been in print at least thirty years. He is sometimes also inaccurate; but his inaccuracy evidently often proceeds rather from haste than ignorance. Thus in his preface he talks about "Miss Muloch's 'History of Christian Names,'" a sentence in which there is a little nest of blunders. So, too, at page 144 he misquotes Piers Plowman:—

[22] "Our English Surnames: Their Sources and Significations." By Charles Wareing Bardsley, M.A. London: Chatto and Windus. 1874.

"Death cam dryvynge after,
And al to duste passed
Kynges and Knyghtes."

By writing "passed" for "pashed," Mr. Bardsley weakens the whole force of a magnificent passage. "Pash," we may notice, is used by Shakspeare. "With my armed fist, I'll pash him over the face," says Ajax in "Troilus and Cressida" (act ii. sc. 3), and the word is still a provincialism in the North East of Yorkshire, especially in the saying, "He'll pash oop all afore him." Again, we think Mr. Bardsley is hardly correct, when he makes Ashurst and Ashley (pp. 92, 93), to be connected with ash, the tree. We, on the other hand, should be disposed to refer both words to the Welsh *wysg*, a current. Mr. Bardsley should turn to Mr. Isaac Taylor's "Words and Places," where under Esk he will find a vast amount of information on the subject. Mr. Bardsley may be able, we are aware, to quote authorities in favour of the ash-tree derivation, but he should have given us the choice of the other derivation. Again, we do not feel quite sure that Mr. Bardsley is right in translating "Wonte" by weasel (p. 118). Is it not rather a mole, still preserved in our South country provincialism "wont," or "want," as Mr. Bardsley himself notices at pages 202 and 413? But these are very small blemishes where there are so many merits. The book is a mine of information and amusement, and we can strongly recommend it both to circulating libraries and to schools.

Dr. Mackay's "Lost Beauties of the English Language"* is a well-intentioned book. But it must be used with great caution. Generally speaking, the advice "verbum insolitum tanquam scopulum vitare," cannot with impunity be neglected. The man makes his style. Carlyle uses words which no one else dare to use. They are right and proper in his pages, though even with him they not seldom wear an air of affectation and extravagance. Our poets, too, especially Tennyson, Browning, Rossetti, Morris, and many others, have of late years given new life to many a long-forgotten word. Mr. Furnivall and Mr. Skeat, too, in prose have shown us the wonderful resources of our English language. But after all, each one must choose for himself. Words are to the literary artist what colours are to the painter. Language, too, has its own laws. Some years since there was a great controversy as to which was most proper for the English people to use "to telegram," or "to telegraph," or "to telegrapheme." We forget now which we were ordered to use. But since that day an unsuspected word has sprung up, and beaten all three out of the field. Both in the United States and in England the commercial world now says "to wire." The doctrine of the "survival of the fittest" holds good in language. Dr. Mackay's book may with discrimination be used as a sort of gradus. Still it should not be allowed to lie about. We should be afraid of its effects upon any young writer, especially in the *Daily*

* "Lost Beauties of the English Language: an Appeal to Authors, Poets, Clergymen, and Public Speakers." By Charles Mackay, LL.D., &c. London: Chatto and Windus. 1874.

Telegraph, who discovered that, according to Dr. Mackay, "gutter-slush" and "jobber-noule" were among the lost beauties of the English language. But Dr. Mackay does not often fall into such mistakes. He has evidently taken much trouble with his work, and we have to thank him for having given us in such a convenient form so many words which illustrate both the great beauty and the great wealth of our mother-tongue.

Many, however, of the words which Dr. Mackay gives us amongst the lost beauties of the English language are still in common use amongst our peasantry. We are, therefore, especially glad to receive that portion of "The Transactions of the Manchester Literary Club,"[15] which deals with the Lancashire Glossary. The Committee of the Glossary have now fairly got to work. Mr. Nodal, the chairman, gives an account of what has been already done. We are glad to see that both he and Dr. Ernest Adams have adopted Mr. Skeat's plan of registering every word in each district, in opposition to that proposed by the *Saturday Review*. As Dr. Adams rightly says, "to limit a county glossary to the words peculiar to that county alone would be absurd, and it would also be impossible for them to say what words did not exist in other counties" (p. 21). Both he and Mr. Nodal also touched upon that most difficult of all questions, the pronunciation. We would suggest that if Mr. Ellis's Glossic Code could not be adopted in full—and we certainly think there are great difficulties in the way—some modification of it might be adopted. Mr. Ellis himself might be asked to draw up a more simple code for general use. It would, of course, be a great advantage if all the English dialects could be compiled under one system of pronunciation. We feel quite sure, by our own experience and that of others, that Mr. Ellis very much underrates the difficulties of his Glossic for ordinary capacities, especially in the country. Our fear is, that many persons who would gladly contribute to the work of collecting provincialisms, will be repelled by the labour of mastering so intricate a system of sound-symbols. As an example of the wealth of the Lancashire dialect, Mr. Nodal mentioned that in the Fylde district there were no less than three or four different pronunciations, and almost as many different dialects. But the most curious point remains to be mentioned—that "where a river was fordable, or crossed by a bridge, the dialect was the same on both sides of the river; but as soon as the river becomes unfordable, the dialect changed on both sides" (p. 24) The Society has begun its work well. It needs only to be carried on with the same spirit, and success is certain.

We gladly welcome the first volume of the "English Dialect Society."[16] It belongs to series B, and contains seven reprints of scarce and valuable glossaries. Before we notice them, however, we must

---

[15] "Transactions of the Manchester Literary Club. Session 1873-4. The Glossary of the Lancashire Dialect." Manchester: Alexander Ireland and Co. 1874.

[16] "English Dialect Society. Series B. Reprinted Glossaries." Edited by the Rev. Walter W. Skeat, M.A. London: Trübner and Co. 1873.

say a few words upon the general Introduction, written, we presume, by the editor, Mr. Skeat. It is full of valuable matter. Most important is Mr. Skeat's advice to word-collectors. He warns them not to omit words because they are common to several districts. "Quite common words," he most rightly says, "will acquire a new value and interest when duly labelled with the localities in which they are used, or when the pronunciation of them (often different in different districts) can be supplied." On the other hand, Mr. Skeat also warns word-collectors of precisely the opposite error of supposing that some word is peculiar to their own district, and to no other. He gives a very good instance of this from Mr. J. P. Morris's Furness Glossary. Mr. Morris rightly pointed out that the Furness *to year*, for this year, is used by Chaucer. But, rejoins Mr. Skeat, Chaucer was better acquainted with the Southern than the Northern Dialect, and we are not therefore surprised at the word turning up in Pegge's MS. Kentish Glossary, which was secured last year for the English Dialect Society at Sir Frederick Madden's sale. Again, Mr. Skeat most properly warns the word-collector against etymology. This is no part of his work. His duty is to register, and to register only. As Mr. Skeat says, "he, and only he, can supply the *true sense*, the *true use*, the *exact locality*, the statements as to whether it is *common* or *uncommon*, as to what *class of people* use it, and the like *practical details* which form the only true scientific basis for study." The italics, we may remark, are Mr. Skeat's. This work of simply registering may appear very humble, but it will be more valuable just now than any amount of etymology. The remaining portion of Mr. Skeat's Introduction is taken up with an account of the work which is in hand for the Society. We have only to say that the advice which he gives is excellent, and that further it is highly to his credit to have brought out the present instalment in so short a time. We now come to the Reprints of various Glossaries in the present volume, which have all been edited by Mr. Skeat. The first is a reprint of a glossary at the end of Hutton's "Tour to the Caves in the Environs of Ingleborough and Settle, in the West Riding of Yorkshire." [1781.] Hutton's book has long been very scarce, and the present handsome reprint is therefore a great boon. Mr. Skeat's work, as editor, we need not say, is most carefully done. We have collated the reprint with the original. Mr. Skeat has corrected one or two misspellings and misprints, such as "twinters" for "twinter," and re-arranged some of the words, but has in all cases given the reader due notice. The next series of reprints is taken from Marshall's volumes of "Rural Economy" of different counties. Marshall's volumes are not expensive, but are excessively cumbrous, so that these reprints in so handy a form will be very welcome. Marshall's West Devonshire Glossary has the advantage of being annotated by Mr. Shelly, who has also marked some of the pronunciation in glossic. This, too, we have collated with the original. The only remark we have to offer to the editor is whether it would not be as well for the English Dialect Society to adhere to one system of writing botanical scientific names. Marshall is not very particular, nor were botanists particular in his day. Mr.

Shelly's notes are excellent. Thus he corrects Marshall's statement that "Fairies" in the Devonshire dialect mean squirrels. Mr. Shelly adds that they mean polecats. And it is worth noticing that the French *belette* is derived by Diez from bella, and that our own urchin means both a hedgehog and a fairy. The last reprint in the volume is that of Dr. Willan's Glossary of the "Mountainous District of the West Riding of Yorkshire." As this glossary appeared in the seventeenth volume of "Archæologia," it was practically inaccessible, and the present re-issue, therefore, is not amongst the least of the many benefits in the present volume. This reprint, too, has the advantage of being annotated by Mr. F. K. Robinson, the well-known compiler of the "Whitby Glossary." We have, too, collated this with the original, and can bestow the same unqualified praise on the editor's work. In one or two places, where a word like "Arles" had been misplaced under "Arr," it is restored to its proper position. Altogether the present volume may be taken as an earnest of the future success of the English Dialect Society. We shall look forward with great interest to the next volume of reprints. Amongst them we would venture to suggest the glossary from Meriton's "Praise of Yorkshire Ale," [1697], and the still rarer, "The Obliging Husband and Imperious Wife, or, the West Country Clothier" [1717], in the Devonshire Dialect.

Lastly, we have a quantity of children's books. We do not exactly know whether they are part of the late Christmas literature, or whether the publishers intend them for Easter. Certainly they are of a much tamer character than the generality of Christmas books, and are most of them intended for girls. Perhaps boys read most at Christmas and girls at Easter. We do not pretend to have read the history of Elsie[97] as she is portrayed in three different volumes. By the help, however, of the illustrations, and by dips here and there, we can safely give a favourable account. "The Fairy Family"[98] consists not only of prose, but of verse of a much higher character than we generally find in such books. The illustrations and "getting up" are also remarkably good. "Fables and Fancies"[99] deserves the same high praise, whilst Lady Barker's "Sybill's Book"[100] has already, we believe, become a classic in the nursery and schoolroom.

---

[97] I. "Elsie Densmore." By Martha Farquharson. London: Henry S. King and Co. II. "Elsie's Girlhood." By Martha Farquharson. Same Publishers. III. "Elsie's Holidays at Rowlands." By Martha Farquharson. Same Publishers.

[98] "The Fairy Family: a Series of Ballads and Metrical Tales, Illustrating the Fairy Mythology of Europe." By Archibald Maclaren. London: Macmillan and Co. 1874.

[99] "Fables and Fancies." By Denis Francis. With Illustrations by J. B. Zwecker and Others. London: W. Isbister and Co. 1874.

[100] "Sybill's Book." By Lady Barker, Author of "Stories About." London: Macmillan and Co. 1874.

ART.

THE publishers of the present series of "The Works of James Gillray the Caricaturist,"[1] have had in view the production of a volume which should offer a popular, and at the same time a fairly complete picture of the activity and times of the artist, who in 1770, found political caricature in its struggling infancy, and whose unwearied pencil during the course of forty years brought the art to its fullest maturity. A selection from Gillray's caricatures was first published in parts by Messrs. Miller, Rodwell and Martin, and Blackwood of Edinburgh, about 1818, but the undertaking was never completed, and the series ended with Part IX. In 1830 Thomas McClean, who had secured a large proportion of the original copperplates of Gillray's works, brought out a set of impressions from them in a collected form in two volumes. Next, Mr. Henry Bohn, having become the possessor of the original copperplates of the series first published by Mrs. Humphrey, which had been reprinted in the edition of 1830, and having also obtained several large important plates chiefly published by Fores of Piccadilly, rearranged them in two divisions, and issued them in 1851 in one thick folio volume, the coarser subjects being collected in a supplementary form. Mr. Bohn also secured the co-operation of Mr. Thomas Wright, who with the assistance of Mr. R. H. Evans, prepared an account of the caricatures in an octavo volume to accompany the plates. But the form in which Gillray's Works were thus preserved was too costly for the general public, and it is for the general public that the present work is intended. Such subjects as would be likely to puzzle the average reader by their too distant allusion, or to offend him by their coarseness, have been suppressed, whilst in many cases only the more pungent portions of certain caricatures are given, in order to make room for the introduction of a wider selection than either of the hitherto published editions affords. This selection gathered from the best public and private sources is accompanied by a summary of events illustrated by the caricatures, and particulars regarding the personages depicted in them. It will be seen that the present publication does not afford the materials necessary for original study of Gillray's work. The reduced size of many of the cuts, and the partial selection made from others, preclude the possibility of our basing on them any estimate of Gillray's peculiar gift. For such a purpose as this, examination of impressions taken from the original copperplates can alone suffice. The volume before us is intended for and adapted to the service of the general reader, and not only contains all the information which he can possibly require, but is calculated to afford valuable assistance to special students of the time, and to be a useful introduction to the study of works which preserve the designs in their original dimensions. The engravings are carefully arranged in chronological

[1] "The Works of James Gillray, the Caricaturist; with the History of His Life and Times." Edited by Thomas Wright, M.A., F.R.S. London: Chatto and Windus.

order, and the execution of the accompanying text, which deals with the Works and Times of the artist, leaves nothing to be desired; it is full of information on every point which suggests itself, thorough, complete, well ordered, and written in simple and intelligible English. The introduction, which contains a short biography of Gillray, is scarcely so good in workmanship, and would seem to have been done by a different hand. The writer displays a slight tendency to phrase-making, and falls into the faults common to modern biographers. He incorporates picturesque guesses with his facts, and where matter is deficient supplies its place by the introduction of facts which are hardly relevant. The care and spirit with which the illustrations selected have been reproduced deserves the highest commendation. Achitophel in the Dumps (Fox seated desponding on a braying Ass) p. 71; Pitt as Fawning Bill, p. 90; Madame Schwellenberg gliding into Paradise, p. 137; Flemish characters; Sin, Death, and the Devil (Queen Charlotte, Pitt, and Thurlow), p. 146; and The Gout, p. 204; are designs distinguished by such fine qualities of expression, draughtmanship, and invention as render them interesting in themselves as works of art. We may say of the artist with George Cruikshank, "He that did these things was a great man, sir,—a very great man, sir!" We have noted however but few instances where all is noteworthy, for even such cuts as have no special artistic value are of the highest interest as pictures of contemporary life and manners, and the full series taken in conjunction with the explanatory text, form an attractive as well as a most desirable contribution to our knowledge of the political history of the period.

"A Gallery of Illustrious Literary Characters (1830-1838),"[a] is the title of a republication of sketches by Maclise, accompanied by notes written for the most part by William Maginn, which appeared originally in the pages of *Fraser's Magazine*. Some of these sketches reach excellence of a very high order, the best seem to be those which present the faintest traces of intentional caricature. Caricature in the hands of a born caricaturist is but rarely cruel, the victim himself may generally see his presentment without much suffering; but caricature in the hands of those not to the manner born, becomes a dangerous weapon, never unsheathed except with intent to kill. Throughout the long series of Gillray's works which we have just passed in review, we find scarcely a trace of personal animosity; his pencil is always good-humoured even when it is least flattering, but Maclise, whose daily studies would induce a habit of mind quite foreign to the attitude of the genuine caricaturist, now and then handles the unaccustomed tools with a cruel severity of intention, unredeemed by any touch of sympathy or compassion. The ghastly drawing of old Samuel Rogers, from which Goethe turned in humane disgust, and the equally offensive sketch of Harriet Martineau, are just specimens of

---

[a] "A Gallery of Illustrious Literary Characters (1830-38)." Drawn by the late Daniel Maclise, R.A. Accompanied with Notices, chiefly by the late William Maginn, LL.D. Republished from *Fraser's Magazine*. Edited by William Bates, B.A. London: Chatto and Windus.

what might have become in the hands of Gillray merely happy hits, but which the serious pencil of Maclise endues with a horrible bitterness. The blows are too weighty for joke, and amusing irony passes into the expression of brutal malevolence. By far the greater portion however of this Gallery, is filled by sketches of pure character, drawn with a master's force in design and power of abstraction. Extreme simplicity of line, and skilful science of arrangement command attention, and in every instance the power shown of distinctly individualizing the type is of a high order. Godwin is a fine example of subtle expression; the sketch of John Soane the architect; of Coleridge, infirm and aged, the Coleridge sheltered by Gillman through the last sad stage; of Cruikshank mounted on a beer barrel sketching the humours of the tavern; these are pictures which do indeed help us to realize facts. Lastly, let us name that which is perhaps the finest in the whole collection, the warning figure of Talleyrand sleeping after dinner by the fire, sleeping the heavy sleep of worn out decrepitude. His book has fallen from his nerveless hands between his feet, the candles which light his desolate slumbers gutter miserably down, whilst from the shelf above watch the busts of men once actors with him in the busy theatre from which they have passed into the shades whither he too is beckoned. Of Maginn's accompanying notes, Mr. Bates, the present editor, speaks in terms of high encomium, terms which are certainly not warranted either by their manner or their matter. He tells us that they are "pregnant with learning, and all aglow with the lambent humour of Aristophanes and Rabelais;" but a reader of even average cultivation will, we think, fail to detect the learning, whilst any person of taste must too surely be annoyed and offended by the all-pervading tone of slangy and rollicking cleverness, which enriches most of the articles with specimens of "bad style." Maginn himself, if he wrote the notice of Miss Martineau, had every reason to desire that his name should be suppressed.

Mr. Redgrave's "Dictionary of Artists of the English School"[a] is a most useful contribution to art-literature, the need of which has long made itself sensibly felt. It is the first work in the form of a dictionary which has been devoted exclusively to artists of the English School. Mr. Redgrave has included painters, sculptors, architects, engravers, and ornamentists; the materials have been collected with diligence, and no source of information has been neglected. Of course in the first essay towards the production of an *ouvrage d'ensemble*, lacunæ are sure to be discovered; but Mr. Redgrave seems to have done everything in his power to make the book as complete as possible. He has wisely included amongst his English artists, not only such foreigners as came to this country in their early youth, and who, like Fuseli, learnt their art here, practised it here, and died here, but also any foreign artists who have held any public employment or appointment here, or who have been connected with

---

[a] "A Dictionary of Artists of the English School: Painters, Sculptors, Architects, Engravers, and Ornamentists." By Samuel Redgrave. London: Longmans, Green, and Co. 1874.

the art institutions of the country, as for instance Dassier, Engraver to the Royal Mint in 1755, and Angelica Kauffman. The length of the notices does not vary in accordance with the importance of the artist noticed. To those who may object that names have been inserted of those who have left little behind them, or that a full account is given of the life of an obscure man, whilst those of greater men are passed over in a few short lines, Mr. Redgrave explains that in each case he has been guided by the materials at his disposal. Sometimes ample information exists concerning an indifferent artist, when a few meagre particulars are all that can be gleaned concerning one of eminence. In each case he has carefully collected, and faithfully preserved for us all that could be saved from oblivion, and in so doing has not only produced a convenient handbook but has brought together the materials for future use and study.

In Miss Tytler's "Modern Painters and their Paintings"[4] we find that notice of Reynolds and Romney, which she so strangely omitted from her "Old Masters and their Pictures," a volume which we reviewed last quarter. Why Miss Tytler put Greuze into the Old Masters and reserved his English contemporaries to swell the ranks of the Modern Painters is a puzzle which is wholly unexplained. The style in which the history of modern painting is told is by no means so simple and agreeable as that in which the authoress wrote her former volume. In the present instance, she has had to take as her authorities contemporary writers, and has been unable to resist the temptation of endeavouring to rival them in the "tall" phrase-making popular with some of our art-critics.

The second instalment of Theodor Simons' "Culturbilder aus Altrömischer Zeit"[5] has now reached us. The present number contains "Ein Gastmahl bei Lucullus," and "Ein Hochzeitsfest im Romischen Karthago." The lively descriptions of the text are based on very thorough antiquarian research, and the author in his notes give us many valuable references. The pictures of peaceful domestic life with which he deals in the present part do not afford, either to himself or to his illustrator, the same brilliant opportunity for dramatic display which were opened out to them by the gladiatorial show and the chariot race on which they spent their energies in their first number (*West. Rev.*, April, 1873). We are consequently inclined to see the shortcomings of their work even more forcibly than before, when a certain amount of exciting dash, which befitted the subject, carried the eye captive. Nothing short of genuine art can give meaning and reality to quiet passages of subdued action the movement of which has to be indicated by the modulation of a gesture. Alexander Wagner is not equal to such a task as this, and in his Robing of the Bride we at once perceive his lack of sympathetic and refined intention.

The first edition of Professor Streckfuss's "Lehrbuch der Perspec-

---

[4] "Modern Painters and their Paintings." For the Use of Schools. By Sarah Tytler. London: Strahan and Co. 1873.

[5] "Aus Altrömischer Zeit Culturbilder." Von Theodor Simons. Mit Illustrations von Alexander Wagner. Lieferung II. Berlin: Gebrüder Paetel. 1874.

tive"[6] appeared as far back as 1858. Later, the author published two supplements, in which he introduced further simplifications of his original methods, and also added several new diagrams. He has now entirely recast the work and improved it, adapting it carefully both for the purposes of self-instruction and for the use of schools. The atlas which accompanies the text furnishes the learner with all the help which he can possibly require, in a compact and simple form. The extreme pains which have been bestowed, indeed, on the simplification of every problem, on the reduction of the number of working lines, and on rendering the working out of each diagram perfectly intelligible to the learner ought to insure the success of the work.

The numbers of "The Picture Gallery,"[7] published by Sampson Low and Marston, for October, November, and December of the past year, maintain their wonted excellence. The December number is specially attractive, containing a charming reproduction of Sir Joshua Reynolds' Countess Spencer. The text is hardly up to the merit of the photographs.

"Gleanings for the Drawing-room"[8] is a book intended for the less educated portion of the religious public.

---

[6] "Lehrbuch der Perspective zum Schulgebrauche und Selbstunterrichte." Prof. Wilhelm Streckfuss. Mit einem Atlas. Second Edition. Breslau: Trewendt. 1874.

[7] "The Picture Gallery." Vol. II., Nos. 10, 11, 12. London: Sampson Low, Marston, and Co. 1873.

[8] "Gleanings for the Drawing-room in Prose and Verse." With Illustrations after Sir Edwin Landseer, Birket Foster, &c. London: Partridge and Co.

INDEX.

**** All Books must be looked for under the Author's name.*

END OF VOL. XLV.

www.ingramcontent.com/pod-product-compliance
Lightning Source LLC
Chambersburg PA
CBHW022123020426
42334CB00015B/741

* 9 7 8 3 7 4 1 1 7 8 7 5 7 *